Principles
of
Compiler Design

Principles
of
Compiler Design

ALFRED V. AHO

Bell Laboratories
Murray Hill, New Jersey

JEFFREY D. ULLMAN

Princeton University
Princeton, New Jersey

ADDISON-WESLEY PUBLISHING COMPANY
Reading, Massachusetts • Menlo Park, California
London • Amsterdam • Don Mills, Ontario • Sydney

This book is in the
ADDISON-WESLEY SERIES IN
COMPUTER SCIENCE AND INFORMATION PROCESSING

Michael A. Harrison
Consulting Editor

Reproduced by Addison-Wesley from camera-ready copy supplied by the authors.

ISBN 0-201-00022-9
BCDEFGHIJK-HA-7987

Preface

This book is intended as a text for an introductory course in compiler design at the Junior, Senior, or first-year graduate level. The emphasis is on solving the problems universally encountered in designing a compiler, regardless of the source language or the target machine.

Although few people are likely to implement or even maintain a compiler for a major programming language, many people can profitably use a number of the ideas and techniques discussed in this book in general software design. For example, the finite-state techniques used to build lexical analyzers have also been used in text editors, bibliographic search systems, and pattern recognition programs. Context-free grammars and syntax-directed translation schemes have been used to build text processors of many sorts, such as the mathematical typesetting system used to produce this book. Techniques of code optimization also have applicability to program verifiers and to programs that produce "structured" programs from unstructured ones.

Use of the Book

We have attempted to cover the major topics in compiler design in depth. Advanced material, however, has been put into separate chapters, so that courses on a variety of levels can be taught from this book. A brief synopsis of the chapters and comments on their appropriateness in a basic course is therefore appropriate.

Chapter 1 introduces the basic structure of a compiler, and is essential to all courses.

Chapter 2 covers basic concepts and terminology in programming languages. In courses we have taught, this material was covered in prerequisite courses, but if that is not the case, this material too is essential.

Chapter 3 covers lexical analysis, finite-state techniques, and the scanner generator. It is one of our favorite chapters, but if time does not permit, all but Sections 3.1 and 3.2 could be skipped.

Chapters 4, 5, and 6 cover parsing. The first of these introduces basic notions and is essential. One may then choose either 5 or 6 if both cannot be covered. Chapter 5 discusses the most common kinds of parsers — operator precedence and recursive descent. Chapter 6 covers LR parsing,

iii

which we believe to be the method of choice.

In Chapter 7 we introduce the principal ideas connected with intermediate-code generation. We use the syntax-directed approach and give translation schemes for the most basic programming language constructs — simple assignments and simple control structures. We regard all this material as essential.

Chapter 8 is a continuation of Chapter 7, covering the translation of additional language constructs such as array and structure references. Chapter 8 may be omitted if time presses.

Chapter 9 covers symbol tables. On the assumption that a course in data structures is a prerequisite to a course on compilers, Section 9.2 may be skipped.

Chapter 10 is on run-time organization. We introduce the subject by discussing the run-time implementation of the programming language C, which is easier to implement than other recursive languages such as ALGOL or PL/I. A possible candidate for omission is Section 10.3 on FORTRAN COMMON and EQUIVALENCE statements.

Chapter 11 discusses error recovery, another essential topic.

Chapters 12, 13, and 14 are on the subject of code optimization. The essentials are introduced in Chapter 12, and a first course will probably not go into the material of 13 and 14.

Finally, Chapter 15 covers object code generation. We have presented only the most universally applicable ideas, and most of what we do cover is appropriate for a first course. If forced to cut, however, we would omit Sections 15.5 and 15.6.

This book also contains sufficient material to make up an advanced course on compiler design. For example, at Princeton and Stevens we taught a graduate course to students who had had an elementary compiler course and a course in automata and language theory. There we covered scanner generators from Chapter 3, LR parsers and parser generators from Chapter 6, code optimization from Chapters 12, 13, and 14, and some topics in code generation from Chapter 15.

The Compiler Project

Appendix B contains a modular implementation project in which the student produces a compiler front end (lexical analyzer, parser, bookkeeping routines, and an intermediate code generator). The intermediate code may be interpreted, giving experience in run-time storage management. Unfortunately, we find that the typical one-semester course does not normally provide enough time for adding object code generation to this project, although such a module can easily be attached if time permits.

Also in Appendix B is a description of a simple language, a "subset" of PASCAL, which can be used in the project if desired. We regret that to make the job simple enough for a term project we have had to take out a

number of the elegant features of PASCAL, including data type definitions and block structure (although recursion remains). An SLR(1) grammar for the language is given, along with directions for converting it to operator-precedence or LL(1) form if one of those types of parser is desired.

Exercises

We have traditionally rated exercises with stars. Zero-starred exercises are suitable for elementary courses, singly-starred exercises are intended for more advanced courses, and doubly-starred exercises are food for thought.

Acknowledgments

The manuscript at various stages was read by a number of people who gave us valuable comments. In this regard we owe a debt of gratitude to Brenda Baker, David Copp, Bruce Englar, Hania Gajewska, Sue Graham, Matt Hecht, Ellis Horowitz, Steve Johnson, Randy Katz, Ken Kennedy, Brian Kernighan, Doug McIlroy, Marshall McKusick, Arnaldo Moura, Tom Peterson, Dennis Ritchie, Eric Schmidt, Ravi Sethi, Tom Szymanski, Ken Thompson, and Peter Weinberger.

This book was phototypeset by the authors using the excellent software available on the UNIX operating system. We would like to acknowledge the people who made it possible to do so. Dennis Ritchie and Ken Thompson were the creators and principal implementors of UNIX. Joe Ossanna wrote TROFF, the program which formats text for the phototypesetter. Brian Kernighan and Lorinda Cherry produced EQN, the preprocessor which enables mathematical text to be typeset conveniently. Mike Lesk implemented both the MS macro package, which greatly simplifies the specification of page layouts, and TBL, the preprocessor used to prepare the tables in this book.

The authors would particularly like to thank Carmela Scrocca who so expertly typed the manuscript and prepared it for photocomposition. The authors would also like to acknowledge the support services provided by Bell Laboratories during the preparation of the manuscript.

A. V. A.
J. D. U.

Contents

CHAPTER 1

Introduction
to
Compilers

The purpose of this book is two-fold. We hope to acquaint the reader with the basic constructs of modern programming languages and to show how they can be efficiently implemented in the machine language of a typical computer. We shall also show how tools can be developed and used to help construct certain translator components. These tools not only facilitate the construction of compilers, but they can also be used in a variety of applications not directly related to compiling.

1.1 Compilers and Translators

A *translator* is a program that takes as input a program written in one programming language (the *source language*) and produces as output a program in another language (the *object* or *target language*). If the source language is a high-level language such as FORTRAN, PL/I, or COBOL, and the object language is a low-level language such as an assembly language or machine language, then such a translator is called a *compiler*.

Executing a program written in a high-level programming language is basically a two-step process, as illustrated in Fig. 1.1. The source program must first be *compiled*, that is, translated into the object program. Then the resulting object program is loaded into memory and executed.

Compilers were once considered almost impossible programs to write. The first FORTRAN compiler, for example, took 18 man-years to implement (Backus et al. [1957]). Today, however, compilers can be built with much less effort. In fact, it is not unreasonable to expect a fairly substantial compiler to be implemented as a student project in a one-semester compiler design course. The principal developments of the past twenty years which led to this improvement are:

1

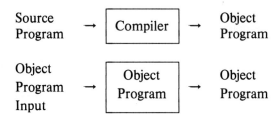

Fig. 1.1. Compilation and execution.

- The understanding of how to organize and modularize the process of compilation,
- The discovery of systematic techniques for handling many of the important tasks that occur during compilation,
- The development of software tools that facilitate the implementation of compilers and compiler components.

These are the developments we shall consider in this book. This chapter provides an overview of the compilation process and introduces the major components of a compiler.

Other Translators

Certain other translators transform a programming language into a simplified language, called *intermediate code,* which can be directly executed using a program called an *interpreter.* We may think of the intermediate code as the machine language of an abstract computer designed to execute the source code. For example, SNOBOL is often interpreted, the intermediate code being a language called Polish postfix notation (see Section 7.4). In some cases, the source language itself can be the intermediate language. For example, most *command languages,* such as JCL, in which one communicates directly with the operating system, are interpreted with no prior translation at all.

Interpreters are often smaller than compilers and facilitate the implementation of complex programming language constructs. However, the main disadvantage of interpreters is that the execution time of an interpreted program is usually slower than that of a corresponding compiled object program.

There are several other important types of translators, besides compilers. If the source language is assembly language and the target language is machine language, then the translator is called an *assembler.* The term *preprocessor* is sometimes used for translators that take programs in one high-level language into equivalent programs in another high-level language. For example, there are many FORTRAN preprocessors that map "structured" versions of FORTRAN into conventional FORTRAN.

1.2 Why do we Need Translators?

The answer to this question is obvious to anyone who has programmed in machine language. With machine language we must communicate directly with a computer in terms of bits, registers, and very primitive machine operations. Since a machine language program is nothing more than a sequence of 0's and 1's, programming a complex algorithm in such a language is terribly tedious and fraught with opportunities for mistakes. Perhaps the most serious disadvantage of machine-language coding is that all operations and operands must be specified in a numeric code. Not only is a machine language program cryptic, but it also may be impossible to modify in a convenient manner.

Symbolic Assembly Language

Because of the difficulties with machine language programming, a host of "higher-level" languages have been invented to enable the programmer to code in a way that resembles his own thought processes rather than the elementary steps of the computer. The most immediate step away from machine language is symbolic assembly language. In this language, a programmer uses mnemonic names for both operation codes and data addresses. Thus a programmer could write ADD X, Y in assembly language, instead of something like 0110 001110 010101 in machine language (where 0110 is the hypothetical machine operation code for "add" and 001110 and 010101 are the addresses of X and Y).

A computer, however, cannot execute a program written in assembly language. That program has to be first translated to machine language, which the computer can understand. The program that performs this translation is the assembler.

Macros

Many assembly (and programming) languages provide a "macro" facility whereby a macro statement will translate into a sequence of assembly language statements and perhaps other macro statements before being translated into machine code. Thus, a macro facility is a text replacement capability. There are two aspects to macros: definition and use. To illustrate the utility of macros, consider a situation in which a machine does not have a single machine- or assembly-language statement that adds the contents of one memory address to another, as did our hypothetical assembly instruction ADD X, Y, above. Instead, suppose the machine has an instruction LOAD, which moves a datum from memory to a register, an instruction ADD, which adds the contents of a memory address to that of a register, and an instruction STORE, which moves data from a register to memory. Using these instructions, we can create, with a *macro definition,* a "two-address add" instruction as follows.

```
    MACRO       ADD2    X, Y
                LOAD    Y
                ADD     X
                STORE   Y
ENDMACRO
```

The first statement gives the name ADD2 to the macro and defines its dummy arguments, known as *formal parameters,* X and Y. The next three statements define the macro, that is, they give its translation. We assume that the machine has only one register, so the question of what registers LOAD and STORE refer to needs no elaboration.

Having defined ADD2 in this way, we can then use it as an ordinary assembly language operation code. For example, if the statement ADD2 A, B is encountered somewhere after the definition of ADD2, we have a *macro use.* Here, the macro processor substitutes for ADD2 A, B the three statements which form the definition of ADD2, but with the *actual parameters* A and B replacing the formal parameters X and Y, respectively. That is, ADD2 A, B is translated to

```
            LOAD        B
            ADD         A
            STORE       B
```

High-Level Languages

Symbolic assembly programs are easier to write and understand than machine-language programs primarily because numerical codes for addresses and operators are replaced by more meaningful symbolic codes. Nevertheless, even with macros, there are severe drawbacks to writing in assembly language. The programmer must still know the details of how a specific computer operates. He must also mentally translate complex operations and data structures into sequences of low-level operations which use only the primitive data types that machine language provides. The programmer must also be intimately concerned with how and where data is represented within the machine. Although there are a few situations in which such detailed knowledge is essential for efficiency, most of the programmer's time is unnecessarily wasted on such intricacies.

To avoid these problems, high-level programming languages were developed. Basically, a high-level programming language allows a programmer to express algorithms in a more natural notation that avoids many of the details of how a specific computer functions. For example, it is much more natural to write the expression A+B than a sequence of assembly language instructions to add A and B. COBOL, FORTRAN, PL/I, ALGOL,† SNOBOL, APL, PASCAL, LISP and C are some of the more common high-level languages, and we assume the reader is familiar with at least one of these languages. References for these languages and others are found in the bibliographic notes of Chapter 2.

A high-level programming language makes the programming task simpler, but it also introduces some problems. The most obvious is that we need a program to translate the high-level language into a language the machine can understand. In a sense, this program, the compiler, is completely analogous to the assembler for an assembly language.

A compiler, however, is a substantially more complex program to write than an assembler. Some compilers even make use of an assembler as an appendage, with the compiler producing assembly code, which is then assembled and loaded before being executed in the resulting machine-language form.

Before discussing compilers in detail, however, we should know the types of constructs typically found in high-level programming languages. The form and meaning of the constructs in a programming language have a strong impact on the overall design of a compiler for that language. Chapter 2 of this book reviews the main concepts concerning programming languages.

1.3 The Structure of a Compiler

A compiler takes as input a source program and produces as output an equivalent sequence of machine instructions. This process is so complex that it is not reasonable, either from a logical point of view or from an implementation point of view, to consider the compilation process as occurring in one single step. For this reason, it is customary to partition the compilation process into a series of subprocesses called *phases,* as shown in Fig. 1.2. A phase is a logically cohesive operation that takes as input one representation of the source program and produces as output another representation.

---

† Throughout this book, ALGOL refers to ALGOL 60 rather than ALGOL 68.

Source Program

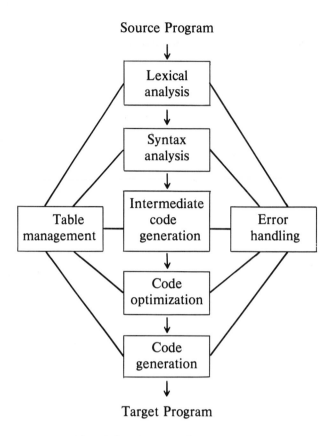

Fig. 1.2. Phases of a compiler.

The first phase, called the *lexical analyzer,* or *scanner,* separates characters of the source language into groups that logically belong together; these groups are called *tokens.* The usual tokens are keywords, such as DO or IF, identifiers, such as X or NUM, operator symbols such as $<=$ or $+$, and punctuation symbols such as parentheses or commas. The output of the lexical analyzer is a stream of tokens, which is passed to the next phase, the *syntax analyzer,* or *parser.* The tokens in this stream can be represented by codes which we may regard as integers. Thus, DO might be represented by 1, $+$ by 2, and "identifier" by 3. In the case of a token like "identifier," a second quantity, telling which of those identifiers used by the program is represented by this instance of token "identifier," is passed along with the integer code for "identifier."

The syntax analyzer groups tokens together into syntactic structures. For example, the three tokens representing A$+$B might be grouped into a syntactic structure called an *expression*. Expressions might further be combined to form statements. Often the syntactic structure can be regarded as a tree whose leaves are the tokens. The interior nodes of the tree represent strings of tokens that logically belong together.

The *intermediate code generator* uses the structure produced by the syntax analyzer to create a stream of simple instructions. Many styles of intermediate code are possible. One common style uses instructions with one operator and a small number of operands. These instructions can be viewed as simple macros like the macro ADD2 discussed in Section 1.2. The primary difference between intermediate code and assembly code is that the intermediate code need not specify the registers to be used for each operation.

Code optimization is an optional phase designed to improve the intermediate code so that the ultimate object program runs faster and/or takes less space. Its output is another intermediate code program that does the same job as the original, but perhaps in a way that saves time and/or space.

The final phase, *code generation,* produces the object code by deciding on the memory locations for data, selecting code to access each datum, and selecting the registers in which each computation is to be done. Designing a code generator that produces truly efficient object programs is one of the most difficult parts of compiler design, both practically and theoretically.

The *table-management,* or *bookkeeping,* portion of the compiler keeps track of the names used by the program and records essential information about each, such as its type (integer, real, etc.). The data structure used to record this information is called a *symbol table.*

The *error handler* is invoked when a flaw in the source program is detected. It must warn the programmer by issuing a diagnostic, and adjust the information being passed from phase to phase so that each phase can proceed. It is desirable that compilation be completed on flawed programs, at least through the syntax-analysis phase, so that as many errors as possible can be detected in one compilation. Both the table management and error handling routines interact with all phases of the compiler.

Passes

In an implementation of a compiler, portions of one or more phases are combined into a module called a *pass.* A pass reads the source program or the output of the previous pass, makes the transformations specified by its phases, and writes output into an intermediate file, which may then be read by a subsequent pass. If several phases are grouped into one pass, then the operation of the phases may be interleaved, with control alternating among several phases.

The number of passes, and the grouping of phases into passes, are usually dictated by a variety of considerations germane to a particular language and machine, rather than by any mathematical optimality criteria. Appendix A shows the overall structure of several existing compilers.

The structure of the source language has a strong effect on the number of passes. Certain languages require at least two passes to generate code easily. For example, languages such as PL/I or ALGOL 68 allow the declaration of a name to occur after uses of that name. Code for expressions containing such a name cannot be generated conveniently until the declaration has been seen.

The environment in which the compiler must operate can also affect the number of passes. A multi-pass compiler can be made to use less space than a single-pass compiler, since the space occupied by the compiler program for one pass can be reused by the following pass. A multi-pass compiler is, of course, slower than a single-pass compiler, because each pass reads and writes an intermediate file. Thus, compilers running on computers with small memory would normally use several passes while, on a computer with a large random access memory, a compiler with fewer passes would be possible.

Reducing the Number of Passes

Since each phase is a transformation on a stream of data representing an intermediate form of the source program, the reader may wonder how several phases can be combined into one pass without the reading and writing of intermediate files. In some cases one pass produces its output with little or no memory of prior inputs. Lexical analysis is typical. In this situation, a small buffer serves as the interface between passes. In other cases, we may merge phases into one pass by means of a technique known as "backpatching," which is discussed in Section 7.8. In general terms, if the output of a phase cannot be determined without looking at the remainder of the phase's input, the phase can generate output with "slots" which can be filled in later, after more of the input is read.

While we cannot give an example of backpatching as it pertains to compilers until we have described in some detail what the phases do, an example from assemblers will serve as a paradigm. An assembler might have a statement like

GOTO L

which precedes a statement with label L. A two-pass assembler uses its first pass to enter into its symbol table a list of all identifiers (statement labels and data names) together with the machine address (relative to the beginning of the program), to which these identifiers correspond. Then a second pass replaces mnemonic operation codes, such as GOTO, by their machine-language equivalent and replaces uses of identifiers by their machine addresses.

A one-pass assembler, on the other hand, could generate a skeleton of the GOTO machine instruction the first time it saw GOTO L. It could then append the machine address for this instruction to a list of instructions to be backpatched once the machine address for L is determined. For example, when the assembler encounters a statement such as

L: ADD X

it scans the list of statements referring to L and places the machine address for statement L: ADD X in the address field of each such instruction. Subsequent assembly instructions referring to L can have the value for L substituted immediately.

In a compiler, most of the backpatching that needs to be done is done over relatively short distances. For example, labels normally need to be backpatched as above only within one procedure or subroutine. We shall see other examples of backpatching in Chapter 7; and Chapter 10 contains other examples where output can be generated on a procedure-by-procedure basis.

The distance over which backpatching occurs is important since the code to be backpatched must remain accessible until backpatching is complete. Even though the object program may fit in memory when it is produced, intermediate forms of the source program may be too big to fit in memory all at once, especially as a substantial portion of memory may be occupied by the compiler program itself.

It is worth noting that programming languages with the structure of ("standard") ALGOL, where each program is a single procedure, do not lend themselves to one-pass compiling, since, for example, forward jumps may traverse the entire length of the program. In contrast, languages like PL/I or FORTRAN lend themselves to a programming style in which large programs can be created as a sequence of relatively small procedures or subroutines. In these cases, most backpatching can be done on a procedure-by-procedure basis, and the loader can be used to link the procedures together (thus providing a hidden extra pass not thought of as part of the compiler). In fact for this reason, among others, most ALGOL implementations add to the "standard" by allowing programs to consist of a sequence of procedures which may be linked.

In this book we shall not consider how much processing should be done in one pass or how big a given pass should be. The answer to this question is too dependent on the particular environment of a given compiler. Rather, we shall study each phase of the compilation process shown in Fig.

1.2 as a process in itself, investigating algorithms and tradeoffs that are applicable to the phase alone. The reader should bear in mind, however, that, in any real compiler, all phases must act in concert, and that a strategy adopted for one phase can affect the type of processing that must be done in a subsequent phase. We now turn to a more detailed look at each of the phases shown in Fig. 1.2.

1.4 Lexical Analysis

The lexical analyzer is the interface between the source program and the compiler. The lexical analyzer reads the source program one character at a time, carving the source program into a sequence of atomic units called *tokens*. Each token represents a sequence of characters that can be treated as a single logical entity. Identifiers, keywords, constants, operators, and punctuation symbols such as commas and parentheses are typical tokens. For example, in the FORTRAN statement

$$\text{IF (5 .EQ. MAX) GO TO 100} \qquad (1.1)$$

we find the following eight tokens: IF; (; 5; .EQ.; MAX;); GOTO; 100.

What is called a token depends on the language at hand and, to some extent, on the discretion of the compiler designer; but in general each token is a substring of the source program that is to be treated as a single unit. For example, it is not reasonable to treat M or MA (of the identifier MAX above) as an independent entity.

There are two kinds of token: specific strings such as IF or a semicolon, and classes of strings such as identifiers, constants, or labels. To handle both cases, we shall treat a token as a pair consisting of two parts: a token type and a token value. For convenience, a token consisting of a specific string such as a semicolon will be treated as having a type (the string itself) but no value. A token such as the identifier MAX, above, has a type "identifier" and a value consisting of the string MAX. Frequently, we shall refer to the type or value as the token itself. Thus, when we talk about identifier being a token, we are referring to a token type; when we talk about MAX being a token, we are referring to a token whose value is MAX.

The lexical analyzer and the following phase, the syntax analyzer, are often grouped together into the same pass. In that pass, the lexical analyzer operates either under the control of the parser or as a coroutine with the parser. The parser asks the lexical analyzer for the next token, whenever the parser needs one. The lexical analyzer returns to the parser a code for the token that it found. In the case that the token is an identifier or another token with a value, the value is also passed to the parser. The usual method of providing this information is for the lexical analyzer to call a bookkeeping routine which installs the actual value in the symbol table if it is not already there. The lexical analyzer then passes the two components of the token to the parser. The first is a code for the token type (identifier), and the second is the value, a pointer to the place in the symbol table reserved for the specific value found.†

Finding Tokens

To find the next token, the lexical analyzer examines successive characters in the source program, starting from the first character not yet grouped into a token. The lexical analyzer may be required to search many characters beyond the next token in order to determine what the next token actually is.

Example 1.1. Suppose the lexical analyzer has last isolated the left parenthesis as a token in statement (1.1). We may represent the situation as follows.

$$\text{IF(5.EQ.MAX)GOTO100}$$
$$\uparrow$$

The string to the left of the arrow represents the symbols already broken up into tokens by the lexical analyzer. pointer. Note that blanks have been removed, since they are ignored in FORTRAN.

When the parser asks for the next token, the lexical analyzer reads all the characters between 5 and Q, inclusive, to determine that the next token is just the constant 5. The reason it has to scan as far as it does is that until it sees the Q, it is not sure it has seen the complete constant; it could be working on a floating-point constant such as 5.E−10. After determining that the next token is the constant 5, the lexical analyzer repositions its input pointer at the first dot, the character following the token.

$$\text{IF(5.EQ.MAX)GOTO100}$$
$$\uparrow$$

The lexical analyzer may return token type "constant" to the parser. The value associated with this "constant" could be the numerical value 5 or a pointer to the string 5. When statement (1.1) is completely processed by the lexical analyzer, the token stream might look like

$$\textbf{if } (\text{ [const, 341] } \textbf{eq } \textbf{[id}, \text{ 729]) } \textbf{goto } \textbf{[label}, \text{ 554]} \qquad (1.2)$$

Here we use boldface codes to represent the token types. Parentheses represent their own codes. The tokens having an associated value are

---

† We shall see in Section 10.1 that in some cases it is impossible for the lexical analyzer to install the identifier in the symbol table, and the identifier itself must be passed to the parser.

represented by pairs in square brackets. The second component of the pair can be interpreted as an index into the symbol table where information about constants, variables, and labels is kept. The relevant entries of the symbol table are suggested in Fig. 1.3. □

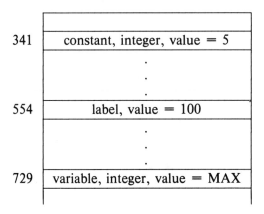

Fig. 1.3. Symbol table.

1.5 Syntax Analysis

The parser has two functions. It checks that the tokens appearing in its input, which is the output of the lexical analyzer, occur in patterns that are permitted by the specification for the source language. It also imposes on the tokens a tree-like structure that is used by the subsequent phases of the compiler.

For example, if a PL/I program contains the expression

$$A + / B$$

then after lexical analysis this expression might appear to the syntax analyzer as the token sequence

id + / id

On seeing the /, the syntax analyzer should detect an error situation, because the presence of these two adjacent binary operators violates the formation rules of a PL/I expression.

The second aspect of syntax analysis is to make explicit the hierarchical structure of the incoming token stream by identifying which parts of the token stream should be grouped together. For example, the expression

$$A \; / \; B * C$$

has two possible interpretations:

a) divide A by B and then multiply by C (as in FORTRAN); or

b) multiply B by C and then use the result to divide A (as in APL).

Each of these two interpretations can be represented in terms of a *parse tree,* a diagram which exhibits the syntactic structure of the expression. Parse trees that reflect orders (a) and (b) are shown in Fig. 1.4(a) and (b), respectively. Note how in each case the operands of the first operation to be performed meet each other at a lower level than that at which they meet the remaining operand.

The language specification must tell us which of interpretations (a) and (b) is to be used, and in general, what hierarchical structure each source program has. These rules form the syntactic specification of a programming language. We shall see in Chapter 4 that *context-free grammars* are particularly helpful in specifying the syntactic structure of a language. Moreover, efficient syntactic analyzers can be constructed automatically from certain types of context-free grammars. This matter is pursued in further detail in Chapters 5 and 6.

Example 1.2. While the exact parsing of a token stream depends on the grammar chosen, a plausible grammar for FORTRAN might impose the tree structure of Fig. 1.5 on the token stream (1.2) discussed in Example 1.1. □

1.6 Intermediate Code Generation

On a logical level the output of the syntax analyzer is some representation of a parse tree. The intermediate code generation phase transforms this parse tree into an intermediate-language representation of the source program.

Three-Address Code

One popular type of intermediate language is what is called "three-address code." A typical three-address code statement is

$$A := B \; \textbf{op} \; C$$

where A, B, and C are operands and **op** is a binary operator.

The parse tree in Fig. 1.4(a) might be converted into the three-address code sequence

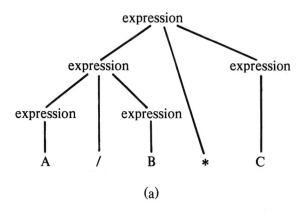

(a)

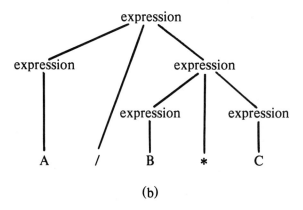

(b)

Fig. 1.4. Parse trees.

$$T_1 := A / B$$
$$T_2 := T_1 * C$$

where T_1 and T_2 are names of temporary variables.

In addition to statements that use arithmetic operators, an intermediate language needs unconditional and simple conditional branching statements, in which at most one relation is tested to determine whether or not a branch is to be made. Higher-level flow of control statements such as

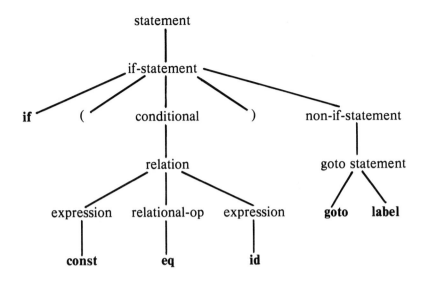

Fig. 1.5. Parse of if-statement (1.2).

while-do statements, or if-then-else statements, are translated into these lower-level conditional three-address statements.

Example 1.4. Consider the following while-statement

$$\textbf{while } A > B \text{ \& } A < = 2*B - 5 \textbf{ do}$$
$$A := A + B;$$

which has the corresponding token stream

$$\textbf{while } [\textbf{id}, n_1] > [\textbf{id}, n_2] \text{ \& } [\textbf{id}, n_1] \leqslant [\textbf{const}, n_3] * [\textbf{id}, n_2]$$
$$- [\textbf{const}, n_4] \textbf{ do } [\textbf{id}, n_1] \leftarrow [\textbf{id}, n_1] + [\textbf{id}, n_2];$$

Here n_1, n_2, n_3, and n_4 stand for pointers to the symbol table entries for A, B, 2 and 5, respectively. The parse tree for this statement might plausibly be the one shown in Fig. 1.6. We use "exp" for "expression," "relop" for "relational operator," and we indicate parenthetically the particular name or constant to which each instance of token **id** and **const** refer.

The actual algorithms by which parse trees such as Fig. 1.6 can be translated to intermediate code will not be discussed until Chapter 7. However, we can now show what the intermediate code should look like. A straightforward algorithm for translation would produce intermediate code like that shown in Fig. 1.7. The jumps over jumps, such as in the first two

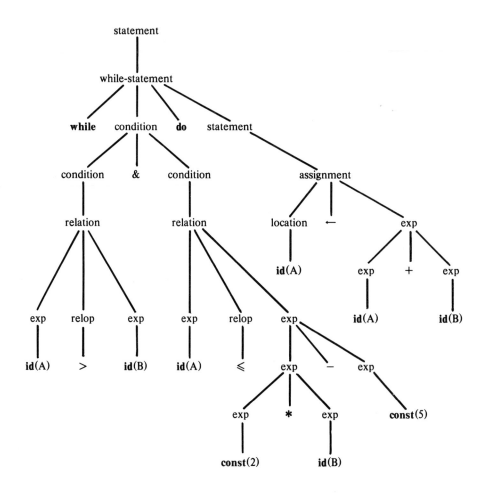

Fig. 1.6. Parse tree for while-statement.

statements, can be cleaned up during the code-optimization or code-generation phase. □

Most compilers do not generate a parse tree explicitly but rather go to intermediate code directly as syntax analysis takes place. We have chosen to talk of syntax analysis as producing a parse tree explicitly because we want to be able to evaluate several parsing algorithms in Chapters 5 and 6, without cluttering the analysis with details of intermediate-code generation.

Chapters 7 and 8 talk about intermediate-code generation by *syntax-directed translation,* a technique in which the actions of the syntax analysis

```
L1:     if A > B goto L2
        goto L3
L2:     T₁ := 2 * B
        T₂ := T₁ - 5
        if A ⩽ T₂ goto L4
        goto L3
L4:     A := A + B
        goto L1
L3:
```

Fig. 1.7. Intermediate code for while-statement.

phase guide the translation. These two chapters show how to define intermediate-language constructs in terms of the syntactic constructs found in a programming language. They also show how the intermediate code can be generated as syntax analysis takes place.

1.7 Optimization

Object programs that are frequently executed should be fast and small. Certain compilers have within them a phase that tries to apply transformations to the output of the intermediate code generator, in an attempt to produce an intermediate-language version of the source program from which a faster or smaller object-language program can ultimately be produced. This phase is popularly called the *optimization phase*.

The term "optimization" in this context is a complete misnomer, since there is no algorithmic way of producing a target language program that is the best possible under any reasonable definition of "best." Optimizing compilers merely attempt to produce a better target program than would be produced with no "optimization." A good optimizing compiler can improve the target program by perhaps a factor of two in overall speed, in comparison with a compiler that generates code carefully but without using the specialized techniques generally referred to as code optimization.

Local Optimization

There are "local" transformations that can be applied to a program to attempt an improvement. For example, in Fig. 1.6 we saw two instances of jumps over jumps in the intermediate code, such as

$$\begin{aligned} &\textbf{if } A > B \textbf{ goto } L2 \\ &\textbf{goto } L3 \end{aligned} \qquad (1.3)$$

L2:

This sequence could be replaced by the single statement

$$\textbf{if } A \leqslant B \textbf{ goto } L3 \qquad (1.4)$$

Sequence (1.3) would typically be replaced in the object program by machine statements which:

1. compare A and B to set the condition codes,

2. jump to L2 if the code for $>$ is set, and

3. jump to L3.

Sequence (1.4), on the other hand, would be translated to machine instructions which:

4. compare A and B to set the condition codes, and

5. jump to L3 if the code for $<$ or $=$ is set.

If we assume $A > B$ is true half the time, then for (1.3) we execute (1) and (2) all the time and (3) half the time, for an average of 2.5 instructions. For (1.4) we always execute two instructions, a 20% savings. Also, (1.4) provides a 33% space saving if we crudely assume that all instructions require the same space.

Another important local optimization is the elimination of common subexpressions. Provided A is not an alias for B or C, the assignments

$$A := B + C + D$$
$$E := B + C + F$$

might be evaluated as

$$T_1 := B + C$$
$$A := T_1 + D$$
$$E := T_1 + F$$

taking advantage of the common subexpression B+C. Common subexpressions written explicitly by the programmer are relatively rare, however. A more productive source of common subexpressions arises from computations generated by the compiler itself. Chief among these is subscript calculation. For example, the assignment

$$A[I] := B[I] + C[I]$$

will, if the machine memory is addressed by bytes and there are, say, four bytes per word, require 4∗I to be computed three times. An optimizing compiler can modify the intermediate program so that the calculation of 4∗I is done only once. Note that it is impossible for the programmer to specify that this calculation of 4∗I be done only once in the source program, since these address calculations are not explicit at the source level.

Loop Optimization

Another important source of optimization concerns speedups of loops. Loops are especially good targets for optimization because programs spend most of their time in inner loops. A typical loop improvement is to move a computation that produces the same result each time around the loop to a point in the program just before the loop is entered. Then this computation is done only once each time the loop is entered, rather than once for each iteration of the loop. Such a computation is called *loop invariant*.

Chapter 12 introduces the various aspects of code optimization − local optimization, loop optimization, and the analysis of the flow of control and data. Chapter 13 considers control-flow analysis, loops, and loop optimization in detail; Chapter 14 covers data-flow analysis, the gathering and utilization of information about the use of data throughout the program.

1.8 Code Generation

The code-generation phase converts the intermediate code into a sequence of machine instructions. A simple-minded code generator might map the statement A:=B+C into the machine code sequence

LOAD B
ADD   C
STORE A

However, such a straightforward macro-like expansion of intermediate code into machine code usually produces a target program that contains many redundant loads and stores and that utilizes the resources of the target machine inefficiently.

To avoid these redundant loads and stores, a code generator might keep track of the run-time contents of registers. Knowing what quantities reside in registers, the code generator can generate loads and stores only when necessary.

Many computers have only a few high-speed registers in which computations can be performed particularly quickly. A good code generator would therefore attempt to utilize these registers as efficiently as possible. This aspect of code generation, called *register allocation,* is particularly difficult to do optimally, but some heuristic approaches can give reasonably good results. Chapter 15 discusses some basic strategies for code generation and register allocation.

1.9 Bookkeeping

A compiler needs to collect information about all the data objects that appear in the source program. For example, a compiler needs to know whether a variable represents an integer or a real number, what size an array has, how many arguments a function expects, and so forth. The information about data objects may be explicit, as in declarations, or implicit, as in the first letter of an identifier or in the context in which an identifier is used. For example, in FORTRAN, A(I) is a function call if A has not been declared to be an array.

The information about data objects is collected by the early phases of the compiler — lexical and syntactic analysis — and entered into the symbol table. For example, when a lexical analyzer sees an identifier MAX, say, it may enter the name MAX into the symbol table if it is not already there, and produce as output a token whose value component is an index to this entry of the symbol table. If the syntax analyzer recognizes a declaration **integer** MAX, the action of the syntax analyzer will be to note in the symbol table that MAX has type "integer." No intermediate code is generated for this statement.

The information collected about the data objects has a number of uses. For example, if we have the expression A+B, where A is of type integer and B of type real, and if the language permits an integer to be added to a real, then on most computers code must be generated to convert A from type integer to type real before the addition can take place. The addition must be done in floating point, and the result is real. If mixed-mode expressions of this nature are forbidden by the language, then the compiler must issue an error message when it attempts to generate code for this construct.

The term *semantic analysis* is applied to the determination of the type of intermediate results, the check that arguments are of types that are legal for an application of an operator, and the determination of the operation denoted by the operator (e.g., + could denote fixed or floating add, perhaps logical "or," and possibly other operations as well). Semantic analysis can be done during the syntax analysis phase, the intermediate code generation phase, or the final code generation phase.

1.10 Error Handling

One of the most important functions of a compiler is the detection and reporting of errors in the source program. The error messages should allow the programmer to determine exactly where the errors have occurred. Errors can be encountered by virtually all of the phases of a compiler. For example,

1. The lexical analyzer may be unable to proceed because the next token in the source program is misspelled.

2. The syntax analyzer may be unable to infer a structure for its input because a syntactic error such as a missing parenthesis has occurred.

3. The intermediate code generator may detect an operator whose operands have incompatible types.

4. The code optimizer, doing control flow analysis, may detect that certain statements can never be reached.

5. The code generator may find a compiler-created constant that is too large to fit in a word of the target machine.

6. While entering information into the symbol table, the bookkeeping routine may discover an identifier that has been multiply declared with contradictory attributes.

Whenever a phase of the compiler discovers an error, it must report the error to the error handler, which issues an appropriate diagnostic message. Once the error has been noted, the compiler must modify the input to the phase detecting the error, so that the latter can continue processing its input, looking for subsequent errors.

Good error handling is difficult because certain errors can mask subsequent errors. Other errors, if not properly handled, can spawn an avalanche of spurious errors. Techniques for error recovery are discussed in Chapter 11.

1.11 Compiler-Writing Tools

A number of tools have been developed specifically to help construct compilers. These tools range from scanner and parser generators to complex systems, variously called *compiler-compilers, compiler-generators,* or *translator-writing systems,* which produce a compiler from some form of specification of a source language and target machine. The input specification for these systems may contain:

1. a description of the lexical and syntactic structure of the source language,

2. a description of what output is to be generated for each source language construct, and

3. a description of the target machine.

In many cases the specification is merely a collection of programs fitted together into a framework by the compiler-compiler. Some compiler-compilers, however, permit a portion of the specification of a language to be nonprocedural rather than procedural. For example, instead of writing a program to perform syntax analysis, the user writes a context-free grammar and the compiler-compiler automatically converts that grammar into a program for syntax analysis.

While a number of useful compiler-compilers exist, they have limitations. The chief problem is that there is a tradeoff between how much work the compiler-compiler can do automatically for its user and how flexible the system can be. For example, it is tempting to assume that lexical analyzers for all languages are really the same, except for the particular keywords and signs recognized. Many compiler-compilers do in fact produce fixed lexical analysis routines for use in the generated compiler. These routines differ only in the list of keywords recognized, and this list is supplied by the user. This approach is quite valid, but may be unworkable if it is required to recognize nonstandard tokens such as identifiers that may include characters other than letters and digits. More general approaches to the automatic generation of lexical analyzers exist, such as those described in Chapter 3, but these require the user to supply more input to the compiler-compiler, i.e., to do more work.

The principal aids provided by existing compiler-compilers are:

1. *Scanner generators.* The "built-in" approach described above and regular expression based techniques described in Chapter 3 are the most common approaches.

2. *Parser generators.* Almost every compiler-compiler provides one. The reason is twofold. First, while parsing represents only a small part of compiler construction, having a fixed framework in which parsing is done can be a great aid in the organization of the entire compiler. Second, the parsing phase is unique among the compiler phases in that a notation exists — the context-free grammar described in Chapter 4 — which is sufficiently nonprocedural to reduce the work of the compiler writer significantly, sufficiently general to be of use in any compiler, and sufficiently developed to permit efficient implementations to be generated automatically.

One significant advantage of using a parser generator is increased reliability. A mechanically-generated parser is more likely to be correct than
one produced by hand. We discuss one parser generator in Chapter 6.

3. *Facilities for code generation.* Often a high-level language especially suitable for specifying the generation of intermediate, assembly, or object code
is provided by the compiler-compiler. The user writes routines in this
language and, in the resulting compiler, the routines are called at the
correct times by the automatically generated parser. A common feature of
compiler-compilers is a mechanism for specifying decision tables that select
the object code. These tables become part of the generated compiler, along
with an interpreter for these tables, supplied by the compiler-compiler.

The bibliographic notes of this chapter contain references to a number
of compiler-compiler systems. Chapter 3 and 6 provide references to
scanner and parser generators.

1.12 Getting Started

Although a compiler is just another program in a system, it usually is an
important program that will be used by many people. Therefore, before
writing any code a would-be compiler designer should give some thought to
the following issues.

A new compiler may be for a new source language, or produce new
object code, or both. If the source language is new, how will it be used?
Should compilation speed be of greater importance than the quality of output code? How important are good error diagnostics and good error
recovery?

The nature of the target machine and operating environment likewise
should be considered, for they have a strong influence on what the compiler will look like and what code generation strategies it should use. In
terms of writing the compiler, the implementation language, the programming environment, and the available tools are most important, for they
determine how quickly the compiler can be built. For example, it is pain-
fully obvious that systems programming languages, such as BLISS, C, and
PASCAL, are much better-suited to compiler construction than are APL,
COBOL, or FORTRAN.

Compiler-writing, like any other large software effort, is an exercise in
compromise. The design, therefore, should be such that change and
modification can be readily accommodated throughout the birth and life of
the compiler. The use of some of the compiler-building tools we discuss
can be a significant help in this direction.

Bootstrapping

A compiler is characterized by three languages: its source language, its object language, and the language in which it is written. These languages may all be quite different. For example, a compiler may run on one machine and produce object code for another machine. Such a compiler is often called a *cross-compiler*. Many minicomputer and microprocessor compilers are implemented this way; they run on a bigger machine and produce object code for the smaller machine.

Sometimes we hear of a compiler being implemented in its own language. This naturally raises the question, "How was the first compiler compiled?" This question may sound like "Who was the first parent?" but it is not nearly as hard.

Suppose we have a new language L, which we want to make available on several machines, say A and B. As a first step we might write for machine A a small compiler C_A^{SA}† that translates a subset S of language L into the machine or assembly code of A. This compiler can first be written in a language that is already available on A (the assembly language of A if need be).

We then write a compiler C_S^{LA} in the simple language S. This program, when run through C_A^{SA}, becomes C_A^{LA}, the compiler for the complete language L, running on machine A, and producing object code for A. The process is shown in Fig. 1.8.

$$ C_S^{LA} \quad \rightarrow \quad \boxed{C_A^{SA}} \quad \rightarrow \quad C_A^{LA} $$

Fig. 1.8. Bootstrapping a compiler.

Now suppose we want to produce another compiler for L to run on machine B and to produce code for B. If C_S^{LA} has been designed carefully and machine B is not that different from machine A, it should be far less work to convert C_S^{LA} into a compiler C_L^{LB} which produces object code for B than it is to write a new compiler from scratch. Note that we can now use the full language L to implement C_L^{LB}.

---

† We use the notation C_Z^{XY} to stand for a compiler for language X, written in language Z, and producing object code in language Y. We use A and B to stand for the machine codes of computers A and B.

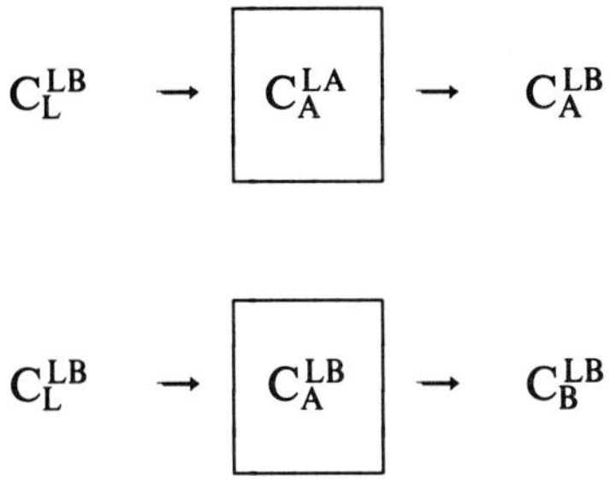

$$C_L^{LB} \quad \rightarrow \quad \boxed{C_A^{LA}} \quad \rightarrow \quad C_A^{LB}$$

$$C_L^{LB} \quad \rightarrow \quad \boxed{C_A^{LB}} \quad \rightarrow \quad C_B^{LB}$$

Fig. 1.9. Bootstrapping a compiler to a second machine.

Using C_L^{LB} to produce C_B^{LB}, a compiler for L on B, is now a two-step process, as shown in Fig. 1.9. We first run C_L^{LB} through C_A^{LA} to produce C_A^{LB}, a cross-compiler for L which runs on machine A but produces code for machine B. Then we run C_L^{LB} through this cross-compiler to produce the desired compiler for L that runs on machine B and produces object code for B.

Bibliographic Notes

As the division line between assemblers and compilers is not a sharp one, pronouncing a particular piece of software "the first compiler" is somewhat akin to determining "the first human species." The first compilers were developed during the mid-to-late 1940's and the early 1950's, and the reader interested in the history of the subject is referred to Sammet [1968, 1972], Bauer [1974], and Knuth and Trabb Pardo [1976].

There are a number of widely-circulated books covering various aspects of compiler design. These include Randell and Russell [1964], Hopgood [1969], Cocke and Schwartz [1970], Gries [1971], Bauer and Eickel [1974], and Lee [1974].

Some of the mathematics underlying compiler design is covered in Aho and Ullman [1972b, 1973a] and Lewis, Rosenkrantz, and Stearns [1976]. Rosen [1967] and Pollack [1972] are compendia of fundamental papers in the field.

Feldman and Gries [1968] survey the early compiler-compilers. Some of the more popular systems described in the literature are BMCC (Brooker *et al.* [1963], Rosen [1964]), META (Schorre [1964]), TGS (Cheatham [1965]), TMG (McClure [1965]), COGENT (Reynolds [1965]), XPL (McKeeman, Horning, and Wortman [1970]), and CDL (Koster [1974]).

CHAPTER 2

Programming
Languages

This chapter reviews many of the basic constructs found in high-level programming languages. Most of this chapter should be familiar to those who have experience with several different programming languages.

2.1 High-Level Programming Languages

A programming language is a notation with which people can communicate algorithms to computers and to one another. Hundreds of programming languages exist. They differ in their degree of closeness to natural or mathematical language on one hand and to machine language on the other. They differ also in the type of problem for which they are best suited. Some of the aspects of high-level languages which make them preferable to machine or assembly language are the following.

1. *Ease of understanding.* A high-level language program is generally easier to read, write, and prove correct than is an assembly-language program, because a high-level language usually provides a more natural notation for describing algorithms than does assembly language. Even among high-level languages, some are easier to use than others. Part of this has to do with the operators, data structures, and flow of control features provided in a language. A good programming language should provide features for modular design of easy-to-understand programs. Subroutines and powerful operators are essential here, and orderly data structures and the ability to create such structures are important, too. A good language should also enable control flow to be specified in a clean, understandable manner.

2. *Naturalness.* Much of the understandability of a high-level programming language comes from the ease with which one can express an algorithm in that language. Some languages are clearly more suitable than others in this regard for differing problem domains. FORTRAN was designed for numerical and mathematical computations, COBOL for business applications and SNOBOL for string manipulation. One would not write a complex numerical calculation in COBOL or SNOBOL, even though, theoretically, a

26

program written in one of these languages can be simulated, with varying degrees of efficiency, by a program written in any of the other languages.

3. *Portability.* Users must often be able to run their programs on a variety of machines. Languages such as FORTRAN or COBOL have relatively well-defined "standard versions," and programs conforming to the standard should run on any machine. There are pitfalls that come up unexpectedly, however. For example, a programmer using a 40-bit word-length machine may choose 10^{10} for a constant used only as a "very large number." However, if he tries to run his program on a machine with a 32-bit word length, he will find that this constant is too large to fit in one word, and he will not be able to run his program without change. PL/I, with its ability to declare arbitrary precision for constants, avoids this pitfall to some extent, although the hypothetical programmer mentioned above might find his program slowed down when he moved to the 32-bit machine, if arithmetic on constants requiring two words was slower than arithmetic on one-word constants.

4. *Efficiency of use.* This area covers a number of aspects of both program and language design. One would like to be able to translate source programs into efficient object code. One would also like the compilation process itself to be efficient. In both cases, the design of the language can affect how easily the computation can be done. But it is often more important that the programmer be able to implement programs in a way that makes efficient use of his time. To the latter end, a high-level programming language should have facilities for defining data structures, macros, subroutines, and the like. The operating system and programming environment can also be as important as the language in reducing programming time.

No matter what language is being used, certain styles of programming lend themselves to producing readable and well-structured programs. However, particular high-level language features facilitate reliable programming. Some such features are:

- data structures;

- scope rules that allow modifications to be made to a piece of a program without unwittingly affecting other portions of the same program;

- flow-of-control constructs that clearly identify the looping structures in a program;

- subroutines, allowing a program to be designed in small pieces.

A compiler can also assist in producing reliable programs. For example, a compiler could check that the types of operands are compatible, and could often warn the user if there is a possibility that a variable is used before being defined or if an array reference could be out of bounds.

2.2 Definitions of Programming Languages

It would be desirable to have a notation, with the following features, that could be used to define programming languages.

1. A language designer could simply and clearly express what programs are valid and what these programs mean.

2. A programmer could determine what programs he could write and what they do.

3. A compiler designer could determine what source programs a compiler should accept and what object code the compiler should produce for them.

Unfortunately, no widely accepted notation of this nature exists. This section mentions some of the difficulties in finding such a notation.

Syntax

A program in any language can be viewed as a string of characters chosen from some set, or *alphabet,* of characters. But how do we prescribe which strings of characters represent valid programs? The rules that tell us whether a string is a valid program or not are called the *syntax* of the language. It is often almost impossible to state concisely and precisely what strings are valid programs, just as it is hard to state which sentences of English are proper and which are not. However, in Chapters 3 through 6 we shall find that certain notations, namely regular expressions and context-free grammars, are useful not only for specifying much of the syntax of programming languages, but also for helping in the construction of their compilers.

Semantics

Once we know that we have a valid program, how do we specify what the program does? It is essential to know what a program means if we are to compile it faithfully into a machine language program that does what the programmer expects. The rules that give meaning to programs are called the *semantics* of the programming language. The semantics of a programming language is much harder to specify than is its syntax. No completely satisfactory means for specifying semantics in a way that helps construct a correct compiler for the language has been found.

Example 2.1. To see some of the subtleties that enter into the specification of the meaning of a language, consider some of the possible meanings that can be attached to the following for-statement, written in an ALGOL-like syntax.

for I := 1 step 10−J until 10∗J do J := J+1

One possible meaning, as in PL/I, is that the limit 10∗J and increment 10−J are to be evaluated once before the loop. Then, if J = 5 before the loop, we would run through ten times and exit. A completely different meaning occurs if we are required to evaluate the limit and increment every time through the loop. Then the loop would never terminate if J = 5 initially, as the increment would soon become negative, driving I down, while J increased.

A third interpretation is given by languages, such as ALGOL, which prescribe that when the increment is negative, the test made for termination of the loop is not I>10∗J, but rather I<10∗J. In that case, the loop would terminate as soon as J reached 11. From this example we can see that the language designer, the user, and the compiler designer must all agree on what a language means, or otherwise chaos would result. □

This example may seem far-fetched, and the reader may argue that a programmer writing such a statement deserves whatever he gets. Yet there are other details of programming languages where knowledge of the exact semantics of the language is essential in everyday use. For example, in Section 2.11 we shall discuss parameter-passing conventions, and the convention used in a given language must be understood clearly by anyone using subroutines. We must, therefore, consider some of the possible approaches to the specification of semantics of languages that have been proposed.

1. *Interpretive* (or *operational*) *semantics.* A machine language has its semantics defined by the computer itself. A machine language program "means" exactly what the computer does when the program is run. With a high-level language, however, we cannot let the computer define the language's semantics, since we cannot "run programs and see" until we have a compiler; we cannot have a compiler we know is correct until we have defined what programs mean. The interpretive approach to defining the semantics of programming languages is to postulate an abstract machine and provide rules for executing programs on this abstract machine. These rules then define the meaning of programs the way the real machine did for assembly language programs. Usually, the abstract machine is characterized

by a *state,* consisting of all data objects, their values, and the program with its program counter (indicator of the "current" step of the program). The semantic rules specify how the state is transformed by the various programming language constructs. The Vienna Definition Language (VDL), described in Wegner [1972], is one example of a language definition facility based on interpretive semantics.

2. *Translation.* The translation of assembly language into machine language, being so direct and comprehensible, forms a useful semantic specification for an assembly language. To an extent, such an approach can be carried over to higher-level languages. We can give rules which associate with each valid program a sentence in a language whose semantics we already understand. For example, we could use a mathematical language such as lambda calculus, or we could use a specific machine language as the well-understood language. In the latter case, the compiler for the language on that specific machine becomes the semantic definition of the language.

3. *Axiomatic definition.* We can define rules that relate the data before and after execution of each program construct. We can then use the rules to prove theorems about the input-output relation of a program. This approach has the advantage that it can be used to define semantics for a part rather than for all of a language. It also has been widely studied in relation to proofs of program correctness.

4. *Extensible definition.* In this approach we define certain primitive operations and define the meaning of the language in terms of these primitives. LISP is the major example of this type of language definition.

5. *Mathematical* (or *denotational*) *semantics.* Mathematical objects corresponding to programs are defined, and rules are given translating programs to these abstract objects.

In this book we shall not attempt to define programming-language semantics formally at all, since none of these methods has gained universal acceptance. Rather we shall introduce terminology that lets us talk about the most common choices for the meaning of common programming constructs. For us, then, the definition of a programming language will be a series of choices made by the language designer. To help us think about such choices, we shall take an overview of programming languages from the point of view that programming languages consist of a hierarchy of concepts. The remaining sections of this chapter will discuss each level of the hierarchy, giving the common options at each level.

The Hierarchical Structure of Programming Languages

A programming language is a notation for specifying a sequence of operations to be carried out on data objects. Both the data objects and the operations can be grouped into a hierarchy that looks like the tree of Fig. 2.1. Not all languages have every one of these features, and some languages, such as ALGOL 68, permit statements to be in expressions. Nevertheless, the units in this hierarchy are so common that they should be familiar to all.

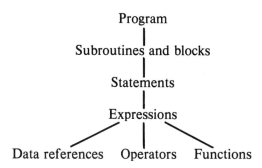

Fig. 2.1. Hierarchy of program elements.

At the top of the hierarchy is the program itself. The program is the basic execution unit. Next comes an entity that can be compiled but not necessarily executed — the subroutine or block. These are units which may have their own data (*local names*). Subroutines differ from blocks by being callable from other portions of a program. Both subroutines and blocks are composed of statements. In turn, statements are fashioned from expressions, which are made up of operators, function calls, and references to data.

Having had this top-down view, we shall now study the hierarchy of elements bottom-up. Our intent is to build an understanding of each construct from an understanding of its constituent parts. The next section covers syntactic issues at all levels, with emphasis on the lowest levels, where they are most evident. The balance of the chapter will discuss semantic issues primarily.

Each construct in a programming language has both a *logical* (abstract) meaning and an *implementation.* The logical meaning is the way we think of the construct in mathematical terms, while the implementation is its representation inside the computer. For a simple example, names denoting reals are, on the logical level, placeholders for real numbers. On the implementation level, they denote a word, or sequence of words, of memory wherein a sequence of bits is kept. These bits are interpreted in a specific way (e.g., sign bit, exponent bits, and mantissa bits) and have a value that is of limited range and precision.

2.3 The Lexical and Syntactic Structure of a Language

Consider a string such as A*B+C. This string contains five symbols that can be grouped together in various ways. For example, this entire string might be considered to be one identifier. More likely, however, it would be considered to be three identifiers separated by two operators and interpreted as (A*B)+C or as A*(B+C). Which of these two is correct depends on the language definition. The lexical structure of a language determines what groups of symbols are to be treated as identifiers and operators. The syntactic structure determines how these lexical constructs are to be grouped together into larger structures called *syntactic categories*.

Alphabets

The set of symbols used in a programming language is called its *character set* or *alphabet*. As with natural languages, there is considerable variety in the alphabets of programming languages. The typical machine language usually has an alphabet of only 0 and 1. Figure 2.2 shows the alphabet sizes of some common programming languages.

Language	Alphabet size	Alphabetic characters	Numeric characters	Others
ALGOL 60	114	52	10	52
COBOL	51	26	10	15
FORTRAN	47	26	10	11
PL/I (60 characters)	60	29	10	21

Fig. 2.2. Alphabet sizes of some common languages.

The FORTRAN alphabet, for example, consists of the 26 upper case characters A, B, ..., Z, the ten digits 0, 1, ..., 9 and eleven other characters: blank, +, −, *, /, =, (,), comma, period, and $.

The reason the ALGOL character set is so large is that it includes not only primitive symbols such as punctuation symbols, brackets, and operators, but also keywords such as **for**, **begin**, and so on. The keywords are considered single symbols in the ALGOL reference language although, in any implementation of ALGOL they would be composed of individual characters from a smaller alphabet.

Tokens

The string representing a program can be partitioned at the lowest level into a sequence of substrings called *tokens*. Each token is a sequence of characters whose significance is possessed collectively rather than individually. While that which is called a token depends on the language at hand, most languages treat the following as tokens:

1. constants, e.g., 1, 2.3, 4.5E6,

2. identifiers, e.g., A, H2035B, SPEED,

3. operator symbols, e.g., $+$, $-$, $**$, $:=$, .EQ.,

4. keywords, e.g., IF, GOTO, SUBROUTINE,

5. punctuation symbols, e.g., parentheses, brackets, comma and semicolon.

Higher Level Constructs

Syntactic structures are groupings of tokens. Most languages contain expressions, which are sequences of operator and operand tokens (constants and identifiers), e.g., $A+2.0*B$. There is considerable variety in the types of expression found in programming languages, and we shall discuss the common forms and their semantics in Section 2.6.

Expressions, together with the assignment operator, punctuation symbols, and keywords, form the building blocks for the higher-level constructs such as statements, blocks, and programs. We shall discuss statement syntax and semantics in Section 2.8 and programs in Section 2.9.

Lexical Conventions

The physical presentation of programs can affect the difficulty of lexical analysis. Some languages, such as FORTRAN, require certain statement elements to be written in restricted positions on the input line. The fixed format is reminiscent of assembly languages, where the position of a token conveyed information regarding its role in the statement. The trend in high-level language design is toward free-format input, allowing statements to be positioned anywhere in the input line. These languages help avoid syntax errors due to improper positioning of tokens and permit source programs to be laid out so that they are easy to read and they show the program structure by their indentation. The cost, in terms of the additional time to compile a free-format language, is negligible.

Blanks are another lexical issue worth mentioning. In some programming languages, such as FORTRAN or ALGOL 68, blanks are not significant except in literal character-string data. They can be added or removed from a program to help improve the program's readability. This treatment of blanks complicates the task of identifying the tokens in a program, as we shall see in Chapter 3. In other languages, blanks are used as token separators, and their presence or absence affects the syntactic structure placed on a program. SNOBOL, for example, uses the blank as the string-concatenation operator.

2.4 Data Elements

One of the basic building blocks of a programming language is the set of primitive data elements to which operators can be applied, and out of which more complex data structures can be built. This section introduces the typical data elements provided by most programming languages. The next section discusses methods of grouping these data elements into data structures and the following section discusses the operators which can be applied to these data elements.

There is considerable variation among programming languages in the sets of basic data elements. The ones commonly found are the following.

1. *Numerical data.* These include integers, reals, complex numbers, and multiple precision versions of these types.

2. *Logical data.* Most languages have a logical (Boolean) data type and/or a bit string data type. Either can be subjected to the logical operations **(and, or, not)**.

3. *Character data.* Some languages permit characters and strings of characters as a data type. These strings may be of fixed length or, in more versatile languages, their length may vary during computation.

4. *Pointers.* These are data elements whose values are other data elements. While the syntax may vary, the general idea is that we may write statement P:=**addr**(X) to mean that P will now point to X, that is, P's value will be the variable X. We may then write Y := *P to mean that the value of Y is to become the value of the object pointed to by P (X in this case). Pointers are useful in allowing the programmer to create his own data structures, although their indiscriminate use can make programs hard to read or debug, just as the indiscriminate use of goto's does.

5. *Labels.* In some languages, data whose value is a statement or position in the program is permitted.

We assume that the reader is familiar with the use and usual computer implementation of these basic data elements. Figure 2.3 shows some of the data types that may be defined in four common programming languages.

ALGOL
        integer, real, Boolean
FORTRAN
        integer, real, double precision (real), complex, logical
PASCAL
        integer, real, Boolean, char, scalar, subrange, pointer
PL/I
        number (with four orthogonal attributes)
                mode: real or complex
                scale: fixed-point or floating-point
                base: decimal or binary
                precision: number of digits
        character string, bit string, pointer,
        area, offset, label, entry, format, task, event

Fig. 2.3. Elementary data types.

Identifiers and Names

On the logical level, each programming language manipulates and uses *objects* (or *values*), which are data elements such as integers or reals, or are more complex items such as arrays or procedures. It is customary to view the computer as consisting of an abstract *store,* consisting of cells in which a value of any type may be kept. Each cell has a *name,* which is usually a variable of the programming language. Each name, in turn, is denoted by an *identifier,* which is a string of characters. The set of legal identifiers varies from language to language; letters followed by sequences of letters and/or digits is typical. The same identifier may denote different names at different places in the program or at different times during execution. For example, WINK may be an identifier found in declarations in several different subroutines, and in each subroutine a different name is denoted by WINK.

The distinction between identifiers and names may appear subtle and, in fact, we shall often refer to identifier WINK as a name if the particular name denoted by this instance of WINK is understood or irrelevant. However, there are times when the distinction must be made, for example, when we discuss scopes of names in Section 2.10.

Each name possesses a value and attributes. On the logical or abstract level, a value is the contents of the placeholder with that name. This value may be numerical, or it could be an input-output relationship if the name is a procedure, for example. The attributes of a name determine the possible values that the name may have, the operations that may be applied to the value, and the effect of those operations. We shall discuss the important kinds of attributes shortly.

On the implementation level, a name is represented by a portion of the computer's memory, a bit, byte, word, or several words. This location contains a sequence of bits indicating the value of the name, and sometimes a *data descriptor* (or *dope vector*), which indicates how the bit string is to be decoded. The data descriptor is necessary for data whose size, shape, or type changes while the computer is running. Examples are variable length character strings and arrays whose size is adjustable.

It is important to note that a name may represent different locations at different times as the program is running. For example, a recursive procedure in which an integer NUM is declared may have several instances of NUM in memory at once during the running of the program. The name NUM refers to the location of the most recently activated instance.

Conversely, the same location may have several names. An example occurs when procedure F(X) is called by F(A). The name A of the calling procedure may denote the same location as name X of F, depending on the parameter-passing convention of the language (see Section 2.11). Another example is locations in FORTRAN COMMON blocks, which may have different names in several subroutines.

Attributes

The attributes of a name determine its properties. The most important attribute of a name is its *type*, which determines what values it may have, possibly the way its value is to be represented in the computer, and the operations to which it may be subjected. Figure 2.3 showed the different kinds of values numerical data could have in PL/I. There are also other attributes in PL/I which affect the way in which memory is used to represent data. An example is the ALIGNED attribute, which causes the datum to be allocated memory beginning at a word boundary (for rapid access to the item).

Other attributes of a name may determine its *scope*, that is, when its value is accessible. For example, the scope of an ALGOL name is the block or procedure in which it is declared, and it has a memory location only when that block or procedure is being executed.

Declarations

The attributes of a name are determined implicitly, explicitly, or in some cases by default. For example, in FORTRAN, any identifier beginning with I, J, . . . , N is implicitly an integer. Generally, the attributes of a name can be set by means of an explicit declaration. For example, numbers in

PL/I can have combinations of four kinds of attributes — mode, scale, base and precision (see Fig. 2.3). The declaration

DECLARE A DECIMAL FLOAT(10)

declares A to be of scale floating-point, in the decimal base and of precision 10 (decimal) digits. By default, the mode is real rather than complex, since no declaration of a mode was given. The value of A might be represented by eight bytes of memory (as in the compiler for PL/C, e.g.), with portions of those bytes set aside for the sign, the exponent, and the fractional part.

In any implementation, arithmetic operations on A will have to take into account the fact that this representation is being used. The compiler must be capable of generating operations on data with any combination of the attributes permissible for the language at hand. It must also be able to generate conversions of data from one set of attributes to another and to cause these conversions to be performed when an operation on two items with different attributes is required. Thus, when many attributes are permitted in a language, even compiling arithmetic expressions becomes a nontrivial task.

Binding Attributes to Names

The act of associating attributes to a name is often referred to as *binding* the attributes to the name. Most binding of attributes is done during compilation (*at compile time*) when the attributes become known as the compiler reads declarations. This situation is called *static binding*. Most languages allow only static binding. Some languages, such as SNOBOL, allow *dynamic binding,* or binding of attributes while the program is running (*at run time*). (Throughout this book "static" means "done at compile time" and "dynamic" means "done at run time.")

If attributes are bound to a name by a declaration, then those attributes are fixed in advance and cannot be changed while the program is running. In such languages (e.g., PASCAL) it is possible to do extensive *type checking* at compile time, making sure that no operations performed are semantically meaningless (e.g., multiplying together two pointers). In addition, static binding of attributes generally permits a more efficient implementation of operators, since we do not have to examine data at run time to see what machine operations to perform.

In APL, for example, dynamic binding of attributes to names is permitted. It is possible to use a name as an integer on one line and in the next line as an array. SETL is another example of a language using dynamic binding. There, names can have values which are sets or lists, as well as the usual primitive data types. When dynamic binding is used, operations on data may involve a check to determine what the current type of the name is. In this case, all names must have data descriptors as part of their values, and the implementation of operations often involves a subroutine call whose first action is to examine the data descriptors of its arguments to see how the operator is to be applied. Thus, dynamic binding of attributes to names can be of convenience to the user but can result in a less efficient implementation than if static binding were required. In languages with dynamic binding, code-optimization techniques that attempt to replace dynamic checks by equivalent static ones are particularly important, but efficient ways of doing so are still in the research stage.

2.5 Data Structures

In this section we shall consider some basic data structures on both the logical and implementation level. On the logical level, a data structure is a set of primitive data elements and other data structures, together with a set of structural relations among its components. Often, a data structure is defined recursively. Here are two examples.

1. *Lists.* On the logical level, a list is either null or a data element followed by a list. The basic operations on lists are the insertion, deletion or substitution of an element, and the determination of whether a given element is on the list.

2. *Trees.* A tree T can be recursively defined as a collection of elements (*nodes*) with the following structural relationship.

   a) One element r is called the *root* of T.

   b) The remaining nodes can be partitioned into $k \geqslant 0$ subtrees $T_1, T_2, \ldots, T_k$ such that the root of T_i is a *child* of r.

Often, an order is ascribed to the children of each node. The order is indicated by listing the children of each node from left to right in the sequence in which they are to appear.

Other common data structures are arrays, queues, stacks, strings, and graphs. We assume that the reader has encountered these data structures before, at least on the logical level.

A number of functions are commonly associated with data structures. There are functions which create instances of the data structure (*constructors*), dismantle data structures to make their storage area available again (*destructors*), and access data structures (*selectors*).

Associated with a data element in a structure is its name, its value, and its relative position in the structure. Given a name, we might want to refer to either its value or its position. For example, if A is an array, then A[I] is a name for one of its elements. In the assignment B := A[I], the name

A[I] refers to the value of A[I], while in A[I] := C, the name A[I] refers to the position of the I*th* element of A.

Let us now take up the implementation of data structures by a compiler. An implementation of a language on a particular computer is invariably an approximation to the logical definition of the language. A real computer imposes limits on how large integers, pointers, arrays, strings, and so on, can be, while often no such limit is implied by the logical definition of these elements. Even less obvious is the effect of differing word sizes on the layout of data structures in memory. For example, in many machines, data must be aligned with certain byte or word boundaries, forcing data elements to have slightly different relative positions in different implementations.

Arrays

An array is a collection of elements of some fixed type, laid out in a *k*-dimensional rectangular structure. A measure of the distance along each dimension is called an *index,* or *subscript,* and the elements are found at integer points from some lower limit to some upper limit, along each dimension. For example, ANS ("standard") FORTRAN permits arrays only of one to three dimensions, with a lower limit of 1 for each dimension. Many other languages permit arbitrary upper and lower limits for each index and arbitrary numbers of dimensions, although each implementation imposes a limit on these quantities.

An element of an array is named by giving the name of the array and the values of its indices, as $A[i_1, ..., i_k]$. The upper and lower bounds and the total number of elements in an array may be known at compile time (a *fixed-size* array) or determined at run time (an *adjustable* array). We shall consider fixed-size arrays first, since their implementation is easier.

a) *Fixed-size one-dimensional arrays.* If the size of the array is known at compile time, then it is expedient to implement the array as a block of consecutive words in memory. If it takes *k* memory units† to store each data element, then A[i], the *i*th element of array A, begins in location

$$BASE + k*(i-LOW)$$

where LOW is the lower bound on the subscript and BASE is the lowest numbered memory unit allocated to the array. That is, BASE is the location of A[LOW].

---

† A *memory unit* is the amount of storage by which addresses are counted, i.e., a word in a word-addressed memory or a byte in a byte-addressed memory.

A data descriptor for a one-dimensional array would contain the following information:

i)   the data type (i.e., one-dimensional array),

ii) the element type (e.g., integer or character),

iii) the number of memory units per element,

iv) the lower limit on subscript range, and

v)   the upper limit on subscript range.

In the case where everything is of fixed size, all this information is available in the symbol table at compile time. Thus the compiler can generate a reference to any element of an array by determining its offset from the base of the array.

b) *Fixed-size multidimensional arrays.* Consider the 2×3 array A shown in Fig. 2.4.

A[1,1]	A[1,2]	A[1,3]
A[2,1]	A[2,2]	A[2,3]

Fig. 2.4. Two-dimensional array.

A two-dimensional array is normally stored in one of two forms, either *row-major* (row-by-row) or *column major* (column-by-column). FORTRAN uses column-major form; PL/I uses row-major form. Figure 2.5 shows the implementation of A in (a) row-major form and (b) column-major form.

```
A[1,1] ⎫                    A[1,1] ⎫ First column
A[1,2] ⎬ First row          A[2,1] ⎭
A[1,3] ⎭                    A[1,2] ⎫ Second column
A[2,1] ⎫                    A[2,2] ⎭
A[2,2] ⎬ Second row         A[1,3] ⎫ Third column
A[2,3] ⎭                    A[2,3] ⎭

    (a) Row-major              (b) Column major
```

Fig. 2.5. Representing a two-dimensional array.

Another implementation of two-dimensional arrays is by *edge-vectors*. In this implementation each row is represented as a one-dimensional array. The two-dimensional array is represented by a one-dimensional array of pointers to the arrays for the rows.

In the case of a two-dimensional array stored in row-major form, with lower limit 1 in each dimension, the location for $A[i, j]$ can be calculated by the formula

$$\text{BASE} + k*((i-1)*r + j - 1)$$

where k is the number of memory units per element and r is the number of elements per row. In column-major form the formula is

$$\text{BASE} + k*((j - 1)*c + i - 1)$$

where c is the number of elements per column.

We can generalize row- or column-major form to many dimensions and to arrays whose lower limits are other than 1. The generalization of row-major form is to store the elements in such a way that, as we scan down the block of storage, the rightmost subscripts appear to vary fastest, like the numbers on an odometer. Column major form generalizes to the opposite arrangement, with the leftmost subscripts varying fastest. The general formulas for the location of an element in a multidimensional array stored in row-major or column-major form can be found in Section 8.1. The edge-vector representation can similarly be generalized to many dimensions. A k-dimensional array is represented by a one-dimensional array of pointers to representations for $(k-1)$-dimensional arrays.

c) *Adjustable arrays.* Many languages, such as ALGOL and PL/I, but not FORTRAN, permit the size of arrays to be specified dynamically, that is, at run time. APL allows even the number of dimensions to vary at run time. In such situations, a dynamic storage allocation scheme, as discussed in Section 2.12, is needed to provide the necessary storage. The accessing formulas are the same as for fixed-size arrays, but the upper and lower limits are part of the data descriptor, which must be found with the array elements themselves.

Record Structures

An important class of data structures is the record structure, found in COBOL or PL/I, for example. Logically, a record structure is a tree, with the fields (second-level structures) of the record being the children of the root, the subfields (third-level structures) being children of these, and so on. Perhaps the paradigm of a record structure is a mailing list. Suppose we wish to store the names and addresses of a collection of people, as in

MR. ALAN TURING
172 THE GRADUATE COLLEGE
PRINCETON, N. J. 08540

A PL/I structure to accommodate these names and addresses might be declared as follows:

```
1 FRIENDS(1000),
     2 NAME,
               3 TITLE CHARACTER(6),
               3 FIRST CHARACTER(15),
               3 LAST CHARACTER(15),
     2 ADDRESS,
               3 STREET CHARACTER(30),
               3 TOWN CHARACTER(15),
               3 STATE CHARACTER(15),
               3 ZIP FIXED DECIMAL(5);
```

Record structures are implemented as a block of memory. To determine how much storage is necessary, and what the accessing functions for the various fields are, we must determine the *width* and *offset* for each field. Assuming memory units are bytes, a field of characters has width equal to the number of characters. In general, any field which is a primitive data element will have width equal to the amount of storage needed for that data element. Assuming one word of four bytes is sufficient for 5 decimal digits, the field ZIP above might be given one word. If so, it has width 4.

The offset of a field f is the sum of the widths of the preceding fields contained along with f in the field of next higher level than f. Thus, TITLE has offset zero from the beginning of NAME, the field of next higher level containing TITLE, while LAST has offset 21, the sum of the widths of TITLE and FIRST. The width of a field that is composed of subfields is the sum of the widths of those subfields. Note that if a subfield is an array, its width is the width of one element multiplied by the number of elements in the array. Continuing our example, we find the NAME field has width 36, and the ADDRESS field has width 64. The offset of ADDRESS is 36 from the field FRIEND. Each FRIEND has width 100, and there are 1000 of them, for a total of 100000 bytes of storage.

The data descriptor for a record structure must include the offset for each field and must include the width of each field that is an array. Also included is the data type for each field consisting of primitive data elements. Usually this data descriptor need not be included with the structure.

We shall not give detailed accessing formulas for record elements here. Sections 8.5 and 8.6 contain algorithms for record accessing. Here let us content ourselves with an example.

Example 2.2. Suppose we had the assignment

$$X = FRIEND(123).ADDRESS.STATE$$

That is, we want the state of friend number 123. Since the FRIEND array begins with FRIEND(1), the location of the beginning of FRIEND(123) will be BASE (the first location of the array) plus the product 100 (the width of a FRIEND) times (123 − 1), that is, BASE + 12200. Then we must add the offset for ADDRESS relative to the beginning of a FRIEND. The offset of ADDRESS is 36. Next, we add the offset of STATE relative to the beginning of ADDRESS. That offset is 45. Thus, the desired string is in bytes BASE + 12281 through BASE + 12295. □

Character Strings

These are really one-dimensional arrays whose elements are characters. They may thus be represented as arrays. If a language, like SNOBOL, does not require a declared limit on the length of a string, then dynamic storage allocation must be used. In a language like PL/I, where strings may vary only up to some predetermined limit, a block of storage of the maximum possible size may be allocated for each name whose value is a character string. A data descriptor consisting of the number of characters currently in the string is essential and must appear with the string if the length varies.

List Structures

LISP is an example of a language that allows arbitrary list structures. These lists are formed from elements which are records with two fields, called CAR and CDR for traditional reasons.† Each of these fields contains either an *atom* (primitive data type such as integer or character), the null pointer, or the address of another record.

For example, the linear list A, B, C can be created by using three records. CAR of each contains A, B, and C, respectively. CDR of the first points to the second, CDR of the second points to the third, and CDR of the third has a null pointer, as shown in Fig. 2.6.

Trees can be represented by taking one record for each node. CAR of a node has a pointer to the leftmost child, or a null pointer if there are no children. CDR has a pointer to the *right sibling,* the node with the same parent and immediately to the right, if there is one. While this arrangement may appear awkward, one can move down the tree easily. For

---

† CAR and CDR stand for "contents of the address (resp. decrement) register." This terminology refers to particular collections of bit positions in the memory words of an IBM 7090 computer.

CAR CDR

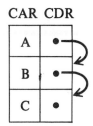

Fig. 2.6. Array representation of LISP list structures.

example, to go to the second child of a node, follow CAR, then CDR.

The implementation of this sort of list structure is not difficult if one thinks of all memory as an array of records. The record has four fields; two are CAR and CDR, and the others are bits telling whether given CAR's and CDR's are atoms or pointers. It is also useful to have a bit that may be used for the purposes of *garbage collection*. That is, as a LISP program runs, it tends to use and discard records, causing it to run out of space even though not all of memory may be in use. A garbage collection scans all records, determining which are in use, and making an *available space list* of those which may be reused. We refer the reader to Knuth [1968] or Horowitz and Sahni [1976] for algorithms for garbage collection.

Stacks

A stack is a linear list that we operate on only at the beginning or *top* end. We may *push* a new element onto the stack, making it the first element on the list. For example, pushing D onto the list A, B, C yields the list D, A, B, C. We may also *pop* elements from the top by removing them. If we pop the stack A, B, C, we get B, C.

There are two ways that stacks appear in programming languages. First, a language like PL/I permits the programmer to define stacks as a data type using the CONTROLLED attribute and the ALLOCATE (push) and FREE (pop) operations. In PL/I, the elements of a stack will appear in available storage, with pointers linking them. If we know in advance the limit to which a stack will grow, we can use a simpler implementation. Use a block of storage in which an array of the maximum number of elements can be put. Use a pointer to one of these elements to indicate the current top element. Push an element onto the stack by moving the pointer to the next higher place and putting the element there. Pop an element by moving the pointer to the next lower place.

There are also stacks that the user cannot explicitly manipulate in many programming languages. Virtually any language that allows recursive procedures uses a *run-time stack* on which the data associated with procedures is kept. Run-time stacks will be considered in Sections 2.12, 10.1 and 10.2.

2.6 Operators

The richness of a language is determined by its operators. This section discusses some of the operators found in many high-level languages.

Arithmetic Operators

We are all familiar with the arithmetic operators $+$, $-$, $*$, $/$ and $**$ or $\uparrow$ (for exponentiation). The operator $-$ can be either *unary* (taking one argument, as in $-X$) or *binary* (taking two arguments, as in $X-Y$). The other operators are binary only, although some languages permit unary $+$.

A unary operator may precede its operand, as unary minus does, in which case it is called a *prefix* operator. In some cases, a unary operator may follow its operand, and we call it *postfix*. For example, the language C allows $++$ as both a prefix and postfix unary operator; when X and Y are integer variables, $X = ++Y$ means the same as

$$Y = Y + 1$$
$$X = Y$$

and $X = Y++$ means the same as

$$X = Y$$
$$Y = Y + 1$$

A binary operator can come before, between, or after its operands, in which case it is called *prefix, infix,* or *postfix,* respectively. Virtually all binary operators in programming languages are infix, but when we study translation of programming languages in Chapter 7 we shall see the importance of postfix forms.

Arithmetic Expressions

Operators can be composed to create expressions. Typical rules used to create expressions from operands and operators are:

1. A single data reference is an expression. A data reference is just the name of a data element, for example, an identifier, a constant, or an array element name like A[I].

2. If θ is a binary infix operator and E_1 and E_2 are expressions, then $E_1 \, \theta \, E_2$ is an expression.

3. If θ is a unary prefix operator and E is an expression, then θE is an expression. If θ is unary postfix, then $E\theta$ is an expression.

4. If E is an expression, then so is (E).

Thus, for example, A and B are each expressions because they are names. A + B and −A are expressions by rules (2) and (3), respectively. (A + B) is an expression by rule (4); −A ∗ (A + B) is an expression by rule (2) again.

Relational Operators

A relational operator takes a pair of expressions as operands and returns a logical value, **true** or **false**. There are six common relational operators: $\leqslant$, $<$, $=$, $\neq$, $\geqslant$ and $>$.

Logical Operators

A logical or Boolean operator has arguments with logical values, and the operator itself returns a logical value. The logical operators **and, or, not**, and "exclusive or" are common in many programming languages. Relational operators and logical operators can be combined with arithmetic operators arbitrarily, as long as the types of results match the required types of operands. For example,

$$(A + B) \textbf{ and } (X < Y)$$

is a legal expression in some language only if in that language the integer sum A + B may be interpreted as a logical value.

String Operators

Concatenation, substring formation, and pattern matching are the principal operations on strings. PL/I, SNOBOL, and text editors are examples of languages permitting operations on strings.

The *concatenation* operator maps a pair of strings into the single string formed by juxtaposing the first and the second strings. ‖ is the symbol used in PL/I for concatenation; e.g., $'abc' \, \| \, 'de' = 'abcde'$. Also used is a substring operator that produces a certain consecutive portion of a string. For example, the substring of length three beginning at position two of $'abcde'$ is $'bcd'$. In connection with substring computations, SNOBOL in particular has elaborate pattern-matching operators to define the desired substring.

Associativity and Precedence

When we combine operators to form expressions, the order in which the operators are to be applied may not be obvious. For example, $a + b + c$ can be interpreted as $((a + b) + c)$ or as $(a + (b + c))$. We say that $+$ is *left-associative* if operands are grouped left to right as in $((a + b) + c)$. We say it is *right-associative* if it groups in the opposite direction, as in $(a + (b + c))$.

The expression $a + b * c$ can also be grouped in these two ways, but the associativities of $+$ and $*$ do not tell us which grouping is to be preferred. We therefore need the notion of *precedence levels* to indicate which operands are allowed to group their operands first. Normally, $*$ is given higher precedence than $+$, meaning that $a + b * c$ is grouped by first finding operands to the left and right of $*$, then doing the same for $+$. That is, the grouping $(a + (b * c))$ is correct.

Every language ascribes some precedence level and associativity to its operators. APL uses the simple rule that all operators have the same precedence level and the operators are collectively right-associative in the absence of parentheses. Thus, $a * (b + c) * d + e$ would be evaluated as $(a * ((b + c) * (d + e)))$.

The precedence levels of operators in ALGOL, FORTRAN, and PL/I are shown in Fig. 2.7. The operators are listed in order of precedence, from highest to lowest, with operators of equal precedence grouped together. The languages differ in the rules for the associativity of certain operators. ALGOL evaluates all binary operators left-associatively. FORTRAN lets the compiler designer choose the associativity, and PL/I evaluates all binary operators left-associatively, except for exponentiation, which is right-associative, i.e., $a ** b ** c$ means $(a ** (b ** c))$.

Different operators on the same precedence level are treated as if they were the same operator, that is, they are normally associated left to right. Thus $a + b - c / d * e$ is evaluated as $((a + b) - ((c / d) * e))$. Beware of the treatment of unary minus. In many languages (such as FORTRAN and PL/I†), $-I**2$ means $-(I**2)$, while in some (such as ALGOL 68), the unary minus binds more tightly than exponentiation.

Algebraic Properties of Operators

Many operators obey certain algebraic laws, which make some simplifications of expressions by the compiler possible and enable the compiler to produce more efficient object code than would be possible otherwise. In ordinary arithmetic, addition and multiplication are *commutative*,

---

† In PL/I the operators at the highest precedence level in Fig. 2.7 bind from right to left.

$$
\begin{array}{ccc}
\uparrow & ** & **,\ \text{unary}\ +,\ \text{unary}\ -,\ \neg \\
\times, /, \div & *, / & *, / \\
+, - & +, - & +, - \\
<, =, >, \leqslant, \neq, \geqslant & \left.\begin{cases}.\text{LT}.,.\text{EQ}.,.\text{GT}., \\ .\text{LE}.,.\text{NE}.,.\text{GE}.\end{cases}\right. & \| \\
\neg & .\text{NOT}. & \left\{\begin{matrix}<, =, >, <=, >=, \\ \neg<, \neg=, \neg>\end{matrix}\right\} \\
\wedge & .\text{AND}. & \\
\vee & .\text{OR}. & \& \\
\supset & & | \\
\equiv & &
\end{array}
$$

ALGOL　　　　　FORTRAN　　　　　PL/I

Fig. 2.7. Operator precedences.

meaning that $E_1 + E_2 = E_2 + E_1$ for any expressions E_1 and E_2, and likewise for multiplication. Addition and multiplication are also *associative,* meaning $(E_1 + E_2) + E_3 = E_1 + (E_2 + E_3)$. Also, multiplication *distributes* over addition, meaning $E_1 * (E_2 + E_3) = E_1 * E_2 + E_1 * E_3$.

On a real computer, the commutative laws usually hold (although there are exceptions). The associative and distributive laws, on the other hand, rarely hold for computer arithmetic. For example, $(a + b) + c$ may not give the same result as $a + (b + c)$, because an overflow may occur in one expression but not the other. Also one ordering of the operations may cause the loss of many significant digits while the other does not. Nevertheless, many languages permit arbitrary reordering of computations using the associative and commutative laws, unless the user specifically prohibits it. For example, in FORTRAN, parentheses must be used to force expressions to be evaluated in a particular order.

Other Operators

Languages provide a variety of other operators besides the arithmetic, relational, and logical ones we have studied. The most commonly used operator by far is assignment, which we discuss in the next section. Other important operators include:

1. *Conditionals.* An assignment like A := **if** B **then** C **else** D in ALGOL assigns A the value of C or D, if B is true or false, respectively.

2. *Selectors.* The primary example is the subscripting operator, usually denoted by enclosing a list of array indices in parentheses. Brackets instead of parentheses are used in ALGOL and some other languages to distinguish

an array element name from a procedure call. We shall use brackets to indicate subscripts, except in cases where we are talking about a particular language that uses parentheses. Another important example of a selector is the dot in PL/I, used to combine field names in record structures.

Note that operators like subscripting and conditionals have a syntax unlike the usual binary infix notation. In particular, the conditional takes three arguments, and we call it a *ternary* operator. The subscripting operator is *variadic,* or *polyadic,* meaning that it may take any number of operands — one array name and the rest subscripts. Variadic operators require careful treatment in compilation, and it is useful to think of subscripting as consisting of one operator that attaches the array name to the complete list of subscripts and to consider that there is a list-forming operator, which combines a single subscript with a list of subscripts to form a longer list. Section 8.1 discusses subscripting in more detail.

Coercion of Types

If a programming language permits operators to have operands with differing types, as most do, then the language must provide rules to specify what the type of the result is. The translation of the operator, which the compiler must provide, includes any necessary conversions from one type to another, and this implied change in type is called a *coercion.* If the language does not permit some operator to have operands of mixed types, then the compiler must detect the situation when it occurs and produce an error message.

Implementation of Operators

Many of the common operators on primitive data types are implemented by corresponding machine operations. These normally include the arithmetic operators on integers and reals, and the logical operators on Boolean values. Relational operators are often implemented by comparison instructions and conditional jumps. Other operators require sequences of several machine steps or subroutine calls. These include string-processing operators and arithmetic operators on long operands or complex numbers. On small machines, even multiplication and division may require implementation by subroutines. The variability of instruction repertoires from machine to machine makes it difficult to find general strategies for code generation. In Chapter 15 we shall have more to say about the implementation of operators when we discuss code generation.

2.7 Assignment

Assignment is by far the most common operation appearing in programs. Perhaps this fact partially explains the varying syntax for this operator. Figure 2.8 summarizes the assignment operators used in various languages. In this book, unless we are talking about a specific language, we shall use :=
to denote the assignment operator. This enables us to use = unambiguously for the equality relation.

ALGOL   A := B
APL   A ← B
BASIC   LET A = B
COBOL   MOVE B TO A
FORTRAN   A = B

Fig. 2.8. Various forms of the assignment operator.

l- and r-values

We have seen that the location and value represented by a name are two distinct concepts. This is most apparent in a simple assignment A := B, whose meaning is "put the value of B in the location denoted by A." That is, even though A and B have no distinguishing marks, the position of B on the right side of the assignment symbol tells us that its value is meant. Similarly, the position of A on the left tells us that its location is meant. Thus we refer to the value associated with a name as its *r-value,* the *r* standing for "right," and we call the location denoted by a name its *l-value,* the *l* standing for "left."

We can determine the *l-* and *r*-values of expressions as follows. In most languages, although there are exceptions to be discussed subsequently, an expression consisting of a single name has the same *l-* and *r*-value as that name. The *r*-value of an expression with operators is the value produced by applying the operators just as one would expect. However, not every expression has an *l*-value. For example, A+B is rarely permitted on the left side of an assignment statement. In general, an expression has an *l*-value only if it denotes a location. Some additional examples should clarify the matter.

Example 2.3.

1. Every name has an *l*-value, namely the location or locations reserved for its value.

2. If A is an array name, the *l*-value of A[I] is the location or locations reserved for the I*th* element of the array. The *r*-value of A[I] is the value stored there.

3. The constant 2 has an *r*-value but no *l*-value. Note that 2 does not represent memory location 2 in a typical programming language.

4. If P is a pointer, its *r*-value is the location to which P points and its *l*-value is the location in which the value of P itself is stored. □

Two interesting exceptions to these generalities are BLISS and ALGOL 68. In BLISS a name always denotes an *l*-value on both the left and right sides of an assignment statement. The unary prefix . operator produces the *r*-value of a given *l*-value, so to add B to C and assign the result to A we must write A ← .B+.C. The assignment A ← B sets the *r*-value of A equal to the *l*-value of B, i.e., it makes A point to B.

ALGOL 68 makes the distinction between the *l*-value and *r*-value of a variable by requiring every variable to have a mode which begins with the word **ref** (for reference). For example, an integer variable has the mode **ref int** and is said to *refer to an object of mode* **int**. In an integer assignment, the left side must be, or be convertible to, an object of mode **ref int**. The right side must be, or be convertible to, an object of mode **int**.

Thus an integer variable in itself represents only its *l*-value. If that variable is used on the right side of an assignment where its *r*-value is needed, then a type conversion automatically takes place, converting its mode from **ref int** to **int**. This coercion is called *dereferencing*.

Implementation of Assignment

One of the many ways in which a compiler can implement the assignment A := B is the following:

1. The compiler generates code to compute the *r*-value of B into some register *r*.

2. If the data types of A and B are incompatible, the compiler generates code to convert the type of B to a type appropriate for A.

3. If necessary, the compiler generates code to determine the *l*-value of A. For most languages and computers, no code is needed here if A is of primitive type.

4. Finally the compiler generates code to store the contents of register *r* into the *l*-value of A.

Example 2.4. Suppose we have the assignment X[I] := Y[J], and our computer is one in which memory units are bytes, with four bytes per word. Suppose also that X and Y are integer arrays in fixed locations, whose indices start at zero and whose elements require one word each. Then the r-value of Y[J] can be computed by a sequence such as†

```
LOAD    J, r₂              /* load J into r₂ */
MULT    #4, r₂             /* multiply r₂ by 4 */
LOAD    Y(r₂), r₁
```

which brings the r-value of Y[J] to register r_1. To compute the l-value of X[I], we have only to compute the offset from the base of the array X by a sequence such as:

```
LOAD    I, r₂
MULT    #4, r₂
```

Then, to store into X[I] we execute a STORE instruction with address equal to the base of array X, indexed by what we computed in register 2. The entire sequence of steps would be:

```
LOAD    J, r₂
MULT    #4, r₂
LOAD    Y(r₂), r₁
LOAD    I, r₂
MULT    #4, r₂
STORE   r₁, X(r₂)   □
```

Assignment as an Operator

Certain languages such as ALGOL 68, BLISS, and C treat the assignment operator as any other binary infix operator, giving it precedence lower than that of arithmetic, relational, or logical operators. For example, in C one can write expressions such as

$$A = (B = C + D) + (E = F + G)$$

The r-value of $E_1 = E_2$, if E_1 and E_2 are expressions and $=$ is the assignment operator, is the same as the r-value of E_2; the expression has no l-value. In C, $=$ has lower precedence than $+$, so the above expression can be interpreted as:

---

† We use an assembly code style similar to that of the PDP-11, where the last argument is the destination or place to hold the result of an operation.

```
B = C + D
E = F + G
A = B + E
```

There is no uniformity among languages as to which side of an assignment is to be evaluated first. ALGOL 60 stipulates left to right evaluation whereas ALGOL 68 and C specifically define the order to be undefined.

Certain languages such as ALGOL and PL/I allow the same value to be assigned to several variables in the same statement, although they do not allow the general use of assignment as a binary operator.

More General Assignment

Certain languages such as PL/I, APL, and ALGOL 68 permit assignments of the form A := B, where A and B can be complex data structures rather than primitive data elements. There is usually a requirement that A and B be *conformable* (of the same size, type, and structure). For example, if A is an array, then A = 0 in PL/I initializes all elements of the array to 0. If B is an array of the same size and shape as A, then A = B assigns each element of A the value of the corresponding element of B. Note that in the assignment A = 0 there is an implicit type conversion of the integer constant 0 to the appropriate array constant, the type of which is inferred from the type of A.

2.8 Statements

The elementary actions of evaluation, assignment, and control of evaluation order are specified by the statements of a programming language. Statements can have rather diverse forms and meanings.

Simple and Compound Statements

A *simple* statement is one that does not contain any embedded statements. Read, assignment, and goto are three examples of simple statements. In certain languages, a program may be regarded as a sequence of simple statements (e.g., BASIC, SNOBOL, APL).

A *compound* statement is one that may contain one or more embedded statements. The logical IF in FORTRAN:

    IF (condition) statement

is an example of a compound statement. Compound statements enable computations that logically belong together to be grouped together syntactically. This ability helps make programs readable.

Some examples of compound statements from PASCAL are:

1. **if** condition **then** statement

2. **if** condition **then** statement **else** statement

3. **begin** statement; statement; · · · ; statement **end**

4. **while** condition **do** statement

5. **for** identifier := initial-value **to** final-value **do** statement

The usual meanings of these statements should be clear. The if-then- and if-then-else-statements allow all actions that apply for a value of the condition to be grouped together. The compound statement (3) permits a sequence of statements to be used wherever one may appear. The while-statement is a way to establish loops with arbitrary loop-control conditions. Note that the test for the condition is performed before the statement, allowing the loop to be executed zero times if necessary.

Of course, in other languages that have compound statements, the syntax may vary widely from these examples. Another common arrangement is to put an endmarker keyword like **fi** or **endif** after the if-statement and **od** or **endwhile** after the while-statement. Then a list of statements may appear wherever a statement is indicated in (1), (2), (4) and (5), with no need for **begin ... end** brackets in statement lists.

Types of Statements

Most of the statements in programming languages fall into one of the following major categories.

1. *Computation statements.* These are statements that apply operators to operands to compute new values. The assignment statement is the prime example.

2. *Sequence-control statements.* In most languages, control automatically flows from one statement to the next. Certain statements such as **goto, break, call,** and **return** deliberately alter the flow of control. There has been considerable debate as to what statements are best suited for creating easy to understand flow-of-control patterns in programs. The goto-statement has been the focus of much of this controversy. Used indiscriminately, **goto** permits arbitrary flow-of-control patterns, including those that are difficult to comprehend.

3. *Structural statements.* Certain statements such as END serve to group simple statements into structures.

4. *Declaration statements.* These statements generally produce no executable code. Their semantic effect is to inform the compiler about the

attributes of names encountered in the program. The compiler "implements" a declaration statement by storing the attribute information contained therein in the symbol table and then consulting this information whenever the declared names are used in the program.

5. *Input and output statements.* These statements serve the role indicated by their names. In many languages they are implemented by library subroutines made available by the operating system to control input/output devices and convert data to or from human-readable form. In a variety of languages we see *formats,* which are strings of information about how data is to be interpreted (for a read) or expressed (for a write). As in FORTRAN, formats may syntactically be statements. They are neither executed by the compiler in the sense declarations are, nor are they compiled. Rather they are passed essentially intact by the compiled program to a library routine, which interprets them as if they were statements from a simple interpreted language.

We discuss the translation of common programming language statements into three-address code, or another intermediate form, in Chapters 7 and 8. We discuss the generation of machine code from the three-address statements in Chapter 15.

2.9 Program Units

We now move to the highest levels of the hierarchy of programming language constructs: blocks, procedures, and programs. By considering three languages for their program structure, we introduce the basic terminology of program units.

FORTRAN

In FORTRAN, a program consists of one main program and zero or more subprograms. The subprograms can be subroutines, functions, or block data. Both the main program and the subprograms can be separately compiled, a facility which promotes the modular construction of programs. The main program and each subroutine or function consists of a sequence of declarations and a sequence of executable statements.

Global data, that is, data available to more than one unit, can be obtained through the COMMON declaration statement. Other names are *local* to each program unit, in the sense that they are not known or usable outside the unit in which they are declared. If an identifier is declared in two different subprograms, it represents two different names which are not related; and assigning a value to one does not affect the other.

ALGOL

In ALGOL, a program is a *block,* a program subunit that has the ability to declare its own names. The chief characteristics of blocks in general are a bracketing structure (**begin** and **end** in ALGOL and many other languages) for delimiting the extent of the block and a method for declaring local names, that is, names known only inside the block. Certain blocks in an ALGOL program may be declared to be procedures, that is, subunits which may be called by other procedures or the program itself, and to which parameters may be passed.

ALGOL is a *block-structured language,* meaning that blocks or procedures may be nested inside other blocks or procedures. In fact, in ALGOL a block may appear in any place a statement can. It is not possible for two blocks B_1 and B_2 to overlap in such a way that B_1 begins, then B_2 does, but B_1 ends before B_2 ends. Block structure allows the same identifier to be used in different blocks to denote different names, even though one block is nested within the other. The rules governing the scope of names in block-structured languages are:

1. A name declared within block B is valid only within B.

2. If block B' is nested within B, then any name valid for B is also valid for B', unless the identifier for that name is redeclared in B'.

Rules (1) and (2) imply that if an identifier X appears in a declaration more than once in a program, then a use of X refers to the declaration of X in the block that most closely surrounds that use of X and which has a declaration of X. Figure 2.9 illustrates this point. It shows the nesting structure of blocks in an ALGOL program and where various declarations are valid. Subscripts are used on X and Y in Fig. 2.9 to indicate the block in which the declaration is made. That is, the subscripts on identifiers X and Y indicate the different names these identifiers represent.

Block structure lends itself to efficient use of storage. The fact that a name A is known inside a block but not outside it allows us to allocate storage for A when the block is entered and to free the storage when the block is left. For example, in Fig. 2.9, X from block 3 could share the same memory space with Y from block 4. We shall have more to say about this sort of storage handling in Section 2.12 and Chapter 10.

PL/I

PL/I combines characteristics of both FORTRAN and ALGOL in its program structure. A PL/I program consists of a set of external procedures, one of which is distinguished as the main program. Each external procedure may be compiled separately, and like ALGOL procedures, may have

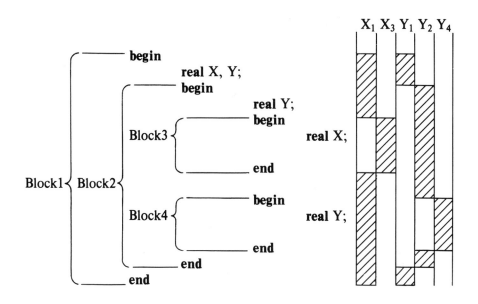

Fig. 2.9. ALGOL program structure.

blocks and internal procedures nested within it. The capability of simultaneous execution of two or more procedures is present in PL/I through a type of subprogram called a *task*, a subject which we shall not discuss here.

2.10 Data Environments

Suppose we have a statement A := B + 1 in a program. How is the value of B determined? First, we realize that the identifier B may occur in many different places in the program. It might refer in some of these places to a local or global variable; it might be a formal parameter or the name of a parameterless procedure. In each case, different rules apply to determine the appropriate value of B at a given time during the execution of the program. We call the association of identifiers with the names they currently denote the *environment* of a statement, block, or subprogram.

Binding Identifiers to Names

To properly translate a program to machine code we must associate with each mention of an identifier in the program a location which this identifier represents. The association is a two-stage process. First we must determine the name represented by the identifier (*bind* the identifier to a name) and then we must bind the name to a location. We discuss binding of identifiers here; the binding of names is covered in Section 2.12 and Chapters 10 and 15.

In many languages, the binding of an identifier depends only on its position in the program. The compiler may then determine the binding, and languages such as FORTRAN, ALGOL, and PL/I in which this is possible are said to use *static* binding of identifiers to names. In this case, the binding of names to locations may be static or dynamic. We discuss the options in Section 2.12. In other languages, such as SNOBOL, LISP, and APL, the name denoted by an identifier may not be known until run time. Such languages are said to require *dynamic* binding of identifiers.

Scope Rules

The *scope* of a name is the portion of the program over which it may be used. The rules that determine the scope of a name can be static or dynamic. Static scope rules define the scope of a name in terms of the syntactic structure of the program. That is, one can tell just by looking at the program, but without running it, to what name a particular use of an identifier refers.

We have already seen how the blocks in ALGOL determine the scope of names. The scope of a name declared in a particular block consists of that block, exclusive of any blocks nested within it that declare the same identifier. For example, in Fig. 2.9, the scope of the Y declared in block 2 consists of blocks 2 and 3, but not block 4, because the latter declares its own Y.

As a consequence of this scope rule, a mention of an identifier A refers to the declaration of A in that block which has a declaration of A and most closely surrounds the mention of A. We call this rule the "most closely nested" rule. It is the one followed by ALGOL, PL/I, and many other languages.

There are also languages with dynamic binding of identifiers to names, and these languages use scope rules which are dynamic, in the sense that the region of a program over which a name is valid can vary while the program is running. The rules used by SNOBOL, APL, and LISP are essentially the same. It is required that a name A refer to the declaration of A in the most recently initiated, but not yet terminated block or procedure having a declaration of A. For example, if, as the program runs, procedure P enters block *B* nested within P, and *B* subsequently calls procedure Q, then a mention of identifier X during this execution of Q refers to (1) the declaration of X by Q if there is one, (2) otherwise, the declaration of X by *B*, if there is one, or (3) otherwise, the declaration of X by P if there is one. It does not matter what the relative positions of P, *B* and Q are in the physical presentation of the program.

2.11 Parameter Transmission

The ability to define and call procedures is a great asset in a programming language. Procedures:

1. permit modular design of programs, by allowing large tasks to be broken into smaller units,

2. permit economy in the size of programs and in the total programming effort, since similar computations need be specified only once, and

3. add extensibility to a language, since operators can be defined in terms of procedures, which can then be used as functions within expressions.

One problem arising from the introduction of procedures is that a method of transmitting information to and from procedures must be defined and established. The usual method of communication between two procedures, one of which calls the other, is through global variables and parameters of the called procedure. This section discusses various ways of passing information to a called procedure through its parameters. It is important to know what parameter passing convention a language (or compiler) uses, because the value of a program can depend on the convention used.

Parameters

As with macros, we need to make a distinction between the definition of a procedure and its use. Suppose the sequence

> **integer procedure** DIVIDE(X, Y) **integer** X, Y;
>   **if** Y = 0 **then return** 0
>   **else return** X/Y

defines a procedure called DIVIDE. X and Y in this definition are called *formal parameters,* or just *formals.* (FORTRAN calls them "dummy arguments" and PL/I calls them "parameters.")

In a use of this procedure, as in

> A := DIVIDE(B, C)

B and C are called *actual parameters,* or *actuals* (in FORTRAN and PL/I, "arguments"). The terms B and C could be expressions, rather than simple variables.

In general, the formal parameters of a procedure definition are placeholders for values which will be supplied when the procedure is called. The actual parameters provide the values to be substituted for the formal parameters, and any implementation of a procedure must provide a way of associating the actual parameters of the call with the formals. If, as in our example above, the procedure is a function that returns a value to the calling program, we must also provide a method for the calling procedure to receive the value returned. In general, this additional linkage of data presents no special problems. The compiler can treat this situation as if there were an additional formal and actual parameter associated with the function procedure.

There are three common methods of passing parameters. They are: call-by-reference, call-by-value, and call-by-name.

Call-by-Reference

When parameters are passed by reference (also known as call-by-address or call-by-location), the calling program passes to the subroutine a pointer to the r-value of each actual parameter. The value of the pointer (the address of the actual parameter) is put in a known place determined by the language implementation, so that the calling procedure can know where to put the pointers, and the called procedure can know where to find them.

If an actual parameter is a simple variable or any expression having an l-value, then that l-value itself is passed. However, if the actual parameter is an expression, like $A + B$ or 2, which generally has no l-value, then the expression is evaluated in a new location, and the l-value of that location is passed. A reference to a formal parameter in the called procedure becomes, in machine code, an indirect reference through the pointer passed to the called procedure.

```
procedure SWAP(X, Y) integer X, Y;
    begin
        integer TEMP;
        TEMP := X;
        X := Y;
        Y := TEMP
    end
```

Fig. 2.10. The procedure SWAP.

Example 2.5. Consider the procedure SWAP(X, Y) in Fig. 2.10. A call to SWAP with actual parameters I and A[I], i.e., SWAP(I, A[I]), would have the same effect as the following sequence of steps.

1. Place the addresses (*l*-values) of I and A[I] in known locations, say ARG1 and ARG2.

2. Set TEMP to the contents of the location pointed to by ARG1 (i.e., set TEMP equal to I_0, where I_0 is the initial value of I). This step corresponds to TEMP := X in the definition of SWAP.

3. Set I to the contents of the location pointed to by ARG2, that is, I := A[I_0]. This corresponds to X := Y in SWAP.

4. Set the contents of the location pointed to by ARG2 equal to the value of TEMP, that is, set A[I_0] = I_0. This step corresponds to Y := TEMP. □

Call-by-reference is specified in the definitions of a number of languages, such as PL/I.

Call-by-Value

This is, in a sense, the simplest possible method of passing parameters. The actual parameters are evaluated and their *r*-values are passed to the subroutine in locations determined by the language implementation. The effect is that of initializing the formal parameters of the subroutine with the *r*-values of the actual parameters. The procedure can then be implemented as though its formals were ordinary variables.

Note, however, that it is now impossible to change values in the calling program, unless we explicitly pass pointers as actual parameters. The corresponding formal parameters must be declared to be pointers and be used as pointers in the called procedure. For example, the call of the procedure SWAP(I, A[I]) would be equivalent to the sequence of steps:

$$T_1 := I$$
$$T_2 := A[I]$$
$$TEMP := T_1$$
$$T_1 := T_2$$
$$T_2 := TEMP$$

where T_1 and T_2 are names local to SWAP. Thus, SWAP would do nothing to data other than its own if called by value. To make SWAP work correctly we would have to declare X and Y to be pointers and use statements such as TEMP := *X.

A generalization of call-by-value is *copy-restore* (*copy-in, copy-out,* or *value-result) linkage*. Before the call, the actual parameters are evaluated. The *r*-values of the actuals are passed to the called procedure as in call-by-value. In addition, however, the *l*-values of those actual parameters having *l*-values are also determined before the call. When the call returns, the current values of the formal parameters (which were initialized to the *r*-values of the actuals) are copied back into the *l*-values of the actuals, using the *l*-values computed before the call.

The reader should verify that SWAP(I, A[I]) will work correctly using copy-restore linkage. The important point is that the location of A[I] is computed and preserved by the calling program before the call. Thus, the final value of formal parameter Y, which will be the initial value of I, is copied into the correct location, even though, should we compute the location of A[I] after the call, we would get a different result (because the value of I has changed).

Call-by-value is the method of parameter passing used in the language C, and certain ALGOL parameters (declared **value**) are also passed this way. Copy-restore is utilized in some FORTRAN implementations.

Call-by-Name

Call-by-name, the method specified for ALGOL, is a mechanism of substantial power and theoretical interest, but it is unfortunately hard to implement. The basic idea is to leave the actual parameters unevaluated until they are needed and to evaluate them anew each time they are needed. The usual implementation of this idea is to pass to the called procedure parameterless subroutines, commonly called *thunks,* which can evaluate the *l*-value or *r*-value of an actual parameter. This mechanism will be discussed in detail in Section 10.2.

The traditional way of defining the meaning of call-by-name is by the ALGOL *copy rule,* which states that the called procedure is to be implemented as if it were a macro, that is, as if the procedure itself were substituted for the call, with actual parameters literally substituted for formal parameters. Any local name of the called procedure having the same identifier as a name mentioned in the actual parameters must be given a distinct identifier before the substitution of actuals for formals. Also, the actual parameters must be surrounded by parentheses if necessary to preserve their integrity.

Example 2.6. The call to SWAP(I, A[I]) from Example 2.5 would be implemented as though it were

```
TEMP := I;
I := A[I];
A[I] := TEMP
```

Thus, under call-by-name, SWAP sets I to A[I], as we would expect, but has the unexpected result of setting $A[A[I_0]]$ — rather than $A[I_0]$ — to I_0, where I_0 is the initial value of I. This phenomenon occurs because the location of X in the assignment X := TEMP of SWAP is not evaluated until needed, whereupon the value of I has already changed. It is interesting to note that a correctly working version of SWAP apparently cannot be written if call-by-name is used (see Fleck [1976]). □

2.12 Storage Management

This section discusses issues in programming language design that affect the utilization of storage by a running program. There are a number of elements to which storage must be allocated in order to execute the object program. Most obvious is the storage required for the object program and the user-defined data structures, variables, and constants. Less obvious is the need for space for procedure-linkage information, the temporaries required for expression evaluation and parameter transmission, and the space allocated for input/output buffers. Let us consider the ways in which various languages arrange to have space made available to the object program and how it may be arranged to have that space used economically.

Static Storage Allocation

If the size of every data item can be determined by the compiler (for example, no strings or arrays of adjustable length are permitted in the language), and if recursive procedure calls are not permitted, then the space for all programs and data can be allocated at compile time, i.e., statically. Moreover, the association of names to locations can also be done statically in this case. Static allocation has the virtues that it is easy to implement efficiently and requires no *run-time support* (library routines loaded with the object program) for allocating storage.

This method is used in FORTRAN. Each subroutine can be compiled separately and the space needed for its arrays computed. Note that the only time a size need not be specified for an array occurs when that array is a formal parameter. In that case, no storage need be allocated for the array at all. Since there is no recursion in FORTRAN, each subprogram can store its *return address* (place to which the return is to go) in a private location. Thus in FORTRAN, the space required for a program is just the sum of the space needed for the subprograms, their data and linkage information (return address), and any library routines used. This space never changes as the program is running.

Dynamic Storage Allocation

If a programming language permits either recursive procedures or data structures whose size is adjustable, then some sort of dynamic storage management is necessary. There are two kinds of dynamic storage allocation prevalent — stack allocation and heap allocation; some languages use a combination of both.

Stack allocation is useful for handling recursive procedures. As each procedure is called, it places its data on top of a stack, and when the procedure returns, it pops its data off the stack. Virtually any language with recursive procedures is required to use some sort of stack at run time.

Heap allocation is useful for implementing data whose size varies as the program is running, for example, strings in SNOBOL or lists in LISP. It involves taking a large block of memory and dividing it into variable-length blocks, some used for data and some free. When a piece of data is created, we must find a free block of sufficient size. When data is no longer needed, its block becomes free. We shall discuss the mechanics of stack and heap allocation shortly.

Stack Allocation of Storage

The basic idea is to start with a region of consecutive words of memory. This region will be used as a stack, in the sense that allocated storage will always be added to the top by incrementing a stack pointer. Released storage will always be removed from the top by decrementing the stack pointer. While such a storage-management scheme could not be used to handle arbitrary allocations and releases of storage, the last-in first-out mode of operation corresponds exactly to the storage requirements of block-structured languages.

We can collect all the fixed-size storage required by variables declared in one procedure into a single chunk of storage called an *activation record*. The activation record might contain the following items:

1. Storage for simple names, and pointers to arrays and other data structures local to the procedure.

2. Temporaries for expression evaluation and parameter passing.

3. Information regarding attributes for local names and formal parameters, when these cannot be determined at compile time.

4. The return address.

5. A pointer to the activation record of the caller.

It is customary and useful to place immediately above the activation record data whose size cannot be determined until the procedure is called. Figure 2.11 shows the format for a typical activation record, including two adjustable-length arrays. Pointers to the locations of these arrays are stored at a fixed position in the activation record. Thus, the compiler can generate code to access them indirectly through the top-of-stack pointer and the pointer for the array itself, even though it cannot know precisely where the arrays begin. All other data is accessed indirectly, through the top-of-stack pointer. Note that these arrays are actually above the activation record, not part of it.

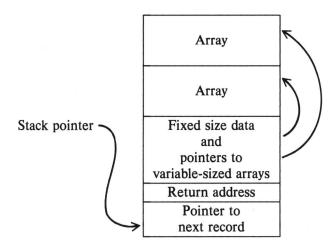

Fig. 2.11. Activation record.

When a procedure P calls procedure Q, the activation record for Q and space for its adjustable-size data is pushed onto the stack. When Q returns, the return address is fetched from the activation record. Then the activation record for Q is effectively removed from the stack by lowering the stack pointer to the activation record for P immediately below.

Example 2.7. Consider the block-structured program suggested by Fig. 2.12. Dealing with blocks is similar to dealing with procedures, in that blocks may have local data as procedures do, and the stack mechanism can be used for allocation of storage for a block's data as well.

When A begins execution, its activation record is placed on top of the stack as in Fig. 2.13(a). The stack contents when B and C initiate are

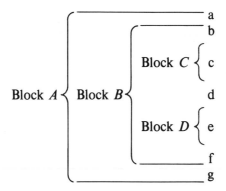

Fig. 2.12. Block-structured program.

shown in Fig. 2.13(b) and (c), respectively. The stack contents for points (d) through (g) of Fig. 2.12 are shown in Fig. 2.13(d) through (g), respectively. □

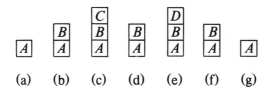

(a)   (b)   (c)   (d)   (e)   (f)   (g)

Fig. 2.13. Behavior of stack.

Recursion and Displays

When a language has recursive procedures, we may find that several activation records for the same block or procedure can appear simultaneously on the run-time stack. This situation is not anomalous, as each record represents a different "activation" of the procedure, with distinct data. If the language is one like C which provides that a procedure can reference only its local data (found in the top activation record) and global data (allocated statically), then the fact that more than one activation record for a procedure appears on the stack presents no serious problem.

In languages like ALGOL, however, data accessible to a block or procedure includes data from a variety of other blocks and procedures. If more than one activation of a procedure (or block) exists, then it is to the topmost (most recently activated) copy that a reference to that procedure's local data refers.[†] But how is the topmost activation record for a procedure or block to be found?

One method useful for ALGOL or other languages using static binding of identifiers to names under the most-closely-nested rule is the *display*. In addition to the stack of activation records, which may contain any number of activation records for a block or procedure, there is a list of pointers, called the display. The display has a pointer to the correct activation record for every procedure in the environment of the currently active procedure. Recall that under the most-closely-nested rule, the names valid at a point in the program are those defined by each block or procedure that surrounds the point.

The activation record for blocks nested within an active procedure can be found a fixed distance up the stack from the activation record for that procedure. The order from the top of the display list is that the more closely the procedure surrounds the active point, the higher its pointer is on the display. Figure 2.14 shows a typical display. The implementation and use of a display is covered in detail in Section 8.2.

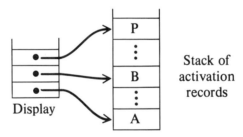

Fig. 2.14. A display.

Stack Allocation with Dynamic Binding

An entirely different problem occurs in a language like SNOBOL which allows recursive procedure calls and uses dynamic binding of identifiers to names. Recall that the usual dynamic binding rule is that a reference to an identifier refers to the most recently initiated active declaration of that identifier. If the activation record for each procedure contained a list of all its declared identifiers, we could search down the stack for the topmost record having a value for the desired identifier. However, this search could

---

† Certain exceptions may occur if procedure-valued parameters are permitted. See Section 10.2.

be time consuming.

An alternative is to eschew a stack of activation records. Rather, the compiler can create a stack for each identifier that is mentioned in the program. When a procedure initiates, it must push down a new value for each local identifier, and when the procedure returns, pop those values off the stacks. Then, any reference to any identifier refers to whatever value is currently on top of the stack for that identifier.

Heap Allocation

In languages like LISP and SNOBOL, where data is constantly being created, destroyed, and modified in size, it is inconvenient to place variable-length data on the stack. In contrast, in languages like PL/I and ALGOL, we can determine the maximum size of a data structure when the procedure or block is entered, even though we cannot necessarily do so at compile time. In that case, stack allocation of adjustable-length data is feasible. But what if we can never know how big a data structure will become during one activation of the procedure declaring it?

One useful run-time organization is the *heap,* a large block of storage that may be partitioned at will into smaller blocks. The typical situation is illustrated in Fig. 2.15. There we see pointers from fixed locations representing three names X, Y, and Z. These fixed locations might be allocated statically or they might be on a stack. They point to blocks of memory in the heap, and the value of each name, including a data descriptor giving the block's length, is kept in the block. The portions of the heap not currently in use are linked together in an *available space list.* That is, each free block contains a pointer to the next free block and information regarding how long the free block is.

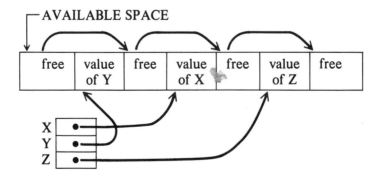

Fig. 2.15. Heap allocation.

The question of efficient heap management is a somewhat specialized issue in data structure theory. We shall therefore not go into great detail here regarding how space is to be allocated within the heap. We shall merely touch upon the key problems. First, how are we to know when a value stored in the heap is no longer in use? PL/I, for example, requires the programmer to deallocate space explicitly, but in languages like SNO-BOL and LISP, a library routine loaded with each program is charged with determining when a block of storage is free.

One method is to attach a *use count* to every block, telling how many pointers point to it. When the use count reaches zero, the block is made free. The implementation of SNOBOL allows an assignment such as X = Y to be performed by making the pointer for string X point to the value of Y; LISP allows arbitrary pointer configurations for its list structures. Thus use counts above one are quite normal.

Another problem in heap management is *fragmentation*. When we free a block, we must do something to attach it to adjacent free blocks, if any. The penalty for not doing so is that storage will fragment, that is, the available space list will consist of many little blocks, none of which is sufficient to hold a large block of data. When no sufficiently large block of the heap is available, a library routine loaded with the program must merge adjacent free blocks into larger blocks. It may even be necessary to move data around in the heap to make a large consecutive free block.

The typical LISP implementation takes another point of view regarding heap management. No attempt at keeping use counts is made. Rather, when there is no more available space, each block is checked to see whether there is a path of pointers from the location associated with some name to that block. If not, the block is placed on the available space list. This process is called *garbage collection*.

Exercises

2.1 Which of the following expressions have *l*-values? Which have *r*-values? Assume * is the "indirection" operator and & the "address of" operator.

a)   A[I+1]
b)   *A
c)   &A
d)   &(*A)
e)   *(&A)
f)   *(&(&A))

2.2 What is printed by the program in Fig. 2.16, assuming (a) call-by-name, (b) call-by-reference, (c) copy-restore linkage, (d) call-by-value?

```
procedure PROC(X, Y, Z);
begin
      Y := Y + 1;
      Z := Z + X;
end  PROC;
begin
      A := 2;
      B := 3;
      PROC(A+B, A, A);
      print A
end
```

Fig. 2.16. Example program.

2.3 Suppose A[−4:5,−3:3] is a 10×7 integer array, whose first subscript ranges from −4 to +5, and whose second ranges from −3 to 3. Write code to assign A[I,J] := 0, assuming A is stored in row-major form beginning at location 1000 in a byte-addressed machine with six bytes per word.

2.4 Let +, *, and ↑ stand for addition, multiplication, and exponentiation, but with nonstandard precedences and associativities. Evaluate 1+1*2↑1*1↑2 on the assumption that

   a)   The order of precedence is +(highest), *, and ↑, with all operators left-associative.

   b)   The order of precedence is ↑, +, *, with all operators right-associative.

*2.5 Certain languages, like LISP, have the facility to create new procedures at run time. This ability requires dynamic binding of names to memory locations and, in fact, can require the use of a tree of activation records rather than a stack. A reference to X by a procedure P is in the closest ancestor (in the tree) of P's activation record having a declaration of X. The binding rule we shall consider, known as *deep* or *funarg* binding, is that whenever a procedure P is created, its activation record becomes a child of the activation record of the function creating P. For the purposes of this exercise, let us simply assume names of types real and function. All functions, whether defined by the programmer or created at run time, take at most one argument and return one value, either a function or a real. We shall use one operator ○, standing for composition of functions. Consider the collection of programs shown in Fig. 2.17.

a)   What value is printed by MAIN?

b)   When A is computed by MAIN, what is the tree of activation records?

c)   Is it always possible to remove an activation record when a function returns?

```
function F(X);
    function X, Y;
    Y := X ○ H; /* creates Y when executed */
    return Y
end F;

function H( );
    return SIN
end H;

function G(Z);
    function Z, W;
    W := ARCTAN ○ Z; /* creates W when executed */
    return W
end G;

function MAIN( );
    real A;
    function U, V;
    V := F(G);
    U := V( );
    A := U(π /2);
    print A
end MAIN
```

Fig. 2.17. A collection of functions.

**2.6 An alternative to deep binding, known as *shallow* binding, does not create an activation record for a procedure P until P is called, at which time the activation record for P becomes a child of the activation record for the procedure calling it.

> a) In the collection of functions in Fig. 2.17, what is the sequence of activation record trees when MAIN is called?
>
> b) Is a stack sufficient to hold activation records when shallow binding is used?

Bibliographic Notes

Programming languages were being considered as early as the mid 1940's, although languages such as FORTRAN and ALGOL were not developed until the late 1950's. See Sammet [1968, 1972] and Knuth and Trabb Pardo [1976] for historical remarks. Elson [1973], Nicholls [1975], and Pratt [1975] discuss issues of programming languages as well as giving overviews of several common languages. Galler and Perlis [1970] and Wegner [1968] also discuss programming language concepts.

Historical or other information about the programming languages discussed in this book can be found in the following sources. ALGOL 60: Naur [1963]; ALGOL 68: Van Wijngaarden [1975], Pagan [1976]; APL: Iverson [1962]; BLISS: Wulf et al. [1975]; C: Ritchie, Kernighan, and Lesk [1975]; FORTRAN: Backus et al. [1957], ANSI [1966, 1976b]; LISP: McCarthy et al. [1965]; PASCAL: Wirth [1971], Jensen and Wirth [1975]; PL/I: ANSI [1976a]; SETL: Schwartz [1973]; SIMULA: Birtwistle *et al.* [1973]; SNOBOL: Griswold, Poage, and Polonsky [1971].

Britton *et al.* [1976] and Jones and Muchnick [1976] discuss implementation of a variety of binding strategies, and Shaw [1974] evaluates the cost of programming-language features in terms of compilation difficulty.

To read more on semantics of programming languages, the reader can consult Manna [1974], Marcotty, Ledgard, and Bochmann [1977] and some of the basic papers such as Hoare [1969] on the axiomatic approach, Reynolds [1972] on the interpretive approach, and Scott [1970] for the mathematical, lattice-theoretic approach.

CHAPTER 3

Lexical
Analysis

As we indicated in Section 1.4, the function of the lexical analyzer is to read the source program, one character at a time, and to translate it into a sequence of primitive units called tokens. Keywords, identifiers, constants, and operators are examples of tokens.

This chapter discusses the problem of designing and implementing lexical analyzers. We shall see that there are several aspects to this problem. First we need some method of describing the possible tokens that can appear in the input stream. For this purpose we introduce regular expressions, a notation that can be used to describe essentially all the tokens of programming languages.

Second, having decided what the tokens are, we need some mechanism to recognize these tokens in the input stream. In this chapter we see that *transition diagrams* and *finite automata* are convenient ways of designing token recognizers. In addition to locating tokens in the input, we also need some mechanism to perform various actions as the tokens are recognized. For example, an action might enter the value of the token into a table, generate some output, or produce a diagnostic message. We shall discuss how actions can be incorporated into the framework of transition diagrams and finite automata.

One advantage of using regular expressions to specify tokens is that from a regular expression we can automatically construct a recognizer for tokens denoted by that regular expression. Near the end of this chapter we discuss a system for automatically generating lexical analyzers from regular expression-like specifications. Such a system alleviates much of the drudgery of implementing lexical analyzers and can be used in a variety of other stream-processing applications.

This chapter is organized so that hand implementation of lexical analyzers may be studied by reading Sections 3.1 and 3.2, with the study of automatic generation of lexical analyzers in the remaining sections left to a second reading of the book. Section 3.7 discusses a high-level language for specifying lexical analyzers and Section 3.9 gives some applications of this language to tasks other than compiling.

73

3.1 The Role of the Lexical Analyzer

The lexical analyzer could be a separate pass, placing its output on an intermediate file from which the parser would then take its input. More commonly, however, the lexical analyzer and parser are together in the same pass; the lexical analyzer acts as a subroutine or coroutine, which is called by the parser whenever it needs a new token. This organization eliminates the need for the intermediate file. In this arrangement, the lexical analyzer returns to the parser a representation for the token it has found. The representation is an integer code if the token is a simple construct such as a left parenthesis, comma, or colon. The representation is a pair consisting of an integer code and a pointer to a table if the token is a more complex element such as an identifier or constant. The integer code gives the token type; the pointer points to the value of that token. Pairs are also returned whenever we wish to distinguish between instances of a token. For example, we may treat "operator" as a token and let the second component of the pair indicate whether the operator found is $+$, $*$, and so on.

The Need for Lexical Analysis

The purpose of splitting the analysis of the source program into two phases, lexical analysis and syntactic analysis, is to simplify the overall design of the compiler. It is easier to specify the structure of tokens than the syntactic structure of the source program. Consequently, we can construct a more specialized, and hence more efficient, recognizer for tokens than for syntactic structures.

By including certain constructs in the lexical rather than the syntactic structure, we can greatly simplify the design of the syntax analyzer. In the next chapter we shall see how context-free grammars can be used to specify the syntactic structure of a programming language. Using a grammar, we can treat the entire syntactic-analysis process uniformly, possibly at the expense of introducing a few difficult-to-recognize tokens into the lexical analyzer. Thus the decision as to what to treat as a token is often a compromise between complicating either the lexical analyzer or the syntactic analyzer, usually resolved in favor of complicating the former.

Other functions sometimes performed by a lexical analyzer are keeping track of line numbers, producing an output listing if necessary,† stripping out white space (such as redundant blanks and tabs), and deleting comments.

---

† In an interactive environment there is little need for a compiler to produce a listing. The job is better relegated to a general purpose print utility.

Input Buffering

The lexical analyzer scans the characters of the source program one at a time to discover tokens. Often, however, many characters beyond the next token may have to be examined before the next token itself can be determined. For this and other reasons, it is desirable for the lexical analyzer to read its input from an input buffer. There are many schemes that can be used to buffer input (see Knuth [1968], e.g.), and we shall discuss only one here. Figure 3.1 shows a buffer divided into two halves of, say, 100 characters each. One pointer marks the beginning of the token being discovered. A lookahead pointer scans ahead of the beginning point, until the token is discovered. We view the position of each pointer as being between the character last read and the character next to be read. In practice, each buffering scheme adopts one convention; either a pointer is at the symbol last read or the symbol it is ready to read.

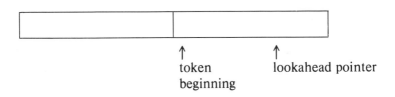

token   lookahead pointer
beginning

Fig. 3.1. Input buffer.

The distance which the lookahead pointer may have to travel past the actual token may be large. For example, in a PL/I program we may see

DECLARE(ARG1, ARG2, . . . , ARGn)

without knowing whether DECLARE is a keyword or an array name until we see the character that follows the right parenthesis. In either case, the token itself ends at the second E. If the lookahead pointer travels beyond the buffer half in which it began, the other half must be loaded with the next characters from the source file.

Since the buffer of Fig. 3.1 is of limited size, there is an implied constraint on how much lookahead can be used before the next token is discovered. For example, in Fig. 3.1 if the lookahead traveled to the left half and all the way through the left half to the middle, we could not reload the right half, because we would lose characters that had not yet been grouped into tokens. While we can make the buffer larger if we choose or use another buffering scheme, we cannot ignore the fact that lookahead is limited.

Preliminary Scanning

There are certain processes that are best performed as characters are moved
from the source file to the buffer. For example, we may delete comments.
In a language like FORTRAN which ignores blanks, we can delete them
from the character stream except in literals. In other languages, we may
collapse strings of several blanks to one blank. A count of lines may be
kept by checking for newline characters.

All these processes may be carried out with an extra buffer into which
the source file is read and then copied, with modification, into the buffer of
Fig. 3.1. Alternatively, the condensation of the text may be carried out in
place in the buffer of Fig. 3.1. Preprocessing the character stream being
subjected to lexical analysis saves the trouble of moving the lookahead
pointer back and forth over comments or strings of blanks.

3.2 A Simple Approach to the Design of Lexical Analyzers

One way to begin the design of any program is to describe the behavior of
the program by a flowchart. This approach is particularly useful when the
program is a lexical analyzer, because the action taken is highly dependent
on what characters have been seen recently. Remembering previous characters by the position in a flowchart is a valuable tool, so much so that a
specialized kind of flowchart for lexical analyzers, called a *transition diagram,*
has evolved. In a transition diagram, the boxes of the flowchart are drawn
as circles and called *states.* The states are connected by arrows, called *edges.*
The labels on the various edges leaving a state indicate the input characters
that can appear after that state.

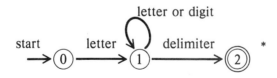

Fig. 3.2. Transition diagram for identifier.

Figure 3.2 shows a transition diagram for an identifier, defined to be a
letter followed by any number of letters or digits. The starting state of the
transition diagram is state 0, the edge from which indicates that the first
input character must be a letter. If this is the case, we enter state 1 and
look at the next input character. If that is a letter or digit, we re-enter state
1 and look at the input character after that. We continue this way, reading

letters and digits, and making transitions from state 1 to itself, until the next input character is a delimiter for an identifier, which here we assume is any character that is not a letter or a digit. On reading the delimiter, we enter state 2.

To turn a collection of transition diagrams into a program, we construct a segment of code for each state. The first step to be done in the code for any state is to obtain the next character from the input buffer. For this purpose we use a function GETCHAR, which returns the next character, advancing the lookahead pointer at each call. The next step is to determine which edge, if any, out of the state is labeled by a character or class of characters that includes the character just read. If such an edge is found, control is transferred to the state pointed to by that edge. If no such edge is found, and the state is not one which indicates that a token has been found (indicated by a double circle), we have failed to find this token. The lookahead pointer must be retracted to where the beginning pointer is, and another token must be searched for, using another transition diagram. If all transition diagrams have been tried without success, a lexical error has been detected, and an error correction routine must be called (see Section 11.2).

Consider again the transition diagram in Fig. 3.2. The code for state 0 might be:

> state 0: C := GETCHAR( );
>   **if** LETTER(C) **then goto** state 1
>   **else** FAIL( )

Here LETTER is a procedure which returns **true** if and only if C is a letter. FAIL is a routine which retracts the lookahead pointer and starts up the next transition diagram, if there is one, or calls the error routine. The code for state 1 is:

> state 1: C := GETCHAR( );
>   **if** LETTER(C) **or** DIGIT(C) **then goto** state 1
>   **else if** DELIMITER(C) **then goto** state 2
>   **else** FAIL( )

DIGIT is a procedure which returns **true** if and only if C is one of the digits 0, 1, . . . , 9. DELIMITER is a procedure which returns **true** whenever C is a character that could follow an identifier. If we define a delimiter to be any character that is not a letter or digit, then the clause "**if** DELIMITER(C) **then**" need not be present in state 1. To detect errors more effectively we might define a delimiter more precisely (e.g., blank, arithmetic or logical operator, left or right parenthesis, equals sign, colon, semicolon, or comma), depending on the language being compiled.

State 2 indicates that an identifier has been found. Since the delimiter is not part of the identifier, we must retract the lookahead pointer one character, for which we use a procedure RETRACT. We use a * to indicate states on which input retraction must take place. We must also install the newly-found identifier in the symbol table if it is not already there, using the procedure INSTALL. In state 2 we return to the parser a pair consisting of the integer code for an identifier, which we denote by **id**, and a value that is a pointer to the symbol table returned by INSTALL. The code for state 2 is:

> state 2: RETRACT( );
>   **return** (**id**, INSTALL( ))

If blanks must be skipped in the language at hand, we should include in the code for state 2 a step that moved the beginning pointer to the next non-blank.

Token	Code	Value
begin	1	—
end	2	—
if	3	—
then	4	—
else	5	—
identifier	6	Pointer to symbol table
constant	7	Pointer to symbol table
<	8	1
<=	8	2
=	8	3
<>	8	4
>	8	5
>=	8	6

Fig. 3.3. Tokens recognized.

Example 3.1. Let us consider an extended example of transition diagrams, those for a subset of the tokens of the language in Appendix B. Figure 3.3 lists the tokens that we shall consider, together with the code for the token type and the value returned if any. Figure 3.4 indicates the transition diagrams recognizing keywords (the first five tokens in Fig. 3.3), identifiers, constants, and relops (the last six tokens in Fig. 3.3).

A more efficient program can be constructed from a single transition diagram than from a collection of diagrams, since there is no need to backtrack and rescan using a second transition diagram. In Fig. 3.4 we have combined all keywords into one transition diagram. However, if we attempt to combine the diagram for identifiers with that for keywords, difficulties arise. For example, on seeing the three letters BEG, we could not tell whether to be in state 3 or state 24. Section 3.8 shows how these difficulties can be surmounted and gives a general algorithm to combine any collection of transition diagrams into a single diagram.

In Fig. 3.4, each keyword is treated as a separate token, whereas all relops are combined into one token class, with the associated token value distinguishing one relop from another. Which approach we choose is a matter of taste. The utility of treating relational operators as one token will be seen when we study the translation of expressions in Chapter 7. As all relational expressions have similar forms of translations, we are able to express the translation formula once, using the value as a parameter, rather than repeating the translation formula six times, once for each relop.

Let us now consider an example of the action of the lexical analyzer constructed from the transition diagram of Fig. 3.4. On seeing IFA followed by a blank, the lexical analyzer would traverse states 0, 15, and 16, then fail and retract the input to I. It would then start up the second transition diagram at state 23, traverse state 24 three times, go to state 25 on the blank, retract the input one position, install IFA in the symbol table, and return to the parser. □

Implementation of a Transition Diagram

Let us briefly consider what the code for states such as those found in Fig. 3.4 should look like. If the language in which we are writing our lexical analyzer has a case-statement, we can use such a statement for each state, with one case for each edge leaving the state. Presumably, case statements are handled reasonably efficiently in the programming language in which the compiler is being written. If we do not have a case statement, we should use one of several strategies, depending on the kinds of transitions out of the state.

One kind of state is typified by state 0 in Fig. 3.4. This state has several transitions out and would have more if all keywords were being recognized. To implement this state, we generate code that calls GETCHAR and converts the resulting character to an integer, which will presumably be in some small range such as 0–127. Then we produce code that uses that integer to index into an array of labels. Each label marks the location of the piece of program for the next state. Thus, in Fig. 3.4, the label indexed by B would point to code for state 1. The label for E would point to the program for state 7, and so on. The labels for characters that did not begin a keyword would all be the same and would point to code which implemented the transition diagram for identifier.

keywords:

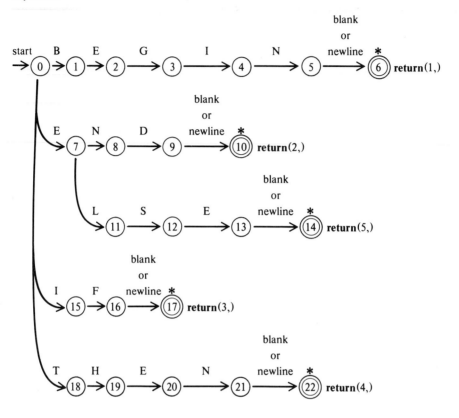

identifier:

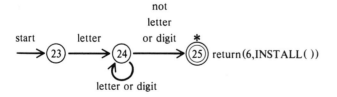

constant:

relops:

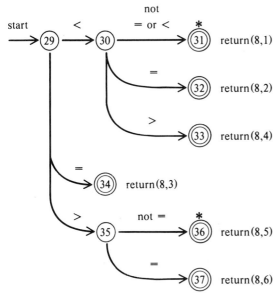

Fig. 3.4. Transition diagrams.

A second kind of state is typified by state 1. Its code would call GETCHAR and test whether the character returned were E, jumping to the code for state 2 if so. If not, it would retract the input pointer and start up the transition diagram for identifiers.

A third kind of state is typified by state 23. There, after calling GETCHAR, the code would test whether the character returned lies in one of several ranges. Exactly how many ranges are needed to recognize letters depends on whether only upper-case letters, or both upper- and lower-case letters, are sought and whether the character code is ASCII, EBCDIC, or another code. For example, in ASCII we can detect upper-case letters by testing whether the code for the character lies numerically between the code for A and the code for Z.†

Section 3.8 discusses the automatic implementation of the programs associated with states. There we shall see how a tool for generating lexical analyzers can generate efficient implementations for states regardless of which type they are.

Reserved Words

One method, called the *reserved word* strategy, is frequently used in practice. We may dispense with the part of a transition diagram for recognizing keywords if we treat keywords as identifiers and enter them initially into the symbol table, with an indicator that they are keywords and with the codes for their tokens. When the lexical analyzer recognizes an identifier and finds its symbol table location, it can then determine whether that identifier is, in fact, a keyword and return the correct code for that token. With this strategy, keywords cannot be used as identifiers.

In practice, it is convenient to write a little subroutine to enter the keywords and their associated integer codes into the symbol table. The use of the subroutine helps to avoid some rather difficult-to-catch bugs that can result from incorrect table entries.

3.3 Regular Expressions

We shall now begin the discussion of the design of a program for generating lexical analyzers automatically. We first introduce a very useful notation, called regular expressions, suitable for describing tokens. We later show how regular expressions can be converted automatically into finite automata, which are just formal specifications for transition diagrams. Still later we shall discuss the implementation of finite automata by programs.

---

† In EBCDIC, the other common character code, this test does not work, because letters of the same case are not consecutively numbered.

Strings and Languages

Let us first introduce a few basic terms dealing with languages. We shall use the term *alphabet* or *character class* to denote any finite set of symbols. The terms "symbol" and "character" will be used synonymously, and we presume they are terms understood by the reader.

Example 3.2. The set $\{0,1\}$ is an alphabet. It consists of the two symbols, 0 and 1, and it is often called the *binary alphabet*. Two important examples of programming language alphabets are the ASCII and EBCDIC character sets.   □

A *string* is a finite sequence of symbols, such as 001. *Sentence* and *word* are synonyms for string. The *length* of a string x, usually denoted $|x|$, is the total number of symbols in x. For example, 01101 is a string of length 5. A special string is the *empty string*, which we shall denote by ϵ. This string is of length zero.

If x and y are strings, then the *concatenation* of x and y, written $x \cdot y$ or just xy, is the string formed by following the symbols of x by the symbols of y. For example, $abc \cdot de = abcde$. That is, if $x = abc$ and $y = de$, where a, b, c, d, and e are symbols, then $xy = abcde$. The concatenation of the empty string with any string is that string; more formally, $\epsilon x = x\epsilon = x$.

We may think of concatenation as a sort of "product."† It thus makes sense to talk of exponentiation of strings as representing an iterated product. For example, $x^1 = x$, $x^2 = xx$, $x^3 = xxx$, and so on. In general, x^i is the string x repeated i times. As a useful convention, we take x^0 to be ϵ for any string x. Thus, ϵ plays the role of 1, the multiplicative identity, if we think of concatenation as a product operator.

If x is some string, then any string formed by discarding zero or more trailing symbols of x is called a *prefix* of x. For example, *abc* is a prefix of *abcde*. A *suffix* of x is a string formed by deleting zero or more of the leading symbols of x; *cde* is a suffix of *abcde*. A *substring* of x is any string obtained by deleting a prefix and a suffix from x. Thus, for any string x, both x and ϵ are prefixes, suffixes, and substrings of x. Moreover, any prefix or suffix of x is a substring of x, but a substring need not be a prefix or a suffix. For example, *cd* is a substring of *abcde* but not a prefix or a suffix. We say a nonempty string y is a *proper* prefix, suffix, or substring of x if it is a prefix, suffix, or substring of x, and $y \neq x$.

We use the term *language* to mean any set of strings formed from some specific alphabet. This is an enormously broad definition. Simple sets such as ϕ, the *empty set*, having no members, or $\{\epsilon\}$, the set containing only the

---

† But beware that concatenation is not commutative as arithmetic multiplication is. For example, dog·house $\neq$ house·dog.

empty string, are languages under this definition. So too are the set of all valid FORTRAN programs and the set of all English sentences. Note that our definition of "language" does not assign any meaning to strings in the language. In Chapter 7 we shall discuss syntax-directed translation as one method of associating meaning with languages.

The notation of concatenation can also be applied to languages. If L and M are languages, then $L \cdot M$, or just LM, is the language consisting of all strings xy which can be formed by selecting a string x from L, a string y from M, and concatenating them in that order. That is,

$$LM = \{xy \mid x \text{ is in } L \text{ and } y \text{ is in } M\}$$

We call LM the *concatenation* of L and M.

Example 3.3. Let L be $\{0, 01, 110\}$ and let M be $\{10, 110\}$. Then $LM = \{010, 0110, 01110, 11010, 110110\}$. For example, 11010 can be written as the concatenation of 110 from L and 10 from M. 0110 can be written as either $0 \cdot 110$ or $01 \cdot 10$; either way, it is a string from L followed by one from M.

In analogy with strings, we use L^i to stand for $LL \cdots L$ (i times). It is logical to define L^0 to be $\{\epsilon\}$, since $\{\epsilon\}$ is the identity under concatenation of languages. That is,

$$\{\epsilon\}L = L\{\epsilon\} = L$$

for all languages L.

The union of languages L and M is given by

$$L \cup M = \{x \mid x \text{ is in } L \text{ or } x \text{ is in } M\}$$

We may draw an analogy between union and addition, if concatenation is analogous to multiplication. Then ϕ, the empty set, is the identity under union (analogous to zero), since

$$\phi \cup L = L \cup \phi = L$$

and

$$\phi L = L\phi = \phi$$

The latter follows since any string in the concatenation of ϕ with L must be formed from x in ϕ and y in L. But there is no x in ϕ, the empty set.

There is another operation on languages which plays an important role in specifying tokens. This is the *closure* or "any number of" operator. We use L^* to denote the concatenation of language L with itself any number of times. That is, we define

$$L^* = \bigcup_{i=0}^{\infty} L^i$$

Example 3.4. Let D be the language consisting of the strings 0, 1, ..., 9, that is, each string is a single decimal digit. Then D^* is all strings of digits, including the empty string. For another example, if $L = \{aa\}$, then L^* is all strings of an even number of a's, since $L^0 = \{\epsilon\}$, $L^1 = \{aa\}$, $L^2 = \{aaaa\}$, and so on. If we wished to exclude ϵ, we could write $L \cdot (L^*)$ to denote that language. That is,

$$L \cdot (L^*) = L \cdot \bigcup_{i=0}^{\infty} L^i = \bigcup_{i=0}^{\infty} L^{i+1} = \bigcup_{i=1}^{\infty} L^i$$

by using the fact that concatenation distributes over union. We shall often use the shorthand L^+ for $L \cdot (L^*)$. The unary postfix operator $^+$ is called *positive closure* and denotes "one or more instances of." □

Definition of Regular Expressions

With these definitions we are ready to describe regular expressions, the notation we shall use to define the class of languages known as regular sets. Recall that a token is either a single string (such as a punctuation symbol) or one of a collection of strings of a certain type (such as an identifier). If we view the set of strings in each token class as a language, we can use the regular-expression notation to describe tokens.

Consider the example of identifiers in a programming language. In several languages, an identifier is defined to be a letter followed by zero or more letters or digits. Saying this in English is not that cumbersome, but it is rather difficult to construct automatically a lexical analyzer from this type of English language description.

In regular expression notation we could write

identifier = letter (letter | digit)*

The vertical bar means "or," that is, union, the parentheses are used to group subexpressions, and the star is the closure operator meaning "zero or more instances." We shall soon see that from a description of this nature we can automatically construct a program that recognizes identifiers.

What we call the *regular expressions over alphabet* Σ are exactly those expressions that can be constructed from the following rules.† Each regular expression *denotes* a language, and we give the rules for construction of the

---

† For technical reasons, ϕ is normally considered a regular expression denoting the empty set. We choose not to do so here for simplicity.

denoted languages along with the regular-expression construction rules.

1. ϵ is a regular expression denoting $\{\epsilon\}$, that is, the language containing only the empty string.

2. For each a in Σ, a is a regular expression denoting $\{a\}$, the language with only one string, that string consisting of the single symbol a.

3. If R and S are regular expressions denoting languages L_R and L_S, respectively, then:

    i) $(R)\,|\,(S)$ is a regular expression denoting $L_R \cup L_S$.
    ii) $(R)\cdot(S)$ is a regular expression denoting $L_R \cdot L_S$.
    iii) $(R)^*$ is a regular expression denoting L_R^*.

We have shown regular expressions formed with parentheses wherever possible. In fact, we eliminate them when we can, using the precedence rules that * has highest precedence, then comes ·, and | has lowest precedence. We also remove the · operator, allowing juxtaposition to stand for concatenation. Note that these conventions are consistent with the notion that concatenation is a "product" and union a "sum."

We have just seen an example of a *recursive definition,* in that "regular expression" is defined in terms of primitive regular expressions (the *basis* of the definition) and compound regular expressions (the *induction* rules). Rules (1) and (2) above form the basis and rule (3) the inductive portion.

Example 3.5. In what follows, let us assume that our alphabet Σ is $\{a, b\}$. The regular expression a denotes $\{a\}$, which is different from just the string a. It should be clear from context whether we are talking about a as a regular expression or as a string.

1. The regular expression a^* denotes the closure of the language $\{a\}$, that is,

$$a^* = \bigcup_{i=0}^{\infty} \{a^i\}$$

the set of all strings of zero or more a's. The regular expression aa^*, which by our precedence rules is parsed $a(a)^*$, denotes the strings of one or more a's, by an argument similar to that followed in Example 3.4. We may use the shorthand a^+ for aa^*.

2. What does the regular expression $(a\,|\,b)^*$ denote? We see that $a\,|\,b$ denotes $\{a, b\}$, the language with two strings a and b. Thus $(a\,|\,b)^*$ denotes

$$\overset{\infty}{\underset{i=0}{\cup}} \{a, \ b\}^i$$

which is just the set of all strings of a's and b's, including the empty string. The reader should verify that $(a^*b^*)^*$ denotes the same set.

3. The expression $a \,|\, ba^*$ is grouped $a \,|\, (b(a)^*)$ and denotes the set of strings consisting of either a single a or a b followed by zero or more a's.

4. The expression $aa \,|\, ab \,|\, ba \,|\, bb$ denotes all strings of length two, so $(aa \,|\, ab \,|\, ba \,|\, bb)^*$ denotes all strings of even length. Note that ϵ is a string of even length, zero.

5. $\epsilon \,|\, a \,|\, b$ denotes strings of length zero or one.

6. $(a \,|\, b)(a \,|\, b)(a \,|\, b)$ denotes strings of length three. Thus $(a \,|\, b)(a \,|\, b)(a \,|\, b)(a \,|\, b)^*$ denotes strings of length three or more, and

$$\epsilon \,|\, a \,|\, b \,|\, (a \,|\, b)(a \,|\, b)(a \,|\, b)(a \,|\, b)^*$$

denotes all strings whose length is not two. □

Example 3.6. The tokens discussed in Example 3.1 can be described by regular expressions as follows.

$$
\begin{aligned}
\text{keyword} \quad &= \text{BEGIN} \,|\, \text{END} \,|\, \text{IF} \,|\, \text{THEN} \,|\, \text{ELSE} \\
\text{identifier} \quad &= \text{letter (letter} \,|\, \text{digit)}^* \\
\text{constant} \quad &= \text{digit}^+ \\
\text{relop} \quad &= {<} \,|\, {<=} \,|\, {=} \,|\, {<>} \,|\, {>} \,|\, {>=}
\end{aligned}
$$

where letter stands for $A \,|\, B \,|\, \cdots \,|\, Z$ and digit stands for $0 \,|\, 1 \,\cdots\, |\, 9$. We shall see that it is possible to construct the transition diagrams of Fig. 3.4 directly from these expressions. We need the theory of finite automata and their implementation, and we defer the actual construction until Section 3.8. □

If two regular expressions R and S denote the same language, we write $R = S$ and say that R and S are *equivalent*. For example, we previously observed that $(a \,|\, b)^* = (a^*b^*)^*$.

There are a number of useful algebraic laws obeyed by the regular-expression operators, and these can be used to manipulate regular expressions into equivalent forms. For any regular expressions R, S, and T, the following axioms hold:

1. $R \,|\, S = S \,|\, R$ ($|$ is commutative)
2. $R \,|\, (S \,|\, T) = (R \,|\, S) \,|\, T$ ($|$ is associative)
3. $R(ST) = (RS)T$ ($\cdot$ is associative)

4. $R(S \mid T) = RS \mid RT$
    and $(S \mid T)R = SR \mid TR$ ($\cdot$ distributes over $\mid$)
5. $\epsilon R = R\epsilon = R$ (ϵ is the identity for concatenation)

3.4 Finite Automata

A *recognizer* for a language L is a program that takes as input a string x and answers "yes" if x is a sentence of L and "no" otherwise. Clearly, the part of a lexical analyzer that identifies the presence of a token on the input is a recognizer for the language defining that token.

Suppose we have specified a language by a regular expression R, and we are given some string x. We want to know whether x is in the language L denoted by R. One way to attempt this test is to check that x can be decomposed into a sequence of substrings denoted by the primitive subexpressions in R.

Example 3.7. Suppose R is $(a \mid b)^*abb$, the set of all strings ending in *abb*, and x is the string *aabb*. We see that $R = R_1R_2$, where $R_1 = (a \mid b)^*$ and $R_2 = abb$. We can verify that a is an element of the language denoted by R_1 and that *abb* similarly matches R_2. In this way we show that *aabb* is in the language denoted by R. $\square$

Nondeterministic Automata

A better way to convert a regular expression to a recognizer is to construct a generalized transition diagram from the expression. This diagram is called a (*nondeterministic*) *finite automaton*. It cannot in general be easily simulated by a simple program, but a variant called a *deterministic finite automaton* can be simulated easily, and as we shall see, is constructible from the nondeterministic finite automaton. A nondeterministic finite automaton recognizing the language $(a \mid b)^*abb$ is shown in Fig. 3.5.

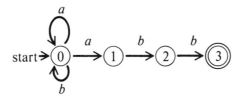

Fig. 3.5. A nondeterministic finite automaton.

As can be seen, the nondeterministic finite automaton (hereafter abbreviated NFA) is a labeled directed graph. The nodes are called *states,* and the labeled edges are called *transitions.* The NFA looks almost like a transition diagram, but edges can be labeled by ϵ as well as characters, and the same character can label two or more transitions out of one state. One state (0 in Fig. 3.5) is distinguished as the *start state,* and one or more states may be distinguished as *accepting states* (or *final states*) (in Fig. 3.5, state 3 is accepting, as indicated by the double circle).

The transitions of an NFA can be conveniently represented in tabular form by means of a *transition table.* The transition table for the NFA of Fig. 3.5 is shown in Fig. 3.6. In the transition table, there is a row for each state and a column for each admissible input symbol and ϵ, if necessary. The entry for row i and symbol a is the set of possible next states for state i on input a.

State	Input symbol	
	a	b
0	{0,1}	{0}
1	—	{2}
2	—	{3}

Fig. 3.6. Transition table.

The NFA *accepts* an input string x if and only if there is a path from the start state to some accepting state, such that the labels along that path spell out x. The NFA of Fig. 3.5 will accept the input strings *abb, aabb, babb, aaabb,....* For example, *aabb* is accepted by the path from 0, following the edge labeled a to state 0 again, then to states 1, 2 and 3 via edges labeled a, b and b, respectively.

This path can be formally represented by the following sequence of *moves:*

State	Remaining Input
0	*aabb*
0	*abb*
1	*bb*
2	*b*
3	ϵ

Initially the NFA is in state 0 "reading" the first input symbol a. In the first move, the NFA re-enters state 0 and advances to the next input symbol, reflecting the transition from state 0 to state 0 on input symbol a. The NFA is again in state 0 reading an a as the input symbol. In the second move, the NFA may enter state 1 (as well as state 0) and again advance to the next input symbol. Continuing in this fashion, the NFA enters the final configuration in which it is in state 3 (among other states) and no more characters are left to be read on the input.

The *language defined by* an NFA is the set of input strings it accepts. It is not hard to show that the NFA of Fig. 3.5 accepts $(a|b)$ *abb*.

Example 3.8. In Fig. 3.7 we see an NFA to recognize $aa^*|bb^*$. String *aaa* is accepted by going through states 0, 1, 2, 2, and 2. The labels of these edges are ϵ, *a*, *a*, and *a*, whose concatenation is *aaa*. Note that ϵ's "disappear" in a concatenation. □

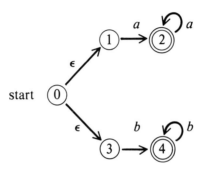

Fig. 3.7. NFA accepting $aa^*|bb^*$.

Deterministic Automata

Note that the NFA of Fig. 3.5 has more than one transition from state 0 on input *a*; that is, it may go to state 0 or 1. Similarly, the NFA of Fig. 3.7 has two transitions on ϵ from state 0. These situations, in which the transition function is multivalued, are the reason why it is hard to simulate an NFA with a computer program. The definition of acceptance merely asserts that there must be some path labeled by the input string in question leading from the start state to an accepting state. But if there are many paths with the same label string, we may have to consider them all before we find one that leads to an accepting state or determine that no path leads to acceptance. Fortunately, there is a deterministic version of the finite automaton which can be simulated in a straightforward manner, since a deterministic finite automaton has at most one path from the start state labeled by any string. We say a finite automaton is *deterministic* if

1. It has no transitions on input ϵ.
2. For each state s and input symbol a, there is at most one edge labeled a leaving s.

Example 3.9. In Fig. 3.8 we see a deterministic finite automaton (DFA for short) accepting the language $(a \mid b)^*abb$, which is the same language as that accepted by the NFA of Fig. 3.5. □

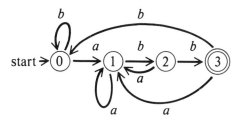

Fig. 3.8. DFA accepting $(a \mid b)^*abb$.

Since there is at most one transition out of any state on any input symbol, a DFA is easier to simulate by a program than is an NFA. To simulate a DFA we can create a piece of program for each state, that piece of program determining the proper transition to make on the current input symbol.

Fortunately, for each NFA we can find a DFA accepting the same language. The number of states of the DFA could be exponential in the number of states of the NFA, but in practice this worst case occurs rarely. The next algorithm gives the NFA-to-DFA construction. The general idea is that after reading input $a_1 a_2 \cdots a_n$, the DFA is in a state which represents the set of states of the NFA which are reachable from the NFA's start state along a path labeled $a_1 a_2 \cdots a_n$. Since the states of the DFA represent subsets of the set of all states of the NFA, this algorithm is often called the *subset construction*.

Algorithm 3.1. Constructing a deterministic finite automaton from a nondeterministic one.

Input. An NFA N.

Output. A DFA D accepting the same language.

Method. Each state of D is a set of states which N could be in after reading some sequence of input symbols. Thus D is able to simulate "in parallel" all possible moves N can make on a given input string. The initial state of D is the set consisting of s_0, the initial state of N, together with all states of

N that can be reached from s_0 by means of ϵ-transitions only. The accepting states of D are those sets of states that contain at least one accepting state of N.

For convenience, let us define the function ϵ-CLOSURE(s) to be the set of states of N built by applying the following rules:

1. s is added to ϵ-CLOSURE(s).
2. If t is in ϵ-CLOSURE(s), and there is an edge labeled ϵ from t to u, then u is added to ϵ-CLOSURE(s) if u is not already there. Rule 2 is repeated until no more states can be added to ϵ-CLOSURE(s).

Thus, ϵ-CLOSURE(s) is just the set of states that can be reached from s on ϵ-transitions alone. If T is a set of states, then ϵ-CLOSURE(T) is just the union over all states s in T of ϵ-CLOSURE(s).

The computation of ϵ-CLOSURE(T) is a typical process of searching a graph for nodes reachable from a given set of nodes. In this case the nodes of T are the given set, and the graph consists of the ϵ-labeled edges of the transition diagram only. A simple algorithm to compute ϵ-CLOSURE(T) uses a stack of nodes known to be in ϵ-CLOSURE(T), but whose ϵ-labeled transitions out have not yet been consulted. Such a procedure is shown in Fig. 3.9.

```
begin
    push all states in T onto STACK;
    ε-CLOSURE(T) := T;
    while STACK not empty do
        begin
            pop s, the top element of STACK, off of STACK;
            for each state t with an edge from s to t labeled ε do
                if t is not in ε-CLOSURE(T) do
                    begin
                        add t to ε-CLOSURE(T);
                        push t onto STACK
                    end
        end
end
```

Fig. 3.9. Computation of ϵ-CLOSURE.

The states of D and their transitions are constructed as follows. Initially, let ϵ-CLOSURE(s_0) be a state of D. This state is the start state of D. We assume each state of D is initially "unmarked." Then perform the algorithm of Fig. 3.10. □

> **while** there is an unmarked state $x = \{s_1, s_2, \ldots, s_n\}$ of D **do**
>   **begin**
>   mark x;
>   **for** each input symbol a **do**
>   **begin**
>   let T be the set of states to which there is
>   a transition on a from some state s_i in x;
> $y := \epsilon\text{-CLOSURE}(T)$;
>   **if** y has not yet been added to the
>   set of states of D **then**
>   make y an "unmarked" state of D and
>   add a transition from x to y labeled a
>   **end**
>   **end**

Fig. 3.10 The subset construction.

Example 3.10. Figure 3.11 shows another NFA N accepting the language $(a \mid b)^*abb$. It happens to be the one we would obtain if we applied an algorithm, yet to be specified, to construct an NFA from that regular expression.

Let us apply Algorithm 3.1 to N. The initial state of the equivalent DFA is ϵ-CLOSURE(0), which is $A = \{0, 1, 2, 4, 7\}$, since these are exactly the states reachable from state 0 via a path in which every edge is labeled ϵ. Note that 0 is reached from itself by such a path, the path having no edges.

The algorithm of Fig. 3.10 tells us to set x to A and compute T, the set of states of N having transitions on a from members of A. Among the states 0, 1, 2, 4 and 7, only 2 and 7 have such transitions, to 3 and 8, so

$$y = \epsilon\text{-CLOSURE}(\{3, 8\}) = \{1, 2, 3, 4, 6, 7, 8\}$$

Let us call this set B. Among the states in A, only 4 has a transition on b to 5, so the DFA has a transition on b from A to

$$C = \epsilon\text{-CLOSURE}(\{5\}) = \{1, 2, 4, 5, 6, 7\}$$

If we continue this process with the now unmarked sets B and C, we shall eventually reach the point where all sets that are states of the DFA are marked. This is certain since there are "only" 2^{11} different subsets of the set of eleven states, and a set, once marked, is marked forever. The five different sets of states we actually construct are:

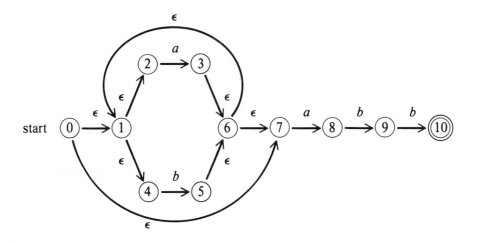

Fig. 3.11. NFA N for $(a \mid b)$ *abb.

$$A = \{0, 1, 2, 4, 7\} \qquad D = \{1, 2, 4, 5, 6, 7, 9\}$$
$$B = \{1, 2, 3, 4, 6, 7, 8\} \quad E = \{1, 2, 4, 5, 6, 7, 10\}$$
$$C = \{1, 2, 4, 5, 6, 7\}$$

The transition table of the resulting DFA is shown in Fig. 3.12. It should be noted that the DFA of Fig. 3.8 also accepts $(a \mid b)$ *abb and has one fewer state. We shall discuss the question of minimization of the number of states of a DFA in Section 3.6. □

	State	Input	
		a	b
(Start)	A	B	C
	B	B	D
	C	B	C
	D	B	E
(Accept)	E	B	C

Fig. 3.12. Transition table for Fig. 3.11.

3.5 From Regular Expressions to Finite Automata

We have already mentioned that determining whether a string is in the language denoted by a regular expression is a task easily performed by a deterministic finite automaton. We have also stated that a regular expression is a natural notation for describing the language of a token, and that we were going to give a method of going from the description, the regular expression, to the program, that is, the deterministic finite automaton. Already we know how to build a DFA from an NFA, and this is convenient, because it is also relatively easy to go from a regular expression to an NFA. The direct construction of a DFA from a regular expression is somewhat harder.

We shall now give an algorithm that produces an NFA from a regular expression. This is not the best possible algorithm, in the sense that some special-case modifications would produce an NFA with fewer states from the same regular expression. However, the algorithm is simple to implement in the form in which we present it, and in the next section we show how to reduce the number of states of a DFA to the smallest possible number.

Algorithm 3.2. Constructing an NFA from a regular expression.

Input. A regular expression R over alphabet Σ.

Output. An NFA N accepting the language denoted by R.

Method. We first decompose R into its primitive components. For each component we construct a finite automaton inductively, as follows. Parts (1) and (2) form the basis and part (3) is the induction.

1.   For ϵ we construct the NFA

2.   For a in Σ we construct the NFA

Each time we need a new state, we give that state a new name. Even if a appears several times in the regular expression R, we give each instance of a a separate finite automaton with its own states. In this way, no two states generated either for the basis components or for the inductively constructed components to follow have the same name.

3. Having constructed components for the basis regular expressions, we
    proceed to combine them in ways that correspond to the way compound
    regular expressions are formed from smaller regular expressions.

For all regular expressions we construct an NFA with one initial and
one final state, and with the extra properties that no more than two edges
leave any state, and that no edge enters the initial state or leaves the final
state. The limit of two on the number of edges leaving each state is a convenience that allows an efficient representation of the transition function of
the automaton. We observe that each of the above properties holds for the
basis automata constructed in (1) and (2).

Now suppose we are given NFA's N_1 and N_2 for regular expressions R_1
and R_2. For the regular expression $R_1|R_2$ we construct the composite
NFA

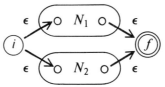

where i is a new initial state and f a new final state. There is a transition on
ϵ from the new initial state to the initial states of N_1 and N_2. There is an
ϵ-transition from the final states of N_1 and N_2 (which are no longer final in
the composite NFA) to the new final state f. Note that any path from i to
f must go through either N_1 or N_2; no mixtures of the states of these two
automata is possible. Thus it is not hard to see why the composite automa-
ton accepts $R_1|R_2$.

For the expression R_1R_2 we construct the composite NFA.

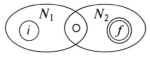

The initial state of N_2 is identified with the accepting state of N_1, in the
sense that the latter disappears, and all transitions from the former now
come from the final state of N_1. The initial state of N_1 becomes the initial
state of the composite machine, and the final state of the composite is the
final state of N_2. A path from i to f must go first through N_1, then through
N_2, so the label of that path will be a string in the language of R_1 followed
by a string in the language of R_2. Thus each such string is in the concatenation of the two languages. Note that since no edge enters the initial state
of N_2 or leaves the final state of N_1, there can be no a path from i to f that
travels from N_2 back to N_1.

For the expression R_1^* we construct the composite NFA

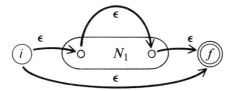

where i is a new initial state and f a new final state. In this new automaton, we can go from i to f directly, along a path labeled ϵ, representing the fact that ϵ is in R_1^*, or we can go through N_1 one or more times.

We can easily check that the above constructions are correct, in the sense that if N_1 and N_2 accept the languages of R_1 and R_2, respectively, then the composite automaton accepts the language $R_1|R_2$, R_1R_2, or R_1^* for each of the three constructions given in part (3). Moreover, on the assumption that N_1 and N_2 have the various properties stated before the constructions (one final state, e.g.), it can be checked that the composite automata will possess those properties. □

Example 3.11. Let us construct an NFA for the regular expression $R = (a|b)^*abb$. Figure 3.13 shows the decomposition of R into its primitive components.

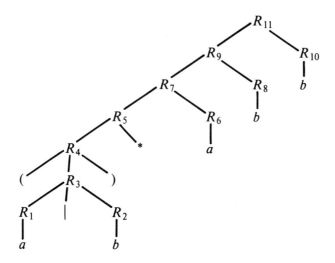

Fig. 3.13. Decomposition of $(a|b)^*abb$.

For the first primitive component R_1, the first a, we construct the primitive NFA

$$N_1: \quad (2) \xrightarrow{a} (3)$$

(The significance of this choice of state numbers will become clear shortly.) For R_2 we construct

$$N_2: \quad (4) \xrightarrow{b} (5)$$

We can now combine N_1 and N_2 using the rule for union to obtain the NFA N_3 for $R_3 = R_1 | R_2$.

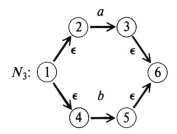

N_4, the NFA for $R_4 = (R_3)$ is the same as N_3. Then, N_5, the automaton for $R_5 = R_4^*$ is:

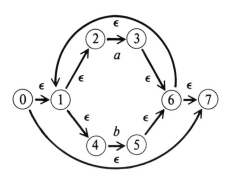

The primitive machine for $R_6 = a$ is

$$N_6: \quad (7') \xrightarrow{a} (8)$$

To obtain the machine for $R_7 = R_5 R_6$, we merely identify states 7 and 7' to obtain N_7:

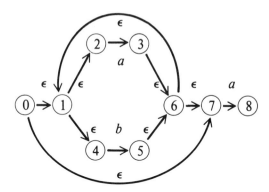

Continuing in this fashion, we obtain the NFA for $R_{11} = (a|b)$ *abb which was first exhibited in Fig. 3.11. □

In many cases, simplifications of the inductive NFA constructions in Algorithm 3.2 can be made. In particular, we could merge the initial and final states of the two automata in the construction for union. The reason we did not do so is that this construction causes certain states to have more than two transitions out. While this is not a fatal problem, there is a great convenience in having this limitation on transitions. In particular, note that every NFA constructed by Algorithm 3.2 has either one or two out-transitions labeled ϵ or one transition labeled by a real symbol. Thus we can represent each state by a triple of the form (symbol, nextstate1, nextstate2).

3.6 Minimizing the Number of States of a DFA

The DFA of Fig. 3.12 constructed from the NFA of Fig. 3.11 is not the smallest possible. In particular, we gave, in Fig. 3.8, another DFA with only four states that also accepted $(a|b)$ *abb. Part of the reason for this nonminimality of the subset construction lies in the fact that we did not include in Algorithm 3.1 some obvious state identifications that could be made. Suppose we call a state of an NFA *important* if it has a non-ϵ out-transition. If we take a look at the subset construction in Fig. 3.10, we see that it is only the important states in a subset of NFA states x that determine the DFA state to which x goes on input a. Thus two different subsets can be identified as one state of the DFA being constructed, provided:

1. they have the same important states and
2. they either both include or both exclude accepting states of the NFA.

Example 3.12. In the case of the NFA *N* of Fig. 3.11, the important states
are 2, 4, 7, 8, and 9. Thus, in the DFA constructed, we can identify the
nonaccepting states $A = \{0, 1, 2, 4, 7\}$ and $C = \{1, 2, 4, 5, 6, 7\}$, since
each contains the important NFA states 2, 4, and 7 only. Note that $E = \{1, 2, 4, 5, 6, 7, 10\}$, which has the same important states as these, cannot
be identified with them because *E* is an accepting state of the DFA. □

The next algorithm gives a more general way of reducing the number
of states of a DFA. Suppose that we have a DFA *M* and that *S* is *M*'s set
of states, and Σ its set of input symbols. We assume that every state has a
transition on every input symbol. If that were not the case, just introduce a
new "dead state" *d*, with transitions from *d* to *d* on all inputs, and add a
transition from state *s* to *d* on input *a* if there was no transition from *s*
labeled *a*.

We say that string *w* *distinguishes* state *s* from state *t* if, by starting the
DFA *M* in state *s* and feeding it input *w*, we wind up in a final state while,
by starting in state *t* and feeding it input *w*, we wind up in a nonfinal state,
or vice versa. For example, ε distinguishes any final state from any
nonfinal state, and in the DFA of Fig. 3.12, states *A* and *B* are distinguished by the input *bb*, since *A* goes to the nonfinal *C* on input *bb*,
while *B* goes to accepting state *E* on that input.

Our algorithm to minimize the number of states of a DFA works by
finding all groups of states that can be distinguished by some input string.
Those groups of states that cannot be distinguished are then merged into a
single state for the entire group. The algorithm works by keeping a partition of the set of states such that each group of states consists of states
which have not yet been distinguished from one another, and such that any
pair of states chosen from different groups have been found distinguishable
by some input.

Initially, there are only two groups, the final states and the nonfinal
states. The fundamental step is to take some group of states, say
$A = \{s_1, s_2, ..., s_k\}$ and some input symbol *a*, and look at what transitions
states $s_1, ..., s_k$ have on input *a*. If these transitions are to states that fall
into two or more different groups of the current partition, then we must
split *A* so that the transitions from the subsets of *A* are all confined to a
single group of the current partition. Suppose, for example, that s_1 and s_2
go to states t_1 and t_2 on input *a*, and t_1 and t_2 are in different groups. Then
we must split *A* into at least two subsets so that one subset contains s_1 and
the other s_2. Note that t_1 and t_2 are distinguished by some string *w* and
that s_1 and s_2 are distinguished by string *aw*.

We repeat this process of splitting groups until no more groups need to be split. While we have justified why states that have been split into different groups really can be distinguished, we have not indicated why states that are not split into different groups are certain not to be distinguishable by any input string. Such is the case, however, and we leave a proof of that fact to the reader interested in the theory. Also left to the interested reader is a proof that the DFA constructed by taking one state for each group of the final partition and then throwing away the dead state and states not reachable from the initial state has as few states as any DFA accepting the same language.

Algorithm 3.3. Minimizing the number of states of a DFA.

Input. A DFA M with set of states S, inputs Σ, transitions defined for all states and inputs, initial state s_0, and set of final states F.

Output. A DFA M' accepting the same language as M and having as few states as possible.

Method.

1. We construct a partition Π of the set of states. Initially, Π consists of two groups, the final states F, and the nonfinal states $S - F$. Then we construct a new partition Π_{new} by the procedure of Fig. 3.14. Π_{new} will always be a *refinement* of Π, meaning that Π_{new} consists of the groups of Π, each split into one or more pieces. If $\Pi_{new} \neq \Pi$, we replace Π by Π_{new} and repeat the procedure of Fig. 3.14. If $\Pi_{new} = \Pi$, then no more changes can ever occur, so we terminate this part of the algorithm. Note that since each Π_{new} has at least as many groups as the previous one, and we halt when equality occurs, we must get a Π for which $\Pi_{new} = \Pi$.

> **for** each group G of Π **do**
> > **begin**
> > > partition G into subgroups such that two states s and t
> > > of G are in the same subgroup if and only if for all
> > > input symbols a, states s and t have transitions
> > > to states in the same group of Π;
> > > /* at worst, a state will be in a subgroup by itself */
> > > place all subgroups so formed in Π_{new}
> > **end**

Fig. 3.14. Construction of Π_{new}.

2. When the final partition Π has been constructed in step (1), pick a *representative* for each group, that is, an arbitrary state in the group. The representatives will be the states of the reduced DFA M'. Let s be a representative state, and suppose on input a there is a transition of M from s to t. Let r be the representative of t's group (r may be t). Then M' has a transition from s to r on a. Let the initial state of M' be the representative of the group containing the initial state s_0 of M, and let the final states of M' be the representatives which are in F. Note that each group of Π either consists only of states in F or has no states in F.

3. If M' has a *dead state*, that is, a state d which is not final and with transitions to itself on all input symbols a, then remove d from M'. Also remove any states not reachable from the initial state. Any transitions to d from other states become undefined. □

Example 3.13. Let us reconsider the DFA represented in Fig. 3.12. The initial partition Π consists of two groups, $(ABCD)$, consisting of the nonfinal states and (E), the final states. To construct Π_{new} by the algorithm of Fig. 3.14, we first consider (E). Since this consists of one state, it cannot be further split, so we place (E) in Π_{new}. Now consider $(ABCD)$. On input a, each of these states goes to B, so they could all be placed in one group as far as input a is concerned. However, on input b, A, B, and C go to members of the group $(ABCD)$ of Π, while D goes to E, a member of another group. Thus, in Π_{new} $(ABCD)$ must be split into two groups (ABC) and (D). The new value of Π is thus $(ABC)(D)(E)$.

Constructing the next Π_{new}, we again have no splitting on input a, but (ABC) must be split into two groups $(AC)(B)$, since on input b, A and C each go to C, while B goes to D, a member of a group of Π different from that of C. Thus the next value of Π is $(AC)(B)(D)(E)$. When we construct Π_{new} from this, we cannot split any of the groups consisting of a single state. The only possibility is that (AC) could be split. But A and C go to the same state, B, on input a, and they go to the same state, C, on input b. Hence, $\Pi_{new} = \Pi$ here, and the final partition Π from step (1) of Algorithm 3.3 is $(AC)(B)(D)(E)$.

Let us now choose representatives. Of course B, D, and E represent the groups containing only themselves. Let us choose A to represent the group (AC). Then the transition table for the reduced automaton is shown in Fig. 3.15.

For example, E goes to C on input b in the automaton of Fig. 3.12. Since A is the representative of the group for C, we have a transition from E to A on input b in Fig. 3.15. A similar change has taken place in the entry for A on input b, and all other transitions are copied from Fig. 3.12.

		a	b
(Start)	A	B	A
	B	B	D
	D	B	E
(Accept)	E	B	A

Fig. 3.15. Reduced automaton.

There is no dead state in Fig. 3.15, and all states are reachable from the initial state A. The automaton of Fig. 3.15 is the one whose transition diagram was shown in Fig. 3.8. □

3.7 A Language for Specifying Lexical Analyzers

We shall now study the question of how one builds a lexical analyzer from a specification of tokens in the form of a list of regular expressions. The discussion centers around the design of an existing tool, called LEX (Lesk [1975]), for automatically generating lexical analyzers. If the compiler writer does not have a tool like LEX, he may still follow a mental process similar to the method by which LEX constructs a lexical analysis program from its input.

A LEX source program is a specification of a lexical analyzer, consisting of a set of regular expressions together with an action for each regular expression. The action is a piece of code which is to be executed whenever a token specified by the corresponding regular expression is recognized. Typically, an action will pass an indication of the token found to the parser, perhaps with side effects such as making an entry in the symbol table. The output of LEX is a lexical analyzer program constructed from the LEX source specification.

We can view LEX as a compiler for a stylized language, a language that is very good for writing lexical analyzers and some other tasks of a text-processing nature. Unlike most programming languages, a source program for LEX does not supply all the details of the intended computation. Rather, LEX itself supplies with its output a program that simulates a finite automaton. This program takes a transition table as data. The transition table is that portion of LEX's output that stems directly from LEX's input. The situation is depicted in Fig. 3.16, where the lexical analyzer L is the transition table plus the program to simulate an arbitrary finite automaton expressed as a transition table. Only L is to be included in the compiler being built.

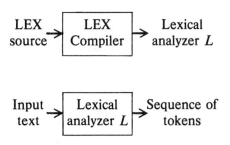

Fig. 3.16. The role of LEX.

Auxiliary Definitions

A LEX source program consists of two parts, a sequence of *auxiliary definitions* followed by a sequence of *translation rules*. The auxiliary definitions are statements of the form

$$D_1 = R_1$$
$$D_2 = R_2$$
$$\cdot$$
$$\cdot$$
$$\cdot$$
$$D_n = R_n$$

where each D_i is a distinct name, and each R_i is a regular expression whose symbols are chosen from $\Sigma \cup \{D_1, D_2, \ldots, D_{i-1}\}$, i.e., characters or previously defined names. The D_i's are shorthand names for regular expressions. Σ is our input symbol alphabet, e.g., the ASCII or EBCDIC character sets. To avoid confusion, lower-case strings are used as names for the D_i's, the regular expression names.

Example 3.14. We can define the class of identifiers for a typical programming language with the following sequence of auxiliary definitions.

letter $= A | B | \cdots | Z$
digit $= 0 | 1 | \cdots | 9$
identifier $=$ letter (letter | digit)*

For a more elaborate example of the use of auxiliary definitions, let us consider the definition of FORTRAN arithmetic constants. Having had the definition of digit above, we can define

integer = digit$^+$
sign = + | − | ϵ
signed-integer = sign integer

Then we can define a decimal (as opposed to exponential) real number to be

decimal = signed-integer . integer
| signed-integer .
| sign . integer

Next, an exponential-form real number is a decimal or signed integer followed by E and a signed-integer. That is

exponential = (decimal | signed-integer) E signed-integer

Finally, a real number is defined by

real = decimal | exponential ☐

By restricting ourselves in each R_i to the symbols of Σ and the previously defined names for regular expressions, we make sure that each R_i defines a regular set. That is, we can construct a regular expression over Σ for any R_i by repeatedly replacing regular-expression names by the expressions they denote.† The reader should note that if auxiliary regular-expression definitions were allowed to refer to one another at will, including references to following definitions, then we could not necessarily expand all names to regular expressions over Σ. These kinds of mutually recursive definitions do form an important part of the theory of parser design, and we shall encounter them when we discuss grammars in the next chapter.

Translation Rules

The translation rules of a LEX program are statements of the form

---

† In the case that an auxiliary definition D_i is a set of characters, like letter and digit from Example 3.14, it is useful to keep D_i as a "symbol" and have one transition on D_i in the NFA's constructed, rather than replacing D_i by transitions on each of the symbols for which D_i stands. When we construct the DFA we can take account of the fact that D_i stands for a collection of characters.

$$P_1 \quad \{A_1\}$$
$$P_2 \quad \{A_2\}$$

.

.

.

$$P_m \quad \{A_m\}$$

where each P_i is a regular expression called a *pattern,* over the alphabet consisting of Σ and the auxiliary definition names. The patterns describe the form of the tokens. Each A_i is a program fragment describing what action the lexical analyzer should take when token P_i is found. The A_i's are written in a conventional programming language; however, rather than using any particular language here, we shall use our informal "pseudo-language" which should be clear to everyone. To create the lexical analyzer L, each of the A_i's must be compiled into machine code, just like any other program written in the language of the A_i's.

The lexical analyzer L created by LEX behaves in the following manner. L reads its input, one character at a time, until it has found the longest prefix of the input which matches one of the regular expressions, P_i. Once L has found that prefix, L removes it from the input and places it in a buffer called TOKEN. (Actually, TOKEN may be a pair of pointers to the beginning and end of the matched string in the input buffer itself.) L then executes the action A_i. After completing A_i, L returns control to the parser. When requested to, L repeats this series of actions on the remaining input.

It is possible, however, that none of the regular expressions denoting the tokens matches any prefix of the input. In that case, an error has occurred, and L presumably transfers control to some error handling routine (see Chapter 11). It is also possible that two or more patterns match the same longest prefix of the remaining input. If that is the case, L will break the tie in favor of that token which came first in the list of translation rules.

Example 3.15. Let us consider the collection of tokens defined in Fig. 3.3. We shall give a LEX specification for these tokens here, and in the next section, see how the lexical analyzer recognizing these tokens would be produced by LEX. The lexical analyzer produced by LEX always returns a single quantity, the token type, to the parser. To pass a value as well, it sets a global variable called LEXVAL. The program shown in Fig. 3.17 is a LEX program defining the desired lexical analyzer.

Suppose the lexical analyzer resulting from the above rules is given input BEGIN followed by blank. Both the first and sixth patterns match

AUXILIARY DEFINITIONS

letter = A | B | ... | Z
digit = 0 | 1 | ... | 9

TRANSLATION RULES

BEGIN	{**return** 1}
END	{**return** 2}
IF	{**return** 3}
THEN	{**return** 4}
ELSE	{**return** 5}
letter(letter | digit)*	{LEXVAL := INSTALL(); **return** 6}
digit$^+$	{LEXVAL := INSTALL(); **return** 7}
<	{LEXVAL := 1; **return** 8}
<=	{LEXVAL := 2; **return** 8}
=	{LEXVAL := 3; **return** 8}
<>	{LEXVAL := 4; **return** 8}
>	{LEXVAL := 5; **return** 8}
>=	{LEXVAL := 6; **return** 8}

Fig. 3.17. LEX program.

BEGIN, and no pattern matches a longer string. Since the pattern for keyword BEGIN precedes the pattern for identifiers in the above list, the conflict is resolved in favor of the keyword. In general, LEX's ambiguity resolving strategy makes it easy to reserve keywords by listing them ahead of the pattern for identifiers.

For another example, suppose <= are the first two characters read. While pattern < matches the first character, it is not the longest pattern matching a prefix of the input. Thus LEX's strategy that the longest prefix matching a pattern is selected makes it easy to resolve the conflict between < and <= in the expected manner — by choosing <= as the next token. □

The Lookahead Operator

Let us also mention at this point that certain programming languages require a "lookahead" feature in order to specify their lexical analyzers correctly. A popular example from FORTRAN is the statement

$$DO\ 10\ I = 1.25$$

where we cannot tell until we see the decimal point that this is not a DO statement, but rather an assignment to an identifier DO10I. We shall use / as an operator in regular expressions indicating that the token, if found, ends at the point of the /. Then a specification for the keyword DO could be

$$DO\ /\ (\ letter\ |\ digit\ )\ *\ =\ (\ letter\ |\ digit\ )\ *\ ,$$

With this specification, the lexical analyzer would look ahead to the comma to be sure that we did not have an assignment statement. Then only the characters D and O, preceding the /, would be removed from the input and placed in the buffer TOKEN.

Example 3.16. Another subtle example from FORTRAN is the recognition of the keyword IF. The problem is that

$$IF(I, J) = 3$$

is perfectly good FORTRAN, but not an IF statement. One way to specify the context of the keyword IF is to note that the IF statement has the form

IF (condition) statement

Also, every unlabeled FORTRAN statement begins with a letter. Finally, we note that every right parenthesis used for subscripting or operand grouping must be followed by an operator symbol such as =, +, or comma, or the end of the statement. Surely such a right parenthesis cannot be followed by a letter. Thus to confirm that IF is a keyword rather than an array name we scan forward for a right parenthesis followed by a letter before we see a newline character (we assume continuation cards "cancel" the previous newline character). Thus the pattern for keyword IF could be written

IF/ '(' any * ')' letter

Here, the auxiliary definition "any" stands for any character except newline. □

We might observe that another way to handle the problem posed by the IF statement is to introduce a test to see whether IF has been declared an array, after seeing IF(. Scan for the full pattern indicated above only if it has been so declared. Such tests make automatic implementation of the lexical analyzer generated by LEX harder, and they may even cost time in the long run, since frequent checks must be made by the program simulating a transition diagram to determine whether any such tests must be made.

3.8 Implementation of a Lexical Analyzer

It should be apparent that LEX can build from its input a lexical analyzer that behaves roughly like a finite automaton. The idea is to construct a nondeterministic finite automaton N_i for each token pattern P_i in the translation rules, using Algorithm 3.2, and then link these NFA's together with a new start state as shown in Fig. 3.18. Next we convert this NFA to a DFA, using the subset construction, Algorithm 3.1.

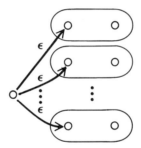

Fig. 3.18. NFA recognizing several tokens simultaneously.

There are several nuances in this procedure of which the reader should be aware. First, there are in the combined NFA several different "accepting states." That is, the accepting state of each N_i indicates that its own token, P_i has been found. When we convert to a DFA, the subsets we construct may include several different final states. Moreover, the final states lose some of their significance, since we are looking for the longest prefix of the input which matches some pattern. After reaching a final state, the lexical analyzer must continue to simulate the DFA until it reaches a state with no next state for the current input symbol. Let us say we reach *termination* when we meet an input symbol from which the DFA cannot proceed. We must presume that the programming language is designed so that a valid program cannot entirely fill the input buffer (see Section 3.1) without reaching termination. For example, each compiler puts a restriction on the length of an identifier, and violations of this limit will be detected when the input buffer overflows, if not sooner.

Upon reaching termination, it is necessary to review the states of the DFA which we have entered while processing the input. Each such state represents a subset of the NFA's states, and we look for the last DFA state which includes a final state for one of the pattern-recognizing NFA's N_i. That final state indicates which token we have found. If none of the states which the DFA has entered includes any final states of the NFA, then we have an error condition. If the last DFA state to include a final NFA state in fact includes more than one final state, then the final state for the pattern listed first has priority.

Example 3.17. A simple example should make these ideas clear. Suppose we have the following LEX program.

AUXILIARY DEFINITIONS

   (none)

TRANSLATION RULES

a	{}/* Actions are omitted here */
abb	{}
a^*b^+	{}

The three tokens above are recognized by the simple automata of Fig. 3.19(a), among others.

We may convert the NFA's of Fig. 3.19(a) into one NFA as described above. The result is shown in Fig. 3.19(b). Then this NFA may be converted to a DFA using Algorithm 3.1. We show the resulting transition table in Fig. 3.20, where the states of the DFA have been named by lists of the states of the NFA.

The last column in Fig. 3.20 indicates the token which will be recognized if that state is the last state entered that recognizes any token at all. In all cases but the last line, state 68, the token recognized is the only token whose final state is included among the NFA states forming the DFA state. For example, among NFA states 2, 4, and 7, only 2 is final, and it is the final state of the automaton for regular expression a in Fig. 3.19(a). Thus, DFA state 247 recognizes token a. In the case of DFA state 68, both 6 and 8 are final states of their respective nondeterministic automata. Since the translation rules of our LEX program mention abb before a^*b^+, NFA state 6 has priority, and we announce that abb has been found in DFA state 68.

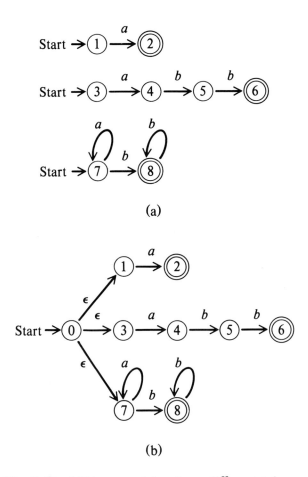

(a)

(b)

Fig. 3.19. NFA recognizing three different tokens.

Suppose that the first input characters are *aba*. The DFA of Fig. 3.20 starts off in state 0137. On input *a* it goes to state 247. Then on input *b* it progresses to state 58, and on input *a* it has no next state. We have thus reached termination, progressing through the DFA states 0137, then 247, then 58. The last of these includes the final NFA state 8 from Fig. 3.19(a). Thus the action for state 58 of the DFA is to announce that the token a^*b^+ has been recognized, and to select *ab*, the prefix of the input that led to state 58, as TOKEN.

It is worth mentioning what would happen if DFA state 58, the last state entered before termination, had not included a final state of some

State	a	b	token found
0137	247	8	none
247	7	58	a
8	-	8	a*b+
7	7	8	none
58	-	68	a*b+
68	-	8	abb

Fig. 3.20. Transition table for DFA.

NFA. In that case we would consider the DFA state previously entered, 247 in this case, and recognize the token a, which state 247 calls for. The prefix a would in that case be TOKEN. □

The role of the action A_i associated with the regular expression P_i should be clear. When an instance of a token P_i is recognized on the input, the lexical analyzer makes the input prefix recognized be TOKEN and proceeds to execute the program A_i. Note that A_i is not executed just because the DFA enters a state which includes the accepting state for P_i. A_i is only executed if P_i turns out to be the longest pattern on the input.

Example 3.18. In Fig. 3.21 we see the NFA's for the patterns of Example 3.15, linked together with a new initial state, as Fig. 3.18 suggests. Simpler NFA's than would be constructed by Algorithm 3.2 are used for identifiers and constants. The DFA constructed from Fig. 3.21 is shown in Fig. 3.22. Each state of the deterministic automaton is a subset of the states of the nondeterministic automaton. State s_0 is the set of nondeterministic states {0, 1, 7, 11, 14, 19, 24, 26, 28, 30, 33, 35, 38, 40}.

The states marked # have transitions to state {25} on all letters and digits for which no transition is shown. Note that character classes letter and digit have not been expanded but are treated as symbols, for which a range test on input characters will be made.

On an input such as THE followed by a nonletter or digit, the DFA winds up in state {17, 25}, which contains accepting state 25 of the nondeterministic automaton. That state signals that an identifier has been found and the appropriate action, as indicated in Example 3.15, is taken.

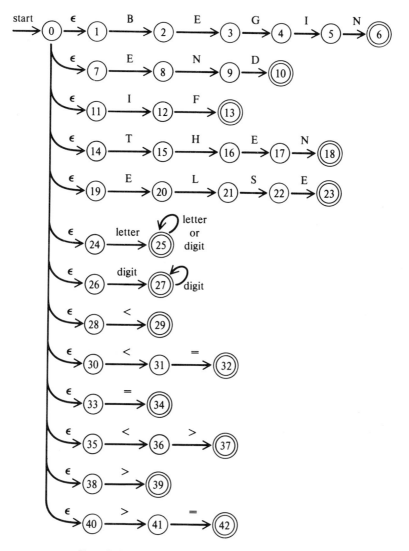

Fig. 3.21. Combined NFA for tokens.

On input <A, the lexical analyzer goes to state {29, 31, 36} on <, from which no transition on A is possible. Of the three NFA states, only 29 is accepting and it indicates that the token < has been found. Again the action specified by Example 3.15 is taken. □

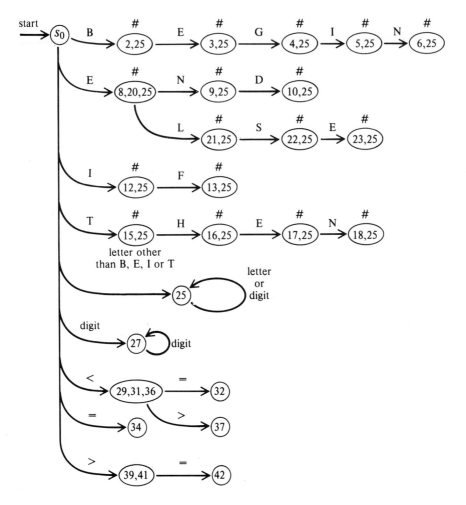

Fig. 3.22. DFA constructed from Fig. 3.20.

State Minimization

The reader should also be made aware of the modification which must be made to the state minimization procedure of Algorithm 3.3, if we are to apply it to the DFA's constructed as above. We must begin Algorithm 3.3 with an initial partition which places in different groups all states indicating different tokens.

Example 3.19. In the case of the DFA of Fig. 3.20, the initial partition would group 0137 with 7, since they each gave no indication of a token recognized; 8 and 58 would also be grouped, since they each indicated token a^*b^+. Other states would be in groups by themselves. Then we immediately discover that 0137 and 7 belong in different groups since they go to different groups on input a. Likewise, 8 and 58 do not belong together because of their transitions on input b. Thus the DFA of Fig. 3.20 is the minimum-state automaton doing its job.   □

Implementing the Lookahead Operator

Recall from Section 3.7 that the lookahead operator, /, is necessary in many situations, since the pattern that indicates the presence of a particular token may extend beyond the token itself. When converting a pattern with / to an NFA, treat the / as if it were ϵ, so we do not actually look for / on the input. However, if the pattern is recognized by a DFA constructed from this NFA and others, the end of the token is not the position of the NFA's final state. Rather it is at the last occurrence of the state of this NFA having the transition on the (imaginary) / .

Example 3.20. The NFA recognizing the pattern for IF given in Example 3.16 is shown in Fig. 3.23. If this NFA is combined with others into a DFA, a state of the DFA containing state 6 indicates the presence of keyword IF. However, we find the token IF by scanning backwards for a DFA state containing state 2.   □

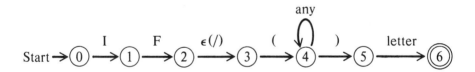

Fig. 3.23. NFA recognizing FORTRAN keyword IF.

Representing a Transition Diagram as a Data Structure

The actual representation in the computer's memory of the transition table of the DFA deserves mention. The process of lexical analysis occupies a reasonable portion of the compiler's time, since it is the only process that must look at the input one character at a time. Therefore a fast implementation should be selected. A two-dimensional array, indexed by states and characters, is the fastest, but it can take up too much space (say several hundred states by 128 characters).

A more compact but slower scheme is to list the transitions out of each state, with a "default" at the end of the list. For example, in state {8,20,25} of Fig. 3.22 there would be separate entries for N and L to {9,25} and {21,25}, respectively, and if neither of these characters was present, the default, state {25}, would apply. We shall discuss this type of representation more extensively in connection with parsers, in Section 6.8.

A more subtle compaction scheme involves the data structure depicted in Fig. 3.24. The structure consists of four arrays indexed by state numbers.[†] The BASE array is used to determine the base location of the entries for each state stored in the NEXT and CHECK arrays. The DEFAULT array is used to determine an alternative base location in case previous base locations have been invalid.

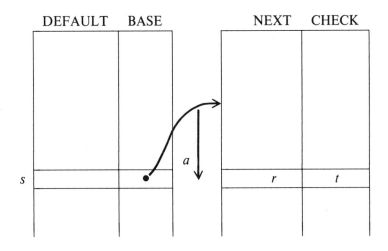

Fig. 3.24. Data structure for representing transition tables.

To compute the transition for state s on input symbol a, we first consult the pair of arrays NEXT and CHECK. In particular, we find their entries for state s in location $l = BASE[s]+a$, where character a is treated as an integer. We take NEXT[l] to be the next state for s on input a if CHECK[l] = s. If not, we determine $q = DEFAULT[s]$ and repeat the entire procedure recursively, using q in place of s.

[†]There would be in practice another array indexed by s, giving the token, recognized, if any, when state s is entered. This information is derived from the NFA states making up DFA state s.

This procedure is summarized in Fig. 3.25.

> **procedure** NEXTSTATE(s, a);
> **if** CHECK[BASE[s] + a] = s **then**
>   **return** NEXT[BASE[s] + a]
> **else**
>   **return** NEXTSTATE(DEFAULT[s], a)

Fig. 3.25. Computing transitions.

The intended use of the structure of Fig. 3.24 is to make the NEXT-CHECK arrays short, by taking advantage of the similarities among states. For example, consider state {25} of Fig. 3.22. This state might have all its transitions entered directly into the NEXT-CHECK array. That is, the number of DFA state {25} might be 18 if we counted from the top of Fig. 3.22. Thus we could set BASE[18] to 0, set CHECK[i] to 18 for $0 \leqslant i \leqslant 127$, set NEXT[$i$] to 18 if the ith character is a letter or digit, and make NEXT[i] undefined (e.g., give it a value higher than any state number) if character i is not a letter or digit. So far, we have saved nothing. In fact, we have used twice as much space as would be necessary for state {25} if we used the state × symbol matrix implementation.

However, the savings occur when we represent the many keyword-recognizing states in Fig. 3.22. These states behave almost like state {25}, but they go to different states on one or two characters. For example, suppose state {8, 20, 25} is indexed 6 in the numbering of DFA states. Then we may choose a value for BASE[6] and enter 6 into CHECK[BASE[6]+N] and CHECK[BASE[6]+L].[†] The next states on N and L for 6, the DFA index for state {8, 20, 25}, are entered into the corresponding entries of the NEXT array. Then, 18, the index for state {25}, is entered in DEFAULT[6]. The algorithm of Fig. 3.21 will make the right transitions on N and L and otherwise cause {8, 20, 25} to behave like state {25}, which is correct. If the input a is any character but N or L in state {8, 20, 25}, we shall not find CHECK[BASE[6]+a] = 6, and so must follow the default state's action.

State {8, 20, 25} has used only two entries in the NEXT-CHECK arrays. While we may not be able to choose BASE values so that no NEXT-CHECK entries remain unused, experience shows that a simple algorithm setting the BASE to the lowest number such that the special entries can be filled in without conflicting with existing entries is fairly good

---

† N and L here represent the numerical values of their codes.

and utilizes little more space than the minimum possible.

3.9 The Scanner Generator as Swiss Army Knife

While regular expressions are of great use in the design and implementation of a compiler, uses of regular expressions are certainly not limited to compiler writing. In fact, pattern matching based on regular expression recognition is useful wherever text processing is done. In this section we shall mention a few of these uses.

Example 3.21. Certain pattern-recognition problems can be reduced to the recognition of regular expressions. For example, Jarvis [1976] used LEX to recognize imperfections in printed circuits. The typical imperfection in a metal lead looks like Fig. 3.26, where the strip of metal narrows too much to pass current without resistance. The circuits are digitally scanned and lines converted to a series of line segments at different angles. It is then a simple matter to write a regular expression which denotes "bumps" in lines. The alphabet for this expression is a small number of angles; the line segments are represented by the angle which best approximates their true angle. □

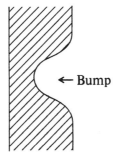

Fig. 3.26. Narrowing of a metal lead.

Example 3.22. Certain classes of regular expressions are useful in bibliographic search applications. A common problem in this area is to search a citation index for patterns consisting of keywords and phrases. For expressions of this form, an especially efficient algorithm for constructing a DFA is possible, but in any event, the time actually spent constructing the DFA is negligible. What is important is that a DFA can search for all keywords in a single pass, rather than having to search sequentially for each keyword in turn (Aho and Corasick [1975]). □

Example 3.23. Many text formatting systems based on card input are in existence. Among other jobs, they adjust line lengths and handle capitalization. The latter task is necessary because card input normally allows capital letters only, while the output text will usually be lower-case. A useful strategy is to capitalize the beginning of sentences automatically and allow other letters to be made capital by preceding them by $. In general, we can identify the end of a sentence by a period followed by either two or more blanks (⊔ in what follows) or by some number of blanks and a newline character (**n** in what follows). However, we should allow after the period any sequence of single or double quotes and right parentheses. Moreover, the first letter of the next sentence could be preceded by any sequence of quotes and left parentheses. Finally, we wish to assume that a new sentence begins whenever we see a paragraph command, which we take to be .PP followed by a newline. The following is a LEX program that translates card input to unformatted text with the proper capitalization. Note that letters preceded by $ will be caught by the second pattern before they could be recognized by the third pattern.

AUXILIARY DEFINITIONS

letter = A | B | ... | Z
open = " | ' | (
close = " | ' |)
any = "any character"

TRANSLATION RULES

(.PP**n** | . close*⊔*(⊔⊔ | **n**))open*letter
        {transmit entire string recognized}

$ letter   {transmit the letter only}

letter   {translate the letter into corresponding lower case letter}

any   {transmit the character}   □

Text Editing

The design and implementation of many text editors has also been influenced by the regular expression notation. There is an important difference between lexical analysis and text editing, however. The lexical analyzer will run many times on long inputs (programs). It therefore pays to make the lexical analyzer as efficient as possible. Hence we convert a regular expression to a DFA, and we implement the DFA as efficiently as is feasible. But a typical text-editing operation is to search a single line for one instance of a pattern and replace it by another string. The time we spend processing the regular-expression pattern to convert it to a form, such as a DFA, suitable for scanning the input line could far exceed the time actually spent scanning the line.

To make the whole process efficient we must balance the time spent processing the pattern and doing the scanning. A reasonable compromise, proposed by Thompson [1968], is to convert the regular expression to an NFA. The process of scanning the input is then one of directly simulating the NFA. As we scan the line, a list of "current" states is kept, beginning with the ϵ-CLOSURE of the start state. If a is the next input character, we create a new list of all states with a transition on a from a state of the old list. The old list is then discarded and we compute the ϵ-CLOSURE of the new list. If the final state is not on the new list, we repeat the process with the next character.

The reason this process is efficient for short lines is that while we are actually undergoing the subset construction, we construct only those states of the DFA which would be entered by the DFA reading the line scanned. This may be a small fraction of all the DFA's states. We begin to lose by this strategy if the length of the line exceeds the number of states of the DFA, for then we shall have to construct each DFA state more than once on the average.

Exercises

3.1 Write regular expressions for the following patterns. Use auxiliary definitions where convenient.

   a) The set of words having a, e, i, o, and u appearing in that order, although not necessarily consecutively.

   b) The set of chess moves, such as $p-k4$ or $kbp \times qn$.

   c) PL/I comments, that is, strings without $*/$ surrounded by $/*$ and $*/$.

3.2 Construct nondeterministic and deterministic finite automata for the regular expressions of Exercise 3.1.

*3.3 Suppose we have the sequence of auxiliary definitions:

$$A_0 = a \mid b$$
$$A_1 = A_0 A_0$$
$$A_2 = A_1 A_1$$
$$\vdots$$
$$A_n = A_{n-1} A_{n-1}$$

followed by the pattern A_n.

a) Informally describe the set of strings denoted by the pattern (as a function of n).
b) If we substitute out all auxiliary definitions in the pattern, how long is the regular expression?
c) If we convert the regular expression from (b) into an NFA, how many states are there?
d) If we convert the NFA of (c) into a DFA, how many states are there?
e) Show that $2^n + 1$ states are necessary for any NFA (and hence for any DFA) recognizing A_n.
f) Show that $2^n + 1$ states are sufficient for a DFA (and hence for an NFA) to recognize A_n.

**3.4 (a)–(d) Repeat Exercise 3.3 (a)–(d) for the pattern

$$(a|b) *aA_n.$$

e) Show that 2^{2^n+1} states are necessary for any DFA recognizing $(a|b) *aA_n$.
f) Show that 2^{2^n+1} states are sufficient for a DFA to recognize $(a|b) *aA_n$.
g) Show that $2^n + 2$ states are sufficient for an NFA to recognize $(a \mid b) *aA_n$.

3.5 There are eight relational operators in PL/I (see Fig. 2.7, Section 2.6). However, these operators denote only six different relations. For example, $\neg<$ and $>=$ are both the same as the FORTRAN .GE. .

a) Write seven translation rules which recognize PL/I relational operators and convert them to the corresponding FORTRAN operators, copying all other input characters to the output without change. Note that the last translation rule should have pattern "any character," and its action is to print that character.
b) Convert your translation rules from (a) into a single DFA. Indicate which states call for an action, and indicate which action is called for.

*3.6 Suppose a picture is encoded as an $n \times m$ matrix M of "light intensities." M_{ij} is a number from 0 to 15, with 0 = black and 15 = white. M may be stored row by row, with rows terminated by newline (**n**) characters. Call this string v_M. For example, if M is

$$
\begin{array}{cccc}
0 & 0 & 2 & 6 \\
0 & 1 & 4 & 7 \\
1 & 8 & 8 & 6
\end{array}
$$

then v_M is 0026 **n** 0147 **n** 1886. We can also encode M by its differences along rows, d_M. For example, for M above, d_M is 0+2+4 **n** +1+3+3 **n** +70−2. If we replace positive numbers by + and negative numbers by − in d_M we get the sequence of changes, d'_M. In this case, $d'_M = 0++ $ **n** $ +++ $ **n** $ +0-$. Suppose a *feature* is defined to be a nonempty sequence of increasing values of intensity, followed by from zero to three unchanging values of intensity followed by at least one decreasing value of intensity, all on one row.

a) Write a LEX program to find maximal features in d'_M and surround them by parentheses. A *maximal* feature is not a proper substring of any other feature.

b) Implement your LEX program as a DFA.

c) Suppose we wished to produce d'_M from v_M. Write a LEX program to do so.

d) How feasible is your solution to (c) as n, the number of intensity levels, gets large? *Hint:* Show that by the proper use of auxiliary definitions, the LEX program need have length only $O(n \log n)$. How does this compare with more obvious methods of converting v_M to d'_M?

e) Repeat (c) and (d) for the conversion of v_M to d_M.

3.7 Use the method of Section 3.8 to represent the DFA's of Exercise 3.2.

*3.8 For which of the following regular sets could a recognizer based on the methods of this chapter be implemented on a computer of modest cost?

a) The set of strings of letters containing exactly one instance of each letter.

b) The set of strings of letters with no repeated letter.

c) The set of strings with at least one repeated letter.

*3.9 Suppose that, instead of attempting to build a DFA for a regular set, we attempted to simulate an NFA. For which of the sets in Exercise 3.8 would NFA simulation be feasible?

3.10 Algorithm 3.2 gave constructions for NFA's recognizing $R_1|R_2$, R_1R_2 and R_1^*, given NFA's for R_1 and R_2. Several other operators have similar constructions. Give constructions preserving the properties of NFA's in Algorithm 3.2 (e.g., one final state) for the operators

    a) R_1^+

    b) R_1?, which stands for $R_1|\epsilon$.

*3.11 Show that the class of regular sets is closed under union, intersection, and complementation. That is, if R and S are regular sets, show that $R \cup S$, $R \cap S$, and R' are also regular sets. (R', the complement of R, is the set of all strings from its alphabet that are not in R.)

3.12 A DFA may be constructed directly from a regular expression as follows. Add a unique endmarker $ to the right end of the regular expression. Then associate a unique index with each alphabetic character (including $) in the regular expression. For example, a, b, c and $ of $a(b|c)^*$$ would have indices 1, 2, 3, and 4, respectively. Each state of the DFA is the set of indices of symbols that are currently *active*, that is, symbols which can be seen next when the DFA is in that state. For example, the initial state of the DFA for $a(b|c)^*$$ would be $\{1\}$ since only a is initially active. State $\{1\}$ would have a transition on a to state $\{2,3,4\}$ since on seeing an a, the DFA can next expect to see a b or a c or the right endmarker.

    a) Give rules to construct the initial set of active symbols of any regular expression.

    b) Give an algorithm to compute the transition function on sets of active symbols.

    c) Use (a) and (b) to derive an algorithm to constructing a DFA directly from a regular expression.

3.13 Give an algorithm to simulate an NFA reading an input string. What is the time and space complexity of your algorithm as a function of the size of the DFA and the length of the input string? (See Thompson [1968] for one solution to this problem.)

*3.14 Show that a deterministic finite automaton can be constructed from a regular expression of the form $\text{any}^*(x_1|x_2| \cdots |x_n)\text{any}^*$ in time linearly proportional to the sum of the lengths of the x_i's, where "any" stands for any symbol. (See Aho and Corasick [1975], Boyer and Moore [1976], and Knuth, Morris, and Pratt [1974] for discussion of efficient string matching algorithms.)

Bibliographic Notes

Regular expressions were first studied by Kleene [1956], and finite automata by Huffman [1954] , Moore [1956], and Rabin and Scott [1959]. The theory of finite automata, regular expressions, and regular sets is well developed. Minsky [1967], Hopcroft and Ullman [1969], and Salomaa [1973] discuss the principal results and provide additional references. The construction of DFA's from regular expressions is discussed in McNaughton and Yamada [1960].

Regular expressions and finite automata have been used in many applications other than compiling. Thompson [1968] describes a regular-expression recognition algorithm used in the QED text editor. Bullen and Millen [1972] describe the use of regular expressions to microprogram file-searching processes. They use the "derivatives of regular expressions" method of Brzozowski [1964]. Aho and Corasick [1975] describe an application of finite automata to a bibliographic search system. Knuth, Morris, and Pratt [1974] describe an efficient algorithm for construction of a DFA from a regular expression which is a single keyword. Gates and Poplawski [1973] show how finite state machines can be used to translate structure references in PL/I. Naur [1976] discusses the use of finite state machines in the general setting of control record processing.

Several systems have been built to construct lexical analyzers automatically from regular expression specifications. Johnson *et al.* [1968] discuss one such system. LEX, the language discussed in Sections 3.7 and 3.8, is based on a lexical analyzer generator of the same name due to Lesk [1975]. The compact implementation scheme of Fig. 3.23 was suggested by S. C. Johnson.

CHAPTER 4

The
Syntactic Specification
of
Programming Languages

The last chapter showed that the lexical structure of tokens could be specified by regular expressions and that from a regular expression we could automatically construct a lexical analyzer to recognize the tokens denoted by the expression. In this and the next two chapters we shall give a similar treatment of syntax analysis. For the syntactic specification of a programming language we shall use a notation called a context-free grammar (grammar, for short), which is also sometimes called a BNF (Backus-Naur Form) description. This notation has a number of significant advantages as a method of specification for the syntax of a language.

- A grammar gives a precise, yet easy to understand, syntactic specification for the programs of a particular programming language.

- An efficient parser can be constructed automatically from a properly designed grammar. Certain parser construction processes can reveal syntactic ambiguities and other difficult-to-parse constructs which might otherwise go undetected in the initial design phase of a language and its compiler.

- A grammar imparts a structure to a program that is useful for its translation into object code and for the detection of errors.

In this chapter we shall describe how a grammar defines a language and consider what features of programming languages can, and cannot, be specified by context-free grammars. The next chapter discusses some popular parsing strategies, and Chapter 6 presents a method of automatically constructing efficient parsers for many programming-language grammars.

125

4.1 Context-Free Grammars

It is natural to define certain programming-language constructs recursively. For example, we might state:

> If S_1 and S_2 are statements and E is an expression, then
> "**if** E **then** S_1 **else** S_2" is a statement.   (4.1)

or:

> If S_1, S_2, ... , S_n are statements, then
> "**begin** S_1; S_2; $\cdots$; S_n **end**" is a statement.   (4.2)

As a third example:

> If E_1 and E_2 are expressions, then "E_1+E_2" is an expression.   (4.3)

If we use the syntactic category "statement" to denote the class of statements and "expression" to denote the class of expressions, then (4.1) can be expressed by the *rewriting rule* or *production*

> statement $\rightarrow$ **if** expression **then** statement **else** statement   (4.4)

We may read this formation rule exactly as we read (4.1), or we may say "One way to form a statement is to concatenate the keyword **if** with an expression, the keyword **then**, a statement, the keyword **else**, and another statement."

Similarly, (4.3) can be written as

> expression $\rightarrow$ expression + expression   (4.5)

and read "One way to form an expression is to take two smaller expressions and connect them with a plus sign."

Assertion (4.2) presents a small problem. We could write:

> statement $\rightarrow$ **begin** statement; statement; $\cdots$; statement **end**

but the use of ellipses ($\cdots$) would create problems when we attempt to define translations based on this description. For this reason, we require that each rewriting rule have a known number of symbols, with no ellipses permitted.

To express (4.2) by rewriting rules, we can introduce a new syntactic category "statement-list" denoting any sequence of statements separated by semicolons. Then one set of rewriting rules expressing (4.2) is:

> statement $\rightarrow$ **begin** statement-list **end**
>
> statement-list $\rightarrow$ statement   (4.6)
>
> | statement ; statement-list

The vertical bar means "or." Thus, the rules for statement-list can be read "A statement-list is either a statement or a statement followed by a semicolon followed by a statement-list." Put another way, "Any sequence of statements separated by semicolons is a statement-list." Since these are the only rules for statement-list, we may also state: "A string of characters is a statement-list if and only if it is a sequence of statements separated by semicolons."

A set of rules such as (4.6) is an example of a grammar. In general, a grammar involves four quantities: *terminals, nonterminals,* a *start symbol,* and *productions.*

The basic symbols of which strings in the language are composed we shall call *terminals.* The word "token" is a synonym for "terminal" when we are talking about programming languages. In the example above, certain keywords, such as **begin** and **else,** are terminals, as are punctuation symbols such as ';' and operators such as '+'.

Nonterminals are special symbols that denote sets of strings. The terms "syntactic variable" and "syntactic category" are synonyms for "nonterminal." In the examples above, the syntactic categories statement, expression, and statement-list are nonterminals; each denotes a set of strings. One nonterminal is selected as the *start symbol,* and it denotes the language in which we are truly interested. The other nonterminals are used to define other sets of strings, and these help define the language. They also help provide a hierarchical structure for the language at hand.

The *productions (rewriting rules)* define the ways in which the syntactic categories may be built up from one another and from the terminals. Each production consists of a nonterminal, followed by an arrow (sometimes the symbol ::= is used in place of the arrow), followed by a string of nonterminals and terminals. Lines (4.4) and (4.5) above are productions. The rules in (4.6) represent the three productions

$$\text{statement} \rightarrow \textbf{begin}\ \text{statement-list}\ \textbf{end}$$

$$\text{statement-list} \rightarrow \text{statement}$$

$$\text{statement-list} \rightarrow \text{statement ; statement-list}$$

Example 4.1. Consider the following grammar for simple arithmetic expressions. The nonterminal symbols are expression and operator, with expression the start symbol. The terminal symbols are

$$\textbf{id} \quad + \quad - \quad * \quad / \quad \uparrow \quad (\quad)$$

The productions are:

$$\text{expression} \rightarrow \text{expression operator expression}$$

$$\text{expression} \rightarrow (\text{ expression })$$

$$\text{expression} \rightarrow - \text{ expression}$$

$$\text{expression} \rightarrow \textbf{id}$$

$$\text{operator} \rightarrow +$$

$$\text{operator} \rightarrow -$$

$$\text{operator} \rightarrow *$$

$$\text{operator} \rightarrow /$$

$$\text{operator} \rightarrow \uparrow \qquad \square$$

Notational Conventions

To avoid always having to state "these are nonterminals," "these terminals," and so on, we shall employ some notational shorthands. These shorthands are summarized here:

1. These symbols are usually nonterminals:
    i)   lower-case names such as expression, statement, operator, etc.;
    ii)   italic capital letters near the beginning of the alphabet;
    iii)   the letter S, which, when it appears, is usually the start symbol.

2. These symbols are usually terminals:
    i)   single lower-case letters $a, b, c, \ldots$;
    ii)   operator symbols such as $+, -$, etc.;
    iii)   punctuation symbols such as parentheses, comma, etc.;
    iv)   the digits $0, 1, \ldots, 9$;
    v)   boldface strings such as **id** or **if**.

3. Capital symbols near the end of the alphabet, chiefly X, Y, Z, represent *grammar symbols,* that is, either nonterminals or terminals.

4. Small letters near the end of the alphabet, chiefly $u, v, \ldots, z$, represent strings of terminals.

5. Lower-case Greek letters, α, β, γ, for example, represent strings of grammar symbols. Thus a generic production could appear as $A \rightarrow \alpha$, indicating that there is a single nonterminal A on the left of the arrow (the *left side* of the production) and a string of grammar symbols α to the right of the arrow (the *right side* of the production).

6. If $A \rightarrow \alpha_1$, $A \rightarrow \alpha_2$, ..., $A \rightarrow \alpha_k$ are all productions with A on the left (we call them *A-productions*), we may write $A \rightarrow \alpha_1|\alpha_2| \cdots |\alpha_k$. We call α_1, α_2, ..., α_k the *alternates* for A.

7. Unless otherwise stated, the left side of the first production is the start symbol.

Example 4.2. Using these shorthands, we could write the grammar of Example 4.1 concisely as

$$E \rightarrow E A E \mid (E) \mid -E \mid \mathbf{id}$$

$$A \rightarrow + \mid - \mid * \mid / \mid \uparrow$$

Our conventions tell us that E and A are nonterminals, with E the start symbol. The remaining symbols are terminals. □

4.2 Derivations and Parse Trees

How does a context-free grammar define a language? The central idea is that productions may be applied repeatedly to expand the nonterminals in a string of nonterminals and terminals. For example, consider the following grammar for arithmetic expressions

$$E \rightarrow E+E \mid E*E \mid (E) \mid -E \mid \mathbf{id} \qquad (4.7)$$

The nonterminal E is an abbreviation for expression. The production $E \rightarrow -E$ signifies that an expression preceded by a minus sign is also an expression. This production can be used to generate more complex expressions from simpler expressions by allowing us to replace any instance of an E by $-E$. In the simplest case we can replace a single E by $-E$. We can describe this action by writing

$$E \Rightarrow -E$$

which is read as "E derives $-E$." The production $E \rightarrow (E)$ tells us that we could also replace one instance of an E in any string of grammar symbols by (E); e.g.,

$$E*E \Rightarrow (E)*E \text{ or } E*E \Rightarrow E*(E).$$

We can take a single E and repeatedly apply productions in any order to obtain a sequence of replacements. For example,

$$E \Rightarrow -E \Rightarrow -(E) \Rightarrow -(\mathbf{id})$$

We call such a sequence of replacements a *derivation* of $-(\mathbf{id})$ from E. This derivation provides a proof that one particular instance of an expression is the string $-(\mathbf{id})$.

In a more abstract setting, we say that $\alpha A\beta \Rightarrow \alpha\gamma\beta$ if $A \rightarrow \gamma$ is a production and α and β are arbitrary strings of grammar symbols. If $\alpha_1 \Rightarrow \alpha_2 \Rightarrow \cdots \Rightarrow \alpha_n$, we say α_1 *derives* α_n. The symbol $\Rightarrow$ means "derives in one step." Often we wish to say "derives in zero or more steps." For this purpose we can use the symbol $\overset{*}{\Rightarrow}$. Thus

1. $\alpha \overset{*}{\Rightarrow} \alpha$ for any string α, and

2. If $\alpha \overset{*}{\Rightarrow} \beta$ and $\beta \Rightarrow \gamma$, then $\alpha \overset{*}{\Rightarrow} \gamma$.

Likewise, we use $\alpha \overset{+}{\Rightarrow} \beta$ to mean "α derives β in a derivation of one or more steps."

Given a context-free grammar G with start symbol S we can use the $\overset{*}{\Rightarrow}$ relation to define $L(G)$, the *language generated by* G. Strings in $L(G)$ may contain only terminal symbols of G. We say a string of terminals w is in $L(G)$ if and only if $S \overset{+}{\Rightarrow} w$. The string w is called a *sentence* of G. If $S \overset{*}{\Rightarrow} \alpha$, where α may contain nonterminals, then we say α is a *sentential form* of G.

Example 4.3. The string $-(\mathbf{id}+\mathbf{id})$ is a sentence of grammar (4.7) because

$$E \Rightarrow -E \Rightarrow -(E) \Rightarrow -(E+E)$$
$$\Rightarrow -(\mathbf{id}+E) \Rightarrow -(\mathbf{id}+\mathbf{id})$$

The strings $E, -E, -(E), \ldots, -(\mathbf{id}+\mathbf{id})$ appearing in this derivation are all sentential forms of this grammar.

We can write $E \overset{*}{\Rightarrow} -(\mathbf{id}+\mathbf{id})$. It is not hard to show that the language of grammar (4.7) is the set of all arithmetic expressions involving the binary operators $+$ and $*$, the unary operator $-$, and the operand $\mathbf{id}$. □

There is often a degree of arbitrariness in the choice of replacement made in a derivation. Of course, we may choose any alternate for a nonterminal being replaced. But in addition, at any step of the derivation we may choose which nonterminal we wish to replace. For example, the derivation of Example 4.3 could continue from $-(E+E)$ as follows:

$$-(E+E) \Rightarrow -(E+\mathbf{id}) \Rightarrow -(\mathbf{id}+\mathbf{id}) \qquad (4.8)$$

Each nonterminal in (4.8) is replaced by the same right side as in Example 4.3, but the order of replacements is different.

To understand how certain parsers work we need to consider derivations in which only the leftmost nonterminal in a sentential form is replaced at each step. Such derivations are termed *leftmost*. The derivation in Example 4.3 is leftmost. Analogously, *rightmost* derivations are those in which the rightmost nonterminal is replaced at each step.

Parse Trees

We can create a graphical representation for derivations that filters out the choice regarding replacement order. This representation is called the *parse tree,* and it has the important purpose of making explicit the hierarchical syntactic structure of sentences that is implied by the grammar.

Each interior node of the parse tree is labeled by some nonterminal A, and the children of the node are labeled, from left to right, by the symbols in the right side of the production by which this A was replaced in the derivation. For example, if $A \rightarrow XYZ$ is a production used at some step of a derivation, then the parse tree for that derivation will have the subtree

The leaves of the parse tree are labeled by nonterminals or terminals and, read from left to right, they constitute a sentential form, called the *yield* or *frontier* of the tree. For example, the parse tree for $-(\mathbf{id}+\mathbf{id})$ implied by the derivation of Example 4.3 is shown in Fig. 4.1.

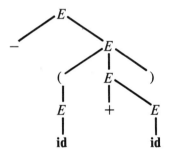

Fig. 4.1 Parse tree.

For a precise description of parse tree construction, consider a derivation $\alpha_1 \Rightarrow \alpha_2 \Rightarrow \cdots \Rightarrow \alpha_n$, where α_1 is a single nonterminal A. We construct a parse tree whose yield is α_i for each sentential form α_i in this derivation. The process is an induction on i. For the basis, the tree for $\alpha_1 = A$ is a single node labeled A. To do the induction, suppose we have already constructed the parse tree whose yield is $\alpha_{i-1} = X_1 X_2 \cdots X_k$. (Recalling our conventions, each X_i is either a nonterminal or a terminal.) Suppose α_i is derived from α_{i-1} by replacing X_j, a nonterminal, by $\beta = Y_1 Y_2 \cdots Y_r$. That is, at the ith step of the derivation, production $X_j \rightarrow \beta$ is applied to α_{i-1} to derive $\alpha_i = X_1 X_2 \cdots X_{j-1} \beta X_{j+1} \cdots X_k$.

To model this step of the derivation, we find the jth leaf from the left in the current parse tree. This leaf is labeled X_j. We give this leaf r children, labeled $Y_1, Y_2, \ldots, Y_r$, from the left. As a special case, if $r = 0$, i.e., $\beta = \epsilon$, then we give the jth leaf one child labeled ϵ.

Example 4.4. Consider the derivation of Example 4.3. The sequence of parse trees constructed from this derivation is shown in Fig. 4.2. In the first step of the derivation, $E \Rightarrow -E$. To model this step in the creation of the parse tree, we add two children, labeled $-$ and E, to the root E of the initial tree to create the second tree.

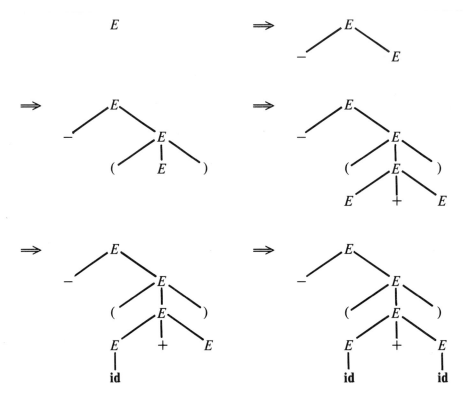

Fig. 4.2 Building parse trees.

In the second step of the derivation, $-E \Rightarrow -(E)$. Consequently we add three children, labeled (, E, and), to the leaf labeled E of the second tree to obtain the third tree with yield $-(E)$. Continuing in this fashion we obtain the complete parse tree as the sixth tree. □

As we have mentioned, the parse tree ignores variations in the order in which symbols are replaced. For example, if the derivation of Example 4.3 were continued as in line (4.8), the same final parse tree of Fig. 4.2 would result. These variations in the order in which productions are applied can also be eliminated by considering only leftmost (or rightmost) derivations. It is not hard to see that every parse tree has associated with it a unique leftmost and a unique rightmost derivation (see Section 5.1). However, we should not assume that every sentence necessarily has only one parse tree or only one leftmost or rightmost derivation.

Example 4.5. Let us again consider the arithmetic expression grammar (4.7), with which we have been dealing. The sentence **id + id ∗ id** has the two distinct leftmost derivations:

$$
\begin{array}{ll}
E \Rightarrow E + E & \quad E \Rightarrow E \ast E \\
\quad \Rightarrow \textbf{id} + E & \quad\quad \Rightarrow E + E \ast E \\
\quad \Rightarrow \textbf{id} + E \ast E & \quad\quad \Rightarrow \textbf{id} + E \ast E \\
\quad \Rightarrow \textbf{id} + \textbf{id} \ast E & \quad\quad \Rightarrow \textbf{id} + \textbf{id} \ast E \\
\quad \Rightarrow \textbf{id} + \textbf{id} \ast \textbf{id} & \quad\quad \Rightarrow \textbf{id} + \textbf{id} \ast \textbf{id}
\end{array}
$$

with the two corresponding parse trees shown in Fig. 4.3. □

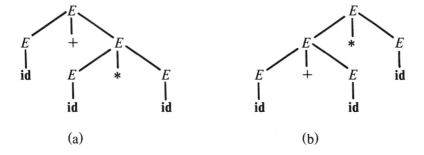

(a) (b)

Fig. 4.3. Two parse trees for **id + id ∗ id**.

Note that, in some sense, the parse tree of Fig. 4.3(a) is "correct" in that it reflects the commonly assumed "precedence" of + and ∗, while the tree if Fig. 4.3(b) does not. It is customary to treat operator ∗ as having higher precedence than +, so Fig. 4.3(a), which groups the operands of ∗ before those of +, corresponds to the structure we would normally attribute to an expression like *a + b ∗ c.*

Ambiguity

A grammar that produces more than one parse tree for some sentence is said to be *ambiguous*. Put another way, an ambiguous grammar is one that produces more than one leftmost or more than one rightmost derivation for some sentence. For certain types of parsers, it is desirable that the grammar be made unambiguous, for if it is not, we cannot uniquely determine which parse tree to select for a sentence. In the sections to follow we shall see techniques for constructing unambiguous grammars. For some applications we shall also consider methods whereby we can use certain ambiguous grammars, together with *disambiguating rules* that "throw away" undesirable parse trees, leaving us with only one tree for each sentence.

Example 4.6. Consider the following grammar for arithmetic expressions involving $+, -, *, /,$ and $\uparrow$ (exponentiation)

$$
\begin{aligned}
E \rightarrow\ &E + E \mid E - E \\
&\mid E * E \mid E / E \\
&\mid E \uparrow E \mid (E) \\
&\mid -E \mid \mathbf{id}
\end{aligned}
\tag{4.9}
$$

This grammar, like (4.7), is ambiguous. However, we can disambiguate both these grammars by specifying the associativity and precedence of the arithmetic operators. Suppose we wish to give the operators the following precedences in decreasing order:

$$
\begin{aligned}
&- \quad \text{(unary minus)} \\
&\uparrow \\
&* \quad / \\
&+ \quad -
\end{aligned}
$$

Suppose further we wish $\uparrow$ to be right-associative [e.g., $a \uparrow b \uparrow c$ is to mean $a \uparrow (b \uparrow c)$] and the other binary operators to be left-associative [e.g., $a - b - c$ is to mean $(a - b) - c$]. These precedences and associativities are the ones customarily used in mathematics and in many, but not all, programming languages [e.g., $a + -b \uparrow c + d * e$ is interpreted as $(a + ((-b) \uparrow c)) + (d * e)$]. These rules concerning the associativity and precedence of operators are sufficient to disambiguate both grammars (4.7) and (4.9). For each sentence of these two grammars there is exactly one parse tree that groups operands of operators according to these associativity and precedence rules. For example, Fig. 4.3(b) would not be a valid parse tree for $\mathbf{id} + \mathbf{id} * \mathbf{id}$ according to these rules because there $+$ appears to have higher precedence than $*$.

We can also rewrite a grammar to incorporate the associativity and precedence rules into the grammar itself. To illustrate what is involved, let us
transform (4.9) into an equivalent unambiguous grammar that obeys the
associativity and precedence rules given above. We begin by introducing
one nonterminal for each precedence level. A subexpression that is essentially indivisible we shall call an *element*. An element is either a single
identifier or a parenthesized expression. We therefore have the productions

$$\text{element} \rightarrow \text{(expression)} \mid \textbf{id}$$

Next, we introduce the category of *primaries*, which are elements with
zero or more of the operator of highest precedence, the unary minus. The
rule for primary is:

$$\text{primary} \rightarrow -\text{primary} \mid \text{element}$$

Then we construct *factors* as sequences of one or more primaries connected
by exponentiation signs. That is:

$$\text{factor} \rightarrow \text{primary} \uparrow \text{factor} \mid \text{primary}$$

Note that the choice of the right side primary $\uparrow$ factor rather than
factor $\uparrow$ primary forces expressions like $a \uparrow b \uparrow c$ to group from the right as
$a \uparrow (b \uparrow c)$.

Then we introduce *terms*, which are sequences of one or more factors
connected by the *multiplicative operators*, namely * and /, and finally *expressions*, which are sequences of one or more terms connected by the *additive
operators*, + and binary −. The productions for term are

$$\text{term} \rightarrow \text{term} * \text{factor}$$
$$\mid \text{term} / \text{factor}$$
$$\mid \text{factor}$$

These productions cause terms to be grouped from the left [e.g., $a * b * c$
means $(a * b) * c$]. The final, unambiguous grammar is:

$$\text{expression} \rightarrow \text{expression} + \text{term}$$
$$\mid \text{expression} - \text{term}$$
$$\mid \text{term}$$
$$\text{term} \rightarrow \text{term} * \text{factor}$$
$$\mid \text{term} / \text{factor}$$
$$\mid \text{factor}$$
$$\text{factor} \rightarrow \text{primary} \uparrow \text{factor}$$

$$| \text{ primary}$$
$$\text{primary} \rightarrow -\text{primary}$$
$$| \text{ element}$$
$$\text{element} \rightarrow (\text{ expression })$$
$$| \textbf{ id} \qquad \qquad \square$$

4.3 Capabilities of Context-Free Grammars

Context-free grammars are capable of describing most, but not all, of the syntax of programming languages. In this section we shall try to indicate what programming language constructs can, and cannot, be described by context-free grammars.

Regular Expressions vs. Context-Free Grammars

Regular expressions, as we have seen, are capable of describing the syntax of tokens. Any syntactic construct that can be described by a regular expression can also be described by a context-free grammar. For example, the regular expression $(a|b)(a|b|0|1)^*$ and the context-free grammar

$$S \rightarrow aA \,|\, bA$$
$$A \rightarrow aA \,|\, bA \,|\, 0A \,|\, 1A \,|\, \epsilon$$

describe the same language. This grammar was constructed from the obvious NFA for the regular expression using the following construction: For each state there is a nonterminal symbol. If state A has a transition to state B on symbol a, introduce production $A \rightarrow aB$. If A goes to B on input ϵ, introduce $A \rightarrow B$. If A is an accepting state, introduce $A \rightarrow \epsilon$. Make the start state of the NFA be the start symbol of the grammar.

Since every regular set can be described by a context-free grammar, we may reasonably ask, "Why bother with regular expressions?" There are several reasons. First, the lexical rules are usually quite simple and we don't need a notation as powerful as context-free grammars. With the regular expression notation it is a bit easier to understand what set of strings is being defined than it is to grasp the language defined by a collection of productions. Second, it is easier to construct efficient recognizers from regular expressions than from context-free grammars. Third, separating the syntactic structure of a language into lexical and nonlexical parts provides a convenient way of modularizing the front end of a compiler into two manageable-sized components.

There are no firm guidelines as to what to put into the lexical rules, as opposed to the syntactic rules. Regular expressions are most useful for describing the structure of lexical constructs such as identifiers, constants, keywords and so forth. Context-free grammars, on the other hand, are most useful in describing nested structures such as balanced parentheses, matching **begin-end**'s, corresponding **if-then-else**'s and so on. These nested structures cannot be described by regular expressions.

Examples of Context-Free Grammars

Let us consider some examples of grammar fragments for common programming language constructs.

Example 4.7. Consider the grammar (4.10)

$$S \rightarrow (S)S \mid \epsilon \qquad (4.10)$$

This simple grammar generates all strings of balanced parentheses, and only those. To see this, we shall show that every sentence derivable from S is balanced, and that every balanced string is derivable from S. To show that every sentence derivable from S is balanced, a simple inductive proof on the number of steps in a derivation suffices. The only string of terminals derivable from S in one step is the empty string, which surely is balanced.

Now if we assume that all derivations of fewer than n steps produce balanced sentences, consider a leftmost derivation of exactly n steps. Such a derivation must be of the form

$$S \Rightarrow (S)S \stackrel{*}{\Rightarrow} (x)S \stackrel{*}{\Rightarrow} (x)y$$

The derivations of x and y from S take fewer than n steps so, by the inductive hypothesis, x and y are balanced. Therefore the string $(x)y$ must be balanced.

We have thus shown that any string derivable from S is balanced. We must next show that every balanced string is derivable from S. We now use induction on the length of a string. The empty string is derivable from S. Assume that every balanced string of length less than $2n$ is derivable from S, and consider a balanced string w of length $2n$, $n \geqslant 1$. Surely w begins with a left parenthesis. Let (x) be the shortest prefix of w having an equal number of left and right parentheses. Then w can be written as $(x)y$ where both x and y are balanced. Since x and y are of length less than $2n$, they are derivable from S by the inductive hypothesis. Thus, we can find a derivation of the form

$$S \Rightarrow (S)S \stackrel{*}{\Rightarrow} (x)S \stackrel{*}{\Rightarrow} (x)y$$

proving that $w = (x)y$ is also derivable from S.

This example shows the two things we must do in order to prove that a grammar generates a language L. We must show that every sentence generated by the grammar is in L, and we must show that every string in L can be generated by the grammar. □

We have already seen a grammar for arithmetic expressions. The following grammar fragment (4.11) generates conditional statements.

$$\text{stat} \rightarrow \textbf{if} \text{ cond } \textbf{then} \text{ stat}$$

$$| \ \textbf{if} \text{ cond } \textbf{then} \text{ stat } \textbf{else} \text{ stat} \qquad\qquad (4.11)$$

$$| \ \text{other-stat}$$

Thus the string

$$\textbf{if } C_1 \textbf{ then } S_1$$

$$\textbf{else if } C_2 \textbf{ then } S_2 \textbf{ else } S_3$$

would have the parse tree shown in Fig. 4.4.

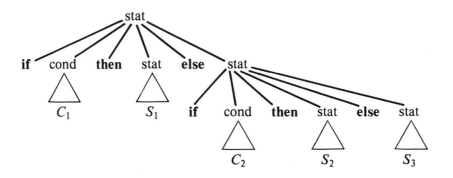

Fig. 4.4. Parse tree.

Grammar (4.11) is ambiguous, however, since the string

$$\textbf{if } C_1 \textbf{ then if } C_2 \textbf{ then } S_1 \textbf{ else } S_2 \qquad\qquad (4.12)$$

has the two parse trees shown in Fig. 4.5.

In all programming languages with conditional statements of this form, the first parsing is preferred. The general rule is "Each **else** is to be matched with the closest previous unmatched **then**."

We could incorporate this disambiguating rule directly into the grammar if we wish. For example, we could rewrite grammar (4.11) as the following

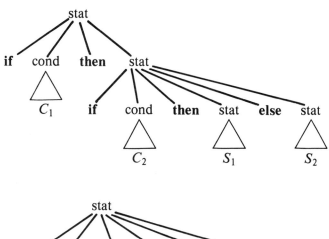

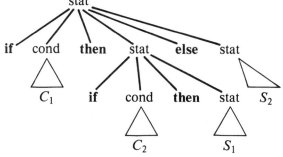

Fig. 4.5. Two parse trees for ambiguous sentence.

unambiguous grammar.

$$\text{stat} \rightarrow \text{matched-stat}$$
$$| \text{ unmatched-stat}$$
$$\text{matched-stat} \rightarrow \textbf{if } \text{cond } \textbf{then } \text{matched-stat } \textbf{else } \text{matched-stat}$$
$$| \text{ other-stat}$$
$$\text{unmatched-stat} \rightarrow \textbf{if } \text{cond } \textbf{then } \text{stat}$$
$$| \textbf{ if } \text{cond } \textbf{then } \text{matched-stat } \textbf{else } \text{unmatched-stat}$$

This grammar generates the same set of strings as (4.11), but it allows only one parsing for string (4.12), namely the one that associates each **else** with the previous unmatched **then**.

Non-Context-Free Language Constructs

It should come as no surprise that for some languages we can find no context-free grammar at all. However, it turns out that there are some surprisingly simple abstract languages that are not context-free, and that these languages represent constructs of real programming languages. Let us now consider some problems that come up if we try to specify too much of the details of a language in syntax.

Example 4.8. The language $L_1 = \{wcw \mid w \text{ is in } (a \mid b)^*\}$ is not a context-free language. That is, L_1 consists of all words composed of a repeated string of a's and b's separated by a c, such as *aabcaab*. The problem of recognizing L_1 can be embedded in the problem of checking that identifiers are declared before use. That is, the first w in wcw represents the declaration of an identifier w. The second w represents its use. While it is beyond the scope of this book to prove it, the non-context-freedom of L_1 directly implies the non-context-freedom of ALGOL, which does require declaration before use and allows identifiers of arbitrary length, when ALGOL is described down to the level of individual characters.

Thus, the syntax of ALGOL, which is normally defined by a context-free grammar, does not get down to the level of characters in a name. Instead, all names are represented by a token such as **id**, and it is left to the bookkeeping phase of the compiler to keep track of declarations and uses of particular names. This method is used to keep track of identifiers in all languages, even if declarations are not required and/or identifiers are of limited length. □

Example 4.9. The language $L_2 = \{a^n b^m c^n d^m \mid n \geq 1 \text{ and } m \geq 1\}$ is not context-free. That is, L_2 consists of words in $a^*b^*c^*d^*$ such that the number of a's and c's are equal and the number of b's and d's are equal. (Recall a^n means a written n times.) L_2 is embedded in languages which require that procedures be declared with the same number of formal parameters as there are actual parameters in their use. That is, a^n and b^m could represent the formal parameter lists in two procedures declared to have n and m arguments, respectively. Then c^n and d^m represent the actual parameter lists in calls to these two procedures.

Again note that the typical syntax of procedure definitions and uses does not concern itself with counting the number of parameters. For example, the CALL statement in a FORTRAN-like language might be described

$$\text{statement} \rightarrow \text{CALL } \textbf{id} \text{ (expression list)}$$

$$\text{expression list} \rightarrow \text{expression list, expression}$$

$$\mid \text{ expression}$$

with suitable productions for expression. Checking that the number of actual parameters in the call is correct is usually done during semantic analysis. □

Example 4.10. The language $L_3 = \{a^n b^n c^n \mid n \geq 0\}$, that is, strings in $a^* b^* c^*$ with equal numbers of a's, b's and c's, is not context-free. An example of a problem which embeds L_3 is the following. Typeset text uses italics where ordinary typed text uses underlining. In converting a file of text destined to be printed on a line printer to text suitable for a photo-typesetter, one has to replace underlined words by italics. An underlined word is a string of letters followed by an equal number of backspaces and an equal number of underscores. If we regard a as any letter, b as back-space, and c as underscore, the language L_3 represents underlined words. The conclusion is that we cannot use a grammar to describe underlined words, and more importantly, we cannot use a parser-generating tool based solely on context-free grammars to create a program to convert underlined words to italics. This situation is unusual, in that most simple text-processing programs can be written easily with the aid of a scanner genera-tor like LEX of Chapter 3, which is even less powerful than a parser gen-erator. □

It is interesting to note that languages very similar to L_1, L_2, and L_3 are context-free. For example, $L_1' = \{wcw^R \mid w$ is in $(a \mid b)^* \}$, where w^R stands for w reversed, is context-free. It is generated by the grammar

$$S \to aSa \mid bSb \mid c$$

$L_2' = \{a^n b^m c^m d^n \mid n \geq 1$ and $m \geq 1\}$ is context-free, generated by

$$S \to aSd \mid aAd$$
$$A \to bAc \mid bc$$

Also, $L_2'' = \{a^n b^n c^m d^m \mid n \geq 1$ and $m \geq 1\}$ is context-free, with grammar

$$S \to AB$$
$$A \to aAb \mid ab$$
$$B \to cBd \mid cd$$

Finally, $L_3' = \{a^n b^n \mid n \geq 1\}$ is context-free, with grammar

$$S \to aSb \mid ab$$

It is worth noting that L_3' is an example of a language not definable by any regular expression. To see this, suppose L_3' were the language of regular expression R. Then we could construct a DFA A accepting L'_3. A must have some finite number of states, say k. Consider the sequence of states $s_0, s_1, s_2, \ldots, s_k$ entered by A given inputs $\epsilon, a, aa, \ldots$. In general, s_i is the state entered by A having read i a's. Then as there are only k different states, two states among $s_0, s_1, \ldots, s_k$ must be the same, say $s_i = s_j$. Then an additional sequence of i b's takes s_i to an accepting state f, since $a^i b^i$ is in L'_3. But then there is also a path from the initial state s_0 to s_i to f labeled $a^j b^i$, as shown in Fig. 4.6.

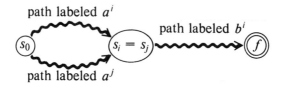

Fig. 4.6. The DFA A.

Thus A also accepts $a^j b^i$, which is not in L'_3, contradicting the assumption that L'_3 is the language accepted by A.

Colloquially, we say that "finite automata cannot count," meaning they cannot accept a language like L'_3 which requires that they count the number of a's exactly. Similarly, we say "grammars can count two things but not three," since with a context-free grammar we can define L'_3 but not L_3.

Exercises

4.1 a) Write a grammar whose sentences are the regular expressions over the alphabet $\{a, b\}$.

   b) Suppose concatenation may optionally be indicated by an explicit dot, as $a \cdot b$, for example. Modify your grammar from (a) to permit this extension.

   c) Modify your grammar from (b) to permit the unary postfix operations $+$ and $?$. (r^+ usually stands for rr^* and $r?$ for $r \mid \epsilon$).

   d) Make your grammars unambiguous if they are not already so.

4.2 A *list structure* may be defined as follows:

   i) Λ is a (*null*) list structure.

   ii) a (an *atom*) is a list structure.

   iii) If $l_1, l_2, \ldots, l_k$ are list structures, $k \geq 1$, then $(l_1, l_2, \ldots, l_k)$ is a list structure.

   a) Construct a grammar for list structures.

b) Draw a parse tree for $(((a,a), \Lambda, (a)), a)$ in your grammar from part (a).

4.3 The following grammar fragment is proposed to remedy the ambiguity in the **if** $\cdots$ **then** $\cdots$ **else** grammar (4.11).

$$stat \rightarrow \textbf{if } cond \textbf{ then } substat \textbf{ else } stat$$

$$| \textbf{ if } cond \textbf{ then } stat$$

$$substat \rightarrow \textbf{if } cond \textbf{ then } substat \textbf{ else } stat$$

Show that this grammar fragment is unambiguous, if stat, substat, and cond are given productions which allow them to derive terminal strings.

**4.4 The following is a simple grammar for declarations of a single identifier:

$$stat \rightarrow \textbf{declare id } options$$

$$options \rightarrow option\ options \mid \epsilon$$

$$option \rightarrow mode \mid scale \mid precision \mid base$$

$$mode \rightarrow \textbf{real} \mid \textbf{complex}$$

$$scale \rightarrow \textbf{fixed} \mid \textbf{floating}$$

$$precision \rightarrow \textbf{single} \mid \textbf{double}$$

$$base \rightarrow \textbf{binary} \mid \textbf{decimal}$$

a) Show how the above grammar can be generalized to permit n options A_i, $1 \leqslant i \leqslant n$, each of which can be either a_i or b_i.
b) The above grammar permits redundant or contradictory declarations such as

declare X real fixed real floating

We could insist that the syntax of the language forbid such declarations. We are thus left with a finite number of token sequences that are syntactically correct. Surely the legal declarations form a context-free language, and even a regular set. Write a grammar for declarations with n options, each option appearing at most once.
c) Show that a grammar written out in answer to (b) must have length at least 2^n symbols.
d) What does (c) say about the feasibility of enforcing non-redundancy and non-contradiction among options in a declaration via the syntactic definition of a language?

*4.5 There are a number of common shorthands used in the definition of languages. Square brackets are often used to denote an optional part of a production. For example, we might write

statement → **if** expression **then** statement [**else** statement]

In general, $A \rightarrow \alpha\ [\ \beta\ ]\ \gamma$ means the same as $A \rightarrow \alpha B \gamma$ and $B \rightarrow \beta \mid \epsilon$.

Curly brackets are often used to denote a phrase which may be repeated zero or more times, as in

statement → **begin** statement { ; statement } **end**

In general, $A \rightarrow \alpha\ \{\ \beta\ \}\ \gamma$ means the same as $A \rightarrow \alpha B \gamma$ and $B \rightarrow \beta B \mid \epsilon$.

In a sense, $[\ \beta\ ]$ stands for the regular expression $\beta \mid \epsilon$, and $\{\ \beta\ \}$ stands for β^*. We may generalize these notations to allow any regular expression of grammar symbols on the right side of productions.

a) Give a set of productions generating the same strings as $A \rightarrow B^*\ a\ (C \mid D)$.
b) Show how to replace any production $A \rightarrow r$, where r is a regular expression, by a finite collection of context-free productions.

Bibliographic Notes

The original source for the notion of context-free grammars is Chomsky [1956] and Chomsky [1959]. These grammars were advanced as a way of defining natural languages rather than computer languages. The ALGOL 60 report (Naur [1963]) used BNF to define the syntax of ALGOL, and was the first use of a grammar-like construct to define a programming language. The equivalence of BNF and context-free grammars was noted shortly thereafter, and the theory of context-free languages received much attention. A key early paper in context-free language theory is Bar Hillel, Perles, and Shamir [1961], which gives a technique for proving that languages such as L_1, L_2, and L_3 described in Section 4.3 are not context-free. Some texts which delve into this and other aspects of context-free language theory are Ginsburg [1966], Hopcroft and Ullman [1969], and Salomaa [1973]. Another type of grammar, which was introduced for the specification of ALGOL 68, is the W-grammar. See Cleaveland and Uzgalis [1977] for an introduction.

CHAPTER 5

Basic
Parsing
Techniques

Chapter 4 showed how a context-free grammar can be used to define the syntax of a programming language. This chapter shows how to check whether an input string is a sentence of a given grammar and how to construct, if desired, a parse tree for the string. As every compiler performs some type of syntax analysis, usually after lexical analysis, the input to a parser is typically a sequence of tokens. The output of the parser can be of many different forms. This chapter assumes for simplicity that the output is some representation of the parse tree. Chapters 7 and 8 show how to attach "semantic" rules to the productions of a grammar to produce other kinds of outputs.

This chapter discusses the two most common forms of parsers — operator precedence and recursive descent. Operator precedence is especially suitable for parsing expressions, since it can use information about the precedence and associativity of operators to guide the parse. Recursive descent uses a collection of mutually recursive routines to perform the syntax analysis. The great bulk of compilers in existence in the early 1970's use one or both of these methods (McClure, [1972]). A common situation is for operator precedence to be used for expressions and recursive descent for the rest of the language.

The primary advantage of these methods is that they are easy to implement by hand. But there are some drawbacks as well. Operator precedence has the curious property that if one is not careful, one can recognize inputs that are not in the language of the underlying grammar. Likewise, recursive descent, particularly when augmented with backtracking, can produce rather unexpected results.

Fortunately, there are two newer methods gaining popularity that are both more general than the older methods and more firmly grounded in grammar theory. Moreover, with the proper tools (parser generators) the newer methods are easier to use than the more classical approaches. The first of these methods, LL parsing, will be mentioned in this chapter, as it

145

is really a table-based variant of recursive descent. The second method, LR parsing, is the subject of Chapter 6, where its most important variants will be discussed.

5.1 Parsers

A *parser* for grammar G is a program that takes as input a string w and produces as output either a parse tree for w, if w is a sentence of G, or an error message indicating that w is not a sentence of G. Often the parse tree is produced in only a figurative sense; in reality, the parse tree exists only as a sequence of actions made by stepping through the tree construction process. This chapter discusses the operation of two basic types of parsers for context-free grammars — bottom-up and top-down. As indicated by their names, bottom-up parsers build parse trees from the bottom (leaves) to the top (root), while top-down parsers start with the root and work down to the leaves. In both cases the input to the parser is being scanned from left to right, one symbol at a time.

The bottom-up parsing method we discuss is called "shift-reduce" parsing because it consists of shifting input symbols onto a stack until the right side of a production appears on top of the stack. The right side may then be replaced by (*reduced to*) the symbol on the left side of the production, and the process repeated.

Unfortunately, if $A \rightarrow XYZ$ is a production, then not every time that XYZ is on top of the stack is it correct to reduce XYZ to A; there may be occasions where it is necessary to continue to shift input symbols on top of XYZ. Designing an algorithm from a grammar so that shift-reduce decisions are made properly is the fundamental problem of bottom-up parser construction. In Section 5.3 we show how to construct one kind of shift-reduce parser called an operator-precedence parser. Chapter 6 discusses LR parsers, a more general type of shift-reduce parser.

The top-down parsing method we discuss is called recursive descent parsing. Section 5.5 shows how to construct a tabularized form of recursive descent parser called a predictive parser. Section 5.5 concludes with a discussion of LL parsers, a special kind of predictive parser.

Representation of a Parse Tree

Chapter 7 discusses the type of output typically produced by a parser in a compiler. In this chapter we shall treat the output of a parser as a representation of a parse tree for the input, if the input is syntactically well formed. There are two basic types of representations we shall consider — implicit and explicit. The sequence of productions used in some derivation is an example of an implicit representation. A linked list structure for the parse tree is an explicit representation.

Recall that a derivation in which the leftmost nonterminal is replaced at every step is said to be leftmost. If $\alpha \Rightarrow \beta$ by a step in which the leftmost nonterminal in α is replaced, we write $\alpha \underset{lm}{\Rightarrow} \beta$. Every leftmost step, using our notational conventions, has the form $wA\gamma \underset{lm}{\Rightarrow} w\delta\gamma$ in which w consists of terminals only. If α derives β by a leftmost derivation, we write $\alpha \underset{lm}{\overset{*}{\Rightarrow}} \beta$. If $S \underset{lm}{\overset{*}{\Rightarrow}} \alpha$, then we say α is a *left-sentential form* of the grammar at hand. An analogous definition holds for rightmost derivation, where the rightmost nonterminal is replaced at every step. Rightmost derivations are sometimes called *canonical* derivations.

Every sentence of a language has both a leftmost and a rightmost derivation, as well as many others. To find one leftmost derivation for a sentence w, we can take any derivation for w and construct from it the corresponding parse tree T. From T we can then construct a leftmost derivation by traversing the tree top-down. We begin with the start symbol S, which corresponds to the root of T. We then construct the leftmost derivation

$$S = \alpha_1 \underset{lm}{\Rightarrow} \alpha_2 \underset{lm}{\Rightarrow} \cdots \underset{lm}{\Rightarrow} \alpha_n = w$$

corresponding to T, one step at a time, using the following procedure.

If the root labeled S has children labeled A, B, and C, we create the first step of the leftmost derivation by replacing S by the labels of its children; i.e., $S \underset{lm}{\Rightarrow} ABC$. Here S is α_1 and ABC is α_2.

If the node for A has children labeled XYZ in T, we create the next step of the derivation by replacing A by the labels of its children; i.e., $ABC \underset{lm}{\Rightarrow} XYZBC$. Here $XYZBC$ is α_3. We continue in this fashion by finding the node corresponding to the leftmost nonterminal D of α_i and replacing D by its children in T to obtain α_{i+1}, for each $i = 1, 2, \ldots, n-1$.

If we were to construct a parse tree in preorder[†], then the order in which the nodes are created corresponds to the order in which the productions are applied in a leftmost derivation.

Example 5.1. Consider the grammar

[†] A *preorder* traversal of a tree is defined recursively as follows. (1) If a tree consists of one leaf, visit the leaf. (2) If a tree has root n, with children $n_1, n_2, \ldots, n_k$ in order from the left, visit n, then visit the subtree rooted at n_1 in preorder, then visit the subtree rooted at n_2 in preorder, and so on.

(1) $S \rightarrow i\, C\, t\, S$

(2) $S \rightarrow i\, C\, t\, S\, e\, S$ (5.1)

(3) $S \rightarrow a$

(4) $C \rightarrow b$

Here i, t, and e stand for **if, then,** and **else,** C and S for "conditional" and "statement."

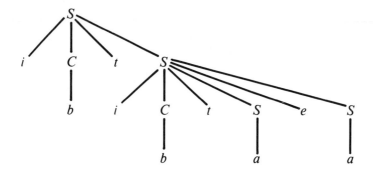

Fig. 5.1. Parse tree T.

We shall construct a leftmost derivation for the sentence $w = i\,b\,t\,i\,b\,t\,a\,e\,a$. A parse tree T for w is shown in Fig. 5.1. The leftmost derivation corresponding to this parse tree is found to be

$$S \underset{lm}{\Rightarrow} i\, C\, t\, S$$

$$\underset{lm}{\Rightarrow} i\, b\, t\, S$$

$$\underset{lm}{\Rightarrow} i\, b\, t\, i\, C\, t\, S\, e\, S$$

$$\underset{lm}{\Rightarrow} i\, b\, t\, i\, b\, t\, S\, e\, S$$

$$\underset{lm}{\Rightarrow} i\, b\, t\, i\, b\, t\, a\, e\, S$$

$$\underset{lm}{\Rightarrow} i\, b\, t\, i\, b\, t\, a\, e\, a$$

The portions of the parse tree corresponding to the first four steps of this derivation are shown in Fig. 5.2.

(a) $S \Rightarrow i\,C\,t\,S$

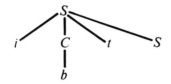

(b) $S \Rightarrow i\,C\,t\,S \Rightarrow i\,b\,t\,S$

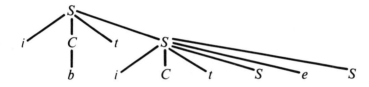

(c) $S \Rightarrow i\,C\,t\,S \Rightarrow i\,b\,t\,S \Rightarrow i\,b\,t\,i\,C\,t\,S\,e\,S$

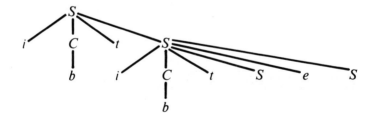

(d) $S \Rightarrow i\,C\,t\,S \Rightarrow i\,b\,t\,S \Rightarrow i\,b\,t\,i\,C\,t\,S\,e\,S \Rightarrow i\,b\,t\,i\,b\,t\,S\,e\,S$

Fig. 5.2. Constructing a leftmost derivation.

A rightmost derivation can be constructed from a parse tree analogously. At each step we replace the rightmost nonterminal by the labels of its children. For example, the first two steps of a rightmost derivation constructed from the tree in Fig. 5.1 would be $S \implies iCtS \implies iCtiCtSeS$. □

It should now be clear that a leftmost (or rightmost) derivation is equivalent to a parse tree, in that we can easily convert a leftmost (or rightmost) derivation to a parse tree, or a parse tree to a leftmost (or rightmost) derivation.

5.2 Shift-Reduce Parsing

In this section we discuss a bottom-up style of parsing called shift-reduce parsing. This parsing method is bottom-up because it attempts to construct a parse tree for an input string beginning at the leaves (the bottom) and working up towards the root (the top). We can think of this process as one of "reducing" a string w to the start symbol of a grammar. At each step a string matching the right side of a production is replaced by the symbol on the left.

For example, consider the grammar

$$S \rightarrow aAcBe$$
$$A \rightarrow Ab \mid b$$
$$B \rightarrow d$$

and the string $abbcde$. We want to reduce this string to S. We scan $abbcde$ looking for substrings that match the right side of some production. The substrings b and d qualify. Let us choose the leftmost b and replace it by A, the left side of the production $A \rightarrow b$. We obtain the string $aAbcde$. We now find that Ab, b, and e each match the right side of some production. Suppose this time we choose to replace the substring Ab by A, the left side of the production $A \rightarrow Ab$. We now obtain $aAcde$. Then replacing d by B, the left side of the production $B \rightarrow d$, we obtain $aAcBe$. We can now replace this entire string by S.

Each replacement of the right side of a production by the left side in the process above is called a *reduction*. Thus, by a sequence of four reductions we were able to reduce $abbcde$ to S. These reductions, in fact, traced out a rightmost derivation in reverse.

Informally, a substring which is the right side of a production such that replacement of that substring by the production left side leads eventually to a reduction to the start symbol, by the reverse of a rightmost derivation, is called a "handle." The process of bottom-up parsing may be viewed as one of finding and reducing handles.

We must not be misled by the simplicity of this example. In many cases the leftmost substring β which matches the right side of some production $A \rightarrow \beta$ is not a handle because a reduction by the production $A \rightarrow \beta$ may yield a string which cannot be reduced to the start symbol. For example, if we replaced b by A in the second string $aAbcde$ we would obtain a string $aAAcde$ which cannot be subsequently reduced to S. For this reason, we must give a more precise definition of a handle. We shall see that if we write a rightmost derivation in reverse, then the sequence of replacements made in that derivation naturally defines a sequence of correct replacements that reduce the sentence to the start symbol.

Handles

A *handle* of a right-sentential form γ is a production $A \rightarrow \beta$ and a position of γ where the string β may be found and replaced by A to produce the previous right-sentential form in a rightmost derivation of γ. That is, if $S \overset{*}{\underset{rm}{\Rightarrow}} \alpha A w \underset{rm}{\Rightarrow} \alpha \beta w$, then $A \rightarrow \beta$ in the position following α is a handle of $\alpha \beta w$. The string w to the right of the handle contains only terminal symbols.

In the example above, $abbcde$ is a right-sentential form whose handle is $A \rightarrow b$ at position 2. Likewise, $aAbcde$ is a right-sentential form whose handle is $A \rightarrow Ab$ at position 2.

Sometimes we shall say "the substring β is a handle of $\alpha \beta w$" if the position of β and the production $A \rightarrow \beta$ we have in mind are clear. If a grammar is unambiguous, then every right-sentential form of the grammar has exactly one handle.

Figure 5.3 portrays the handle β in the parse tree of a right-sentential form $\alpha \beta w$. The handle represents the leftmost complete subtree consisting of a node and all its children. In Fig. 5.3, A is the leftmost node with all its children in the tree.

Example 5.2. Consider the following grammar

$$
\begin{array}{lll}
(1) & E \rightarrow E + E & \\
(2) & E \rightarrow E * E & \\
(3) & E \rightarrow (E) & (5.2) \\
(4) & E \rightarrow \mathbf{id} &
\end{array}
$$

and consider the rightmost derivation

$$
\begin{aligned}
E &\underset{rm}{\Rightarrow} \underline{E + E} \\
&\underset{rm}{\Rightarrow} E + \underline{E * E}
\end{aligned}
$$

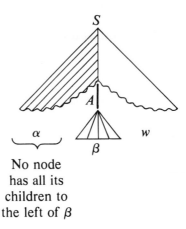

No node
has all its
children to
the left of β

Fig. 5.3. The handle in a parse tree.

$$\underset{rm}{\Longrightarrow} E + E * \underline{\mathbf{id}_3}$$

$$\underset{rm}{\Longrightarrow} E + \underline{\mathbf{id}_2} * \mathbf{id}_3$$

$$\underset{rm}{\Longrightarrow} \underline{\mathbf{id}_1} + \mathbf{id}_2 * \mathbf{id}_3$$

We have subscripted the **id**'s for notational convenience and underlined a handle of each right-sentential form. For example, $\mathbf{id}_1$ is a handle of the right-sentential form $\mathbf{id}_1 + \mathbf{id}_2 * \mathbf{id}_3$ because **id** is the right side of the production $E \rightarrow \mathbf{id}$, and replacing $\mathbf{id}_1$ by E produces the previous right-sentential form $E + \mathbf{id}_2 * \mathbf{id}_3$. Note that the string appearing to the right of a handle contains only terminal symbols.

Because grammar (5.2) is ambiguous, there is another rightmost derivation of the same string. This derivation begins $E \Longrightarrow E * E$ and produces another set of handles. In particular, $E + E$ is a handle of $E + E * \mathbf{id}_3$ according to this derivation, just as $\mathbf{id}_3$ by itself is a handle of this same right sentential form according to the derivation above.   □

Handle Pruning

A rightmost derivation in reverse, often called a *canonical reduction sequence,* is obtained by "handle pruning." That is, we start with a string of terminals w which we wish to parse. If w is a sentence of the grammar at hand, then $w = \gamma_n$, where γ_n is the nth right-sentential form of some as yet unknown rightmost derivation

$$S = \gamma_0 \underset{rm}{\Rightarrow} \gamma_1 \underset{rm}{\Rightarrow} \gamma_2 \underset{rm}{\Rightarrow} \cdots \underset{rm}{\Rightarrow} \gamma_{n-1} \underset{rm}{\Rightarrow} \gamma_n = w.$$

To reconstruct this derivation in reverse order, we locate the handle β_n in γ_n and replace β_n by the left side of some production $A_n \rightarrow \beta_n$ to obtain the $(n-1)$st right-sentential form γ_{n-1}. Note that we have not yet told how handles are to be found, but we shall give methods of doing so in this chapter and the next.

We then repeat this process. That is, we locate the handle β_{n-1} in γ_{n-1} and reduce this handle to obtain the right-sentential form γ_{n-2}. If by continuing this process we produce a right-sentential form consisting only of the start symbol S, then we halt and announce successful completion of parsing. The reverse of the sequence of productions used in the reductions is a rightmost derivation for the input string.

Example 5.3. Consider the grammar (5.2) of Example 5.2 and the input string $\textbf{id}_1 + \textbf{id}_2 * \textbf{id}_3$. The following sequence of reductions reduces $\textbf{id}_1 + \textbf{id}_2 * \textbf{id}_3$ to the start symbol E:

Right-sentential form	Handle	Reducing production
$\textbf{id}_1 + \textbf{id}_2 * \textbf{id}_3$	$\textbf{id}_1$	$E \rightarrow \textbf{id}$
$E + \textbf{id}_2 * \textbf{id}_3$	$\textbf{id}_2$	$E \rightarrow \textbf{id}$
$E + E * \textbf{id}_3$	$\textbf{id}_3$	$E \rightarrow \textbf{id}$
$E + E * E$	$E * E$	$E \rightarrow E * E$
$E + E$	$E + E$	$E \rightarrow E + E$
E		

The reader should observe that the sequence of right-sentential forms in this example is just the reverse of the sequence in the rightmost derivation in Example 5.2. Again, recall that there is another rightmost derivation in which $\textbf{id}_1 + \textbf{id}_2$ comes from a single E, and this rightmost derivation implies a different sequence of handles. □

Stack Implementation of Shift-Reduce Parsing

There are two problems that must be solved if we are to automate parsing by handle pruning. The first is how to locate a handle in a right-sentential form, and the second is what production to choose in case there is more than one production with the same right side. Before we get to these questions, let us first consider the type of data structures to use in a handle-pruning parser.

A convenient way to implement a shift-reduce parser is to use a stack and an input buffer. We shall use $ to mark the bottom of the stack and the right end of the input.

	Stack	Input
	$	w $

The parser operates by shifting zero or more input symbols onto the stack until a handle β is on top of the stack. The parser then reduces β to the left side of the appropriate production. The parser repeats this cycle until it has detected an error or until the stack contains the start symbol and the input is empty:

	Stack	Input
	$S	$

In this configuration the parser halts and announces successful completion of parsing.

Example 5.4. Let us step through the actions a shift-reduce parser might make in parsing the input string $id_1 + id_2 * id_3$ according to grammar (5.2), using the derivation of Example 5.2. The sequence is shown in Fig. 5.4. Note that because grammar (5.2) has two rightmost derivations for this input there is another sequence of steps a shift-reduce parser could take. □

	Stack	Input	Action
(1)	$	$id_1 + id_2 * id_3$$	shift
(2)	id_1	$+ id_2 * id_3$$	reduce by $E \rightarrow id$
(3)	E	$+ id_2 * id_3$$	shift
(4)	$E +$	$id_2 * id_3$$	shift
(5)	$E + id_2$	$* id_3$$	reduce by $E \rightarrow id$
(6)	$E + E$	$* id_3$$	shift
(7)	$E + E *$	$id_3$$	shift
(8)	$E + E * id_3$	$	reduce by $E \rightarrow id$
(9)	$E + E * E$	$	reduce by $E \rightarrow E * E$
(10)	$E + E$	$	reduce by $E \rightarrow E + E$
(11)	E	$	accept

Fig. 5.4. Shift-reduce parsing actions.

While the primary operations of the parser are shift and reduce, there are actually four possible actions a shift-reduce parser can make: (1) shift, (2) reduce, (3) accept, and (4) error.

1. In a *shift* action, the next input symbol is shifted to the top of the stack.

2. In a *reduce* action, the parser knows the right end of the handle is at the top of the stack. It must then locate the left end of the handle within the stack and decide with what nonterminal to replace the handle.

3. In an *accept* action, the parser announces successful completion of parsing.

4. In an *error* action, the parser discovers that a syntax error has occurred and calls an error recovery routine.

There is an important fact that justifies the use of a stack in shift-reduce parsing: the handle will always eventually appear on top of the stack, never inside. This fact becomes obvious when we consider the possible forms of two successive steps in any rightmost derivation. These two steps can be of the form

$$(1) \quad S \underset{rm}{\overset{*}{\Rightarrow}} \alpha A z$$
$$\underset{rm}{\overset{*}{\Rightarrow}} \alpha \beta B y z$$
$$\underset{rm}{\overset{*}{\Rightarrow}} \alpha \beta \gamma y z$$

or

$$(2) \quad S \underset{rm}{\overset{*}{\Rightarrow}} \alpha B x A z$$
$$\underset{rm}{\overset{*}{\Rightarrow}} \alpha B x y z$$
$$\underset{rm}{\overset{*}{\Rightarrow}} \alpha \gamma x y z$$

In case (1), A is replaced by βBy, and then the rightmost nonterminal B in that right side is replaced by γ. In case (2), A is again replaced first, but this time the right side is a string y of terminals only. The next rightmost nonterminal, B, will be somewhere to the left of y.

Let us consider case (1) in reverse, where a shift-reduce parser has just reached the configuration

Stack	Input
$\$\alpha\beta\gamma$	$yz\$$

The parser now reduces the handle γ to B to reach the configuration

Stack	Input
$\$\alpha\beta B$	$yz\$$

Since B is the rightmost nonterminal in $\alpha\beta Byz$, the right end of the handle of $\alpha\beta Byz$ cannot occur inside the stack. The parser can therefore shift the string y onto the stack to reach the configuration

Stack	Input
$\$\alpha\beta By$	$z\$$

in which βBy is the handle, and it gets reduced to A.

In case (2), in configuration

Stack	Input
$\$\alpha\gamma$	$xyz\$$

the handle γ is on top of the stack. After reducing the handle γ to B, the parser can shift the string xy to get the next handle y on top of the stack:

Stack	Input
$\$\alpha Bxy$	$z\$$

Now the parser reduces y to A.

In both cases, after making a reduction the parser had to shift zero or more symbols to get the next handle onto the stack. It never had to go into the stack to find the handle. It is this aspect of handle pruning that makes a stack a particularly convenient data structure for implementing a shift-reduce parser. The next section of this chapter and all of Chapter 6 are devoted to methods whereby shift-reduce-accept-error decisions can be made.

Constructing a Parse Tree

It is often useful to construct a parse tree explicitly. This can be done quite simply as we perform shift-reduce parsing. The strategy is to build parse trees bottom-up. With each symbol on the stack we associate a pointer to a tree whose root is that symbol and whose yield is the string of terminals which have been reduced to that symbol, perhaps by a long series of reductions. At the end of the shift-reduce parse, the start symbol remaining on the stack will have the entire parse tree associated with it. The bottom-up tree construction process has two aspects.

1. When we shift an input symbol a onto the stack we create a one-node tree labeled a. Both the root and the yield of this tree are a, and the yield truly represents the string of terminals "reduced" (by zero reductions) to the symbol a.

2. When we reduce $X_1 X_2 \cdots X_n$ to A, we create a new node labeled A. Its children, from left to right, are the roots of the trees for $X_1, X_2, \ldots, X_n$. If for all i the tree for X_i has yield x_i, then the yield for the new tree is $x_1 x_2 \cdots x_n$. This string has in fact been reduced to A by a series of reductions culminating in the present one. As a special case, if we reduce ϵ to A we create a node labeled A with one child labeled ϵ.

(a) After shifting id_1.   (b) After reducing id_1 to E.

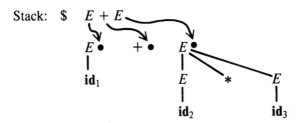

(c) After reducing $id_1 + id_2 * id_3$ to $E + E$.

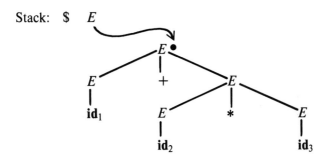

(d) At completion.

Fig. 5.5. Parse tree construction.

Example 5.5. Consider the sequence of steps depicted in Fig. 5.4. At line
(2) the stack and sequence of trees — one tree consisting of one node — is
shown in Fig. 5.5(a). At line (3), the **id** at the top is reduced to E. A
node labeled E is created, and its one child is the node pointed to by the **id**
removed from the stack. The result is shown in Fig. 5.5(b). After a
sequence of shifts and reductions we arrive at the situation shown in Fig.
5.5(c), which corresponds to line (10) of Fig. 5.4. At that point, $E + E$ is

reduced to E. We create a new node labeled E, and this node receives three children, the nodes pointed to by the three top positions on the stack. The result is shown in Fig. 5.5(d) and corresponds to line (11) of Fig. 5.4.
□

5.3 Operator-Precedence Parsing

For a certain small class of grammars we can easily construct efficient shift-reduce parsers by hand. These grammars have the property (among other essential requirements) that no production right side is ϵ or has two adjacent nonterminals. A grammar with the latter property is called an *operator grammar*.

Example 5.6. The following grammar for expressions

$$E \rightarrow E A E \mid (E) \mid -E \mid \textbf{id}$$
$$A \rightarrow + \mid - \mid * \mid / \mid \uparrow$$

is not an operator grammar, because the right side EAE has two (in fact three) consecutive nonterminals. However, if we substitute for A each of its alternates, we obtain the following operator grammar:

$$E \rightarrow E + E \mid E - E \mid E * E \mid E / E \mid E \uparrow E \mid (E) \mid -E \mid \textbf{id} \quad (5.3)$$

□

We shall now describe an easy-to-implement parsing technique called operator-precedence parsing. Historically, the operator-precedence technique was first described as a manipulation on tokens without any reference to an underlying grammar. In fact, once we finish building an operator-precedence parser from a grammar, we may effectively ignore the grammar, using the nonterminals on the stack only as placeholders for the nodes of a parse tree being constructed in the bottom-up fashion just described.

As a general parsing technique, operator-precedence parsing has a number of disadvantages. For example, it is hard to handle tokens like the minus sign which has two different precedences (depending on whether it is unary or binary). Worse, since the relationship between a grammar for the language being parsed and the operator-precedence parser itself is tenuous, one cannot always be sure the parser accepts exactly the desired language. Finally, only a small class of grammars can be parsed using operator-precedence techniques.

Nevertheless, because of its simplicity, numerous compilers using operator-precedence parsing techniques for expressions have been successfully built. Often these parsers use recursive descent, described in the next section, for statements and higher-level constructs. Operator-precedence parsers have even been built for entire languages. SNOBOL, being virtually "all operators," is an example of a language for which operator precedence works well.

In operator-precedence parsing, we use three disjoint *precedence relations*, $<\cdot$, $\doteq$ and $\cdot>$, between certain pairs of terminals. These precedence relations guide the selection of handles. If $a <\cdot b$, we say a "yields precedence to" b; if $a \doteq b$, a "has the same precedence as" b; if $a \cdot> b$, a "takes precedence over" b. We should caution the reader that while these relations may appear similar to the arithmetic relations "less than," "equal to" and "greater than," the precedence relations have quite different properties. For example, we could have $a <\cdot b$ and $a \cdot> b$ for the same language, or we might have none of $a <\cdot b$, $a \doteq b$, and $a \cdot> b$ holding for some terminals a and b.

There are two common ways of determining what precedence relation should hold between a pair of terminals. The first method we discuss is intuitive and is based on the traditional notions of associativity and precedence of operators. For example, if $*$ is to have higher precedence than $+$, we make $+ <\cdot *$ and $* \cdot> +$. This approach will be seen to resolve the ambiguities of grammar (5.3) and to enable us to write an operator-precedence parser for it (although the unary minus sign causes problems).

The second method of selecting operator-precedence relations is to first construct an unambiguous grammar for the language, a grammar which reflects the correct associativity and precedence in its parse trees. This job is not difficult for expressions; Example 4.6 provided the paradigm. For the other common source of ambiguity, the dangling **else**, the grammar in Appendix B, which uses the nonterminal restricted-statement to generate statements other than the **if** $\cdots$ **then** statement, is a useful model. Having obtained an unambiguous grammar, there is a mechanical method for constructing operator-precedence relations from it. These relations may not be disjoint, and they may parse a language other than that generated by the grammar, but with the standard sorts of arithmetic expressions, few problems are encountered in practice.

Using Operator-Precedence Relations

The intention of the precedence relations is to delimit the handle of a right-sentential form, with $<\cdot$ marking the left end, $\doteq$ appearing in the interior of the handle, if any, and $\cdot>$ marking the right end. To be more precise, suppose we have a right-sentential form of an operator grammar. The fact that no adjacent nonterminals appear on the right sides of productions implies that no right-sentential form will have two adjacent nonterminals either. Thus, we may write the right-sentential form as $\beta_0 a_1 \beta_1 \cdots a_n \beta_n$, where each β_i is either ϵ (the empty string) or a single nonterminal. Suppose that between a_i and a_{i+1} exactly one of the relations $<\cdot$, $\doteq$, and $\cdot>$ holds. Further, we use \$ to mark each end of the string, and define $\$ <\cdot b$ and $b \cdot> \$$ for all terminals b.

Now suppose we remove the nonterminals from the string and place the correct relation, $<\cdot$, $\doteq$, or $\cdot>$, between each pair of terminals and between the endmost terminals and the \$'s marking the ends of the string. For example, suppose we initially have the right-sentential form **id** + **id** * **id** and the precedence relations are those given in Fig. 5.6.

	id	**+**	*****	**\$**
id		$\cdot>$	$\cdot>$	$\cdot>$
+	$<\cdot$	$\cdot>$	$<\cdot$	$\cdot>$
*	$<\cdot$	$\cdot>$	$\cdot>$	$\cdot>$
\$	$<\cdot$	$<\cdot$	$<\cdot$	

Fig. 5.6. Operator precedence relations.

Then the string with the precedence relations inserted is:

$$\$ <\cdot \mathbf{id} \cdot> + <\cdot \mathbf{id} \cdot> * <\cdot \mathbf{id} \cdot> \$ \qquad (5.4)$$

For example, $<\cdot$ is inserted between \$ and **id** since $<\cdot$ is the entry in row \$ and column **id**. Now the handle can be found by the following process.

1. Scan the string from the left end until the leftmost $\cdot>$ is encountered. In (5.4) above, this occurs between the first **id** and $+$.
2. Then scan backwards (to the left) over any $\doteq$'s until a $<\cdot$ is encountered. In (5.4), we scan backwards to \$.
3. The handle contains everything to the left of the first $\cdot>$ and to the right of the $<\cdot$ encountered in step (2), including any intervening or surrounding nonterminals. (The inclusion of surrounding nonterminals is necessary so that two adjacent nonterminals do not appear in a right-sentential form.) In (5.4) the handle is the first **id**.

If we are dealing with grammar (5.3), we then reduce **id** to E. At this point we have the right-sentential form $E+\mathbf{id}*\mathbf{id}$. After reducing the two remaining **id**'s to E by the same steps, we obtain the right-sentential form $E+E*E$. Consider now the string $\$+*\$$ obtained by deleting the nonterminals. Inserting the precedence relations, we get

$$\$ <\cdot + <\cdot * \cdot> \$$$

indicating that the left end of the handle lies between $+$ and $*$ and the right end between $*$ and \$. These precedence relations indicate that, in the right-sentential form $E+E*E$, the handle is $E*E$. Note how the E's surrounding the $*$ become part of the handle.

Since the nonterminals do not influence the parse, we need not worry about distinguishing among them. A single marker "nonterminal" can be kept on the stack of a shift-reduce parser to indicate placeholders for nodes of the parse tree being constructed or to indicate a variety of possible translations, as discussed in Chapter 7.

It may appear from the discussion above that the entire right-sentential form must be scanned at each step to find the handle. Such is not the case if the precedence relations are used to guide the actions of a shift-reduce parser. If the precedence relation $<\cdot$ or $\doteq$ holds between the topmost terminal symbol on the stack and the next input symbol, the parser shifts. The parser has not yet found the right end of the handle. If the relation $\cdot>$ holds, a reduction is called for. Now the parser has found the right end of the handle, and the precedence relations can be used to find the left end of the handle in the stack.

If no precedence relation holds between a pair of terminals (indicated by a blank entry in Fig. 5.6), then a syntactic error has been detected and an error recovery routine, such as the one described in Chapter 11, is invoked.

Operator-Precedence Relations from Associativity and Precedence

We are always free to create operator-precedence relations any way we see fit and hope that a shift-reduce parser will work properly when guided by them. For a language of arithmetic expressions such as that generated by grammar (5.3) we can use the following heuristic to produce a useful set of precedence relations. Note that grammar (5.3) is ambiguous, and right-sentential forms could have many handles. Our rules are designed to select the "proper" handles to reflect a given set of associativity and precedence rules for binary operators.

1. If operator θ_1 has higher precedence than operator θ_2, make $\theta_1 \cdot> \theta_2$ and $\theta_2 <\cdot \theta_1$. For example, if $*$ has higher precedence than $+$, make $* \cdot> +$ and $+ <\cdot *$. These relations ensure that, in an expression of the form $E+E*E+E$, the central $E*E$ is the handle that will be reduced first.

2. If θ_1 and θ_2 are operators of equal precedence (they may in fact be the same operator), then make $\theta_1 \cdot> \theta_2$ and $\theta_2 \cdot> \theta_1$ if the operators are left-associative, or make $\theta_1 <\cdot \theta_2$ and $\theta_2 <\cdot \theta_1$ if they are right-associative. For example, if $+$ and $-$ are left-associative, then make $+ \cdot> +$, $+ \cdot> -$, $- \cdot> -$, and $- \cdot> +$. If $\uparrow$ is right associative, then $\uparrow <\cdot \uparrow$. These relations ensure that $E-E+E$ will have handle $E-E$ selected and $E\uparrow E\uparrow E$ will have the last $E\uparrow E$ selected.

3. Make $\theta <\cdot \text{ id}$, $\text{id} \cdot> \theta$, $\theta <\cdot$ (, ($<\cdot \theta$,) $\cdot> \theta$, $\theta \cdot>$), $\theta \cdot>$ \$ and \$ $<\cdot \theta$ for all operators θ. Also, let

($\doteq$)	\$ $<\cdot$ (	\$ $<\cdot$ **id**
($<\cdot$ (	**id** $\cdot>$ \$	) $\cdot>$ \$
($<\cdot$ **id**	**id** $\cdot>$)	) $\cdot>$)

These rules ensure that **id** will be reduced to E wherever found and (E) will be reduced to E wherever found. Also, \$ will serve as both left and right endmarker, causing handles to be found between \$'s wherever possible.

Example 5.7. The operator-precedence relations for grammar (5.3), assuming

1. $\uparrow$ is of highest precedence and right-associative,
2. $*$ and $/$ are of next highest precedence and left-associative, and
3. $+$ and $-$ are of lowest precedence and left-associative,

are shown in Fig. 5.7. (Blanks denote error entries.) The reader should try out the table to see that it works correctly, ignoring problems with unary minus for the moment. Try input **id**$*$(**id**$\uparrow$**id**)$-$**id**$/$**id**, for example. □

	$+$	$-$	$*$	$/$	$\uparrow$	**id**	(	)	\$
$+$	$\cdot>$	$\cdot>$	$<\cdot$	$<\cdot$	$<\cdot$	$<\cdot$	$<\cdot$	$\cdot>$	$\cdot>$
$-$	$\cdot>$	$\cdot>$	$<\cdot$	$<\cdot$	$<\cdot$	$<\cdot$	$<\cdot$	$\cdot>$	$\cdot>$
$*$	$\cdot>$	$\cdot>$	$\cdot>$	$\cdot>$	$<\cdot$	$<\cdot$	$<\cdot$	$\cdot>$	$\cdot>$
$/$	$\cdot>$	$\cdot>$	$\cdot>$	$\cdot>$	$<\cdot$	$<\cdot$	$<\cdot$	$\cdot>$	$\cdot>$
$\uparrow$	$\cdot>$	$\cdot>$	$\cdot>$	$\cdot>$	$<\cdot$	$<\cdot$	$<\cdot$	$\cdot>$	$\cdot>$
id	$\cdot>$	$\cdot>$	$\cdot>$	$\cdot>$	$\cdot>$			$\cdot>$	$\cdot>$
(	$<\cdot$	$<\cdot$	$<\cdot$	$<\cdot$	$<\cdot$	$<\cdot$	$<\cdot$	$\doteq$	
)	$\cdot>$	$\cdot>$	$\cdot>$	$\cdot>$	$\cdot>$			$\cdot>$	$\cdot>$
\$	$<\cdot$	$<\cdot$	$<\cdot$	$<\cdot$	$<\cdot$	$<\cdot$	$<\cdot$		

Fig. 5.7. Operator precedence relations.

Handling Unary Operators

If we have a unary operator such as $\neg$ (logical negation), which is not also a binary operator, we can easily incorporate it into the above scheme for creating operator-precedence relations. Supposing $\neg$ to be a unary prefix operator, we make $\theta <\cdot \neg$ for any operator θ, whether unary or binary. We make $\neg \cdot> \theta$ if $\neg$ has higher precedence than θ and $\neg <\cdot \theta$ if not. For example, if ¬ has higher precedence than &, and & is left-associative, we would group $E\&\neg E\&E$ as $(E\&(\neg E))\&E$, by these rules. The rule for unary postfix operators is analogous and is left as an exercise.

The situation changes when we have an operator like the minus sign − which is both unary prefix and binary infix. Even if we give unary and binary minus the same precedence, the table of Fig. 5.7 will fail to parse strings like **id∗−id** correctly. The best approach in this case is to use the lexical analyzer to distinguish between unary and binary minus, by having it return a different token when it sees unary minus. Unfortunately, the lexical analyzer cannot use lookahead to distinguish the two; it must remember the previous token. In FORTRAN, for example, a minus sign is unary if the previous token was an operator, a left parenthesis, a comma, or an assignment symbol.

Operator-Precedence Grammars

If we use an unambiguous operator grammar for arithmetic expressions or for a variety of other programming-language constructs, and our grammar satisfies certain conditions, we can construct a reliable operator-precedence table for the grammar. The resulting parser might accept strings not in the language of the grammar, but in practical cases that does not usually happen. Example 4.6 gives a typical construction of an unambiguous grammar for arithmetic expressions, although that grammar, which includes the unary minus operator, will turn out not to be an operator-precedence grammar (one for which the following construction works), unless unary minus is regarded as a distinct token.

We shall now define the term "operator-precedence grammar," show how to compute its precedence relations, and explain the details of shift-reduce parsing using precedence relations. To begin, let G be an ϵ-free operator grammar (i.e., no right side is ϵ and no production has a pair of adjacent nonterminals). For each two terminal symbols a and b, we say:

i) $a \doteq b$ if there is a right side of a production of the form $\alpha a \beta b \gamma$, where β is either ϵ or a single nonterminal. That is $a \doteq b$ if a appears immediately to the left of b in a right side, or if they appear separated by one nonterminal. For example, in grammar (5.1) of Example 5.1, the production $S \rightarrow iCtSeS$ implies that $i \doteq t$ and $t \doteq e$.

ii) $a <\!\!\cdot\, b$ if for some nonterminal A there is a right side of the form $\alpha a A \beta$, and $A \xrightarrow{+} \gamma b \delta$, where γ is either ϵ or a single nonterminal. That is, $a <\!\!\cdot\, b$ if a nonterminal A appears immediately to the right of a and derives a string in which b is the first terminal symbol. For example, in grammar (5.1), we have i immediately to the left of C in $S \rightarrow iCtS$, and $C \xrightarrow{+} b$, so $i <\!\!\cdot\, b$. The derivation is one step, and

$\gamma = \epsilon$ here. Also, define $\$ <\cdot b$ if there is a derivation $S \overset{+}{\Rightarrow} \gamma b \delta$ and γ is ϵ or a single nonterminal.

iii) $a \cdot > b$ if for some nonterminal A there is a right side of the form $\alpha A b \beta$, and $A \overset{+}{\Rightarrow} \gamma a \delta$, where δ is either ϵ or a single nonterminal. That is, $a \cdot > b$ if a nonterminal appearing immediately to the left of b derives a string whose last terminal is a. For example, in grammar (5.1), $S \rightarrow iCtS$ and $C \overset{+}{\Rightarrow} b$ imply $b \cdot > t$. Also, define $a \cdot > \$$ if $S \overset{+}{\Rightarrow} \gamma a \delta$ and δ is either ϵ or a single nonterminal.

Intuitively, $a \doteq b$ means that a and b are part of one right side. If during parsing they appear together on the stack, with a below b, and if b is included in the handle, then a must also be included. This explains why, when searching the stack for a handle, we moved down the stack, past $\doteq$'s, to find a $<\cdot$ to mark the left end of the handle.

If $a \cdot > b$, then by rule (iii) above there is a parse tree that looks like Fig. 5.8(a). Thus, it appears that a could be the rightmost terminal of the handle (the handle shown here is a C-production).

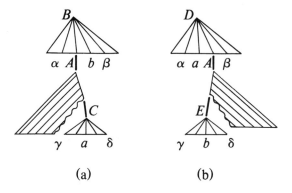

(a)   (b)

Fig. 5.8. Parse trees indicating $a \cdot > b$ and $a <\cdot b$.

Finally, $a <\cdot b$ indicates that there could be a parse tree like that of Fig. 5.8(b). In that picture, b is the leftmost terminal of a handle, this time indicated as an E-production. This fact shows why we used $<\cdot$, while scanning the stack for a handle, to indicate that the left end of the handle had been found.

Of course, just because the precedence relations make it appear that the left/middle/right of a handle has been found does not mean that we truly have the handle. The collection of productions that imply the precedence relations may be different from the production which is actually the handle.

We may, however, define a small but useful class of grammars for which appearances are never deceiving: what looks like a handle really is.

Definition. An *operator-precedence grammar* is an ϵ-free operator grammar in which the precedence relations $<\cdot$, $\doteq$, and $\cdot>$ constructed as above are disjoint. That is, for any pair of terminals a and b, never more than one of the relations $a <\cdot b$, $a \doteq b$, and $a \cdot> b$ is true.

Example 5.8. Let us consider a simplification of the operator grammar (5.3) in which there are only the operators $+$ and $*$.

$$E \rightarrow E + E \mid E * E \mid (E) \mid \textbf{id} \tag{5.5}$$

This grammar is not an operator-precedence grammar because two precedence relations hold between certain pairs of terminals. We shall show that two precedence relations hold between $+$ and $+$.

In rule (iii) defining the $\cdot>$ relation, we could let the right side $\alpha A b \beta$ be $E+E$. That is, $\alpha = \epsilon$, $A = E$, $b = +$, and $\beta = E$. Then the derivation $A \overset{+}{\Longrightarrow} \gamma a \delta$ could be the one-step derivation $E \Longrightarrow E+E$, where $\gamma = E$, $a = +$ and $\delta = E$. We have thus shown the relation $+ \cdot> +$.

We can similarly apply rule (ii), the definition of $<\cdot$. Let right side $\alpha a A \beta$ be $E+E$ again; here a is $+$ and A is E. The derivation $E \overset{+}{\Longrightarrow} E+E$ shows that E can derive strings whose first terminal is $+$. Thus, $+ <\cdot +$. Since both $+ <\cdot +$ and $+ \cdot> +$, (5.5) is not an operator-precedence grammar.

Using the construction in Example 4.6, we can transform grammar (5.5) into an equivalent grammar that is both operator-precedence and unambiguous. It is:

$$E \rightarrow E + T \mid T$$
$$T \rightarrow T * F \mid F \tag{5.6}$$
$$F \rightarrow (E) \mid \textbf{id}$$

Here E, T, and F stand for expression, term, and factor as in Example 4.6.

This grammar is clearly an operator grammar. To see that at most one precedence relation holds between any pair of symbols, we shall construct the matrix of all precedence relations for grammar (5.6). Before doing so, however, let us first deduce, for each nonterminal, those terminals that can be the first or last terminal in a string derived from that nonterminal. All derivations from F will have the symbols (or **id** as the first terminal, and the symbols) or **id** as the last. A derivation from T could begin $T \Longrightarrow T * F$, showing that $*$ could be both first and last terminal. Or a derivation could begin $T \Longrightarrow F$, meaning that every first or last terminal derivable from F is also a first or last terminal derivable from T. Thus, the symbols $*$, (, and **id** can be first and $*$,), and **id** can be last in a derivation from T. A similar argument applies to E, and we see that $+$, $*$, $($, or **id** can be first and $*$, $+$, $)$, or **id** can be last. These facts are summarized in Fig. 5.9.

Nonterminal	First terminal	Last terminal
E	$*$, $+$, $($, **id**	$*$, $+$, $)$, **id**
T	$*$, $($, **id**	$*$, $)$, **id**
F	$($, **id**	$)$, **id**

Fig. 5.9. First and last terminals.

Now, to compute the $\doteq$ relation, we look for right sides with two terminals separated by nothing or by a nonterminal. Only one right side, (E), qualifies, so we determine $(\doteq)$.

Next, consider $<\!\cdot$. We look for right sides with a terminal immediately to the left of a nonterminal to play the roles of a and A in rule (ii). For each such pair, a is related by $<\!\cdot$ to any terminal which can be first in a string derivable from A. The candidates in the grammar (5.6) are $+$ and T in the right side $E+T$, $*$ and F in $T*F$, and $($ and E in (E). The first of these gives $+ <\!\cdot *$, $+ <\!\cdot ($, and $+ <\!\cdot$ **id**. The $*$:F pair gives $* <\!\cdot ($ and $* <\!\cdot$ **id**. The $($:E pair gives $(<\!\cdot *$, $(<\!\cdot +$, $(<\!\cdot ($, and $(<\!\cdot$ **id**. We then add the relationships $\$ <\!\cdot *$, $\$ <\!\cdot +$, $\$ <\!\cdot ($, and $\$ <\!\cdot$ **id**, since $\$$ must be related by $<\!\cdot$ to all possible first terminals derivable from the start symbol E.

Symmetrically we can construct the $\cdot\!>$ relation. We look for right sides with a nonterminal immediately to the left of a terminal, to play the roles of A and b of rule (iii). Then, every terminal that could be the last in a string derivable from A is related by $\cdot\!>$ to b. In our example (5.6), the pairs corresponding to A and b are E:$+$, T:$*$, and E:$)$. Thus, we have the relations $* \cdot\!> +$, $+ \cdot\!> +$, $) \cdot\!> +$, **id** $\cdot\!> +$, $* \cdot\!> *$, $) \cdot\!> *$, **id** $\cdot\!> *$, $* \cdot\!>)$, $+ \cdot\!>)$, $) \cdot\!>)$, and **id** $\cdot\!>)$. We add the relations $* \cdot\!> \$$, $+ \cdot\!> \$$, $) \cdot\!> \$$, and **id** $\cdot\!> \$$ according to rule (iii). The precedence relations for grammar (5.6) are shown in Fig. 5.10.   □

Let us now develop the algorithm necessary to construct precedence relations. If we observe the methodology used in Example 5.8, we notice we first constructed two sets LEADING(A) and TRAILING(A) for each nonterminal A, defined by:

LEADING$(A) = \{a | A \xRightarrow{+} \gamma a \delta$, where γ is ϵ or a single nonterminal$\}$

TRAILING$(A) = \{a | A \xRightarrow{+} \gamma a \delta$, where δ is ϵ or a single nonterminal$\}$

	+	*	(	)	id	$
+	·>	<·	<·	·>	<·	·>
*	·>	·>	<·	·>	<·	·>
(	<·	<·	<·	≐	<·	
)	·>	·>		·>		·>
id	·>	·>		·>		·>
$	<·	<·	<·		<·	

Fig. 5.10. Operator-precedence relations.

We determined the $<·$ relation by looking in each right side for adjacent symbols $··· aA ···$. Then a was related by $<·$ to each b in LEADING(A). The TRAILING sets similarly helped compute the $·>$ relations.

Let us therefore begin with an algorithm to compute LEADING. The computation is based on two rules.

1. a is in LEADING(A) if there is a production of the form $A → \gamma a \delta$, where γ is ϵ or a single nonterminal.
2. If a is in LEADING(B), and there is a production of the form $A → B\alpha$, then a is in LEADING(A).

Our computational method will be to construct a Boolean array $L[A, a]$, where $L[A, a]$ is to be set to **true** if and only if terminal a is in LEADING(A), for nonterminal A. We initialize $L[A, a]$ to be **true** if and only if it so follows from rule (1) above. We keep a stack of pairs (B, a) such that $L[B, a]$ has been set to **true**, but the pair (B, a) has not been used in rule (2) to find new pairs (A, a) such that a is in LEADING(A). The details are given in Algorithm 5.1.

Algorithm 5.1. Computation of LEADING.

Input. A context-free grammar G.

Output. The Boolean array $L[A, a]$ in which the entry for indices A and a is **true** if and only if a is in LEADING(A).

Method. We need a procedure INSTALL(A, a), which sets $L[A, a]$ to **true**, and if it was not previously **true**, places (A, a) on STACK, a stack of nonterminal-terminal pairs that have not yet been used in rule (2) above to find new pairs.

procedure INSTALL$(A,\ a)$;
if not $L[A,\ a]$ **then**
    begin
        $L[A,\ a] :=$ **true**;
        push $(A,\ a)$ onto STACK
    end

The main procedure is given in Fig. 5.11.   □

      begin /∗ initialize L according to rule (1) ∗/
(1)   **for** each nonterminal A and terminal a **do** $L(A,\ a) :=$ **false**;
(2)   **for** each production of the form $A \rightarrow a\alpha$ or $A \rightarrow Ba\alpha$ **do**
          INSTALL$(A,\ a)$;
          /∗ main loop considers each $(B,\ a)$ on STACK to add
          new pairs $(A,\ a)$ by rule (2) ∗/
      while STACK not empty **do**
          begin
(3)   pop top pair $(B,\ a)$ from STACK;
(4)   **for** each production of the form $A \rightarrow B\alpha$ **do**
               INSTALL$(A,\ a)$
          end
    end

Fig. 5.11. Computing LEADING.

The algorithm for calculating TRAILING is analogous to Algorithm 5.1, and we leave the necessary modifications as an exercise. The complete algorithm for finding precedence relations can now be stated.

Algorithm 5.2. Computing operator-precedence relations.

Input. An operator grammar G.

Output. The relations $<\!\cdot$, $\doteq$, and $\cdot\!>$ for G.

Method.
1. Compute LEADING(A) and TRAILING(A) for each nonterminal A.
2. Execute the program of Fig. 5.12, examining each position of the right side of each production.
3. Set $\$ <\!\cdot\ a$ for all a in LEADING(S) and set $b \cdot\!> \$$ for all b in TRAILING(S), where S is the start symbol of G.   □

> **for** each production $A \rightarrow X_1 X_2 ... X_n$ **do**
>   **for** $i := 1$ **to** $n-1$ **do**
>   **begin**
>   **if** X_i and X_{i+1} are both terminals **then** set $X_i \doteq X_{i+1}$;
>   **if** $i \leqslant n-2$ and X_i and X_{i+2} are terminals
>   and X_{i+1} is a nonterminal **then**
>   set $X_i \doteq X_{i+2}$;
>   **if** X_i is a terminal and X_{i+1} is a nonterminal **then**
>   **for** all a in LEADING(X_{i+1}) **do** set $X_i <\cdot a$;
>   **if** X_i is a nonterminal and X_{i+1} is a terminal **then**
>   **for** all a in TRAILING(X_i) **do** set $a \cdot> X_{i+1}$
>   **end**

Fig. 5.12. Calculation of operator-precedence relations.

The Operator-Precedence Parsing Algorithm

Now let us explore how a shift-reduce parser is built from precedence relations that are constructed from an operator-precedence grammar. Consider the grammar (5.6), whose precedence relations appear in Fig. 5.10. Suppose we are given the expression **id** + **id** to parse. We set up the stack and input as:

Stack		Input
$	$<\cdot$	**id** + **id** $

Since the $<\cdot$ relation applies between the symbol on top of the stack and the first input symbol, we shift, giving:

$ $<\cdot$ **id**	$\cdot>$	+ **id** $

Now, the precedence relation $\cdot>$ holds between the symbol on top of the stack and the current input symbol. Thus we have found the right end of the handle. The left end of the handle is found by going into the stack, looking for the first $<\cdot$ relation. Thus, $<\cdot$ and $\cdot>$ frame the right side to be reduced; it is **id**. We know there is one production with that right side, namely $F \rightarrow$ **id**. We reduce, leaving:

$ F	$<\cdot$	+ **id** $

Following the rules that determine whether to shift or reduce, the next few steps are:

$$\begin{array}{llll}
\$ <\cdot\ F + & <\cdot & \textbf{id}\ \$ \\
\$ <\cdot\ F + <\cdot\ \textbf{id} & \cdot> & \$ \\
\$ <\cdot\ F + F & \cdot> & \$
\end{array}$$

Now we are told to reduce. The handle indicated by the precedence relations is $F+F$. But there is no production with that right side.

If one remembers that the shift-reduce parser is supposed to trace out a rightmost derivation in reverse, one can see what went wrong. The lower (leftmost) F on the stack should have been reduced to T and then to E, and the other F should have been reduced to T. Then we would have $E+T$ on the stack, and this could be reduced correctly to E, completing the parse. We note that all the missed reductions are of the form $A \rightarrow B$ for nonterminals A and B. Such a production is called a *single* production, because its right side is a single nonterminal. As the operator-precedence parsing method examines terminals only and ignores the nonterminals, it is no surprise that we could not detect the need for reductions by single productions.

One commonly used solution to the problem is to ignore the nonterminals as far as parsing is concerned. We assume that reductions by single productions could be made as needed. Then we keep only terminals on the stack and make only those reductions that do not involve single productions. The disadvantage of this method is that we lose the power the nonterminals have to warn us that pieces of the input do not fit together properly, and in fact, we may wind up accepting an input that was not a sentence of the operator-precedence grammar. However, any sentence will be parsed by this method. In the next chapter we shall discuss a shift-reduce parsing method that does parse all sentences and only sentences.

Algorithm 5.3. Operator-precedence parsing algorithm.

Input. The precedence relations from some operator-precedence grammar and an input string of terminals from that grammar.

Output. Strictly speaking, there is no output. We could construct a *skeletal* parse tree as we parse, with one nonterminal labeling all interior nodes and the use of single productions not shown. Alternatively, the sequence of shift-reduce steps could be considered the output.

Method. Let the input string be $a_1 a_2 \cdots a_n \$$. Initially, the stack contains $\$$. Execute the program of Fig. 5.13.

If a parse tree is desired, we must create a node for each terminal shifted onto the stack at line (4). Then, when the loop of lines (6) − (7) reduces by some production, we create a node whose children are the nodes corresponding to whatever is popped off the stack. After line (7) we place on the stack a pointer to the node created. This means that some of the

(1)	**repeat forever**
(2)	**if** only $ is on the stack and only $ is on the input **then**
	accept and **break**
	else
	begin
(3)	let a be the topmost terminal symbol on the stack
	and let b be the current input symbol;
(4)	**if** $a <\cdot b$ or $a \doteq b$ **then** shift b onto the stack
(5)	**else if** $a \cdot> b$ **then** /* reduce */
(6)	**repeat** pop the stack
(7)	**until** the top stack terminal is related by $<\cdot$
	to the terminal most recently popped
(8)	**else** call the error correcting routine
	end

Fig. 5.13. Operator precedence parsing algorithm.

"symbols" popped by line (6) will be pointers to nodes. The comparison of line (7) continues to be made between terminals only; pointers are popped with no comparison being made.   □

Example 5.9. Consider grammar (5.6) again; Fig. 5.10 gives the operator-precedence relations. Let **id** + **id** be the input. The stack, input, and trees constructed are shown in Fig. 5.14. □

Precedence Functions

Compilers using operator-precedence parsers need not store the table of precedence relations. In most cases, the table can be encoded by two *precedence functions* f and g, which map terminal symbols to integers. We attempt to select f and g so that, for symbols a and b,

1. $f(a) < g(b)$ whenever $a <\cdot b$,
2. $f(a) = g(b)$ whenever $a \doteq b$,
3. $f(a) > g(b)$ whenever $a \cdot> b$

Thus the precedence relation between a and b can be determined by a numerical comparison between $f(a)$ and $g(b)$. Note, however, that error entries in the precedence matrix are obscured, since one of (1), (2), or (3) holds no matter what $f(a)$ and $g(b)$ are. The loss of error detection capability is generally not considered serious enough to prevent the using of precedence functions where possible; errors can still be caught when a reduction is called for and no handle can be found (see Section 11.3).

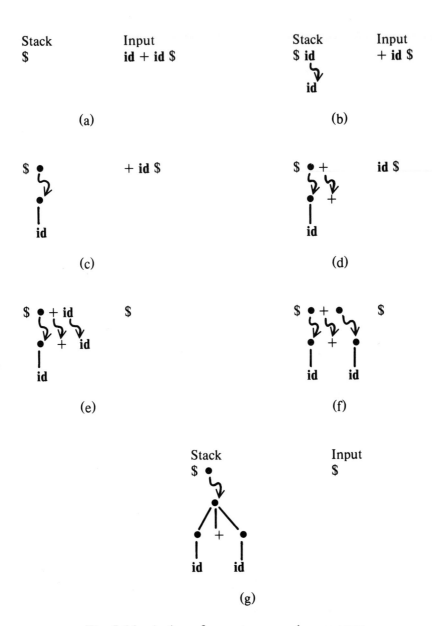

Fig. 5.14. Action of operator-precedence parser.

Not every table of precedence relations has precedence functions to encode it, but in practical cases the functions usually exist.

Example 5.10. Consider the precedence table of Fig. 5.10. A suitable pair of precedence functions is:

	+	*	(	)	id	$
f	2	4	0	4	4	0
g	1	3	5	0	5	.0

For example, $* <\cdot \text{id}$, and $f(*) < g(\text{id})$. Note that $f(\text{id}) < g(\text{id})$ suggests that $\text{id} <\cdot \text{id}$; but, in fact, no precedence relation holds between id and id. Other error entries in Fig. 5.10 are similarly replaced by one or another precedence relation. □

A simple method for finding precedence functions for a table, if such functions exist, is the following.

1. Create symbols f_a and g_a for each a that is a terminal or $.

2. Partition the created symbols into as many groups as possible, in such a way that if $a \doteq b$, then f_a and g_b are in the same group. Note that we may have to put symbols in the same group even if they are not related by $\doteq$. For example, if $a \doteq b$ and $c \doteq b$, then f_a and f_c must be in the same group, since they are both in the same group as g_b. If, in addition, $c \doteq d$, then f_a and g_d are in the same group even though $a \doteq d$ may not hold.

3. Create a directed graph whose nodes are the groups found in (2). For any a and b, if $a <\cdot b$, place an edge from the group of g_b to the group of f_a. If $a \cdot> b$, place an edge from the group of f_a to that of g_b. Note that an edge or path from f_a to g_b means that $f(a)$ must exceed $g(b)$; a path from g_b to f_a means that $g(b)$ must exceed $f(a)$.

4. If the graph constructed in (3) has a cycle, then no precedence functions exist. If there are no cycles, let $f(a)$ be the length of the longest path beginning at the group of f_a; let $g(a)$ be the length of the longest path from the group of g_a.

Example 5.11. Consider the matrix of Fig. 5.6. There are no $\doteq$ relationships, so each symbol is in a group by itself. Fig. 5.15 shows the graph constructed as above.

There are no cycles, so precedence functions exist. As $f_\$$ and $g_\$$ have no out-edges, $f(\$) = g(\$) = 0$. The longest path from g_+ has length 1, so $g(+) = 1$. There is a path from g_{id} to f_* to g_* to f_+ to g_+ to $f_\$$, so $g(\text{id}) = 5$. The resulting precedence functions are:

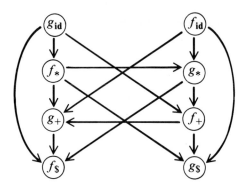

Fig. 5.15. Graph representing precedence functions.

	id	+	*	$
f	4	2	4	0
g	5	1	3	0

□

5.4 Top-Down Parsing

We now turn to another, rather different, parsing strategy, called top-down parsing. We first discuss a general form of top-down parsing that may involve backtracking, that is, making repeated scans of the input. We then discuss a special case, called recursive-descent parsing, which eliminates the need for backtracking over the input.

Top-down parsing can be viewed as an attempt to find a leftmost derivation for an input string. Equivalently, it can be viewed as attempting to construct a parse tree for the input starting from the root and creating the nodes of the parse tree in preorder. For example, consider the grammar

$$S \rightarrow cAd$$

$$A \rightarrow ab \mid a \qquad\qquad (5.7)$$

and the input $w = cad$. To construct a parse tree for this sentence top-down, we initially create a tree consisting of a single node labeled S. An input pointer points to c, the first symbol of w. We then use the first production for S to expand the tree and obtain

The leftmost leaf, labeled c, matches the first symbol of *w*, so we now advance the input pointer to *a*, the second symbol of *w*, and consider the next leaf, labeled *A*. We can then expand *A* using the first alternate for *A* to obtain the tree

We now have a match for the second input symbol.

We now consider *d*, the third input symbol, and the next leaf, labeled *b*. Since *b* does not match *d*, we report failure and go back to *A* to see whether there is another alternate for *A* that we have not tried but which might produce a match.

In going back to *A* we must reset the input pointer to position 2, the position it had when we first came to *A*. We now try the second alternate for *A* to obtain the tree

The leaf *a* matches the second symbol of *w* and the leaf *d* matches the third symbol. Since we have now produced a parse tree for *w*, we halt and announce successful completion of parsing.

An easy way to implement such a parser is to create a procedure for each nonterminal. In the case of this simple grammar, generating only two strings, there is no need for recursion among the procedures, but in practical cases, where grammars derive an infinite number of strings, recursive procedures are essential.

In many compiler-writing systems based on top-down parsing with backtrack [e.g. META (Schorre, 1964) or TMG (McClure, 1965)], an interpreter is used to simulate a collection of recursive procedures. In Section 5.5 we shall discuss predictive parsers, which, in effect, enable us to interpret recursive procedures having no backtrack.

```
procedure S( );
begin
    if input symbol = 'c' then
        begin
            ADVANCE( );
            if A( ) then
                if input symbol = 'd' then
                    begin ADVANCE( ); return true end
        end;
        return false
end
```

(a) Procedure S.

```
procedure A( );
begin
    isave := input-pointer;
    if input symbol = 'a' then
        begin
            ADVANCE( );
            if input symbol = 'b' then
                begin ADVANCE( ); return true end
        end
    input-pointer := isave;
        /* failure to find ab */
    if input-symbol = 'a' then
        begin ADVANCE( ); return true end
    else return false
end
```

(b) Procedure A.

Fig. 5.16. Recursive procedures for top-down parsing.

Example 5.12. Let us suppose the procedure ADVANCE moves the input pointer to the next input symbol. "Input symbol" is the one currently pointed to by the input pointer. Figure 5.16 gives the procedures for S and A corresponding to the informal discussion above. Procedures return value **true** (success) or **false** (failure), depending on whether or not they have found on the input a string derived by the corresponding nonterminal. Note that, on failure, each procedure leaves the input pointer where it was when the procedure it failed, and that on success it moves the input pointer over the substring recognized. □

There are several difficulties with top-down parsing as just presented. The first concerns left-recursion. A grammar G is said to be *left-recursive* if it has a nonterminal A such that there is a derivation $A \overset{+}{\Rightarrow} A\alpha$ for some α. A left-recursive grammar can cause a top-down parser to go into an infinite loop. That is, when we try to expand A, we may eventually find ourselves again trying to expand A without having consumed any input. This cycling will surely occur on an erroneous input string, and it may also occur on legal inputs, depending on the order in which the alternates for A are tried. Therefore, to use top-down parsing, we must eliminate all left-recursion from the grammar. We shall show how to do this shortly.

A second problem concerns backtracking. If we make a sequence of erroneous expansions and subsequently discover a mismatch, we may have to undo the semantic effects of making these erroneous expansions. For example, entries made in the symbol table might have to be removed. Since undoing semantic actions requires a substantial overhead, it is reasonable to consider top-down parsers that do no backtracking. The recursive-descent and predictive parsers discussed next are types of top-down parsers that avoid backtracking. They compensate somewhat for the lack of back-tracking by using the next input symbol to guide parsing actions.

A third problem with top-down backtracking parsers is that the order in which alternates are tried can affect the language accepted. For example, if, in grammar (5.7), we used a and then ab as the order of the alternates for A, we could fail to accept $cabd$. That is, with parse tree

and ca already matched, the failure of the next input symbol, b, to match, would imply that the alternate cAd for S was wrong, leading to rejection of $cabd$.

Yet another problem is that when failure is reported, we have very little idea where the error actually occurred. In the form given here, a top-down parser with backtrack simply returns failure no matter what the error is.

Elimination of Left-Recursion

If we have the left-recursive pair of productions $A \rightarrow A\alpha \mid \beta$, where β does not begin with an A, then we can eliminate the left-recursion by replacing this pair of productions with

$$A \rightarrow \beta A'$$

$$A' \rightarrow \alpha A' \mid \epsilon$$

Notice that we do not change the set of strings derivable from A. Figure 5.17 illustrates the nature of this transformation. Parse tree (a) is in the original grammar, (b) in the new.

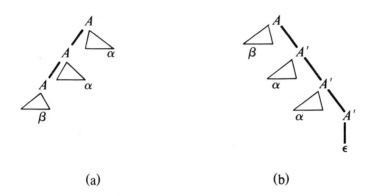

(a)   (b)

Fig. 5.17. Equivalent parse trees.

Example 5.13. Consider the following grammar

$$E \rightarrow E + T \mid T$$
$$T \rightarrow T * F \mid F \qquad\qquad (5.8)$$
$$F \rightarrow (E) \mid \textbf{id}$$

Eliminating the *immediate left-recursion* (productions of the form $A \rightarrow A\alpha$), we obtain

$$E \rightarrow TE'$$
$$E' \rightarrow +TE' \mid \epsilon$$
$$T \rightarrow FT' \qquad\qquad (5.9)$$
$$T' \rightarrow *FT' \mid \epsilon$$
$$F \rightarrow (E) \mid \textbf{id} \qquad\qquad \square$$

In general, to eliminate immediate left-recursion among all A-productions we group the A productions as

$$A \rightarrow A\alpha_1 \mid A\alpha_2 \mid \cdots \mid A\alpha_m \mid \beta_1 \mid \beta_2 \mid \cdots \mid \beta_n$$

where no β_i begins with an A. Then we replace the A-productions by

$$A \rightarrow \beta_1 A' \mid \beta_2 A' \mid \cdots \mid \beta_n A'$$
$$A' \rightarrow \alpha_1 A' \mid \alpha_2 A' \mid \cdots \mid \alpha_m A' \mid \epsilon$$

This process will eliminate all immediate left-recursion (provided no α_i is ϵ), but it will not eliminate left-recursion involving derivations of two or more steps. For example, consider

$$S \rightarrow Aa \mid b$$
$$A \rightarrow Ac \mid Sd \mid e \qquad\qquad (5.10)$$

The nonterminal S is left-recursive because $S \Rightarrow Aa \Rightarrow Sda$.

It is possible, although difficult, to eliminate all left-recursion from any grammar. Here we shall present an algorithm to eliminate left-recursion that is guaranteed to work if the grammar has no cycles (derivations of the form $A \overset{+}{\Rightarrow} A$) or ϵ-productions (productions of the form $A \rightarrow \epsilon$). The algorithm is presented in Fig. 5.18. Note that the resulting non-left-recursive grammar may have ϵ-productions.

1. Arrange the nonterminals of G in some order $A_1, A_2, \ldots, A_n$.
2. **for** $i := 1$ **to** n **do**
    begin
     for $j := 1$ **to** $i-1$ **do**
      replace each production of the form $A_i \rightarrow A_j \gamma$
      by the productions $A_i \rightarrow \delta_1 \gamma \mid \delta_2 \gamma \mid \cdots \mid \delta_k \gamma$,
      where $A_j \rightarrow \delta_1 \mid \delta_2 \mid \cdots \mid \delta_k$ are all the
      current A_j-productions;
     eliminate the immediate left-recursion among the
      A_i-productions
    end

Fig. 5.18. Algorithm to eliminate left-recursion from a grammar with no cycles or ϵ-productions.

Example 5.14. Let us apply this procedure to grammar (5.10). We order the nonterminals S, A. There is no immediate left-recursion among the S-productions. We then substitute the S-productions in $A \rightarrow Sd$ to obtain the following A-productions.

$$A \rightarrow Ac \mid Aad \mid bd \mid e$$

Eliminating the immediate left-recursion among the A-productions yields the following grammar.

$$S \rightarrow Aa \mid b$$
$$A \rightarrow bdA' \mid eA'$$
$$A' \rightarrow cA' \mid adA' \mid \epsilon \qquad\qquad \square$$

Recursive-Descent Parsing

In many practical cases a top-down parser needs no backtrack. In order that no backtracking be required, we must know, given the current input symbol a and the nonterminal A to be expanded, which one of the alternates of production $A \rightarrow \alpha_1 \mid \alpha_2 \mid \cdots \mid \alpha_n$ is the unique alternate that derives a string beginning with a. That is, the proper alternate is detectable by looking at only the first symbol it derives. For example, control constructs, with their distinguishing keywords, are detectable in this way. Suppose we have productions:

$$\text{statement} \rightarrow \textbf{if} \text{ condition } \textbf{then} \text{ statement } \textbf{else} \text{ statement}$$

$$\mid \textbf{while} \text{ condition } \textbf{do} \text{ statement}$$

$$\mid \textbf{begin} \text{ statement-list } \textbf{end}$$

Then the keywords **if**, **while**, and **begin** tell us which alternate is the only one that could possibly succeed if we are to find a statement.

One nuance concerns the empty string. If one alternate for A is ϵ, and none of the other alternates derives a string beginning with a, then on input a we may expand A by $A \rightarrow \epsilon$, that is, we succeed without further ado in recognizing an A.

A parser that uses a set of recursive procedures to recognize its input with no backtracking is called a *recursive-descent* parser. The recursive procedures can be quite easy to write and fairly efficient if written in a language that implements procedure calls efficiently.

To avoid the necessity of a recursive language, we shall also consider a tabular implementation of recursive descent, called predictive parsing, where a stack is maintained by the parser, rather than by the language in which the parser is written.

Example 5.15. Let us consider grammar (5.9), which is suitable for a non-backtracking recursive-descent parser. The procedures making up this parser are shown in Fig. 5.19. The same conventions as in Example 5.12 are used, but there is no need for the procedures to return an indication of success or failure, since the calling procedure has no intention of trying another alternate. Rather, on failure, an error-correcting routine, which we here name ERROR, can be invoked. Section 11.3 discusses the sorts of error actions that could be taken to resume parsing. □

Left-Factoring

Often the grammar one writes down is not suitable for recursive-descent parsing, even if there is no left-recursion. For example, if we have the two productions

```
procedure E( );
begin
    T( );
    EPRIME( )
end;

procedure EPRIME( );
if input-symbol = '+' then
    begin
        ADVANCE( );
        T( );
        EPRIME( )
    end;

procedure T( );
begin
    F( );
    TPRIME( )
end;

procedure TPRIME( );
if input-symbol = '*' then
    begin
        ADVANCE( );
        F( );
        TPRIME( )
    end;

procedure F( );
if input-symbol = 'id' then
    ADVANCE( )
else if input-symbol = '(' then
    begin
        ADVANCE( );
        E( );
        if input-symbol = ')' then
            ADVANCE( )
        else ERROR( )
    end
else ERROR( )
```

Fig. 5.19. Mutually recursive procedures to recognize
arithmetic expressions.

statement → **if** condition **then** statement **else** statement

| **if** condition **then** statement

we could not, on seeing input symbol **if**, tell which to choose to expand statement. A useful method for manipulating grammars into a form suitable for recursive-descent parsing is *left-factoring,* the process of factoring out the common prefixes of alternates.

If $A \to \alpha\beta \mid \alpha\gamma$ are two A-productions, and the input begins with a nonempty string derived from α, we do not know whether to expand A to $\alpha\beta$ or to $\alpha\gamma$. We may defer the decision by expanding A to $\alpha A'$. Then, after seeing the input derived from α, we expand A' to β or to γ. That is, left-factored, the original productions become

$$A \to \alpha A'$$
$$A' \to \beta \mid \gamma$$

Example 5.16. Consider again the grammar

$$S \to iCtS \mid iCtSeS \mid a$$
$$C \to b$$

which abstracts the dangling **else** problem. Left-factored, this grammar becomes:

$$S \to iCtSS' \mid a$$
$$S' \to eS \mid \epsilon$$
$$C \to b$$

Thus we may expand S to $iCtSS'$ on input i, and wait until $iCtS$ has been seen to decide whether to expand S' to eS or to ϵ.   □

Transition Diagrams

Just as a transition diagram was seen in Section 3.2 to be a useful plan, or flowchart, for a lexical analyzer, we can use a transition diagram as a plan for a recursive-descent parser. Several differences are immediately apparent. In the case of the parser, there is one transition diagram for each nonterminal. The labels of edges are not characters but tokens or nonterminals. A transition on a token (terminal) means we should take that transition if that token is the next input symbol. Edges may also be labeled by nonterminals A, implying that the transition diagram for A should be "called."

There is no guarantee that one can correctly choose a path through a transition diagram, although if we eliminate left-recursion and then left-factor, we have a fair chance of success if we do the following for each nonterminal A:

1. Create an initial and final (return) state.
2. For each production $A \rightarrow X_1 X_2 \cdots X_n$, create a path from the initial to the final state, with edges labeled $X_1, X_2, \ldots, X_n$.

Example 5.17. Grammar (5.9) has the collection of transition diagrams shown in Fig. 5.20. If we interpret the edges out of the initial state for E' as saying: take the transition on $+$ whenever that is the next input and take the transition on ϵ otherwise, and make the analogous assumption for T', we have a program that functions as a correct recursive-descent parser for grammar (5.9).   □

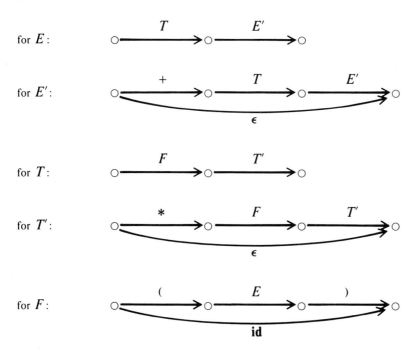

Fig. 5.20. Transition diagrams.

It should be observed that if there is "nondeterminism" in which there are two transitions out of some state labeled by the same symbol, or there are transitions labeled by a terminal symbol and a nonterminal symbol, then we cannot necessarily apply the subset construction of Chapter 3 to make the transition diagrams deterministic. Intuitively, the reason the subset construction does not work is that it cannot remember how many recursive calls are made. In cases with nondeterminism, the method fails to produce a recursive-descent parser, but it may be used to help design one with backtrack.

It is possible to simplify transition diagrams by substituting diagrams in one another. For example, in Fig. 5.20, the call of E' on itself can be replaced by a jump to the beginning of the diagram for E', as shown in Fig. 5.21(a).

Fig. 5.21(b) shows an equivalent transition diagram for E'. We may then substitute the diagram of Fig. 5.21(b) for the transition on E' in the diagram for E, yielding the diagram of Fig. 5.21(c). Lastly, we observe that the first and third nodes in Fig. 5.21(c) are equivalent and we merge them.

The same techniques apply to the diagrams for T and T'. The resulting set of diagrams is shown in Fig. 5.21(d).

5.5 Predictive Parsers

A predictive parser is an efficient way of implementing recursive-descent parsing by handling the stack of activation records explicitly. We can picture a predictive parser as in Fig. 5.22.

The predictive parser has an input, a stack, a parsing table, and an output. The input contains the string to be parsed, followed by $, the right endmarker. The stack contains a sequence of grammar symbols, preceded by $, the bottom-of-stack marker. Initially, the stack contains the start symbol of the grammar preceded by $. The parsing table is a two-dimensional array $M[A, a]$, where A is a nonterminal, and a is a terminal or the symbol $.

The parser is controlled by a program that behaves as follows. The program determines X, the symbol on top of the stack, and a, the current input symbol. These two symbols determine the action of the parser. There are three possibilities.

1. If $X = a = $, the parser halts and announces successful completion of parsing.

2. If $X = a \neq $, the parser pops X off the stack and advances the input pointer to the next input symbol.

3. If X is a nonterminal, the program consults entry $M[X, a]$ of the parsing table M. This entry will be either an X-production of the grammar or an error entry. If $M[X, a] = \{X \rightarrow UVW\}$, the parser replaces X on top of the stack by WVU (with U on top). As output, the grammar does the semantic action associated with this production, which, for the time being, we shall assume is just printing the production used. If $M[X, a] = $ **error**, the parser calls an error recovery routine.

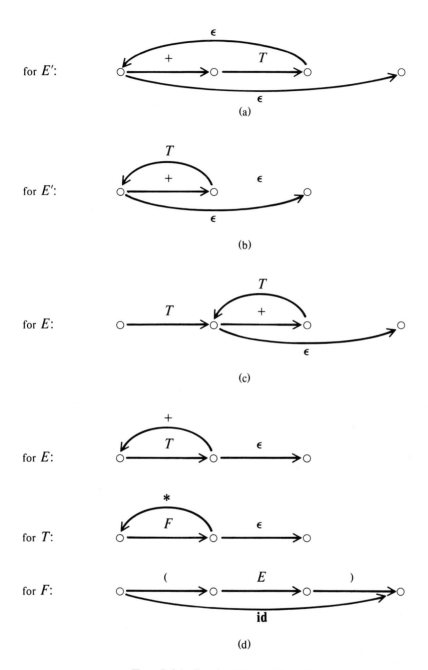

for E':

(a)

for E':

(b)

for E:

(c)

for E:

for T:

for F:

(d)

Fig. 5.21. Revised transition diagrams.

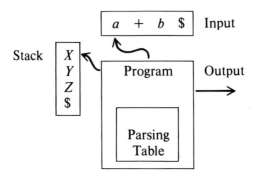

Fig. 5.22. Model of a predictive parser.

We shall describe the behavior of the parser in terms of its configurations, which give the stack contents and the remaining input. Initially, the parser is in configuration

Stack	Input
$ S	w $

where S is the start symbol of the grammar and w is the string to be parsed. The program that utilizes the predictive parsing table to produce a parse is shown in Fig. 5.23.

Example 5.18. Consider grammar (5.9) from Example 5.13. A predictive parsing table for this grammar is shown in Fig. 5.24. Blanks are error entries. Note that we have not yet indicated how these entries could be selected, but we shall do so shortly.

With input **id + id * id** the predictive parser would make the sequence of moves in Fig. 5.25.

If we observe the actions of this parser carefully, we see that it is tracing out a leftmost derivation for the input. The productions output are those of a leftmost derivation. The input symbols that have already been scanned, followed by the grammar symbols on the stack (from top to bottom), make up the left-sentential forms in the derivation. □

FIRST and FOLLOW

Now let us consider how to fill in the entries of a predictive parsing table. We need two functions associated with a grammar G. These functions, FIRST and FOLLOW, will indicate the proper entries in the table for G, if such a parsing table for G exists. If α is any string of grammar symbols, let *FIRST*(α) be the set of terminals that begin strings derived from α. If $\alpha \stackrel{*}{\Longrightarrow} \epsilon$, then ϵ is also in FIRST(α).

repeat
   begin
      let X be the top stack symbol and a the next input symbol;
      if X is a terminal or $ **then**
         if $X = a$ **then**
            pop X from the stack and remove a from the input
         else
            ERROR( )
      else /* X is a nonterminal */
         if $M[X, a] = X \rightarrow Y_1 Y_2 \cdots Y_k$ **then**
            begin
               pop X from the stack;
               push $Y_k, Y_{k-1}, \ldots, Y_1$ onto the stack, Y_1 on top
            end
         else
            ERROR( )
   end
until
   $X = $ /* stack has emptied */

Fig. 5.23. Predictive parsing program.

	id	+	*	(	)	$
E	$E \rightarrow TE'$			$E \rightarrow TE'$		
E'		$E' \rightarrow +TE'$			$E' \rightarrow \epsilon$	$E' \rightarrow \epsilon$
T	$T \rightarrow FT'$			$T \rightarrow FT'$		
T'		$T' \rightarrow \epsilon$	$T' \rightarrow *FT'$		$T' \rightarrow \epsilon$	$T' \rightarrow \epsilon$
F	$F \rightarrow$ **id**			$F \rightarrow (E)$		

Fig. 5.24. Parsing table for grammar (5.9).

Define $FOLLOW(A)$, for nonterminal A, to be the set of terminals a that can appear immediately to the right of A in some sentential form, that is, $S \overset{*}{\Rightarrow} \alpha A a \beta$ for some α and β. If A can be the rightmost symbol in some sentential form, then ϵ is in FOLLOW(A).

To compute FIRST(X) for all grammar symbols X, apply the following rules until no more terminals or ϵ can be added to any FIRST set.

Stack	Input	Output
$E	id + id * id$	
$E'T	id + id * id$	$E \rightarrow TE'$
$E'T'F	id + id * id$	$T \rightarrow FT'$
$E'T'$id	id + id * id$	$F \rightarrow$ id
$E'T'	+ id * id$	
$E'	+ id * id$	$T' \rightarrow \epsilon$
$E'T+	+ id * id$	$E' \rightarrow +TE'$
$E'T	id * id$	
$E'T'F	id * id$	$T \rightarrow FT'$
$E'T'$id	id * id$	$F \rightarrow$ id
$E'T'	* id$	
$E'T'F*	* id$	$T' \rightarrow *FT'$
$E'T'F	id$	
$E'T'$id	id$	$F \rightarrow$ id
$E'T'	$	
$E'	$	$T' \rightarrow \epsilon$
$	$	$E' \rightarrow \epsilon$

Fig. 5.25. Moves by predictive parser.

1. If X is terminal, then FIRST(X) is $\{X\}$.

2. If X is nonterminal and $X \rightarrow a\alpha$ is a production, then add a to FIRST(X). If $X \rightarrow \epsilon$ is a production, then add ϵ to FIRST(X).

3. If $X \rightarrow Y_1 Y_2 \cdots Y_k$ is a production, then for all i such that all of $Y_1, \ldots, Y_{i-1}$ are nonterminals and FIRST(Y_j) contains ϵ for $j = 1, 2, \ldots, i-1$ (i.e. $Y_1 Y_2 \cdots Y_{i-1} \overset{*}{\Rightarrow} \epsilon$), add every non-$\epsilon$ symbol in FIRST(Y_i) to FIRST(X). If ϵ is in FIRST(Y_j) for all $j = 1, 2, \ldots, k$, then add ϵ to FIRST(X).

Now, we can compute FIRST for any string $X_1 X_2 \cdots X_n$ as follows. Add to FIRST($X_1 X_2 \cdots X_n$) all the non-ϵ symbols of FIRST(X_1). Also add the non-ϵ symbols of FIRST(X_2) if ϵ is in FIRST(X_1), the non-ϵ symbols of FIRST(X_2) if ϵ is in both FIRST(X_1) and FIRST(X_2), and so on. Finally, add ϵ to FIRST($X_1 X_2 \cdots X_n$) if, for all i, FIRST(X_i) contains ϵ.

To compute FOLLOW(A) for all nonterminals A, apply the following rules until nothing can be added to any FOLLOW set.

1. ϵ is in FOLLOW(S), where S is the start symbol.

2. If there is a production $A \rightarrow \alpha B\beta$, then everything in FIRST(β) but ϵ is in FOLLOW(B). Note that ϵ may still wind up in FOLLOW(B) by rule (3).

3. If there is a production $A \rightarrow \alpha B$, or a production $A \rightarrow \alpha B\beta$ where FIRST(β) contains ϵ (i.e., $\beta \overset{*}{\Rightarrow} \epsilon$), then everything in FOLLOW(A) is in FOLLOW(B).

Example 5.19. Consider again grammar (5.9)

$$E \rightarrow TE'$$
$$E' \rightarrow +TE' \mid \epsilon$$
$$T \rightarrow FT'$$
$$T' \rightarrow *FT' \mid \epsilon$$
$$F \rightarrow (E) \mid \mathbf{id}$$

Then:

$$\text{FIRST}(E) = \text{FIRST}(T) = \text{FIRST}(F) = \{(, \mathbf{id}\}.$$
$$\text{FIRST}(E') = \{+, \epsilon\}$$
$$\text{FIRST}(T') = \{*, \epsilon\}$$
$$\text{FOLLOW}(E) = \text{FOLLOW}(E') = \{), \epsilon\}$$
$$\text{FOLLOW}(T) = \text{FOLLOW}(T') = \{+,), \epsilon\}$$
$$\text{FOLLOW}(F) = \{+, *,), \epsilon\}$$

For example, **id** and left parenthesis are added to FIRST(F) by rule (2) in the definition of FIRST. Then by rule (3) with $i = 1$, the production $T \rightarrow FT'$ implies that **id** and left parenthesis are in FIRST(T) as well.

To compute FOLLOW sets, we put ϵ in FOLLOW(E) by rule (1). By rule (2) applied to production $F \rightarrow (E)$, the right parenthesis is also in FOLLOW(E). By rule (3) applied to production $E \rightarrow TE'$, ϵ and right parenthesis are in FOLLOW(E'). Since $E' \overset{*}{\Rightarrow} \epsilon$, they are also in FOLLOW(T). For a last example of how the FOLLOW rules are applied, the production $E \rightarrow TE'$ implies, by rule (2), that everything other than ϵ in FIRST(E') must be placed in FOLLOW(T). We have already seen that ϵ is in FOLLOW(T) anyway. $\square$

Construction of Parsing Tables

The following algorithm can be used to construct a predictive parsing table for a grammar G. The idea behind the algorithm is simple. Suppose $A \rightarrow \alpha$ is a production with a in FIRST(α). Then, whenever the parser has A on top of the stack with a the current input symbol, the parser will expand A by α. The only complication occurs when $\alpha = \epsilon$ or $\alpha \stackrel{*}{\Rightarrow} \epsilon$. In this case, we should also expand A by α if the current input symbol is in FOLLOW(A), or if the $ on the input has been reached and ϵ is in FOLLOW(A).

Algorithm 5.4. Constructing a predictive parsing table.

Input. Grammar G.

Output. Parsing table M.

Method.

1. For each production $A \rightarrow \alpha$ of the grammar, do steps 2 and 3.
2. For each terminal a in FIRST(α), add $A \rightarrow \alpha$ to $M[A, a]$.
3. If ϵ is in FIRST(α), add $A \rightarrow \alpha$ to $M[A, b]$ for each terminal b in FOLLOW(A). If ϵ is in FIRST(α) and in FOLLOW(A), add $A \rightarrow \alpha$ to $M[A, \$]$.
4. Make each undefined entry of M **error**. □

Example 5.20. Let us apply Algorithm 5.4 to grammar (5.9). Since FIRST$(TE') = $ FIRST$(T) = \{(, \textbf{id}\}$, production $E \rightarrow TE'$ causes $M[E, (]$ and $M[E, \textbf{id}]$ to acquire the entry $E \rightarrow TE'$.

Production $E' \rightarrow +TE'$ causes $M[E', +]$ to acquire $E' \rightarrow +TE'$. Production $E' \rightarrow \epsilon$ causes $M[E',)]$ and $M[E', \$]$ to acquire $E' \rightarrow \epsilon$ since FOLLOW$(E') = \{), \epsilon\}$.

The parsing table produced by Algorithm 5.4 for G was shown in Fig. 5.24.   □

LL(1) Grammars

Algorithm 5.4 can be applied to any grammar G to produce a parsing table M. For some grammars, however, M may have some entries that are multiply-defined. For example, if G is left-recursive or ambiguous, then M will have at least one multiply-defined entry.

Example 5.21. Consider the grammar from Example 5.16.

$$S \rightarrow iCtSS' \mid a$$
$$S' \rightarrow eS \mid \epsilon \qquad\qquad\qquad (5.11)$$
$$C \rightarrow b$$

The parsing table for grammar (5.11) is shown in Fig. 5.26.

	a	b	e	i	t	$
S	$S \to a$			$S \to iCtSS'$		
S'			$S' \to \epsilon$ $S' \to eS$			$S' \to \epsilon$
C		$C \to b$				

Fig. 5.26. Parsing table.

The entry for $M[S', e]$ contains both $S' \to eS$ and $S' \to \epsilon$, since FOLLOW$(S') = \{e, \epsilon\}$. The grammar is ambiguous and the ambiguity is manifested by a choice in what production to use when an e (**else**) is seen. We can resolve the ambiguity if we choose $S' \to eS$. This choice corresponds to associating **else**'s with the closest previous **then**'s. Note that the choice $S' \to \epsilon$ would prevent e from ever being put on the stack or removed from the input, and is therefore surely wrong. □

There arises the question of what should be done when a parsing table has multiply-defined entries. The easiest recourse is to transform the grammar by eliminating all left-recursion and then left-factoring whenever possible, hopefully to produce a grammar for which the parsing table has no multiply-defined entries.

A grammar whose parsing table has no multiply-defined entries is said to be $LL(1)$. It can be shown that Algorithm 5.4 produces a parsing table for every LL(1) grammar, and that this table parses all and only the sentences of the grammar. It can also be shown that a grammar G is LL(1) if and only if whenever $A \to \alpha \mid \beta$ are two distinct productions of G the following conditions hold:

1. There is no terminal a such that α and β derive strings beginning with a.
2. At most one of α and β can derive the empty string.
3. If $\beta \overset{*}{\Rightarrow} \epsilon$, then α does not derive any strings beginning with a terminal in FOLLOW(A).

Clearly, the grammar of Example 5.19 for arithmetic expressions is LL(1). The grammar (5.11) of Example 5.21 modeling **if-then-else** statements is not.

Unfortunately, there are some grammars for which no amount of rewriting will yield an LL(1) grammar. Grammar (5.11) is one such example. As we saw, we can still parse (5.11) with a predictive parser by arbitrarily making $M[S', e] = \{S' \to eS\}$. In general, however, there are no universal rules by which multiply-defined entries can be made single-valued without affecting the language recognized by the parser.

Exercises

5.1 Consider the following grammar for list structures:

$$S \rightarrow a \,|\, \wedge \,|\, (\,T\,)$$
$$T \rightarrow T\!,S \,|\, S$$

In the above grammar, find leftmost and rightmost derivations for
a) $(a, (a, a))$ b) $(((a, a), \wedge, (a)), a)$

5.2 For the rightmost derivations of Exercise 5.1
   a) indicate the handle of each right-sentential form,
   b) show the steps of a shift-reduce parser corresponding to these rightmost derivations.
   c) indicate how the parse tree is constructed bottom-up during the shift-reduce parse of (b).

5.3 a) Compute LEADING and TRAILING for the grammar of Exercise 5.1.
   b) Compute the operator-precedence relations for this grammar. Is it an operator-precedence grammar?
   c) Find precedence functions for the relations computed in (b).

5.4 a) Eliminate left recursion from the grammar of Exercise 5.1.
   b) Write recursive routines for your nonterminals in (a) and show the steps of a top-down parser with backtrack on the strings in Exercise 5.1.
   c) Left factor the grammar of part (b).
   d) Repeat part (b) for your grammar from part (c). Is there any difference in the speed of the parse, compared with your grammar from (a)?
   e) Is your grammar from (c) an LL(1) grammar? If so, give the predictive parsing table.

5.5 The following is an LL(1) grammar for regular expressions over alphabet $\{a, b\}$, with $+$ standing for the union operator $(\,|\,)$ and $\in$ for the symbol ϵ.

$$E \rightarrow TE'$$
$$E' \rightarrow +E \,|\, \epsilon$$
$$T \rightarrow FT'$$
$$T' \rightarrow T \,|\, \epsilon$$
$$F \rightarrow PF'$$
$$F' \rightarrow *F' \,|\, \epsilon$$
$$P \rightarrow (E) \,|\, a \,|\, b \,|\, \epsilon$$

a) Compute FIRST and FOLLOW for each nonterminal of the above grammar.

b) Show that the grammar is LL(1).

c) Construct the predictive parsing table for the grammar.

d) Construct a recursive-descent parser for the grammar.

**5.6 Consider the following grammar:

$$S \rightarrow aSa \mid aa$$

Clearly the grammar generates all even length strings of a's except for the empty string.

a) By tracing through the steps of a top-down parser (with backtrack) which tries the alternate aSa before aa, show that S succeeds on 2, 4 or 8 a's, but fails on 6 a's.

b) What strings cause the parser to succeed?

5.7 There is a precedence-based parsing method, called *simple precedence*, which many regard as an improvement on operator-precedence because one cannot parse a nonsentence.[†] Suppose we have a grammar with no empty right sides. We may define three precedence relations $<\cdot_s$, $\doteq_s$, and $\cdot>_s$ between pairs of grammar symbols, both terminals and nonterminals.

1. We say $X \doteq_s Y$ if there is a production right side of the form $\alpha XY\beta$ for some strings α and β. For example, in the grammar of Exercise 5.1, the production $S \rightarrow (T)$ tells us that $(\doteq_s T$ and $T \doteq_s)$.

2. We say $X <\cdot_s Y$ if there is a production right side $\alpha XA\beta$ for some nonterminal A and strings α and β, and there is a derivation of one or more steps $A \overset{+}{\Rightarrow} Y\gamma$ for some γ. Note the collection of Y's such that $A \overset{+}{\Rightarrow} Y\gamma$ is computable by a method akin to the way FIRST was calculated in Section 5.5. The absence of ϵ-productions makes matters easier here, in fact. For example, in the grammar of Exercise 5.1, $\alpha XA\beta$ could be (T), where $T = A$. Then the derivation

$$T \Rightarrow T,S \Rightarrow S,S \Rightarrow a,S$$

tells us that $(<\cdot_s T$, $(<\cdot_s S$, and $(<\cdot_s a$.

---

† We agree, but we have chosen not to cover simple precedence in detail because the LR grammars discussed in the next chapter properly include the simple precedence grammars, and there are many natural constructs, such as arithmetic expressions, for which only awkward simple precedence grammars exist. Moreover, some types of LR parsers are not much harder to construct than simple precedence parsers.

3. We say $X \cdot>_s a$ if there is a right side $\alpha A Y \beta$ such that a is in FIRST(Y), and there is a derivation of one or more steps $A \overset{+}{\Rightarrow} \gamma X$ for some γ. FIRST is the function from Section 5.5, and the set of X such that $A \overset{+}{\Rightarrow} \gamma X$ for some γ is computable by an algorithm similar to the computation of FIRST. For example, production $S \rightarrow (T)$ and the derivation $T \Rightarrow S \Rightarrow a$ tells us $S \cdot>_s)$ and $a \cdot>_s)$. Note that $T = A$ and $Y = a$ here. Also, do not forget that in the definition of $\cdot>_s$, Y may be a nonterminal, and there may be many terminals a in FIRST(Y).

4. We say $\$ <\cdot_s X$ if $S \overset{+}{\Rightarrow} X\alpha$ for some α, and $X \cdot>_s \$$ if $S \overset{+}{\Rightarrow} \alpha X$ for some α.

We define a grammar to be a *simple precedence grammar* if it has no ϵ-productions, no two productions have the same right side, and the relations $<\cdot_s$, $\doteq_s$, and $\cdot>_s$ are disjoint.

a) Compute the simple precedence relations for the grammar of Exercise 5.1. Is it a simple precedence grammar?

b) The following grammar generates the same language:

$$S \rightarrow a \mid \wedge \mid (R)$$
$$T \rightarrow S, T \mid S$$
$$R \rightarrow T$$

Verify that the table of simple precedence relations in Fig. 5.27 is correct for this grammar.

c) Is the grammar of (b) a simple precedence grammar?

d) Find precedence functions to encode Fig. 5.27.

5.8 A simple precedence parser behaves exactly as an operator-precedence parser does, but nonterminals are kept on the stack and enter into the relations. If X is the top stack symbol and a the next input symbol, the parser shifts if $X <\cdot_s a$ or if $X \doteq_s a$. The parser reduces if $X \cdot>_s a$. In the latter case, suppose $X_1 X_2 \cdots X_n$ is the entire stack, where $X_n = X$. The handle is $X_i X_{i+1} \cdots X_n$ if $X_{i-1} <\cdot_s X_i \doteq_s X_{i+1} \doteq_s \cdots \doteq_s X_n$. Note how the condition that no two productions have the same right side ensures that the non-terminal replacing $X_i X_{i+1} \cdots X_n$ in the reduction can be determined. Simulate the simple precedence parser using Fig. 5.27 on the strings in Exercise 5.1.

	R	S	T	a	$\wedge$	$,$	$($	$)$	$\$$
R								$\doteq_s$	
S						$\doteq_s$		$\cdot\!>_s$	
T								$\cdot\!>_s$	
a						$\cdot\!>_s$		$\cdot\!>_s$	$\cdot\!>_s$
$\wedge$						$\cdot\!>_s$		$\cdot\!>_s$	$\cdot\!>_s$
$,$		$<\!\cdot_s$	$\doteq_s$	$<\!\cdot_s$	$<\!\cdot_s$		$<\!\cdot_s$		
$($	$\doteq_s$	$<\!\cdot_s$	$<\!\cdot_s$	$<\!\cdot_s$	$<\!\cdot_s$		$<\!\cdot_s$		
$)$						$\cdot\!>_s$		$\cdot\!>_s$	$\cdot\!>_s$
$\$$				$<\!\cdot_s$	$<\!\cdot_s$		$<\!\cdot_s$		

Fig. 5.27. Simple precedence relations.

Bibliographic Notes

The operator-precedence idea and the use of precedence functions are from Floyd [1963]. There are a variety of other bottom-up parsing strategies that have been used in compilers and/or compiler-writing systems. Simple, or Wirth-Weber precedence, introduced in Exercise 5.7, was first used in the implementation of the language EULER (Wirth and Weber [1966]). Bounded-context parsing (Floyd [1964], Graham [1964]) generalizes simple- and operator-precedence parsers, and LR parsers (Knuth [1965]) in turn generalize bounded-context parsers. The LR parsers are the subject of the next chapter, where we shall consider the important developments that followed Knuth's 1965 paper. A number of other generalizations of precedence parsing ideas have been used. McKeeman, Horning and Wortman [1970] used a variant called mixed-strategy precedence in their XPL compiler writing system. Ichbiah and Morse [1970] used weak precedence in their compiler generator.

The recursive-descent parser is attributed to Lucas [1961] and Conway [1963]. Top-down parsing with backtrack has been used in a number of compilers and in several compiler writing systems such as META (Schorre [1964]) and TMG (McClure [1965]). A solution to Exercise 5.6 can be found in Birman and Ullman [1973], along with some of the theory of these parsers. LL parsers were defined by Lewis and Stearns [1968]. Knuth [1971a] is another source on these parsers and the slightly more general predictive parsers. Lewis and Rosenkrantz [1971] and Lewis, Rosenkrantz, and Stearns [1976] describe their use in compilers. Foster [1968], Wood [1969], and Stearns [1971] describe algorithms to transform grammars to LL(1) form. The theory of LL(1) grammars is developed in Rosenkrantz and Stearns [1970].

All the above methods have the property that they work on only a subset of the context-free grammars. There is an efficient general method that works on all context-free grammars, due to Earley [1968]. This algorithm takes time at most proportional to the square of the input length on unambiguous grammars and the cube of the input length on ambiguous ones. While most programming languages can be parsed by the more efficient but less general methods mentioned above, Earley's algorithm is useful for extensible languages, where the complete grammar is not known in advance.

There is another algorithm due to Valiant [1975] which asymptotically and in the worst case is more efficient than Earley's. Valiant's algorithm takes time proportional to $n^{2.81}$ on an input of length n. However, the method is too complicated to be a serious candidate for implementation. Descriptions of all the parsing algorithms mentioned above (with the exception of Valiant's), and others, can be found in Aho and Ullman [1972b, 1973a].

CHAPTER 6

Automatic Construction
of
Efficient Parsers

This chapter shows how to construct efficient bottom-up parsers for a large class of context-free grammars. These parsers are called LR parsers because they scan the input from *l*eft-to-right and construct a *r*ightmost derivation in reverse. LR parsers are attractive for a variety of reasons.

- LR parsers can be constructed to recognize virtually all programming-language constructs for which context-free grammars can be written.
- The LR parsing method is more general than operator precedence or any of the other common shift-reduce techniques discussed in the last chapter, yet it can be implemented with the same degree of efficiency as these other methods. LR parsing also dominates the common forms of top-down parsing without backtrack.
- LR parsers can detect syntactic errors as soon as it is possible to do so on a left-to-right scan of the input.

The principal drawback of the method is that it is too much work to implement an LR parser by hand for a typical programming-language grammar. One needs a specialized tool — an LR parser generator. Fortunately, many such generators are available, and we shall discuss the design of one in this chapter. With such a generator, one can write a context-free grammar and have the generator automatically produce a parser for that grammar. If the grammar contains ambiguities or other constructs that are difficult to parse in a left-to-right scan of the input, then the parser generator can locate these constructs and inform the compiler designer of their presence.

Logically, an LR parser consists of two parts, a driver routine and a parsing table. The driver routine is the same for all LR parsers; only the parsing table changes from one parser to another. The schematic form of an LR parser is shown in Fig. 6.1. As the driver routine is simple to implement, we shall often consider the LR parser-construction process as one of producing the parsing table for a given grammar as in Fig. 6.1(a).

197

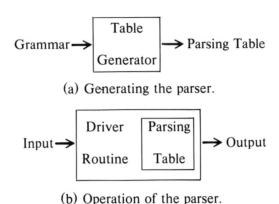

(a) Generating the parser.

(b) Operation of the parser.

Fig. 6.1. Generating an LR parser.

There are many different parsing tables that can be used in an LR parser for a given grammar. Some parsing tables may detect errors sooner than others, but they all accept the same sentences, exactly the sentences generated by the grammar. In this chapter we shall give three different techniques for producing LR parsing tables. The first method, called simple LR (SLR for short), is easiest to implement. Unfortunately, it may fail to produce a table for certain grammars on which the other methods succeed. The second method, called canonical LR, is the most powerful and will work on a very large class of grammars. Unfortunately, the canonical LR method can be very expensive to implement. The third method, called lookahead LR (LALR for short), is intermediate in power between the SLR and the canonical LR methods. The LALR method will work on most programming-language grammars and, with some effort, can be implemented efficiently. We then show how ambiguous grammars can be used to simplify the description of languages and produce efficient parsers.

6.1 LR Parsers

Figure 6.2 depicts an LR parser. The parser has an input, a stack, and a parsing table. The input is read from left to right, one symbol at a time. The stack contains a string of the form $s_0X_1s_1X_2s_2 \cdots X_ms_m$, where s_m is on top. Each X_i is a grammar symbol and each s_i is a symbol called a *state*. Each state symbol summarizes the information contained in the stack below it and is used to guide the shift-reduce decision. In an actual implementation, the grammar symbols need not appear on the stack. We include them there only to help explain the behavior of an LR parser. The parsing table consists of two parts, a parsing action function ACTION and a goto function GOTO.

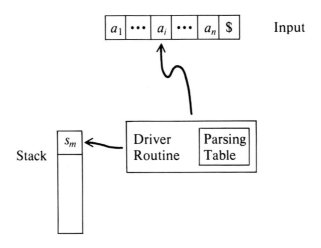

Fig. 6.2. LR parser.

The program driving the LR parser behaves as follows. It determines s_m, the state currently on top of the stack, and a_i, the current input symbol. It then consults ACTION$[s_m, a_i]$, the parsing action table entry for state s_m and input a_i. The entry ACTION$[s_m, a_i]$ can have one of four values:

1. shift s
2. reduce $A \rightarrow \beta$
3. accept
4. error

The function GOTO takes a state and grammar symbol as arguments and produces a state. It is essentially the transition table of a deterministic finite automaton whose input symbols are the terminals and nonterminals of the grammar.

A *configuration* of an LR parser is a pair whose first component is the stack contents and whose second component is the unexpended input:

$$(s_0 \; X_1 \; s_1 \; X_2 \; s_2 \; \cdots \; X_m \; s_m, \; a_i \; a_{i+1} \; \cdots \; a_n \; \$)$$

The next move of the parser is determined by reading a_i, the current input symbol, and s_m, the state on top of the stack, and then consulting the parsing action table entry ACTION$[s_m, a_i]$. The configurations resulting after each of the four types of move are as follows:

1. If ACTION$[s_m, a_i]$ = shift s, the parser executes a shift move, entering the configuration

$$(s_0 \; X_1 \; s_1 \; X_2 \; s_2 \; \cdots \; X_m \; s_m \; a_i \; s, \; a_{i+1} \; \cdots \; a_n \; \$)$$

Here the parser has shifted the current input symbol a_i and the next state $s = \text{GOTO}[s_m, a_i]$ onto the stack; a_{i+1} becomes the new current input symbol.

2. If $\text{ACTION}[s_m, a_i] = $ reduce $A \rightarrow \beta$, then the parser executes a reduce move, entering the configuration

$$(s_0\ X_1\ s_1\ X_2\ s_2\ \ldots\ X_{m-r}\ s_{m-r}\ A\ s,\ \ a_i\ a_{i+1}\ \ldots\ a_n\ \$)$$

where $s = \text{GOTO}[s_{m-r}, A]$ and r is the length of β, the right side of the production. Here the parser first popped $2r$ symbols off the stack (r state symbols and r grammar symbols), exposing state s_{m-r}. The parser then pushed both A, the left side of the production, and s, the entry for $\text{ACTION}[s_{m-r}, A]$, onto the stack. The current input symbol is not changed in a reduce move. For the LR parsers we shall construct, $X_{m-r+1} \cdots X_m$, the sequence of grammar symbols popped off the stack, will always match β, the right side of the reducing production.

3. If $\text{ACTION}[s_m, a_i] = $ accept, parsing is completed.

4. If $\text{ACTION}[s_m, a_i] = $ error, the parser has discovered an error and calls an error recovery routine.

The LR parsing algorithm is very simple. Initially the LR parser is in the configuration $(s_0, a_1\ a_2\ \ldots\ a_n\ \$)$ where s_0 is a designated initial state and $a_1 a_2 \ldots a_n$ is the string to be parsed. Then the parser executes moves until an accept or error action is encountered. All our LR parsers behave in this fashion. The only difference between one LR parser and another is the information in the parsing action and goto fields of the parsing table.

Example 6.1. Figure 6.3 shows the parsing action and goto functions of an LR parser for the grammar

(1) $E \rightarrow E + T$
(2) $E \rightarrow T$
(3) $T \rightarrow T * F$
(4) $T \rightarrow F$
(5) $F \rightarrow (E)$
(6) $F \rightarrow \text{id}$

The codes for the actions are:

1. si means shift and stack state i,
2. rj means reduce by production numbered j,
3. acc means accept,
4. blank means error.

Note that the value of $\text{GOTO}[s, a]$ for terminal a is found in the action field connected with the shift action on input a for state s. The goto field gives $\text{GOTO}[s, A]$ for nonterminals A. Also, bear in mind that we have not yet

State	Action						Goto		
	id	+	*	(	)	$	E	T	F
0	s5			s4			1	2	3
1		s6				acc			
2		r2	s7		r2	r2			
3		r4	r4		r4	r4			
4	s5			s4			8	2	3
5		r6	r6		r6	r6			
6	s5			s4				9	3
7	s5			s4					10
8		s6			s11				
9		r1	s7		r1	r1			
10		r3	r3		r3	r3			
11		r5	r5		r5	r5			

Fig. 6.3. Parsing table.

explained how the entries for Fig. 6.3 are selected; we shall deal with this issue shortly.

Consider the moves made by the parser on input **id** * **id** + **id**. The sequence of stack and input contents is shown in Fig. 6.4.

	Stack	Input
(1)	0	**id** * **id** + **id** $
(2)	0 **id** 5	* **id** + **id** $
(3)	0 F 3	* **id** + **id** $
(4)	0 T 2	* **id** + **id** $
(5)	0 T 2 * 7	**id** + **id** $
(6)	0 T 2 * 7 **id** 5	+ **id** $
(7)	0 T 2 * 7 F 10	+ **id** $
(8)	0 T 2	+ **id** $
(9)	0 E 1	+ **id** $
(10)	0 E 1 + 6	**id** $
(11)	0 E 1 + 6 **id** 5	$
(12)	0 E 1 + 6 F 3	$
(13)	0 E 1 + 6 T 9	$
(14)	0 E 1	$

Fig. 6.4. Moves of LR parser on **id** * **id** + **id**.

For example, at line (1) the LR parser is in state 0 with **id** the first input symbol. The action in row 0 and column **id** of the action field of Fig.

6.3 is s5, meaning shift and cover the stack with state 5. That is what has happened at line (2): the first token **id** and the state symbol 5 have both been pushed onto the stack, and **id** has been removed from the input.

Then, $*$ becomes the current input symbol, and the action of state 5 on input $*$ is to reduce by $F \to$ **id**. Two symbols are popped off the stack (one state symbol and one grammar symbol). State 0 is then exposed. Since the goto of state 0 on F is state 3, F and 3 are pushed onto the stack. We now have the configuration in line (3).

Each of the remaining moves are determined similarly.   □

LR Grammars

Our primary question is, "How do we construct an LR parsing table from a grammar?" A grammar for which we can construct a parsing table in which every entry is uniquely defined is said to be an *LR grammar*. Unfortunately, there are context-free grammars which are not LR, but these can generally be avoided for typical programming-language constructs. Intuitively, in order for a grammar to be LR, it is sufficient that a left-to-right parser be able to recognize handles when they appear on top of the stack.

An LR parser does not have to scan the entire stack to know when the handle appears on top. Rather, the state symbol on top of the stack contains all the information it needs. It is a remarkable fact that if it is possible to recognize a handle knowing only what is in the stack, then a finite automaton can, by reading the stack from bottom to top, determine what handle, if any, is on top of the stack. The driver routine of an LR parser is essentially such a finite automaton. It need not, however, read the stack on every move. The state symbol stored on top of the stack is the state the handle-recognizing finite automaton would be in if it had read the stack from bottom to top. Thus, the LR parser can determine from the state on top of the stack everything that it needs to know about what is in the stack.

Another source of information than an LR parser can use to help make its shift-reduce decisions is the next k input symbols. In practice, $k=0$ or $k=1$ is sufficient, and we shall only consider LR parsers with $k \leqslant 1$ here. A grammar that can be parsed by an LR parser examining up to k input symbols on each move is called an *LR(k) grammar*.

It is worth noting that the LR requirement that we be able to recognize the occurrence of the right side of a production, having seen what is derived from that right side, is far less stringent than the requirement for a predictive parser, namely that we be able to recognize the apparent use of the production seeing only the first symbol it derives. Thus, it should be no surprise that LR parsers are more general than predictive parsers.

Some Non-LR Constructs

As we have mentioned, there are context-free grammars that are not LR. In this section we shall give some examples of syntactic constructs that give rise to non-LR grammars. Intuitively, a grammar is non-LR(1) if every shift-reduce parser for that grammar can reach a configuration in which the parser, knowing the entire stack contents and the next input symbol, cannot decide whether to shift or to reduce, or cannot decide which of several reductions to make.

An ambiguous grammar can never be LR. For example, suppose we have a grammar with productions (among others)

$$S \rightarrow iCtS \mid iCtSeS$$

modeling the dangling-else construct. If we have a bottom-up parser in configuration

Stack	Input
$\cdots iCtS$	$e \cdots \$$

we cannot tell whether $iCtS$ is the handle no matter what appears below it on the stack. There are two choices. It might be correct to reduce $iCtS$ to S or it might be correct to shift e and then to look for another S to finally complete the alternate $iCtSeS$. Thus, we cannot tell whether to shift or reduce in this case, so the grammar is not LR(1). More generally, no ambiguous grammar, as this one certainly is, can be LR(k) for any k.

We should mention, however, that the LR parsing technique can be easily adapted to parse certain ambiguous grammars, such as the if-then-else grammar above. When we construct an LR parser for a grammar containing the two productions above, there will be a state with a parsing action conflict: on e, either shift or reduce by $S \rightarrow iCtS$. If we resolve the conflict in favor of shifting, the parser will behave naturally. We shall discuss the parsing of ambiguous grammars in Section 6.6.

Another common cause of non-LR-ness occurs when we know we have a handle, but what we see on the stack is not sufficient to tell what production should be used in a reduction. The next example illustrates this situation.

Example 6.2. Suppose we have a lexical analyzer which returns token **id** for all identifiers, regardless of usage. Suppose also that our language invokes procedures by giving their names, with parameters surrounded by parentheses, and that arrays are referenced by the same syntax. Since the translation of indices in array references and parameters in procedure calls are different, we shall want to use different productions to generate lists of actual parameters and indices (see Section 8.2 for a discussion of the need for this distinction). Our grammar might therefore have (among others) productions such as:

(1) statement → **id** (parameter-list)
(2) statement → expression := expression
(3) parameter-list → parameter-list, parameter
(4) parameter-list → parameter
(5) parameter → **id**
(6) expression → **id** (expression-list)
(7) expression → **id**
(8) expression-list → expression-list, expression
(9) expression-list → expression

A statement beginning with A(I, J) would appear as the token stream **id (id , id)** to the parser. After shifting the first three tokens onto the stack, a shift-reduce parser would be in configuration

$$\text{Stack} \qquad \text{Input}$$
$$\cdots \text{ id(id} \quad \text{, id)} \cdots \text{\$}$$

It is evident that the **id** on top of the stack must be reduced, but to what? The correct choice is production (5) if A is a procedure and (7) if A is an array. The stack does not tell which; only the symbol table does.

One solution is to change the token **id** in production (1) to **procid** and to use a more sophisticated lexical analyzer that returns token **procid** when it recognizes an identifier which is the name of a procedure. Doing this would require the lexical analyzer to consult the symbol table before returning a token.

If we made this modification, then on processing A(I, J) the parser would be either in the configuration

$$\text{Stack} \qquad \text{Input}$$
$$\cdots \textbf{ procid(id} \quad \text{, id)} \cdots \text{\$}$$

or in the configuration above. In the former case we choose reduction by production (5); in the latter case by production (7). Notice how the symbol third from the top of the stack determines the reduction to be made, even though it is not involved in the reduction. This is an example of the power of the LR method, utilizing information down in the stack to guide the parse. □

6.2 The Canonical Collection of LR(0) Items

This section begins to show how to construct a "simple" LR parser for a grammar, if such a parser exists. The central idea is the construction of a DFA from the grammar. In the next section we show how to turn this DFA into an LR parsing table. The DFA recognizes *viable prefixes* of the grammar, that is, prefixes of right-sentential forms that do not contain any symbols to the right of the handle.[†] A viable prefix is so called because it is

---

† This is not the same as the language generated by the grammar.

always possible to add terminal symbols to the end of a viable prefix to obtain a right-sentential form. Therefore, there is apparently no error as long as the portion of the input seen to a given point can be reduced to a viable prefix.

We define an *LR(0) item* (*item* for short) of a grammar G to be a production of G with a dot at some position of the right side. Thus, production $A \rightarrow XYZ$ generates the four items

$$A \rightarrow \cdot XYZ$$

$$A \rightarrow X \cdot YZ$$

$$A \rightarrow XY \cdot Z$$

$$A \rightarrow XYZ \cdot$$

The production $A \rightarrow \epsilon$ generates only one item, $A \rightarrow \cdot$. Inside the computer, items are easily represented by pairs of integers, the first giving the number of the production and the second the position of the dot.

Intuitively, an item indicates how much of a production we have seen at a given point in the parsing process. For example, the first item above would indicate that we are expecting to see a string derivable from XYZ next on the input. The second item would indicate that we have just seen on the input a string derivable from X and that we next expect to see a string derivable from YZ.

We group items together into sets, which give rise to the states of an LR parser. The items can be viewed as the states of an NFA recognizing viable prefixes, and the "grouping together" is really the subset construction discussed in Chapter 3.

One collection of sets of items, which we call the *canonical I R (0)* collection, provides the basis for constructing a class of LR parsers called simple LR (SLR). To construct the canonical LR(0) collection for a grammar, we need to define an augmented grammar and two functions, CLOSURE and GOTO.

If G is a grammar with start symbol S, then G', the *augmented grammar* for G, is G with a new start symbol S' and production $S' \rightarrow S$. The purpose of this new starting production is to indicate to the parser when it should stop parsing and announce acceptance of the input. This would occur when the parser was about to reduce by $S' \rightarrow S$.

CLOSURE

If I is a set of items for a grammar G, then the set of items CLOSURE(I) is constructed from I by the rules:

1. Every item in I is in CLOSURE(I).

2.   If $A \rightarrow \alpha \cdot B\beta$ is in CLOSURE(I) and $B \rightarrow \gamma$ is a production, then add
the item $B \rightarrow \cdot \gamma$ to I, if it is not already there.

Intuitively, $A \rightarrow \alpha \cdot B\beta$ in $CLOSURE(I)$ indicates that, at some point in the
parsing process, we next expect to see a string derivable from $B\beta$ as input.
If $B \rightarrow \gamma$ is a production, we would also expect to see a string derivable
from γ at this point. It is for this reason that we also include $B \rightarrow \cdot \beta$ in
$CLOSURE(I)$.

Example 6.3. Consider the augmented grammar

$$E' \rightarrow E$$
$$E \rightarrow E + T \mid T$$
$$T \rightarrow T * F \mid F \tag{6.1}$$
$$F \rightarrow (E) \mid \mathbf{id}$$

If I is the set of one item $\{[E' \rightarrow \cdot E]\}$, then CLOSURE($I$) contains the items

$$E' \rightarrow \cdot E$$
$$E \rightarrow \cdot E + T$$
$$E \rightarrow \cdot T$$
$$T \rightarrow \cdot T * F$$
$$T \rightarrow \cdot F$$
$$F \rightarrow \cdot (E)$$
$$F \rightarrow \cdot \mathbf{id}$$

That is, $E' \rightarrow \cdot E$ is in CLOSURE(I) by rule (1). Since there is an E
immediately to the right of a dot, by rule (2) we are forced to add the E-
productions with dots at the left end, that is, $E \rightarrow \cdot E + T$ and $E \rightarrow \cdot T$. Now
there is a T immediately to the right of a dot, so we add $T \rightarrow \cdot T * F$ and
$T \rightarrow \cdot F$. Next, the F to the right of a dot forces $F \rightarrow \cdot (E)$ and $F \rightarrow \cdot \mathbf{id}$ to
be added. No other items are put into CLOSURE(I) by rule (2).   □

The function CLOSURE can be computed as in Fig. 6.5.

A convenient way to implement the function CLOSURE is to keep a
Boolean array ADDED, indexed by the nonterminals of G, such that
ADDED[B] is set to **true** if and when we add the items $B \rightarrow .\gamma$ for each
B-production $B \rightarrow \gamma$. Note that if one B-production is added to I with the
dot at the left end, then all B-productions will be similarly added to I. In
fact, it is not necessary in some circumstances to actually list the items
$B \rightarrow .\gamma$ added to I by CLOSURE. A list of the nonterminals B whose productions were so added will suffice.

```
procedure CLOSURE(I);
begin
    repeat
        for each item A → α·Bβ in I and each production
            B → γ in G such that B → ·γ is not in I
            do add B → ·γ to I
    until no more items can be added to I;
    return I;
end
```

Fig. 6.5. Computation of CLOSURE.

GOTO

The second useful function is GOTO(I, X) where I is a set of items and X is a grammar symbol. GOTO(I, X) is defined to be the closure of the set of all items $[A \rightarrow \alpha X \cdot \beta]$ such that $[A \rightarrow \alpha \cdot X\beta]$ is in I. Intuitively, if I is the set of items that are valid for some viable prefix γ, then GOTO(I, X) is the set of items that are valid for the viable prefix γX.

Example 6.4. If I is the set of items $\{[E' \rightarrow E\cdot], [E \rightarrow E\cdot + T]\}$, then GOTO(I, +) consists of

$$E \rightarrow E + \cdot T$$

$$T \rightarrow \cdot T * F$$

$$T \rightarrow \cdot F$$

$$F \rightarrow \cdot (E)$$

$$F \rightarrow \cdot \text{id}$$

That is, we examine I for items with + immediately to the right of the dot. $E' \rightarrow E\cdot$ is not such an item, but $E \rightarrow E\cdot + T$ is. We move the dot over the + to get $\{E \rightarrow E + \cdot T\}$ and take the closure of this set. □

The Sets-of-Items Construction

We are now ready to give the algorithm to construct C, the canonical collection of sets of LR(0) items for an augmented grammar G'; the algorithm is shown in Fig. 6.6.

Example 6.5. The canonical collection of sets of items for grammar (6.1) of Example 6.3 is shown in Fig. 6.7. The GOTO function for this set of items is shown as the transition diagram of a deterministic finite automaton D in Fig. 6.8. □

procedure ITEMS(G');
begin
    $C := \{\text{CLOSURE}(\{S' \rightarrow \cdot S\})\}$;
    repeat
        for each set of items I in C and each grammar symbol X
            such that GOTO(I, X) is not empty and is not in C
            do add GOTO(I, X) to C
    until no more sets of items can be added to C
end

Fig. 6.6 The sets-of-items construction.

I_0: $E' \rightarrow \cdot E$
      $E \rightarrow \cdot E + T$
      $E \rightarrow \cdot T$
      $T \rightarrow \cdot T * F$
      $T \rightarrow \cdot F$
      $F \rightarrow \cdot (E)$
      $F \rightarrow \cdot \textbf{id}$

I_1: $E' \rightarrow E \cdot$
      $E \rightarrow E \cdot + T$

I_2: $E \rightarrow T \cdot$
      $T \rightarrow T \cdot * F$

I_3: $T \rightarrow F \cdot$

I_4: $F \rightarrow (\cdot E)$
      $E \rightarrow \cdot E + T$
      $E \rightarrow \cdot T$
      $T \rightarrow \cdot T * F$
      $T \rightarrow \cdot F$
      $F \rightarrow \cdot (E)$
      $F \rightarrow \cdot \textbf{id}$

I_5: $F \rightarrow \textbf{id} \cdot$

I_6: $E \rightarrow E + \cdot T$
      $T \rightarrow \cdot T * F$
      $T \rightarrow \cdot F$
      $F \rightarrow \cdot (E)$
      $F \rightarrow \cdot \textbf{id}$

I_7: $T \rightarrow T * \cdot F$
      $F \rightarrow \cdot (E)$
      $F \rightarrow \cdot \textbf{id}$

I_8: $F \rightarrow (E \cdot)$
      $E \rightarrow E \cdot + T$

I_9: $E \rightarrow E + T \cdot$
      $T \rightarrow T \cdot * F$

I_{10}: $T \rightarrow T * F \cdot$

I_{11}: $F \rightarrow (E) \cdot$

Fig. 6.7. Collection of sets of items.

If each state of D is a final state and I_0 is the initial state, then D recognizes exactly the viable prefixes of grammar (6.1). This is no accident. For every grammar G, the GOTO function of the canonical collection of sets of items defines a deterministic finite automaton that recognizes the viable

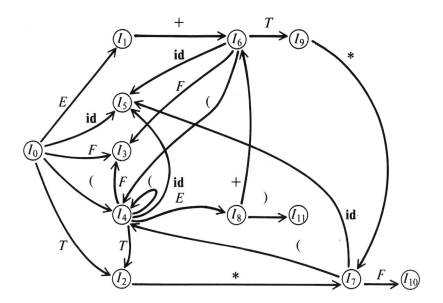

Fig. 6.8. Deterministic finite automaton D.

prefixes of G. In fact, one can visualize a nondeterministic finite automaton N whose states are the items themselves. There is a transition from $A \to \alpha \cdot X\beta$ to $A \to \alpha X \cdot \beta$ labeled X, and there is a transition from $A \to \alpha \cdot B\beta$ to $B \to \cdot \gamma$ labeled ϵ. Then CLOSURE(I) for set of items (states of N) I is exactly the ϵ-CLOSURE of a set of NFA states defined in Section 3.4. GOTO(I, X) gives the transition from I on symbol X in the DFA constructed from N by the subset construction. Viewed in this way, the procedure ITEMS(G') above is just the subset construction itself applied to the NFA N constructed from G' as we have described.

Valid Items

We say item $A \to \beta_1 \cdot \beta_2$ is *valid* for a viable prefix $\alpha\beta_1$ if there is a derivation $S' \overset{*}{\underset{rm}{\Rightarrow}} \alpha Aw \overset{*}{\underset{rm}{\Rightarrow}} \alpha\beta_1\beta_2 w$. In general an item will be valid for many viable prefixes. The fact that $A \to \beta_1 \cdot \beta_2$ is valid for $\alpha\beta_1$ tells us a lot about whether to shift or reduce when we find $\alpha\beta_1$ on the parsing stack. In particular, if $\beta_2 \neq \epsilon$, then it suggests that we have not yet shifted the handle onto the stack, so shift is our move. If $\beta_2 = \epsilon$, then it looks as if $A \to \beta_1$ is the handle, and we should reduce by this production. Of course, two valid items may tell us to do different things for the same viable prefix. Some of these conflicts can be resolved by looking at the next input symbol, but we should not suppose that all parsing action conflicts can be resolved if the LR method is used to construct a parsing table for an arbitrary grammar.

We can easily compute the set of valid items for each viable prefix that can appear on the stack of an LR parser. In fact, it is a major theorem of LR parsing theory that the set of valid items for a viable prefix γ is exactly the set of items reached from the initial state along a path labeled γ in the DFA constructed from the canonical collection of sets of items with transitions given by GOTO. In essence, the set of valid items embodies all the useful information that can be gleaned from the stack. While we shall not prove this theorem here, we shall give an example.

Example 6.6. Let us consider grammar (6.1) again, whose sets of items and GOTO function are exhibited in Figs. 6.7 and 6.8. The string $E + T *$ is a viable prefix of (6.1). The automaton of Fig. 6.8 will be in state I_7 after having read $E + T *$. State I_7 contains the items

$$T \rightarrow T * \cdot F$$

$$F \rightarrow \cdot (E)$$

$$F \rightarrow \cdot \mathbf{id}$$

which are precisely the items valid for $E + T *$. To see this, consider the following three rightmost derivations

(1) $E' \Rightarrow E$

        $\Rightarrow E + T$

        $\Rightarrow E + T * F$

        $\Rightarrow E + T * \mathbf{id}$

        $\Rightarrow E + T * F * \mathbf{id}$

(2) $E' \Rightarrow E$

        $\Rightarrow E + T$

        $\Rightarrow E + T * F$

        $\Rightarrow E + T * (E)$

(3) $E' \Rightarrow E$

        $\Rightarrow E + T$

        $\Rightarrow E + T * F$

        $\Rightarrow E + T * \mathbf{id}$

The first derivation shows the validity of $T \rightarrow T * \cdot F$, the second the validity of $F \rightarrow \cdot(E)$, and the third the validity of $F \rightarrow \cdot \textbf{id}$ for the viable prefix $E + T *$. It can be shown that there are no other valid items for $E + T *$, and we leave a proof to the interested reader. □

In summary, when we construct C, the canonical collection of sets of items for an augmented grammar G', the sets of items become the states of a deterministic finite automaton D that recognizes the viable prefixes of G'. The GOTO function on C becomes the state transition function of D. In the next section we show how to convert D into an LR parsing table for G'.

6.3 Constructing SLR Parsing Tables

This section shows how to construct the SLR parsing action and goto functions from the deterministic finite automaton that recognizes viable prefixes. It will not produce uniquely-defined parsing action tables for all grammars but does succeed on many grammars for programming languages. Given a grammar G, we augment G to produce G', and from G' we construct C, the canonical collection of sets of items for G'. We construct ACTION, the parsing action function, and GOTO, the goto function, from C using the following "simple" LR (SLR for short) parsing table construction technique. It requires us to know FOLLOW(A) for each nonterminal A of a grammar (see Section 5.5).

Algorithm 6.1. Construction of an SLR parsing table.

Input. C, the canonical collection of sets of items for an augmented grammar G'.

Output. If possible, an LR parsing table consisting of a parsing action function ACTION and a goto function GOTO.

Method. Let $C = \{I_0, I_1, \ldots, I_n\}$. The states of the parser are $0, 1, \ldots, n$, state i being constructed from I_i. The parsing actions for state i are determined as follows:

1. If $[A \rightarrow \alpha \cdot a\beta]$ is in I_i and GOTO(I_i, a) $= I_j$, then set ACTION$[i, a]$ to "shift j." Here a is a terminal.
2. If $[A \rightarrow \alpha \cdot]$ is in I_i, then set ACTION$[i, a]$ to "reduce $A \rightarrow \alpha$" for all a in FOLLOW(A).
3. If $[S' \rightarrow S \cdot]$ is in I_i, then set ACTION$[i, \$]$ to "accept."

If any conflicting actions are generated by the above rules, we say the grammar is not SLR(1).[†] The algorithm fails to produce a valid parser in this case.

[†] Recall that the 1 in SLR(1) indicates that one input symbol is used to help resolve conflicts.

The goto transitions for state i are constructed using the rule:

4. If GOTO(I_i, A) = I_j, then GOTO[i, A] = j.
5. All entries not defined by rules (1) through (4) are made "error."
6. The initial state of the parser is the one constructed from the set of items containing [$S' \rightarrow \cdot S$].   □

The parsing table consisting of the parsing action and goto functions determined by Algorithm 6.1 is called the *SLR table for G*. An LR parser using the SLR table for G is called the SLR parser for G, and a grammar having an SLR parsing table is said to be *SLR(1)*.

Example 6.7. Let us construct the SLR table for grammar (6.1). The canonical collection of sets of items for (6.1) was shown in Fig. 6.7. Consider I_0:

$$E' \rightarrow \cdot E$$

$$E \rightarrow \cdot E + T$$

$$E \rightarrow \cdot T$$

$$T \rightarrow \cdot T * F$$

$$T \rightarrow \cdot F$$

$$F \rightarrow \cdot (E)$$

$$F \rightarrow \cdot \mathbf{id}$$

The item $F \rightarrow \cdot (E)$ gives rise to the entry ACTION[0, (] = shift 4, the item $F \rightarrow .\mathbf{id}$ to the entry ACTION[0, $\mathbf{id}$] = shift 5.
    Consider I_1:

$$E' \rightarrow E \cdot$$

$$E \rightarrow E \cdot + T$$

The first item yields ACTION[1, \$] = accept, the second yields ACTION[1, +] = shift 6.
    Consider I_2:

$$E \rightarrow T \cdot$$

$$T \rightarrow T \cdot * F$$

Since FOLLOW(E) = {\$, +,)}, the first item makes ACTION[2, \$] = ACTION[2, +] = ACTION[2,)] = reduce $E \rightarrow T$. The second item makes ACTION[2, *] = shift 7. Continuing in this fashion we obtain the parsing action and goto tables which were shown in Fig. 6.3.   □

Example 6.8. Every SLR(1) grammar is unambiguous, but there are many unambiguous grammars that are not SLR(1). Consider the grammar with productions

$$S \rightarrow L = R$$
$$S \rightarrow R$$
$$L \rightarrow * R \qquad\qquad (6.2)$$
$$L \rightarrow \textbf{id}$$
$$R \rightarrow L$$

We may think of L and R as standing for l-value and r-value, respectively, and $*$ as an operator indicating "contents of." The canonical collection of sets of LR(0) items for grammar (6.2) is shown in Fig. 6.9.

I_0: $S' \rightarrow \cdot S$ $S \rightarrow \cdot L = R$ $S \rightarrow \cdot R$ $L \rightarrow \cdot * R$ $L \rightarrow \cdot \textbf{id}$ $R \rightarrow \cdot L$	I_5: $L \rightarrow \textbf{id} \cdot$ I_6: $S \rightarrow L = \cdot R$ $R \rightarrow \cdot L$ $L \rightarrow \cdot * R$ $L \rightarrow \cdot \textbf{id}$
I_1: $S' \rightarrow S \cdot$	I_7: $L \rightarrow * R \cdot$
I_2: $S \rightarrow L \cdot = R$ $R \rightarrow L \cdot$	I_8: $R \rightarrow L \cdot$ I_9: $S \rightarrow L = R \cdot$
I_3: $S \rightarrow R \cdot$	
I_4: $L \rightarrow * \cdot R$ $R \rightarrow \cdot L$ $L \rightarrow \cdot * R$ $L \rightarrow \cdot \textbf{id}$	

Fig. 6.9. Canonical sets of items for grammar (6.2).

Consider I_2. The first item makes ACTION[2, =] be "shift 6." Since FOLLOW(R) contains =, (consider $S \Rightarrow L = R \Rightarrow * R = R$), the second item sets ACTION[2, =] to "reduce $R \rightarrow L$." Thus entry ACTION[2, =] is multiply defined. Since there is both a shift and a reduce entry in ACTION[2, =], state 2 has a *shift-reduce* conflict on input symbol =.

Grammar G is not ambiguous. This shift-reduce conflict arises from the fact that the SLR parser construction method is not powerful enough to remember enough left context to decide what action the parser should take on input = having seen a string reducible to L. The next two sections discuss more powerful methods for constructing LR parsing tables. It should be pointed out, however, that there are unambiguous grammars for which every LR parser construction method will produce a parsing action table with parsing action conflicts. Such grammars can usually be avoided in programming language applications.

6.4 Constructing Canonical LR Parsing Tables

In the SLR method, state i calls for reduction by $A \rightarrow \alpha$ if set of items I_i contains item $[A \rightarrow \alpha\cdot]$ and a is in FOLLOW(A). In some situations, however, when state i appears on top of the stack, the viable prefix $\beta\alpha$ on the stack is such that βA cannot be followed by a in a right-sentential form. Thus, the reduction by $A \rightarrow \alpha$ would be invalid on input a.

For example, reconsider Example 6.8, where in state 2 we had item $R \rightarrow L\cdot$, which could correspond to $A \rightarrow \alpha$ above, and a could be the $=$ sign, which is in FOLLOW(R). Thus, the SLR parser calls for reduction by $R \rightarrow L$ in state 2 with $=$ as the next input (the shift action is also called for because of item $S \rightarrow L \cdot = R$ in state 2). However, there is no right-sentential form of the grammar in Example 6.8 that begins $R = \cdots$. Thus state 2, which is the state corresponding to viable prefix L, among others, should not really call for reduction of that L to R.

It is possible to carry more information in the state that will allow us to rule out some of these invalid reductions by $A \rightarrow \alpha$. By splitting states when necessary, we can arrange to have each state of an LR parser indicate exactly which input symbols can follow a handle α for which there is a possible reduction to A.

The extra information is incorporated into the state by redefining items to include a terminal symbol as a second component. The general form of an item becomes $[A \rightarrow \alpha\cdot\beta, \; a]$, where $A \rightarrow \alpha\beta$ is a production and a is a terminal or the right endmarker \$. We call such an object an *LR(1) item*. The 1 refers to the length of the second component, called the *lookahead* of the item. The lookahead has no effect in an item of the form $[A \rightarrow \alpha\cdot\beta, \; a]$, where β is not ϵ, but an item of the form $[A \rightarrow \alpha\cdot, \; a]$ calls for a reduction by $A \rightarrow \alpha$ only if the next input symbol is a. Thus, we are compelled to reduce by $A \rightarrow \alpha$ only on those input symbols a for which $[A \rightarrow \alpha\cdot, \; a]$ is an LR(1) item in the state on top of the stack.

Formally, we say LR(1) item $[A \rightarrow \alpha\cdot\beta, \; a]$ is *valid* for viable prefix γ if there is a derivation $S \overset{*}{\underset{rm}{\Rightarrow}} \delta Aw \underset{rm}{\Rightarrow} \delta\alpha\beta w$, where

1. $\gamma = \delta\alpha$, and
2. Either a is the first symbol of w, or w is ϵ and a is \$.

Example 6.9. Let us consider the grammar

$$S \rightarrow BB$$
$$B \rightarrow aB \mid b$$

There is a rightmost derivation $S \overset{*}{\underset{rm}{\Rightarrow}} aaBab \underset{rm}{\Rightarrow} aaaBab$. We see that item $[B \rightarrow a \cdot B, a]$ is valid for viable prefix $\gamma = aaa$ by letting $\delta = aa$, $A = B$, $w = ab$, $\alpha = a$, and $\beta = B$ in the above definition.

There is also a rightmost derivation $S \overset{*}{\underset{rm}{\Rightarrow}} BaB \underset{rm}{\Rightarrow} BaaB$. From this derivation we see that item $[B \rightarrow a \cdot B, \$]$ is valid for viable prefix Baa. □

The method for constructing the collection of sets of valid LR(1) items is essentially the same as the way we built the canonical collection of LR(0) sets of items in Section 6.2. We need two procedures, CLOSURE and GOTO, similar to those of Section 6.2.

To appreciate the definition of the CLOSURE operation, consider an item of the form $[A \rightarrow \alpha \cdot B\beta, a]$ in the set of items valid for some viable prefix γ. Then there is a rightmost derivation $S \overset{*}{\underset{rm}{\Rightarrow}} \delta Aax \underset{rm}{\Rightarrow} \delta\alpha B\beta ax$, where $\gamma = \delta\alpha$. Suppose βax derives terminal string by. Then for each production of the form $B \rightarrow \eta$ for some η, we have derivation $S \overset{*}{\underset{rm}{\Rightarrow}} \gamma Bby \underset{rm}{\Rightarrow} \gamma\eta by$. Thus, $[B \rightarrow \cdot\eta, b]$ is valid for γ. Note that b can be the first terminal derived from β, or it is possible that β derives ϵ in the derivation $\beta ax \overset{*}{\Rightarrow} by$, and b can therefore be a. To summarize both possibilities we say that b can be any terminal in FIRST(βax), where FIRST is the function from Section 5.5. Note that x cannot contain the first terminal of by, so FIRST(βax) = FIRST(βa). We now give the LR(1) sets of items construction.

Algorithm 6.2. Construction of the sets of LR(1) items for a grammar G.

Input. A grammar G.

Output. The sets of LR(1) items which are the sets of items valid for one or more viable prefixes of G.

Method. The procedures CLOSURE and GOTO and the main routine for constructing the sets of items are shown in Fig. 6.10.   □

Example 6.10. Consider the following augmented grammar.

$$S' \rightarrow S$$
$$S \rightarrow CC$$
$$C \rightarrow cC \mid d$$

We begin by computing the closure of $\{[S' \rightarrow \cdot S, \$]\}$. To close, we match the item $[S' \rightarrow \cdot S, \$]$ with the item $[A \rightarrow \alpha \cdot B\beta, a]$ in the procedure CLOSURE. That is, $A = S'$, $\alpha = \epsilon$, $B = S$, $\beta = \epsilon$, and $a = \$$. CLOSURE tells us to add $[B \rightarrow \cdot\gamma, b]$ for each production $B \rightarrow \gamma$ and terminal b in FIRST(βa). In terms of the present grammar, $B \rightarrow \gamma$ must be $S \rightarrow CC$, and since β is ϵ and a is $\$$, b may only be $\$$. Thus we add $[S \rightarrow \cdot CC, \$]$.

procedure CLOSURE(I);
begin
   repeat
      for each item $[A \rightarrow \alpha \cdot B\beta,\ a]$ in I, each
          production $B \rightarrow \gamma$, and each terminal b in FIRST(βa)
          such that $[B \rightarrow \cdot\gamma,\ b]$ is not in I **do**
             add $[B \rightarrow \cdot\gamma,\ b]$ to I;
   until no more items can be added to I;
   return I
end;

procedure GOTO($I,\ X$);
begin
   let J be the set of items $[A \rightarrow \alpha X \cdot \beta,\ a]$, such that
      $[A \rightarrow \alpha \cdot X\beta,\ a]$ is in I;
   return CLOSURE(J)
end;

begin
   $C := \{\text{CLOSURE}(\{S' \rightarrow \cdot S,\ \$\})\}$;
   repeat
      for each set of items I in C and each grammar
          symbol X such that GOTO($I,\ X$) is not empty
          and not already in C **do**
             add GOTO($I,\ X$) to C
   until no more sets of items can be added to C
end

Fig. 6.10. LR(1) sets-of-items construction.

We continue to compute the closure by adding all items $[C \rightarrow \cdot\gamma,\ b]$ for b in FIRST($C\$$). That is, matching $[S \rightarrow \cdot CC,\ \$]$ against $[A \rightarrow \alpha \cdot B\beta,\ a]$ we have $A = S$, $\alpha = \epsilon$, $B = C$, $\beta = C$, and $a = \$$. Since C does not derive the empty string, FIRST($C\$$) = FIRST(C). Since FIRST(C) contains terminals c and d, we add items $[C \rightarrow \cdot cC,\ c]$, $[C \rightarrow \cdot cC,\ d]$, $[C \rightarrow \cdot d,\ c]$ and $[C \rightarrow \cdot d,\ d]$. None of the new items has a nonterminal immediately to the right of the dot, so we have completed our first set of LR(1) items. The initial set of items is:

I_0: $S' \rightarrow \cdot S,\ \$$

     $S \rightarrow \cdot CC,\ \$$

     $C \rightarrow \cdot cC,\ c/d$

     $C \rightarrow \cdot d,\ c/d$

(The brackets have been omitted for notational convenience.) We use the notation $[C \rightarrow \cdot cC, c/d]$ as a shorthand for the two items $[C \rightarrow \cdot cC, c]$ and $[C \rightarrow \cdot cC, d]$.

Now we compute $GOTO(I_0, X)$ for the various values of X. For $X = S$ we must close the item $[S' \rightarrow S\cdot, \$]$. No additional closure is possible, since the dot is at the right end. Thus we have the next set of items:

$$I_1: \quad S' \rightarrow S\cdot, \$$$

For $X = C$ we close $[S \rightarrow C\cdot C, \$]$. We add the C-productions with second component $\$$ and then can add no more, yielding:

$$I_2: \quad S \rightarrow C\cdot C, \$$$
$$C \rightarrow \cdot cC, \$$$
$$C \rightarrow \cdot d, \$$$

Next, let $X = c$. We must close $\{[C \rightarrow c\cdot C, c/d]\}$. We add the C-productions with second component c/d, yielding:

$$I_3: \quad C \rightarrow c\cdot C, c/d$$
$$C \rightarrow \cdot cC, c/d$$
$$C \rightarrow \cdot d, c/d$$

Finally, let $X = d$, and we wind up with the set of items:

$$I_4: \quad C \rightarrow d\cdot, c/d$$

We have finished considering GOTO on I_0. We get no new sets from I_1, but I_2 has GOTO's on C, c, and d. On C we get:

$$I_5: \quad S \rightarrow CC\cdot, \$$$

no closure being needed. On c we take the closure of $\{[C \rightarrow c\cdot C, \$]\}$, to obtain:

$$I_6: \quad C \rightarrow c\cdot C, \$$$
$$C \rightarrow \cdot cC, \$$$
$$C \rightarrow \cdot d, \$$$

Note that I_6 differs from I_3 only in second components. We shall see that it is common for several sets of LR(1) items for a grammar to have the same first components and differ in their second components. When we construct the collection of sets of LR(0) items for the same grammar, each set of LR(0) items will coincide with the set of first components of one or more sets of LR(1) items. We shall have more to say about this phenomenon when we discuss LALR parsing.

Continuing with the GOTO function for I_2, GOTO(I_2, d) is easily seen to be:

$$I_7:\ C \to d\cdot,\ \$$$

Turning now to I_3, the GOTO's of I_3 on c and d are I_3 and I_4, respectively. GOTO(I_3, C) is:

$$I_8:\ C \to cC\cdot,\ c/d$$

I_4 and I_5 have no GOTO's. The GOTO's of I_6 on c and d are I_6 and I_7, respectively, and GOTO(I_6, C) is:

$$I_9:\ C \to cC\cdot,\ \$$$

The remaining sets of items yield no GOTO's, so we are done. Figure 6.11 shows the ten sets of items with their GOTO's.   □

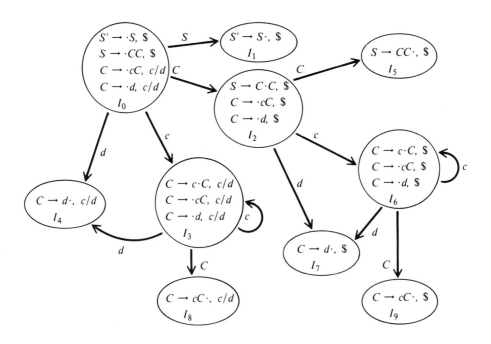

Fig. 6.11. GOTO graph.

We now give the rules whereby the LR(1) parsing action and goto functions are constructed from the sets of LR(1) items. The action and goto functions are represented by a table as before. The only difference is in the values of the entries.

Algorithm 6.3. Construction of a canonical LR parsing table.

Input. A grammar G augmented by production $S' \rightarrow S$.

Output. If possible, the canonical LR parsing action function ACTION and goto function GOTO.

Method.
1. Construct $C = \{I_0, I_1, \ldots, I_n\}$, the collection of sets of LR(1) items for G.
2. State i of the parser is constructed from I_i. The parsing actions for state i are determined as follows:
    a) If $[A \rightarrow \alpha \cdot a\beta, b]$ is in I_i and GOTO$(I_i, a) = I_j$, then set ACTION$[i, a]$ to "shift j."
    b) If $[A \rightarrow \alpha \cdot, a]$ is in I_i, then set ACTION$[i, a]$ to "reduce $A \rightarrow \alpha$."
    c) If $[S' \rightarrow S \cdot, \$]$ is in I_i, then set ACTION$[i, \$]$ to "accept."

If a conflict results from the above rules, the grammar is said not to be LR(1), and the algorithm is said to fail.

3. The goto transitions for state i are determined as follows: If GOTO$(I_i, A) = I_j$, then GOTO$[i, A] = j$.
4. All entries not defined by rules (2) through (3) are made "error."
5. The initial state of the parser is the one constructed from the set containing item $[S' \rightarrow \cdot S, \$]$. □

The table formed from the parsing action and goto functions produced by Algorithm 6.3 is called the *canonical* LR(1) parsing table. An LR parser using this table is called a canonical LR parser. If the parsing action function has no multiply-defined entries, then the given grammar is called an *LR(1) grammar*.

Example 6.11. The canonical parsing table for the grammar of the previous example is shown in Fig. 6.12. Productions 1, 2, and 3 are $S \rightarrow CC$, $C \rightarrow cC$, and $C \rightarrow d$. □

Every SLR(1) grammar is an LR(1) grammar, but for an SLR(1) grammar the canonical LR parser may have more states than the SLR parser for the same grammar. The grammar of the previous examples is SLR and has an SLR parser with seven states, compared with the ten of Fig. 6.12.

6.5 Constructing LALR Parsing Tables

We now introduce our last parser construction method, the LALR (*lookahead*-LR) technique. This method is, in practice, the method of choice, in that the tables obtained by it are considerably smaller than the canonical LR tables, yet most common syntactic constructs of programming languages can be expressed conveniently by an LALR grammar. The same

State	Action			Goto	
	c	d	$	S	C
0	s3	s4		1	2
1			acc		
2	s6	s7			5
3	s3	s4			8
4	r3	r3			
5			r1		
6	s6	s7			9
7			r3		
8	r2	r2			
9			r2		

Fig. 6.12. Canonical parsing table.

is almost true for SLR grammars, but there are a few constructs that cannot be conveniently handled by SLR techniques (see Example 6.8, e.g.).

For a comparison of parser size, the SLR and LALR tables for a grammar always have the same number of states, and this number is typically several hundred states for a language like ALGOL. The canonical LR table would typically have several thousand states for the same size language. Thus, it is much easier and more economical to construct SLR or LALR tables than the canonical LR tables.

By way of introduction, let us again consider the grammar

$$S' \rightarrow S$$

$$S \rightarrow CC$$

$$C \rightarrow cC \mid d$$

whose sets of LR(1) items were shown in Fig. 6.11. Take a pair of similar looking states, such as I_4 and I_7. Each of these states has only items with first component $C \rightarrow d\cdot$. In I_4, the lookaheads are c or d; in I_7, $ is the only lookahead.

To see the difference between the roles of I_4 and I_7 in the parser, note that our grammar generates the regular set c^*dc^*d. When reading an input $cc...cdcc...cd$, the parser shifts the first group of c's and their following d onto the stack, entering state 4 after reading the d. The parser then calls for a reduction by $C \rightarrow d$, provided the next input symbol is c or d. The requirement that c or d follow makes sense, since these are the symbols that could begin strings in c^*d. If $ follows the first d, we have an input like ccd which is not in the language, and state 4 correctly declares an error if $ is the next input.

The parser enters state 7 after reading the second d. Then, the parser must see $ on the input, or it started with a string not of the form $c*dc*d$. It thus makes sense that state 7 should reduce by $C \rightarrow d$ on input $ and declare error on inputs c or d.

Let us now replace I_4 and I_7 by I_{47}, the union of I_4 and I_7, consisting of the set of three items represented by $[C \rightarrow d\cdot, c/d/\$]$. The goto's on d to I_4 or I_7 from I_0, I_2, I_3 and I_6 now enter I_{47}. The action of state 47 is to reduce on any input. The revised parser behaves essentially like the original, although it might reduce d to C in circumstances where the original would declare error, for example, on inputs like ccd or $cdcdc$. The error will eventually be caught; in fact, it will be caught before any more input symbols are shifted.

More generally, we can look for sets of LR(1) items having the same *core*, that is, set of first components, and we may merge these sets with common cores into one set of items. For example, in Fig. 6.7, I_4 and I_7 are such a pair, with core $\{C \rightarrow d\cdot\}$. I_3 and I_6 is another pair, with core $\{C \rightarrow c\cdot C, C \rightarrow \cdot cC, C \rightarrow \cdot d\}$. There is one more pair, I_8 and I_9, with core $\{C \rightarrow cC\cdot\}$. Note that, in general, a core is a set of LR(0) items for the grammar at hand, and that an LR(1) grammar may produce more than two sets of items with the same core.

Since the core of GOTO(I, X) depends only on the core of I, the goto's of merged sets can themselves be merged. Thus, there is no problem revising the goto function as we merge sets of items. The action functions are modified to reflect the non-error actions of all sets of items in the merger.

Suppose we have an LR(1) grammar, that is, one whose sets of LR(1) items produce no parsing-action conflicts. If we replace all states having the same core with their union, it is possible that the resulting union will have a conflict, but it is unlikely for the following reason: Suppose in the union there is a conflict on lookahead a because there is an item $[A \rightarrow \alpha\cdot, a]$ calling for reduction by $A \rightarrow \alpha$, and there is another item $[B \rightarrow \beta\cdot a\gamma, b]$ calling for a shift. Then some set of items from which the union was formed has item $[A \rightarrow \alpha\cdot, a]$, and since the cores of all these states are the same, it must have an item $[B \rightarrow \beta\cdot a\gamma, c]$ for some c. But then this state has the same shift-reduce conflict on a, and the grammar was not LR(1) as we assumed. Thus, the merging of states with common cores can never produce a shift-reduce conflict that was not present in one of the original states, because shift actions depend only on the core, not the lookahead.

It is possible, however, that a merger will produce a reduce-reduce conflict, as the following example shows.

Example 6.12. Consider the grammar

$$S' \rightarrow S$$
$$S \rightarrow aAd \mid bBd \mid aBe \mid bAe$$

$$A \rightarrow c$$
$$B \rightarrow c$$

generating the four strings *acd, ace, bcd,* and *bce.* The reader can check
that the grammar is LR(1) by constructing its sets of items. Upon doing
so, we find $\{[A \rightarrow c\cdot, d], [B \rightarrow c\cdot, e]\}$ valid for viable prefix *ac* and
$\{[A \rightarrow c\cdot, e], [B \rightarrow c\cdot, d]\}$ valid for *bc.* Neither of these sets has a
conflict, and their cores are the same. However, in their union, which is

$$A \rightarrow c\cdot, \; d/e$$

$$B \rightarrow c\cdot, \; d/e$$

there is a conflict, since reductions by both $A \rightarrow c$ and $B \rightarrow c$ are called for
on inputs *d* and *e.*   □

We are now prepared to give our first of two LALR table construction
algorithms. The general idea is to construct the sets of LR(1) items, and if
no conflicts arise, merge sets with common cores. We then construct the
parsing table from the collection of merged sets of items. The number of
such sets of items will be the same as the number of sets of LR(0) items
and will generally be much smaller than the number of sets of items produced by the canonical LR method. The method we are about to describe
serves primarily as a definition of LALR(1) grammars. Constructing the
entire collection of LR(1) sets of items requires too much space and time
to be used in practice. The reader should see Section 6.9 for an implementation of the LALR table construction algorithm that uses less space.

Algorithm 6.4. An easy, but space consuming LALR table construction.

Input. A grammar G augmented by production $S' \rightarrow S$.

Output. The LALR parsing tables ACTION and GOTO.

Method.

1. Construct $C = \{I_0, I_1, \ldots, I_n\}$, the collection of sets of LR(1) items.

2. For each core present among the sets of LR(1) items, find all sets having that core, and replace these sets by their union.

3. Let $C' = \{J_0, J_1, \ldots, J_m\}$ be the resulting sets of LR(1) items. The
   parsing actions for state i are constructed from J_i in the same manner
   as in Algorithm 6.3. If there is a parsing-action conflict, the algorithm
   fails to produce a parser, and the grammar is said not to be LALR(1).

4. The GOTO table is constructed as follows. If J is the union of one or
   more sets of LR(1) items, i.e., $J = I_1 \cup I_2 \cup \cdots \cup I_m$, then the
   cores of GOTO(I_1, X), GOTO(I_2, X), $\ldots$, GOTO(I_k, X) are the
   same, since $I_1, I_2, \ldots, I_k$ all have the same core. Let K be the union
   of all sets of items having the same core as GOTO(I_1, X). Then

GOTO$(J, X) = K$.   □

The table produced by Algorithm 6.4 is called the *LALR parsing table* for *G*. If there are no parsing-action conflicts, then the given grammar is said to be an *LALR(1) grammar*.

Example 6.13. Consider the grammar

$$S' \rightarrow S$$

$$S \rightarrow CC$$

$$C \rightarrow cC \mid d$$

whose GOTO graph was shown in Fig. 6.11. As we mentioned, there are three pairs of sets of items that can be merged. I_3 and I_6 are replaced by their union:

$$I_{36}: \; C \rightarrow c \cdot C, \; c/d/\$$$

$$C \rightarrow \cdot cC, \; c/d/\$$$

$$C \rightarrow \cdot d, \; c/d/\$$$

I_4 and I_7 are replaced by

$$I_{47}: \; C \rightarrow d\cdot, \; c/d/\$$$

and I_8 and I_9 are replaced by their union:

$$I_{89}: \; C \rightarrow cC\cdot, \; c/d/\$$$

The LALR action and goto functions for the condensed sets of items are shown in Fig. 6.13.

State	Action			Goto	
	c	*d*	$	*S*	*C*
0	s36	s47		1	2
1			acc		
2	s36	s47			5
36	s36	s47			89
47	r3	r3	r3		
5			r1		
89	r2	r2	r2		

Fig. 6.13. LALR parsing table.

To see how the goto's are computed, consider GOTO(I_{36}, C). In the original set of LR(1) items, GOTO$(I_3, C) = I_8$, and I_8 is now part of I_{89}, so we make GOTO(I_{36}, C) be I_{89}. We could have arrived at the same conclusion if we considered I_6, the other part of I_{36}. That is, GOTO(I_6, C) = I_9, and I_9 is now part of I_{89}. For another example, consider GOTO(I_2, c), an entry which is exercised after the shift action of I_2 on input c and which appears in the action field. In the original sets of LR(1) items, GOTO(I_2, c) = I_6. Since I_6 is now part of I_{36}, GOTO(I_2, c) becomes I_{36}. Thus, the entry in Fig. 6.13 for state 2 and input c is made s36, meaning shift and push state 36 onto the stack.   □

When presented with a string from the language c^*dc^*d, both the LR parser of Fig. 6.12 and the LALR parser of Fig. 6.13 make exactly the same sequence of shifts and reductions, although the names of the states on the stack may differ; i.e., if the LR parser puts I_3 or I_6 on the stack, the LALR parser will put I_{36} on the stack. This relationship holds in general for an LALR grammar. The LR and LALR parsers will mimic one another on correct inputs.

However, when presented with an erroneous input, the LALR parser may proceed to do some reductions after the LR parser has declared an error, although the LALR parser will never shift another symbol after the LR parser declares an error. For example, on input ccd followed by $, the LR parser of Fig. 6.12 will put

$$0 \; c \; 3 \; c \; 3 \; d \; 4$$

on the stack, and in state 4 will discover an error, because $ is the next input symbol and state 4 has action error on $. In contrast, the LALR parser of Fig. 6.13 will make the corresponding moves, putting

$$0 \; c \; 36 \; c \; 36 \; d \; 47$$

on the stack. But state 47 on input $ has action reduce $C \rightarrow d$. The LALR parser will thus change its stack to

$$0 \; c \; 36 \; c \; 36 \; C \; 89$$

Now the action of state 89 on input $ is reduce $C \rightarrow cC$. The stack becomes

$$0 \; c \; 36 \; C \; 89$$

whereupon a similar reduction is called for, obtaining stack

$$0 \; C \; 2$$

Finally, state 2 has action error on input $, so only now is the error discovered.   □

6.6 Using Ambiguous Grammars

It is a theorem that every ambiguous grammar fails to be LR, and thus is not in any of the classes of grammars discussed in the last three sections. However, some ambiguous grammars are quite useful in the specification of languages, and this section shows how to deal with them in the framework of LR parsing. For example, we might prefer the natural ambiguous grammar for arithmetic expressions with operators $+$ and $*$:

$$E \rightarrow E + E \mid E * E \mid (E) \mid \textbf{id} \qquad (6.3)$$

assuming that the precedence and associativity of the operators $+$ and $*$ has been specified elsewhere.

There are two reasons why we might want to use this grammar instead of the one in Example 6.1. First, as we shall see, we can easily change the associativities and precedence levels of the operators $+$ and $*$ without disturbing the productions of (6.3) or the number of states in the resulting parser. Second, the parser for the unambiguous grammar of Example 6.1 will spend a substantial fraction of its time reducing by the single productions $E \rightarrow T$ and $T \rightarrow F$, whose sole function is to enforce associativity and precedence information. The parser for (6.3) will not waste time reducing by single productions.

The sets of LR(0) items for (6.3) augmented by $E' \rightarrow E$ are shown in Fig. 6.14. The parsing action conflict in I_1 between accept and shift can be resolved by the SLR approach. Only \$ is in FOLLOW(E'), so acceptance is the unique action for input \$. On the other hand, $+$ and $*$ are the only inputs calling for a shift.

However, the conflict in I_7 between reduction by $E \rightarrow E+E$ and shift on $+$ and $*$ cannot be resolved in an SLR way, because $+$ and $*$ are each in FOLLOW(E). Thus both actions would be called for by the SLR parser on inputs $+$ and $*$. A similar conflict occurs in I_8, between reduction by $E \rightarrow E*E$ and shift on inputs $+$ and $*$. Every LR parser construction method will have these conflicts.

These conflicts, however, can be resolved using the precedence and associativity information for $+$ and $*$. Let us consider an input like $\textbf{id} + \textbf{id} * \textbf{id}$, which causes the parser to enter state 7 after processing $\textbf{id} + \textbf{id}$; in particular the parser reaches a configuration with $0E1+4E7$ on the stack and $* \textbf{id}$ \$ remaining on the input. Assuming that $*$ takes precedence over $+$, we know the parser should shift $*$ onto the stack, preparing to reduce the $*$ and its surrounding $\textbf{id}$'s to an expression. This is what the SLR parser of Fig. 6.3 for the same language would do, and it is what the operator-precedence parser would do. On the other hand, if $+$ takes precedence over $*$, we know the parser should reduce $E+E$ to E. Thus the relative precedence of $+$ followed by $*$ uniquely determines how the parsing action conflict between reducing by $E \rightarrow E+E$ and shifting on $*$ in state 7 should be resolved.

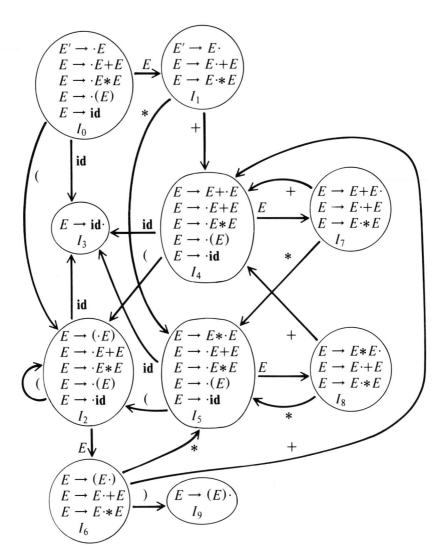

Fig. 6.14. Sets of LR(0) items.

If the input had been **id** + **id** + **id**, instead, the parser would still reach a configuration in which it had $0E1+4E7$ after processing **id** + **id**. On input + there is again a shift-reduce conflict in state 7. Now, however, the associativity of the + operator determines how this conflict should be resolved. If + is left-associative, the correct action is to reduce by $E \rightarrow E+E$. That is, the **id**'s surrounding the first + must be grouped first. Again this choice coincides with what the SLR or operator-precedence parsers would do for the grammar of Example 6.1.

In summary, assuming $+$ is left-associative, the action of state 7 on input $+$ should be to reduce by $E \rightarrow E + E$, and assuming that $*$ takes precedence over $+$, the action of state 7 on input $*$ should be to shift.

Similarly, assuming that $*$ is left-associative and takes precedence over $+$, we can argue that state 8, which can appear on top of the stack only when $E * E$ are the top three grammar symbols, should have action reduce $E \rightarrow E * E$ on both $+$ and $*$ inputs. In the case of input $+$, the reason is that $*$ takes precedence over $+$ and in the case of input $*$, the rationale is that $*$ is left-associative.

Proceeding in this way, we obtain the LR parsing table shown in Fig. 6.15. Productions $1-4$ are $E \rightarrow E + E$, $E \rightarrow E * E$, $E \rightarrow (E)$, and $E \rightarrow$ **id**, respectively. An LR parser using this table would recognize the same language as one using the table in Fig. 6.3, but would do so without making any reductions by single productions. Ambiguous grammars can be handled in a similar way in the context of LALR and canonical LR parsing.

state	action						goto
	id	$+$	$*$	(	)	$	E
0	s3			s2			1
1		s4	s5			acc	
2	s3			s2			6
3		r4	r4		r4	r4	
4	s3			s2			7
5	s3			s2			8
6		s4	s5		s9		
7		r1	s5		r1	r1	
8		r2	r2		r2	r2	
9		r3	r3		r3	r3	

Fig. 6.15. Parsing table from ambiguous grammar.

For another case where ambiguous grammars can be useful descriptors of programming languages, consider a group of productions which might be used to define **if** statements, such as:

> stat $\rightarrow$ **if** cond **then** stat **else** stat
>
> | **if** cond **then** stat
>
> | all other productions for statement

As we noted in Section 4.3, this grammar is ambiguous. To simplify discussion of how this construct should be parsed, let us consider an abstraction of the above grammar, where i stands for **if** cond **then**, e stands for **else**, and *a* stands for "all other productions." We can then write the grammar, with augmenting production $S' \rightarrow S$, as:

$$S' \rightarrow S$$

$$S \rightarrow iSeS \mid iS \mid a \tag{6.3}$$

The sets of LR(0) items for grammar (6.3) are shown in Fig. 6.16. The set of items I_4 yields a shift-reduce conflict, since $S \rightarrow iS \cdot eS$ calls for a shift of *e* while, since *e* is in FOLLOW(S), item $S \rightarrow iS \cdot$ calls for reduction by $S \rightarrow iS$ on input *e*.

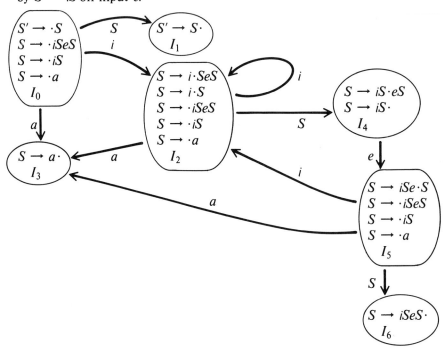

Fig. 6.16. LR(0) states for "dangling-else" grammar.

Translating back to the **if...then...else** terminology, given **if** cond **then** stat on the stack and **else** as the first input symbol, should we shift **else** onto the stack (i.e., shift *e*) or reduce **if** cond **then** stat to stat (i.e. reduce by $S \rightarrow iS$)? The answer is that we should shift **else**, because it is "associated" with the previous **then**. In the terminology of grammar (6.3), the *e* on the input, standing for **else**, can only form part of the right side beginning with the *iS* on the top of the stack. If what follows *e* on the input cannot be parsed as an *S*, completing right side *iSeS*, then it can be shown that there is no other parse possible.

We are drawn to the conclusion that the conflict in I_4 should be resolved in favor of shift on input *e*. The parsing table constructed from the sets of items of Fig. 6.16, using the above resolution of the conflict in I_4 on input e, is shown in Fig. 6.17. Productions 1 through 3 are $S \rightarrow iSeS$, $S \rightarrow iS$, and $S \rightarrow a$, respectively. Note that $FOLLOW(S) = \{e, \$\}$.

state	action				goto
	i	e	a	$\$$	S
0	s2		s3		1
1				acc	
2	s2		s3		4
3		r3		r3	
4		s5		r2	
5	s2		s3		6
6		r1		r1	

Fig. 6.17. LR parsing table for abstract "dangling-else" grammar.

For example, on input *iiaea*, the parser produces the parse shown in Fig. 6.18, corresponding to the correct resolution of the "dangling-else." Note that at line (5), state 4 selects the shift action on input e, whereas at line (9), state 4 calls for reduction by $S \rightarrow iS$ on $\$$ input.

	Stack	Input
(1)	0	*iiaea* $\$$
(2)	0*i*2	*iaea* $\$$
(3)	0*i*2*i*2	*aea* $\$$
(4)	0*i*2*i*2*a*3	*ea* $\$$
(5)	0*i*2*i*2*S*4	*ea* $\$$
(6)	0*i*2*i*2*S*4*e*5	*a* $\$$
(7)	0*i*2*i*2*S*4*e*5*a*3	$\$$
(8)	0*i*2*i*2*S*4*e*5*S*6	$\$$
(9)	0*i*2*S*4	$\$$
(10)	0*S*1	$\$$

Fig. 6.18. Processing of *iiaea*.

6.7 An Automatic Parser Generator

We have seen two examples of how to take a natural, ambiguous grammar and by thinking a bit, resolve conflicts in the manner that reflects our beliefs about precedence and associativity of operators, including the idea that an **else** "associates" with (i.e., is part of the same production as) the

then immediately to its left. These ideas have been incorporated into at least one compiler-writing system, YACC (Johnson [1975]), and we would like to take some time to discuss how YACC allows the user to specify a possibly ambiguous grammar along with precedence and associativity information about operators and how YACC resolves any parsing action conflicts that arise.

To begin, the user provides YACC with a grammar, and YACC builds the LALR(1) states. YACC then attempts to select the parsing actions for each state. If there are no conflicts (i.e., the grammar is LALR(1)), then the user need not supply anything more than his grammar. If the source grammar is ambiguous, however, the user may provide more information to help YACC resolve parsing action conflicts.

Precedence of Terminals and Productions

The philosophy behind conflict resolution in YACC is that each production and each terminal symbol may be given a "precedence." If on input a we have a conflict between reducing by production $A \rightarrow \alpha$ and shifting, we compare the precedence of $A \rightarrow \alpha$ with the precedence of a. If $A \rightarrow \alpha$ has higher precedence than a, we reduce; if not, we shift. YACC has a facility that allows the user to assign a precedence to every production and to every terminal. A more usual way to give precedence to productions is to follow the rule that, in the absence of a specific precedence for the production, the precedence of $A \rightarrow \alpha$ is the same as the precedence of the rightmost terminal of α. Of course, not every terminal and production need be given a precedence; those not involved in conflicts need not have precedences.

Example 6.14. Let us reconsider the grammar $S \rightarrow i S e S \mid i S \mid a$, whose sets of LR(0) items are given in Fig. 6.16. If we simply state that e is of higher precedence than i, then the production $S \rightarrow iS$ has lower precedence than e, since i is the rightmost terminal of the right side iS. Thus, in I_4 the conflict between shifting e and reducing by $S \rightarrow iS$ on input e is resolved in favor of the shift.

We could specify to YACC directly that the precedence of production $S \rightarrow iS$ is lower than the precedence of e by creating a dummy terminal of lower precedence than e, by the following YACC-like notation:[†]

TERMINAL e	/* terminals with precedence are
TERMINAL dummy	listed highest precedence first */
$S \rightarrow iSeS$	/* then come the productions */

[†] Our notation differs from YACC's in a number of respects designed to favor readability over conciseness. In particular, YACC uses a number of shorthands and lists terminals lowest precedence first. The reader interested in using YACC should consult Johnson [1975].

$S \rightarrow iS$ PRECEDENCE dummy   /* the keyword PRECEDENCE gives the production the precedence of "terminal" dummy */

$S \rightarrow a$

Another option, with a different significance, would be to give terminal i or production $S \rightarrow iS$ higher precedence than e. Then we would reduce on input e in I_4. This choice never allows e to be shifted, since, in Fig. 6.17, we note that state 4 is the only state with a shift action on input e, and that action would be changed to reduce by $S \rightarrow iS$. Thus, there is good argument for giving e the higher precedence.   □

Associativity

Let us again look at the ambiguous grammar

$$E \rightarrow E + E \mid E * E \mid (E) \mid \textbf{id}$$

whose sets of items are given in Fig. 6.14. We see that giving precedence to terminals and productions is often not enough. We would logically give $*$ higher precedence than $+$, and this choice would properly resolve the conflict on input $+$ in I_8 of Fig. 6.14. That is, we would reduce by $E \rightarrow E * E$ on input $+$, since production $E \rightarrow E * E$, with rightmost terminal $*$, is given higher precedence than terminal $+$. We would find that the conflict in I_7 on input $*$ was also resolved; we would shift, since production $E \rightarrow E + E$ has lower precedence than terminal $*$.

But what about the conflict in I_7 on input $+$ between shift and reduction by $E \rightarrow E + E$, or the conflict in I_8 on input $*$ between shift and reduction by $E \rightarrow E * E$? In each case the production has the same precedence as the terminal, so we still don't know whether to shift or reduce. What is missing is associativity.

In essence, left-associativity means that ties should be broken in favor of reduce, and right-associativity means break ties in favor of shift. Thus if we declare both $+$ and $*$ to be left-associative, we shall correctly resolve both remaining conflicts in favor of reduce. YACC permits one other kind of associativity, called "nonassociativity." Essentially, *nonassociativity* means that ties are to be "broken" by declaring error. This is the correct decision for binary operators like .EQ. in FORTRAN, where expressions of the form A .EQ. B .EQ. C are not permitted.

It is also useful to be able to declare that two or more terminals have the same precedence. An example would be $+$ and $-$, which are usually treated as having the same precedence and being collectively left-associative; e.g., $a - b + c$ means $(a - b) + c$.

Example 6.15. The following is a declaration in YACC style of some typical arithmetic, relational, and logical operators. Unary minus is of higher precedence than the multiplicative operators but lower than exponentiation.

The relational operators are all of the same precedence and are nonassociative, as in FORTRAN.

TERMINAL	↑	RIGHT	/* exponentiation is right associative and highest in precedence */
TERMINAL	UMINUS		/* UMINUS is a dummy symbol associated with production $E \rightarrow -E$ */
TERMINAL	* /	LEFT	
TERMINAL	+ −	LEFT	
TERMINAL	< = > <= >= <>	NONASSOC	
TERMINAL	¬		
TERMINAL	&	LEFT	
TERMINAL			LEFT	

The production $E \rightarrow -E$, introducing unary minus, would be given the precedence of UMINUS. Thus, for example, in the set of states valid for $-E$, we would correctly reduce by $E \rightarrow -E$ on input symbols like * or /, whereas if $E \rightarrow -E$ were given the precedence of −, we would shift. □

A final conflict resolution technique concerns reduce-reduce conflicts. The rule in YACC is that whichever production is listed first is to be preferred for reduction on inputs for which both reductions would be correct according to the LALR(1) rules.

Example 6.16. Let us consider a preprocessor as an example. Kernighan and Cherry's [1975] equation-typesetting preprocessor, which was used to typeset this book, uses a context-free grammar with, among other unusual operators, a subscript operator **sub** and a superscript operator **sup**. **sub** and **sup** are of equal precedence and right-associative. The expression a **sub** i **sup** 2, however, does not mean a_{i2}, but rather the more usual a_i^2. We must arrange that with E **sub** E **sup** E on the stack we do not reduce E **sup** E to E, but rather reduce by production $E \rightarrow E$ **sub** E **sup** E. We arrange this choice by listing the former production first. The following is a complete specification for expressions of this type. Braces are used by the preprocessor to bracket compound expressions, and c is used here as a token representing any string of text.

TERMINAL   sub   sup   RIGHT

$E \rightarrow E$ **sub** E **sup** E
$E \rightarrow E$ **sub** E
$E \rightarrow E$ **sup** E
$E \rightarrow \{ E \}$

$$E \rightarrow c$$

The parsing table constructed from this grammar, with augmentation, and the YACC resolution rules are shown in Fig. 6.19. Productions are numbered in the order shown above.   □

State	Action						Goto
	sub	sup	{	}	c	$	E
0			s2		s3		1
1	s4	s5				acc	
2			s2		s3		6
3	r5	r5		r5		r5	
4			s2		s3		7
5			s2		s3		8
6	s4	s5		s9			
7	s4	s10		r2		r2	
8	s4	s5		r3		r3	
9	r4	r4		r4		r4	
10			s2		s3		11
11	s4	s5		r1		r1	

Fig. 6.19. Parsing table.

6.8 Implementation of LR Parsing Tables

As we have mentioned, a typical programming language grammar with 50 to 100 terminals and 100 productions may have an LALR parsing table with several hundred states. The action function may easily have 20000 entries, each requiring at least 8 bits to encode. Clearly a more efficient encoding than a two-dimensional array is called for, especially in minicomputers.

Encoding the Action Field

One useful technique is to recognize that usually many rows of the action table are identical. For example, in Fig. 6.19, states 0, 2, 4, 5, and 10 have identical action entries. We can therefore save considerable space, at a negligible cost in time, if we create a pointer for each state into a one-dimensional array. Pointers for states with the same actions point to the same location. To access information from this array, we assign each terminal a number from zero to one less than the number of terminals, and we use this integer as an offset from the pointer value for each state. In a given state, the parsing action for the ith terminal will be found i locations past the pointer value for that state.

Further space efficiency can be achieved at the expense of a somewhat slower parser (generally considered a reasonable trade, since an LR-like parser consumes only a small fraction of the compilation time) by creating a list for the actions of each state. The list consists of pairs of a terminal symbol and an action. The most frequent action for a state can be appended to the end of the list, and in place of a terminal we may use the notation "any," meaning that if the current input symbol has not been found so far on the list, we should do that action no matter what the input is. Moreover, error entries can be replaced by reduce actions, for further uniformity along a row, although replacing them by shift would often cause problems in detecting errors.

Example 6.17. Let us consider the parsing table of Fig. 6.3. First, we note that the actions for states 0, 4, 6, and 7 agree. We can represent them all by the list:

Symbol	Action
id	s5
(	s4
any	error

State 1 has a similar list:

+	s6
$	acc
any	error

In state 2, we can replace the error entries by r2, so reduction by production 2 will occur on any input but *. Thus the list for state 2 is:

*	s7
any	r2

State 3 has only error and r4 entries. We can replace the former by the latter, so the list for state 3 consists of only the pair (any, r4). States 5, 10, and 11 can be treated similarly. The list for state 8 is:

+	s6
)	s11
any	error

and for state 9:

*	s7
any	r1

□

Encoding the Goto Field

We can also encode the GOTO table by a list, but here it appears more efficient to make a list of pairs for each nonterminal A. Each pair is of the form (current-state, next-state), indicating

$$\text{GOTO[current-state, } A] = \text{next-state.}$$

This technique is useful because there tend to be rather few states in any one column of the GOTO table. This stems from the fact that the goto on nonterminal A can only be a state derivable from a set of items in which some items have A immediately to the left of a dot. No set has items with X and Y immediately to the left of a dot if $X \neq Y$.

For more space reduction, we note that the error entries in the goto table are never consulted. We can replace each error entry by the most common non-error entry in its column. This entry becomes the default; it is represented in the list for each column by one pair with "any" in place of current-state.

Example 6.18. Consider Fig. 6.3 again. The column for F has entry 10 for state 7, and all other entries are either 3 or error. We may replace error by 3 and create for column F the list:

Current-state	Next-state	c
7	10	
any	3	

Similarly, a suitable list for column T is:

6	9
any	2

For column E we may choose, either 1 or 8 to be the default; two entries are necessary in either case. For example, we might create for column E the list:

4	8
any	1

$\square$

If the reader totals up the number of entries in the lists created in this example and the previous one, and then adds the pointers from states to action lists and from nonterminals to next-state lists, he will not be impressed with the space savings over the matrix implementation of Fig. 6.3. We should not be misled by this small example, however. For practical grammars, the space needed for the list representation is typically less than ten percent of that needed for the matrix representation. More importantly, the lists take up a small fraction of the main memory of a typical computer. The list representation is somewhat slower than the matrix representation. But while lookup in the parser table is a vital part of the compiling process, it takes only a tiny fraction of the total time, so the compiler is slowed down negligibly by the use of lists rather than matrices.

The double-array data structure discussed in Section 3.8 for implementing transition tables can also be adapted to the implementation of LR parsing tables. Such a scheme is more complex to implement but it combines the time efficiency of the matrix representation with the space efficiency of the list representation. It is the method used in YACC. The reader is referred to Section 3.8 for more details.

6.9 Constructing LALR Sets of Items

Let us briefly give some practical hints regarding how to write a program to construct the LALR sets of items for a grammar. The definition of the LALR sets-of-items construction implies that we should first construct a large collection of sets of items [the $LR(1)$ set] and then shrink that collection by merger [to the size of the $LR(0)$ set]. For economy of space, we would like an alternative approach that would use only an amount of space proportional to the size of the $LR(0)$ collection, rather than that of the $LR(1)$ collection.

Kernels

Our first point applies to all three types of LR parsers mentioned in this chapter. It is not necessary to store all the items in a set; the *kernel*, that is, those items not added in the closure, will do. Recall that we can recognize a kernel item because it is either $[S' \rightarrow \cdot S, \$]$, or it has a symbol to the left of the dot.

We can compute the parsing actions from the kernel alone. Any item calling for a reduction by $A \rightarrow \alpha$ will be in the kernel unless $\alpha = \epsilon$. Reduction by $A \rightarrow \epsilon$ is called for on input a if and only if there is a kernel item $B \rightarrow \beta \cdot C\gamma$, b such that $C \underset{rm}{\overset{*}{\Rightarrow}} A\delta$ for some δ, and a is in $\text{FIRST}(\delta\gamma b)$. The set of nonterminals A such that $C \underset{rm}{\overset{*}{\Rightarrow}} A\delta$ can be precomputed for all nonterminals C. Finally, the shift actions can be determined as follows. We shift on input a if there is a kernel item $[A \rightarrow \alpha \cdot B\beta, b]$ where $B \underset{rm}{\overset{*}{\Rightarrow}} ax$ in a derivation in which the last step does not use an ϵ-production. The set of such a's can also be precomputed for each B.

The goto entries can also be computed from the kernel as follows. If $[A \rightarrow \alpha \cdot X\beta, a]$ is in the kernel of I, then $[A \rightarrow \alpha X \cdot \beta, a]$ is in the kernel of $\text{GOTO}(I, X)$. Item $[A \rightarrow X \cdot \beta, a]$ is also in the kernel of $\text{GOTO}(I, X)$ if there is an item $[B \rightarrow \gamma \cdot D\delta, b]$ in the kernel of I, and $D \underset{rm}{\overset{*}{\Rightarrow}} Az$ for some z. If we precompute for each pair of nonterminals E and F whether $E \underset{rm}{\overset{*}{\Rightarrow}} F\theta$ for some θ, then computing sets of items from kernels only is just slightly less efficient than doing it with closed sets of items.

Propagating Lookaheads

By the above method we can begin computing the LALR(1) sets of items by computing the kernels of the collection of sets of LR(0) items. Then we can expand the LR(0) sets by attaching to each LR(0) item the proper lookahead symbols (second components).

To see how lookahead symbols propagate from a set of items I to GOTO(I, X), consider an LR(0) item $A \rightarrow B \cdot CD$ in the kernel of some set I. Suppose $C \underset{rm}{\overset{*}{\Rightarrow}} E\alpha$ for some α (perhaps $C = E$ and $\alpha = \epsilon$), and $E \rightarrow X\beta$ is a production. Then LR(0) item $E \rightarrow X \cdot \beta$ is in GOTO(I, X). Suppose now that we are computing not LR(0) items, but LR(1) items, and $[A \rightarrow B \cdot CD, a]$ is in set I_1. Then for what values of b will $[E \rightarrow X \cdot \beta, b]$ be in GOTO(I_1, X)? Certainly if some b is in FIRST(αD), then the derivation $C \underset{rm}{\overset{*}{\Rightarrow}} E\alpha$ tells us that $[E \rightarrow X \cdot \beta, b]$ must be in GOTO(I, X). In this case, the value of a is irrelevant, and we say that b, as a lookahead for $E \rightarrow X\beta$, is generated *spontaneously*.

But there is another source of lookaheads for $E \rightarrow X \cdot \beta$. If $\alpha D \overset{*}{\Rightarrow} \epsilon$, then $[E \rightarrow X \cdot \beta, a]$ will also be in GOTO(I_1, X). We say, in this case, that lookaheads *propagate* from $A \rightarrow B \cdot CD$ to $E \rightarrow X \cdot \beta$. A simple way to determine when an LR(1) item in I generates a lookahead in GOTO(I, X) spontaneously, and when lookaheads propagate, is contained in the next algorithm.

Algorithm 6.5. Determining lookaheads

Input. The kernel K of a set of LR(0) items I and a grammar symbol X.

Output. For each item $A \rightarrow \alpha X \cdot \beta$ in the kernel of GOTO(I, X), we produce the set of lookaheads generated spontaneously from items in I and those items in K that propagate lookaheads to $A \rightarrow \alpha X \cdot \beta$ in GOTO(I, X).

Method. The algorithm is given in Fig. 6.20. It uses a dummy lookahead symbol # to detect situations in which lookaheads propagate. □

Now let us consider how we go about finding all the lookaheads associated with all the items in all the kernels of the sets of LR(0) items. First, we know that $ is a lookahead for $S' \rightarrow \cdot S$ in the initial set of LR(0) items. Algorithm 6.5 gives us all the lookaheads generated spontaneously. After listing all those lookaheads, we must allow them to propagate until no further propagation is possible. There are many different approaches, all of which in some sense keep track of "new" lookaheads that have propagated to an item but which have not propagated out. We might, for example, keep a stack of triples consisting of (1) a set of items I, (2) an item $A \rightarrow \alpha \cdot \beta$ in the kernel of I, and (3) a lookahead a for $A \rightarrow \alpha \cdot \beta$ in I which has not yet been allowed to propagate to GOTO(I, X) for the various

for each item $B \to \gamma \cdot \delta$ in K **do**
    begin
        $J' := \text{CLOSURE}(\{[B \to \gamma \cdot \delta, \ \#]\})$
        if $[A \to \alpha \cdot X\beta, \ a]$ is in J', where a is not $\#$, **then**
            lookahead a is generated spontaneously for item
            $A \to \alpha X \cdot \beta$ in GOTO$(I, \ X)$;
        if $[A \to \alpha \cdot X\beta, \ \#]$ is in J', **then**
            lookaheads propagate from $B \to \gamma \cdot \delta$ in I to
            $A \to \alpha X \cdot \beta$ in GOTO$(I, \ X)$
    end

Fig. 6.20. Discovering propagated and spontaneous lookaheads.

grammar symbols X. The next algorithm describes this idea in detail.

Algorithm 6.6. Computing LALR(1) sets of items.

Input. A grammar G augmented by production $S' \to S$.

Output. The LALR(1) sets of items for G.

Method.
1. Construct the kernels of the LR(0) sets of items for G.
2. Use Algorithm 6.5 to determine for each set of LR(0) items I, for each $A \to \alpha \cdot \beta$ in the kernel of I, and for each grammar symbol X, to which items $B \to \gamma \cdot \delta$ in the kernel of GOTO$(I, \ X)$ do lookaheads propagate from $A \to \alpha \cdot \beta$ in I to $B \to \gamma \cdot \delta$ in GOTO$(I, \ X)$. Also determine which lookaheads are generated spontaneously for $B \to \gamma \cdot \delta$ in GOTO$(I, \ X)$.
3. We now create a stack called STACK of triples $(I, \ A \to \alpha \cdot \beta, \ a)$ where I is (a pointer to) a set of LR(0) items, $A \to \alpha \cdot \beta$ is an item in the kernel of I, and a is a terminal symbol such that $[A \to \alpha \cdot \beta, \ a]$ is in the set of LALR(1) items whose core is I. To avoid having the same triple appear twice on the stack, we keep a Boolean array ON, indexed by triples, such that ON$[I, \ A \to \alpha \cdot \beta, \ a]$ is **true** if and only if $(I, \ A \to \alpha \cdot \beta, \ a)$ has ever been on the stack, or equivalently, if a has previously been discovered to be a lookahead for $A \to \alpha \cdot \beta$ in I. We then use a procedure INSERT, shown in Fig. 6.21, to put triples on the stack if they are not already there.

The algorithm in Fig. 6.21 creates a list, for each set of LR(0) items I and for each $A \to \alpha \cdot \beta$ in the kernel of I, of the set of lookaheads for $A \to \alpha \cdot \beta$ in the set of LALR(1) items whose core is I. □

Example 6.19. Let us consider grammar (6.2), whose LR(0) sets of items are shown in Fig. 6.9. To begin, let us observe that there are only two items that cause spontaneous lookahead generation. $S' \to \cdot S$ has lookahead $\$$, of course. By line (3) of Fig. 6.19 we place $(I_0, \ S' \to \cdot S, \ \$)$ on STACK.

procedure INSERT(I, $A \rightarrow \alpha \cdot \beta$, a);
if not ON[I, $A \rightarrow \alpha \cdot \beta$, a] **then**
    begin
        push (I, $A \rightarrow \alpha \cdot \beta$, a) onto STACK;
        ON[I, $A \rightarrow \alpha \cdot \beta$, a] := **true**;
        add a to the list of lookaheads for $A \rightarrow \alpha \cdot \beta$ in I
    end;

	begin
(1)	**for all** I, $A \rightarrow \alpha \cdot \beta$ and a **do** ON[I, $A \rightarrow \alpha \cdot \beta$, a] := **false**;
(2)	STACK := empty;
(3)	INSERT(I_0, $S' \rightarrow \cdot S$, \$);
(4)	**for** each I, $A \rightarrow \alpha \cdot \beta$ and a such that a is spontaneously generated as a lookahead for $A \rightarrow \alpha \cdot \beta$ in I **do**
(5)	INSERT(I, $A \rightarrow \alpha \cdot \beta$, a);
(6)	**while** STACK not empty **do**
	begin
(7)	pop (J, $B \rightarrow \gamma \cdot \delta$, a), the top triple on STACK off of STACK;
(8)	**for** each grammar symbol X **do**
(9)	**for** each $A \rightarrow \alpha \cdot \beta$ in the kernel of GOTO(J, X) such that $B \rightarrow \gamma \cdot \delta$ in J propagates lookaheads to $A \rightarrow \alpha \cdot \beta$ in GOTO(J, X) **do**
(10)	INSERT(GOTO(J, X), $A \rightarrow \alpha \cdot \beta$, a)
	end
end	

Fig. 6.21. LALR(1) Sets of items construction.

The only other item that spontaneously generates lookaheads is $S \rightarrow \cdot L = R$. This item is in I_0, and if we recompute $I_0 = \text{CLOSURE}(\{[S' \rightarrow \cdot S, \#]\})$, as suggested in Algorithm 6.5, we find that $=$ is spontaneously generated as a lookahead for nonkernel items $L \rightarrow \cdot *R$ and $L \rightarrow \cdot \text{id}$. Thus, at line (4) of Fig. 6.19, we place (I_4, $L \rightarrow *\cdot R$, $=$) and (I_5, $L \rightarrow \text{id}\cdot$, $=$) on STACK.

The latter of these does not propagate lookaheads to any item in I_5, and since the dot in $L \rightarrow \text{id}\cdot$ is at the right end, no propagation of lookaheads from $L \rightarrow \text{id}\cdot$ in I_5 to kernel items of other states takes place. We next consider (I_4, $L \rightarrow *\cdot R$, $=$). Consulting lists of information precomputed by Algorithm 6.5, or recomputing closures as in that algorithm, we find that $L \rightarrow *\cdot R$ in I_4 propagates its lookaheads to $L \rightarrow *R\cdot$ in I_7, $R \rightarrow L\cdot$ in I_8, to $L \rightarrow \text{id}\cdot$ in I_5, and to itself in I_4. Thus we push (I_8, $R \rightarrow L\cdot$, $=$) and (I_7, $L \rightarrow *R\cdot$, $=$) onto STACK. We do not push (I_5, $L \rightarrow \text{id}\cdot$, $=$) or

$(I_4, L \rightarrow *\cdot R, =)$, since these have already been on STACK. Neither triple pushed propagates any new lookaheads, since their dots are at the right ends. Thus we eventually expose $(I_0, S' \rightarrow \cdot S, \$)$ on STACK. $S' \rightarrow \cdot S$ in I_0 propagates lookaheads to $S \rightarrow L\cdot = R$ in I_2, $S \rightarrow R\cdot$ in I_3, $R \rightarrow L\cdot$ in I_2. $L \rightarrow *\cdot R$ in I_4, $L \rightarrow \mathbf{id}\cdot$ in I_5, and $S' \rightarrow S\cdot$ in I_1. We thus place

$$(I_2, S \rightarrow L\cdot=R, \$)$$
$$(I_3, S \rightarrow R\cdot, \$)$$
$$(I_2, R \rightarrow L\cdot, \$)$$
$$(I_4, L \rightarrow *\cdot R, \$)$$
$$(I_5, L \rightarrow \mathbf{id}\cdot, \$)$$
$$(I_1, S' \rightarrow S\cdot, \$)$$

on STACK. The first and fourth of these yield new lookahead entries. The first causes us to place $(I_6, S \rightarrow L=\cdot R, \$)$ on STACK, which requires us to place

$$(I_9, S \rightarrow L=R\cdot, \$)$$
$$(I_8, R \rightarrow L\cdot, \$)$$

on STACK. We omit placing $(I_5, L \rightarrow \mathbf{id}\cdot, \$)$ or $(I_4, L \rightarrow *\cdot R, \$)$ on STACK since they have already been pushed once. $(I_9, S \rightarrow L=R\cdot, \$)$ and $(I_8, R \rightarrow L\cdot, \$)$ yield nothing. The next triple on the stack that adds something new is $(I_4, L \rightarrow *\cdot R, \$)$, which causes us to push $(I_7, L \rightarrow *R\cdot, \$)$ on STACK. This last triple propagates nothing, so we are done. The kernels of the ten sets of items and their lookaheads are shown in Fig. 6.22. Note that grammar (6.2) is LALR although it is not SLR. □

I_0: $S' \rightarrow \cdot S$, $\$$

I_1: $S' \rightarrow S\cdot$, $\$$

I_2: $S \rightarrow L\cdot=R$, $\$$
     $R \rightarrow L\cdot$, $\$$

I_3; $S \rightarrow R\cdot$, $\$$

I_4: $L \rightarrow *\cdot R$, $=/\$$

I_5: $L \rightarrow \mathbf{id}\cdot$, $=/\$$

I_6: $S \rightarrow L=\cdot R$, $\$$

I_7: $L \rightarrow *R\cdot$, $=/\$$

I_8: $R \rightarrow L\cdot$, $=/\$$

I_9: $S \rightarrow L=R\cdot$, $\$$

Fig. 6.22. Kernels with lookaheads.

Algorithm 6.6 has been designed for speed but may take up too much space to be practical. In particular, the size of the array ON and the maximum length to which STACK might grow are equal to the sum over all sets of LR(0) items (of which there might be several hundred) of the sum over all kernel items in the set (there might be more than one kernel item; the average is probably around two) of the number of lookaheads for that item (perhaps 10 is typical). The output itself is of this size, although we can represent the lists for each item by bit vectors and so reduce the required space to a reasonable amount.

One commonly used way way to save space is to use pairs $(I, A \rightarrow \alpha \cdot \beta)$ instead of triples. The implication of this choice is that when $(J, B \rightarrow \gamma \cdot \delta)$ is popped off the stack at line (7) of Fig. 6.21, we do not know what lookahead a caused $(J, B \rightarrow \gamma \cdot \delta)$ to be placed on the stack (when a was found to be a lookahead for $B \rightarrow \gamma \cdot \delta$ in J). Thus we must propagate all current lookaheads for $B \rightarrow \gamma \cdot \delta$ in J to the kernel items in GOTO(J, X) for each grammar symbol X. If any symbol b is propagated to any item $A \rightarrow \alpha \cdot \beta$ in GOTO(J, X) such that b was not already on the list for $A \rightarrow \alpha \cdot \beta$ in GOTO(J, X), then (GOTO(J, X), $A \rightarrow \alpha \cdot \beta$) is put on the stack. Thus the same pair may appear on the stack many times, but at most once per lookahead symbol for that pair, and perhaps many fewer times than that. There is some empirical evidence that a queue is superior to a stack here. The reason is that with a queue we may hold off considering pair $(I, A \rightarrow \alpha \cdot \beta)$ until we have many new lookaheads to propagate from that pair. In fact, for this reason, the modification suggested may actually speed up Algorithm 6.6 rather than slow it down.

An alternative approach, used in YACC, is to avoid a stack or queue altogether. Instead, visit each set of items in turn, propagating lookaheads from the items in that set to all its GOTO's. The algorithm terminates when no new symbols are propagated on one full pass through the items. There is similarity between this approach and data flow analysis techniques discussed in Chapter 14.

Exercises

6.1 Consider the grammar

$$S \rightarrow AS \mid b$$

$$A \rightarrow SA \mid a$$

a) List all the LR(0) items for the above grammar.
b) Construct an NFA whose states are the LR(0) items from (a). Show that the canonical collection of LR(0) items for the grammar is the same as the states of the equivalent DFA.

c) Is the grammar SLR? If so, construct the SLR parsing table.

d) Is the grammar LALR? LL(1)?

6.2 The following is an LALR (actually SLR as well) grammar for regular expressions over $\{a,b\}$, using $+$ for union and ϵ for the regular expression ϵ.

$$E \rightarrow E+T \mid T$$
$$T \rightarrow TF \mid F$$
$$F \rightarrow F^* \mid (E) \mid a \mid b \mid \epsilon$$

Construct the LALR sets of items and the parse table for the above grammar.

6.3 We might prefer to generate regular expressions using the ambiguous grammar

$$E \rightarrow E+E \mid EE \mid E^* \mid (E) \mid a \mid b \mid \epsilon$$

a) Give ambiguity-resolving declarations in the style of Section 6.7 that will cause regular expressions to be parsed normally.

b) Construct the LALR parser for the grammar with your ambiguity-resolving rules. Test out the parser to make sure it groups $a+ba^*$ and similar expressions properly.

**6.4 To generate a small NFA from a regular expression, it is useful to identify character strings in the syntax analysis of a regular expression. We might therefore wish to introduce the nonterminal S (not the start symbol), standing for "string," as follows:

$$E \rightarrow E+E \mid EE \mid E* \mid (E) \mid a \mid b \mid \epsilon \mid S$$
$$S \rightarrow aS \mid bS \mid \epsilon$$

a) Give ambiguity-resolving rules that will cause all maximal length strings of two or more consecutive a's and b's to be parsed as an S.

b) Construct the LALR parser for the grammar with your ambiguity rules.

6.5 For the grammars of Exercises 6.1 through 6.4, format their parsing tables according to the method of Section 6.8.

*6.6 Consider the ambiguous grammar G_n for n binary infix operators:

$$E \rightarrow E\theta_1 E \mid E\theta_2 E \mid \cdots \mid E\theta_n E \mid (E) \mid \mathbf{id}$$

Assume that all operators are left-associative and that θ_i takes precedence over θ_j if $i > j$.

a) Construct the LALR sets of items for G_n. How many sets of items are there, as a function of n?

b) Construct the LALR parsing table for G_n and implement it by the representation of Section 6.8. What is the total length of all the lists used in the representation, as a function of n?

c) How many steps does it take to parse **id** θ_i **id** θ_j **id**,

*6.7 Repeat Exercise 6.6 for the family of unambiguous grammars:

$$E_1 \rightarrow E_1 \theta_1 E_2 \mid E_2$$
$$E_2 \rightarrow E_2 \theta_2 E_3 \mid E_3$$
$$\vdots$$
$$E_n \rightarrow E_n \theta_n E_{n+1} \mid E_{n+1}$$
$$E_{n+1} \rightarrow (E_1) \mid \textbf{id}$$

What does your answer to Exercises 6.6 and 6.7 say about the relative space efficiency of parsers for equivalent ambiguous and unambiguous grammars? What about the relative efficiency of constructing the parser? Which is more important?

**6.8 Consider the family of grammars H_n defined by:

$$S \rightarrow A_i b_i \qquad 1 \leqslant i \leqslant n$$
$$A_i \rightarrow a_j A_i \mid a_j \qquad 1 \leqslant i, \; j \leqslant n \text{ and } j \neq i$$

a) Show that H_n has $2n^2 - n$ productions and $2^n + n^2 + n$ sets of LR(0) items. What does this exercise say about the maximum possible size of LR parsers?

b) Is H_n LALR? SLR?

*6.9 Give algorithms to compute for each nonterminal A

a) the set of nonterminals B such that $A \overset{*}{\Longrightarrow} B\alpha$ for some α, and

b) the set of terminals a such that $A \overset{*}{\underset{rm}{\Longrightarrow}} aw$ for some w, where the last step does not use an ϵ-production.

Bibliographic Notes

The fundamental paper on LR parsing is Knuth [1965]. However, the method was not deemed practical because of the size of the parsers generated until Korenjak [1969] gave a method of producing reasonable-sized parsers for practical languages. The SLR and LALR parser-construction algorithms, which are simpler than Korenjak's, are each due to DeRemer [1969, 1971]. Proofs of the validity of these methods can be found in Aho and Ullman [1972a, 1973a]. The simpler but more restrictive LR(0) parser is considered by Geller and Harrison [1973].

The use of ambiguous grammars for LR parsers is due to Aho, Johnson, and Ullman [1975] and Earley [1973]. El Djabri [1973b] shows how operator-precedence techniques can be used to derive LR-like parsers. It is not always possible to be sure that resolving ambiguities does not change the language accepted by the parser. Demers [1974] is an aid to proving that a parser accepts the language it is supposed to accept.

The implementation techniques suggested in Section 6.8 are due to Anderson, Eve, and Horning [1973], Lalonde, Lee, and Horning [1971], and Johnson [1975]. Similar ideas appear in the domain of bounded right-context parsers (Mickunas and Schneider [1973]). Joliat [1974] presents another idea—initially detecting error entries and then coding the tables in a way that takes advantage of the fact that error entries are really "don't care" entries.

The elimination of reductions by single productions (those of the form $A \rightarrow B$) has received much attention. Algorithms that do so have been proposed by Anderson, Eve, and Horning [1973], Aho and Ullman [1973b], Pager [1974], Demers [1975], Backhouse [1976], Joliat [1976], Lalonde [1976], and Soisalon-Soininen [1977]. There have also been attempts to generalize LR parsing to strategies that do not necessarily trace out a rightmost derivation in reverse. Szymanski and Williams [1976] typifies this approach. A general survey of LR parsing can be found in Aho and Johnson [1974].

CHAPTER 7

Syntax-
Directed
Translation

The previous four chapters have discussed regular expressions and context-free grammars, notations with which a compiler designer can express the lexical and syntactic structure of a programming language. In these chapters we saw that one could mechanically construct a program that would act as a recognizer for the set of strings defined by a regular expression or context-free grammar. It would be desirable to have similar notations for the remaining phases of compilation, but unfortunately, no such notations are known.

There is, however, a notational framework for intermediate code generation that is an extension of context-free grammars. This framework, called a *syntax-directed translation scheme,* allows subroutines or "semantic actions" to be attached to the productions of a context-free grammar. These subroutines generate intermediate code when called at appropriate times by a parser for that grammar. The syntax-directed translation scheme is useful because it enables the compiler designer to express the generation of intermediate code directly in terms of the syntactic structure of the source language. Unfortunately, there is no widely-accepted formalism, other than a general programming language, to describe the full range of semantic actions needed to produce intermediate code for typical programming languages.[†]

This chapter introduces the technique of syntax-directed translation. We show how to translate basic programming-language constructs such as arithmetic assignments, Boolean expressions, and flow-of-control statements into intermediate code using this technique. Chapter 8 continues this study of syntax-directed translation, covering more involved programming language constructs such as array references, procedure calls, declarations, switch statements and record-structure references.

---

† There are, however, certain languages such as FSL (Feldman [1966]) or the languages associated with many compiler writing systems (see the bibliographic notes of Chapter 1) which have dictions especially suitable for describing the generation of code.

Because of the great variety of ways in which syntax-directed translation can be used, we have been forced to limit our discussion in several ways. We discuss only translation from token streams to intermediate code, although we could also have discussed translation to machine or assembly code. Translation to the latter forms generally speeds up the compiler, although the translations are more difficult to write, and optimization of machine or assembly code is harder than optimization of intermediate code. We have focussed our discussion on syntax-directed translation done in conjunction with bottom-up parsing. The same ideas carry over to top-down parsing, and we give a brief example in Section 7.11. Finally, we have chosen to emphasize, although not exclusively, one form of intermediate code, called *three-address code,* and to concentrate on one implementation of this form, called *quadruples.*

7.1 Syntax-Directed Translation Schemes

In designing an intermediate-code generator, there are two basic issues. First we must decide what intermediate code we should generate for each programming language construct. Then we must implement an algorithm for generating this code.

Semantic Actions

In this chapter we shall use the formalism of *syntax directed translation schemes* to describe the output we wish to generate for each input construct. A syntax-directed translation scheme is merely a context-free grammar in which a program fragment called an *output action* (or sometimes a *semantic action* or *semantic rule*) is associated with each production. For example, suppose output action α is associated with production $A \rightarrow XYZ$. The action α is executed whenever the syntax analyzer recognizes in its input a substring w which has a derivation of the form $A \Rightarrow XYZ \overset{*}{\Rightarrow} w$. In a bottom-up parser, the action is taken when XYZ is reduced to A. In a top-down parser the action is taken when A, X, Y, or Z is expanded, whichever is appropriate.

The output action may involve the computation of values for variables belonging to the compiler, the generation of intermediate code, the printing of an error diagnostic, or the placement of some value in a table, for example. The values computed by action α quite frequently are associated with the parse tree nodes corresponding to the instance of A to which α is reduced.

A value associated with a grammar symbol is called a *translation* of that symbol. The translation may be a structure consisting of fields of various types. The rules for computing the value of a translation can be as involved as we wish.

We shall usually denote the translation fields of a grammar symbol X with names such as $X.\text{VAL}$, $X.\text{TRUE}$, and so forth. If we have a production with several instances of the same symbol on the right, we shall distinguish the symbols with superscripts. For example, suppose we have the production and semantic action

$$E \rightarrow E^{(1)} + E^{(2)} \quad \{E.\text{VAL} := E^{(1)}.\text{VAL} + E^{(2)}.\text{VAL}\}$$

The semantic action is enclosed in braces, and it appears after the production. Here the semantic action is a formula which states that the translation $E.\text{VAL}$ associated with the E on the left side of the production is determined by adding together the translations associated with the E's on the right side of the production. Note that the terminal symbol $+$ in the production is "translated" into its usual meaning by the semantic rule. This translation is suitable not for a compiler, but for a "desk calculator" program that actually evaluates expressions rather than generating code for them. In most compilers we need an action that generates code to perform the addition.

The action above is typical of many of the semantic actions we shall use. It defines the value of the translation of the nonterminal on the left side of the production as a function of the translations of the nonterminals on the right side. Such a translation is called a *synthesized translation.*

Consider the following production and action

$$A \rightarrow XYZ \quad \{Y.\text{VAL} := 2*A.\text{VAL}\}$$

Here the translation of a nonterminal on the right side of the production is defined in terms of a translation of the nonterminal on the left. Such a translation is called an *inherited translation.*

We shall use synthesized attributes exclusively. They are more natural than inherited translations for mapping most programming language constructs into intermediate code, and they can be implemented simply in conjunction with a bottom-up or top-down parser.

Translations on the Parse Tree

We now consider how the semantic actions define the values of translations. Consider the following syntax-directed translation scheme suitable for a "desk calculator" program, in which $E.\text{VAL}$ is an integer-valued translation.

Production	Semantic Action
$E \rightarrow E^{(1)} + E^{(2)}$	$\{E.\text{VAL} := E^{(1)}.\text{VAL} + E^{(2)}.\text{VAL}\}$
$E \rightarrow \textbf{digit}$	$\{E.\text{VAL} := \textbf{digit}\}$

Here **digit** stands for any digit between 0 and 9. Formally, the values of the translations are determined by constructing a parse tree for an input string and then computing the values the translations have at each node.

For example, suppose we have the input string 1+2+3. A parse tree for this string is shown in Fig. 7.1.

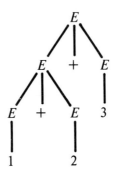

Fig. 7.1. Parse tree for expression $1+2+3$.

Consider the bottom leftmost E. This node corresponds to a use of the production $E \rightarrow 1$. The corresponding semantic action sets $E.\text{VAL}=1$. Thus we can associate the value 1 with the translation $E.\text{VAL}$ at the bottom leftmost E. Similarly, we can associate the value 2 with the translation $E.\text{VAL}$ at the right sibling of this node.

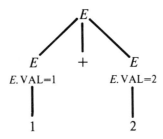

Fig. 7.2. Subtree with previously computed translations.

Now consider the subtree shown in Fig. 7.2. The value of $E.\text{VAL}$ at the root of this subtree is 3, which we calculate using the semantic rule

$$E.\text{VAL} := E^{(1)}.\text{VAL} + E^{(2)}.\text{VAL}$$

In applying this rule we substitute the value of $E.\text{VAL}$ of the bottom leftmost E for $E^{(1)}.\text{VAL}$ and the value of $E.\text{VAL}$ at its right sibling E for $E^{(2)}.\text{VAL}$.

Continuing in this manner we derive the values shown in Fig. 7.3 for the translations at each node of the complete parse tree.

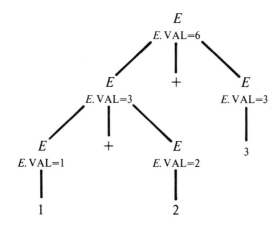

Fig. 7.3. Complete parse tree.

We see from this example that whenever we apply the rule

$$E.\,\mathrm{VAL} := E^{(1)}.\mathrm{VAL} + E^{(2)}.\mathrm{VAL}$$

the values of $E^{(1)}.\mathrm{VAL}$ and $E^{(2)}.\mathrm{VAL}$ have been computed by a previous application of this rule or the rule $E.\,\mathrm{VAL} := \textbf{digit}$. In general, when we define the formulas for computing the values of translations we must make sure that these formulas will work for all possible legal combinations of productions. That is to say, if we have a translation $A.\,\mathrm{VAL}$, then the formulas for all productions with an A on the left side must produce a value that can be used for every occurrence of $A.\,\mathrm{VAL}$ in a semantic rule associated with a production having A on the right.

We should point out that, although we have formally defined the value of a translation for A in terms of a node labeled A in a parse tree, in practice the parse tree often does not need to be constructed. The translation of A could be computed as we perform a reduction to A and its value could be placed on a stack to be accessed later.

7.2 Implementation of Syntax-Directed Translators

A syntax-directed translation scheme is a convenient description of what we would like done. The output defined is independent of the kind of parser used to construct the parse tree or the kind of mechanism used to compute the translations. Thus, a syntax-directed translation scheme provides a method for describing an input-output mapping, and that description is independent of any implementation. Another convenience of this approach is that it is easy to modify. New productions and semantic actions can often be added without disturbing the existing translations being computed.

Having written a syntax-directed translation scheme, our next task is to convert it into a program that implements the input-output mapping described. Ideally we would like to have a generator produce this program automatically. Before we consider this possibility, let us first examine what mechanisms can be used to implement a syntax-directed translator.

A useful, although not essential, requirement is that we have a bottom-up parser for the grammar. Some type of LR(1) parser would be quite adequate for most schemes. However, we must augment the parser with some mechanism for computing the translations. To compute the translation at a node A associated with a production $A \rightarrow XYZ$, we need only the values of the translations associated with nodes labeled X, Y and Z. These nodes will be roots of subtrees in the forest representing the partially constructed parse tree. The nodes X, Y, and Z will become children of node A after reduction by $A \rightarrow XYZ$. Once the reduction has occurred we do not need the translations of X, Y and Z any longer.

One way to implement a syntax-directed translator is to use extra fields in the parser stack entries corresponding to the grammar symbols. These extra fields hold the values of the corresponding translations. Let us suppose the stack is implemented by a pair of arrays STATE and VAL, as shown in Fig. 7.4. Each STATE entry is a pointer (or index) to the LR(1) parsing table. (Note that the grammar symbol is implicit in the state and need not be present explicitly.) It is convenient, however, to refer to the state by the unique grammar symbol which it covers when placed on the parsing stack as described in Chapter 6. If the ith STATE symbol is E, then VAL[i] will hold the value of the translation E.VAL associated with the parse tree node corresponding to this E.

TOP is a pointer to the current top of the stack. We assume semantic routines are executed just before each reduction. Before XYZ is reduced to A, the value of the translation of Z is in VAL[TOP], that of Y in VAL[TOP+1] and that of X in VAL[TOP+2]. After the reduction, TOP is incremented by 2 and the value of A.VAL appears in VAL[TOP].

Example 7.1. We shall now give an example of how a syntax-directed translation scheme can be used to specify a "desk calculator" program and how that translation scheme can be implemented by a bottom-up parser that invokes program fragments to compute the semantic actions.

The desk calculator is to evaluate arithmetic expressions involving integer operands and the operators $+$ and $*$. We assume that an input expression is terminated by $. The output is to be the numerical value of the input expression. For example, for the input expression 23*5+4$, the program is to produce the value 119.

To design such a translator, we must first write a grammar to describe the inputs. We use the nonterminals S (for complete sentence), E (for

STATE   VAL

TOP →

Z	Z.VAL
Y	Y.VAL
X	X.VAL
	.
	.
	.

Fig. 7.4. Stack before reduction.

expression) and I (for integer). The productions are

$$S \rightarrow E\$$$
$$E \rightarrow E+E$$
$$E \rightarrow E*E$$
$$E \rightarrow (E)$$
$$E \rightarrow I$$
$$I \rightarrow I \text{ digit}$$
$$I \rightarrow \text{digit}$$

We assume the usual precedence levels and associativities for the operators $+$ and $*$ (see Example 5.7). The terminals are \$, $+$, $*$, parentheses and **digit**, which we assume stands for any of the digits 0, 1, . . . , 9.

We must now add the semantic actions to the productions. With each of the nonterminals E and I we associate one integer-valued translation, called E.VAL and I.VAL, respectively, which denotes the numerical value of the expression or integer represented by a node of the parse tree labeled E or I. With the terminal **digit** we associate the translation LEXVAL, which we assume is the second component of the pair (**digit**, LEXVAL) returned by the lexical analyzer when a token of type digit is found.

One possible set of semantic actions for the desk calculator grammar is shown in Fig. 7.5. Using this syntax-directed translation scheme, the input 23*5+4\$ would have the parse tree and translations shown in Fig. 7.6.

To implement this syntax-directed translation scheme we need to construct a lexical analyzer and a bottom-up parser, and we must make the parser invoke a program fragment to implement a semantic action just before making each reduction. A compiler-compiler would tie the parser

Production	Semantic Action
(1) $S \rightarrow E \,\$$	{**print** $E.\mathrm{VAL}$}
(2) $E \rightarrow E^{(1)} + E^{(2)}$	{$E.\mathrm{VAL} := E.^{(1)}\mathrm{VAL} + E.^{(2)}\mathrm{VAL}$}
(3) $E \rightarrow E^{(1)} * E^{(2)}$	{$E.\mathrm{VAL} := E.^{(1)}\mathrm{VAL} * E.^{(2)}\mathrm{VAL}$}
(4) $E \rightarrow (E^{(1)})$	{$E.\mathrm{VAL} := E.^{(1)}\mathrm{VAL}$}
(5) $E \rightarrow I$	{$E.\mathrm{VAL} := I.\mathrm{VAL}$}
(6) $I \rightarrow I^{(1)}$ **digit**	{$I.\mathrm{VAL} := 10 * I.^{(1)}\mathrm{VAL} + \mathrm{LEXVAL}$}
(7) $I \rightarrow$ **digit**	{$I.\mathrm{VAL} := \mathrm{LEXVAL}$}

Fig. 7.5. Syntax-directed translation scheme for desk calculator.

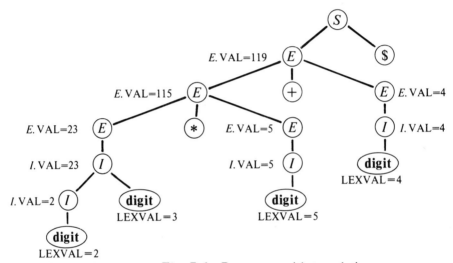

Fig. 7.6. Parse tree with translations.

and the semantic action program fragments together, producing one module.

The construction of the lexical analyzer is easy. We assume the lexical analyzer scans the input and partitions it into tokens, which here are just the terminals of the grammar. Every time the parser calls for a shift and needs the next token, the lexical analyzer skips over blanks to find the next nonblank input symbol, which will be one of the terminals. In the case that one of 0, 1, ... , 9 is the next nonblank, the lexical analyzer returns the token **digit** and a value, denoted LEXVAL, which will be the numerical value of the digit found.

We can use the techniques of Section 6.5 to construct an LR(1) parser for this grammar. To implement the semantic actions we cause the parser to execute the program fragments of Fig. 7.7 just after making the

Production	Program Fragment
(1) $S \rightarrow E \, \$$	**print** VAL[TOP]
(2) $E \rightarrow E + E$	VAL[TOP] := VAL[TOP] + VAL[TOP−2]
(3) $E \rightarrow E * E$	VAL[TOP] := VAL[TOP] * VAL[TOP−2]
(4) $E \rightarrow (E)$	VAL[TOP] := VAL[TOP−1]
(5) $E \rightarrow I$	none
(6) $I \rightarrow I$ **digit**	VAL[TOP] := 10 * VAL[TOP] + LEXVAL
(7) $I \rightarrow$ **digit**	VAL[TOP] := LEXVAL

Fig. 7.7. Implementation of desk calculator.

appropriate reduction.

Figure 7.8 shows the sequence of moves made by the parser on input 23*5+4$. The contents of the STATE and VAL fields of the parsing stack are shown after each move. We have again taken the liberty of replacing stack states by their corresponding grammar symbols. We take the further liberty of using, instead of **digit** on the stack, its associated LEXVAL.

	Input	STATE	VAL	Production Used
(1)	23*5+4$	_	_	
(2)	3*5+4$	2	_	
(3)	3*5+4$	I	2	$I \rightarrow$ **digit**
(4)	*5+4$	I3	2 _	
(5)	*5+4$	I	(23)	$I \rightarrow I$ **digit**
(6)	*5+4$	E	(23)	$E \rightarrow I$
(7)	5+4$	$E*$	(23) _	
(8)	+4$	$E*5$	(23) _ _	
(9)	+4$	$E*I$	(23) _ 5	$I \rightarrow$ **digit**
(10)	+4$	$E*E$	(23) _ 5	$E \rightarrow I$
(11)	+4$	E	(115)	$E \rightarrow E*E$
(12)	4$	$E+$	(115) _	
(13)	$	$E+4$	(115) _ _	
(14)	$	$E+I$	(115) _ 4	$E \rightarrow$ **digit**
(15)	$	$E+E$	(115) _ 4	$E \rightarrow I$
(16)	$	E	(119)	$E \rightarrow E+E$
(17)	_	$E\$$	(119) _	
(18)	_	S	_	$S \rightarrow E\$$

Fig. 7.8. Sequence of moves.

Explanation of the first few moves should make this example clear. Consider the sequence of events on seeing the input symbol 2. In the first move the parser shifts the state corresponding to the token **digit** (whose LEXVAL is 2) onto the stack. (The state is represented by LEXVAL, which is 2.) On the second move the parser reduces by the production $I \rightarrow$ **digit** and then invokes the semantic action I.VAL = LEXVAL. The program fragment implementing this semantic action causes the VAL field of the stack entry for **digit** to acquire the value 2.

The remaining moves should now be clear. Note that after each reduction and semantic action the top of the VAL stack contains the value of the translation associated with the left side of the reducing production.

7.3 Intermediate Code

While the use of syntax-directed translation is not restricted to compiling, the latter is still the subject of this book, so let us now discuss the kinds of syntax-directed translations done most often in compilers. In many compilers the source code is translated into a language which is intermediate in complexity between a (high-level) programming language and machine code. Such a language is therefore called *intermediate code* or *intermediate text*. It is possible to translate directly from source to machine or assembly language in a syntax-directed way but, as we have mentioned, doing so makes generation of optimal, or even relatively good, code a difficult task.

The reason efficient machine or assembly language is hard to generate is that one is immediately forced to choose a particular register to hold the result of each computation, making the efficient use of registers difficult. Therefore one usually chooses for intermediate text a notation in which, as in assembly language, each statement involves at most one arithmetic operation or one test, but where, unlike in assembly language, the register in which each operation occurs is left unspecified. The usual intermediate text introduces symbols to stand for various temporary quantities such as the value of B*C in the source language expression A+B*C. Four kinds of intermediate code often used in compilers are *postfix notation, syntax trees, quadruples,* and *triples.* These forms are the subjects of the next three sections.

7.4 Postfix Notation

The ordinary (*infix*) way of writing the sum of a and b is with the operator in the middle: $a+b$. The *postfix* (or *postfix Polish*[†]) notation for the same expression places the operator at the right end, as $ab+$. In general, if e_1 and e_2 are any postfix expressions, and θ is any binary operator, the result of applying θ to the values denoted by e_1 and e_2 is indicated in postfix notation by $e_1e_2\theta$. No parentheses are needed in postfix notation because the position and arity (number of arguments) of the operators permits only one

---

† Named after the nationality of J. Lukasiewicz, the originator of the notation.

way to decode a postfix expression.

Example 7.2.

1. $(a+b)*c$ in postfix notation is $ab+c*$, since $ab+$ represents the infix expression $(a+b)$.
2. $a*(b+c)$ is $abc+*$ in postfix.
3. $(a+b)*(c+d)$ is $ab+cd+*$ in postfix.   □

Postfix notation can be generalized to k-ary operators for any $k \geqslant 1$. If k-ary operator θ is applied to postfix expressions $e_1, e_2, \ldots, e_k$, then the result is denoted by $e_1 e_2 \cdots e_k \theta$. If we know the arity of each operator, then we can uniquely decipher any postfix expression by scanning it from either end.

For example, consider the postfix string $ab+c*$. The righthand $*$ says that there are two arguments to its left. Since the next-to-rightmost symbol is c, a simple operand, we know c must be the second operand of $*$. Continuing to the left, we encounter the operator $+$. We now know the subexpression ending in $+$ makes up the first operand of $*$. Continuing in this way, we deduce that $ab+c*$ is "parsed" as $(((a,b)+),c)*$.

Example 7.3. Let us introduce a useful 3-ary *(ternary)* operator, the conditional expression. Let **if** e **then** x **else** y denote the expression whose value is x if $e \neq 0$ and y if $e = 0$. Using ? as a ternary postfix operator, we can represent this expression as $exy?$. The postfix form of the expression

$$\textbf{if } a \textbf{ then if } c-d \textbf{ then } a+c \textbf{ else } a*c \textbf{ else } a+b$$

is: $acd-ac+ac*?ab+?$.   □

One language that normally uses a postfix intermediate language is SNOBOL. In fact, SNOBOL is often interpreted rather than compiled. The output of the SNOBOL compiler is the intermediate code itself which is passed to an interpreter, which reads the intermediate code and executes it. (Some SNOBOL compilers exist, producing machine code heavily laced with subroutine calls.)

Evaluation of Postfix Expressions

Having generated postfix notation for an expression, we can evaluate it easily using a stack, either a hardware stack or one implemented in software. The general strategy is to scan the postfix code left to right. We push each operand onto the stack when we see it. If we encounter a k-ary operator, its first (leftmost) argument will be $k-1$ positions below the top on the stack, its last argument will be at the top, and in general, its ith argument is $k-i$ positions below the top. It is then easy to apply the operator to the top k values on the stack. These values are popped and the result of applying the k-ary operator is pushed onto the stack.

Example 7.4. Consider the postfix expression $ab+c*$ from Example 7.2. Suppose a, b, and c have values, 1, 3 and 5 respectively. To evaluate $13+5*$ we perform the following actions:

1. Stack 1.
2. Stack 3.
3. Add the two topmost elements, pop them off the stack, and then stack the result, 4.
4. Stack 5.
5. Multiply the two topmost elements, pop them off the stack, and then stack the result, 20.

The value on top of the stack at the end (here 20) is the value of the entire expression. □

Control Flow in Postfix Code

While postfix notation is useful for intermediate code if the language is mostly expressions, as SNOBOL is, there are problems when more than rudimentary flow of control must be handled. For example, our previous implementation of the conditional **if-then-else** operator causes the second and third arguments always to be evaluated, even though only one of them is used. Therefore, if operands are undefined or have side effects, the postfix implementation described above not only would be inefficient, but might be incorrect.

One solution is to introduce labels and conditional and unconditional jumps into the postfix code. The postfix code can then be stored in a one-dimensional array, with each word of the array being either an operator or operand. Operands are represented by pointers to the symbol table and operators by integer codes. To distinguish operators from operands, we might, for example, use negative integers for operator codes. In this implementation, a label is just an index into the array holding the code.

We also need an unconditional transfer operator **jump** and a variety of conditional jumps such as **jlt** or **jeqz**. The postfix expression l **jump** causes a transfer to label l. Expression e_1 e_2 l **jlt** causes a jump to l if postfix expression e_1 has a smaller value than postfix expression e_2. Expression e l **jeqz** causes a jump to l if e has the value zero. All jump and conditional jump operators cause their operands to be popped off the stack when evaluated, and no value is pushed onto the stack.

Example 7.5. Using the above jump operators, the conditional expression **if** e **then** x **else** y is expressed in postfix by e l_1 **jeqz** x l_2 **jump** l_1: y l_2:. Labels followed by a colon are not actually present in the code but are used to indicate positions in the code. The expression of Example 7.3 would be written

$$al_1 \text{ \textbf{jeqz} } cd-l_2 \text{ \textbf{jeqz} } ac+l_3 \text{ \textbf{jump} } l_2\text{: } ac*l_3 \text{ \textbf{jump} } l_1\text{: } ab+l_3\text{:} \qquad \square$$

Syntax-Directed Translation to Postfix Code

The production of postfix intermediate code for expressions is simple. It is described by the syntax-directed translation scheme in Fig. 7.9. Here E.CODE is a string-valued translation. The value of the translation E.CODE for the first production is the concatenation of the two translations $E^{(1)}$.CODE and $E^{(2)}$.CODE and the symbol **op**, which stands for any operator symbol. In the second rule we see that the translation of a parenthesized expression is the same as that for the unparenthesized expression. The third rule tells us that the translation of any identifier is the identifier itself.

Production	Semantic Action
$E \rightarrow E^{(1)}$ **op** $E^{(2)}$	$E.\text{CODE} := E^{(1)}.\text{CODE} \parallel$ $E^{(2)}.\text{CODE} \parallel \text{'}\textbf{op}\text{'}$
$E \rightarrow (E^{(1)})$	$E.\text{CODE} := E^{(1)}.\text{CODE}$
$E \rightarrow \textbf{id}$	$E.\text{CODE} := \textbf{id}$

Fig. 7.9. Syntax-directed translation scheme for infix-postfix translation.

The semantic actions in this translation scheme have a particularly simple form. The translation of the nonterminal on the left of each production is the concatenation of the translations of the nonterminals on the right in the same order as in the production, followed by some additional string (perhaps the empty string). Such a translation scheme is called *simple postfix*[†] and it can be implemented without a translation stack just by emitting the output string after each reduction.

Production	Program Fragment
$E \rightarrow E^{(1)}$ **op** $E^{(2)}$	{ **print op** }
$E \rightarrow (E^{(1)})$	{ }
$E \rightarrow \textbf{id}$	{ **print id** }

Fig. 7.10. Implementation of infix-postfix translation.

[†] The term "postfix" here refers to the fact that all output is emitted at the end of each production, not to the fact that postfix code is being produced. Simple postfix translations can produce any kind of output.

The program fragments of Fig. 7.10 can be used for the scheme above. Thus when we reduce by the production $E \rightarrow$ **id**, we emit the identifier. On reduction by $E \rightarrow (E)$ we emit nothing. When we reduce by $E \rightarrow E$ **op** E we emit the operator **op**. By so doing we generate the postfix equivalent of the infix expression.

For example, processing the input $a+b*c$, a syntax-directed infix-to-postfix translator based on an LR parser, resolving ambiguities in the usual way, would make the sequence of moves shown in Fig. 7.11. In this example we view a, b, c, $+$, and $*$ as lexical values (analogous to LEXVAL in the desk calculator of Section 7.2) associated with **id** and **op**.

1. shift a
2. reduce by $E \rightarrow$ **id** and print a
3. shift $+$
4. shift b
5. reduce by $E \rightarrow$ **id** and print b
6. shift $*$
7. shift c
8. reduce by $E \rightarrow$ **id** and print c
9. reduce by $E \rightarrow E$ **op** E and print $*$
10. reduce by $E \rightarrow E$ **op** E and print $+$

Fig. 7.11. Sequence of moves.

7.5 Parse Trees and Syntax Trees

The parse tree itself is a useful intermediate-language representation for a source program, especially in optimizing compilers where the intermediate code needs to be extensively restructured. A parse tree, however, often contains redundant information which can be eliminated, thus producing a more economical representation of the source program. One such variant of a parse tree is what is called an (*abstract*) *syntax tree,* a tree in which each leaf represents an operand and each interior node an operator.

Example 7.6. The syntax tree for the expression $a*(b+c)/d$ is shown in Fig. 7.12(a). The syntax tree for statement **if** $a=b$ **then** $a:=c+d$ **else** $b:=c-d$ is shown in Fig. 7.12(b). □

Syntax-Directed Construction of Syntax Trees

Like postfix code, it is easy to define either a parse tree or a syntax tree in terms of a syntax-directed translation scheme. The scheme in Fig. 7.13 defines expressions. $E.\text{VAL}$ is a translation whose value is a pointer to a node in the syntax tree.

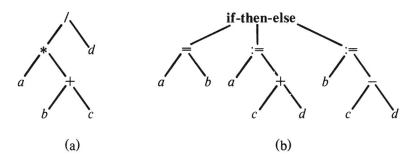

Fig. 7.12. Syntax trees.

Production	Semantic Action
(1) $E \rightarrow E^{(1)}$ **op** $E^{(2)}$	$\{E.\text{VAL} := \text{NODE}(\textbf{op}, E^{(1)}.\text{VAL}, E^{(2)}.\text{VAL})\}$
(2) $E \rightarrow (E^{(1)})$	$\{E.\text{VAL} := E^{(1)}.\text{VAL}\}$
(3) $E \rightarrow -E^{(1)}$	$\{E.\text{VAL} := \text{UNARY}(-, E^{(1)}.\text{VAL})\}$
(4) $E \rightarrow \textbf{id}$	$\{E.\text{VAL} := \text{LEAF}(\textbf{id})\}$

Fig. 7.13. Syntax-directed translation scheme to construct syntax trees.

The function NODE(OP, LEFT, RIGHT) takes three arguments. The first is the name of the operator, the second and third are pointers to roots of subtrees. The function creates a new node labeled by the first argument and makes the second and third arguments the left and right children of the new node, returning a pointer to the created node. The function UNARY(OP, CHILD) creates a new node labeled OP and makes CHILD its child. Again, a pointer to the created node is returned. The function LEAF(ID) creates a new node labeled by ID and returns a pointer to that node. This node receives no children. In practice the label of the leaf would be a representation of a particular name, such as a pointer to the symbol table.

7.6 Three-Address Code, Quadruples, and Triples

We shall now introduce our final category of intermediate code, known as three-address code. This intermediate code is preferred in many compilers, especially those doing extensive code optimization, since it allows the intermediate code to be rearranged in a convenient manner.

Three-Address Code

Three-address code is a sequence of statements, typically of the general form A := B **op** C, where A, B, and C are either programmer-defined names, constants or compiler-generated temporary names; **op** stands for any operator, such as a fixed- or floating-point arithmetic operator, or a logical operator on Boolean-valued data. The reason for the name "three-address code" is that each statement usually contains three addresses, two for the operands and one for the result. Note that no complicated arithmetic expressions are permitted, as there is only one operator per statement. Thus an expression like X + Y * Z would be "unraveled" to yield

$$T_1 := Y * Z$$
$$T_2 := X + T_1$$

where T_1 and T_2 are compiler-generated temporary names. It is this unravelling of complicated arithmetic expressions and of nested flow-of-control statements that makes three-address code more suitable for object-code generation than the source program itself would be.

Additional Three-Address Statements

There are a number of types of three-address statements that involve fewer than three addresses, or in which one of the "addresses" is not a name. In the following paragraphs we catalog the common kinds of three-address statements that we shall use in this book.

1. Assignment statements of the form A := B **op** C, where **op** is a binary arithmetic or logical operation. These instructions have been mentioned in the example above.
2. Assignment instructions of the form A := **op** B, where **op** is a unary operation. Essential unary operations include unary minus, logical negation, shift operators, and conversion operators that, for example, convert a fixed-point number to a floating-point number. An important special case of **op** is the identity function where A := B means that the value of B is assigned to A.
3. The unconditional jump **goto** L. The meaning of this instruction is to execute next the L*th* three-address statement.
4. Conditional jumps such as **if** A **relop** B **goto** L. This instruction applies relational operator **relop** ($<, =, \geqslant$, etc.) to A and B, and executes statement L next if A stands in relation **relop** to B. If not, the three-address statement following **if** A **relop** B **goto** L is executed next, as in the usual sequence.
5. **param** A and **call** P, *n*. These instructions are used to implement a procedure call. The typical use is as the sequence of three-address statements

> **param** A_1
> **param** A_2
> .
> .
> .
> **param** A_n
> **call** P, n

generated as part of a call of procedure $P(A_1, A_2, \ldots, A_n)$. The n in "**call** P, n" is an integer indicating the number of actual parameters in the call. This information is redundant, as n can be computed by counting the number of **param** statements. It is a convenience to have n available with the **call** statement, however. Procedure calls will be discussed in more detail in Section 8.2.

6. Indexed assignments of the form A := B[I] and A[I] := B. The first of these sets A to the value in the location I memory units beyond location B. A[I] = B sets the location I units beyond A to the value of B. In both these instructions, A, B, and I are assumed to refer to data objects and will be represented by pointers to the symbol table.

7. Address and pointer assignments of the form A := **addr** B, A=*B, and *A=B. The first of these sets the value of A to be the location of B. Presumably B is a name, perhaps a temporary, which denotes an expression with an *l-value* such as X[I, J]. A is a pointer name or temporary. That is, the *r*-value of A is the *l-value* (location) of something else. In A:=*B, presumably B is a pointer or a temporary whose *r*-value is a location. The *r-value* of A is made equal to the contents of that location. Finally, *A:=B sets the *r*-value of the object pointed to by A to the *r*-value of B.

The three-address statement is an abstract form of intermediate code. In an actual compiler these statements can be implemented in one of the following ways.

Quadruples

We may use a record structure with four fields, which we shall call OP, ARG1, ARG2, and RESULT. This representation of three-address statements is known as *quadruples*. OP contains an internal code for the operator. There are actually two levels of specificity which the OP field may have. We may, as we translate to intermediate code, determine whether a binary operator like * means fixed- or floating-point multiplication, or perhaps another kind of multiplication, using a different operator code for different meanings. The next section contains an example of how we can determine the meaning for operators like *, introducing coercion of data types where necessary. The alternative is to use only one code for *, leaving it to the object code generation phase to do the semantic checking, introduce the type coercions, and determine what type of multiplication is meant.

A three-address statement A := B **op** C puts B in ARG1, C in ARG2, and A in RESULT. Let us adopt the convention that statements with unary operators like A := −B or A:=B do not use ARG2. Operators like **param** use neither ARG2 nor RESULT. Conditional and unconditional jumps put the target label in RESULT.

Example 7.7. An assignment statement like A := −B∗(C+D) would be translated to three-address statements, using the straightforward algorithm of the next section, as follows.

$$T_1 := -B$$
$$T_2 := C+D$$
$$T_3 := T_1*T_2$$
$$A := T_3$$

These statements are represented by quadruples as shown in Fig. 7.14.   □

	OP	ARG1	ARG2	RESULT
(0)	uminus	B	–	T_1
(1)	+	C	D	T_2
(2)	*	T_1	T_2	T_3
(3)	:=	T_3	–	A

Fig. 7.14. Quadruple representation of three-address statements.

The contents of fields ARG1, ARG2, and RESULT are normally pointers to the symbol-table entries for the names represented by these fields. If so, temporary names must be entered into the symbol table as created. Chapter 10 describes ways in which temporary names can be reused to avoid cluttering up the symbol table.

Triples

To avoid entering temporary names into the symbol table, one can allow the statement computing a temporary value to represent that value. If we do so, three-address statements are representable by a structure with only three fields OP, ARG1 and ARG2, where ARG1 and ARG2, the arguments of OP, are either pointers to the symbol table (for programmer-defined names or constants) or pointers into the structure itself (for temporary values). Since three fields are used, this intermediate code format is known as *triples.*[†]

We use parenthesized numbers to represent pointers into the triple structure, while symbol-table pointers are represented by the names themselves. In practice, the information needed to interpret the different kinds of entries in the ARG1 and ARG2 fields can be encoded into the OP field or some additional fields.

Example 7.8. The three-address code from Example 7.7 can be implemented in triple form as shown in Fig. 7.15.

	OP	ARG1	ARG2
(0)	**uminus**	B	_
(1)	+	C	D
(2)	*	(0)	(1)
(3)	:=	A	(2)

Fig. 7.15. Triple representation of three-address statements.

A ternary operation like A[I] := B actually requires two entries in the triple structure, as shown in Fig. 7.16(a), while A := B[I] is naturally represented as in Fig. 7.16(b).

	OP	ARG1	ARG2
(0)	[ ]=	A	I
(1)	_	B	_

	OP	ARG1	ARG2
(0)	=[ ]	B	I
(1)	:=	(0)	A

(a)   (b)

Fig. 7.16. More triple representations.

Indirect Triples

Another implementation of three-address code which has been considered is that of listing pointers to triples, rather than listing the triples themselves. This implementation is naturally called *indirect triples.*

Example 7.9. Let us use an array STATEMENT to list pointers to triples

---

† Some refer to triples as "two-address code," preferring to identify "quadruples" with the term "three-address code." We shall, however, treat "three-address code" as an abstract notion with various implementations, with triples and quadruples being the principal ones.

in the desired order. Then the three-address statements of Example 7.7 might be represented as in Fig. 7.17. □

	STATEMENT		OP	ARG1	ARG2
(0)	(14)	(14)	uminus	B	–
(1)	(15)	(15)	+	C	D
(2)	(16)	(16)	*	(14)	(15)
(3)	(17)	(17)	:=	A	(16)

Fig. 7.17. Indirect triples representation of three-address statements.

Comparison of Representations: The Use of Indirection

We may regard the difference between triples and quadruples as a matter of how much indirection is present in the representation. When we ultimately produce object code, each datum, temporary or programmer-defined, will be assigned some memory location. This location will be placed in the symbol-table entry for the datum. Using the quadruple notation, the location for each temporary can be immediately accessed via the symbol table, from where it is needed — at the three-address statements defining or using that temporary. If the triples notation is used, we have no idea, unless we scan the code, how many temporaries are active simultaneously, or how many words must be allocated for temporaries; so with triples the assignment of locations to temporaries is usually deferred to code generation.

A more important benefit of quadruples appears in an optimizing compiler, where we often move statements around. Using the quadruple notation, the symbol table interposes an extra degree of indirection between the computation of a value and its use. If we move a statement computing A, the statements using A require no change. However, in the triples notation, moving a statement that defines a temporary value requires us to change all pointers to that statement in the ARG1 and ARG2 arrays. This problem makes triples difficult to use in an optimizing compiler.

Indirect triples present no such problem. To move a statement we simply reorder the STATEMENT list. Since pointers to temporary values refer to the OP-ARG1-ARG2 arrays, which are not changed, none of those pointers need be changed. Thus, indirect triples look very much like quadruples as far as their utility is concerned. The two notations require about the same amount of space and they are equally efficient for reordering of code. As with ordinary triples, allocation of storage to those temporaries needing it must be deferred to the code generation phase. However, indirect triples can save some space compared with quadruples if the same temporary value is used more than once. This is because two or more entries in the STATEMENT array can point to the same line of the OP-

ARG1-ARG2 structure.

Quadruples present the problem that they tend to clutter up the symbol table with temporary names. If we use integer codes for temporaries and do not enter temporaries in the symbol table, we have the same problem as with triples when we assign locations to temporaries. In Chapter 10 we shall discuss methods of reusing temporary names to avoid this disadvantage of quadruples.

Single Array Representations

Both triples and quadruples waste some space, since fields will occasionally be empty. If space is important, one can use a single array and store either triples or quadruples consecutively. Since the operator determines which fields are actually in use, we can decode the single array if we follow each operator by those of ARG1, ARG2 and RESULT (if quadruples are being stored) which are actually in use. For example, the quadruples of Fig. 7.15 can be represented linearly as **uminus**, B, T_1, $+$, C, D, T_2, $*$, T_1, T_2, T_3, $:=$, T_3, A.

The disadvantage of this representation is seen if we try to examine the statements in reverse order, since we cannot tell just by looking at a word whether it represents an operator or operand. This problem is not artificial. For example, we shall see in Chapter 15 how code generation is facilitated if we preprocess triples or quadruples in a backward scan.

7.7 Translation of Assignment Statements

Because of the relative difficulty and importance of translation to three-address code, we shall consider translation of basic programming-language constructs into code of this form here and in the next two sections. Let us now give a syntax-directed translation scheme for simple assignment statements. To simplify the problem we assume that all identifiers denote primitive data types. In Chapter 8 we take up translation of expressions with array and record-structure references. Here, we begin with a simple scheme in which semantic checking is not necessary. Then we consider what happens when operands can have a variety of types. The output of the translation is three-address code in each case; modifications to produce the other kinds of intermediate code are not hard.

Assignment Statements With Integer Types

Let us begin by considering simple assignment statements involving only integer variables. The following grammar describes the form of the assignment statements.

$$A \rightarrow \textbf{id} := E$$

$$E \rightarrow E + E \mid E * E \mid -E \mid (E) \mid \textbf{id}$$

Here A stands for an assignment statement. We show only the two binary operators $+$ and $*$ as examples of the full operator set that would be present in a typical language. Operator associativities and precedences are the usual ones. Example 7.7 showed a typical assignment statement generated by this grammar and gave its translation into three-address code.

In general, the three-address code for **id** $:= E$ consists of code to evaluate E into some name T, followed by the assignment X $:=$ T, where X is the name corresponding to **id** on the left of the assignment. To evaluate an expression of the form $E+E$, for example, we first evaluate the expression on the left, then the expression on the right of the $+$ sign, using two temporary names, say T_1 and T_2, to hold the values of the expressions. We then add T_1 and T_2, giving the result a new temporary name, say T_3.†

There are two levels on which we wish to discuss the translation scheme that reflects the above notion of what the translation of simple assignment statements should be. On the abstract level we can formalize and generalize the above discussion of expressions of the form $E+E$. At the next lower level we discuss how to actually generate the translation as a sequence of three-address statements.

The Abstract Translation Scheme

Abstractly, we wish the translation of E to be a structure with two fields:

1. E.PLACE, the name that will hold the value of the expression, and
2. E.CODE, a sequence of three-address statements evaluating the expression.

For the translation of A there is one field, A.CODE, which is three-address code to execute the assignment. We also use **id**.PLACE to denote the name corresponding to this instance of token **id**.

To create new temporary names we use a function NEWTEMP( ), which returns an appropriate name. We shall assume NEWTEMP( ) returns $T_1, T_2, \ldots$ in response to successive calls. Figure 7.18 shows the abstract translation scheme.

---

† There is good reason for not using one of T_1 and T_2 in place of T_3. If one or both E's in $E+E$ were a single identifier, say Y, the "expression" Y would be "evaluated" with no code at all, and Y would be T_1 or T_2. If we blindly reused one of T_1 and T_2 we might wind up assigning a new value to Y.

Production	Semantic Action
(1) $A \rightarrow$ **id** $:= E$	$\{A.\text{CODE} := E.\text{CODE} \parallel$ **id**.PLACE $\parallel \; ':=' \parallel E.\text{PLACE} \}$
(2) $E \rightarrow E^{(1)} + E^{(2)}$	$\{ \text{T} := \text{NEWTEMP( )};$ $E.\text{PLACE} := \text{T};$ $E.\text{CODE} := E^{(1)}.\text{CODE} \parallel E^{(2)}.\text{CODE} \parallel$ $E.\text{PLACE} \parallel \; ':=' \parallel E^{(1)}.\text{PLACE} \parallel \; '+' \parallel E^{(2)}.\text{PLACE} \}$
(3) $E \rightarrow E^{(1)} * E^{(2)}$	$\{ \text{T} := \text{NEWTEMP( )};$ $E.\text{PLACE} := \text{T};$ $E.\text{CODE} := E^{(1)}\text{CODE} \parallel E^{(2)}.\text{CODE} \parallel$ $E.\text{PLACE} \parallel \; ':=' \parallel E^{(1)}.\text{PLACE} \parallel \; '*' \parallel E^{(2)}.\text{PLACE}$
(4) $E \rightarrow -E^{(1)}$	$\{ \text{T} := \text{NEWTEMP( )};$ $E.\text{PLACE} := \text{T};$ $E.\text{CODE} := E^{(1)}.\text{CODE} \parallel$ $E.\text{PLACE} \parallel \; ':= \; -' \parallel E^{(1)}.\text{PLACE} \}$
(5) $E \rightarrow (E^{(1)})$	$\{ E.\text{PLACE} := E^{(1)}.\text{PLACE};$ $E.\text{CODE} := E^{(1)}.\text{CODE} \}$
(6) $E \rightarrow$ **id**	$\{ E.\text{PLACE} := \textbf{id}.\text{PLACE};$ $E.\text{CODE} := \textbf{null} \}$

Fig. 7.18. Abstract translation scheme.

A More Concrete Translation Scheme

Let us now fill in some of the details regarding the scheme of Fig. 7.18. First, $E.$PLACE and **id**.PLACE can be represented by symbol-table pointers, and these pointers can be stored on the parsing stack of a bottom-up parser along with their corresponding grammar symbols. $E.$CODE and $A.$CODE do not have to be attached to a parse tree either, which is fortunate as it could be quite time-consuming if we had to repeatedly copy sequences of three-address statements as implied by Fig. 7.18. If we look at that scheme, we note that the CODE translations satisfy the conditions introduced in Section 7.4 for a simple postfix translation. That is, CODE for the nonterminal on the left is the concatenation of CODE for each nonterminal on the right, in order, followed by a string, the *tail* of the translation. For example, the tail in rule (4) is "$E.$PLACE $:= - E^{(1)}.$PLACE," and the tail in rule (5) is the empty string.

For notational convenience, we shall use a procedure GEN(A := B + C) to emit the three-address statement A := B + C with actual values substituted for A, B, and C. In practice, GEN would enter the operator +, and the values of A, B, and C into the quadruple array.

We can now modify the scheme of Fig. 7.18 in the following way. We remove the assignments to A.CODE and E.CODE from each rule and replace them by the calls to GEN indicated in Fig. 7.19.

Production	Call to GEN
(1)	GEN(**id**.PLACE := E.PLACE)
(2)	GEN(E.PLACE := $E^{(1)}$.PLACE + $E^{(2)}$.PLACE)
(3)	GEN(E.PLACE := $E^{(1)}$.PLACE * $E^{(2)}$.PLACE)
(4)	GEN(E.PLACE := $-E^{(1)}$.PLACE)
(5)	none
(6)	none

Fig. 7.19. Calls to GEN replacing CODE definitions.

Example 7.10. The action of a bottom-up parser making the proper shift-reduce decisions to reflect the usual associativity and precedence of operators is shown in Fig. 7.20 operating on A := −B*(C+D). The field PLACE is carried along with grammar symbols in the stack but shown on a stack of its own. Generated three-address statements are shown with the step just before they are generated. □

In subsequent translations into three-address code we shall find that the abstract scheme usually has a translation field like CODE which represents the desired output and is in simple postfix form. Other fields are easily carried on the stack. We shall describe the abstract translation only informally and go directly to an implementation using GEN.

Assignment Statements with Mixed Types

In the example above, all **id**'s are assumed to be of the same type. In practice, there would be many different types of variables and constants, so the compiler must either reject certain mixed-mode operations or generate appropriate coercion (mode conversion) instructions.

Example 7.11. Consider the grammar for assignment statements as above, but suppose there are two modes — real and integer, with integers converted to reals when necessary. We can have an additional field in the translation of E, namely E.MODE, whose value is either REAL or INTEGER. The semantic rule for E.MODE associated with the production

$E \rightarrow E + E$, say, is just:

$E \rightarrow E + E$ {**if** $E^{(1)}$.MODE = INTEGER **and** $E^{(2)}$.MODE = INTEGER
then E.MODE := INTEGER
else E.MODE := REAL }

The entire semantic rule for $E \rightarrow E + E$ and most of the other productions must be modified to generate, when necessary, three-address statements of the form A := **inttoreal** B, whose effect is to convert integer B to a real of equal value, called A. We must also include with the operator code an indication of whether fixed- or floating-point arithmetic is intended.

The complete semantic action for a production of the form $E \rightarrow E^{(1)}$ **op** $E^{(2)}$ is listed in Fig. 7.21.

For example, for the input

$$X := Y + I * J$$

assuming X and Y have mode REAL, and I and J have mode INTEGER, the output would look like

Input	Stack	PLACE	Generated Code
A := −B∗(C+D)			
:= −B∗(C+D)	**id**	A	
−B∗(C+D)	**id** :=	A _	
B∗(C+D)	**id** := −	A _ _	
∗(C+D)	**id** := −**id**	A _ _ B	
∗(C+D)	**id** := −E	A _ _ B	$T_1 := -B$
∗(C+D)	**id** := E	A _ T_1	
(C+D)	**id** := $E∗$	A _ T_1 _	
C+D)	**id** := $E∗($	A _ T_1 _ _	
+D)	**id** := $E∗($**id**	A _ T_1 _ _ C	
+D)	**id** := $E∗(E$	A _ T_1 _ _ C	
D)	**id** := $E∗(E+$	A _ T_1 _ _ C _	
)	**id** := $E∗(E+$**id**	A _ T_1 _ _ C _ D	
)	**id** := $E∗(E+E$	A _ T_1 _ _ C _ D	$T_2 := C+D$
)	**id** := $E∗(E$	A _ T_1 _ _ T_2	
	id := $E∗(E)$	A _ T_1 _ _ T_2 _	
	id := $E∗E$	A _ T_1 _ T_2	$T_3 := T_1∗T_2$
	id := E	A _ T_3	A := T_3
	A		

Fig. 7.20. Trace of syntax-directed translation.

$T_1 := I$ **int** $*$ J

$T_2 :=$ **inttoreal** T_1

$T_3 := Y$ **real** $+ T_2$

$X := T_3$

The semantic rule of Fig. 7.21 uses two translation fields $E.\text{PLACE}$ and $E.\text{MODE}$ for the nonterminal E. The translator would therefore need two fields on the translation stack to implement this translation scheme. As the number of modes increases, the number of cases that arise increases quadratically (or worse, if there are operators with more than two arguments). Therefore with large numbers of modes, careful encoding of the semantic rules becomes more important.

```
T := NEWTEMP( );
```
if $E^{(1)}.\text{MODE} = \text{INTEGER}$ **and** $E^{(2)}.\text{MODE} = \text{INTEGER}$ **then**
> **begin**
>> GEN(T := $E^{(1)}$.PLACE **int op** $E^{(2)}$.PLACE);
>> $E.$MODE := INTEGER
>
> **end**

else if $E^{(1)}.\text{MODE} = \text{REAL}$ **and** $E^{(2)}.\text{MODE} = \text{REAL}$ **then**
> **begin**
>> GEN(T := $E^{(1)}$.PLACE **real op** $E^{(2)}$.PLACE);
>> $E.$MODE := REAL
>
> **end**

else if $E^{(1)}.\text{MODE} = \text{INTEGER}$ /* **and** $E^{(2)}.\text{MODE} = \text{REAL}$ */ **then**
> **begin**
>> U := NEWTEMP( );
>> GEN(U := **inttoreal** $E^{(1)}$.PLACE);
>> GEN(T := U **real op** $E^{(2)}$.PLACE);
>> $E.$MODE := REAL
>
> **end**

else /* $E^{(1)}.\text{MODE} = \text{REAL}$ **and** $E^{(2)}.\text{MODE} = \text{INTEGER}$ */
> **begin**
>> U := NEWTEMP( );
>> GEN(U := **inttoreal** $E^{(2)}$.PLACE);
>> GEN(T := $E^{(1)}$.PLACE **real op** U);
>> $E.$MODE := REAL
>
> **end**;

$E.$PLACE := T

Fig. 7.21. Semantic rule for $E \rightarrow E^{(1)}$ **op** $E^{(2)}$.

7.8 Boolean Expressions

In programming languages, Boolean expressions have two primary functions. They are used as conditional expressions in statements that alter the flow of control, such as while- or if-then-statements, and they are also used to compute logical values. Boolean expressions are composed of the Boolean operators (**and**, **or**, and **not**) applied to elements that are Boolean variables or relational expressions. In turn, relational expressions are of the form E_1 **relop** E_2, where E_1 and E_2 are arithmetic expressions. Some languages, such as PL/I, allow more general expressions, where Boolean, arithmetic, and relational operators can be applied to expressions of any type whatever, with no distinction between Boolean and arithmetic values; a coercion is performed when necessary. To get the ideas across, let us assume the restricted form of expressions generated by the following grammar:

$$E \rightarrow E \text{ or } E \mid E \text{ and } E \mid \text{not } E \mid (E)$$
$$\mid \text{ id } \mid \text{ id relop id}$$

where **relop** is any of $<$, $\leqslant$, $=$, $\neq$, $>$, or $\geqslant$. As is customary, we assume that **or** and **and** are left-associative, and that **or** has lowest precedence, then **and**, then **not**.

Methods of Translating Boolean Expressions

There are two principal methods of representing the value of a Boolean expression. The first method is to encode **true** and **false** numerically and to evaluate a Boolean expression analogously to an arithmetic expression. Often 1 is used to denote **true** and 0 to denote **false**, although many other encodings are also possible. For example, we could let any nonzero quantity denote **true** and zero denote **false**, or we could let any nonnegative quantity denote **true** and any negative number denote **false**.

The second principal method of implementing Boolean expressions is by flow of control, that is, representing the value of a Boolean expression by a position reached in a program. This method is particularly convenient in implementing the Boolean expressions in flow of control statements, such as the if-then and while-do statements. However, neither scheme is uniformly superior to the other. For example, the BLISS/11 optimizing compiler (Wulf *et al.* 1975), among others, chooses the appropriate method for each expression individually.

This section considers both methods for the translation of Boolean expressions to three-address code. In addition to the three-address statements used in the previous sections, we shall also use branching statements of the form

> **goto** L
> **if** A **goto** L
> **if** A **relop** B **goto** L

where A and B are simple variables or constants, L is a quadruple label, and **relop** is any of $<$, $\leqslant$, $=$, $\neq$, $>$, or $\geqslant$.

Numerical Representation

Let us first consider the implementation of Boolean expressions using 1 to denote TRUE and 0 to denote FALSE. Expressions will be evaluated from left to right, in a manner similar to arithmetic expressions. For example, the translation for

> A **or** B **and** C

is the three-address sequence

$$T_1 := B \text{ and } C$$

$$T_2 := A \text{ or } T_1$$

We assume **and** and **or** are ultimately implemented by the logical operators of the target machine.

A relational expression such as A $<$ B is equivalent to the conditional statement **if** A $<$ B **then** 1 **else** 0, which can be translated into the three-address code sequence of Fig. 7.22(a).

> (1)   **if** A $<$ B **goto** (4)
> (2)   T := 0
> (3)   **goto** (5)
> (4)   T := 1
> (5)

Fig. 7.22(a). Translation of **if** A $<$ B **then** 1 **else** 0.

Thus the Boolean expression A $<$ B **or** C can be translated into the three-address code sequence shown in Fig. 7.22(b).

The semantic rules for the two productions $E \rightarrow E$ **or** E and $E \rightarrow$ **id relop id** are shown in Fig. 7.23. Similar rules can be defined for

> (1)   **if** A $<$ B **goto** (4)
> (2) $T_1 := 0$
> (3)   **goto** (5)
> (4) $T_1 := 1$
> (5) $T_2 := T_1$ **or** C

Fig. 7.22(b). Translation of A$<$B **or** C.

Production	Semantic Rule
$E \rightarrow E^{(1)}$ **or** $E^{(2)}$	{ T := NEWTEMP( ); E.PLACE := T; GEN(T := $E^{(1)}$.PLACE **or** $E^{(2)}$.PLACE) }
$E \rightarrow$ **id**$^{(1)}$ **relop id**$^{(2)}$	{ T := NEWTEMP( ); E.PLACE := T; GEN(**if id**$^{(1)}$.PLACE **relop id**$^{(2)}$.PLACE **goto** NEXTQUAD+3); GEN(T := 0); GEN(**goto** NEXTQUAD+2); GEN(T := 1) }

Fig. 7.23. Semantic rules.

the other productions. In these rules we assume that quadruples are being generated and that NEXTQUAD indicates the next available entry in the quadruple array. GEN increments NEXTQUAD after producing a quadruple.

If triples are generated, the numbers must be changed, since the three-address statement **if** A $<$ B **goto** L requires two triples:

(1) $<$ A B
(2) **if** (1) L

Control-Flow Representation of Boolean Expressions

In Fig. 7.22(b) the value of T_1 is, in a sense, redundant since we can tell what value T_1 will have by whether we reach statement (2) or statement (4). This suggests that we use the position reached in the program to represent the value of a Boolean expression.

If we evaluate expressions by program position, we may be able to avoid evaluating the entire expression. For example, given the expression A **or** B, if we determine that A is true, then we can conclude that the entire expression is true without having to evaluate B. The semantic definition of the programming language determines whether all parts of a Boolean expression must be evaluated. If the language definition permits portions of a Boolean expression to go unevaluated, then the compiler writer is free to attempt to optimize the evaluation of Boolean expressions by computing only enough of an expression to determine its value. This means that, in an expression such as A **or** B, neither A nor B is necessarily evaluated. If either A or B is an expression with side effects (e.g., contains a function that changes a global variable), then an unexpected answer may be obtained.

In this section we shall consider the translation of Boolean expressions in the context of conditional statements such as

if E then $S^{(1)}$ else $S^{(2)}$

and

while E do S

In these contexts we can associate two kinds of exits with the Boolean expression E, a true exit to statement TRUE and a false exit to statement FALSE. The general forms of the translations for these statements are shown in Fig. 7.24(a) and (b).

In Fig. 7.24(a) we see how control flows in the statement **if E then $S^{(1)}$ else $S^{(2)}$**. The code for the Boolean expression E has jumps out of it to the first statement of the code for $S^{(1)}$ if E is true, and to the first statement of $S^{(2)}$ if E is false.

In Fig. 7.24(b) we see a similar picture of the code for the statement **while E do S**. The code for the Boolean expression E has jumps out of it when E is false; these jumps go to whatever code follows the while-statement. The code for E also has jumps out of it when E is true; these jumps go to the beginning of the code for S.

Example 7.12. As a special case, consider the FORTRAN statement

IF (A .LT. B .OR. C .LT. D) X = Y + Z

We can translate this statement into the following three-address code sequence:

(1)	**if** A < B **goto** (4)	/* condition true in either
(2)	**if** C < D **goto** (4)	of these cases */
(3)	**goto** (6)	/* condition false */
(4)	T := Y + Z	
(5)	X := T	
(6)		

Here (4) is the true exit of the Boolean expression and (6) the false exit. □

An expression E will be translated into a sequence of three-address statements that "evaluate" E. This translation is a sequence of conditional and unconditional jumps to one of two locations. One of these locations is TRUE, the place control is to reach if the value of the expression is true, the other is FALSE, the place control is to reach if the value is false.

Consider an expression of the form $E^{(1)}$ **or** $E^{(2)}$. If $E^{(1)}$ is true, then we immediately know that E itself is true so we can make the location TRUE for $E^{(1)}$ be the same as TRUE for E. If $E^{(1)}$ is false, then we must

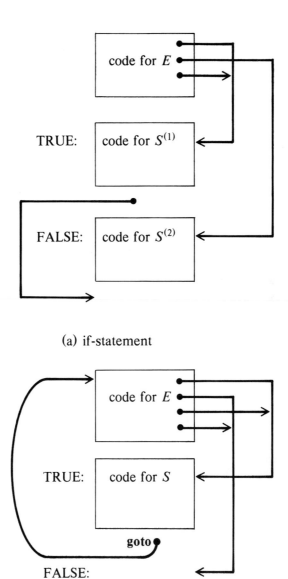

(a) if-statement

(b) while-statement

Fig. 7.24. Form of code for constructs using Boolean expressions.

evaluate $E^{(2)}$, so we make FALSE for $E^{(1)}$ be the first statement in the code for $E^{(2)}$. The true and false exits of $E^{(2)}$ can be made the same as the true and false exits of E, respectively.

Analogous considerations apply to the translation of $E^{(1)}$ **and** $E^{(2)}$. The translation of an expression E of the form **not** E is particularly easy: We just interchange the true and false exits of $E^{(1)}$ to get the true and false exits of E.

Let us now consider a syntax-directed translation scheme that generates quadruples for Boolean expressions in the manner suggested above. One problem that arises when we produce code bottom-up is that we may not have generated the actual quadruples to which the jumps are to be made at the time the jump statements are generated. The code we generate, there-fore, is a series of branching statements with the targets of the jumps tem-porarily left unspecified. Each such quadruple will be on one or another list of quadruples to be filled in when the proper location is found. We call this subsequent filling in of quadruples *backpatching*.

To manipulate the lists of quadruples, we use three functions.

1. MAKELIST(i) creates a new list containing only i, an index into the array of quadruples being generated. MAKELIST returns a pointer to the list it has made.
2. MERGE(p_1, p_2) takes the lists pointed to by p_1 and p_2, concatenates them into one list, and returns a pointer to the concatenated list.
3. BACKPATCH(p, i) makes each of the quadruples on the list pointed to by p take quadruple i as a target.

We can now describe the two translations of E needed to produce the three-address code. These two translations, called E.TRUE and E.FALSE, are pointers to lists of already generated quadruples that must be filled in with the target location, should E be true or false, respectively.

The semantic actions reflect the considerations mentioned above. Con-sider production $E \rightarrow E^{(1)}$ **and** $E^{(2)}$. If $E^{(1)}$ is false, then E is false, so the quadruples on list $E^{(1)}$.FALSE can eventually be filled in with the location which follows the larger expression E in the case that E is false. That is to say, the semantic routine for $E \rightarrow E^{(1)}$ **and** $E^{(2)}$ will, among other things, make $E^{(1)}$.FALSE part of the list E.FALSE.

If $E^{(1)}$ is true, however, we must next test $E^{(2)}$, so the target for the quadruples on list $E^{(1)}$.TRUE must be the beginning of the code generated for $E^{(2)}$. But if we wait until we are about to reduce $E^{(1)}$ **and** $E^{(2)}$ to E, it will be too late to backpatch the $E^{(1)}$.TRUE list, as we will no longer have a record of the number of the first quadruple of $E^{(2)}$.CODE.

One approach is to *factor* the production $E \rightarrow E^{(1)}$ **and** $E^{(2)}$, so that the proper semantic action, backpatching $E^{(1)}$.TRUE, can be done immediately after the code for $E^{(1)}$ has been generated. At that time a pointer NEXTQUAD, which holds the number of the first quadruple to follow, gives the proper value to substitute into quadruples on list $E^{(1)}$.TRUE. That is, we could replace $E \to E$ **and** E by the two productions

$$E \to \text{EAND } E$$

$$\text{EAND} \to E \text{ and}$$

Then we could make a call to BACKPATCH($E^{(1)}$.TRUE, NEXTQUAD) part of the semantic routine for EAND $\to E$ **and**.

An alternative approach, the one we shall adopt here, is to create a marker nonterminal M, with production $M \to \epsilon$ and one translation M.QUAD with semantic routine

$$M \to \epsilon \quad \{M.\text{QUAD} := \text{NEXTQUAD}\}$$

The sole purpose of this production is to cause a semantic action to pick up NEXTQUAD at the appropriate time and preserve it as a translation of its own. The revised grammar is:

$$
\begin{array}{lll}
(1) & E & \to E^{(1)} \text{ or } M \ E^{(2)} \\
(2) & & |\ E^{(1)} \text{ and } M \ E^{(2)} \\
(3) & & |\ \textbf{not } E^{(1)} \\
(4) & & |\ (\ E^{(1)}\ ) \\
(5) & & |\ \textbf{id} \\
(6) & & |\ \textbf{id}^{(1)} \textbf{ relop id}^{(2)} \\
(7) & M & \to \epsilon
\end{array}
$$

The presence of M will not normally cause problems in constructing a bottom-up parser for the (ambiguous) grammar at hand, using the techniques discussed in Section 6.7. If the grammar is converted to an LR(1) grammar, M can still be carried along with no problem. The syntax-directed translation scheme is as follows.

(1) $E \to E^{(1)}$ **or** $M \ E^{(2)}$

    { BACKPATCH ($E^{(1)}$.FALSE, M.QUAD);

    E.TRUE := MERGE($E^{(1)}$.TRUE, $E^{(2)}$.TRUE);

    E.FALSE := $E^{(2)}$.FALSE }

(2) $E \to E^{(1)}$ **and** $M \ E^{(2)}$

    { BACKPATCH($E^{(1)}$.TRUE, M.QUAD);

    E.TRUE := $E^{(2)}$.TRUE;

    E.FALSE := MERGE($E^{(1)}$.FALSE, $E^{(2)}$.FALSE) }

(3) $E \to$ **not** $E^{(1)}$

    { E.TRUE := $E^{(1)}$.FALSE;

    E.FALSE := $E^{(1)}$.TRUE }

(4) $E \to (\ E^{(1)}\ )$

    { E.TRUE := $E^{(1)}$.TRUE;

    E.FALSE := $E^{(1)}$.FALSE }

(5) $E \rightarrow$ **id**
 {   *E*.TRUE := MAKELIST(NEXTQUAD);
    E.FALSE := MAKELIST(NEXTQUAD + 1);
    GEN(**if id**.PLACE **goto** _);
    GEN(**goto** _) }

(6) $E \rightarrow$ **id**$^{(1)}$ **relop id**$^{(2)}$

  {   *E*.TRUE := MAKELIST(NEXTQUAD);
     E.FALSE := MAKELIST(NEXTQUAD + 1);
     GEN(**if id**$^{(1)}$.PLACE **relop id**$^{(2)}$.PLACE **goto** _)
     GEN(**goto** _) }

(7) $M \rightarrow \epsilon$
  {   *M*.QUAD := NEXTQUAD}

Semantic actions (5) and (6) each generate two quadruples, a conditional goto and an unconditional one. Neither has its target filled in. The index of the first generated quadruple is made into a list and *E*.TRUE is given a pointer to that list. The second generated quadruple, "**goto** _", is also made into a list and given to *E*.FALSE.

Example 7.13. Consider the expression

$$P < Q \text{ or } R < S \text{ and } T < U$$

Using the usual order of precedence, the parse tree would look like Fig. 7.25. We have also shown the values of the translations at each node, assuming that NEXTQUAD has the initial value 100 and is incremented with each call to GEN. Note that T, F, and Q have been used to abbreviate field names TRUE, FALSE, and QUAD, respectively.

 Consider the semantic actions occurring as the numbered nodes are "created" in a bottom-up parse. In response to the reduction corresponding to node 1, the two quadruples

    100:   **if** P < Q **goto** _
    101:   **goto** _

are generated. (We arbitrarily start quadruple numbers at 100.) Then, node 2 records the value of NEXTQUAD, which is 102. Node 3 generates the quadruples

    102:   **if** R < S **goto** _
    103:   **goto** _

Node 4 records the current value of NEXTQUAD, which is now 104. Node 5 generates the quadruples

    104:   **if** T < U **goto** _
    105:   **goto** _

Node 6 corresponds to a reduction by $E \rightarrow E^{(1)}$ **and** $M E^{(2)}$. The

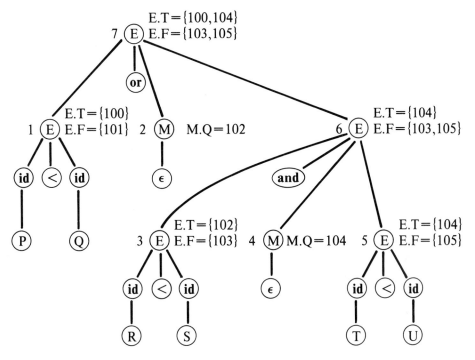

Fig. 7.25. Parse tree for P<Q or R<S and T<U.

corresponding semantic routine calls BACKPATCH({102},104) where {102} as argument denotes a pointer to the list containing only 102, that list being the one pointed to by *E*.TRUE of node 3. This call to BACKPATCH fills in 104 in quadruple 102. The six quadruples generated so far are thus:

```
100:  if P < Q goto _
101:  goto _
102:  if R < S goto 104
103:  goto _
104:  if T < U goto _
105:  goto _
```

Node 7, the root, is created by a reduction by $E \rightarrow E^{(1)}$ **or** $M\ E^{(2)}$. The associated semantic routine calls BACKPATCH({101},102) which leaves the quadruples looking like:

```
100:  if P < Q goto _
101:  goto 102
102:  if R < S goto 104
103:  goto _
104:  if T < U goto _
105:  goto _
```

The entire expression is true if and only if the **goto**'s of quadruples 100 or 104 are reached, and is false if and only if the **goto**'s of quadruples 103 or 105 are reached. These instructions will have their targets filled in later in the compilation, when it is seen what must be done depending on the truth or falsehood of the expression.

Note that the code generated is not optimal, in that quadruple 101 can be eliminated without changing the value of the code. Redundant instructions of this form can be subsequently removed by a simple peephole optimizer (see Section 15.7). Another approach that avoids generating these redundant jumps is to translate a relational expression of the form $id^{(1)} < id^{(2)}$ into the statement

$$\text{if } id^{(1)} \geqslant id^{(2)} \text{ goto } \_$$

with the presumption that when the relation is true we fall through the code. (See Exercise 7.10 for more details.)   □

Mixed Mode Expressions

It is important to realize that we have simplified the grammar for Boolean expressions. In practice, Boolean expressions often contain arithmetic subexpressions as in $(A+B) < C$. In some languages, a Boolean expression is deemed to have a numerical value, for example, with **false** identified with 0 and **true** with 1. In such a language, $(A<B) + (B<A)$ can be considered an arithmetic expression with value 0 if $A = B$, and 1 otherwise.

One can still use the method of representing Boolean expressions by flow of control, even if arithmetic expressions are represented by code to compute their value. For example, consider the representative grammar

$$E \rightarrow E + E \mid E \text{ and } M \ E \mid E \text{ relop } E \mid id$$

$$M \rightarrow \epsilon$$

We may suppose that $E+E$ produces an integer arithmetic result (the inclusion of real or other arithmetic types makes matters more complicated but adds nothing to the instructive value of this example), while expressions E **and** $M \ E$ and E **relop** E produce Boolean values represented by flow of control. Expression E **and** $M \ E$ requires both arguments to be Boolean, but the operations $+$ and **relop** take either type of argument, including mixed ones. $E \rightarrow id$ is also deemed arithmetic, although we could extend this example by allowing Boolean identifiers.

To generate code in this situation, we can use a translation $E.\text{MODE}$, which will be either **arith** or **Bool** depending on which type of expression E is. E will have translations $E.\text{TRUE}$ and $E.\text{FALSE}$ for Boolean expressions and $E.\text{PLACE}$ for arithmetic. Part of the semantic rule for $E \rightarrow E^{(1)} + E^{(2)}$ is shown in Fig. 7.26.

$E \rightarrow E^{(1)} + E^{(2)}$

```
{   E.MODE := arith;
    if (E(1).MODE = arith and E(2).MODE = arith) then
        begin    /* normal arithmetic add */
            T := NEWTEMP( );
            E.PLACE := T;
            GEN(T := E(1).PLACE + E(2).PLACE)
        end
    else if (E(1).MODE = arith and E(2).MODE = Bool) then
        begin
            T := NEWTEMP( );
            E.PLACE := T;
            BACKPATCH(E(2).FALSE, NEXTQUAD);
            GEN(T := E(1).PLACE);
            GEN(goto NEXTQUAD+2);
            BACKPATCH(E(2).TRUE, NEXTQUAD );
            GEN(T := E(1).PLACE + 1)
        end
    else if  · · ·  }
```

Fig. 7.26. Mixed-mode addition.

In the mixed mode case, we generate three quadruples. The first is the place to jump to when $E^{(2)}$ is false, guaranteed by the call to BACKPATCH($E^{(2)}$.PLACE, NEXTQUAD) before the three quadruples are generated. The second is used to jump around the third (an awkwardness which might be ironed out in code optimization). The third quadruple is the target of all jumps on the $E^{(2)}$.TRUE list and causes T to get the value 1 plus the value of $E^{(1)}$. The net effect is that the value of T is the value of E.PLACE if $E^{(2)}$ is false and one more than that if $E^{(2)}$ is true. The semantic rules for the two remaining cases and the other productions are quite similar to what we have already seen, and we leave them for an exercise.

7.9 Statements that Alter the Flow of Control

We now consider the translation of source statements that affect the flow of control in a program. We discuss what code to generate for unconditional jumps and for "structured" flow-of-control constructs such as if-then and while-statements. As in the previous section, we fix our attention on the generation of quadruples, and the notation regarding translation field names and list-handling procedures from that section carries over to this section as well.

Unconditional Jumps

The most elementary programming-language feature for jumps is the label and goto. When a compiler encounters a statement like **goto** L, it looks for the label L in the symbol table. If the jump is backward, that is, L has already been encountered, then the symbol table will have an entry giving the number of the first quadruple generated for the statement labeled L. We generate a **goto** three-address statement with that quadruple number as target.

If the jump is forward, this may be the first occurrence of the label L, and if so we enter L into the symbol table. In any case, if the statement labeled L has not yet been encountered, then we can only generate a **goto** quadruple with unspecified target and add the quadruple generated to a list of quadruples whose target is L. A pointer to this list appears in the symbol table entry for L.

We can describe the syntax of labeled statements with productions such as

$$S \rightarrow \text{LABEL} : S$$

$$\text{LABEL} \rightarrow \textbf{id}$$

The semantic action associated with LABEL $\rightarrow$ **id** is to

1. install that identifier in the symbol table if it is not already there,
2. record that the quadruple referred to by this label is the current value of NEXTQUAD, and finally
3. backpatch the list of **goto**'s whose targets are the label just discovered.

Structured Flow-of-Control Constructs

A more complex example-of-flow of control concerns nested, or structured, control statements. Suppose, for an example, that we have the following productions for statements with the denotations shown:

$$S - \text{statement}$$
$$L - \text{statement list}$$
$$A - \text{assignment statement}$$
$$E - \text{Boolean-valued expression.}$$

(1) $S \rightarrow$ **if** E **then** S
(2) | **if** E **then** S **else** S
(3) | **while** E **do** S
(4) | **begin** L **end**
(5) | A
(6) $L \rightarrow L$; S
(7) | S

Note that there must be other productions, such as those for assignment statements. The productions given, however, will be sufficient to illustrate the techniques used to translate flow of control statements.

We saw in Fig. 7.24 what the structure of the code for an if- or while-statement looks like. What was missing from that picture is the fact that statements as well as expressions can have jumps out of their bodies. These jumps are to whatever code is to be executed after the statement finishes.

For example, in Fig. 7.24(a), jumps out of $S^{(1)}$ or $S^{(2)}$ go to whatever code must follow the if-statement. These jumps becomes jumps out of the if-statement itself. Note that if $S^{(2)}$ were an assignment statement, control could fall out of its code, rather than jumping out. For this reason we make the tacit assumption that the code that follows a given statement in execution also follows it physically in the quadruple array. If that is not true, an explicit jump must be provided.

Similarly, in Fig. 7.24(b), the code for S could have jumps out of it to the beginning of the code for the expression to repeat the while-loop. The jumps out of E when E is false become jumps out of the while-statement taken as a whole.

Our general approach will be to fill in the jumps out of statements when their targets are found. Not only do Boolean expressions need two lists of jumps that occur when the expression is true and when it is false, but statements also need lists of jumps (NEXT lists) to the code that follows them in the execution sequence.

Scheme to Implement the Translation

We shall now describe a syntax-directed translation scheme to generate translations for the flow-of-control constructs given above. The nonterminal E has the two translation fields $E.\text{TRUE}$ and $E.\text{FALSE}$, as discussed in the previous section. L and S each also need a list of unfilled quadruples which must eventually be completed by backpatching. These lists are pointed to by the translation fields $L.\text{NEXT}$ and $S.\text{NEXT}$. $S.\text{NEXT}$ is a pointer to a list of all conditional and unconditional jumps to the quadruple following the statement S in execution order, and $L.\text{NEXT}$ is defined similarly.

The need for such a translation field is apparent when we examine the code we want to produce for the statement **while** E **do** S. The code tests expression E, and, if **true**, executes statement S. Then, after executing statement S, the code jumps back to the test, and not to the quadruple that physically follows the code for S. While we have, in fact, already encountered this target quadruple, we should realize that S may itself be a while-statement perhaps with many levels of nesting. It is therefore important to keep track of which expression is tested after which statement. We could do so with a separate stack, but it is more orderly to utilize the parsing stack for this purpose. We therefore introduce the marker nonterminal M, as in the last section, and write

$$S \rightarrow \textbf{while } M^{(1)} \ E \ \textbf{do } M^{(2)} \ S^{(1)}$$

$$M \rightarrow \epsilon$$

Each M has a translation $M.\text{QUAD}$, which is the number of the first quadruple following. Then when we reduce **while** $M^{(1)} \ E \ \textbf{do} \ M^{(2)} \ S^{(1)}$ to S, we backpatch the list $S^{(1)}.\text{NEXT}$ to make all targets on that list be $M^{(1)}.\text{QUAD}$. As the code for $S^{(1)}$ may also "fall out the bottom," we append a jump to the beginning of the code for E.

$E.\text{TRUE}$ is backpatched to go to the beginning of $S^{(1)}$ by making jumps on the $E.\text{TRUE}$ list go to $M^{(2)}.\text{QUAD}$. Note that by factoring the grammar, the latter backpatching could be done after we see the **do**, thus decreasing the number of quadruples that have to remain in main memory at once.

A more compelling argument for using $S.\text{NEXT}$ and $L.\text{NEXT}$ comes when we consider generating code for the conditional statement **if** E **then** $S^{(1)}$ **else** $S^{(2)}$. When we finish executing $S^{(1)}$, we have no idea where to go next, since it may well be to the quadruple following $S^{(2)}$, whose index is not known until we finish generating code for $S^{(2)}$. The use of the marker nonterminal M solves this problem as well.

One problem remains, however. If we allow the code for $S^{(1)}$ to end by "falling out the bottom" rather than by a jump, as when $S^{(1)}$ is an assignment, we must include at the end of the code for $S^{(1)}$ a jump to $S^{(1)}.\text{NEXT}$. We shall use another marker nonterminal to introduce this jump after $S^{(1)}$.[†] Let nonterminal N be this marker with production $N \rightarrow \epsilon$. N has translation field $N.\text{NEXT}$, which will be a list consisting of the quadruple number of the statement **goto** _ that is generated by the semantic rule for N. We now give the semantic rules for the revised grammar.

(1) $S \rightarrow \textbf{if } E \textbf{ then } M^{(1)} \ S^{(1)} \ N \textbf{ else } M^{(2)} \ S^{(2)}$

> { BACKPATCH($E.\text{TRUE}, \ M^{(1)}.\text{QUAD}$);
> BACKPATCH($E.\text{FALSE}, \ M^{(2)}.\text{QUAD}$);
> $S.\text{NEXT} := \text{MERGE}(S^{(1)}.\text{NEXT}, \ N.\text{NEXT}, \ S^{(2)}.\text{NEXT})$ }

We backpatch the jumps when E is true to the quadruple $M^{(1)}.\text{QUAD}$, which is the beginning of the code for $S^{(1)}$. Similarly, we backpatch jumps when E is false to go to the beginning of the code for $S^{(2)}$. The list $S.\text{NEXT}$ includes all jumps out of $S^{(1)}$ and $S^{(2)}$, as well as the jump

---

[†] An extra translation field for statements and statement lists could indicate whether this jump was actually necessary, but this would not solve the problem of what to do when it was necessary. Adding a jump to every assignment statement is a viable but unattractive and not to be seriously considered alternative.

generated by N.

(2) $N \to \epsilon$

   { N.NEXT := MAKELIST(NEXTQUAD);
   GEN(**goto** _) }

(3) $M \to \epsilon$

   { M.QUAD := NEXTQUAD }

(4) $S \to$ **if** E **then** M $S^{(1)}$

   { BACKPATCH(E.TRUE, M.QUAD);
   S.NEXT := MERGE(E.FALSE, $S^{(1)}$.NEXT) }

(5) $S \to$ **while** $M^{(1)}$ E **do** $M^{(2)}$ $S^{(1)}$

   { BACKPATCH($S^{(1)}$.NEXT, $M^{(1)}$.QUAD);
   BACKPATCH(E.TRUE, $M^{(2)}$.QUAD);
   S.NEXT := E.FALSE
   GEN(**goto** $M^{(1)}$. QUAD) }

(6) $S \to$ **begin** L **end**

   { S.NEXT := L.NEXT }

(7) $S \to A$

   { S.NEXT := MAKELIST( ) }

Here we initialize S.NEXT to an empty list.

(8) $L \to L^{(1)}$; M S

   { BACKPATCH($L^{(1)}$.NEXT, M.QUAD);
   L.NEXT := S.NEXT }

The statement following $L^{(1)}$ in order of execution is the beginning of S. Thus the $L^{(1)}$.NEXT list is backpatched to the beginning of the code for S, which is given by M.QUAD.

(9) $L \to S$

   { L.NEXT := S.NEXT }

Note that no new quadruples are generated anywhere in these semantic rules except for rules (2) and (5). All other code is generated by the semantic actions associated with assignment statements and expressions. What the flow of control does is cause the proper backpatching so that the assignments and Boolean expression evaluations will connect properly.

Example 7.14. Consider the statement

> **while** (A<B) **do**
>
>> **if** (C<D) **then** X := Y + Z   (7.5)

The syntax-directed translation scheme above, coupled with schemes for assignment statements and Boolean expressions, would produce the following code for (7.5).

> 100: **if** (A<B) **goto** 102
> 101: **goto** 107
> 102: **if** (C<D) **goto** 104
> 103: **goto** 100
> 104: T := Y + Z
> 105: X := T
> 106: **goto** 100
> 107:

□

We should mention that, neglecting declarations, a procedure can be treated as a single statement in the grammar above. We could have a production $P \rightarrow S$, whose translation would be a call to

$$\text{BACKPATCH}(S.\text{NEXT, NEXTQUAD})$$

and the generation of a **return** quadruple. If this procedure is the "main program," the **return** three-address statement would eventually be replaced by a system call to gracefully terminate the program.

7.10 Postfix Translations

We have called a translation scheme *postfix* if, for each production $A \rightarrow \alpha$, the translation rule for A.CODE consists of the concatenation of the CODE translations of the nonterminals in α, in the same order as the nonterminals appear in α, followed by a tail of output. We have seen that postfix translations can be implemented by emitting the tail as each production is recognized. Therefore, to reduce space requirements, it is quite useful that CODE be a postfix translation, for if not, we must use a scheme like generation of a parse tree, followed by a walk of the tree, to produce the intermediate-language form of the source program.

Factoring Productions to Achieve Postfix Form

One must sometimes use a little effort to get the grammar into a form such that a postfix translation for code is feasible. The chief technique is factoring, that is, taking a production of the form $A \rightarrow X_1 X_2 \cdots X_n$, introducing a new nonterminal B, and for some i, replacing $A \rightarrow X_1 X_2 \cdots X_n$ by the pair of productions $A \rightarrow BX_{i+1}X_{i+2} \cdots X_n$ and $B \rightarrow X_1X_2 \cdots X_i$. Since there is only one production for B, the two new productions can be used exactly where the old one was, so we have not changed the language. The advantage is that we now reduce $X_1X_2 \cdots X_i$, with the attendant opportunity to generate code or perform other actions.

Example 7.15. We used in several places a marker nonterminal M whose sole purpose was to record a translation $M.\text{QUAD}$ giving the value of NEXTQUAD at a critical time. For example, in Section 7.9 we used the production

$$S \rightarrow \textbf{while } M^{(1)} E \textbf{ do } M^{(2)} S$$

for the **while** statement, so $M^{(1)}$ could record the first quadruple of the code for E, and $M^{(2)}$ the first quadruple of the code for S.

An alternative approach is to rewrite the production as

$$S \rightarrow C \ S$$

$$C \rightarrow W \ E \ \textbf{do}$$

$$W \rightarrow \textbf{while}$$

where C and W are new nonterminals introduced for this purpose. We could give W the translation $W.\text{QUAD}$, which would serve for $M^{(1)}.\text{QUAD}$ and C would have translation $C.\text{QUAD}$ with the same value as $W.\text{QUAD}$. Also, $C.\text{FALSE}$ will be the same as $E.\text{FALSE}$. When we reduce to C, we can backpatch $E.\text{TRUE}$ to position NEXTQUAD immediately, so $M^{(2)}.\text{QUAD}$ is never needed. A suitable syntax-directed translation scheme would be:

$W \rightarrow \textbf{while}$ { $W.\text{QUAD} := \text{NEXTQUAD}$ }

$C \rightarrow W \ E \ \textbf{do}$ { $C.\text{QUAD} := W.\text{QUAD}$;
BACKPATCH($E.\text{TRUE}$, NEXTQUAD);
$C.\text{FALSE} := E.\text{FALSE}$ }

$S \rightarrow C \ S^{(1)}$ { BACKPATCH($S^{(1)}.\text{NEXT}$, $C.\text{QUAD}$);
$S.\text{NEXT} := C.\text{FALSE}$;
GEN(**goto** $C.\text{QUAD}$) }

□

Example 7.16. A more significant example where factoring is useful concerns the for-statement:

$$\textbf{for } L := E^{(1)} \textbf{ step } E^{(2)} \textbf{ to } E^{(3)} \textbf{ do } S$$

where L is any expression with an l-value, usually a variable, called the *index,* and $E^{(1)}$, $E^{(2)}$, and $E^{(3)}$ are expressions, called the *initial value, increment* and *limit,* respectively. A typical such statement is

$$\textbf{for } I := 1 \textbf{ step } 1 \textbf{ until } N \textbf{ do } A[I] := 0 \qquad (7.6)$$

While there are many possible meanings for this statement, let us fix on one which is akin to the PASCAL semantics for this statement or the PL/I semantics for the indexed DO-statement. The keyword **to** in PASCAL indicates that the loop runs until the index exceeds the limit. The increment and limit are evaluated once and for all, before the loop, as is the *l*-value of the index. Semantically, the for-statement is equivalent to the program in Fig. 7.27.

```
begin
    INDEX := addr(L);
    *INDEX := E^(1);
    INCR := E^(2);
    LIMIT := E^(3);
    while *INDEX ≤ LIMIT do
        begin
            code for statement S;
            *INDEX := *INDEX + INCR
        end
end
```

Fig. 7.27. Semantics of for-statement.

We note from Fig. 7.27 that each of the five pieces L, $E^{(1)}$, $E^{(2)}$, $E^{(3)}$, and S appears exactly once, and they appear in the same order as in the for-statement. Thus INDEX is the location of the identifier or array location used for counting; i.e., INDEX is used here as a location, not a value. When we do the counting and test for termination, we must assign and/or use *INDEX, the contents of INDEX. In order that the name INDEX be available where it is needed in Fig. 7.27, it is convenient to factor the for-statement into productions

(1) $F \rightarrow \textbf{for } L$
(2) $T \rightarrow F := E^{(1)} \textbf{ by } E^{(2)} \textbf{ to } E^{(3)} \textbf{ do}$
(3) $S \rightarrow T\, S^{(1)}$

and to use the following syntax-directed translation scheme. As in the previous two sections, we generate quadruples for concreteness.

We assume that $L.\text{INDEX}$ is a pointer to the symbol table entry for a name which plays the role of INDEX in Fig. 7.27. That is, the value of INDEX is the address of the index of the loop. Section 8.1 gives hints on how to generate code to compute the value of INDEX in the case L is an expression with an l-value, such as an array element.

(1) $F \rightarrow$ **for** L

    { F.INDEX := L.INDEX }

F.INDEX is used to record the name INDEX.

(2) $T \rightarrow I$ **by** $E^{(2)}$ **to** $E^{(3)}$ **do**

    { GEN($*F$.INDEX := $E^{(1)}$.PLACE);
      INCR := NEWTEMP( );
      LIMIT := NEWTEMP( );
      GEN(INCR := $E^{(2)}$.PLACE);
      GEN(LIMIT := $E^{(3)}$.PLACE);
      T.QUAD := NEXTQUAD;
      T.NEXT := MAKELIST(NEXTQUAD);
      GEN(**if** $*F$.INDEX $>$ LIMIT **goto** _);
      T.INDEX := F.INDEX;
      T.INCR := INCR }

$E^{(1)}$.PLACE points to the symbol table entry for a name whose r-value is the value of expression $E^{(1)}$. We generate quadruples to assign the values of $E^{(2)}$ and $E^{(3)}$ to new temporaries INCR and LIMIT, respectively. We also generate the first quadruple of the loop, the test to jump out if the index exceeds the limit. Before generating this quadruple, we record the value of NEXTQUAD and make a list consisting of this quadruple, to be backpatched once we find out where to go after the for-loop. T.QUAD and T.NEXT hold these values to be passed to S.

(3) $S \rightarrow T \, S^{(1)}$

    { BACKPATCH($S^{(1)}$.NEXT, NEXTQUAD);
      GEN($*T$.INDEX := $*T$.INDEX $+$ T.INCR);
      GEN(**goto** T.QUAD);
      S.NEXT := T.NEXT }

We backpatch jumps out of $S^{(1)}$ to the code which follows $S^{(1)}$, that is, the statement which increments INDEX. That statement and a statement to jump to T.QUAD, the beginning of the loop, are generated next. Then T.NEXT, the list consisting of the one jump out of the for-loop, is passed to S.NEXT.

Example 7.17. This translation scheme generates the following code for statement (7.6). INDEX is used as a pointer to I, and X_1 and X_2 are used for the values returned by NEWTEMP.

        100:   $*$INDEX := I
        101:   X_1 := 1
        102:   X_2 := N

103:    **if** *INDEX > X_2 **goto** _
104:    code for A[I] := 0

.
.
.

$$\ast INDEX := \ast INDEX + X_1$$
goto 103

Note that we could have used I in place of *INDEX above. However, if the index were an expression, rather than a simple name, we would have to compute its *l*-value and hold it in INDEX. □

7.11 Translation with a Top-Down Parser

It may appear at first glance that more complex translations can be produced in connection with top-down parsing than with bottom-up parsing. More careful thought shows this conclusion is false; in truth, any translation that can be done by a top-down, no-backtrack parser can be done by a bottom-up, no-backtrack parser such as an LR parser. This was proved in a theoretical but realistic setting by Brosgol [1974]. Since the bottom-up parsers work for a larger class of grammars than the top-down parsers do, we feel justified in advocating the use of bottom-up techniques and in presenting translation in those terms.

We should, however, for completeness, discuss how to apply the ideas of this chapter to top-down parsers, such as recursive-descent parsers. In fact, there are certain common situations where the use of such tricks as the introduction of marker nonterminal M to hold a quadruple number, or the factoring discussed in the last section, can be avoided when parsing top-down.

The advantage of a top-down parser is that semantic routines can be called in the middle of productions. Thus, if we are looking for an A, and we expand A by production $A \rightarrow BCD$, we may call a routine immediately, another after recognizing B, another after recognizing C and another after recognizing D. This behavior can also be accomplished in the bottom-up environment. A simple way of gaining control in the middle of a production is to insert markers as follows:

$$A \rightarrow M_1 B M_2 C M_3 D$$

$$M_1 \rightarrow \epsilon$$

$$M_2 \rightarrow \epsilon$$

$$M_3 \rightarrow \epsilon$$

Then, the routine called by a top-down parser immediately upon expansion of A may be called by the bottom-up parser upon reduction to M_1, the routine called after recognition of B could be called after reduction to M_2, and so on.[†]

Let us consider one example of how semantic routines can be attached to a recursive-descent parser.

Example 7.18. Let us consider the grammar for control statements discussed in Section 7.9.

$$
\begin{array}{rl}
(1) & S \rightarrow \textbf{if } E \textbf{ then } S \\
(2) & \quad | \textbf{ if } E \textbf{ then } S \textbf{ else } S \\
(3) & \quad | \textbf{ while } E \textbf{ do } S \\
(4) & \quad | \textbf{ begin } L \textbf{ end} \\
(5) & \quad | A \\
(6) & L \rightarrow L \textbf{ ; } S \\
(7) & \quad | S
\end{array}
$$

In order to parse this grammar with no backtracking we must make several changes. On seeing **if** we do not know which of the first two alternates to use to expand S, so we must left-factor the two right sides, replacing them by:

$$S \rightarrow \textbf{if } E \textbf{ then } S \text{ TAIL}$$

$$\text{TAIL} \rightarrow \textbf{else } S \mid \epsilon$$

Next, we must eliminate the left-recursion in the rules for L, replacing them by

$$L \rightarrow S ; L \mid S$$

then left factor these into:

$$L \rightarrow S \text{ LTAIL}$$

$$\text{LTAIL} \rightarrow ; L \mid \epsilon$$

For each nonterminal we envision a procedure which searches the input and consumes a string derived from that nonterminal. The procedure will generate certain quadruples and return to the procedure from which it was called with its translations as described in Section 7.9. When expanded to **else** S, TAIL will return as value TAIL.NEXT, which is the same as S.NEXT of Section 7.9. When expanded to ; L, LTAIL will return LTAIL.NEXT as value. The procedure S is shown below. To simplify the code, we have omitted steps that remove symbols such as **if** or **while** from the input stream.

---

† In fact, Brosgol's proof that bottom-up can "simulate" top-down simply involves showing that for every grammar that can be parsed top-down, with no backtrack, the grammar formed by adding markers to the beginning of right sides, as above, is LR and, thus can be parsed bottom-up, with the same translation computed as was computed by the top-down parser and translator.

```
procedure S( );
switch (first input token)
    begin
        case 'if':
            begin
                (E.TRUE, E.FALSE) := E( );
                /* E recognizes a Boolean expression and
                   returns E.TRUE and E.FALSE */
                BACKPATCH(E.TRUE, NEXTQUAD);
                /* Note no marker nonterminal is needed.
                   We can backpatch as soon as the expression is found. */
                if next input symbol is 'then' then S⁽¹⁾.NEXT := S( );
                /* S returns S.NEXT */
                else ERROR( );
                if next input symbol is 'else' then
                    begin
                        GEN(goto _ ); /* jump after S⁽¹⁾ */
                        BACKPATCH(E.FALSE, NEXTQUAD);
                        /* NEXTQUAD is now the beginning of the
                           statement following the code for S⁽¹⁾ */
                        S⁽¹⁾.NEXT := MERGE(S⁽¹⁾.NEXT, {NEXTQUAD−1});
                        /* add generated quadruple to S⁽¹⁾.NEXT list */
                        S⁽²⁾.NEXT := S( );
                        /* S returns S.NEXT */
                        return MERGE(S⁽¹⁾.NEXT, S⁽²⁾.NEXT)
                        /* S returns its own S.NEXT list */
                    end
                else /* no else part is present */
                    return MERGE(S⁽¹⁾.NEXT, E.FALSE)
            end  /* 'if' case */
        case 'while':
            begin
                QUAD := NEXTQUAD;
                /* Remember the beginning quadruple for the expression */
                (E.TRUE, E.FALSE) := E( );
                BACKPATCH(E.TRUE, NEXTQUAD);
                if next input symbol is 'do' then
                    begin
                        S.NEXT := S( );
                        BACKPATCH(S.NEXT, QUAD);
                        GEN(goto QUAD);
                        /* S jumps to the code for E after it finishes */
                        return E.FALSE
                        /* S.NEXT for the while-statement is the list E.FALSE */
```

```
              end
            else ERROR( )
        end    /* 'while' case */
    case 'begin':
        begin
            L.NEXT := L( );
            /* L returns L. NEXT */
            return L. NEXT;
        end    /* 'begin' case */
    case 'id': /* do not remove id from the input */
        begin
            A( );
            /* search for assignment statement */
            return MAKELIST( )
            /* return empty list for S. NEXT */
        end    /* 'id' case */
    default: ERROR( )
end    /* switch */
```

Exercises

7.1 Give the parse tree and translations for the expression $(4 * 7 + 19) * 2$ according to the syntax-directed translation scheme of Section 7.1.

7.2 Translate $a*-(b+c)$ into postfix form.

**7.3 If all operators are binary, then a string of operators and operands is a postfix expression if and only if it obeys the following two rules.

i)   There is exactly one fewer operator than operands.
ii) Every nonempty prefix has fewer operators than operands.

a)   Prove the above statement.
b)   Generalize the statement to include k-ary operators, for arbitrary k.

*7.4 Suppose we have a computer with a single register and with assembly-language operations LOAD, STORE, ADD, and MULT with the obvious meanings. Suppose we have the following grammar for assignment statements:

$$A \rightarrow \mathbf{id} := E$$
$$E \rightarrow E + E \mid E * E \mid (E) \mid \mathbf{id}$$

Write a recursive descent parser with semantic routines to translate assignment statements to assembly language.

7.5 Modify your action routines from Exercise 7.4 to take advantage of the commutativity of $+$ and $*$ to generate better code where possible.

7.6 Write quadruples, triples, and indirect triples for the expression $-(a+b)*(c+d)-(a+b+c)$.

7.7 Using the translation schemes of this chapter translate the following program to quadruples.

$$\textbf{while } A < C \textbf{ and } B < D \textbf{ do}$$
$$\textbf{if } A = 1 \textbf{ then } C := C + 1$$
$$\textbf{else while } A \leqslant D \textbf{ do } A := A + 2$$

7.8 The *prefix* form of an expression in which operator θ is applied to expressions $e_1, e_2, \ldots, e_k$ is $\theta f_1 f_2 \cdots f_k$ where f_i is the prefix form of e_i.
a) Give the prefix form of $a*-(b+c)$.
b) Show that there is no postfix translation of infix expressions to prefix form. How would one perform this translation if it were necessary?

**7.9 Prove that any syntax-directed translation scheme based on an LL(1) grammar, in which semantic actions can be called in the middle of productions during the top down parse of the input can be performed bottom-up using an LR(1) grammar and calling semantic routines only after reductions.

*7.10 The second translation scheme in Section 7.8 for Boolean expressions translates $E \rightarrow \textbf{id} < \textbf{id}$ into the pair of statements

$$\textbf{if id}^{(1)} < \textbf{id}^{(2)} \textbf{ goto } \_$$
$$\textbf{goto } \_$$

We could translate instead to

$$\textbf{if id}^{(1)} \geqslant \textbf{id}^{(2)} \textbf{ goto } \_$$

but the resulting code for E would not necessarily cause a jump. That is, when E is true, we can fall through the code.
a) Modify the translation scheme to append a jump to the end of an expression E if the code next executed when E is true does not physically follow the code for E. *Hint.* The problem comes with the **or** operator, where a jump must be inserted after $E^{(1)}$. The solution is found in the handling of **if** $\cdots$ **then** $\cdots$ **else** in Section 7.9.

b) Further modify your translation scheme by adding a translation field E.SAFE, which is true if and only if it is not necessary to add the jump, i.e., the code for E cannot fall through if E is true. Use SAFE to avoid adding superfluous jumps.

7.11 Do the same as Exercise 7.10(b) for the translation scheme of Section 7.9.

*7.12 Write a top-down translation scheme to produce quadruples for Boolean expressions.

Bibliographic Notes

Irons [1961] was among the first to use syntax-directed translation as a method for compiler design. The papers of Samelson and Bauer [1960] and Brooker and Morris [1962] also discuss the idea of a parser calling for semantic actions. The notion of syntax-directed translation was further popularized by the works of Eickel, Paul, Bauer, and Samelson [1963], Cheatham and Sattley [1964], Ingerman [1966], and Feldman [1966]. Lewis and Stearns [1968] developed the early theory of syntax-directed translation.

The translation of Boolean expressions given here is patterned after Arden, Galler, and Graham [1962]. Exercise 7.9, showing that bottom-up parsing and translation "covers" top-down parsing and translation is from Brosgol [1974].

Knuth [1968b] was the first to use the terms "inherited" and "synthesized" to describe translations. Like canonical LR parsing, translations with inherited attributes are not directly implementable in an obvious, efficient way. In fact, Jazayeri, Ogden, and Rounds [1975] prove that the problem of determining whether a translation scheme defines a translation for all parse trees can require an exponential amount of time as a function of grammar size.

As with LR parsers, considerable effort has been devoted to finding restricted classes of translation schemes (analogous to SLR and LALR grammars) for which attributed and synthesized translations can be implemented efficiently. The L-attributed translations of Lewis, Rosenkrantz, and Stearns [1974, 1976] are such a class. Kennedy and Warren [1976] is another approach toward the efficient implementation of these translations, as is Bochmann [1975]. Wilcox [1971] also considers practical classes of syntax-directed translation schemes that generalize the type given in this book.

CHAPTER 8

More About Translation

This chapter discusses the syntax-directed translation of several important programming language constructs not covered in the previous chapter. These are: expressions with array references, procedure calls, declaration statements, case statements, and record structure references.

8.1 Array References in Arithmetic Expressions

In Section 7.7 we discussed the translation of assignment statements having only simple names as operands. In this section we expand on that translation, permitting array references as operands. One approach is to leave a reference such as A[I, J] intact in the intermediate code, leaving it to the code-generation phase to produce object code that computes the offset of A[I, J] from the base of array A and then performs an indexing operation.

A second approach, the one we adopt, is to expand the array references into three-address code that does the offset calculation. This expansion is important if we wish to optimize array references in loops by the optimization techniques discussed in Sections 12.3 and Chapter 13.

A Grammar for Array References

To begin, we need a grammar for assignment statements with subscripted arrays. In developing such a grammar, it is useful to introduce the nonterminal L, standing for an expression that has an l-value. Recall that only an l-valued expression makes sense appearing on the left of an assignment operator. In the present context, the only l-valued expressions are simple names and array references of the form **id**[$E, E, \ldots, E$], where each E is an expression, possibly involving additional array references. A grammar describing assignment statements is:

$$A \rightarrow L := E$$
$$L \rightarrow \textbf{id}[\text{elist}] \mid \textbf{id}$$
$$\text{elist} \rightarrow \text{elist} , E \mid E$$
$$E \rightarrow E + E \mid (E) \mid L$$

296

That is, an assignment statement A is an l-value followed by an assignment symbol followed by an expression E. Note that E effectively means r-value here.

An l-value is either (1) an **id** followed by a bracketed list of expressions (elist) which is the list of indices, or (2) an **id** by itself.

An elist is a list of expressions separated by commas, and an expression is either the sum of two expressions (the sum will have no l-value) or an expression with an l-value. We show only one arithmetic operator, binary $+$, to simplify matters. The generalization to a variety of arithmetic operators should present no serious problem to the reader.

The Code for Static Array References

For simplicity, we assume static allocation of arrays, whose subscripts range from one to some limit known at compile time. Array elements are taken to require one word each. We also assume that the target machine has a word-organized memory, although when we discuss the actual syntax-directed translation scheme for array references, we shall show how to handle the case of byte-organized memories in a simple and natural way.

Consider a two-dimensional 10×20 array named A. We assume A is to be stored statically in a block of 200 words in row major form, that is, with the last subscript varying fastest. Specifically, the order of the elements of A is to be A[1,1], A[1,2], . . . , A[1,20], A[2,1], A[2,2], . . . , A[2,20], . . . , A[10,1], A[10,2], . . . , A[10,20]. Thus if a denotes the location of the first word of the block (i.e., of A[1,1]), then A[i, j] is in location $a+20(i-1)+j-1$ or, grouping differently, $(a-21)+20i+j$. The reason for the latter grouping is that while the values of variables i and j are not known when the reference to A[i, j] is being compiled, the value of $a-21$ may be known. Thus, assuming the usual computer architecture, the machine code to reference A[i, j] will compute $20i+j$ in an index register, then reference location $a-21$ indexed by the contents of this index register.

The value $a-21$ can be computed by the compiler if A is allocated static storage. However, the value of $a-21$ may or may not be known at the time we translate the reference A[i, j]. The availability of base registers can affect how this translation is to be performed.

If base registers are part of the computer's hardware, it is possible to keep all statically allocated data for a procedure in a block of words whose first (*base*) location is held in some known base register. The offset of each name from this base location can be determined as each name is declared. In this case the offset corresponding to $a-21$ is known when a reference to A[i, j] is translated into intermediate code. The three-address code to evaluate A[i, j] into some temporary T would look like this:

code to evaluate i into temporary T_1†

$T_2 := 20*T_1$

code to evaluate j into temporary T_3

$T_4 := T_2 + T_3$

$T := (a-21)[T_4]$‡

On a machine without base registers, however, it may only be sensible to append all statically allocated data to the end of the program. Thus, although the compiler can eventually determine the value of a, it cannot do so until the very end of the compilation, after machine code for the program has been generated. In that case, it makes sense to generate three-address code to "compute" $a-21$, with the understanding that this computation will be carried out during the final code-generation phase, or possibly by the loader, not while the program is actually running. In fact, if negative offsets are forbidden, we would be forced to evaluate $a-21$ at run time even if base registers were used, should that value be negative relative to the base of the data area. The more general sequence of three-address statements is:

code to evaluate i into temporary T_1

$T_2 := 20 * T_1$

code to evaluate j into temporary T_3

$T_4 := T_2 + T_3$

$a := \mathbf{addr}\ (A)$

$T_5 := a-21$

$T := T_5[T_4]$

Because of its greater flexibility and potential for portability, the latter code sequence might well be preferred even if the compiler were written

---

† i or j might stand for an expression. If i is a simple name, T_1 is that name, and no code to evaluate i is present.

‡ We assume a word-organized memory, with one location number per word. If the memory is byte-organized, with each byte numbered, then to get the actual address, both 21 and T_4 would have to be multiplied by the number of bytes per word, and the latter multiplication would be reflected in the three-address statements. For example, if there were 4 bytes per word, the last statement would be replaced by $T_5 := 4*T_4$ and $T := (a-84)[T_5]$.

for a machine whose hardware features make it possible to determine the value of a as we process $A[i, j]$. Although we are presumably writing a compiler for one machine, it is quite possible that compilers for the same language but different machines may be written after this one. If we put a bit of generality into our intermediate language, the entire front end (lexical analyzer, parser and intermediate code generator) and perhaps part of the code optimizer as well, can be carried over to the new compiler with relatively little change.

The k-dimensional Case

Now let us consider a k-dimensional array, where the ith index runs from 1 up to some d_i for each dimension $i = 1, 2, \ldots, k$. The generalization of row major form is to store the array in a block in such a fashion that if we scan the block from top to bottom, and note the indices of the word stored in each location, the rightmost index varies fastest, the second rightmost varies next fastest, and the leftmost index varies most slowly, like the dials of an odometer.

Mathematically, we give element $A[i_1, i_2, \ldots, i_k]$ offset

$$(i_1-1)\,d_2 d_3 \cdots d_k + (i_2-1)\,d_3 d_4 \cdots d_k + \cdots + (i_{k-1}-1)\,d_k + (i_k-1) \quad (8.1)$$

from the first word of the array. We can rewrite (8.1) as

$$(i_1 d_2 d_3 \cdots d_k + i_2 d_3 d_4 \cdots d_k + \cdots + i_{k-1} d_k + i_k)$$
$$- (d_2 d_3 \cdots d_k + d_3 d_4 \cdots d_k + \cdots + d_k + 1) \quad (8.2)$$

Since the d_i's were assumed fixed, the second term of (8.2) can be computed by the compiler. Thus, if a is the address of the first word of the block, then a minus the second term of (8.2) plays the role of "$a-21$" in the example of a 10×20 array considered above, and the first term of (8.2) is the generalization of $20i+j$ of that example. That is, code to access $A[i_1, i_2, \ldots, i_k]$ will consist of code to evaluate the first term of (8.2) using the equivalent formula

$$(\cdots ((i_1 d_2 + i_2)\,d_3 + i_3) \cdots)\,d_k + i_k \quad (8.3)$$

followed by code to "compute" a minus the second term of (8.2) (that code will be evaluated at compile time) followed by an access to the word whose address is equal to the latter value offset by some multiple of (8.3). That multiple is the number of bytes per word in the machine whose object code we are generating. For the purposes of discussion we shall use **bpw** to stand for the number of bytes per word.

The Translations Needed

Our chief problem in generating array references is to relate the computation of (8.3) to the grammar for array references, namely

$$L \rightarrow \text{id}[\text{elist}] \mid \text{id}$$

$$\text{elist} \rightarrow \text{elist}, \ E \mid E$$

In order that the various dimensional limits of the array be available as we group index expressions into an elist, it is necessary that elist have available to it a pointer to the symbol table entry for the array name. It is therefore useful to rewrite the productions as

$$L \rightarrow \text{elist} \ ] \mid \text{id}$$

$$\text{elist} \rightarrow \text{elist} \ , \ E \mid \text{id} \ [\ E$$

That is, the array name is attached to the leftmost index expression rather than being joined to elist when an L is formed.

We use translation elist.ARRAY to denote the symbol-table entry for the array name. We also use elist.NDIM to record the number of dimensions (index expressions) in the elist. Function LIMIT(ARRAY, i) returns d_i, the upper limit along the ith dimension of the array whose symbol-table entry is pointed to by ARRAY. Finally, elist.PLACE denotes the symbol-table entry for a name whose value is computed by the three-address code generated for elist.

An elist which produces the first m indices of a k-dimensional array reference A$[i_1, i_2, \ldots, i_k]$ will generate three-address code to compute

$$(\cdots ((i_1 d_2 + i_2) d_3 + i_3) \cdots) d_m + i_m \qquad (8.4)$$

Thus, when $m = k$ the code will compute (8.3). Note that the i_j's here may really be values of expressions, and code to evaluate those expressions will be interspersed with code to compute (8.3).

An l-value L will have two translations, $L.$PLACE and $L.$OFFSET. In the case that L is a simple name, $L.$PLACE will be a pointer to the symbol-table location for that name, and $L.$OFFSET will be **null**, indicating that the l-value is a simple name rather than an array reference. For **null** we can use a value which is too large or too small to be a possible offset.

The nonterminal E has the same translation $E.$PLACE, with the same meaning as in Section 7.7.

The Syntax-Directed Translation Scheme

We shall now describe the semantic actions in terms of our grammar:

$$
\begin{aligned}
&(1) \quad A \rightarrow L := E \\
&(2) \quad E \rightarrow E + E \\
&(3) \quad \mid (E)
\end{aligned}
$$

(4) | L
(5) $L \rightarrow$ elist]
(6) | **id**
(7)   elist $\rightarrow$ elist , E
(8) | **id** [E

As in the case of expressions without array references, the three-address code itself is produced by the GEN function invoked at each reduction. We assume that the reader can organize fields of the parsing stack to hold the auxiliary translations such as elist.DIM or L.PLACE. Note that the names of translations for different nonterminals sometimes differ, so, for space savings on the stack, some of these names can be made equivalent.

The semantic actions for each production are given below.

(1) $A \rightarrow L := E$

     { **if**(L.OFFSET = **null**) **then** /* L is a simple **id** */
         $GEN(L$.PLACE := E.PLACE);
     else
         GEN(L.PLACE[L.OFFSET] := E.PLACE) }

Here we generate a simple assignment if L is a simple name, and an indexed assignment into the location denoted by L otherwise.

(2) $E \rightarrow E^{(1)} + E^{(2)}$

     { T := NEWTEMP( );
      GEN(T := $E^{(1)}$.PLACE + $E^{(2)}$.PLACE);
      E.PLACE := T }

This code for arithmetic expressions is exactly the same as in Section 7.7.

(3) $E \rightarrow (E^{(1)})$

     { E.PLACE := $E^{(1)}$.PLACE }

(4) $E \rightarrow L$

     { **if**(L.OFFSET = **null**) **then** /* L is a simple **id** */
         E.PLACE := L.PLACE
     else
       begin
          T := NEWTEMP( );
          GEN(T := L.PLACE[L.OFFSET]);
          E.PLACE := T
       end }

If L is an array reference, then when L is reduced to E, we want the r-value. Therefore we use indexing to obtain the contents of the location

L.PLACE[L.OFFSET].

(5) $L \rightarrow$ elist]
$$
\begin{aligned}
&\{ \text{T} := \text{NEWTEMP}(\ ); \\
&\ \text{U} := \text{NEWTEMP}(\ ); \\
&\ \text{GEN}(\text{T} := \text{elist.ARRAY}-C); \\
&\ \text{GEN}(\text{U} := \textbf{bpw} * \text{elist.PLACE}); \\
&\ L.\text{PLACE} := \text{T}; \\
&\ L.\text{OFFSET} := \text{U} \ \}
\end{aligned}
$$

Here C is a constant representing **bpw** multiplied by the second term of
(8.3). U holds **bpw** times the value of elist.PLACE, which is the first term
of (8.3).

(6) $L \rightarrow$ **id**
$$
\begin{aligned}
&\{ L.\text{PLACE} := \textbf{id}.\text{PLACE} \\
&\ \ L.\text{OFFSET} := \textbf{null} \ \}
\end{aligned}
$$

id.PLACE is the location for **id** in the symbol table. A **null** offset indicates
a simple name.

(7) elist $\rightarrow$ elist$^{(1)}$, E
$$
\begin{aligned}
&\{ \text{T} := \text{NEWTEMP}(\ ); \\
&\ \text{GEN}(\text{T} := \text{elist}^{(1)}.\text{PLACE} * \\
&\qquad \text{LIMIT}(\text{elist}^{(1)}.\text{ARRAY}, \text{elist}^{(1)}.\text{NDIM} + 1)); \\
&\ \text{GEN}(\text{T} := \text{T} + E.\text{PLACE}); \\
&\ \text{elist.ARRAY} := \text{elist}^{(1)}.\text{ARRAY}; \\
&\ \text{elist.PLACE} := \text{T}; \\
&\ \text{elist.NDIM} := \text{elist}^{(1)}.\text{NDIM} + 1 \ \}
\end{aligned}
$$

Here T receives the value of (8.4) for $m = \text{elist}^{(1)}.\text{NDIM} + 1$. This value
is computed by taking elist$^{(1)}$.PLACE (which has the value of (8.4) for
$m = \text{elist}^{(1)}.\text{NDIM}$), multiplying it by d_{m+1} and adding i_{m+1} (which is the
value of the name E.PLACE). Note that if elist$^{(1)}$ has m components, then
elist on the left side of the production has $m+1$ components.

(8) elist $\rightarrow$ **id** [E
$$
\begin{aligned}
&\{ \text{elist.PLACE} := E.\text{PLACE}; \\
&\ \text{elist.DIM} := 1; \\
&\ \text{elist.ARRAY} := \textbf{id}.\text{PLACE} \ \}
\end{aligned}
$$

E.PLACE holds both the value of the expression and the value of (8.4) for
$m=1$.

Example 8.1. Let A be a 10×20 array. Therefore, $d_1=10$ and $d_2=20$. Take
bpw to be 4. The assignment $X := A[Y, Z]$ is translated into three-address

code as follows, using the semantic actions above. Figure 8.1 shows a parse tree for the statement, with the translations shown at the nodes. Recall that, in practice, the parse tree would not necessarily be built. More likely, the translations shown would be at the position on the stack corresponding to each node, and the translations would exist exactly when the corresponding node was actually represented by a nonterminal on the stack, which is exactly when their values will eventually be needed.

We use the actual names in place of **id**, and a notation like $E.\text{PLACE} = C$ means that the value of $E.\text{PLACE}$ is an index into the symbol-table location for C. Finally, we assume that temporaries $T_1, T_2, \cdots$ can be generated as needed.

The nodes in Fig. 8.1 are numbered according to the order in which a bottom-up parse would create them. This order is the one in which three-address code is generated for the nodes. Figure 8.2 gives the three-address statements generated in response to the reduction that "creates" each node.   □

8.2 Procedure Calls

Let us consider a grammar for a simple procedure call statement.

$$
\begin{array}{ll}
(1) & S \rightarrow \textbf{call id } (\text{elist}) \\
(2) & \text{elist} \rightarrow \text{elist} , \; E \\
(3) & \text{elist} \rightarrow E
\end{array}
$$

The translation for a call includes what is known as a *calling sequence,* a sequence of actions taken on entry to and exit from each procedure. While calling sequences can differ, even for implementations of the same language, the general idea is that the arguments are evaluated (if they are expressions, not just simple names) and put in a known place so that they may be accessed by the called procedure. Also put in a known place is the *return address,* the location to which the called routine must transfer after it is finished. The return address is usually the location in memory of the machine instruction that follows the call itself. If storage is statically allocated, as in FORTRAN, then the known place could be the code sequence itself, in which case the **param** intermediate statements can represent the placeholders for the parameters. Chapter 10 discusses parameter passing for languages with stack storage allocation.

Let us assume that parameters are passed by reference. If so, when generating three-address code for this type of call, it is sufficient to generate the three-address statements needed to evaluate those arguments that are expressions other than simple names, then follow them by a list of **param** three-address statements, one for each argument. If we do not want to mix the argument-evaluating statements with the **param** statements, we shall have to save the value of $E.\text{PLACE}$, for each expression E in

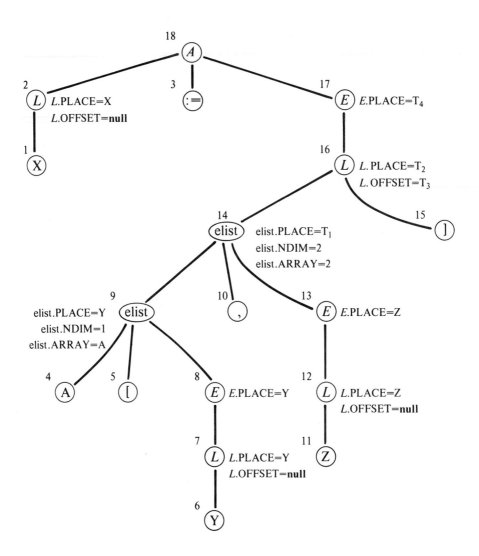

Fig. 8.1. Parse tree for X := A[Y, Z] with translations.

id(*E, E, . . . , E*).†

---

† If parameters are passed to the called procedure by putting them on a stack, there is no reason not to mix evaluation and **param** statements. The effect of **param** in the object code will be to place a parameter on the stack.

Statement   Generated at Node

Statement	Generated at Node
$T_1 := Y * 20$	14
$T_1 := T_1 + Z$	14
$T_2 := A - 84$	16
$T_3 := 4 * T_1$	16
$T_4 := T_2[T_3]$	17
$A := T_4$	18

Fig. 8.2. Three-address code for $X := A[Y, Z]$.

A convenient data structure in which to save these values is the *queue*, a first-in-first-out list. Our semantic routine for elist → elist , E will include a step to store E.PLACE on QUEUE. Then, the semantic routine for S → **call id** (elist) will generate a **param** statement for each item on QUEUE, causing these statements to follow the statements evaluating the argument expressions. Those statements were generated when the arguments themselves were reduced to E. The following syntax-directed translation incorporates these ideas.

(1) S → **call id** (elist)

> { **for** each item p on QUEUE **do**
>   GEN(**param** p);
>   GEN(**call id**.PLACE) }

The code for S is the code for elist, which evaluates the arguments, followed by a **param** p statement for each argument, followed by a **call** statement. A count of the number of parameters is excluded from the **call** statement but could be calculated as we computed elist.DIM in the previous section.

(2)   elist → elist , E

> { append E.PLACE to the end of QUEUE }

(3)   elist → E

> { initialize QUEUE to contain only E.PLACE }

Here QUEUE is emptied and then gets a single pointer to the symbol-table location for the name that denotes the value of E.

Ambiguities Involving Function and Array References

There is an unfortunate situation that arises in FORTRAN and many other languages, one which makes handling of procedures harder than it appears here. In Section 8.1 the semantic action for the production elist → elist , *E* is different from that given above. Since it is essential that the translation of elist depend only on the production used, not on the context (i.e., are we in a call statement or array reference?), we cannot use elist in the productions of the procedure call here. We could instead use another nonterminal "arglist" as follows:

$$S \rightarrow \textbf{call id} \ (\ \text{arglist} \ )$$

$$\text{arglist} \rightarrow \text{arglist} \ , \ E \mid E$$

This modification will work if we are using an LR-type parser, because the parser can "remember" having seen the **call** and can then reduce *E* to arglist rather than elist.

However, it is often not so clear from syntax alone whether we are working on a procedure call or an array reference. For example, some languages use parentheses, rather than brackets, to denote array references, and at the same time use the syntax PROC(ARG1 , . . . , ARGn) for a procedure call, with no keyword to tip us off, the way CALL does in FORTRAN. If we see A(I, J) on the input, we cannot tell whether I, J is an arglist or an elist until we see whether the right parenthesis is followed by a statement delimiter or an assignment operator. In fact, even FORTRAN presents great problems with function invocations. How are we to tell whether the statement B = A(I, J) involves an array reference or a call to function A?

The answer, of course, is that we must consult the symbol table. If A is an array, it will have been declared as such. But this answer is not entirely satisfactory, since the implication is that we must consult the symbol table about A at the time we reduce the first expression I in A(I, J) to elist or arglist. It is true that, when this reduction occurs, the value of the translation **id**.PLACE associated with A will be a pointer to the symbol-table location for A. However, A is not part of the production for arglist or elist.

There is an even more serious grammatical problem. Consider the assignment statement **id** := **id**(**id**). The right side of this statement can be parsed as an array reference or as a function call. Unfortunately, this is not the kind of grammatical ambiguity which can be resolved by the techniques suggested in Section 6.6. One solution is to let the lexical analyzer do the resolution of this ambiguity by consulting the symbol table when it finds the token representing the array or procedure name on the input. Associated with the regular expression for identifiers will be an action which, among other things, consults the symbol table about the identifier it has found. If that identifier is a procedure name, the lexical analyzer passes token **proc** to the parser and otherwise passes **id**. The syntax-directed translation scheme can then be constructed without difficulty.

8.3 Declarations

The simplest form of declaration syntax found in programming languages is a keyword denoting an attribute, followed by a list of names having that attribute. The semantic action associated with a statement of this kind should enter the declared attribute into the symbol-table entry for each name on the list. A grammar for such declarations may include productions of the form

$$D \rightarrow \text{integer namelist}$$
$$| \ \text{real namelist}$$
$$\text{namelist} \rightarrow \text{id , namelist}$$
$$| \ \text{id} \qquad\qquad (8.5)$$

The problem with grammar (8.5) is that one cannot get at the attribute associated with namelist until the entire list of **id**'s has been reduced to namelist. Thus, a syntax-directed translation scheme based on (8.5) cannot make the correct symbol-table entries when **id** or **id** , namelist is reduced to namelist. To avoid this difficulty, we can adopt either of the two techniques introduced in the previous section.

1. We can use special nonterminals to distinguish between lists of reals and integers. For example, we could rewrite (8.5) as:

$$D \rightarrow \text{integer intlist}$$
$$| \ \text{real reallist}$$
$$\text{intlist} \rightarrow \text{id , intlist}$$
$$| \ \text{id}$$
$$\text{reallist} \rightarrow \text{id , reallist}$$
$$| \ \text{id}$$

relying on the memory ability of an LR parser to know whether to reduce the first **id** to intlist or reallist. This approach is undesirable since the number of productions grows as the number of possible attributes.

2. We can let the translation of namelist in (8.5) be just the list of names encountered. Then the semantic action for the first two productions in (8.5) can enter the appropriate attribute into the symbol table for each name on the list.

Following the method used in Section 8.1, we can save the trouble of processing lists in method (2) if we rewrite grammar (8.5) as:

$$D \rightarrow D \text{ , } \textbf{id}$$

$$| \text{ } \textbf{integer id}$$

$$| \text{ } \textbf{real id} \qquad\qquad\qquad (8.6)$$

The semantic actions can now be defined. We give nonterminal D the translation $D.$ATTR. The procedure ENTER(P, A) associates attribute A with the symbol-table entry pointed to by P. As usual, **id**.PLACE points to the symbol-table entry for the name represented by the token **id**.

$D \rightarrow$ **integer id**   { ENTER(**id**.PLACE , **integer**);
                    $D.$ ATTR := **integer** }

$D \rightarrow$ **real id**   { ENTER(**id**.PLACE , **real**);
                    $D.$ ATTR := **real** }

$D \rightarrow D^{(1)}$, **id**   { ENTER(**id**.PLACE , $D^{(1)}.$ATTR);
                    $D.$ ATTR := $D^{(1)}.$ATTR }

8.4 Case Statements

The "switch" or "case" statement is available in a variety of languages; even the FORTRAN computed and assigned goto's can be regarded as varieties of the switch statement. The switch syntax that we shall use is shown in Fig. 8.3.

```
switch expression
    begin
        case value:        statement
        case value:        statement
            .
            .
            .
        case value:        statement
        default:           statement
    end
```

Fig. 8.3. Switch statement.

There is a selector expression, which is to be evaluated, followed by n constant values which that expression might take, perhaps including a *default* "value," which always matches the expression if no other value does. The intended translation of a switch is code to:

1. Evaluate the expression.

2. Find which value in the list of cases is the same as the value of the expression. Recall that the default value matches the expression if none of the values explicitly mentioned in cases does.

3. Execute the statement associated with the value found.

Step (2) is an n-way branch, which can be implemented in one of several ways. If the number of cases is not too great, say 10 at most, then it is reasonable to use a sequence of conditional goto's, each of which tests for an individual value and transfers to the code for the corresponding statement.

A more compact way to implement this sequence of conditional goto's is to create a table of pairs, each pair consisting of a value and a label for the code of the corresponding statement. Code is generated to place at the end of this table the value of the expression itself, paired with the label for the default statement. A simple loop can be generated by the compiler to compare the value of the expression with each value in the table, being assured that if no other match is found, the last (default) entry is sure to match.

If the number of values exceeds 10 or so, it is more efficient to construct a hash table (see Section 9.2) for the values, with the labels of the various statements as entries. If no entry for the value possessed by the switch expression is found, a jump to the default statement can be generated.

There is a common special case in which an even more efficient implementation of the n-way branch exists. If the values all lie in some small range, say i_{min} to i_{max}, and the number of different values is a reasonable fraction of $i_{max}-i_{min}$, then we can construct an array of labels, with the label of the statement for value j in the entry of the table with offset $j-i_{min}$ and the label for the default in entries not filled otherwise. To perform the switch, evaluate the expression to obtain the value j, check that it is in the range i_{min} to i_{max} and transfer indirectly to the table entry at offset $j-i_{min}$. For example, if the expression is of type character, a table of, say, 128 entries (depending on the character set) may be created and transferred through with no range testing.

Syntax-Directed Translation of Case Statements

Consider the following switch statement.

```
switch E
    begin
            case V₁:   S₁
            case V₂:   S₂
                .

                .

                .
            case Vₙ₋₁: Sₙ₋₁
            default:   Sₙ
    end
```

With a syntax-directed translation scheme, it is convenient to translate this case statement into intermediate code that has the form of Fig. 8.4.

```
                code to evaluate E into T
                goto TEST
    L₁:         code for S₁
                goto NEXT
    L₂:         code for S₂
                goto NEXT
                    .

                    .

                    .
    Lₙ₋₁:       code for Sₙ₋₁
                goto NEXT
    Lₙ:         code for Sₙ
                goto NEXT
    TEST:       if T = V₁ goto L₁
                if T = V₂ goto L₂
                    .

                    .

                    .
                if T = Vₙ₋₁ goto Lₙ₋₁
                goto Lₙ
    NEXT:
```

Fig. 8.4. Translation of case statement.

The tests all appear at the end is so that a simple code generator can recognize the multiway branch and generate efficient code for it, using the most appropriate implementation suggested at the beginning of this section.

If we generate the more straightforward sequence shown in Fig. 8.5, the compiler would have to do extensive analysis to find the most efficient implementation. Note that it is inconvenient to place the branching statements at the beginning, because the compiler could not then emit code for each of the S_i's as it saw them.

$$
\begin{aligned}
&\quad\quad \text{code to evaluate E into T} \\
&\quad\quad \textbf{if } T \neq V_1 \textbf{ goto } L_1 \\
&\quad\quad \text{code for } S_1 \\
&\quad\quad \textbf{goto } NEXT \\
L_1:&\quad\quad \textbf{if } T \neq V_2 \textbf{ goto } L_2 \\
&\quad\quad \text{code for } S_2 \\
&\quad\quad \textbf{goto } NEXT \\
L_2:& \\
&\quad\quad . \\
&\quad\quad . \\
&\quad\quad . \\
L_{n-2}:&\quad\quad \textbf{if } T \neq V_{n-1} \textbf{ goto } L_{n-1} \\
&\quad\quad \text{code for } S_{n-1} \\
&\quad\quad \textbf{goto } NEXT \\
L_{n-1}:&\quad\quad \text{code for } S_n \\
NEXT:&
\end{aligned}
$$

Fig. 8.5. Another translation of case statement.

To translate into the form of Fig. 8.4, when we see the keyword **switch**, we generate two new labels TEST and NEXT, and a new temporary T. Then as we parse the expression E, we generate code to evaluate E into T. After processing E, we generate the jump **goto** TEST.

Then as we see each **case** keyword, we create a new label L_i and enter it into the symbol table. We place on a stack, used only to store cases, a pointer to this symbol-table entry and the value V_i of the case constant. (If this switch is embedded in one of the statements internal to another switch, we place a marker on the stack to separate cases for the interior switch from those for the outer switch.)

We process each statement **case** V_i: S_i by emitting the newly created label L_i, followed by the code for S_i, followed by the jump **goto** NEXT. Then when the keyword **end** terminating the body of the switch is found, we are ready to generate the code for the n-way branch. Reading the pointer-value pairs on the case stack from the bottom to the top, we can generate a sequence of three-address statements of the form

$$\textbf{case } V_1 \; L_1$$
$$\textbf{case } V_2 \; L_2$$

.

.

.

$$\textbf{case } V_{n-1} \; L_{n-1}$$
$$\textbf{case } T \; L_n$$
$$\textbf{label } \text{NEXT}$$

where T is the name holding the value of the selector expression E, and L_n is the label for the default statement. The **case** V_i L_i three-address statement is a synonym for **if** $T = V_i$ **goto** L_i in Fig. 8.4, but the **case** is easier for the final code generator to detect as a candidate for special treatment. At the code-generation phase, these sequences of **case** statements can be translated into an n-way branch of the most efficient type, depending on how many there are and whether the values fall into a small range.

8.5 Record Structures

Record structures as found in COBOL, PL/I, PASCAL, and C are important language features used to aggregate data. This section considers the translation of C-like record structures into intermediate code; the next section considers the additional work necessary to handle PL/I-like structures, principally the interpretation of partially qualified references (e.g., A.C instead of A.B.C).

Types in C

The *basic types* in C are characters, integers, reals, and double precision reals. From these, we can recursively create new types as follows:

1. An array of elements of a given type (basic or not) is a type.
2. A pointer to any type is a type.
3. A procedure returning an item of any specified type is a type.
4. A structure consisting of a list of fields, each of some particular type, is a type. The field types may include pointers to structures of the type being defined, of a type previously defined, or of a type to be defined.

Any structure type can be given a name. The reader familiar with ALGOL 68 may notice a resemblance of C types to ALGOL 68 modes. Some examples of C types and the syntax used for defining them follow.

Example 8.2.
1. Identifier P may be declared to be a pointer to an integer by writing **int** *P.

2. A linked list of integers may be declared by:

struct LIST_TYPE {
    int DATA;
    struct LIST_TYPE *NEXT;
} LIST[1000];

This declaration defines an array of records called LIST; the array contains 1000 records, numbered 0 to 999.[†] The type name given to the records is LIST_TYPE. This name may be used to specify a pointer to a record of this structure type or to declare other names besides LIST to have this type. A record of type LIST_TYPE consists of an integer field named DATA and a pointer field named NEXT, which points to a record of type LIST_TYPE.

3. An array giving student names (first name: 15 characters, middle initial: 1 character, and last name: 15 characters) and grades (20 assignments) could be defined by:

struct {
    struct {
        char FIRST[15];
        char MIDDLE;
        char LAST[15];
    } NAME;
    int GRADE[20];
} CLASS[100];

Note that a structure definition can be nested within another structure definition. The inner structure is the type declaration for field NAME. This declaration plays the same syntactic role as **int** does for GRADE. Note also that neither structure is given a type name, which is optional. The above declaration is equivalent to the PL/I declaration

DECLARE
    1 CLASS(100),
        2 NAME,
            3 FIRST CHAR(15),
            3 MIDDLE CHAR,
            3 LAST CHAR(15),
        2 GRADE(20) FIXED BINARY;

□

---

† All arrays in C are numbered beginning at 0.

Translating Structure Declarations

Let us now design a grammar for structure declarations. The question of the type of object a pointer points to is important both for catching accidental misuses of pointers at compile time and for interpreting addition of constants to pointers (in C, p=p+1 means add to p the number of memory units taken by an object of the type that p points to). As all pointers occupy the same amount of memory, we may simplify the syntax of structure definitions and treat all declarations of pointers the same. Also for simplicity we shall dispense with type names and types involving functions. Types can thus be defined by the following productions:

$$\text{type} \rightarrow \textbf{struct} \; \{ \; \text{fieldlist} \; \}$$
$$| \; \textbf{ptr}$$
$$| \; \textbf{char}$$
$$| \; \textbf{int}$$
$$| \; \textbf{float}$$
$$| \; \textbf{double}$$

$$\text{fieldlist} \rightarrow \text{fieldlist field ;}$$
$$| \; \text{field ;}$$

$$\text{field} \rightarrow \text{type } \textbf{id}$$
$$| \; \text{field [} \textbf{integer} \text{]}^\dagger$$

C does not permit multiple subscripts. However, a field MAT which is a 10×20 matrix of characters could be declared **char** MAT[10][20].

Field names in C are stored in a symbol table, and an offset is associated with each one. That offset is the number of memory units preceding the field in any structure in which it is declared. Note that the same field name may be used in two different structures, but it is an error if the same field name has two different associated offsets or types. In order to compute the offset associated with a field name we must know the *width* (number of memory units) of previous fields in the structure. Thus the width of a type must also be computed, as the type determines the width of a field. If a name is an array declaration, the number of elements must be computed, as this figure also affects the width of the field with that name.

Let us use the translation WIDTH for field, fieldlist, and type, with the obvious meaning. We shall also use the translation field.NAME to remember the field name. Procedure D_ENTER(NAME, SIZE) increases the number of dimensions for NAME by one and enters the last dimension as SIZE in the symbol table entry for NAME. Procedure W_ENTER(NAME, WIDTH) enters WIDTH as the width of each element of NAME. If NAME is not an array, then its width is the number of

---

† Note that **int** is a keyword, while **integer** is used here as a token type denoting any string of digits.

locations taken by data of NAME's type. Finally, procedure O_ENTER(NAME, OFFSET) makes OFFSET the number for which field name NAME stands. This information, also, is recorded in the symbol-table entry for NAME. We use **id**.NAME for the name associated with this instance of the token **id** and **integer**.VAL for the numerical value of an integer. The translation rules follow.

> field → type **id**
>> { field.WIDTH := type.WIDTH;
>> field.NAME := **id**.NAME;
>> W_ENTER(**id**.NAME, type.WIDTH) }

> field → field$^{(1)}$ [**integer**]
>> { field.WIDTH := field$^{(1)}$.WIDTH * **integer**.VAL
>> field.NAME := field$^{(1)}$.NAME;
>> D_ENTER(field$^{(1)}$.NAME, **integer**.VAL) }

The width of a fieldlist is the sum of the widths of the fields in the list, as reflected by the next rules.

> fieldlist → field ;
>> { O_ENTER(field.NAME, 0);
>> fieldlist.WIDTH := field.WIDTH }

> fieldlist →fieldlist$^{(1)}$ field ;
>> { fieldlist.WIDTH := fieldlist$^{(1)}$.WIDTH + field.WIDTH†
>> O_ENTER(field.NAME, fieldlist$^{(1)}$.WIDTH) }

> type → **struct** '{' fieldlist '}'
>> { type.WIDTH := fieldlist.WIDTH }

For the other productions for type we set type.WIDTH to the width appropriate for each primitive type. For example,

> type → **char**   { type.WIDTH := 1 }

If pointers take four memory units:

> type → **ptr**   { type.WIDTH := 4 }

and so on.

---

† If fields must start on a word boundary, this formula must be modified to take that fact into account, adding enough so that the field may begin on such a boundary.

Structure References

C provides two methods of accessing structures. If P is a pointer to a record of a particular structure type, and FIELD is a field name for that structure, then P→FIELD denotes the value of that field in the record pointed to by P. In C, since field names are shorthands for offsets, the *l*-value of P→FIELD is just the *r*-value of P plus the constant offset represented by FIELD. The *r*-value of P→FIELD is the contents of that location, of course. Translation of the → operator is thus easy.

The other way to reference structures is by the . operator. If RECORD is a record of a certain structure type and FIELD is a field name for that type, then RECORD.FIELD denotes the *l*- or *r*-value of that field. If the type of FIELD is itself a structure, and SUBFIELD is a field within that structure, then RECORD.FIELD.SUBFIELD denotes the value of that subfield, and so on. The *l*-value of such an expression is computed by adding the *l*-value of RECORD to the offsets of FIELD and SUBFIELD.

One complication occurs with both the → and . notations, when either record names or field names have subscripts. For example the *l*-value of RECORD[10].FIELD[20] is computed by taking the *l*-value of RECORD[10] and adding to it the offset of FIELD plus 20 times the width of the elements of FIELD. The *l*-value of RECORD[10] is the *l*-value of RECORD plus 10 times the width of a structure of whose type RECORD is.

Example 8.3. Referring to Example 8.2(3), consider the *l*-value of CLASS[50].NAME.LAST[13]. If characters have width 1 and integers have width 4, then the width of a record with the given structure is $15+1+15+20*4 = 111$. The offset of NAME is 0 and the offset of LAST (within the substructure consisting of FIRST, MIDDLE, and LAST) is 16. If CLASS has *l*-value 1000, then CLASS[50].NAME.LAST[13] has *l*-value $1000+111*50+0+16+1*13 = 6579$.

In many machines, however, integers must begin at a word boundary (multiples of 4, in this example). In that case, when we compute widths of a fieldlist, we must round up to the next multiple of 4 whenever a fieldlist is followed by a field whose type is integer or a structure containing an integer.

For example, in the fieldlist for class, composed of NAME and GRADE, since GRADE is an integer, we must increase the width of NAME to 32. Thus the width of a CLASS record is 112 bytes, not 111, and CLASS[50].NAME.LAST[13] has *l*-value 6629. We leave as an exercise the revision of the syntax-directed translation scheme above to compute field widths on this new basis. It is convenient to introduce an additional translation to indicate whether a type, field, or fieldlist has to be aligned on a word boundary. □

8.6 PL/I-Style Structures

Structures in PL/I are similar to C structures introduced in the last section, but there are two important differences.

1. The same field name may be repeated in different contexts and need not have the same width or offset in different contexts. This forces us to create a symbol-table entry for each instance of each field name.

2. References to structure components may be elliptical as long as they are unambiguous. That is, some field names can be omitted, and we need not give more of the path from the root of the structure tree to the desired component than is necessary to specify that component. This requirement forces us to represent structures by linking their field names in the symbol table into a tree structure that mimics the structure itself. Moreover, given a field name F we must be able to find all the fields with name F. This information is needed when we search for the node in the forest of structures that a given structure reference represents. It is also needed so we can check that such a node is unique.

3. The scope rules of a block-structured language apply to field names as they do to other names in PL/I.

The symbol-table entries for field names will have the width, offset, and dimension information described in the previous section. The symbol table will also have space for pointers representing the tree and for linking fields with identical names. As a field may have an arbitrary number of subfields, we shall adopt the "leftmost child — right sibling" representation of trees, that is, the binary-tree representation discussed in Knuth [1968]. It is also convenient to have each node point to its parent.

Example 8.4. The following is a PL/I structure declaration.

```
DECLARE   1   PERSON (1000),
              2   FATHER,
                  3   FIRST,
                  3   LAST,
              2   MOTHER
                  3   FIRST,
                  3   LAST,
              2   ADDRESS,
                  3   STREET,
                  3   CITY,
          1   HOME (1000),
              2   STREET,
              2   CITY,
              2   RESIDENT,
```

                                3   FIRST,
                                3   LAST;

Some unambiguous references are

                    PERSON.MOTHER.LAST
                    RESIDENT.LAST
                    HOME.STREET
                    PERSON.CITY

However, the reference CITY is ambiguous; it could mean HOME.CITY or
PERSON.ADDRESS.CITY. The forest representing these structures is
shown in Fig. 8.6. We use dashed lines to link fields with the same name,
solid lines for leftmost child and right sibling links, and wavy lines for
parent links.   □

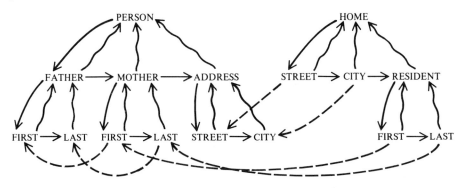

Fig. 8.6.   Forest representing PL/I structures.

Creating Structure Representations from Declarations

In essence, a PL/I structure definition is an alternating list of level numbers
and field names. (We ignore type declarations and dimensions, which must
be stored in the symbol table along with the field names.) When we see a
pair *l* NAME, where *l* is the level number and NAME the field name, we
must create a new entry in the symbol table. This entry is a field name and
the associated identifier is NAME. The first thing we do is link this entry
to the list of other fields with identifier NAME (the dashed lines in Fig.
8.6).

We assume that the symbol table is such that if we search for an entry
for identifier NAME, we first encounter the most recent declaration of
NAME. The hash-table organization described in Section 9.2 has this property, and the linear list organization can also be searched in a suitable
manner. It is convenient to search most recent declarations first so that
when a match for a field reference is first encountered, it is in the closest

surrounding block having a matching declaration.

Next, we must determine where NAME fits into the forest of fields being constructed. The rule to be followed is that a field name at level l is an ancestor of all fields following it until a field at level l or less is encountered. Note that the level of a child may exceed the level of its parent by more than one and that siblings need not have the same level number. For example,

> DECLARE 1 A,
> 7 B,
> 4 C;

means the same as

> DECLARE 1 A,
> 2 B,
> 2 C;

To build the forest, we must record the previous field name, so let us assume that P points to the symbol-table entry for the previous field name. For convenience, assume that P initially points to a dummy field name at level zero. This field will have as children the roots of the structure at level 1; for example, in Fig. 8.6 HOME will be the right sibling of PERSON, and both will be children of the dummy node.

If P points to a field, let its level (recorded in the symbol table) be l_{old} and its field name be OLDNAME (also recorded in the symbol table). Let l_{parent} be the level of OLDNAME's parent in the tree. Then take the appropriate one of the following actions.

1. If $l_{parent} < l \leq l_{old}$, then make NAME the right sibling OLDNAME. Give NAME the same parent as OLDNAME.

2. If $l > l_{old}$, make NAME the leftmost child of OLDNAME.

3. If $l \leq l_{parent}$, then NAME is the child of some ancestor of OLDNAME. Make P point to the parent of OLDNAME and repeat the process.

Finally, set P to the symbol-table entry for NAME, preparing to process the next field declaration. The entire algorithm is given as the routine ENTER in Fig. 8.7. Certain fields in the symbol table, namely LEVEL, PARENT, SIBLING, and LCHILD have their obvious meaning. LEVEL(P), for example, means the level of the entry pointed to by P (what we have called l_{old}). We also assume that Q points to the entry in the symbol table being created for NAME, and the link to the next field with the identifier NAME has already been inserted.

```
procedure ENTER( );
begin LOOP:
    if l ⩽ LEVEL(P) and l > LEVEL(PARENT(P)) then
        /* NAME is a sibling of OLDNAME */
        begin
            SIBLING(P) := Q;
            PARENT(Q) := PARENT(P);
            SIBLING(Q) := LCHILD(Q) := null
        end
    else if l > LEVEL(P) then
        /* NAME is the leftmost child of OLDNAME */
        begin
            LCHILD(P) := Q;
            PARENT(Q) := P;
            SIBLING(Q) := LCHILD(Q) := null
        end
    else/* l ⩾ LEVEL(PARENT(P)) and NAME is a child
            of some ancestor of OLDNAME */
        begin
            P := PARENT(P);
            goto LOOP
        end;
    LEVEL(Q) := l;
    P := Q  /* make NAME the "previous" entry */
end
```

Fig. 8.7. Entering NAME at level l into the forest.

Handling Elliptical Structure References

A structure reference is of the form $F_n.F_{n-1}.\cdots.F_1$, where each F_i is a field name. Subscripts may be interspersed with the F_i's, but we shall ignore these for the moment. In PL/I we must first look for a path in the structure forest from some node labeled F_1 to a root, such that the path reads $F_1, F_2, \ldots, F_n$. However, some of the labels of the implied path may be left out of the structure reference so, failing to find a complete match, we must then look for a path from a node labeled F_1 to a root such that the path is labeled by a supersequence of $F_1, F_2, \ldots, F_n$. A *supersequence* is formed from a given sequence by inserting objects anywhere into the sequence. For example, A,B,C,D,E is a supersequence of B,E. Moreover, our search must proceed from inner to outer blocks. A match is not made ambiguous by another match in a surrounding block, even if the latter match is exact.

Fortunately, our search is simplified by the fact that if $X_1, X_2, \ldots, X_m$ is a supersequence of $Y_1, Y_2, \ldots, Y_r$, then we can discover that fact by searching for the lowest i_1 such that $Y_1 = X_{i_1}$. Then look for the lowest i_2, such that $i_2 > i_1$ and $Y_2 = X_{i_2}$, and so on. Thus, the method below succeeds in finding a path labeled by a supersequence of $F_1, F_2, \ldots, F_n$ and checking for ambiguity of the structure reference $F_n.F_{n-1}.\cdots.F_1$. We want as output that field named F_1 which is unambiguously specified by this reference. If the reference is meaningless or ambiguous, we want an error message.

The method we suggest goes as follows. Let P point, in turn, to each symbol-table entry for field name F_1.[†] We have assumed that these entries are linked in the symbol table so this search can be done efficiently. Apply the procedure SUBSEQ(P, 1) of Fig. 8.8 to each such entry. The first time SUBSEQ returns **true** we have the desired field. If SUBSEQ returns **true** zero times or more than once, we have a meaningless or ambiguous reference. However, a reference that matches precisely a path to the root is not made ambiguous by another path that is a proper supersequence.

procedure SUBSEQ(P, i) /* P points to a symbol-table entry;
       i indexes the fields of the reference $F_n.F_{n-1}.\cdots.F_1$ */
if $i = n + 1$ **then return true** /* success */
else if P = **null then return false** /* failure; no more path in the forest */
else if F_i = NAME(P) **then** /* field matched */
      return SUBSEQ(PARENT(P), $i + 1$)
else return SUBSEQ(PARENT(P), i)

Fig. 8.8. Testing if a sequence of field names is a subsequence of the names on a path in the forest.

The LIKE Attribute

A shorthand found in PL/I for describing structures concerns the keyword LIKE. If one substructure is identical to another, then the second may be declared LIKE the first.

Example 8.5. The structure of Example 8.4 could be expressed as follows:

    DECLARE   1   PERSON (1000),
                     2   FATHER,
                         3   FIRST,
                         3   LAST,

[†] As PL/I has block structure, not all field names F may be currently active. These can be deleted from the list of names with identifier F. This matter is discussed more fully in Section 9.3.

```
          2   MOTHER LIKE FATHER,
          2   ADDRESS,
              3   STREET,
              3   CITY,
      1   HOME (1000),
          2   STREET,
          2   CITY,
          2   RESIDENT LIKE FATHER;                    □
```

To implement the LIKE feature, we need a field in the symbol-table entries that enable us to link an entry to any other entries declared LIKE it.

Example 8.6. The forest for the declaration of Example 8.5 would appear as in Fig. 8.9. Wavy lines indicate LIKE links.   □

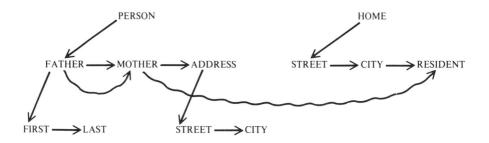

Fig. 8.9. Forest with links for LIKE relationships.

We can modify the procedure SUBSEQ of Fig. 8.8 to check whether the entry pointed to by P has a chain of LIKE pointers to any other entries, and if so, to call itself on each of these entries in turn. SUBSEQ must also be modified to return a path in the forest that represents a supersequence of $F_n, F_{n-1}, \ldots, F_1$ rather than just an indication that one exists starting at a particular node labeled F_1.

Handling Subscripts

A structure reference may include subscripts, like PERSON.CITY(500). These subscripts should be stored aside while the missing fields in the reference, if any, are inserted. Note that the subscripts need not be attached to the field that they modify, but must appear in their proper order. Once the complete reference, say $X_m.X_{m-1}. \cdots .X_1$ is discovered by the methods discussed previously, the list of subscripts, say $I_1, I_2, \ldots, I_k$ can be matched with these. That is, each field X_i has been declared to have a certain number of dimensions. If X_m has two dimensions, then I_1 and I_2 are its subscripts. If X_{m-1} has no dimension, but X_{m-2} has one, then that dimension is I_3, and so on. The number of dimensions required by the X's should be k, or it is an error.

Note that the process of matching subscripts to field names cannot be done simply using syntax-directed processing. In fact, the whole matter of handling elliptical references is not appropriate for syntax-directed translation. The compiler must gather a structure reference and its associated subscripts in a table and process the entire reference after it has been seen.

Exercises

8.1 Translate the following assignment statement to intermediate code using the scheme of Section 8.1.

$$A[I, J] := B[I, J] + C[A[K, L]] + D[I+J]$$

8.2 Several languages have declarations in which the attribute follows the list of names, as in

$$D \rightarrow \text{namelist } \textbf{integer}$$
$$| \text{ namelist } \textbf{real}$$
$$\text{namelist} \rightarrow \textbf{id} \text{ , namelist}$$
$$| \textbf{ id}$$

Rewrite this grammar so that it may be easily translated into a series of actions that enter attribute information into a symbol table. Give the appropriate semantic actions.

*8.3 Some languages, such as PL/I, permit a list of names to be given a list of attributes and also permit declarations to be nested within one another. The following grammar abstracts the problems inherent in the PL/I declaration syntax.

$$D \rightarrow \text{namelist attrlist}$$
$$| \text{ (} D \text{) attrlist}$$
$$\text{namelist} \rightarrow \textbf{id} \text{ , namelist}$$
$$| \textbf{ id}$$
$$\text{attrlist} \rightarrow A \text{ attrlist}$$
$$| A$$
$$A \rightarrow \textbf{fixed} \mid \textbf{float} \mid \textbf{binary} \mid \textbf{decimal} \mid \textbf{real} \mid \textbf{complex}$$

The meaning of $D \rightarrow (D)$ attrlist is that all names mentioned in the declaration inside parentheses are given the attributes on attrlist, no matter how many levels of nesting there are. Note that a declaration of n names and m attributes may cause nm pieces of information to be entered into the symbol table. Give a syntax-directed translation scheme for declarations defined by this grammar.

8.4 a) Write a grammar for case statements of the type discussed in Section 8.4. Assume the nonterminal statement can derive a case statement or "other statement."

b) Write a syntax-directed translation scheme to go along with your grammar from part (a), producing three-address code.

c) Use your translation scheme to translate the case statement of Fig. 8.10.

> **switch** A+B
>   **begin**
>   **case** 2: X := Y
>   **case** 5:
>   **switch** X
>   **begin**
>   **case** 0: A := B+1
>   **case** 1: A := B+3
>   **default** : A := 2
>   **end**
>   **case** 9: X := Y−1
>   **default** : X := Y+1
>   **end**

Fig. 8.10. A case statement.

8.5 Using the syntax-directed translation scheme of Section 8.5, and the structure declaration (3) of Example 8.2:

a) Show the parse tree for the structure declaration.

b) Show the symbol-table entries made in response to the declaration. Assume a machine with four bytes per word, requiring integers to begin at a word boundary.

8.6 Show the symbol table entries for the PL/I structure declaration of Fig. 8.11. Assume a machine with two bytes per word and eight bits per byte. Assume a FLOAT takes two words as a default, and fixed and floating point numbers must be aligned on a word boundary.

8.7 Show the layout of storage for the structure of Fig. 8.11.

8.8 Determine the offset from the base of the TEAM structure

```
DECLARE     1   PLAYER (1000),
            2      NUMBER FIXED DECIMAL (2),
            2      BAT_AV FLOAT,
            2      SALARY FIXED DECIMAL (6),
            1   TEAM (24),
            2      NAME CHAR (30),
            2      MANAGER LIKE PLAYER,
            2      CAPTAIN LIKE PLAYER;
```

Fig. 8.11. A structure.

represented by CAPTAIN.SALARY(10).

*8.9 All our calculations of offsets for field names were based on the assumption that any data element could start on any word boundary. In general, however, if a field F consists of subfields $F_1, F_2, \ldots, F_n$ that can only begin once every $k_1, k_2, \ldots, k_n$ bytes, then an F can only begin once every k bytes, where k is the least common multiple of $k_1, k_2, \ldots, k_n$. Suppose we have a machine with two types of data — the *glorp*, which can only begin at bytes 0, 3, 6, . . . and the *nerd*, which can only begin at bytes 0, 5, 10, ...

a) How many bytes are taken by the structure declaration of Fig. 8.12?

b) Can you find a rearrangement of the subfields in Fig. 8.12 that saves space?

```
DECLARE     1   A (100),
            2      B (10),
            3         C GLORP (2),
            3         D NERD (3),
            2      E GLORP (4);
```

Fig. 8.12. Fanciful structure.

*8.10 Give an efficient algorithm to format a structure under the generalized "word boundary" constraints of Exercise 8.9, so that each data element begins at an appropriate position.

*8.11 We shall see in Section 10.1 that it is sometimes useful for **param** statements in a procedure call to come out in reverse order, that is, with the first actual parameter appearing last. Modify the scheme of Section 8.2 to make this happen. Can we avoid the use of a list like QUEUE to store the temporaries holding the values of the parameters?

8.12 In Section 7.11 we discussed a translation scheme in which the non-terminal L, standing for l-value, was assumed to have a translation $L.\text{INDEX}$ whose r-value was the l-value of a name used to index a for-loop. Show how to modify the translation scheme of Section 8.1 so that L there has such a translation.

Bibliographic Notes

The general references for Chapter 7 are also appropriate for this chapter. The implementation of structure references is discussed by Gates and Poplawski [1973] and Abrahams [1974].

There are many other interesting programming-language constructs whose translation we have not had the space to discuss. The reader is referred to Randell and Russell [1964] and Grau, Hill, and Langmaack [1967] for detailed discussion of implementation of ALGOL 60 constructs, to Freiburghouse [1969] for PL/I, to Wirth [1971] for PASCAL, and to Branquart *et al.* for ALGOL 68.

CHAPTER 9

Symbol
Tables

A compiler needs to collect and use information about the names appearing in the source program. This information is entered into a data structure called a symbol table. The information collected about a name includes the string of characters by which it is denoted, its type (e.g., integer, real, string), its form (e.g., a simple variable, a structure), its location in memory, and other attributes depending on the language.

Each entry in the symbol table is a pair of the form (name, information). Each time a name is encountered, the symbol table is searched to see whether that name has been seen previously. If the name is new, it is entered into the table. Information about that name is entered into the table during lexical and syntactic analysis.

The information collected in the symbol table is used during several stages in the compilation process. It is used in semantic analysis, that is, in checking that uses of names are consistent with their implicit or explicit declarations. It is also used during code generation. There we need to know how much and what kind of run-time storage must be allocated to a name.

There are also a number of ways in which the symbol table can be used to aid in error detection and correction. For example, we can record whether an error message such as "variable A undefined" has been printed out before, and refrain from doing so more than once. Additionally, space in the symbol table can be used for code-optimization purposes, such as to flag temporaries that are used more than once (see Chapter 12).

This chapter discusses the principal ways of organizing and accessing symbol tables. The primary issues in symbol-table design are the format of the entries, the method of access, and the place where they are stored (primary or secondary storage). Block-structured languages impose another problem in that the same identifier can be used to represent distinct names with nested scopes. In compilers for such languages, the symbol-table mechanism must make sure that the innermost occurrence of an identifier is always found first, and that names are removed from the active portion of the symbol table when they are no longer active.

327

9.1 The Contents of a Symbol Table

In the abstract, a symbol table is merely a table with two fields, a name field and an information field. We require several capabilities of the symbol table. We need to be able to

1. determine whether a given name is in the table,
2. add a new name to the table,
3. access the information associated with a given name, and
4. add new information for a given name,
5. delete a name or group of names from the table.

In a compiler, the names in the symbol table denote objects of various sorts. There may be separate tables for variable names, labels, procedure names, constants, field names (for structures) and other types of names, depending on the language. It is often useful to have more than one table, because the amount of space needed per name may vary considerably, depending on the usage of the name. However, one table can suffice, especially if the formats of the information entries may vary. Depending on how lexical analysis is performed, it may be useful to enter keywords into the symbol table initially. If the language does not *reserve* keywords (forbid the use of keywords as identifiers), then it is essential that keywords be entered into the symbol table and that they have associated information warning of their possible use as a keyword.

We assume the reader is familiar with the common data structures that can be used to implement symbol tables. The chief alternatives are linear lists, hash tables, and various sorts of tree structures. At issue is the speed with which an entry can be added or accessed. A linear list is slow to access but simple to implement. A hash table is fast but more complex. Tree structures give intermediate performance. We shall discuss several alternative implementations briefly in the next section.

To appreciate the level of detail that goes into the symbol-table contents, let us consider the data that can be associated with a name in the symbol table. This information includes:

1. The string of characters denoting the name. If the same identifier can be used in more than one block or procedure, then an indication of which block or procedure this name belongs to must also be given.
2. Attributes of the name, such as those mentioned in Section 2.4, and also information identifying what use is being made of the name (e.g., is it a label, a formal parameter, an array).
3. Parameters, such as the number of dimensions of arrays and the upper and lower limits along each dimension.
4. (Possibly) an offset describing the position in storage to be allocated for the name.

This information is entered into the symbol table at various times. Attributes are entered in response to declarations as discussed in Section 8.3. The syntax of the language may also implicitly declare variables to play certain roles. For example, labels are often followed by a colon and a statement, so one action associated with a production like

$$\text{statement} \rightarrow \textbf{id} : \text{statement} \qquad (9.1)$$

is to enter into the symbol table the fact that the name corresponding to this **id** is a label. Similarly, the syntax of procedure declarations tells us that certain names are formal parameters.

The symbol-table entry itself can in many cases be set up by a call to a routine such as INSTALL of Chapter 3, which was invoked by the lexical analyzer upon finding an identifier. Some languages, however, permit one identifier to denote several names of different types, even within the same block or procedure. For example, XYZ could be a label, a real variable, and a field name. In that case, the lexical analyzer can only return to the parser the identifier itself, rather than a pointer to the symbol table. The parser must cause a record in the symbol table to be created for XYZ when it discovers the syntactic role played by this instance of XYZ.

For example, on reducing by production (9.1) above, the action would be to install XYZ into a table of labels if XYZ were the string associated with this instance of XYZ and there was not already a label XYZ for the current block or procedure. A similar action would be taken on reduction by a production like

$$\text{statement} \rightarrow \textbf{goto id}$$

Names and Symbol-Table Records

The simplest way to implement a symbol table is as a linear array of *records*, one record per name. A record normally consists of a known number of consecutive words of memory. The identifier could be stored in the record, as in Fig. 9.1(a). This method is appropriate if there is a modest upper limit on the length of an identifier. For example, IBM FORTRAN permits identifiers of up to eight characters, which is the number of characters which will fit in two words of an IBM 370 series machine. Figure 9.1(a) shows an appropriate format for this case, with an identifier filled out with blanks to make eight characters.

In the case of ALGOL, with no limit on the length of an identifier, or in PL/I, with the rarely approached limit of 31, it would be better to use the indirect scheme of Fig. 9.1(b). In the record for DIMPLE we find a pointer to another array of characters (the *string table*) and a count (6) giving the length of the identifier. The pointer gives the position of the first character of the identifier. This indirect scheme permits the size of the name field in the symbol table itself to remain a constant.

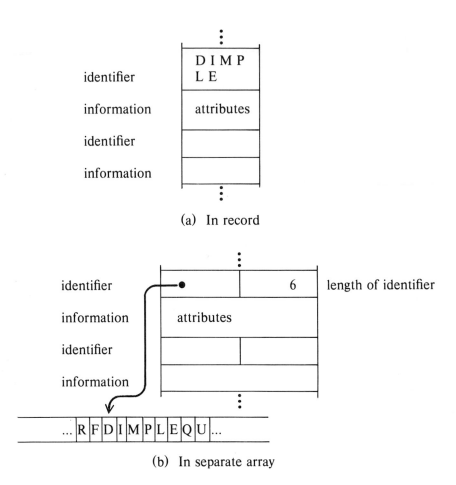

(a) In record

(b) In separate array

Fig. 9.1. Storing the identifier name.

It is worth mentioning that the complete identifier denoting a name must be stored, to ensure that all uses of the same name can be associated with the same symbol-table record.

We must, however, distinguish different names denoted by the same identifier. The techniques needed to do so are discussed in Section 9.3. Until then, it is convenient to assume that the correspondence between identifiers and the names they denote is determined by the symbol-table entry and lookup routines, without, for the moment, specifying how this association is done.

Reusing Symbol-Table Space

The identifier used by the programmer to denote a particular name must be preserved in the symbol table until no further references to that identifier can possibly denote the same name (e.g., in FORTRAN, for the duration of the subroutine in which the name is declared). This is essential so that all uses of the identifier can be associated with the same symbol-table entry, and hence the same name. However, a compiler can be designed to run in less space if the space used to store identifiers can be reused in subsequent passes. For example, the space taken by the string table in Fig. 9.1(b) could be used for other purposes during subsequent passes of the compiler.

One exception concerns external names. When a name is declared external to the program being compiled, the corresponding identifier must be preserved. To record external names while overwriting other names, the compiler must, when it first finds a declaration that NAME is external, make a copy of NAME in another small (presumably) array of characters. Then the pointer to the identifier in the record for NAME is made to point to the new copy of NAME. We can thus do away with the original copy of NAME after the program has been scanned once.

We can arrange to reclaim the space used to store identifiers in Fig. 9.1(a) as well. (In fact, the first words of records in Fig. 9.1(b) can also be reclaimed in the following way.) Instead of storing records in one array, use two, as suggested in Fig. 9.2. If DIMPLE is the ith name found, place it in words $2i-1$ and $2i$ of array IDENTIFIERS. Supposing five words to be

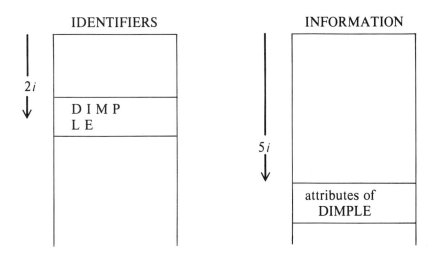

Fig. 9.2. Two-array symbol-table scheme.

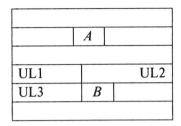

Fig. 9.3. Part of a symbol-table record for FORTRAN.

used for information, the attributes of DIMPLE will be found in words $5i-4$ through $5i$ of array INFORMATION. The internal representation of DIMPLE is no longer a pointer to the symbol table, but rather an integer index, i in this case, which can be used to access either array.

Array Names

Let us consider for a moment how information about array names is to be stored. If the language places a limit on the number of dimensions, then all subscript information can, in principle, be placed in the symbol-table record itself.

Example 9.1. ANS FORTRAN limits us to three dimensions, and in each case, the lower limit is one. Thus, the information associated with array subscripting might appear as in Fig. 9.3. The portion of the word denoted A consists of two bits which indicate the number of dimensions; 00 means the name is not an array. Note that the rest of the word containing A need not be wasted. It could contain other information, such as the type of the name (integer, logical, subroutine, etc.) or whether the name is a formal parameter, in common, or equivalenced. In another designated part of the record will be space for three values, UL1, UL2 and UL3, as needed, to indicate the upper limits along each dimension.

In FORTRAN, all upper limits of arrays must be declared and be integers, except in one special case — if the array is a formal parameter. In that case, an upper limit may be another formal parameter. For that possibility, we must provide three bits, denoted B in Fig. 9.3, to indicate whether any of the three possible limits are formal parameters. If the ith limit is such, then the ith bit of B will be 1 and ULi will be a pointer to the symbol-table record for the formal parameter representing the upper limit. Thus, given the declaration

    SUBROUTINE XYZ(ARY,N)
    INTEGER N
    REAL ARY(10,N,N)

the record for this declaration of ARY would have $B=011$ (in binary) and
$UL1 = 10$ (in decimal). UL2 and UL3 would each point to the record for
the name N. □
    The situation regarding array limits in PL/I is, as one might expect,
somewhat more difficult to handle. There, the upper and lower limits of a
dynamically allocated array can be any expression evaluatable at run time,
when the storage is allocated for the array. If an expression is a constant,
its value can be stored in the symbol table. If a limit is declared to be an
expression, the compiler must generate code to evaluate that expression
and assign the result to a temporary T. If the array is declared automatic
(allocated on a stack) in some block B, the code to evaluate T is executed
every time B is entered. The representation of the limit in the symbol-table
entry for the array is a pointer to the entry for T. This use of T is similar
in spirit to the use of N in Example 9.1.
    Since the number of dimensions is not limited in PL/I, we cannot store
all information regarding limits in a fixed-size entry. Rather, we may store
the number of dimensions and a pointer to a linked list, each element of
the list holding the upper and lower limit in one dimension, as shown in
Fig. 9.4. What we illustrate as LLi is the lower limit in the ith dimension,
consisting of a bit indicating whether the representation is a constant or a
pointer to another symbol-table entry (like T in the discussion above)
together with that constant or pointer.

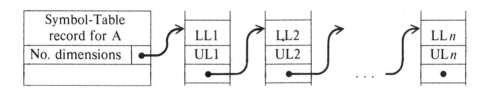

Fig. 9.4. Storage for an array in a language with no limit on dimensions.

    Note that if a formula such as line (8.3) in Section 8.1 is used to evalu-
ate positions in the array, and no array bounds checking is done at run
time, then ULn is not needed. Also, it is useful to have the value of the
first term of line (8.3) available; we might adopt the convention that it
appears in the place ostensibly reserved for the useless ULn. Even if the
first term of (8.3) has to be evaluated on entry to the block, it is reasonable
to generate code to do so and to leave a pointer to the temporary holding
the result in place of ULn.

Also, observe that storing the number of dimensions in the symbol table record is, in principle, unnecessary. We could calculate it by counting the number of elements in the list shown in Fig. 9.4. It is convenient, however, to have the number of dimensions readily available, to check that array references have the proper number of indices. In principle, the presence of a fixed number of bits for the number of dimensions limits the dimensionality of an array. But even without such a count there is a limit, since the supply of records with which to form linked lists of limits is not inexhaustible.

Indirection in Symbol-Table Entries

Let us remark briefly on the virtue of designing symbol-table formats that have pointers to information that is of variable length. We have seen in Fig. 9.1(b) how this use of indirection can save space in representing identifiers over the alternative of allocating in each symbol-table entry the maximum possible amount of space. In Fig. 9.4 we saw how space could be saved when storing array dimensions, compared with selecting a large fixed number of dimensions and allocating space for all array limits in each symbol-table record.

The most significant advantage to using indirection comes when we have a type of information that is applicable to only a minority of the entries. Information about arrays is one example, and in the next chapter we shall see others—for example, the handling of equivalenced and common variables in FORTRAN. It allows for more efficient utilization of space if there is only space for a pointer in the symbol-table entry. Then, if the information is actually present for a given name, the compiler can allocate space for that information in a relatively small (compared with the size of the symbol table) portion of the compiler's data space, and set the symbol-table pointer to the location of that information.

Storage Allocation Information

We mentioned that in certain cases information must appear in the symbol table to denote the locations in storage belonging to data objects at run time. Let us consider names with static storage first. If the object code is assembly language, one can simply, after generating assembly code for the program, scan the symbol table and generate assembly-language data definitions for each name, to be appended to the executable portion of the assembly-language program. In this case the compiler need never worry about storage locations for the various names.

If machine code is to be generated by the compiler, however, then the position of each data object relative to a fixed origin such as the end of the program must be ascertained. The same remark applies to blocks of data loaded as a module separate from the executable program. For example,

COMMON blocks in FORTRAN are loaded separately, and the position of names relative to the beginning of the COMMON block in which they lie must be determined, regardless of whether it is machine- or assembly-code being generated. To make this determination, we can initialize a counter to zero for each separately loadable module (e.g., SUBROUTINES and COMMON blocks in FORTRAN). Upon encountering a declaration of data object A, we store the value of the appropriate counter in the place in A's symbol-table record reserved for an "offset." Then we increase the counter by the number of words taken up by A.

Example 9.2. Suppose we are compiling a hypothetical language for the PDP-11, and there are five types of variables: LOGICAL, INTEGER, REAL, COMPLEX, and DOUBLE. (This language is not exactly like FORTRAN; there are problems in FORTRAN which we shall discuss in a moment.) LOGICAL data are bits that may be packed (16 to a word in the case of LOGICAL arrays). The remaining types require 1, 2, 4, and 4 words, respectively. If we encounter a subroutine beginning with the declarations

> INTEGER A
> REAL B, C(10)
> LOGICAL D(20)
> DOUBLE E, F

we assign A offset 0, B offset 1, and C offset 3. The counter is at 23 after processing C. We give D offset 23 and increment the counter by $\lceil 20/16 \rceil$ to 25, since two words must be used to store array D. E and F are given offsets 25 and 29, respectively. □

In FORTRAN we can give each name an offset either from the end of its routine or from the beginning of its common block. The principles are as suggested in Example 9.2, but we must wait until all declarations have been encountered for a routine before computing offsets. If we encounter the declaration INTEGER A, we may be tempted to give A the offset that is the "current" value of the counter for the "current" subroutine and to increment that counter by one. However, we could see later on the declaration DIMENSION A(100), which would affect the values of offsets for names declared after A. Or, we might see COMMON A, in which case A would not be given an offset associated with the "current" routine at all, but rather with the unlabeled COMMON block. The approach suggested by Example 9.2 needs to be modified for FORTRAN in that we must assign offsets for names after all declarations for a subroutine have been seen and EQUIVALENCE statements have been processed. We shall discuss the handling of equivalences between names in Section 10.3.

In the case of names whose storage is allocated on a stack, the compiler need not allocate storage at all. However, the compiler must plan out the activation record for each procedure, and to do so it needs to store in the symbol table an offset from the base of the activation record for each local name. In many languages this calculation can be done "on the fly," keeping a count for each procedure, assigning that count as the offset when each new name is encountered, and incrementing the count by the size of the value of the name.

A sensible way to allocate space in an activation record is depicted in Fig. 9.5. For each array declaration we simply allocate one word for a pointer to a place above the activation record where the actual array and its data descriptor will be found. This method allows adjustable length arrays whose size cannot be determined until the block or procedure is actually entered at run time. The method is the same as was discussed in Section 2.12.

extra space for arrays and structures
space for simple names and pointers to arrays, structures, etc.
fixed data — e.g., return address, pointer to next activation record

Fig. 9.5. An activation record.

9.2 Data Structures for Symbol Tables

During compilation the symbol table is searched every time an identifier is encountered. Data are added if a new name or new information about an existing name is discovered. Thus, in designing a symbol-table mechanism, we would like a scheme that allows us to add new entries and find existing entries in a table efficiently.

The three symbol-table mechanisms we discuss in this section are linear lists, trees, and hash tables. We shall evaluate each scheme on the basis of the time required to add n entries and make m inquiries. A linear list is the simplest scheme to implement, but its performance becomes poor when m and n get large. A binary search tree gives better performance at some increase in implementation difficulty. Hashing schemes provide the best performance for somewhat greater programming effort and some extra space.

Lists

The conceptually simplest and easiest-to-implement data structure for a symbol table is the linear list of records depicted in Fig. 9.6. We use a single array, or equivalently several arrays (as discussed in connection with Fig. 9.2) to store names and their associated information. New names are added to the list in the order in which they are encountered. To retrieve information about a name, we search from the beginning of the array up to the position marked by pointer AVAILABLE, which indicates the beginning of the empty portion of the array. When the name is located, the associated information can be found in the words following next. If we reach AVAILABLE without finding the name, we have a fault — the use of an undefined name.

To insert a new name, we must scan down the list to be sure it is not already there. If it is, we have another fault — a multiply-defined name. If not, we store the new name in the words immediately following AVAILABLE and increase that pointer by the width of a symbol-table record.

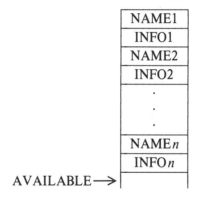

Fig. 9.6. A linear list of records.

If the symbol table contains n names, the work necessary to insert a new name is proportional to n. To find data about a name we shall, on the average, search $n/2$ names, so the cost of an inquiry is also proportional to n. To insert n names and m inquiries the total work is $cn(n+m)$, where c is a constant representing the time necessary for a few machine operations. In a medium-sized program we might have $n=100$ and $m=1000$, so several hundred thousand machine operations are utilized in bookkeeping. That may not be painful, since we are talking about less than a second of time. However, if n and m are multiplied by 10, the cost is multiplied by 100, and the bookkeeping time becomes prohibitive.

Despite the quadratic growth of bookkeeping cost with program size, a linear list is useful in compilers in which small jobs dominate the mix of compiled programs. One advantage of the list organization is that the minimum possible space is taken. In a simple (nonoptimizing) compiler, the space taken by the symbol table may consume most of the space used for the compiler's data. If space is at a premium, it may well pay to use the inefficient list organization for the symbol table.

Self-Organizing Lists

At the cost of a little extra space we can use a trick that will often save a substantial fraction of the time spent in searching the symbol table. We add a LINK field to each record, and we search the list in the order indicated by the LINK's. Figure 9.7(a) shows an example of a four-name symbol table. FIRST gives the position of the first record on the linked list, and each LINK field indicates the next record on the list. In Fig. 9.7(a), the order is NAME3, NAME1, NAME4, NAME2.

When a name is referenced or its record is first created, we move the record for that name to the front of the list by moving pointers. Figure 9.7(b) shows the effect of moving NAME4 to the front of the list. In general, if we search for and find NAMEi, we remember the previous name on the list, say NAMEp. We temporarily remove entry i from the list by making LINKp point where LINKi points. Then we make LINKi point where FIRST points, and finally, we move NAMEi to the front of the list by making FIRST point to NAMEi.

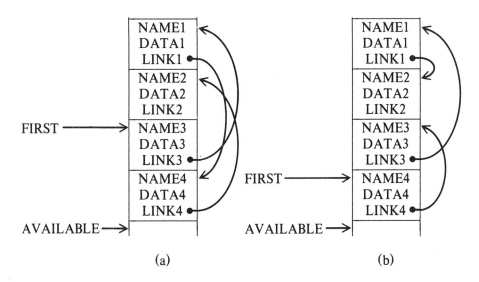

(a)   (b)

Fig. 9.7. Self-organizing symbol table.

The motivation for using the self-organizing list is that the names referenced frequently will tend to be at the front of the list, where they will be found quickly. Moreover, if a small set of names is heavily used in a small section of the program, these names will rise to the top while that section is being processed by the compiler. In a sense, the organization we have described "adapts" or organizes itself in response to local vagaries in the frequency of referencing particular names. If references are random, the self-organizing list will cost time and space. Experience has shown, however, that real programs do not reference names randomly, and a time savings will result on the average.

Search Trees

A more efficient approach to symbol-table organization is to add two link fields, LEFT and RIGHT, to each record. We use these fields to link the records into a binary search tree. This tree has the property that all names NAMEj accessible from NAMEi by following the link LEFTi and then following any sequence of links will precede NAMEi in alphabetical order (symbolically, NAMEj < NAMEi). Similarly, all names NAMEk accessible starting with RIGHTi will have the property that NAMEi < NAMEk. Thus if we are searching for NAME and have found the record for NAMEi, we need only follow LEFTi if NAME < NAMEi and need only follow RIGHTi if NAMEi < NAME. Of course, if NAME = NAMEi we have found what we are looking for. Figure 9.8 gives an algorithm to look for NAME in a binary search tree, where P is initially a pointer to the root.

(1) **while** P $\neq$ **null do**
(2)   **if** NAME = NAME(P) **then** $\cdots$ /* NAME found,
            take action on success */
(3)   **else if** NAME < NAME(P) **then** P := LEFT(P)
            /* visit left child */
(4)   **else** /* NAME(P) < NAME */ P := RIGHT(P)
            /* visit right child */
        /* if we fall through the loop, we have failed to find NAME */

Fig. 9.8. Binary tree search routine.

If NAME is found at line (2), P points to NAME's record. If we fall through the loop, we have failed to find NAME. Should we wish to insert a new record for a new name, we check before assigning to P in lines (3) or (4) that LEFT(P) or RIGHT(P), respectively, is not **null**. If it is **null**, then P points to a record whose left (resp. right) child should be the record for the new name.

If names are encountered in a random order, the average length of a path in the tree will be proportional to log n, where n is the number of names. Since each search follows one path from the root, the expected time needed to enter n names and make m inquiries is proportional to

$(n+m)\log n$. If n is greater than about 50, there are clear advantages to the binary search tree over the linear list and probably over the linked self-organizing list. If efficiency is paramount, however, there is an even better method than the binary search tree, the hash table.

Hash Tables

Many variations of the important searching technique known as hashing have been implemented in compilers. Here we shall consider a rather simple variant. Even this scheme gives us the capability of performing m accesses on n names in time proportional to $n(n+m)/k$, for any constant k of our choosing. Since k can be made as large as we like, this method is generally superior to linear lists or search trees and is the method of choice for symbol tables in most situations, especially if storage is not particularly costly.[†]

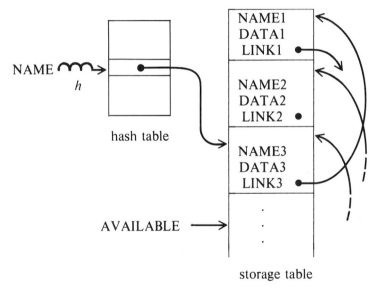

Fig. 9.9 Hash table.

The basic hashing scheme is illustrated in Fig. 9.9. Two tables, a *hash table* and a *storage table*, are used. The hash table consists of k words, numbered $0, 1, \ldots, k-1$. These words are pointers into the storage table to the heads of k separate linked lists (some lists may be empty). Each record in the symbol table appears on exactly one of these lists.

---

† In certain situations, such as block-structured symbol tables discussed in the next section, it may be necessary to perform operations taking time proportional to k. This tends to place a premium on choosing k to be small, say on the order of 100.

To determine whether NAME is in the symbol table, we apply to NAME a *hash function* h such that h(NAME) is an integer between 0 and k−1. It is on the list numbered h(NAME) that the record for NAME belongs. To inquire about NAME, we compute h(NAME) and search that list only. To enter NAME into the symbol table, we create a record for it at the first available place in the storage table and link that record to the beginning of the h(NAME)th list. Since the average list is n/k records long if there are n names in the table, we have cut our searching work down by a factor of k. As k can be as large as we like (the only penalty is that the size of the hash table grows with k), we can choose k sufficiently large that n/k will be small for even very large programs; for example k around 100 will make table lookup a negligible fraction of the total time spent by the compiler.

A great deal of attention has been given to the question of how to design the hash function h such that

1. h will distribute names uniformly among the k lists, and
2. h is easy to compute for names consisting of strings of characters.

One generally suitable approach is to choose k to be a prime. We can interpret strings of characters as integers by breaking them into pieces somewhat shorter than an integer (e.g., chunks of three bytes, filled out with blanks when necessary, if words are four bytes long). Then add the pieces and divide the sum by k. The remainder is an integer from 0 to k−1 and is the value of the hash function applied to the name.

9.3 Representing Scope Information

Most languages have facilities for defining names with limited scopes. Two canonical examples are FORTRAN, where the scope of a name is a single subroutine, and ALGOL, where the scope of a name is the block or procedure in which it is declared. This situation allows the possibility that in the same program the same identifier may be declared several times as distinct names, possibly with different attributes, and usually with different intended storage locations. It is thus the responsibility of the symbol table to keep different declarations of the same identifier distinct.

The usual method of making the distinction is to give a unique number to each program element that may have its own local data. The number of the currently active subprogram (or subprograms in the case of a block-structured language) is computed by semantic rules associated with productions that recognize the beginning and end of a subprogram. The subprogram number is a part of all names declared in that subprogram; the representation of the name inside the symbol table is a pair consisting of the corresponding identifier and the subprogram number. (In some arrangements such as those described in this section, the subprogram number need not actually appear, as it can be deduced from the position of the record in the symbol table.) That is, when we look up a newly-scanned identifier, a match only occurs if the identifiers match character for character, and the associated number in the symbol-table entry is the number of a currently active block or subroutine. Moreover, the subprogram must be the most closely nested of active subprograms declaring that identifier.

Limited scopes give the compiler an opportunity to allow symbol-table entries to share space. The lexical analyzer replaces identifiers with pointers to the symbol table, and these pointers can substitute for the actual names in intermediate code and through code optimization, finally being replaced by run-time locations in the object code. Thus the actual names are needed only when we look up a found identifier in the symbol table to produce a pointer. When the scan of the source program goes beyond the scope of a name, the compiler may erase the characters representing that name.[†] If names are represented in an array of characters as in Fig. 9.1(b), we can reuse portions of that array. Or if names are stored as in Fig. 9.2, we can reuse portions of the array IDENTIFIERS.

Let us briefly reconsider external names, which may not be deleted. As was mentioned in Section 9.1, we must copy external names to a safe area when we see them declared to be external to the current subprogram. One idea is to move them to the high end of the array IDENTIFIERS, placing a pointer to their new location in the record for the attributes of the name. Since one attribute is the property of being external, a bit indicating that fact must already appear in the record, so no confusion should result. If the upper end of IDENTIFIERS is used for external names, we must remember the upper limit of available space in IDENTIFIERS to avoid overprinting external names. If space in the array IDENTIFIERS is likely to be exhausted, we might consider storing it partially in secondary storage. If the pointer-to-string-table method of Fig. 9.1(b) is used, we can move external names to the end of the string table in an analogous manner.

Let us now consider how scopes are to be represented in the symbol table. As is often the case, FORTRAN and ALGOL between them cover most of the common situations.

FORTRAN

A FORTRAN program consists of a main program, subroutines, and functions (call them all *routines*). Each name has a scope consisting of one routine only. We can generate object code for each routine upon reaching the end of that routine. If we do so, it is possible that most of the information in the symbol table can be expunged. We need only preserve names that are external to the routine just processed. These are names of other

---

† If run-time debugging aids are to be provided, however, then these names should be stored in secondary memory at this point.

routines and of common blocks. These names may not truly be external to the entire program being compiled, but must be preserved until the entire collection of routines is processed.

For example, suppose the hashing scheme of Fig. 9.2 is used. We could modify it to look like Fig. 9.10. In each chain, names that are external to the current routine appear first. We append new internal names to the end and new external names to the beginning. When we reach the end of the routine and generate object code for it, we reset the pointer to available storage in the reusable table but not the permanent one. All links in the permanent table that go to the reusable one are set to **null**, and pointers in the hash table that go directly to the reusable table (because there are no permanent identifiers with that hash value) are likewise reset to **null**. Note that this operation takes time that grows with the length of the hash table, suggesting that that table not be too large.

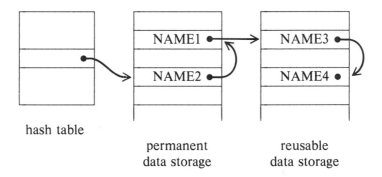

hash table

permanent   reusable
data storage   data storage

Fig. 9.10 Hash table with temporary and permanent storage.

In an optimizing compiler, we might not generate object code on a routine-by-routine basis (see Section 14.8). In that case, we cannot eliminate the data portion of the symbol table for names that are internal to one routine. We may, however, reclaim the space used for the names and links for those names if we keep them separate from the information portion of records. In this case we can use an arrangement like that of Fig. 9.11.

The intermediate code representation of a name must be kept in the permanent area. If we used the location in the name-link storage area to represent a name, such a location may represent several names in different routines, since that area is being reused.

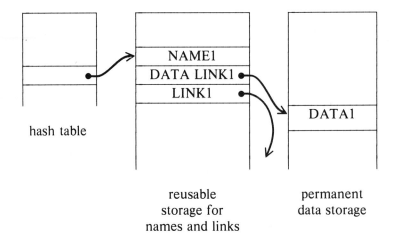

Fig. 9.11. Reusing the storage space for names.

ALGOL

The block structure in ALGOL makes all names local to the block or procedure in which they are declared. Recall the most-closely-nested rule for binding identifiers to declarations (Section 2.10). If we encounter a use of identifier NAME, we must ascertain the closest enclosing block which has a declaration of NAME. (For simplicity, let us call both blocks and procedures "blocks" in what follows.)

Thus, we need a data structure which, as the source program is scanned, makes currently active names available for reference. On the other hand, names no longer active cannot disappear without a trace, as information about them will be needed on subsequent passes. The general idea is to divide the symbol table into two parts, one for active and the other for inactive names. Entries are moved from the first area to the second when their block ends.

Let us consider one common symbol table organization for a block-structured language, depicted in Fig. 9.12. We show the situation which would hold at the point marked "current" in the program of Fig. 9.13. The symbol table itself is divided into two parts. At one end is a region devoted to entries for the names in blocks whose **end** we have already seen — blocks 2 and 3 in this situation. At the other end is data for the currently active blocks — 1 and 4 here. The records for currently active names are linked into chains for each hash value. We also assume that the actual names are represented in a string table. We show one such identifier, called NAME, in Fig. 9.12; it is at the head of the chain for its hash value. To have a permanent target to represent NAME as a pointer in

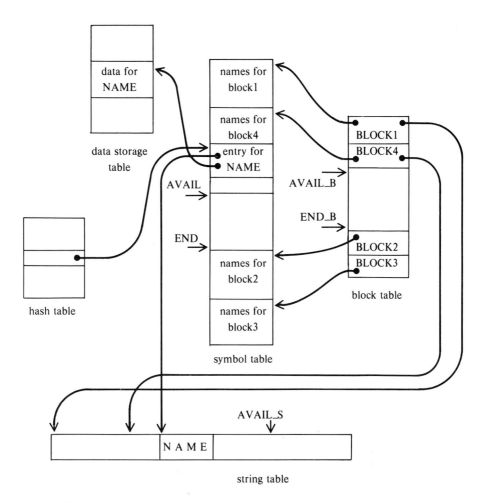

Fig. 9.12. Symbol table organization for ALGOL.

intermediate code, the information for NAME is stored in a permanent data-storage table analogous to the arrangement in Fig. 9.11.

To add a new name, say XYZ, declared in the current block, we search down its chain to make sure it is not already declared in that block. We assume blocks are numbered in the order in which their initial keywords (**begin** or **procedure**) appear, and that the block number appears in the table entry for each name. Thus, when examining the chain for the hash value of XYZ, we should ignore an entry for XYZ with a number other than that of the current block.[†] If we keep the chains ordered, so that the most-recently added name is closest to the beginning, then we may stop our

---

† An alternative way of detecting the fact that a name belongs to the current block is to check that its record appears within the limits indicated by the block record (to be described below)

search as soon as we encounter a name outside the current block. Assuming no other declaration of XYZ in the current block is found, we place XYZ in the first available locations in the string table and make a record for it in the first available place in the symbol table (these places are marked AVAIL and AVAIL_S in Fig. 9.12). The record for XYZ is placed at the beginning of its chain, since the chain is searched from beginning to end.

Suppose now we have a reference to identifier ABC. We hash it and search down its chain for a record with identifier ABC, no matter what active block it may be in. Note that since new declarations are placed at the heads of chains, and as we shall see, no longer active declarations are removed from chains, the first declaration of ABC that we encounter will be the one to which this use of ABC pertains, by the "most closely nested" rule.

Next, let us consider what happens when, during the scan of the source program, a new block is entered. First, note that we have indicated in Fig. 9.12 a "block table" containing some information about each block. This information includes a pointer to the beginning of the region of the symbol table for the names declared in that block. A count of the number of these names is also included but not shown in Fig. 9.12. We also have for each block a pointer to the first byte in the string table for the names declared in that block. If we enter a new block, we create a record for that block at the position indicated by AVAIL_B in the block table, with pointers initialized to the current values of AVAIL_S and AVAIL in the string and symbol tables. In essence, the string table and the tops of the symbol and block tables are all used as stacks.

The most difficult set of operations occurs when we reach the end of a block, say block 4 in Fig. 9.13. Then we must do the following.

1. Transfer the record for block 4 to the position marked END_B in the block storage table of Fig. 9.12. The blocks at the low end of the block table are blocks that are no longer active. The entries in the block table must be preserved until we format the activation record for each block. The formatting can be done now or during the code-generation phase.

2. Transfer the record for each name belonging to block 4 in the symbol table to positions above the point marked END in the symbol table. These records must be detached from the hashing chains, which requires that we scan every chain until we come to a name not in block 4, popping records from the chain as we go.[†] Note that the information in the data storage area is not moved. We presume that pointers to the symbol table which represent names in the intermediate code point to

---

for the current block.

† This scan of the hashing chains could be avoided by recomputing the hash code for each identifier, thus finding the correct chain to scan.

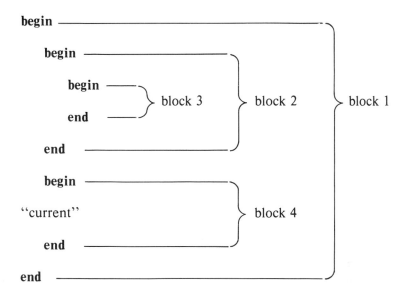

Fig. 9.13 Structure of an ALGOL program.

the data storage record for that name, not the record in the symbol table itself. If we had done the latter, we could not find information about names when we needed it to generate object code, since entries in the symbol table may be overwritten. The arrangement is now as depicted in Fig. 9.14.

3. Position the AVAIL pointer for the string table at the beginning of the space used for block 4. Note that the record for block 4 has a pointer to this position. This action has the effect of erasing all the names for block 4; they are no longer needed. We should be aware that ALGOL permits no external names (in the "standard" version). If we were dealing with a block-structured language that had externals, like PL/I, we would have to make provision to preserve the external names.

Exercises

9.1 Suppose we have a hash table with 10 locations and we wish to enter "names" which are integers, using the hash function $h(i) = i$ mod 10, that is, the remainder when i is divided by 10. Show the links created in the hash and storage tables if the first ten primes 2, 3, 5, . . . , 29 are entered in that order. As you hash more primes into the table, do you expect them to distribute randomly

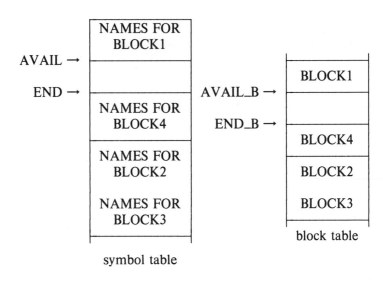

Fig. 9.14. After the end of block 4.

among the ten lists? Why or why not?

*9.2 Suppose a program uses n names, $A_0, A_1, \ldots, A_{n-1}$, and the tth reference, $1 \leqslant t \leqslant 2^n$, is to A_i if the binary representation of t ends in a run of exactly i 1's. For example, if $n=3$ the sequence is $A_1, A_0,$ $A_2, A_0, A_1, A_0, A_3, A_0$. If the self-organizing list of Section 9.2 is used for the symbol table, how far down the organized list does one go on the average to process a name in this sequence? How realistic is this sequence of references? Take a program of your own and see how closely your references to names follows this exponentially decaying distribution.

9.3 Suppose we are given the ALGOL program of Fig. 9.15, and we construct for it a block-structured symbol table using the data structure of Fig. 9.12. Show the contents of the data storage, symbol and block tables, and the string table immediately after the points labeled L1, L2 and L3 in Fig. 9.15.

```
        begin
            integer A, B;
            begin
                real A, C;
            end
            begin
                integer B, D;
L1:             begin
                    real C, E;
L2:             end
            end
L3:     end
```

Fig. 9.15. Block-structured program.

Bibliographic Notes

Data structures for symbol tables and algorithms for searching them are discussed in detail in Knuth [1968, 1973], Aho, Hopcroft, and Ullman [1974], and Horowitz and Sahni [1976]. The lore of hashing is treated in Knuth [1973] and Morris [1968]. The original paper discussing hashing is Peterson [1957]. More on symbol-table organization techniques can be found in Batson [1965] and Price [1971].

CHAPTER 10

Run-time
Storage
Administration

A compiler must allocate resources of the target machine to represent the data objects manipulated by the source program. Elementary data types such as integer, real, and logical variables can usually be represented by equivalent data objects at the machine level. Aggregates, such as arrays, strings, and structures, are usually represented by several words of machine memory.

The rules that define the scope and duration of names in a programming language determine the strategies that can be used to allocate storage to data objects. The simplest strategy is the static allocation scheme used in languages like FORTRAN, where it is possible at compile-time to determine the size and relative position each data object will have at run-time.

A more complex strategy is required for languages like ALGOL, in which a name in a recursive procedure may have more than one activation at a given instant at run time. For languages with recursion, a dynamic allocation scheme involving a stack is usually used. Entry to a new block or procedure causes the allocation of space on a stack, which is then freed on exit from the block or procedure.

A yet more complex strategy is required for languages such as PL/I, which allow the allocation and liberation of memory for some data in a non-nested fashion. For these languages a scheme in which storage can be allocated and freed arbitrarily from an area called a *heap* is often used. The use of a heap was discussed briefly in Section 12.2.

This chapter discusses some of the important ideas involved in run-time storage management for languages with static or stack allocation of storage. Management of heaps is not discussed, since it is more appropriate to a general study of data structure techniques.

10.1 Implementation of A Simple Stack-Allocation Scheme

As an introduction to stack allocation, we are going to consider an implementation of the UNIX programming language C, which allows somewhat simpler implementations than some other stack-oriented languages like ALGOL. The next section will discuss the additional concepts needed for block-structured language implementation.

Data in C can be *global,* meaning it is allocated static storage and available to any procedure, or *local,* meaning it can be accessed only by the procedure in which it is declared. A program consists of a list of global data declarations and procedures; there is no block structure[†] or nesting of procedures. However, recursion is permitted, so local names must be allocated space on a stack.

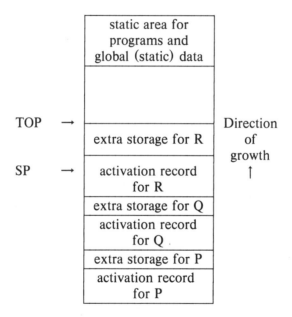

Fig. 10.1. Memory organization for C program.

As mentioned in Chapter 2, with stack allocation of storage each procedure has an activation record on the stack, in which the values of local names are kept. One possible organization of memory is shown in Fig. 10.1. The low-numbered memory locations (the top of Fig. 10.1) contain the code for the various procedures and space for the global (statically allocated) data. Starting from the highest numbered available memory location

---

† This situation is subject to change as the language evolves.

(the bottom of Fig. 10.1) is the *run-time stack*. (This arrangement is peculiar to the implementation of C on the PDP-11 in that there is a gap between the static area and the run-time stack; a more conventional arrangement would store the static area at the bottom of the stack.) Figure 10.1 shows a procedure P (the main program), which has called procedure Q, which, in turn, has called procedure R.

We show two pointers to the stack, which are actually permanently allocated registers. One, called the *stack pointer* (SP), always points to a particular position in the activation record for the currently active procedure. The second, called TOP, always points to the top of the stack. In C, it is often the case that TOP points to the top of the top activation record. However, temporaries used for expression evaluation are allocated storage above the top activation record. If an algorithm for expression evaluation like that of Section 7.6 is used, TOP will always point to the temporary value needed next.

In a language like ALGOL, which permits adjustable arrays, it is customary to allocate space to the array above the fixed-size data and to store a pointer to this space in a fixed position of the activation record. For uniformity, fixed-length arrays are treated this way too. This arrangement allows each activation record to have a fixed size, and all local data can be accessed by going a known distance from the stack pointer. In this situation, SP and TOP often differ widely.

Organization of a C Activation Record

In addition to local data, there are five other items that appear in the activation record.[†]

1. The values of the actual parameters (call-by-value is used in C).
2. The count of the number of arguments.
3. The return address.
4. The return value (all procedures in C may behave like a function and return a value).
5. The value of SP for the activation record below.

Figure 10.2 shows the plan of an activation record. We choose to make SP point to the position just below the local data, so locals are accessed by negative offsets from SP, and parameters by positive offsets. An alternative is to have SP point to the top of the activation record. This scheme is

---

† Our activation record format differs somewhat from that actually used in C implementation, where argument counts and return values are not actually placed on the stack. Also, we have omitted the storage of the contents of the registers just before a call. Return values are actually passed in a register, and argument counts are obtained by a mechanism we shall not discuss. The reader familiar with the PDP-11 is cautioned that our use of the term SP differs from PDP-11 terminology. Actually, the PDP-11 SP register is used for what we call TOP.

useful in base register machines, where only positive offsets from a base register may be used.

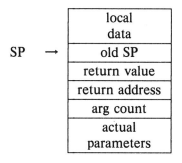

Fig. 10.2. Activation record for a C procedure.

In C, all local data, including arrays, are of fixed size, so the size of the activation record can be computed by the compiler. Hence, a simple local name X can be referenced by X[SP], where X stands for the *offset* of X, the distance of the location for X from the stack pointer. In many compilers for various languages, intermediate code references to a local name on the stack are just written X, leaving it to the code-generation phase to realize that X is on the stack and must be accessed by indexing through the register reserved for SP. It is worth noting here that indexing is actually commutative, and X[SP] refers to the same location as SP[X]. However, since the offset of X is a constant and SP is in a register, the value of X[SP] can be loaded into a register with one instruction, while in a typical machine, computing SP[X] would require loading the offset of X into a register first.

Procedure Calls in C

In Section 8.2 we showed the translation of a procedure call as

$$\textbf{param} \quad T_1$$
$$\cdot$$
$$\cdot$$
$$\cdot$$
$$\textbf{param} \quad T_n$$
$$\textbf{call} \quad P, n$$

Let us consider what actually happens at run-time in response to the **param** and **call** "three-address" statements, that is, what object code should eventually be generated for them. Assuming that TOP points to the lowest-numbered used location on the stack and that memory locations are counted by words, we could translate each **param** T instruction into PUSH(T), where PUSH(X) stands for

TOP := TOP $-$ 1

$*$TOP:= X

The effect of these instructions is to push T onto the run-time stack. Note that on many machines, the decrementation of TOP can be combined with the instruction $*$TOP := X (which is equivalent to 0[TOP] := X). It is most convenient to place the parameters on the stack in the order T_n (lowest) to T_1 (highest), and the scheme of Section 8.2 can be modified easily to put the **param** statements out in reverse order.

The translation of the **call** P,n statement is first to store the argument count n, the return address, and the old stack pointer, and then to jump to the first statement for the procedure called.

PUSH(n)	/$*$ store the argument count $*$/
PUSH(l_1)	/$*$ l_1 is the label of the return address $*$/
PUSH( )	/$*$ leave space for the return value $*$/
PUSH(SP)	/$*$ store the old stack pointer $*$/
goto l_2	/$*$ l_2 is the first statement of the called procedure P $*$/

The first statement of the called procedure must be a special "three-address" statement **procbegin**, which sets the stack pointer to the place holding the old SP (just below the local data), and sets TOP to the top of the activation record. That is:

SP := TOP

TOP := SP $+$ s_P /$*$ s_P, the size of P, is the number of words taken by the local data for P $*$/

As was mentioned earlier, references to local names can be written in the form X[SP], where X is the (negative) offset for the name from the location pointed to by SP. Formal parameters can similarly be referred to by an appropriate positive offset from SP. In particular, the ith formal parameter can be referenced by $(i+3)$[SP].

The return statement in C can have the form

      return (expression)

This statement can be implemented by three-address code to evaluate the expression into a temporary T followed by:

1[SP] := T	/$*$ 1 is the offset for the location of the return value $*$/
TOP := SP $+$ 2	/$*$ TOP now points to the return address $*$/
SP := $*$SP	/$*$ restore SP $*$/
L := $*$TOP	/$*$ the value of L is now the return address $*$/
TOP := TOP $+$ 1	/$*$ TOP points to the argument count $*$/

TOP := TOP + 1 + *TOP   /* *TOP is the number of parameters of P.
We restore TOP to the top of extra storage
for the activation record below */

goto *L

A procedure can also return automatically when its code is completely executed, in which case we must do the same steps but without entering a return value. Presumably a procedure which returns without passing a value back is used as a subroutine rather than as a function. The C **return** statement can be translated into a three-address statement **return** T, which would in turn be translated into code like the above in the object code generation phase. The end of a procedure can be marked by a three-address statement **procend**, which is also translated as above, excluding the storing of a return value.

Who Knows about What?

One might initially be puzzled about why particular combinations of pointers were used to implement stack allocation of storage, or why we selected a particular division of labor between the **call** statement and the **procbegin** statement. In truth, many variations of the scheme we have described are feasible. There is one guiding principle that should be borne in mind, however. Do not expect a procedure to do anything that requires it to know the size of the activation record of another procedure.

In C, as in many other languages, we cannot assume that all procedures are compiled together; they may be on different files and be compiled separately. Thus, when P calls Q, P cannot increment TOP to the top of Q's activation record, because the compiler may not be able to determine the size of that activation record. It must be left for Q to set TOP.

Conversely, when Q is compiled, it may not know about P, so TOP has to be left at a point that makes sense to Q when Q is called. That is, Q knows that TOP will point to the word where the old SP is stored in the activation record for Q, regardless of who calls Q. The passing of parameters requires that both P and Q be able to locate them. Each procedure is able to find the parameters via TOP, which requires that Q reset TOP when it returns, so P can find the return value.

It is interesting to observe what happens if we store temporaries in the activation records and dispense with the "extra space" above activation records. We can then dispense with one of TOP and SP, since they will always differ by s_P. Moreover, we can avoid storing the old SP in an activation record. This is because a called procedure, knowing the width of its own activation record, and being given a count of the number of parameters passed, can reset SP when it is returned to.

10.2 Implementation of Block-Structured Languages

Languages with block structure such as ALGOL or PL/I, present certain complexities not found in C. First, in a block-structured language, not only procedures, but blocks as well, may define their own data. Thus activation records or portions of activation records must be reserved for blocks. Second, many languages, ALGOL and PL/I, for example, permit arrays of adjustable length. Third, and most important, the data-referencing environment of a procedure or block includes all procedures and blocks surrounding it in the program. As discussed in Section 2.9, the compiler for a block-structured language can determine to which declaration of name X a use of X refers, using the most-closely-nested rule. However, to find the location on the stack of the name X in a procedure other than the currently active one requires a network of pointers more complex than the SP-TOP combination used in the previous section.

Displays

Let us ignore blocks for the moment and consider a program to consist of a collection of nested procedure declarations followed by a call on the outermost (parameterless) procedure. During execution, a procedure P can reference a data object in the topmost activation record of any procedure that surrounds P physically in the program. Since the position of an activation record for a procedure may vary, because of the presence of adjustable length arrays, it is necessary to have some method of keeping track of the locations of the various activation records.

One method is to store with each procedure a pointer, called a *static link,* to the topmost activation record of that procedure which physically surrounds it in the program. Then references to nonlocal data (those in the environment of the currently active procedure but not local to it) can be resolved by descending this chain of pointers to find all necessary statically enclosing procedures.

If the nesting level of procedures is deep, however, this method of resolving references to nonlocal data can become expensive. The *display,* introduced in Section 2.12, is a common way of providing more direct access to nonlocal data. A display consists of an array of pointers to the currently accessible activation records of those procedures statically surrounding the one presently active.

There are several places in which the display can be stored. The display might be kept in memory, and all references to activation records would begin by using indirect addressing through the appropriate display pointer. This approach is reasonable on a machine with indirect addressing, although each indirection costs a memory cycle. On machines without indirect addressing, indexing must be used, which makes it useful if the display, pictured as an array, actually is a collection of registers. Note that the compiler can determine the maximum length of this array: it is the maximum nesting depth of procedures in the program. Through code optimization we can arrange that in each procedure only the display pointers needed by that procedure appear in registers.

A simpler arrangement, and the one we choose here, is to store the display on the run-time stack itself and to create a new copy at each block and procedure entry. The top display pointer is stored in a global pointer SP, as in Section 10.1. References to local names, those in the activation record, are made via SP. Nonlocal references are made by the following steps:

1. Use SP and an offset to find the appropriate display pointer in the activation record for the currently active procedure.
2. Use that display pointer plus an offset to find the desired data object in the activation record to which it belongs.

Example 10.1. Figure 10.3 shows the skeleton of a block-structured program. The static environment of Q includes P and MAIN; that of R and P includes only MAIN.

When we execute MAIN, at L5, we call P(w) at L3, which calls Q(z) at L2, which calls R(x, y) at L1. The stack and display are then as shown in Fig. 10.4. (The array of display pointers is shown separately for clarity.) We observe that, since the static environment for R consists only of itself and MAIN, there are but two pointers in the display, to the top activation records for R and MAIN. □

```
            procedure MAIN( );
              procedure P(a);
                procedure Q(b);
L1:               R(x, y);
                end Q;
L2:             Q(z);
              end P;
              procedure R(c, d);
              end R;
L3:           P(w);
L4:           R(u, v);
            end MAIN;
L5:     MAIN();
```

Fig. 10.3. Skeleton ALGOL program.

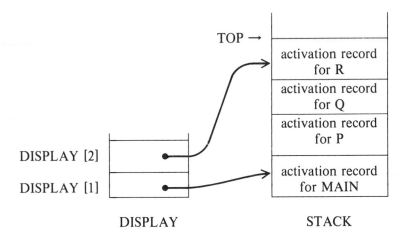

DISPLAY   STACK

Fig. 10.4. Having called R.

Format of Activation Records

Let us discuss the typical layout of activation records for a block-structured language. As in Section 10.1, the activation record contains space for local data, the return address, return value, argument count, actual parameters, and the old value of SP. It also contains pointers on the display other than the top one. If adjustable arrays are permitted, their size cannot be calculated until the procedure is called. It is conventional, therefore, to put only pointers to the array and its data descriptor in the activation record. The array and descriptor are then placed above the activation record, between TOP and SP. The descriptor could, alternatively, appear in the activation record itself.

Example 10.2. Suppose Q calls R(x, y) at L1 of Fig. 10.3, and R has the following declarations of local data.

integer i;
real array A[0:n−1,1:m];
real array B[2:10];

One possible activation-record format for R would be the one shown in Fig. 10.5. Note that the old SP points to the activation record for Q just below, and that activation record has in it display pointers for P and MAIN. □

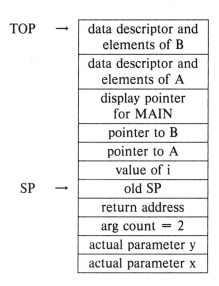

TOP →	data descriptor and elements of B
	data descriptor and elements of A
	display pointer for MAIN
	pointer to B
	pointer to A
	value of i
SP →	old SP
	return address
	arg count = 2
	actual parameter y
	actual parameter x

Fig. 10.5. Activation record for $R(x, y)$.

Procedure Calls

Suppose we are currently executing a procedure such as Q in Fig. 10.3, and we execute a procedure call such as $R(x, y)$ at L1. The *level* of Q, that is, the number of procedures and blocks in its static environment, is three, so while Q is in execution, the display has three pointers, one each to the top activation records of MAIN, P, and Q, in that order from the bottom. However R, at level two, has an environment consisting only of MAIN and itself. Thus, to create the proper display for R, from that of Q, we must replace the pointers to P and Q in the display for Q by a pointer to the record for $R(x, y)$, which we are about to create.

In general, when a procedure P_1 at level l_1 calls P_2 at level l_2, the name P_2 must be part of the static environment of P_1. That is, P_2 must be defined by some procedure P_3 (which may be P_1) at level l_3 in the environment of P_1. Then the environment of P_2 is that portion of the environment of P_1 up to and including P_3, followed by P_2 itself. In the above example of Q calling R, P_1, P_2 and P_3 are Q, R and MAIN, respectively, since R is declared in MAIN.

When P_1 calls P_2, to create the display for P_2 the $l_1 - l_3$ top display pointers must be popped off P_1's display and replaced by a pointer to P_2's activation record. Note that all levels can be computed by the compiler by counting the excess of **begin**'s and **procedure**'s over **end**'s. A global variable may be used by the compiler for this count, which is copied into the symbol table entry for each procedure at the time the declaration of that procedure is encountered. Thus l_1, l_2 and l_3 (which is $l_2 - 1$) are available to the compiler in the symbol table.

If we use the scheme in which the display is kept on the stack, the display for P_2 is constructed by copying the bottom l_3 pointers from the display in P_1's activation record into the activation record for P_2. Note that if $l_1 = l_3$, these pointers include SP. Then SP is set to the activation record created for P_2. The old value of SP is also placed in a special location in P_2's activation record (old SP in Fig. 10.5) regardless of whether $l_1 = l_3$ or not. The purpose of the old SP is to aid in the procedure return; it is not part of the display.

Parameter Passing

The next step in the procedure call is to pass the actual parameters up to the activation record being created. In general, the operand of the **param** three-address statement will be treated as a pointer to the value of the actual parameter (if call-by-reference is used) or as the value itself (if call-by-value or copy-restore linkage is used).

Example 10.3. Suppose we invoke procedure $R(A+B*C, D)$, where A, B, C, and D are integers. A suitable translation of this call into three-address code is:

$$T_1 := B * C$$
$$T_2 := A + T_1$$
param T_2
param D
call R   /* create new display */

We assume that R, the procedure name, will be replaced at the time of code generation by the location in memory of its first statement, just as references to data such as A or T_1 are replaced by their locations.   □

The translation into object code of the statement **param** X is the equivalent of PUSH(**addr**(X)) if call-by-reference is used, and PUSH(X) if call-by-value is used.

Special arrangements must be made to pass parameters of nonsimple types. The principal types of data besides integers, reals, and other simple types are arrays, procedures, and labels. An array is generally passed by giving a pointer to its first location, regardless of the parameter-passing convention used.

Procedure parameters in block-structured languages present more difficulty. Suppose procedure P_2 passes P_1 to Q as an actual procedure-valued parameter, and Q then calls the procedure P_1, by referring to its corresponding formal parameter. Procedure Q may be in the static environment of P_1. If P_1 references a name X local to Q, then is the X referenced the one belonging to this activation of Q?

The answer depends on whether deep or shallow binding of procedure references is used by the language at hand (see Exercises 2.5 and 2.6). If deep binding is used, the environment of P_1 is fixed when it is passed by P_2. Then the most convenient representation of the passed parameter is a pair consisting of the procedure name (first location of its code) and a pointer to the activation record for that procedure R which defines P_2, i.e., the procedure most closely surrounding the definition of P_2.

In a block-structured language with static binding of identifiers to names, P_1 and R must be in the environment of P_2, so the pointer to the appropriate activation record for R must be on P_2's display. Moreover, the levels of P_1, P_2, and R are known to the compiler, so this display pointer may be easily found when P_2 passes P_1 to Q. The calculation is exactly as in our discussion above of the situation in which P_2 calls P_1. When called, the environment of P_1 consists of a newly created activation record for P_1 plus the environment of R, which is the activation record pointed to plus the display pointers in that activation record.

Shallow binding, where the environment of the procedure parameter P_1 is not substituted until it is called, is not appropriate for block-structured languages, since P_1 could be passed to a procedure Q that is not in P_1's static environment. We do see shallow binding used in certain languages, such as SNOBOL, which use dynamic binding of identifiers to names. In that case, no environment pointer need be passed; the environment of P_1 will be established when P_1 is called.

When call-by-name is used to pass parameters, as in ALGOL, all parameters (except array names and procedures) are passed by giving a procedure ("thunk") to evaluate that parameter. The environment of the thunk is itself plus the environment of the procedure P passing it. A suitable representation for the thunk is a pair consisting of the first address for its code and a pointer to the current activation record for P, just as for any procedure passed by P as a parameter.

Finally, we come to label parameters. If P_2 passes label L belonging to procedure P_1 (P_2 may be P_1), we may represent L by a pair consisting of the location of L in the code for P_1 and a pointer to the activation record for P_1 in the environment of P_2. In a block-structured language with static binding of identifiers, P_1 must be in the environment of P_2, so a pointer to the appropriate activation record of P_1 will be found on P_2's display.

Creation of Space for Arrays

If the language permits adjustable-length data, such as adjustable arrays, the activation record for the called procedure is not yet complete, because space for the adjustable-length data has not yet been allocated on the stack. In the running example concerning the creation of the record of Fig. 10.5, suppose TOP now points to the top of the stored display. Space for pointers to arrays appears in the fixed portion of the activation record, but not space for the data descriptors or the arrays themselves.

The translation of an array declaration such as

real array A[0:n−1,1:m];

not only must enter information about A into the symbol table, but also must generate code to calculate A's size and data descriptor at run time. That code must be followed by instructions to decrement TOP by the area needed to hold A and its data descriptor and to enter the data descriptor into the words reserved for that purpose.

Returns

When it is time for procedure Q to return to the procedure P which called it, Q must do the following.

1. Calculate any return value and put the value in its activation record, as in Section 10.1.
2. Obtain the return address from Q's activation record.
3. Set TOP to the value it had before P called Q. This value is a fixed offset from SP, and is the location just below the activation record for Q.
4. Set SP to the value of the old SP found in Q's activation record. Now the situation on the stack is the same as pertained just before P called Q. The top display pointer for P is SP, and the balance of the display is found in the activation record for P pointed to by SP.
5. Jump to the return address to complete the return.

Referencing Data

Let us briefly mention how the values of names stored on the stack can be referenced, for the run-time organization of either this or the previous section. To begin, let us mention that it is reasonable to generate three-address statements like A:=B+C even when A, B, and/or C are names found on the stack. In that case, we leave the creation of the steps which trace display pointers and perhaps other pointers (to arrays) to be handled in the code generation phase. If this option is adopted, then what follows can be used as a description of the object code to be generated. However, it is also legitimate to generate three-address code which does the pointer tracing explicitly. For an optimizing compiler, this option has advantages, but it is not worth the trouble unless extensive optimization is to be attempted. We shall give an example of the advantage of this approach in Chapter 13.

Consider A := B + C where A, B and C are simple names, e.g., integers, with offsets o_A, o_B and o_C, respectively, from the targets of the display pointers for the procedures at levels l_A, l_B and l_C of the current environment. Suppose the display is at offset d from SP. Also assume B is in the current top activation record, but A and C are not. Then suitable code for A:=B+C is

$$T_1 := o_B[SP]$$
$$T_2 := (d-1+l_B-l_C)[SP] \quad /* \text{ get display pointer for record holding C. Note } l_B \text{ is the level of the currently active procedure. } */$$
$$T_3 := o_C[T_2]$$
$$T_4 := T_1 + T_3$$
$$T_5 := (d-1+l_B-l_A)[SP] \quad /* \text{ get display pointer for record holding A } */$$
$$o_A[T_5] := T_4$$

Blocks

Until now, we have considered only procedures in block-structured languages. Languages like ALGOL and PL/I, however, allow the creation of blocks, which are subprograms with their own local data, although they cannot be called from outside. A simple view of blocks is that they are "parameterless procedures," called from only one point (the position in which they appear in the program) and returning only to that point. Thus, they may be given display pointers just as procedures are. Their "invocation" is easy. We know we need not pop any pointers off the stack, as the environment of a block is itself plus the environment of the point in the program immediately before the block. Neither do we have to pass parameters or a return address to a block. We have only to create an activation record for the block, possibly including adjustable-length arrays, and push its pointer onto the display.

However, this method of handling blocks may greatly increase the length of the display. If space on the stack or in registers is at a premium, we can cut down on the size of displays by allocating display pointers for procedures and the outermost block only, keeping the activation records for other blocks within the activation record of the procedure most closely surrounding them.

Example 10.4. Suppose part of an ALGOL program is the procedure of Fig. 10.6. When block B_2 is active, the activation record is as shown in Fig. 10.7(a), and when B_3 is active it is as shown in Fig. 10.7(b). □

A nuance which must be understood concerns jumps out of blocks. It is possible that a jump will cause the termination of more than one block, such as the statement **goto** L in B_2, which terminates both B_2 and B_1. It is therefore not efficient to keep only the old value of TOP in the portion of an activation record reserved for a block. If we did that, a statement such as **goto** L in Fig. 10.6 would require us to "pop" the portion of the record for B_2, then restore TOP as if B_1 were active and then "pop" B_1. We can

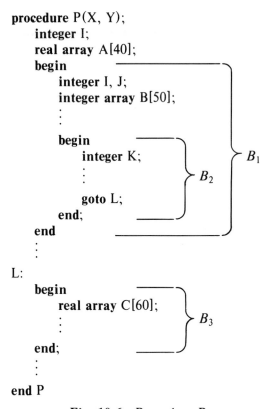

```
procedure P(X, Y);
    integer I;
    real array A[40];
    begin
        integer I, J;
        integer array B[50];
        ⋮

        begin
            integer K;
            ⋮

            goto L;
        end;
    end
    ⋮

L:
    begin
        real array C[60];
        ⋮

    end;
    ⋮

end P
```

Fig. 10.6. Procedure P.

avoid the sequential popping of blocks by storing in P's portion, and in the portion for each block, the value of TOP when that is the currently active block or procedure. Now, the statement **goto** L can be translated simply into code which accesses the value of TOP when P and no internal block is active and sets TOP to that value.

10.3 Storage Allocation in FORTRAN

There are a number of issues concerning the assignment of storage locations to names in FORTRAN. Some, such as storage for temporaries, are typical of the problems raised by any language with static storage allocation. Others, especially the handling of COMMON and EQUIVALENCE declarations, are fairly special to FORTRAN.

Data Areas

To begin with basics, in any language with static storage allocation, the compiler must be able to determine the address that each data object will occupy at run time. Thus the size and relative position of each data object

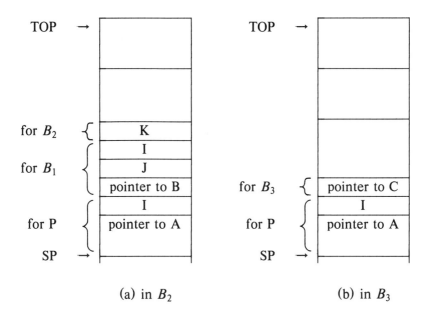

Fig. 10.7. Activation record when B_2 and B_3 are active.

must be known at compile time. For this reason, recursion and adjustable-length arrays are not amenable to static storage allocation.

FORTRAN was designed to permit static storage allocation. A FORTRAN compiler can create a number of *data areas,* blocks of storage in which the values of names can be stored. In FORTRAN, there is one data area for each routine and one data area for each named COMMON block and for blank COMMON, if used. The symbol table must record for each name the data area in which it belongs and its offset in that data area, that is, its position relative to the beginning of the area. The compiler must eventually decide where the data areas go, relative to the executable code and to one another.

For example, in FORTRAN it is reasonable to place the data for each routine immediately after the code for that routine and to follow the routines by the common blocks. On some computer systems it is feasible to leave the relative positions of data areas unspecified and allow the link editor to link data areas and executable code.

The compiler must compute the size of each data area. For the routines' data areas, a single counter suffices, since their sizes are known after each routine is processed. For COMMON blocks, a record for each block must be kept during the processing of all routines, since each routine using a block may have its own idea of how big the block is, and the actual size is the maximum of the sizes implied by the various routines. If routines are separately compiled, the link editor must be able to select the size of a COMMON block to be the maximum of all such blocks with the same name among the pieces of code being linked.

For each data area the compiler creates a *memory map,* which is a description of the contents of the area. This "memory map" might simply consist of an indication in the symbol-table entry for each identifier in the area, of its offset in the area. We need not necessarily have an easy way of answering the question "What are all the names in this data area?" However, in FORTRAN, we know the answer for the routines' data areas, since all names declared in a routine that are not COMMON or equivalenced to a COMMON name are in the routine's data area. COMMON names can have their symbol-table entries linked, with one chain for each COMMON block, in the order of appearance in that block. In fact, as the offsets of names in a data area cannot always be determined until the entire routine is processed (FORTRAN array names can be declared before their dimensions are declared), it is necessary that these chains of COMMON names be created. In a language like PL/I or C, which allows the initialization of names having static storage, it is useful for the compiler to create an actual copy of the data-area contents and to append this copy to the executable code.

Data in COMMON Areas

We shall create, for each block, a record giving the first and last names of the current routine that are declared to be in that COMMON block. When processing a declaration like

COMMON / BLOCK1 / NAME1, NAME2

the compiler must do the following.

1. In the table for COMMON block names, create a record for COMMON block BLOCK1, if none such exists.

2. In the symbol-table entries for NAME1 and NAME2, set a pointer to the symbol-table entry for BLOCK1, indicating that these are in COMMON and members of COMMON block BLOCK1.

3. a)   If the record has just now been created for BLOCK1, set a pointer in that record to the symbol-table entry for NAME1, indicating the first name in this common block. Then link the symbol-table entry for NAME1 to that for NAME2, using a field of the symbol table reserved for linking members of the same COMMON block. Finally, set a pointer in the record for BLOCK1 to the symbol-table entry for NAME2, indicating the

last found member of that block.

b) If, however, this is not the first declaration of BLOCK1, simply link NAME1 and NAME2 to the end of the list of names for BLOCK1. The pointer to the end of the list for BLOCK1, appearing in the record for BLOCK1 is updated, of course.

After a routine has been processed, we are required to apply the equivalencing algorithm, to be discussed shortly. We may discover that some additional names belong in COMMON because they are equivalenced to names which are in COMMON. We shall find that it is not actually necessary to link such a name XYZ to the chain for its COMMON block. A bit in the symbol-table entry for XYZ is set, indicating that XYZ has been equivalenced to something else. A data structure to be discussed will then give the position of XYZ relative to a name actually declared to be in COMMON.

After performing the equivalence operations, we can create a memory map for each COMMON block by scanning the list of names for that block. Initialize a counter to zero, and for each name on the list, make its offset equal to the current value of the counter. Then add to the counter the number of memory units taken by the data object denoted by the name. The COMMON block records can then be deleted and the space reused by the next routine.

If a name XYZ in COMMON is equivalenced to a name not in COMMON, we must determine the maximum offset from the beginning of XYZ for any word of storage needed for any name equivalent to XYZ. For example, if XYZ is a real, equivalenced to A(5,5), where A is a 10×10 array of reals, A(1,1) appears 44 words before XYZ and A(10,10) appears 55 words after XYZ, as shown in Fig. 10.8. The existence of A does not affect the counter for the COMMON block; it is only incremented by one word when XYZ is considered, independent of what XYZ is equivalenced to. However, the end of the data area for the COMMON block must be far enough from the beginning to accommodate the array A. We must therefore keep a quantity which is the largest offset of any word used by a name equivalenced to a member of the COMMON block. In this case, that quantity must be at least the offset of XYZ plus 55. We must also check that the array A does not extend in front of the beginning of the data area; that is, the offset of XYZ must be at least 44. If it is not, we have an error and must produce a diagnostic message.

A Simple Equivalence Algorithm

The first algorithms for processing equivalence statements appeared in assemblers rather than compilers. Since these algorithms can be a bit complex, especially when interactions between COMMON and EQUIVALENCE statements are considered, let us treat first a situation typical of an assembly

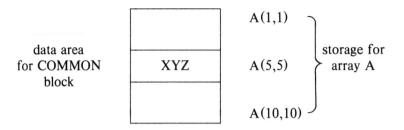

Fig. 10.8. Relation between the effects of COMMON
and EQUIVALENCE statements.

language, where the only EQUIVALENCE statements are of the form

EQUIVALENCE A, B+OFFSET

where A and B are the names of locations. The effect of this statement is
to make A denote the location which is OFFSET memory units beyond the
location for B.

A sequence of EQUIVALENCE statements groups names into
equivalence sets whose positions relative to one another are all defined by
the EQUIVALENCE statements. For example, the sequence of
EQUIVALENCE statements

EQUIVALENCE	A, B+100
EQUIVALENCE	C, D−40
EQUIVALENCE	A, C+30
EQUIVALENCE	E, F

groups names into the sets {A,B,C,D} and {E,F}. E and F denote the same
location. C is 70 locations after B; A is 30 after C and D is 10 after A.

To compute the equivalence sets we create a tree for each set. Each
node of a tree represents a name and contains the offset of that name relative to the name at the parent of this node. The name at the root of a tree
we call the *leader*. The position of any name relative to the leader can be
computed by following the path from the node for that name and adding
the offsets found along the way.

Example 10.5. The equivalence set {A,B,C,D} mentioned above could be
represented by the tree shown in Fig. 10.9. D is the leader, and we can discover that A is located 10 positions before D, since the sum of the offsets
on the path from A to D is $100+(-110) = -10$. □

Let us now give an algorithm for constructing trees for equivalence
sets. The relevant fields in the symbol-table entries are:

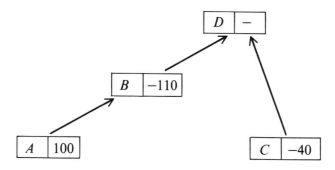

Fig. 10.9. Tree representing equivalence set.

1. PARENT, pointing to the symbol-table entry for the parent, null if the name is a root (or not equivalenced to anything).
2. OFFSET, giving the offset of a name relative to the parent name.

The algorithm we give assumes that any name could be the leader of an equivalence set. In practice, in an assembly language, one and only one name in the set would have an actual location defined by a pseudo-operation, and this name would be made the leader. We trust the reader can see how to modify the algorithm to make one particular name be the leader.

Algorithm 10.1. Construction of equivalence trees.

Input. A list of equivalence-defining statements of the form

$$\text{EQUIVALENCE} \qquad \text{A, B+dist}$$

Output. A collection of trees such that, for any name mentioned in the input list of equivalences, we may, by following the path from that name to the root and summing the OFFSET's found along the path, determine the position of the name relative to the leader.

Method. We repeat the steps of Fig. 10.10 for each equivalence statement EQUIVALENCE A, B+dist, in turn. The justification for the formula in line (12) for the offset of the leader of A relative to the leader of B is as follows. The location of A, say l_A, is equal to c plus the location of the leader of A, say m_A. The location of B, say l_B, equals d plus the location of the leader of B, say m_B. But $l_A = l_B + dist$, so $c + m_A = d + m_B + dist$. Hence $m_A - m_B = d - c + dist$. □

Example 10.6. If we process EQUIVALENCE A, B+100 and EQUIVALENCE C, D−40 we get the configuration shown in Fig. 10.9, but without the OFFSET −110 in the node for B and with no link from B to D. When we process EQUIVALENCE A, C+30 we find that P points to B after the while-loop of line (3) and Q points to D after the while-loop of

```
         begin
(1)          let P and Q point to the nodes for A and B, respectively;
(2)          c:=0; d=0; / * c and d compute the offsets of A and B
                 from the leaders of their respective sets */
(3)          while PARENT(P) ≠ null do
                 begin
(4)                  c := c+OFFSET(P);
(5)                  P := PARENT(P)
                 end; /* move P to the leader of A, accumulating
                     offsets as we go */
(6)          while PARENT(Q) ≠ null do
                 begin
(7)                  d := d + OFFSET(Q);
(8)                  Q := PARENT(Q)
                 end; /* do the same for B */
(9)          if P = Q then /* A and B are already equivalenced */
(10)             if c−d ≠ dist then ...; /* there is an error; A and B
                     are given two different relative positions */
             else/* we must merge the sets of A and B */
                 begin
(11)                 PARENT(P) := Q; /* make the leader of A a child
                         of B's leader */
(12)                 OFFSET(P) := d − c + dist
                 end
     end
```

Fig. 10.10. Equivalence algorithm.

line (6). We also have c=100 and d=−40. Then at line (11) we make D
the parent of B and set the OFFSET field for B to 110, which is
(−40)−(100)+30. □

Algorithm 10.1 could take time proportional to n^2 to process n
equivalences, since in the worst case the paths followed in the loops of
lines (3) and (6) could include every node of their respective trees.
Equivalencing requires only a tiny fraction of the time spent in compilation,
so n^2 steps is not prohibitive, and an algorithm more complex than that of
Fig. 10.10 is probably not justified. However, it happens that there are two
easy things we can do to make Algorithm 10.1 take time that is just about
linear in the number of equivalences it processes. While it is not likely that
equivalence sets will be large enough, on the average, that these improvements need to be implemented, it is worth noting that equivalencing serves
as a paradigm for a number of important processes involving "set merging." For example, a number of efficient algorithms for data flow analysis

depend on fast equivalence algorithms; the interested reader is referred to the bibliographic notes of Chapters 13 and 14.

The first improvement we can make is to keep a count, for each leader, of the number of nodes in its tree. Then, at lines (11) and (12), instead of arbitrarily linking the leader of A to the leader of B, link whichever has the smaller count to the other. This makes sure that the trees grow squat so paths will be short. It is left as an exercise that n equivalences performed in this manner cannot produce paths longer than $\log_2 n$ nodes.

The second idea is known as *path compression*. When following a path to the root in the loops of lines (3) and (6), make all nodes encountered children of the leader if they are not already so. That is, while following the path, record all the nodes $n_1, n_2, \ldots, n_k$ encountered, where n_1 is the node for A or B and n_k is the leader. Then adjust offsets and make $n_1, n_2, \ldots, n_{k-2}$ children of n_k by the steps in Fig. 10.11.

> **begin**
> $h := \text{OFFSET}(n_{k-1})$;
>   **for** $i := k-2$ **to** 1 **by** -1 **do**
>   **begin**
> $\text{PARENT}(n_i) := n_k$;
> $h := h + \text{OFFSET}(n_i)$;
> $\text{OFFSET}(n_i) := h$
>   **end**
> **end**

Fig. 10.11. Adjustment of offsets.

An Equivalence Algorithm for FORTRAN

There are several additional features that must be appended to Algorithm 10.1 to make it work for FORTRAN. First, we must determine whether an equivalence set is in COMMON, which we can do by recording for each leader whether any of the names in its set are in COMMON, and if so, in which block.

Second, in an assembly language, one member of an equivalence set will pin down the entire set to reality by being a label of a statement, thus allowing the addresses denoted by all names in the set to be computed relative to that one location. In FORTRAN, however, it is the compiler's job to determine storage locations, so an equivalence set not in COMMON may be viewed as "floating" until the compiler determines the position of the whole set in its appropriate data area. To do so correctly, the compiler needs to know the extent of the equivalence set, that is, the number of locations which the names in the set collectively occupy. To handle this problem we attach to the leader two fields, LOW and HIGH, giving the offsets relative to the leader of the lowest and highest locations used by any member of the equivalence set. Third, there are minor problems introduced by the fact that names can be arrays and locations in the middle of an array can be equivalenced to locations in other arrays.

Since there are three fields (LOW, HIGH and a pointer to a COMMON block) that must be associated with each leader, we do not want to allocate space for these fields in all symbol-table entries. One course of action is to use the PARENT field from Algorithm 10.1 to point, in the case of the leader, to a record in a new table with three fields, LOW, HIGH, and COMBLK. As this table and the symbol table occupy disjoint areas, we can tell which table a pointer points to. Alternatively, the symbol table can contain a bit indicating whether a name is currently a leader. If space is really at a premium, an alternative algorithm avoiding this extra table at the cost of a bit more programming effort is discussed in the exercises.

Let us consider the calculation that must replace lines (11) and (12) of Fig. 10.10. The situation in which two equivalence sets, whose leaders are pointed to by P and Q, must be merged is depicted in Fig. 10.12(a). The data structure representing the two sets appears in Fig. 10.12(b). First, we must check that there are not two members among the two equivalence sets that are in COMMON. Even if both are in the same block, the FORTRAN standard forbids their being equivalenced. If any one COMMON block contains a member of either equivalence set, then the merged set has a pointer to the record for that block in COMBLK. The code doing this check, assuming the leader pointed to by Q becomes the leader of the merged set, is shown in Fig. 10.13.

In place of lines (11) and (12) of Fig. 10.10 we must also compute the extent of the merged equivalence set. Figure 10.12(a) indicates the formulas for the new values of LOW and HIGH relative to the leader pointed to by Q. Thus we must do:

begin
    LOW(PARENT(Q)) := min(LOW(PARENT(Q)),
        LOW(PARENT(P)) $-$ c + dist + d);
    HIGH(PARENT(Q)) := max(HIGH(PARENT(Q)),
        HIGH(PARENT(P)) $-$ c + dist + d)
end

These statements are followed by lines (11) and (12) of Fig. 10.10 to effect the merger of the two equivalence sets.

Two last details must be covered to make Algorithm 10.1 work for FORTRAN. In FORTRAN, we may equivalence positions in the middle of arrays to other positions in other arrays or to simple names. The offset of an array A from its leader means the offset of the first location of A from the first location of the leader. If a location like A(5,7) is equivalenced to, say, B(20), we must compute the position of A(5,7) relative to A(1,1) and

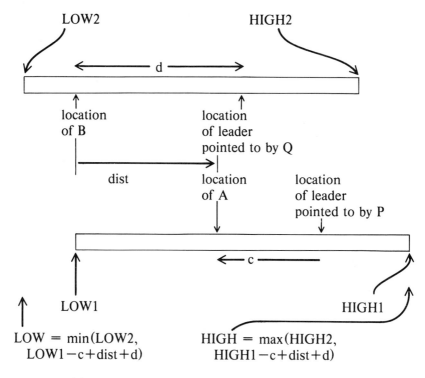

(a) relative positions of equivalence sets

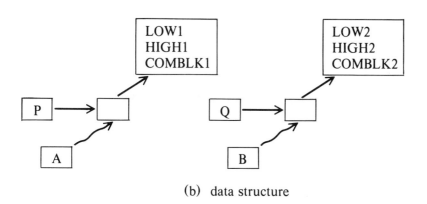

(b) data structure

Fig. 10.12. Merging equivalence sets.

```
begin
    COMBLK1 := COMBLK(PARENT(P));
    COMBLK2 := COMBLK(PARENT(Q));
    if COMBLK1 ≠ null and COMBLK2 ≠ null then · · ·
        /* error; two names in COMMON
        are equivalenced */
    else if COMBLK2 = null then
        COMBLK(PARENT(Q)) := COMBLK1
end
```

Fig. 10.13. Computing COMMON blocks.

initialize c to the negative of this distance in line (2) of Fig. 10.10. Similarly, d must be initialized to the negative of the position of B(20) relative to B(1). The formulas in Section 8.1, together with a knowledge of the size of elements of the arrays A and B, are sufficient to calculate the initial values of c and d.

The last detail to be covered is the fact that FORTRAN allows an EQUIVALENCE which involves many locations, such as

$$\text{EQUIVALENCE } (A(5,7), B(20), C, D(4,5,6))$$

These may be treated as

$$\text{EQUIVALENCE } (B(20), A(5,7))$$
$$\text{EQUIVALENCE } (C, A(5,7))$$
$$\text{EQUIVALENCE } (D(4,5,6), A(5,7))$$

Note that if we do the equivalences in this order, only A becomes the leader of a set of more than one element. A record with LOW, HIGH, and COMBLK can be used many times for "equivalence sets" of a single name.

Mapping Data Areas

We may now describe the rules whereby space in the various data areas is assigned for each routine's names.

1. For each COMMON block, visit all names declared to be in that block, in the order of their declarations (use the chains of COMMON names created in the symbol table for this purpose). Allocate the number of words needed for each name in turn, keeping a count of the number of words allocated, so offsets can be computed for each name. If a name A is equivalenced, the extent of its equivalence set does not matter, but we must check that the LOW value for the leader of A does not

extend past the beginning of the COMMON block. Consult the HIGH value for the leader to put a lower limit on the last word of the block. We leave the exact formulas for these calculations to the reader.

2. Visit all names for the routine in any order.
    a) If a name is in COMMON, do nothing. Space has been allocated in (1).
    b) If a name is not in COMMON and not equivalenced, allocate the necessary number of words in the data area for the routine.
    c) If a name A is equivalenced, find its leader, say L. If L has already been given a position in the data area for the routine, compute the position of A by adding to that position all the OFFSET's found in the path from A to L in the tree representing the equivalence set of A and L. If L has not been given a position, allocate the next HIGH $-$ LOW words in the data area for the equivalence set. The position of L in these words is $-$LOW words from the beginning, and the position of A can be calculated by summing OFFSET's as before.

Temporary Names

We have been going along in the previous chapters assuming that NEWTEMP() generated a new temporary name each time we needed one. It is useful, especially in optimizing compilers, to actually create a distinct name for each temporary; Chapters 12 and 13 give justification for doing so. However, the temporaries used to hold intermediate values in expression calculations will clutter up the symbol table, and it would be a space savings if we could avoid them.

If we, in fact, do enter compiler-generated temporary names into the symbol table, we can make sure they are distinct from any name the programmer might use by beginning the temporary names by a character, such as $, which is illegal in programmer-defined names. We can avoid entering temporaries into the symbol table at all in a FORTRAN compiler by realizing that such temporaries can be of only five types: LOGICAL, INTEGER, REAL, COMPLEX, and DOUBLE PRECISION. They cannot be in COMMON nor can they be equivalenced, be formal parameters or be external. In short, only their type need be recorded. The type of temporary names can be stored along with the three-address statements that use them, saving a symbol-table entry at the cost of some extra space in the area holding intermediate code.

However, we are still left with the problem of allocating storage in data areas for the temporaries used by a routine. Typically, there will be many temporaries used briefly if we generate a new temporary for each intermediate value in an expression. The *scope* of a name is the portion of the program between its definition and last use. Chapter 14 discusses the data-flow analysis necessary to compute the scope of names, which may be complicated in general. In the case of almost all temporaries, however, there is one definition and one use and there is no branching of control possible between definition and use. In such a situation, the scope of a temporary is obvious.

We can, in general, replace two temporaries by one name if their scopes do not overlap. If we compute the scope of each temporary by the methods of Chapter 14, we can allocate storage locations for temporaries by examining each in turn and assigning it the first location such that its scope does not conflict with the scope of any other temporary assigned to that location. If a temporary cannot be assigned to any previously created location, add a new location to the data area for the current routine. In many cases, temporaries can be packed into registers rather than memory locations; this use of registers is a major theme of Chapter 15.

As temporaries of different types are likely to require different numbers of words, it is convenient to use a separate set of locations for temporaries of different types. There is, however, nothing that prevents two adjacent locations from holding one complex-valued temporary at one time and two real valued temporaries at another. In fact, when we discuss stack allocation of temporary storage in the next section, we shall see that this situation is actually quite normal and useful.

Last-in First-out Use of Temporaries

As we have mentioned, the bulk of temporaries denoting data are generated by the translation of expressions, by an algorithm such as that of Section 7.7. The scopes of these names are nested like matching pairs of balanced parentheses, so it is possible to use, as if it were a stack, a small array in a routine's data area to hold temporaries; perhaps use one stack for each simple type of data. Let us assume for simplicity that we are dealing only with integer names. Keep a count c, initialized to zero. Whenever we use a temporary name as an operand, decrement c by 1. Whenever we generate a new temporary name, use $\$c$ and increase c by 1. Note that the "stack" of temporaries is not pushed or popped at run time, although it happens that stores and loads of temporary values are made by the compiler to occur at the "top."

Example 10.7. Consider the assignment

$$X := A*B - C*D + E*F$$

Figure 10.14 shows the sequence of three-address statements that would be generated by the algorithm in Section 7.7, with an indication of the "current" value of c after the generation of each statement. Note that when we compute $\$0 - \$1$, c is decremented to zero, so $\$0$ is again available to hold the result.   □

Statement	Value of c
	0
$0 := A * B	1
$1 := C * D	2
$0 := $0 + $1	1
$1 := E * F	2
$0 := $0-$1	1
X := $0	0

Fig 10.14. Three-address code with stacked temporaries.

We should be aware that in some languages temporaries may be assigned and/or used more than once, for example, in a conditional assignment. These temporaries cannot be assigned names in the last-in first-out manner described above. Since they tend to be rare, we could assign all such temporary values names of their own, perhaps later analyzing their scopes and packing them. The same problem of temporaries defined or used more than once occurs when we perform code optimization such as combining common subexpressions or moving a computation out of a loop (see Chapter 12). A reasonable strategy is to create a new name whenever we create an additional definition or use for a temporary or move its computation. Again, we can pack these new names later with some effort.

10.4 Storage Allocation in Block-Structured Languages

The basic ideas introduced in the previous section for laying out data areas apply to block-structured languages as well. In languages with block structure, however, such as PL/I or ALGOL, little or no data will be put in the static areas for each procedure. In ALGOL, for example, only names declared to have an **own** attribute are allocated space in a static area. The bulk of data is allocated on a stack. Activation records are another kind of data area, and they may be formatted as static data areas are.

We keep a count, initially zero, of memory units allocated in the activation record. As we see declarations of names we enter the current count into the symbol table entry for each name. Then we increment the count by the number of memory units taken by the name declared. The only major difference concerns array names. As we saw in Fig. 10.5, we usually wish to store only a pointer in the activation record. Thus, when an array is declared, the count is incremented by the size of a pointer rather than by the size of the array itself.

Stacking Temporaries

Temporaries used to evaluate expressions can be stored with other fixed-size data on the stack. However, another method is quite useful for handling temporaries that are used in a last-in first-out way, especially for machines that allow automatic incrementation of index registers. To create a new temporary, store its value in the word pointed to by the TOP pointer, and increment the TOP pointer. When using the value of a temporary, we retrieve the value pointed to by the TOP pointer and decrement that pointer. This operation can also be done in one instruction on these machines.

A word of caution should be issued regarding temporaries for languages with stack storage. The semantics of these languages normally require temporaries to be treated as local names of the routine for which they are created. We may not, therefore, use static storage for them.

Example 10.8. Suppose we (foolishly) write a recursive program to sum the first n squares as:

> **procedure** SUMSQ(n);
> **if** $n=1$ **return** 1
> **else return** $n*n+$SUMSQ($n-1$)

We would need to create a temporary for $n*n$ (and for $n-1$ if call by reference were used), and this temporary would need a different location for each call to SUMSQ.

If the above method of handling temporaries were used, each value of the temporary for $n*n$ would appear above the area used for the values of arrays in Fig. 10.5. Above the temporary would appear the actual parameter for the next call to SUMSQ. □

We may attempt to save space on the stack by allocating static storage for those temporaries whose scope does not include any procedure call. Note that in the obvious implementation of SUMSQ from Example 10.8, the value of $n*n$ is computed, and then SUMSQ($n-1$) is computed, and these values are added. Thus, the value of $n*n$ must be preserved across a procedure call, and we must put it on the stack. However, the temporary which holds the value of SUMSQ($n-1$) is used immediately and need not be preserved across any procedure call. Thus one location for SUMSQ($n-1$) may be placed in a static data area.[†] In fact, this data area can be reused by each procedure and need have size equal to the maximum required by any procedure, rather than the sum of the requirements.

[†] In practice, the object code would not refer to this static location, but rather would take the return value off the stack directly.

Exercises

10.1 Suppose P(X,Y) is a C procedure, and it is called by P(A+B,C). Show the intermediate code generated for the call and return. Make arbitrary assumptions about the locations of A, B, and C in the activation record of the calling procedure.

10.2 Suppose the procedure shown in Fig. 10.15 is written in a block-structured language, declared at nesting level three and called by COMB(A+B, C). Select a format for the activation records of the procedure COMB. Write intermediate-code versions of the calls and the return.

procedure COMB(n, m);
begin
        integer n, m;
        if $m \leqslant 0$ **or** $m \geqslant n$ **then return** 1
        else return COMB(n−1, m)+COMB(n−1, m−1)
end

Fig. 10.15. The procedure COMB.

10.3 Suppose we have the following sequence of declarations in a FORTRAN program.

```
SUBROUTINE SUB(X,Y)
INTEGER A, B(20), C(10,15), D, E
COMPLEX F, G
COMMON /CBLK/ D, E, F
EQUIVALENCE G, B(2)
EQUIVALENCE D, F, B(1)
```

Show the contents of the data areas for SUB and CBLK (at least the portion of CBLK's area accessible from SUB). Why is there no space for X and Y?

10.4 A useful data structure for equivalence computations is the *ring structure*. We use one pointer and an offset field in each symbol table entry to link members of an equivalence set. This structure is suggested in Fig. 10.16, where A, B, C, and D are equivalent, and E and F are equivalent, with the location of B 20 words after that of A, and so on.

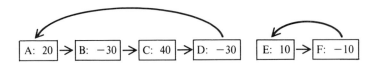

| A: 20 | → | B: −30 | → | C: 40 | → | D: −30 | | E: 10 | → | F: −10 |

Fig. 10.16. Ring structures.

a) Give an algorithm to compute the offset of X relative to Y, assuming X and Y are in the same equivalence set.

b) Give an algorithm to compute LOW and HIGH, as defined in Section 10.3, relative to the location of some name Z.

c) Give an algorithm to process

$$\text{EQUIVALENCE U, V}$$

Do not assume that U and V are necessarily in different equivalence sets.

10.5 The algorithm to map data areas given in Section 10.3 requires that we verify that LOW for the leader of A's equivalence set does not cause the space for the equivalence set of A to extend before the beginning of the COMMON block and that we calculate HIGH for the leader of A to increase the upper limit of the COMMON block, if necessary. Give formulas in terms of NEXT, the offset of A in the COMMON block, and LAST, the current last word of the block, to make the test and to update LAST if necessary.

10.6 Suppose we have an expression, all of whose operands are integers. Give an algorithm to determine the minimum number of distinct temporary names needed to evaluate the expression, assuming no algebraic laws may be applied to alter the expression. For example, A + B * C requires one temporary (for B * C). (A + B) * (C+D)+E requires two, one for C+D and the other for both A+B and (A+B) * (C+D).

Bibliographic Notes

The idea of the display is from Dijkstra [1960]. It has been developed in Randell and Russell [1964] and Gries, Paul, and Wiehle [1965]. Our approach is patterned after the latter paper. Pratt [1975] and Nicholls [1975] discuss other varieties of dynamic storage allocation.

Equivalence algorithms have been described by Arden, Galler, and Graham [1961] and Galler and Fischer [1964]; we have adopted the latter approach. The efficiency of equivalence algorithms is discussed in Fischer

[1972], Hopcroft and Ullman [1973], and Tarjan [1975]. Ershov [1966] discusses the packing of temporaries to save space.

CHAPTER 11

Error Detection
and
Recovery

Programs submitted to a compiler often have errors of various kinds. A good compiler, therefore, should direct attention to as many errors as is reasonably possible. Thus, with regard to errors, the compiler must be an effective communications device; it should deliver comments to the user in a language and manner the user can understand.

The compiler should be able not only to detect errors but also to *recover* from them. That is, even in the presence of errors, the compiler should scan the entire program and try to compile all of it, if for no other reason than to detect as many errors as possible. The problem of recovery is most acute when the lexical analyzer or parser finds an error and cannot proceed. Then the compiler must modify the input so the correct portions of the program can be pieced together and successfully processed, at least through the syntax analysis phase.

Good error detection and diagnostic facilities in a compiler require considerable forethought; their inclusion should be considered from the very beginning in the design of a compiler. This chapter discusses the nature and sources of common errors in programs, and mechanisms by which each phase of the compiler can detect errors and recover from them.

11.1 Errors

There are a variety of ways in which a compiler can react to mistakes in the source program. Obviously unacceptable modes of behavior are to produce a system crash, to emit invalid output, or to merely quit on the first detected error. At the very least, a compiler should attempt to recover from each error and continue analyzing its input. It is in the method of recovery and the type of continuation that compilers differ. A simple compiler may stop all activities other than lexical and syntactic analysis after the detection of the first error. A more complex compiler may attempt to *repair* the error, that is, transform the erroneous input into a similar but legal input on which normal processing can be resumed. An even more sophisticated compiler may attempt to *correct* the erroneous input by making a guess as to what the user intended.

"Detection," "recovery," "repair," and "correction" are just terms used to describe positions in the spectrum of possible reactions to errors. Almost all compilers recover from common errors and continue syntax checking. A few student-job oriented compilers, such as PL/C and DITRAN, attempt repair in order to compile the rest of the source program and to execute the resulting object program. The goal is to detect as many errors as possible in one run, including errors detectable only at run time.

No compiler can do true correction, and there are convincing reasons why a compiler ought not try. One reason is that to do correction a compiler must know the intent of the programmer. However, the true intent is often completely obscured by the errors in the source program. Since completely accurate error correction can be done only by the programmer, it is a task most compilers should not waste time attempting.

Reporting Errors

The manner in which a compiler reports errors can greatly affect how pleasant and economical it is to use its language on a given machine. Good error diagnostics can significantly help reduce debugging and maintenance effort, an activity that often dominates the cost of constructing reliable programs. Good error diagnostics should possess a number of properties:

- The messages should pinpoint the errors in terms of the original source program, rather than in terms of some internal representation that is totally mysterious to the user.
- The error messages should be tasteful and understandable by the user (e.g., "missing right parenthesis in line 5" rather than a cryptic error code such as "OH17".)
- The messages should be specific and should localize the problem (e.g., "ZAP not declared in procedure BLAH" rather than "missing declaration").
- The messages should not be redundant. If a variable ZAP is undeclared, that should be said once, not every time ZAP appears in the program.

Sources of Error

It is difficult to give a precise classification scheme for programming errors. One way to classify errors is according to how they are introduced. If we look at the entire process of designing and implementing a program, we see that errors can arise at every stage of the process.

- At the very onset, the design specifications for the program may be inconsistent or faulty.

- The algorithms used to meet the design may be inadequate or incorrect ("algorithmic errors").
- The programmer may introduce errors in implementing the algorithms, either by introducing logical errors or by using the programming-language constructs improperly ("coding errors").
- Keypunching or transcription errors can occur when the program is typed onto cards or into a file.
- The program may exceed a compiler or machine limit not implied by the definition of the programming language. For example, an array may be declared with too many dimensions to fit in the symbol table, or an array may be too large to be allocated space at run time.
- Finally, although it should not happen, a compiler can insert errors as it translates the source program into an object program ("compiler errors").

The source of the error determines to some degree the likelihood with which a compiler can repair the error. On algorithmic errors a compiler can do little. On coding errors a compiler may do better, but some coding errors are very difficult to correct. For example if a programmer wrote in PL/I

$$\text{DO WHILE } (0 < I < 10)$$

chances are, he did not understand that $0 < I < 10$ will always evaluate to **true**, but did he mean DO I $= 1$ TO 9, or DO WHILE $(0 < I \ \& \ I < 10)$?

With transcription errors there is much more redundancy and hence much more opportunity for a compiler to effect a good repair. Typical of these errors are the following:

- the insertion of an extraneous character or token,
- the deletion of a required character or token,
- the replacement of a correct character or token by an incorrect character or token,
- the transposition of two adjacent characters or tokens.

Note that a replacement error and a transposition error can each be treated as special cases of an insertion error followed by a deletion error.

From the point of view of the compiler writer, it is convenient to classify errors as being either syntactic or semantic. We define a *syntactic error* to be an error detectable by the lexical or syntactic phase of the compiler. Other errors detectable by the compiler are termed *semantic errors*.

Syntactic Errors

Here are a few common examples of syntactic errors.

1. Missing right parenthesis:

   MIN(A, 2 ∗ (3 + B)

2. Extraneous comma:

   DO 10, I = 1, 100

3. Colon in place of semicolon:

   I = 1:
   J = 2;

4. Misspelled keyword:

   F: PORCEDURE OPTIONS (MAIN)

5. Extra blank:

   /∗ COMMENT ∗ /

(1) is an example of a deletion error, (2) and (5) insertion errors, (3) a replacement error, and (4) a transposition error. On error (5) a naive compiler might attempt to treat a large portion of the remainder of the program as a comment.

In each of the examples above, it is easy for a human being to determine the type of error and the position at which it occurs. Often, however, it is difficult to say exactly how many errors there are or where they have occurred, without knowing the intent of the programmer.

For example, consider the statement

A := B − C ∗ D + E)

We know an error has occurred, but we can't be certain whether the error is the extraneous right parenthesis, or whether a left parenthesis has been left out before the B, the C, the D, or conceivably the E.

Quite frequently we cannot detect that an error has occurred until long after it has taken place. For example, in the PL/I program fragment

      IFA = B THEN
             SUM = SUM + A;
      ELSE   (11.1)
             SUM = SUM − A;

The obvious error is a missing blank between the keyword IF and the name A. No error is discernible, however, until the keyword THEN has been read, since the compiler can treat IFA = B as an assignment statement. Because B can be replaced by an expression, this example shows that the detection of an error may occur an arbitrarily long distance after the place where the error actually occurred.

Minimum Distance Correction of Syntactic Errors

One theoretical way of defining errors and their location is the *minimum Hamming distance* method. We define a collection of error transformations. We then say that a program P has k errors if the shortest sequence of error transformations that will map any valid program into P has length k.

For example, if we let our error transformations be the insertion of a single character or the deletion of a single character, then the program fragment (11.1) is distance one from:

$$\text{IF } A = B \text{ THEN}$$
$$\qquad \text{SUM} = \text{SUM} + A;$$
$$\text{ELSE} \qquad\qquad\qquad\qquad\qquad\qquad (11.2)$$
$$\qquad \text{SUM} = \text{SUM} - A;$$

because (11.1) can be mapped into (11.2) by the insertion of a blank between IF and A. Fragment (11.2) is a minimum-distance correction of (11.1), since there can be no legal program at distance less than one from an illegal program.

Although minimum-distance error correction is a convenient theoretical yardstick, it is not generally used in practice because it is too costly to implement. However, we shall in several examples use the minimum-distance criterion for local corrections. That is, various error-repair strategies rely on changing a small portion of a program containing an error into a string that is legal, at least in the local context, and that is at a minimum distance from the original. For example, an LR parser reaching an error action might modify the next three symbols on its input as little as necessary, to obtain an input on which the parser can eventually make three more shift moves.

Henceforth, when we speak of "minimum distance" we shall mean the least number of insertions, deletions, and symbol modifications necessary to transform one string into another. The strategies proposed will not depend exactly on how distance is calculated. For example, we could include transposition of adjacent symbols as a modification at distance one.

Semantic Errors

Semantic errors can be detected both at compile time and at run time. The most common semantic errors that can be detected at compile time are errors of declaration and scope. Typical examples are undeclared or multiply-declared identifiers. Leaving out the declaration of one identifier can spawn a multiplicity of "undeclared identifier" error messages unless some provision is made to enter a special "error flag" for that identifier in the symbol table.

Type incompatibilities between operators and operands, and between formal and actual parameters are another common source of semantic errors that can be detected in many languages at compile time. The amount of type checking that can be done, however, depends on the language at hand. Some languages (such as BLISS) have only one data type, so no type disagreements can arise. Other languages (such as PAS-CAL) have many types, but the type of every name and expression must be calculable at compile time. Such languages are said to be *strongly typed.* Consequently, a PASCAL compiler can do vigorous type checking at compile-time and so catch many potential errors.

Languages such as PL/I define type conversions which automatically occur between operators and operands of disparate types. In such languages automatic type conversion eliminates the possibility of general semantic error detection.

Dynamic Errors

In some languages certain kinds of errors can only be detected at run time. For example, languages such as APL and SNOBOL have several types, and the type of a name can change at run time. Some type checking for languages such as these must therefore be postponed to run time.

Another common kind of error detection usually done at run time, if at all, is range checking for certain values, particularly array subscripts and case statement selectors. A subscript out of range could cause an arbitrary memory location to be overwritten. An arbitrary value in a case statement (or computed goto) could cause a jump to an unknown memory location.

Errors Seen by Each Phase

Each phase of a compiler expects its input to follow a certain specification. When the input does not, the phase has detected an inconsistency or an error, which it should report to the user. Moreover, in order to continue processing its input, the phase has to recover from each error it detects. Thus we can also classify errors as being lexical-phase, syntactic-phase, or semantic-phase errors, depending on which compiler phase detects them. In the following three sections, we shall discuss recovery techniques that a lexical analyzer, a syntactic analyzer, and a semantic analyzer can use in response to errors seen in their respective inputs. Figure 11.1 shows the plan of the error detection and recovery portion of the compiler. It consists of routines to recover from lexical and syntactic errors, a routine to detect semantic errors and a routine to print diagnostics. The diagnostic routine communicates with the symbol table to avoid printing redundant messages. The message printer must defer its diagnostics until after a complete line of source text has been read and listed (if a listing is produced by the compiler).

We might mention that after detecting and reporting an error, a phase can either repair the error or pass it along to subsequent modules. If a phase attempts repair, it should take precautions that the repair does not

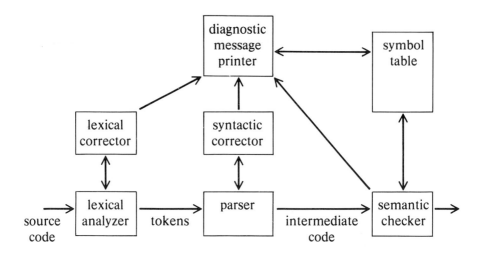

Fig. 11.1. Plan of an error detector/corrector.

introduce a flurry of other errors (and along with them an avalanche of spurious error messages). On the other hand if a phase transmits errors without repair, then all subsequent phases should be prepared to deal with the erroneous inputs passed along. A reasonable precaution is for the compiler to inhibit error messages following a lexical or syntactic error until several tokens from the source have successfully been processed, at least through the parser.

11.2 Lexical-Phase Errors

The function of the lexical analyzer is to carve the stream of characters constituting the source program into a sequence of tokens. Each token class has a specification which is typically a regular set. If, after some processing, the lexical analyzer discovers that no prefix of the remaining input fits the specification of any token class, it can invoke an error-recovery routine that can take a variety of remedial actions.

Unfortunately, there is no one remedial action that will ideally suit all situations. The problem of recovering from lexical errors is further hampered by the lack of redundancy at the lexical level of a language. The simplest expedient is to skip erroneous characters until the lexical analyzer can find another token. This action will likely cause the parser to see a deletion error.

Example 11.1. We shall consider an example of a mistake which leads to a lexical error as well as syntactic and semantic errors. We shall also see some of the ways an error recovery mechanism can perpetuate the parse.

Suppose a FORTRAN programmer writes a statement of the form

IF (long condition .OR. X .LT. Y) GOTO 30

which spills onto a second card after the X. In keypunching the second card, suppose the programmer misplaces the continuation symbol 1 in column 8. Then the lexical analyzer, after reading token X, finds an end-of-statement (the end of a line not followed by a continuation), which is really a token in FORTRAN, playing roughly the same syntactic role as the semicolon in many languages. Since a statement has not been found, there is a syntactic error, and the parser must take some recovery action. For example, it could print a diagnostic message and assume that a statement has been found, reducing everything on the line beginning with IF . . . to the nonterminal "statement."

Then the lexical analyzer must process the continuation

1 .LT. Y) GOTO 30

The token 1. is found next by the lexical analyzer. Supposing that this lexical analyzer does not distinguish reals from variable names, calling them all **id**'s, there is no error detectable by the lexical analyzer or parser at this point. To the compiler it looks as though the continuation is going to be an assignment statement. This erroneous interpretation is not going to be dispelled until semantic analysis. (By that time the compiler should realize that these errors are probably generated by itself.)

The next token read from the input is **id**, namely the "variable" LT. Since the parser cannot accept two identifiers in a row, it attempts some recovery, which might logically be to insert an = sign (the only other token that could follow an initial **id** in a statement is a left parenthesis, which is statistically less probable than an = sign). Thus the parser thinks it has an assignment statement beginning **id** = **id**.

The lexical analyzer now searches for the next token, which must begin with .Y, but it knows of no such token. One possible recovery strategy at this point is to delete the first symbol, dot, and to try again to find a token. This time we find one, the **id** Y. If we had not found a token, we would delete Y and try again at the right parenthesis. The parser again cannot accept two **id**'s in a row, so it takes further corrective action, say inserting a + sign between the two **id**'s. Then the next token, the right parenthesis, causes another syntactic error. At some point the syntactic error corrector will succeed in constructing a (completely erroneous) statement and can get on to the next line, where it will hopefully have better luck. □

Deleting characters indiscriminately from the source program can cause severe difficulties for the syntax analyzer and the remaining phases of the compiler. One way for the lexical analyzer to improve its ability to recover from errors is to have the parser make available to the lexical error recovery routine a list of those tokens that can legitimately appear next in the current context. For example if an LR parser is used, the top state on the parsing stack tells what tokens could cause an action other than error if they appeared next on the input.[†] The error-recovery routine can then decide whether a prefix of the remaining input matches one of these tokens sufficiently closely for the prefix to be treated as that token.

For example, in the situation discussed in Example 11.1, where the lexical analyzer has treated 1. and LT as two **id**'s, and the parser has corrected this to **id** = **id**, an LR parser would expect only the end-of-statement token, a left parenthesis, or an operator token. The lexical analyzer could then avoid treating Y, the right parenthesis, GOTO, or 30 as tokens and would reach the end-of-statement without further ado.

Minimum-Distance Matching

There are a number of situations in which, suspecting a misspelling, we may avoid additional errors by using minimum-distance matching to correct the spelling of a token. For example, suppose we know the next token is supposed to be a keyword but x, the next sequence of alphabetic symbols on the input, is not a keyword. We could determine which keyword is closest to x under some reasonable error metric. On the other hand, if we suspect "identifier" x is a misspelling because no declaration for x is present in the symbol table, we could try to find an identifier in the symbol table that is closest to x. Other situations in which misspellings can be suspected are invalid operators (like .EG. for .GE. in FORTRAN relational expressions), unknown array names in array references, invalid labels in gotos, and so forth.

The problem of finding a word from a given collection that is closest to a given string x has been studied in detail, and a number of general algorithms are known for metrics such as the fewest number of insertion, deletion, and replacement errors.

In most compilers it is rarely worth implementing a general algorithm for minimum-distance error matching. A simple heuristic is easier to implement and runs faster. Assuming that most spelling errors result from one application of an error transformation such as inserting an extra character, deleting a character, modifying a character, or transposing two adjacent characters, a simple strategy is to see whether any word from the permissible collection can be transformed into the erroneous string x by a single error transformation. Several obvious tests can be used to determine quickly which words might be possible sources of x. For example, we could eliminate as candidates words whose length differed from that of x by more than one. Morgan [1970] discusses the subject in greater detail.

[†] These are the tokens for which an action other than error appears in the action field of the row of the parse table for that state.

11.3 Syntactic-Phase Errors

Often much of the error detection and recovery in a compiler is centered around syntax analysis. One reason is the high degree of precision we can achieve in the syntactic specification of programming languages using context-free grammars. From a grammar we can generate a parser that recognizes exactly the language specified by that grammar. Violations of the syntactic specification will be caught automatically by the parser. Although a considerable amount of theoretical and practical effort has been expended in exploring recovery and repair techniques for syntactic errors, the optimal strategy for any programming language is still an open question.

A parser detects an error when it has no legal move from its current configuration, which is determined by its state, its stack contents and the current input symbol. To recover from an error a parser should ideally locate the position of the error, correct the error, revise its current configuration, and resume parsing. All existing methods approximate this ideal and will resume parsing, but there is never a guarantee that the error has been successfully corrected.

Time of Detection

The LL(1) and LR(1) parsers discussed in Chapters 5 and 6 have the *valid prefix property*: they will announce error as soon as a prefix of the input has been seen for which there is no valid continuation. This is the earliest time at which a parser that reads its input from left-to-right can announce error. On the other hand, operator-precedence parsers and a variety of other types of parser do not necessarily have this property.

The advantage of using a parser with the valid prefix property is that it reports error as soon as possible and limits the amount of erroneous output it passes to subsequent phases of the compiler. Note that even the valid prefix property is no assurance that the parser will detect the error where it has actually occurred.

Panic Mode

Since the details of the recovery methods vary somewhat depending on the type of parsing technique used, we shall examine methods for recovering from syntactic errors using operator-precedence, LL, and LR parsers. Before doing so we might mention a crude but effective systematic method of error recovery in any kind of parsing, the so-called "panic mode" of recovery. In panic mode a parser discards input symbols until a "synchronizing" token, usually a statement delimiter such as semicolon or **end**, is encountered. The parser then deletes stack entries until it finds an entry such that it can continue parsing, given the synchronizing token on the input. Two virtues of this recovery method are that it is simple to implement and, unlike some insertion schemes, it can never get into an infinite loop.

Error Recovery in Operator-Precedence Parsing

There are two points in the parsing process at which an operator-precedence parser can discover syntactic errors:

1. If no precedence relation holds between the terminal on top of the stack and the current input symbol.[†]
2. If a handle has been found, but there is no production with this handle as a right side.

Recall that the operator-precedence parser, Algorithm 5.3, appears to reduce handles composed of terminals only. While nonterminals are treated anonymously, however, they must have places held for them on the parsing stack if we are to translate the source program rather than just parse. The placeholder may be a pointer to a node of the parse tree or a record containing translations of the nonterminal. Thus when we talk about a handle matching a production's right side, we mean that the terminals are the same and the positions occupied by nonterminals are the same.

We should observe that there are no other points at which errors could be detected. When scanning down the stack to find the left end of the handle (in steps 6 and 7 of Fig. 5.13, the operator-precedence parsing algorithm), we are sure to find a $<\!\cdot$ relation, since $ marks the bottom of stack and is related by $<\!\cdot$ to any symbol that could appear immediately above it on the stack. Note also that we never allow adjacent symbols on the stack in Fig. 5.13 unless they are related by $<\!\cdot$ or $\doteq$. Thus steps (6) and (7) must succeed in making a reduction.

Just because we find a sequence of symbols $a \; <\!\cdot \; b_1 \doteq b_2 \doteq \cdots \doteq b_k$ on the stack, however, does not mean that $b_1 b_2 \cdots b_k$ is the string of terminal symbols on the right side of some production. We did not check for this condition in Fig. 5.13, but we clearly can do so, and in fact we must do so if we wish to associate semantic rules with reductions. Thus case (2) above gives us an opportunity to detect errors in Fig. 5.13 modified at steps (6) and (7) to determine what production is the handle in a reduction.

Handling Errors During Reductions

We may divide the error detection and recovery routine into several pieces. One piece handles errors of type (2). For example, this routine might pop symbols off the stack just as in steps (6) and (7) of Fig. 5.13. However, as there is no production to reduce by, no semantic actions are taken; a diagnostic message is printed instead. To determine what the diagnostic should

---

[†] In compilers using precedence functions to represent the precedence tables, this source of error detection may be unavailable.

say, the routine handling case (2) must decide what production the right side being popped "looks like." For example, suppose abc is popped, and there is no production right side consisting of a, b and c together with zero or more nonterminals. Then we might consider if deletion of one of a, b, and c yields a legal right side (nonterminals omitted). For example, if there were a right side $aAcB$, we might issue the diagnostic

ILLEGAL b ON LINE (line containing b).[†]

We might also consider changing or inserting a terminal. Thus if $abAdc$ were a right side, we might issue a diagnostic

MISSING d ON LINE (line containing c).

We may also find that there is a right side with the proper sequence of terminals, but the wrong pattern of nonterminals. For example, if abc is popped off the stack with no intervening or surrounding nonterminals, and abc is not a right side but $aAbc$ is, we should issue the diagnostic

MISSING A ON LINE (line containing b).

Here A stands for the syntactic category represented by nonterminal A, e.g., expression or statement.

In general, the difficulty of determining appropriate diagnostics when no legal right side is found depends upon whether there are a finite or infinite number of possible strings that could be popped in lines (6) and (7) of Fig. 5.13. Any such string $b_1 b_2 \cdots b_k$ must have $\doteq$ relations holding between adjacent symbols, so $b_1 \doteq b_2 \doteq \cdots \doteq b_k$. If an operator precedence table tells us that there are only a finite number of sequences of terminals related by $\doteq$, then we can handle these strings on a case-by-case basis. For each such string x we can determine in advance a minimum-distance legal right side y and issue a diagnostic implying that x was found when y was intended.

It is easy to determine all strings which could be popped from the stack in steps (6) and (7) of Fig. 5.13. These are evident in the directed graph whose nodes represent the terminals, with an edge from a to b if and only if $a \doteq b$. Then the possible strings are the labels of the nodes along paths in this graph. Paths consisting of a single node are possible. However, in order for a path $b_1 b_2 \cdots b_k$ to be "poppable" on some input, there must be a symbol a (possibly \$) such that $a <\cdot b_1$. Call such a b_1 *initial*. Also, there must be a symbol c (possibly \$) such that $b_k \cdot> c$. Call b_k *final*. Only then could a reduction be called for and $b_1 b_2 \cdots b_k$ be the sequence of symbols popped. If the graph has a path containing a cycle from an initial to a final node, then there are an infinity of strings which might be popped.

---

† If it is too troublesome to remember the points at which line breaks occurred, the phrase "at or near (current line)" can be used.

Otherwise there are only a finite number.

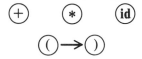

Fig. 11.2. Graph for precedence matrix of Fig. 5.10.

Example 11.2. Consider the precedence matrix of Fig. 5.10, whose graph is shown in Fig. 11.2. There is only one edge, because the only pair related by $\doteq$ is the left and right parenthesis. The initial symbols are $+$, $*$, $($, and **id**. The final symbols are $+$, $*$, $)$, and **id**. Thus the only paths from an initial to a final node are $+$, $*$, **id**, and $($, $)$. There are but a finite number, and each corresponds to the terminals of some production's right side. Thus the error checker for reductions need only check that the proper set of nonterminal markers appears among the terminal strings being reduced. Specifically, the checker does the following:

1. If $+$ or $*$ is reduced, it checks that nonterminals appear on both sides. If not, it can issue the diagnostic

    MISSING EXPRESSION

2. If **id** is reduced, it checks that there is no nonterminal to the right or left. If there is, it can warn

    TWO EXPRESSIONS NOT CONNECTED BY OPERATOR

3. If $(\ )$ is reduced, it checks that there is a nonterminal between the parentheses. If not, it can say

    NULL EXPRESSION BETWEEN PARENTHESES

Also it must check that no nonterminal appears on either side of the parentheses. If one does, it issues the same diagnostic as in (2).

In operator-precedence parsing, nonterminals are anonymous to the parser. Consequently, the appearance of a nonterminal on the stack where one is expected does not imply that it is the correct nonterminal. For the usual sorts of expressions, however, this aspect of operator-precedence parsing does not cause erroneous inputs to be parsed without detection of a syntax error.

The case where there are an infinity of strings that may be popped cannot be handled on a case-by-case basis. We might use a general routine to determine whether some production right side is close (say distance 1 or 2, where distance is measured in terms of tokens, rather than characters, inserted, deleted, or changed) to the popped string and if so, issue a specific diagnostic on the assumption that that production was intended. If no production is close to the popped string, we can issue a general diagnostic to the effect that "something is wrong in the current line." Fortunately, this case is rare in practice.

Handling Shift-Reduce Errors

We must now discuss the other way in which the operator-precedence parser detects errors. When consulting the precedence matrix to decide whether to shift or reduce (line 4 of Fig. 5.13), we may find that no relation holds between the top stack symbol and the first input symbol. For example, suppose a and b are the two top stack symbols (b is at the top), c and d are the next two input symbols, and there is no precedence relation between b and c. To recover, we must take one of the usual steps: change symbols, insert symbols onto the input or stack, or delete symbols from the input or stack. If we insert or change, we must be careful that we do not get into an infinite loop, where, for example, we perpetually insert symbols at the beginning of the input without being able to reduce or to shift any of the inserted symbols.

One approach which will assure us no infinite loops is to guarantee that after recovery the current input symbol can be shifted (if the current input is $, guarantee that no symbol is placed on the input, and the stack is eventually shortened). For example, if $a \lessdot c$ † we might pop b from the stack. Another choice is to delete c from the input if $b \lessdot d$. A third choice is to find a symbol e such that $b \lessdot e \lessdot c$ and insert e in front of c on the input. More generally, we might insert a string of symbols such that $b \lessdot e_1 \lessdot e_2 \lessdot \cdots \lessdot e_n \lessdot c$, if a single symbol for insertion could not be found. The exact action chosen should reflect what error is likely in each case.

For each blank entry in the precedence matrix we must specify an error-recovery routine; the same routine could be used in several places. Then when the parser consults the entry for a and b in step (4) of Fig. 5.13, and no precedence relation holds between a and b, it finds a pointer to the error-recovery routine for this error.

Example 11.3. Consider the precedence matrix of Fig. 5.10, which is reproduced as Fig. 11.3 with blank entries filled in with the names of error handling routines.

The substance of the error handlers is as follows:

---

† We use $\lessdot$ to mean $\lessdot$ or $\doteq$.

	+	*	(	)	id	$
+	·>	<·	<·	·>	<·	·>
*	·>	·>	<·	·>	<·	·>
(	<·	<·	<·	≐	<·	e1
)	·>	·>	e2	·>	e2	·>
id	·>	·>	e2	·>	e2	·>
$	<·	<·	<·	e3	<·	e4

Fig. 11.3. Operator precedence matrix with error entries.

e1: /* called when expression ends with a left parenthesis */
   pop (from the stack
   issue diagnostic: ILLEGAL LEFT PARENTHESIS

e2: /* called when **id** or) is followed by **id** or (*/
   insert + onto the input
   issue diagnostic: MISSING OPERATOR

e3: /* called when expression begins with a right parenthesis */
   delete) from the input
   issue diagnostic: ILLEGAL RIGHT PARENTHESIS

e4: /* called when expression is null */
   insert **id** onto the input
   issue diagnostic: MISSING EXPRESSION

Let us consider how our error-handling mechanism would treat a typical erroneous string. Suppose a chimpanzee is typing at an IBM 029 keypunch and wishes to type the expression D + E. When typing the E, however, his tail momentarily rests on the shift key, causing a right parenthesis to be typed instead. Thus the lexical analyzer passes the sequence of tokens **id** +) to the parser. The first actions taken by the parser are to shift **id**, reduce it (we use E for anonymous nonterminals on the stack), and then to shift the +. We now have configuration

         stack   input
         $E+   )$

Since + ·>) a reduction is called for, and the handle is +. The error checker for reductions is required to inspect for E 's to left and right. Finding one missing, it issues the diagnostic

                  MISSING EXPRESSION

and does the reduction anyway.
   Our configuration is now

         $E   )$

There is no precedence relation between $ and), and the entry in Fig. 11.3 for this pair of symbols is e3. Routine e3 causes diagnostic

ILLEGAL RIGHT PARENTHESIS

to be printed and removes the right parenthesis from the input. We are now left with the final configuration for the parser:

$$\$E \qquad\qquad \$$$

□

Error Recovery in LR Parsing

An LR parser will detect an error when it consults the parsing action table and finds an error entry. Errors never result from consultation of the goto table. Unlike an operator-precedence parser, an LR parser will announce error as soon as there is no valid continuation for the portion of the input thus far scanned.

An exhaustive method of designing an error recovery procedure for an LR parser is to examine each error entry in the parsing table and to decide on the basis of language usage the most likely programmer error that would give rise to that error. An appropriate recovery procedure can then be constructed. This procedure is useful for the most common errors.

Alternatively, a systematic way of recovering would be to scan down the stack until a state s with a goto on a particular nonterminal A is found. Zero or more input symbols are then discarded until a symbol a is found that can legitimately follow A. The parser then stacks the state GOTO[s, A] and resumes normal parsing. There might be more than one choice for the nonterminal A. Normally these would be nonterminals representing major program pieces, such as a statement. For example, if A is the nonterminal statement, a might be semicolon or **end**, in which case the resemblance of this approach to "panic mode" should be noticed.

The above method of recovery attempts to isolate the phrase containing the syntactic error. The parser determines that a string derivable from A contains an error. Part of that string has already been processed and the result of this processing is a sequence of states on top of the stack. The remainder of the string is still on the input, and the parser attempts to skip over the remainder of this string by looking for a symbol on the input that can legitimately follow A. By removing states from the stack, skipping over the input, and pushing GOTO[s, A] on the stack, the parser pretends that it has found an instance of A and resumes normal parsing.

Automatic Error Recovery in YACC

A variant of this method is used in the YACC compiler-compiler. Here the user can identify "major" nonterminals such as those for "program," "block," or "statement." The user then adds to the grammar error productions of the form $A \rightarrow$ **error** α, where A is a major nonterminal and α is any string of grammar symbols, possibly empty.

When the parser generated by YACC encounters an error, it finds the topmost state on its stack whose underlying set of items includes an item of the form $A \rightarrow \cdot$ **error** α. The parser then "shifts" **error**, as though it saw the token **error** on its input. In the usual case where α is ϵ, a reduction to A occurs immediately. The parser then invokes the semantic action associated with the production $A \rightarrow$ **error** (which might be a user-specified error-recovery routine). The parser then discards input symbols until it finds a symbol with which parsing can proceed. For example, an error production of the form $A \rightarrow$ **error**; would specify to the parser that it should skip to the next semicolon on seeing an error in an instance of A. The semantic routine for $A \rightarrow$ **error**; would not need to manipulate the input, but could call for a diagnostic message and set a flag to inhibit generation of object code, for example.

Ad-hoc Error Recovery for LR Parsers

Compared with operator-precedence parsers, the design of specific error-handling routines for an LR parser is relatively easy. In particular, we do not have to worry about faulty reductions; any reduction called for by an LR parser is surely correct. Thus we may fill in each blank entry in the action field with a pointer to an error routine that will take an appropriate action selected by the compiler designer. The actions will include insertion or deletion of symbols from the stack or the input or both, or alteration and transposition of input symbols, just as for the operator-precedence parser. Like that parser, we must make our choices without allowing the possibility that the LR parser will get into an infinite loop. A strategy which assures that at least one input symbol will be removed or eventually shifted, or that the stack will eventually shrink if the end of the input has been reached, is sufficient in this regard. Popping a stack state which covers a nonterminal should be avoided, because this eliminates a construct which has already been successfully parsed.

Example 11.4. Figure 6.15 is an LR parser which recognizes the same expression language as the operator-precedence parser considered in Example 11.3. We reproduce this LR parse table, with error routines introduced, in Fig. 11.4. We have also taken each state which calls for a particular reduction on some input symbols and replaced error entries for that state by the reduction. This has the effect of postponing the error detection until one or more reductions are made, but the error will still be caught before a shift.

state	action						goto
	id	+	*	(	)	$	E
0	s3	e1	e1	s2	e2	e1	1
1	e3	s4	s5	e3	e2	acc	
2	s3	e1	e1	s2	e2	e1	6
3	r4	r4	r4	r4	r4	r4	
4	s3	e1	e1	s2	e2	e1	7
5	s3	e1	e1	s2	e2	e1	8
6	e3	s4	s5	e3	s9	e4	
7	r1	r1	s5	r1	r1	r1	
8	r2	r2	r2	r2	r2	r2	
9	r3	r3	r3	r3	r3	r3	

Fig. 11.4. LR parsing table with error routines.

The error routines are as follows:

e1: /* This routine is called from states 0, 2, 4 and 5, all of which expect the beginning of an operand, either an **id** or a left parenthesis. Instead, an operator, + or *, or the end of the input was found. */
push an imaginary **id** onto the stack and cover it with state 3 (the goto of states 0, 2, 4 and 5 on **id**)[†]
issue diagnostic: MISSING OPERAND

e2: /* This routine is called from states 0, 1, 2, 4 and 5 on finding a right parenthesis. */
remove the next input symbol (right parenthesis)
issue diagnostic: UNBALANCED RIGHT PARENTHESIS

e3: /* This routine is called from states 1 or 6 when expecting an operator and an **id** or right parenthesis is found. */
push + onto the stack and cover it with state 4.
issue diagnostic: MISSING OPERATOR

e4: /* This routine is called from state 6 when the end of the input is found. State 6 expects an operator or a right parenthesis. */
push a right parenthesis onto the stack and cover it with state 9.
issue diagnostic: MISSING RIGHT PARENTHESIS

[†] Note that in practice grammar symbols are not placed on the stack. It is useful to imagine them there to remind us of the symbols which the states "represent."

On the erroneous input **id** +) discussed in Example 11.3, the sequence of configurations entered by the parser is shown in Fig. 11.5. □

stack	input	
0	**id**+)\$	
0**id**3	+)\$	
0E1	+)\$	
0E1+4	)\$	
0E1+4	\$	/* right parenthesis removed by routine e2. diagnostic UNBALANCED RIGHT PARENTHESIS issued. */
0E1+4**id**3	\$	/* **id** pushed onto stack by routine e1. diagnostic MISSING OPERAND issued. */
0E1+4E7	\$	
0E1	\$	/* parsing completed */

Fig. 11.5. Trace of LR(1) parse and error recovery.

Error Recovery in LL Parsing

Simple error-correction strategies for LL parsers substantially parallel the strategies for LR. First of all, there is a "panic mode" of correction for an LL parser. On finding an error we skip on the input to the next of a selected set of synchronizing tokens such as semicolon. Then we pop the stack until a symbol X that derives the synchronizing token (often X will be the synchronizing token itself) appears on top of the stack. If X is not the synchronizing token itself, then X will have to be expanded, and symbols popped in a predetermined way, until the synchronizing token appears on top of the stack.

Note that unlike for the LR parser, there is no harm in popping nonterminals off the stack in an LL parser, because these do not represent successfully parsed constructs, but rather constructs which we had hoped to find on the input.

An alternative approach is to fill in the LL parsing table's blank entries with pointers to error routines. These routines have most of the same options as in prior examples of error-recovery mechanisms. The input may have symbols changed, inserted, or deleted. We may also pop from the stack. It is questionable whether we should permit alteration of stack symbols or the pushing of new symbols onto the stack, since then the steps carried out by the parser might not correspond to the derivation of any word in the language at all. In any event we must be sure that there is no possibility of an infinite loop. Again, being sure that any recovery action eventually results in an input symbol being consumed or the stack being shortened if the end of the input has been reached, is a good way to protect against such loops. We shall give an example of an LL parser with error recovery routines; this parser accepts the same language as the parsers considered in the previous two examples.

Stack symbol	Input symbol					
	id	**+**	*****	**(**	**)**	**$**
E	$E \rightarrow TE'$	e1	e1	$E \rightarrow TE'$	e1	e1
E'	$E' \rightarrow \epsilon$	$E' \rightarrow +TE'$	$E' \rightarrow \epsilon$	$E' \rightarrow \epsilon$	$E' \rightarrow \epsilon$	$E' \rightarrow \epsilon$
T	$T \rightarrow FT'$	e1	e1	$T \rightarrow FT'$	e1	e1
T'	$T' \rightarrow \epsilon$	$T' \rightarrow \epsilon$	$T' \rightarrow *FT'$	$T' \rightarrow \epsilon$	$T' \rightarrow \epsilon$	$T' \rightarrow \epsilon$
F	$F \rightarrow \mathbf{id}$	e1	e1	$F \rightarrow (E)$	e1	e1
id	pop					
+		pop				
*			pop			
(				pop		
)	e2	e2	e2	e2	pop	e2
$	e3	e3	e3	e3	e3	accept

Fig. 11.6. LL parser with error entries.

Example 11.5. The LL parser of Fig. 5.24 is reproduced as Fig. 11.6 with error routines inserted. The table includes the pop actions which match an input symbol against an identical terminal on the stack. Note that some entries have still been left blank. These are entries which can obviously never be exercised, even on erroneous input. For example, + can only appear on the stack when we expand by $E \rightarrow +TE'$. But we only expand by $E \rightarrow +TE'$ when + is the next input symbol. Thus no match of + on the stack against the next input symbol is necessary.

We have also inserted expansions by $E' \rightarrow \epsilon$ and $T' \rightarrow \epsilon$ in certain places where an error could be detected. This change may postpone some error detection, but cannot cause an error to be missed. The actions taken by the error routines are as follows:

e1: /* This routine is called when an operand, beginning with either an **id** or a left parenthesis is expected, but an operator, left parenthesis or the end of input is found. */
push **id** onto the input
issue diagnostic: MISSING OPERAND

e2: /* Here we have a right parenthesis on top of the stack but not on the input. */
pop the right parenthesis from the stack
issue diagnostic: MISSING RIGHT PARENTHESIS

e3: /* The stack has been emptied, but input remains. */
   issue diagnostic: UNEXPECTED (current input symbol)
   remove all remaining symbols from the input

On the erroneous input **id** +) the parser and error recovery mechanism of Fig. 11.6 behaves as in Fig. 11.7. □

stack	input	
$E	**id**+)$	
$E'T	**id**+)$	
$E'T'F	**id**+)$	
$E'T'**id**	**id**+)$	
$E'T'	+)$	
$E'	+)$	
$E'T+	+)$	
$E'T	)$	
$E'T	**id**)$	/* **id** inserted onto input by routine e1. Issue diagnostic: MISSING OPERAND */
$E'T'F	**id**)$	
$E'T'**id**	**id**)$	
$E'T'	)$	
$E'	)$	
$	)$	
$	$	/* Right parenthesis removed from input by routine e3. Issue diagnostic: UNEXPECTED RIGHT PARENTHESIS */

Fig. 11.7. Trace of LL(1) parse and error recovery.

11.4 Semantic Errors

We have already mentioned the primary sources of semantic errors: undeclared names and type incompatibilities. The only point we wish to consider here is the recovery from such errors and the suppression of extraneous and duplicate error messages.

Recovery from an undeclared name is rather straightforward. The first time we encounter an undeclared name we make an entry for that name in the symbol table with appropriate attributes. The attributes can often be determined by the context in which the name is used. A flag in the symbol-table entry is set to indicate that the entry was made in response to a semantic error rather than a declaration.

One of the attributes of an undeclared or misdeclared name ought to be a list of ways (and possibly places) in which the name is erroneously used, e.g. as a real or as a procedure name. Each time the name is used incorrectly, a check of this list is made to determine whether a previous instance of this erroneous usage has been detected. If so, no new error message is printed. If not, an error message is printed and the new erroneous usage is added to the list.

Misspelled identifiers, particularly those for arrays, structures, and procedures, can give rise to extraneous error messages unless special precautions are taken. For example, suppose ARAY[I, J, K] is encountered and ARAY is not a valid array name. Several error messages can be generated. On encountering ARAY we print an error message to the effect that this identifier is undeclared. Then on processing the subscripts we discover that since ARAY has not been declared, the number of subscripts does not match the dimension of the array.

Again the easiest way to handle this situation is to create an entry for ARAY in the symbol table with appropriate attributes. One error message is generated on inserting ARAY into the symbol table. Subsequent references to ARAY cause no error messages to be printed.

Exercises

11.1 Trace out the behavior of the operator-precedence, LR, and LL error-correcting parsers described in Section 11.3 on inputs:

a) $(id + (* id)$
b) $* + id) + (id *$

11.2 The following grammar is operator-precedence and SLR(1).

$$S \rightarrow \text{if } e \text{ then } S \text{ else}$$
$$| \text{ while } e \text{ do } S$$
$$| \text{ begin } L \text{ end}$$
$$| s$$
$$L \rightarrow S ; L \mid S$$

Construct error-correcting parsers of the operator-precedence and LR type for this grammar.

11.3 The grammar in Exercise 11.2 can be made LL by left-factoring the productions for L as:

$$L \rightarrow SL'$$
$$L' \rightarrow ;S \mid \epsilon$$

Construct for the revised grammar an error-correcting LL parser.

11.4 Simulate your error correctors of Exercises 11.2 and 11.3 on input **if** *e* **begin** *s* ; *e* **end else end**.

11.5 Write operator-precedence, LL, and LR "panic mode" error correctors for the grammars of Exercises 11.2 and 11.3, based on using semicolon and **end** as synchronizing symbols. Simulate your error correctors on the input of Exercise 11.4.

*11.6 In Section 11.3 we proposed a graph-oriented method for determining the set of strings which could be popped from the stack in a reduce move of an operator-precedence grammar.

    a) Give an algorithm for finding a regular expression denoting all such strings.

    b) Give an algorithm to tell whether the set of such strings is finite or infinite, listing them if finite.

    c) Apply your algorithms from (a) and (b) to the grammar of Exercise 11.2.

**11.7 We made the claim for each of the error-correcting parsers designed in Section 11.3 that any error correction eventually resulted in at least one more symbol being removed from the input or the stack being shortened if the end of the input has been reached. The corrections chosen, however, did not all cause an input symbol to be consumed immediately, but possibly only after a number of stack moves. Can you prove that no infinite loops are possible for the parsers of Figs. 11.3, 11.4 and 11.6? *Hint:* It helps to observe that for the operator-precedence parser, consecutive terminals on this stack are related by $\lessdot$, even if there have been errors. For the LR parser, the stack will still contain a viable prefix, even in the presence of errors.

**11.8 We mentioned, in connection with Fig. 11.6, that certain blank entries need not be filled in, since they could never be exercised. Are there other error entries in that parser or the parsers of Figs. 11.3 and 11.4 which can never be exercised? Give a general algorithm for detecting unreachable error entries in operator-precedence, LR, and LL parsing tables.

11.9 The LR parser of Fig. 11.4 handles the four situations in which the top state is 4 or 5 (which occur when + and * are on top of the stack, respectively) and the next input is + or * in exactly the same way: by calling e1, which inserts an **id** between them. We could easily envision an LR parser for expressions involving the full set of arithmetic operators behaving in the same fashion: insert **id** between the adjacent operators. In certain languages (such as PL/I but not FORTRAN or ALGOL) it would be wise to treat, in a special way, the case in which / is on top of the stack and * is the next input. Why? What would be a reasonable course of action for the error corrector to take?

*11.10 Error detection in simple-precedence parsers (introduced in Exercise 5.7) is similar, but not identical, to error detection in operator-precedence parsers.

a) At what stages can a simple-precedence parser (see Exercise 5.8) detect errors?

b) For the simple-precedence matrix of Fig. 5.27 suggest error routines that recover from errors in a safe manner (no infinite loops).

*11.11 Construct an algorithm that takes as input two strings and produces as output the fewest number of insertions and deletions required to map one string into the other.

Bibliographic Notes

Irons [1963] was among the first to consider a grammar-based approach to syntactic error recovery. Since that time a number of papers have been written giving various techniques for syntactic error-recovery techniques: Barnard [1976], Graham and Rhodes [1975], James [1972], James and Partridge [1973], LaFrance [1970], Leinius [1970], Levy [1971], and Fischer, Milton, and Quiring [1977]. "Error productions" were employed by Wirth [1968] for handling errors in PL360. Horning [1974] discusses in more detail how a compiler should report errors to the user.

The design of error-repairing compilers is discussed by Conway and Maxwell [1963], Moulton and Muller [1967], and Conway and Wilcox [1973]. The treatment of spelling errors is considered in Freeman [1964] and Morgan [1970]. Algorithms for general minimum-distance error correction are given in Aho and Peterson [1972], Lyon [1974], and Wagner [1974]. Fredman [1975], Hunt and Szymanski [1977], and Wagner and Fischer [1974] give algorithms for computing the Hamming distance between two strings.

An answer to parts of Exercise 11.8 may be found in El Djabri [1973a], and Aho and Ullman [1972c, 1973b]. Hunt and McIlroy [1976] describe an efficient solution to Exercise 11.11.

Wagner [1973] and Heaps and Radhakrishnan [1977] discuss compaction techniques for the storage of diagnostic messages within compilers.

CHAPTER 12

Introduction
to
Code Optimization

The source program, the input to a compiler, is a specification of some computation. The object program, the output of the compiler, is supposed to be another specification of the same computation. For each source program there are infinitely many object programs that implement the same computation, in the sense that they produce the same output when presented with the same input. Some of these object programs may be better than others with regard to such criteria as size or speed. The term "code optimization" refers to techniques a compiler can employ in an attempt to produce a better object language program than the most obvious for a given source program.

The quality of an object program is generally measured by its size or its running time. For large computations, running time is particularly important. For small computers, size may be as important as time, or even more so. Likewise, in a paged environment space savings often imply time savings as well. In this book we shall usually use running time as the cost function, although the techniques we propose often save space as well.

It should be clearly stated at the outset that the term "optimization" is a misnomer. It is theoretically impossible for a compiler to produce the best possible object program for every source program under any reasonable cost function. Therefore, a more accurate term for code optimization would be "code improvement." Tradition, however, has given us the term "code optimization."

There are many aspects to code optimization. The primary questions are how beneficial a given optimization is and how much it costs to implement. In some situations it is unnecessary to consider any optimization; a quick and straightforward translation of the source program is sufficient. Typical of this situation is a "student job" which will be run a few times and then discarded. Exactly the opposite is true of a program which is to be run an indefinitely large number of times. Virtually any amount of time spent improving the running time of the program will be paid back by even a small percentage speedup each time the program is run.

In most cases, however, a program will not run indefinitely without being changed and recompiled. It is economic therefore to have available an "optimizing" compiler which makes only well-judged attempts to improve the code it produces. It is important that the optimizing compiler attempt transformations that are likely to improve the code without costing too much time at compilation. The equation to bear in mind is that the running time we expect to save over the expected number of runs of the optimized object program must exceed the time spent by the compiler doing the optimization. The trend is to make available for each programming language several compilers, or options within one compiler, that spend varying amounts of time improving the code they generate and produce code of increasing quality. In this way the user can decide how much time he wishes to spend optimizing his program.

In this and the next two chapters we discuss some of the important optimization techniques that are useful in designing optimizing compilers for languages such as FORTRAN and PL/I. Techniques of this nature can speed up the object program by a factor of two or three over the speed of an object program produced by a straightforward compiler. This factor, while not spectacular, is important for many frequently executed programs, such as systems programs. It can make the difference between having to write a time-critical program in assembly code or being able to use a high-level language. While we shall not discuss it here, similar techniques have been applied to "very high-level languages" such as "AI-languages" like SAIL and set-theoretic languages like SETL. These languages emphasize ease of use rather than efficient implementation. Optimization techniques applied to these languages can yield order-of-magnitude improvements in the running time and appear to be essential if large programs are to be routinely written in these languages. The bibliographic notes discuss some of the work being done in this area.

Three criteria that we have applied to the selection of optimizing transformations discussed in this chapter are:

1. Does the optimization capture most of the potential improvement without an unreasonable amount of effort, either by the compiler implementer or by the compiler itself?

2. Does the optimization preserve the meaning of the source program? No optimization should map a correct program into an incorrect one.

3. Does the optimization, at least on the average, reduce the time or space taken by the object program?

12.1 The Principal Sources of Optimization

Code-optimization techniques are generally applied after syntax analysis, usually both before and during code generation. The techniques consist of detecting patterns in the program and replacing these patterns by equivalent but more efficient constructs. These patterns may be local or global, and the replacement strategy may be machine-dependent or machine-independent.

Intertwined with code optimization is code generation. It does not make sense to do a good job of code optimization without also doing a good job of code generation. The richest source of optimization is in the efficient utilization of the registers and instruction set of a machine. This aspect of optimization is closely connected with code generation, and many issues in this area are highly machine dependent. We shall discuss this kind of optimization when we discuss code generation in Chapter 15.

Inner Loops

After register allocation, the next important class of optimization techniques concerns the handling of inner loops. It is a generally accepted phenomenon that most of the execution time is spent in relatively little of the program. The so called "90-10 rule" states that 90% of the time is spent in 10% of the code. Thus, the most heavily-traveled parts of a program, the inner loops, are an obvious target for optimization. Typical loop optimizations are the removal of loop-invariant computations and the elimination of induction variables. We shall give examples of these optimizations shortly.

Language Implementation Details Inaccessible to the User

Some programming languages allow a programmer to write source programs that get compiled into reasonably efficient object programs; in these languages the optimizations can be done by the programmer at the source level. Other languages may not permit certain kinds of optimizations to be specified at the source level. Array references are a case in point. In FOR-TRAN and similar languages, the fact that array references are made by indexing, rather than by pointer or address calculation prevents the programmer from dealing with offset calculations in arrays. This almost forces the code generated by a compiler to be suboptimal if no optimization is used. Moreover, it is hard to design a programming language that is easy to use, yet requires the user to specify array references in such a manner that no optimization is necessary for intelligently-written programs.

A similar phenomenon occurs with procedure calls. The user of a language has little control over procedure linkage or the storage of registers before a call. Optimization is needed to make procedure calls reasonably efficient, although optimizing compilers in the past have tended to ignore this potential optimization.

Further Optimizations

Additional important sources of optimization are the identification of common subexpressions and replacement of run-time computations by compile-time computations, that is, the substitution of values for names whose values are constant. The term *constant folding* is used for the latter optimization. Common subexpressions are not always due to programmer sloppiness. A single assignment like

$$A[I+1] := B[I+1] \qquad (12.1)$$

is easier to understand than a pair of statements like

$$J := I + 1$$
$$A[J] := B[J] \qquad (12.2)$$

so a programmer might prefer (12.1) to (12.2). It is the compiler's job to make the object code look as if it came from (12.2), by identifying the common subexpression $I+1$. In fact, if the object code is for a byte-addressable machine, there will be an offset such as $4*(I+1)$ computed twice in the three-address code resulting from (12.1) by the code generation algorithm discussed in Section 8.1. Worse, even for a word-addressable machine, a statement like $A[I, J] := A[I, J] + 1$ results in two computations of the l-value of $A[I, J]$ using standard code-generation algorithms.

Organization of the Chapters on Code Optimization

We shall divide the subject of code optimization into three interrelated areas. One is *local* optimizations, those performed within a *straight-line* (or *basic*) *block* of code (a block with no jumps in except at the beginning and no jumps out except at the end). The second is loop optimization, and the third is *data flow analysis* — the transmission of useful relationships from all parts of the program to the places where the information can be of use. The processing of straight-line blocks is vital to both loop optimization and data-flow analysis. We require data-flow analysis for efficient loop optimization as well as for some of the code-generation algorithms discussed in Chapter 15. Loop and local optimization in turn provide motivation for the data-flow analysis we discuss.

This chapter samples each of these three areas. We cover straight-line blocks in detail and give examples of loop optimizations and data-flow analyses. Chapter 13 covers loop optimization in more detail and Chapter 14 discusses algorithms for data-flow analysis. Another form of local optimization, called "peephole" optimization, which views only small, but possibly widely-separated, pieces of object code, is discussed in Section 15.7.

Algorithm Optimization

Before we leave this section we should point out that the most important source of improvement in the running time of a program often lies beyond the reach of the compiler. We are referring to algorithm improvement. Suppose we have a simple sorting program, say bubblesort, for which a non-optimizing compiler produces an object program B with a running time of $100n^2$ microseconds, where n is the number of items to be sorted. Suppose for this same sorting program an optimizing compiler produces an object program B_o whose running time is $50n^2$ microseconds.

On the other hand consider what happens if we implement an order $n \log n$ running-time algorithm, such as quicksort, for the same problem. Suppose the non-optimizing compiler produces, from a source program implementing quicksort, an object program Q that has a running time of $500n \log_2 n$ microseconds. The following table shows the running times for these three object programs for two values of n.

	n	
	100	1000
Original B	1 sec	100 sec
Optimized B_o	.5 sec	50 sec
Q	.1 sec	1.5 sec

While B_o and Q are equal in running time at $n = 14$ (.01 sec.), the unoptimized Q is 5 times faster than the optimized bubblesort for $n=100$ and 33 times faster for $n=1000$. As n increases the results become even more spectacular. This simple example vividly illustrates the importance of implementing the proper algorithm at the source program level. No amount of code optimization can rescue a bad algorithm. However, true algorithm substitution is not seriously suggested as a "code-optimization technique," at least for FORTRAN, ALGOL or similar languages. The bibliographic notes contain references to attempts at what amounts to algorithm optimization that have been made for "very high-level languages."

12.2 Loop Optimization

This section presents an extended example of the kinds of optimizations that can be performed in a loop. Techniques for detecting loops and implementing these optimizations will be discussed in Chapter 12.

Consider the following fragment of code; it computes the dot product of two vectors A and B of length 20.

```
    begin
        PROD := 0;
        I := 1;
        do
            begin
                PROD := PROD + A[I] * B[I];
                I := I + 1                           (12.3)
            end
        while I ⩽ 20
    end
```

A list of three-address statements performing the computation of (12.3) for a machine with four bytes/word is shown in Fig. 12.1.† It is desirable, although not essential, to perform loop optimizations on the intermediate text rather than on the source program. The code of Fig. 12.1 has actually had some optimization applied to it. For example, we use $I := I + 1$ instead of $T := I + 1; I := T$, and the fact that $4 * I$ is a common subexpression has been detected.

(1)	PROD := 0	
(2)	I := 1	
(3)	$T_1 := 4 * I$	
(4)	$T_2 := \mathbf{addr}(A) - 4$	
(5)	$T_3 := T_2[T_1]$	/* compute A[I] */
(6)	$T_4 := \mathbf{addr}(B) - 4$	
(7)	$T_5 := T_4[T_1]$	/* compute B[I] */
(8)	$T_6 := T_3 * T_5$	
(9)	PROD := PROD + T_6	
(10)	I := I + 1	
(11)	**if** I ⩽ 20 **goto** (3)	

Fig. 12.1. Three-address code computing dot product.

---

†Here and throughout the chapters on code optimization we use three-address statements which we assume are being implemented as quadruples, with a new temporary created for each intermediate value. The same techniques for optimization can be used, with minor modification, on other representations, such as triples, indirect triples, or quadruples with reused temporary names.

Basic Blocks

Our first step is to break the code of Fig. 12.1 into *basic blocks,* that is sequences of consecutive statements which may be entered only at the beginning, and when entered are executed in sequence without halt or possibility of branch (except at the end of the basic block). A useful algorithm for partitioning a sequence of three-address statements into basic blocks is the following.

Algorithm 12.1. Partition into basic blocks.

Input. A sequence of three-address statements.

Output. A list of basic blocks with each three-address statement in exactly one block.

Method.

1. We first determine the set of *leaders,* the first statements of basic blocks. The rules we use are the following.

    i)   The first statement is a leader.
    ii) Any statement which is the target of a conditional or unconditional goto is a leader.
    iii) Any statement which immediately follows a conditional goto is a leader.

2. For each leader construct its basic block, which consists of the leader and all statements up to but not including the next leader or the end of the program. Any statements not placed in a block can never be executed and may now be removed, if desired.

Example 12.1. In Fig. 12.1, statement (1) is a leader by rule (i) and statement (3) is a leader by rule (ii). By rule (iii) the statement following (11) (recall that Fig. 12.1 is just a fragment of a program) is a leader. The basic block beginning at statement (1) runs to statement (2), since (3) is a leader. The basic block with leader (3) runs to (11), that is, it is the balance of the fragment.   □

Flow Graphs

It is useful to portray the basic blocks and their successor relationships by a directed graph called a *flow graph.* The nodes of the flow graph are the basic blocks. One node is distinguished as *initial;* it is the block whose leader is the first statement. There is a directed edge from block B_1 to block B_2 if B_2 could immediately follow B_1 during execution, that is, if

1. there is a conditional or unconditional jump from the last statement of B_1 to the first statement of B_2, or
2. B_2 immediately follows B_1 in the order of the program, and B_1 ends in a conditional jump.

We say that B_1 is a *predecessor* of B_2, and B_2 is a *successor* of B_1.

Example 12.2. The flow graph of the program of Fig. 12.1 is shown in Fig. 12.2. B_1 is the initial node. □

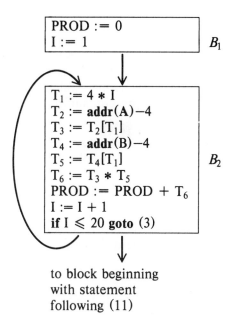

Fig. 12.2. Flow graph.

Basic blocks can be represented by a variety of data structures. For example, after partitioning the three-address statements by Algorithm 12.1, each basic block could be represented by a record consisting of a count of the number of quadruples in the block, followed by a pointer to the leader (first quadruple) of the block, and by the lists of predecessors and successors of the block. As we perform code optimization, however, we may move quadruples from block to block or create new blocks, so an extension of the quadruple array is necessary if the quadruples in each block are to be kept in consecutive storage. An alternative is to make a linked list of the quadruples in each block.

The quadruple numbers in conditional and unconditional jump statements may cause some problem. For example, if block B_2 in Fig. 12.2 were moved elsewhere in the quadruple array or were shrunk, the (3) in **if** $I \leqslant 20$ **goto** (3) would have to be changed. A good idea is to make a jump to quadruple i at the end of a block point to the record for the block whose leader is quadruple i. It is important to remember that an edge of the flow graph from block B to block B' does not tell whether the conditional jump at the end of B (if there is a conditional jump there) goes to the leader of B' if the condition is satisfied or if the condition is not satisfied. Making goto's point to blocks rather than quadruples enables us to recover that information when we need it.

Loops

In Fig. 12.2 there is one loop, and it is easily seen to consist of block B_2 only. In general, the questions of what constitutes a loop, and how one can find them in a flow graph are a bit subtle, and we shall examine them further in the next chapter. For the present, suffice it to say that a loop is a collection of nodes that

1. is *strongly connected,* that is, from any node in the loop to any other, there is a path of length one or more, wholly within the loop, and
2. has a unique *entry,* a node in the loop such that the only way to reach a node of the loop from a node outside the loop is to first go through the entry.

In the example of Fig. 12.2, B_2 is clearly a loop by itself, since condition (2) is trivially satisfied for any one-node loop.

Code Motion

The running time of a program may be improved if we decrease the length of one of its loops, especially an inner loop, even if we increase the amount of code outside the loops. This statement assumes that the loop in question is executed at least once on the average. We must beware of a loop whose body is rarely executed, such as a "blank stripper"

while CHAR $= '\ '$ **do** CHAR $:=$ GETCHAR( )

Here, GETCHAR( ) is assumed to return the next character on an input file. In many situations it might be quite normal that the condition CHAR $= '\ '$ is false the first time around, in which case the statement CHAR $:=$ GETCHAR( ) would be executed zero times.

An important source of modifications of the above type is called *code motion,* where we take a computation that yields the same result independent of the number of times through the loop (a *loop invariant computation*) and place it before the loop. (Note that the notion "before the loop" assumes the existence of an entry for the loop.)

Example 12.3. In Fig. 12.2, the assignments $T_2 :=$ **addr**$(A)-4$ and $T_4 :=$ **addr**$(B)-4$ are presumably loop-invariant computations. If A and B are statically allocated arrays, then their location will not change throughout the execution of the loop, so T_2 and T_4 have the same value each time through. Of course, in this case, T_2 and T_4 can be computed at compile time, so the cost of the computation at run time is zero anyway. However, if A and B were allocated on a stack, **addr**(A) and **addr**(B) and hence T_2 and T_4, might require computation at run time, although the locations of A and B would not change during the execution of the loop, and T_2 and T_4 would still be loop-invariant computations. It should be remarked that if A and B were allocated in a heap subject to garbage collection, then **addr**(A) and **addr**(B) might change during execution of the loop, and T_2 and T_4 would not then be loop-invariant.

Assuming **addr**(A) and **addr**(B) to be loop-invariant, we may remove the computations of T_2 and T_4 from the loop by creating a new block B_3, which consists of the assignments to T_2 and T_4. There is an edge from B_3 to B_2, the entry block of the loop.

All edges from outside the loop that formerly went to the entry of the loop now go to B_3. Here, the edge $B_1 \rightarrow B_2$ becomes $B_1 \rightarrow B_3$ by the above rule. The new flow graph is shown in Fig. 12.3. We have replaced **goto** (3) by **goto** B_2, since quadruple (3) is the leader of B_2. Also note that in this special case, B_1 and B_3 could be combined, since B_1 is B_3's only predecessor and B_3 is B_1's only successor.

Note that the loop, which is executed 20 times, has been reduced from 9 statements to 7, although the total number of statements in the program has not decreased. If the assignments to T_2 and T_4 must be executed at run time we have cut the total number of statements executed from 182 to 144. □

Induction Variables

There is another important optimization which may be applied to the flow graph of Fig. 12.3, one that will actually decrease the total number of instructions as well as speeding up the loop. We note that the purpose of I is to count from 1 to 20 in the loop, while the purpose of T_1 is to step through the arrays, four bytes at a time, since we are assuming four bytes/word. The values of I and T_1 remain in lock-step. That is, at the assignment $T_1 := 4 * I$, I takes on the values 1, 2, . . . , 20 each time through the beginning of loop. Thus, T_1 takes the values 4, 8, . . . , 80 immediately after each assignment to T_1. That is, both I and T_1 form arithmetic progressions. We call such identifiers induction variables.[†] As the

---

† In Section 13.5 we shall take a somewhat more general view of induction variables, although those whose values form an arithmetic progression are most common in practice.

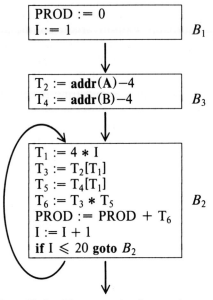

Fig. 12.3. Flow graph after code motion.

relationship $T_1 = 4 * I$ surely holds after the assignment to T_1, and T_1 is not changed elsewhere in the loop, it follows that after statement $I := I + 1$ the relationship $T_1 = 4 * I - 4$ must hold. Thus, at the statement **if** $I \leqslant 20$ **goto** B_2, we have $I \leqslant 20$ if and only if $T_1 \leqslant 76$. When there are two or more induction variables in a loop we have an opportunity to get rid of all but one, and we call this process *induction variable elimination*.

Example 12.4. We may suppose that the value of I is not needed after the loop terminates (although we could not be sure without checking the entire program; we shall see how to make this check in Section 12.5). If so, then we may eliminate I from blocks B_1, B_2, and B_3 entirely by replacing it by T_1. That is, the test **if** $I \leqslant 20$ **goto** B_2 is replaced by **if** $T_1 \leqslant 76$ **goto** B_2. Since we know T_1's values form an arithmetic progression with difference 4 at the assignment $T_1 := 4 * I$, we may replace this statement by $T_1 := T_1 + 4$. The only problem is that T_1 has no value when we enter B_2 from B_3. We therefore place an assignment to T_1 in a new block between B_3 and the loop entry B_2 (we could also place this assignment in B_3 in this flow graph). The assignment must be such that T_1 has the proper value, 4, the first time $T_1 := T_1 + 4$ is executed. It is not hard to deduce that this new block B_4 must contain the assignment $T_1 := 0$. Now all mention of I may be eliminated. The resulting flow graph is shown in Fig. 12.4.   □

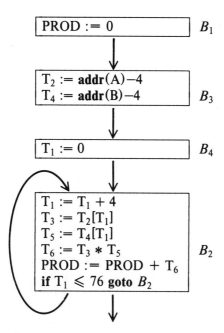

Fig. 12.4. Flow graph after eliminating induction variable I.

We see in Fig. 12.4 that there are now only six statements in the loop, so the number of instructions executed has been reduced from the 144 of Fig. 12.3 to 124. It is important to realize that the reason we are able to improve the code to this extent lies not in the notion that the original source code of (12.3) is faulty; in fact, it is fine. The programmer could not get at the details of array handling, but the optimizing compiler could. It is primarily the ability of the optimizing compiler to properly handle array references in loops that accounts for its ability to improve code beyond the obvious intermediate code generated from perfectly good source code written in a higher-level language.

Reduction in Strength

It is also worth noting that the multiplication step $T_1 := 4 * I$ in Fig. 12.3 was replaced by an addition step $T_1 := T_1 + 4$. This replacement will speed up the object code if addition takes less time than multiplication, as is the case in many machines. The replacement of an expensive operation by a cheaper one is termed *reduction in strength*.

A dramatic example of reduction in strength is the replacement of the string-concatenation operator ‖ in the PL/I statement

$$L = LENGTH \ (S1 \ ‖ \ S2)$$

by an addition

$$L = \text{LENGTH (S1)} + \text{LENGTH (S2)}$$

The extra length determination and addition are far cheaper than the string concatenation. Another example of reduction in strength is the replacement by a shift of the multiplication of an integer by a power of two. This optimization could be applied to the multiplication step $T_1 := 4 * I$ in Fig. 12.3.

12.3 The DAG Representation of Basic Blocks

There are some very local transformations that we have not explained how to make. For example, in the code of Fig. 12.1, we used T_1 to index both A and B, while the compiler using the algorithm for translating array references given in Section 8.1 would create two different temporaries. Again, in Fig. 12.3 we made the claim that the value of I computed by the statement $I := I + 1$ would be used only in the statements $T_1 := 4 * I$ and **if** $I \leqslant 20$ **goto** B_2. Part of this assertion was the claim that "we may suppose" I was not used after control left the loop of B_2. In reality the compiler would have to check that I was not used there, using data-flow analysis techniques to be discussed in Section 12.5. However, even examining block B_2 to determine which statements use the value of I defined at $I := I + 1$ is nontrivial for the compiler, although the determination is easy if we visually inspect the code.

A useful data structure for automatically analyzing basic blocks is a directed acyclic graph (hereafter called a *DAG*). A DAG is a directed graph with no cycles which gives a picture of how the value computed by each statement in a basic block is used in subsequent statements in the block. Constructing a DAG from three-address statements is a good way of determining common subexpressions within a block, determining which names are used inside the block but evaluated outside the block, and determining which statements of the block could have their value used outside the block.

A *computation DAG* (or just *DAG*) is a directed acyclic graph with the following labels on nodes:

1. Leaves are labeled by unique identifiers, either variable names or constants. It is convenient to use leaf labels like **addr**(A) to denote the *l*-value of A, while other identifiers are assumed to denote *r*-values. The leaves represent initial values of names, and we shall subscript them with 0 to avoid confusion with labels denoting "current" values of names as in (3) below.
2. Interior nodes are labeled by an operator symbol.

3. Nodes are also optionally given an extra set of identifiers for labels. The intention is that interior nodes represent computed values, and identifiers labeling a node are deemed to have that value.

It is important not to confuse DAG's with flow graphs. Each node of a flow graph can be represented by a DAG, since each node of the flow graph stands for a basic block. Also note that the DAG representation of a basic block is nothing more nor less than an optimized version of the "triples" form of intermediate code discussed in Section 7.6.

$$
\begin{array}{ll}
(1) & S_1 := 4 * I \\
(2) & S_2 := \textbf{addr}(A) - 4 \\
(3) & S_3 := S_2[S_1] \\
(4) & S_4 := 4 * I \\
(5) & S_5 := \textbf{addr}(B) - 4 \\
(6) & S_6 := S_5[S_4] \\
(7) & S_7 := S_3 * S_6 \\
(8) & S_8 := PROD + S_7 \\
(9) & PROD := S_8 \\
(10) & S_9 := I + 1 \\
(11) & I := S_9 \\
(12) & \textbf{if } I \leqslant 20 \textbf{ goto } (1)
\end{array}
$$

Fig. 12.5. Three-address code for block B_2.

Example 12.5. Figure 12.5 shows the three-address code corresponding to block B_2 of Fig. 12.2 which would be generated directly from the program fragment of (12.3) by a typical compiler. Numbers starting from (1) have been used for convenience. The corresponding DAG is shown in Fig. 12.6. We shall discuss the significance of the DAG after giving an algorithm to construct it. For the time being let us observe that each node of the DAG represents a formula in terms of the leaves, that is, the values possessed by variables and constants upon entering the block. For example, the node labeled S_6 in Fig. 12.6 represents the formula

$$(\textbf{addr}(B) - 4)[4 * I]$$

that is, the value of the word whose address is $4 * I$ bytes offset from address $\textbf{addr}(B) - 4$, which is the intended value of S_6.   □

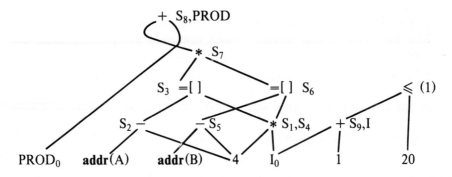

Fig. 12.6. DAG for block of Fig. 12.5.

DAG Construction

To construct a DAG we look at each statement of the block in turn. If we see a statement like A := B + C we look for the nodes which represent the "current" values of B and C. These could be leaves, or they could be interior nodes of the DAG if B and/or C had been evaluated by previous statements of the block. We then create a node labeled + and give it two children; the left child is the node for B, the right the node for C. Then we label this node A. However, if there is already a node denoting the same value as B + C, we do not create a node, but rather give this existing node the additional label A.

Two details should be mentioned. First, if A (not A_0) had previously labeled some other node, we remove that label, since the "current" value of A is the node just created. Second, for an assignment such as A := B we do not create a new node. Rather, we append label A to the node for the "current" value of B.

We shall now give the algorithm to compute a DAG from a block. The reader should be warned that this algorithm may not operate correctly if there are assignments to arrays, if there are indirect assignments through pointers in the block, or if one memory location can be referred to by two or more names, due to EQUIVALENCE statements or the correspondences between actual and formal parameters of a procedure call. We shall discuss the modifications necessary to handle these situations at the end of this section.

Algorithm 12.2. Constructing a DAG.

Input. A basic block.

Output. A DAG with the following information.

1. A *label* for each node. For leaves the label is an identifier (constants permitted), and for interior nodes, an operator symbol.
2. For each node a (possibly empty) list of *attached identifiers* (constants not permitted here).

Method. We assume the appropriate data structures are available to create nodes with one or two children, with "left" and "right" children in the latter case. Also available in the structure is a place for a label for each node and the facility to create a linked list of attached identifiers for each node.

In addition to these components we need to maintain the set of all identifiers (including constants) for which there is a node associated. The node could be either a leaf labeled by that identifier or an interior node with that identifier on its attached identifier list. We assume the existence of a function NODE(IDENTIFIER) which, as we build the DAG, returns the most recently created node associated with IDENTIFIER. Intuitively, NODE(IDENTIFIER) is the node of the DAG which represents the value which IDENTIFIER has at the current point in the DAG construction process. In practice, an entry in the symbol-table record for IDENTIFIER would indicate the value of NODE(IDENTIFIER).

The DAG construction process is to do the following steps (1) through (3) for each statement of the block, in turn. Initially we assume there are no nodes, and NODE( ) is undefined for all arguments. Suppose the "current" three address statement is either (i) A := B **op** C, (ii) A := **op** B, or (iii) A := B.[†] We refer to these as cases (i), (ii), and (iii). We treat a relational operator like **if** I $\leqslant$ 20 **goto** as case (i), with A undefined.

1. If NODE(B) is undefined, create a leaf labeled B, and let NODE(B) be this node. In case (i), if NODE(C) is undefined, create a leaf labeled C and let that leaf be NODE(C).

2. In case (i), determine if there is a node labeled **op**, whose left child is NODE(B) and whose right child is NODE(C). (This is to catch common subexpressions.) If not, create such a node. In either event, let *n* be the node found or created. In case (ii), determine whether there is a node labeled **op**, whose lone child is NODE(B). If not, create such a node, and let *n* be the node found or created. In case (iii), let *n* be NODE(B).

3. Append A to the list of attached identifiers for the node *n* found in (2). Delete A from the list of attached identifiers for NODE(A). Finally, set NODE(A) to *n*.   □

[†] Operators are assumed to have at most two arguments. The generalization to three or more arguments is straightforward.

Example 12.6. Let us return to the block of Fig. 12.5 and see how the DAG of Fig. 12.6 is constructed for it. The first statement is $S_1 := 4 * I$. In step (1) we must create leaves n_1 and n_2 labeled 4 and I_0. (We use the subscript 0, as before, to help distinguish labels from attached identifiers in pictures, but the subscript is not really part of the label.) In step (2) we create a node n_3 labeled $*$, and in step (3) we attach identifier S_1 to it. Figure 12.7(a) shows the DAG at this stage; $NODE(4) = n_1$, $NODE(I) = n_2$, and $NODE(S_1) = n_3$.

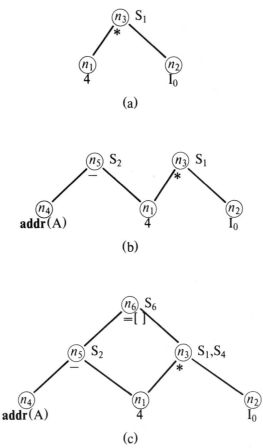

Fig. 12.7. Steps in the DAG construction process.

Next we proceed to statement $S_2 := \mathbf{addr}(A) - 4$. We must create a node n_4 for $\mathbf{addr}(A)$, but $NODE(4) = n_1$, so we do not create another node here. In step (2) we create n_5 with a minus sign for a label, and we attach S_2 to it in step (3), setting $NODE(S_2)$ to n_5. The current DAG is shown in Fig. 12.7(b). At the third statement we find $NODE(S_2) = n_5$ and $NODE(S_1) = n_3$, so we create a node n_6 labeled with the $=[\ ]$ operator symbol. The children of n_6 are n_5 and n_3, and we set $NODE(S_3) = n_6$.

Then we come to statement (4) $S_4 := 4 * I$. We find $NODE(4) = n_1$, and $NODE(I) = n_2$. The operator is $*$, and we find there is a node, namely n_3, which has operator $*$ and children n_1 and n_2 in that order. Thus we do not create a new node for statement (4), but rather append S_4 to the list of attached identifiers for n_3 and set $NODE(S_4) = n_3$. The resulting DAG is shown in Fig. 12.7(c). In the next section we shall discuss an easy way of determining the fact that node n_3, for $4 * I$, already exists.

We invite the reader to complete the construction of the DAG. We shall mention only the steps taken for statement (11) $I := S_9$. This being an instance of case (iii), we find $NODE(S_9)$, which turns out to be n_{14}. We append I to the list of identifiers for n_{14}, which then becomes S_9, I. We set $NODE(I) = n_{14}$. Along with statement (9) this is one of only two statements where the value of $NODE(\ )$ changes for an identifier. That is, previously, $NODE(I)$ was n_2. It is this change which ensures that n_{14}, not n_2, is the left child of the $\leqslant$ operator node constructed for step (12). □

Applications of DAG's

There are several pieces of useful information which we can obtain as we are performing Algorithm 12.2. First, we note that we automatically detect common subexpressions. Second, we can determine which identifiers have their values used in the block; they are exactly those for which a leaf is created in step (1) at some time. Third, we can determine which statements compute values which could be used outside the block. They are exactly those statements S whose node n constructed or found in step (2) still has $NODE(A) = n$ at the end of the DAG construction, where A is the identifier assigned by statement S. (Equivalently, A is still an attached identifier for n.)

Example 12.7. In Example 12.6, all statements meet the above constraint because the only times $NODE(\ )$ is redefined − for PROD and I − the previous value of $NODE(\ )$ was a leaf. Thus all interior nodes can have their value used outside the block. Now, suppose there were some statement $s < 11$ which assigned a value to I. Then at statement s we would create some node m and set $NODE(I) = m$. However, at step (11) we would redefine $NODE(I) = n_{14}$. Thus the value computed at statement S could not be used outside the block. □

Another important use to which the DAG may be put is to reconstruct a simplified list of quadruples taking advantage of common subexpressions and not performing assignments of the form $A := B$ unless absolutely necessary. That is, whenever a node has more than one identifier on its attached list, we check which, if any, of those identifiers are needed outside the block. This requires a data-flow analysis called "live variable analysis" discussed in Section 14.4. However, in many cases we may assume no temporary name such as $S_1, S_2, \ldots, S_9$ in Fig. 12.5 is needed outside the block. (But beware of how logical expressions are translated; one expression may wind up spread over several basic blocks.)

We may in general evaluate the interior nodes of the DAG in any order that is a *topological sort* of the DAG. This means that a node cannot be evaluated until all of its children that are interior nodes have been evaluated. As we evaluate a node, we assign its value to one of its attached identifiers A, preferring one whose value is needed outside the block. We may not, however, choose A if there is another node m whose value was also held by A such that m has been evaluated and is still "live." Here, we define m to be live if its value is needed outside the block or if m has a parent which has not yet been evaluated.

If there are additional attached identifiers $B_1, B_2, \ldots, B_k$ for a node n whose values are also needed outside the block, we assign to them with statements $B_1 := A$, $B_2 := A, \ldots, B_k := A$. If n has no attached identifiers at all (this could happen if, say, n was created by an assignment to A, but A was subsequently reassigned), we create a new temporary name to hold the value of n. The reader should beware that in the presence of pointer or array assignments, not every topological sort of a DAG is permissible; we shall attend to this matter shortly.

Example 12.8. Let us reconstruct a basic block from the DAG of Fig. 12.6, ordering nodes in the same order as their creation. We assume none of the temporaries, S_i, are needed outside the block. We begin with the node representing $4 * I$. This node has two identifiers attached, S_1 and S_4. Let us pick S_1 to hold the value $4 * I$, so the first statement is

$$S_1 := 4 * I$$

just as before. Similarly, the second statement evaluates the node labeled S_2 and is

$$S_2 := \mathbf{addr}(A) - 4$$

The third statement evaluates the node labeled S_3 and is

$$S_3 := S_2 [S_1]$$

The next nodes created were the ones labeled S_5 and S_6. Note that the original statement numbered (4) did not create a node. Thus we next generate statements

$$S_5 := \mathbf{addr}(B) - 4$$
$$S_6 := S_5[S_1]$$

The latter statement uses S_1 as an argument rather than S_4 as the original did, because S_1 is the name chosen to carry the value $4 * I$.

Next we evaluate the node labeled S_7, with

$$S_7 := S_3 * S_6$$

and then the node labeled S_8, PROD. We select PROD to carry the value, since that identifier and not S_8 will (presumably) be needed outside the block. S_8, like S_4, disappears. The next statement is thus

$$PROD := PROD + S_7$$

Similarly we choose I rather than S_9 to carry the value $I + 1$ and generate the last two statements

$$I := I + 1;$$
$$\textbf{if } I \leqslant 20 \textbf{ goto } (1)$$

Notice that the code generated corresponds exactly to statements (3) through (11) of Fig. 12.1 if we replace S_1, S_2, S_3, S_5, S_6, S_7, and **goto** (1) by $T_1, \ldots, T_6$, and **goto** (3), respectively. $\square$

Arrays, Pointers, and Procedure Calls

Consider a basic block

$$X := A[I]$$
$$A[J] := Y$$
$$Z := A[I] \qquad\qquad (12.4)$$

If we used Algorithm 12.2 to construct the DAG for (12.4), we would find A[I] to be a common subexpression, and the "optimized" block would turn out to be

$$X := A[I]$$
$$Z := X \qquad\qquad (12.5)$$
$$A[J] := Y$$

However, (12.4) and (12.5) compute different values for Z in the case $I = J$ and $Y \neq A[I]$. The problem is that when we assign to an array A, we may be changing the r-value of expression A[I], even though **addr**(A) and I do not change. It is therefore necessary that when processing an assignment to array A, we *kill* all nodes labeled =[ ], one of whose descendants is **addr**(A).[†] That is, we make these nodes ineligible to be given an additional identifier label, preventing them from being falsely recognized as common subexpressions. It is thus required that we keep a bit for each node telling whether or not it has been killed. Further, for each array A mentioned in the block, we must have a list of all nodes currently not killed and having **addr**(A) as a descendant, so we can kill those nodes

---

† Note that the argument of =[ ] indicating the array could be **addr**(A) itself, or it could be an expression like **addr**(A) $-$ 4.

should we assign to an element of A.

A similar problem occurs if we have an assignment such as $*P := W$, where P is a pointer. If we do not know what P might point to, every node currently in the DAG being built must be killed. If node n labeled A is killed and there is a subsequent assignment to A, we must create a new leaf for A and use that leaf rather than n. We shall later consider the constraints on the order of evaluation caused by the killing of nodes.

In Section 14.7 we shall discuss methods whereby we could discover that P could only point to some subset of the identifiers. If P could only point to R or S, then only NODE(R) and NODE(S) must be killed. It is also conceivable that we could discover that $I = J$ is impossible in block (12.4), in which case the node for A[I] need not be killed by A[J] := Y. However, the latter type of discovery is not usually worth the trouble.

A procedure call in a basic block kills all nodes, since in the absence of knowledge about the called procedure, we must assume that any variable may be changed as a side effect. Section 14.8 discusses how we may establish that certain identifiers are not changed by a procedure call, and then nodes for these identifiers need not be killed.

If we intend to reassemble the DAG into a basic block and may not want to use the order in which the nodes of the DAG were created, then we must indicate in the DAG that certain apparently independent nodes must be evaluated in a certain order. For example, in (12.4), the statement $Z := A[I]$ must follow A[J] := Y, which must follow X := A[I]. Let us introduce certain edges $n \rightarrow m$ in the DAG that do not indicate that m is an argument of n, but rather that evaluation of n must follow evaluation of m in any computation of the DAG. The rules to be enforced are the following.

1. Any evaluation of or assignment to an element of array A must follow the previous assignment to an element of that array if there is one.
2. Any assignment to an element of array A must follow any previous evaluation of A.
3. Any use of any identifier must follow the previous procedure call or indirect assignment through a pointer if there is one.
4. Any procedure call or indirect assignment through a pointer must follow all previous evaluations of any identifier.

Example 12.9. The DAG for block (12.4) is shown in Fig. 12.8. The dashed line from n_2 to n_1 follows from rule (2). When n_2 is inserted into the DAG, n_1 is killed. The dashed line from n_3 to n_2 is from rule (1). Note that n_3 and n_1 are made distinct nodes because n_1 was killed before n_3 was created.   □

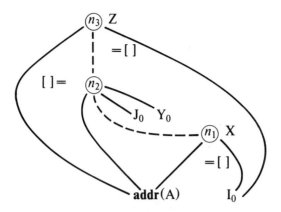

Fig. 12.8. DAG with order constraints.

12.4 Value Numbers and Algebraic Laws

One subtlety glossed over in Algorithm 12.2 occurred in step (2), where we suggested checking whether a node with specified children and a specified operator existed. It might appear that in order to implement this step the entire list of created nodes needs to be examined. Actually, a data structure such as a hash table can be used to enable us to make this determination almost instantaneous, and the idea was termed the *value number method* by Cocke and Schwartz [1970]. A node of the DAG is really just a pointer into an array or arrays holding the information about the node. That is, a node is just a number, either an absolute address or an index into an array, whichever implementation is chosen by the compiler writer. (Nodes represent values computed by the basic block; hence the term "value number.")

Given two nodes n and m we can "hash" the numbers representing n and m to obtain a pointer into a hash table where a list of nodes having n and m as children can be found immediately, save for occasional collisions. We could also involve the operator in the hash address, but it is unlikely that one basic block computes a collection of expressions such as $A + B$, $A - B$, and $A * B$. In at least one case to be discussed, it is useful to group nodes with the same children but distinct operators. Nodes having a single child can similarly be reached by hashing the number representing its lone child.

The Use of Algebraic Identities

In addition to helping us with step (2) of Algorithm 12.2, the value number method is useful in the implementation of certain optimizations based on algebraic laws. For example, if we wish to create a node with left child m and right child n, with operator $*$, we should certainly check whether such a node already exists. But on most machines, multiplication is commutative, so we should also check for a node having operator *, left child n and right child m. Actually, the payoff here is not as great as might be thought, since a programmer rarely writes A * B once and B * A the next time.

A similar optimization can be had by realizing that the relational operators $\leqslant$, $\geqslant$, $<$, $>$, $=$, and $\neq$ can be implemented by subtracting the arguments and performing a test. (This transformation, however, can introduce overflows and underflows where none existed before.) Thus only one node of the DAG need be generated for A−B and A$\leqslant$B, say. If condition codes are used by the target machine, further optimization is possible if we can defer this node to be evaluated last, but that is an issue properly reserved for Chapter 15 on code generation.

The associative law may also be applied to improve the code generated from a DAG. For example, if the source code has

$$A := B + C$$
$$E := C + D + B$$

the DAG of Fig. 12.9(a) could be changed to the one of Fig. 12.9(b), assuming T_2 was not needed outside the block. Both the associative and commutative laws are needed in this example.

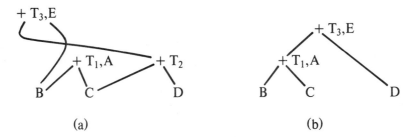

(a)   (b)

Fig. 12.9. Use of associative law.

The reader should be aware that not all languages permit arbitrary reordering of computations. Moreover, the use of algebraic laws could change the value of an expression. For example, if A, B, and C were each almost as large as could be represented on the target machine, then $(A − B) + C$ might be computable while $(A + C) − B$ would produce an overflow. In other situations, both expressions might be evaluable, yet one might cause a loss of significant digits. Because algebraic laws can change the value of a program, it would be desirable to design a compiler so that it is possible to turn off the optimizations due to them.

12.5 Global Data-Flow Analysis

A number of optimizations can be achieved by knowing various pieces of information that can be obtained only by examining the entire program. For example, if a variable A has value 3 every time control reaches a certain point p, then we can substitute 3 for each use of A at p. Knowing that the value of A is 3 at p may require examination of the entire program.

In this section we shall give an informal example of how global data-flow analysis can be used to gather such information. The particular problem we discuss is often called *use-definition* (or *ud-*) *chaining*. Roughly stated, ud-chaining answers the question: Given that identifier A is used at point p, at what points could the value of A used at p have been defined?

By a *use* of identifier A we mean any occurrence of A as an operand. By a *definition* of A we mean either an assignment to A or the reading of a value for A. We have not yet specified how a read operation is to be denoted, but the most likely convention is to have A be the operand of a **param** statement, with the operand of the subsequent **call** being the system read routine.

One more difficulty occurs when A is an array name. The difficulty can be seen when we realize that in the sequence

$$T_1 := 4 * I$$
$$T_2 := \mathbf{addr}(A) - 4$$
$$T_2[T_1] := B$$

the last statement is really an assignment to array A, even though A is not mentioned explicitly. We shall not consider this possibility further since the applications of ud-chaining when the identifier used is an array are not as great as when the identifier is a simple variable.

By a *point* in a program we mean the position before or after any intermediate-language statement. We say control reaches the point just before a statement when that statement is about to be executed, and the point after when that statement has just been executed. We say a definition of a variable A *reaches* a point p if there is a path in the flow graph from that definition to p, such that no other definitions of A appear on the path.

Throughout this discussion we are assuming that all edges in the graph are traversable. This may not be true in practice. For example, we would claim that the definition A := 3 in Fig. 12.10 can reach point p in B_5, even though for no value of A and B will block B_4 actually be reached. In applications of ud-chaining, assuming that a definition can reach a point when it cannot is nonfatal, in the sense that, while we may miss some optimizations, we shall never change what the program is doing. This situation is typical of code optimization. Rarely can we get exact information, but if we are careful, we can tailor our assumptions so that all discrepancies are in the nonfatal (miss an opportunity) direction, rather than the fatal (change what the program does) direction.

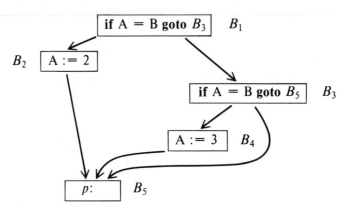

Fig. 12.10. Flow graph.

Reaching Definitions

To determine the definitions that can reach a given point in a program, we first assign a distinct number to each definition. Since each definition is associated with a unique quadruple, the index of that quadruple will do. Then, for each simple variable A, make a list of all definitions of A anywhere in the program. (Recall we are ignoring definitions of array names.)

The next step in ud-chaining is to compute two sets for each basic block B. The first, which we call GEN[B], is the set of generated definitions, those definitions within block B that reach the end of the block. We saw, in our discussion of how DAG's are computed, that GEN[B] can be found by determining for which statements, say A := X + Y, the node of the DAG created for that statement still has A as an attached identifier after completion of the DAG.

The second set needed is KILL[B], which is the set of definitions outside of B that define identifiers that also have definitions within B. We can easily tell which identifiers have definitions within B, and we have already made a list of the definitions of each identifier.

Incidentally, one might suspect that representing GEN[B] and KILL[B] for all blocks B might involve a great deal of space. Actually, since these are all subsets of the set of all definitions, we can use a bit vector representation for these sets, and the amount of space used will not be prohibitive.

The next and most complex step is to compute, for all blocks B, the set IN[B], consisting of all definitions reaching the point just before the first statement of block B. Once we know IN[B] we can determine the definitions which reach any use of identifier A within block B using the following rules. Let u be the statement in question using A.

1. If there are definitions of A within block B prior to statement u, then the last such definition is the only definition of A reaching u.
2. If there are no definitions of A within block B prior to u, then the definitions of A reaching u are these definitions of A that are in IN[B].

To help compute IN we may simultaneously compute OUT[B] for all blocks B. OUT[B] is the set of definitions reaching the point just after the last statement of B. Note that OUT[B] is different from GEN[B], since the latter speaks only of definitions inside B, while OUT[B] (and IN[B] as well) speaks of definitions everywhere.

Data-Flow Equations

There are two sets of equations, called *data-flow equations*, that relate IN's and OUT's. They are, for all blocks B:

(1) OUT[B] = IN[B] − KILL[B] ∪ GEN[B]†

$$(2) \quad \text{IN}[B] = \bigcup_{\substack{P \text{ a pred-} \\ \text{ecessor of } B}} \text{OUT}[P] \qquad\qquad (12.6)$$

Thus rules of group (1) say that a definition d reaches the end of block B if and only if either

i) d is in IN[B], i.e., d reaches the beginning of B, and is not killed by B, or
ii) d is *generated* within B, i.e., it appears in B and its identifier is not subsequently redefined within B.

Rules of group (2) say that a definition reaches the beginning of block B if and only if it reaches the end of one of its predecessors. In the case B has no predecessor (only the initial block or an inaccessible block could have no predecessors), rule (2) says IN[B] is the empty set.

We note that, like KILL and GEN, the sets IN and OUT can be represented by bit vectors. The union operations in rules (1) and (2) can be implemented by logical **or**, a basic operation in most systems-oriented programming languages. The computation of IN[B] − KILL[B] in rule (1) can be implemented by taking the complement of KILL[B] once for each block and then using logical **and** to compute IN[B] ∧ ¬KILL[B].

---

†We take set operations − and ∪ to be equal in precedence and left associative, like arithmetic − and +. This expression is parenthesized (IN[B] − KILL[B]) ∪ GEN[B].

Solving Data-Flow Equations

Since KILL and GEN are known in advance, rules (1) and (2) applied to an n node flow graph yield $2n$ equations in $2n$ unknowns, the IN's and OUT's. An interesting problem encountered when solving equations (12.6) is that the solution is not generally unique.

Example 12.10. To see why the solution to the equations is not always unique, consider the situation in Fig. 12.11, where block B has a loop. That is, B is a predecessor of itself. Suppose there is a solution to (12.6) where $IN[B]$ and $OUT[B]$ have values IN_0 and OUT_0, respectively, and suppose d is a definition not in IN_0, in OUT_0, or in $KILL[B]$. Then we claim $IN[B] = IN_0 \cup \{d\}$ and $OUT[B] = OUT_0 \cup \{d\}$, with each $IN[B']$ or $OUT[B']$ for $B' \neq B$ either unchanged or with d added, as appropriate, also satisfies (12.6).

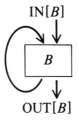

$IN[B]$

B

$OUT[B]$

Fig. 12.11. Block in a Flow Graph.

In proof, suppose d is in $IN[B]$. Then since it is not in $KILL[B]$, it must be in $OUT[B]$ by rule (1). Thus by rule (2), since d is in $OUT[B]$ and B is a predecessor of B, it is consistent to assume that d is in $IN[B]$. Thus there are at least two solutions to the equations.

Note that the existence of a simple loop at B is not essential here. Any path from B back to itself will cause the same problem if d is not killed along the path.   □

Fortunately, there is a *smallest* solution to equations (12.6), in the sense that the values of $IN[B]$ and $OUT[B]$ in the smallest solution are subsets of their values in any other solution. To see that the smallest solution must exist, simply observe that if the values of $IN[B]$ and $OUT[B]$ in two different solutions are intersected, the result will also be a solution to (12.6). More importantly, the smallest solution to (12.6) turns out to be exactly what we want $IN[B]$ and $OUT[B]$ to be. That is, in the smallest solution, $IN[B]$ is the set of definitions that reach the point just before the beginning of B, and $OUT[B]$ is the set of definitions that reach the point just after the end of B. We now give an algorithm to compute these quantities.

Algorithm 12.3. Reaching Definitions.

Input. A flow graph for which KILL[B] and GEN[B] have been computed for each block *B*.

Output. IN[B] and OUT[B] for each block *B*.

Method. We use an iterative approach, starting with the "estimate" IN[B] = ϕ for all *B* and converging to the desired values of IN and OUT. As we must iterate until the IN's (and hence the OUT's) converge, we use a Boolean variable CHANGE to record on each pass through the blocks whether any IN has changed. The algorithm is sketched in Fig. 12.12. □

```
        begin
(1)         for each block B do
                begin
(2)                 IN[B] := φ;
(3)                 OUT[B] := GEN[B]
                end; /* initialize on the assumption IN[B] = φ for all B */
(4)         CHANGE := true; /* to get the while-loop going */
(5)         while CHANGE do
                begin
(6)                 CHANGE := false;
(7)                 for each block B do
                        begin
(8)                         NEWIN :=    U    OUT[P];
                                     P a pred-
                                     ecessor of B

                            /* hold IN[B], computed by rule (2),
                               in a temporary to check for a change */
(9)                         if NEWIN ≠ IN[B] then CHANGE := true;
(10)                        IN[B] := NEWIN;
(11)                        OUT[B] := IN[B] − KILL[B] ∪ GEN[B]
                            /* apply rule (1) */
                        end
                end
        end
```

Fig. 12.12. Algorithm to compute IN and OUT.

Intuitively, Algorithm 12.2 propagates definitions as far as they will go without being killed, in a sense simulating all the possible executions of the program. We shall not prove that Algorithm 12.2 computes IN and OUT correctly. The bibliographic notes of Chapter 14 contain references where proofs of correctness for this and other data-flow analysis algorithms can be found.

We can, however, readily show that the algorithm will eventually halt. An easy induction on the number of times statement (8) is executed shows that IN[B] is always a subset of NEWIN. Thus, the IN's are always increasing, and since they are each subsets of a finite set, they cannot increase in size indefinitely. Thus there must eventually be a pass of the while-loop in which NEWIN $=$ IN[B] for each B at line (9). Then CHANGE will remain **false** and the algorithm terminates.

It may be shown that an upper bound on the number of times around the while-loop is the number of nodes in the flow graph. Intuitively, the reason is that if a definition reaches a point, it can do so along a cycle-free path, and the number of nodes in a flow graph is an upper bound on the number of nodes in a cycle-free path.

In fact, if we properly order the blocks in the for-loop of line (7), there is empirical evidence that the average number of iterations on real programs is under 5 (see Section 14.1). Since the sets can be represented by bit vectors, and the operations on these sets can be implemented by logical operations on the bit vectors, Algorithm 12.2 can be made quite fast. We shall discuss the proper ordering in the for-loop of line (7) and other issues related to this type of algorithm in Chapter 14. Now let us consider an example of Algorithm 12.2.

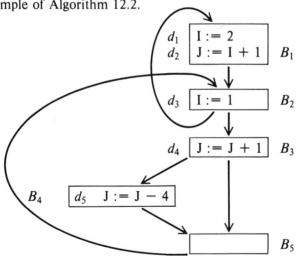

Fig. 12.13. A flow graph.

Example 12.11. Consider the flow graph of Fig. 12.13, where only the definitions of I and J are of interest. We have named these five definitions $d_1, d_2, \ldots, d_5$.

We begin by computing GEN and KILL. In B_1, both I and J are defined, so all definitions of I and J outside B_1 are killed. That is,

KILL$[B_1]$ = $\{d_3, d_4, d_5\}$. GEN$[B_1]$ = $\{d_1, d_2\}$, since each of d_1 and d_2 is the last definition of their respective variables in B_1. In B_2, d_3 kills all definitions of I outside B_2, so KILL$[B_2]$ = $\{d_1\}$, and GEN$[B_2]$ = $\{d_3\}$. The entire list of GEN's and KILL's, including their bit-vector representation (assuming d_i has position i) is shown in Fig. 12.14.

Block B	GEN$[B]$	bit vector	KILL$[B]$	bit vector
B_1	$\{d_1, d_2\}$	11000	$\{d_3, d_4, d_5\}$	00111
B_2	$\{d_3\}$	00100	$\{d_1\}$	10000
B_3	$\{d_4\}$	00010	$\{d_2, d_5\}$	01001
B_4	$\{d_5\}$	00001	$\{d_2, d_4\}$	01010
B_5	ϕ	00000	ϕ	00000

Fig. 12.14. GEN and KILL.

The loop of lines (1) through (3) initializes IN$[B]$ = ϕ and OUT$[B]$ = GEN$[B]$ for each B. Suppose the for-loop of line (7) is executed with $B = B_1, B_2, \ldots, B_5$ in that order. With $B = B_1$ we compute NEWIN = OUT$[B_2]$, since B_2 is the only predecessor of B_1. Thus, NEWIN is set to GEN$[B_2]$ = 00100 (we shall use bit vector notation from here on, with $-$ for "and-not" and $+$ for "or"), so NEWIN $\neq$ IN$[B_2]$. Therefore, CHANGE is immediately set to **true**, and we know we shall go around the while-loop at least once more. We compute

$$\text{OUT}[B_1] = 00100 - 00111 + 11000 = 11000$$

at line (11). Then we consider $B = B_2$. We compute

$$\text{NEWIN} = \text{OUT}[B_1] + \text{OUT}[B_5] = 11000 + 00000 = 11000$$

at line (8), and this becomes the value of IN$[B_2]$. Thus

$$\text{OUT}[B_2] = 11000 - 10000 + 00100 = 01100.$$

For $B = B_3$ we have

$$\text{IN}[B_3] = \text{OUT}[B_2] = 01100$$

and

$$\text{OUT}[B_3] = 01100 - 01001 + 00010 = 00110$$

Then

$$\text{IN}[B_4] = \text{OUT}[B_3] = 00110$$

and

$$\text{OUT}[B_4] = 00110 - 01010 + 00001 = 00101$$

Finally,

$$\text{IN}[B_5] = \text{OUT}[B_3] + \text{OUT}[B_4] = 00110 + 00101 = 00111$$

so

$$\text{OUT}[B_5] = 00111 - 00000 + 00000 = 00111.$$

Figure 12.15 summarizes this computation and the next two iterations of the while-loop. The iteration after that produces the same values for IN and OUT, so the values of IN and OUT shown under "pass 3" in Fig. 12.15 are the correct and final ones.   □

| | initial | | pass 1 | |
block	IN[B]	OUT[B]	IN[B]	OUT[B]
B_1	00000	11000	00100	11000
B_2	00000	00100	11000	01100
B_3	00000	00010	01100	00110
B_4	00000	00001	00110	00101
B_5	00000	00000	00111	00111

| | pass 2 | | pass 3 | |
block	IN[B]	OUT[B]	IN[B]	OUT[B]
B_1	01100	11000	01111	11000
B_2	11111	01111	11111	01111
B_3	01111	00110	01111	00110
B_4	00110	00101	00110	00101
B_5	00111	00111	00111	00111

Fig. 12.15. Computation of IN and OUT.

Computing ud-chains

As mentioned, we can compute ud-chains from the reaching definitions information. If a use of a variable A is preceded in its block by a definition of A, then only the last definition of A in the block prior to this use reaches the use. Thus the list or *ud-chain* for this use consists of only this one definition. If a use of A is preceded in its block B by no definition of A, then the ud-chain for this use consists of all definitions of A in IN[B].

Since the ud-chains take up much space, it is important for an optimizing compiler to format them compactly. Often, the various uses of A will have similar, or even identical ud-chains. Methods for formatting a collection of similar lists have been discussed in Chapters 3 and 6 in connection with action lists for lexical analyzers and parsers, respectively. We trust the reader can use these ideas to advantage for representing ud-chains if he so desires.

Example 12.12. In the flow graph of Fig. 12.13 there are three uses of names: d_2 uses I, and d_4 and d_5 use J. The use of I at d_2 in block B_1 is preceded by a definition of I in B_1, namely d_1. Thus the ud-chain for I in d_2 consists only of d_1.

The use of J at d_4 in B_3 is not preceded by a definition of J in B_3. Thus we consider IN[B_3], which is, from Fig. 12.15, equal to $\{d_2, d_3, d_4, d_5\}$. Of these, all but d_3 is a definition of J, so the ud-chain for J in d_4 is d_2, d_4, d_5.

The use of J at d_5 of block B_4 is not preceded by a definition of J, so we consider IN[B_4] $= \{d_3, d_4\}$. Of these, only d_4 defines J, so the ud-chain for J in d_5 consists of d_4 only. □

Applications of ud-chains

There are a variety of uses to which ud-chaining information can be put. For example, if there is only one definition of name A which reaches a point p, and that definition is A := 3, then we know A has the value 3 at that point, and we can substitute 3 for A if there is a use of A at point p.

Example 12.13. IN[B_5] $= \{d_3, d_4, d_5\}$ in Fig. 12.13. Of the definitions, only d_3: I := 1 is a definition of I. Therefore, if there were a use of I in B_5 that preceded any definition of I in B_5, it could be replaced by a use of the constant 1. □

As a second application of ud-chaining, we can determine whether a particular definition reaches anywhere at all. Recall that in Section 12.3 we discussed reconstructing a more efficient basic block from a DAG, and we said we needed to know whether a particular value could be used after control left the block. Taking the logical "or" of all the IN's gives us this information, although a more efficient way to gather this data will be discussed in Chapter 14.

For a third example of the use of ud-chains, not specifically related to code optimization, we can determine whether for a particular use of a variable A, it is possible that A is undefined at that point. Introduce dummy definitions of all variables prior to the initial block. If the dummy definition of A can reach a point which uses A, the compiler could print a warning that A might be undefined.

Note that we cannot assert that A is undefined at that point, for the path between the dummy definition and the use of A might involve tests that can never be simultaneously satisfied, so that path could never be traversed in a computation by the program. In a similar way, just because two definitions of a name A, say A := 2 and A := 3, reach a point p does

not mean that A does not always have the same value at p. The path from
A := 3 to p, for example, might never get traversed. Figure 12.9 presented
an example of this situation. However, to use ud-chains to detect names
with constant values at a point is entirely within the spirit of code optimization. We can detect many but not all of the useful optimization opportunities without changing what the program computes.

Exercises

12.1 Consider the following matrix multiplication routine:

```
begin
      for i := 1 to n do
            for j := 1 to n do
                  C[i, j] := 0;
      for i := 1 to n do
            for j :=1 to n do
                  for k := 1 to n do
                        C[i, j] := C[i, j] + A[i, k] * B[k, j]
end
```

a) Assuming A, B, and C are allocated static storage and there are
    two bytes per word in a byte-addressed memory, produce
    three-address code for the matrix multiplication program.
b) Partition the program into basic blocks.
c) Find the loops in the flow graph.
d) Move the loop-invariant computations out of the loops.
e) Find the induction variables of each loop and eliminate them
    where possible.
f) Compute reaching definitions and ud-chains for the original
    flow graph from (a) and the final flow graph from (e).

12.2 Construct the DAG for the following basic block.

$$D := B * C$$
$$E := A + B$$
$$B := B * C$$
$$A := E - D$$

12.3 What are the legal evaluation orders and names for the values at
the nodes for the DAG of Exercise 12.2

a) assuming A, B and C are live at the end of the basic block?

b) assuming only A is live at the end?

12.4 If, in Exercise 12.3(b), we are going to generate code for a machine with only one register, which evaluation order is best? Why?

12.5 Construct the DAG for the following code:

$$A[I] := B$$
$$*P := C$$
$$D := A[J]$$
$$E := *P$$
$$*P := A[I]$$

Assume that (a) P can point anywhere, (b) P points to only B or D. Do not forget to show the implied order constraints.

*12.6 If a pointer or array expression such as A[I] or *P is assigned and then used without the possibility of its value having changed in the interim, we can recognize and take advantage of the situation to simplify the DAG. For example, since in the code of Exercise 12.5, P is not assigned between the second and fourth statements, the statement E := *P can be replaced by E := C, since we are sure that whatever P points to has the same value as C, even though we don't know what P points to. Revise the DAG construction algorithm to take advantage of such inferences. Apply your algorithm to the code of Example 12.5.

Bibliographic Notes

There are a number of books available on the general subject of code optimization. These include Cocke and Schwartz [1970], Schaefer [1973], Wulf *et al.* [1975], and Hecht [1977]. The literature also contains descriptions of certain optimizing compilers, such as Ershov [1966], Lowry and Medlock [1969], Busam and Englund [1969], and Abel and Bell [1972]. The reader may also wish to consult current developments in the optimization of very high-level languages such as Earley [1975], Schwartz [1975a,b] and Low and Rovner [1976]. Allen [1975] is a useful bibliography on the subject of code optimization.

Allen [1969] is a fundamental paper on loop optimization; Allen and Cocke [1972] and Waite [1974] are more extensive surveys of techniques in the area. The value number method is from Cocke and Schwartz [1970]. Aho and Ullman [1972a] describe the use of DAG's to represent basic blocks. The scientific study of data-flow analysis techniques may be said to begin with the pair of papers Allen [1970] and Cocke [1970] (since published as Allen and Cocke [1976]), although various methods were in use long before then. Knuth [1971b] contains much useful statistical information on the utility of various optimizations in the context of FORTRAN.

Gajewska [1975] and Palm [1975] contain statistical information pertinent to C optimization. Cocke and Kennedy [1976] discuss the expected gain of certain flow graph optimizations.

CHAPTER 13

More About
Loop
Optimization

Programs spend most of their time going around loops. Loops, therefore, are the most promising sources of speedups in a program, and it behooves an optimizing compiler to generate particularly efficient code for loops. This chapter discusses the important loop optimizations and techniques for implementing them.

The first question to ask is "What is a loop?" Informally, we think of a loop as any cycle in the flow graph of a program. In Section 12.2, however, we saw that a loop should have two properties. First, it should have a single *entry node* (or *header*), such that all paths from outside the loop to any node in the loop go through the entry. This condition is motivated by our desire to have a unique place in which to move loop-invariant computations or initialize induction variables, namely in a block placed outside the loop just in front of the loop entry.

Secondly, a loop should be strongly connected, that is, it should be possible to go from any node of the loop to any other, staying within the loop. The motivation for this condition is that without strong connectedness, at least some of the "loop" could not be executed repetitiously.

Our plan of attack is to describe a method of detecting loops in flow graphs, using the notion of "dominators." Then we consider the notion of a "reducible" flow graph in which detection of loops is easy and loops are well defined. Roughly speaking, a reducible flow graph is one in which every cycle has a unique entry. Empirical evidence suggests that most programs have reducible flow graphs, and there is an interesting relationship between reducible flow graphs and "gotoless" programs.

After presenting the technique for detecting loops, we turn to algorithms for the principal loop optimizations. The spirit will be similar to that of Chapter 12—we cannot achieve true optimality, but we attempt to capture those transformations that give the greatest expected payoff.

13.1 Dominators

We say node *d* of a flow graph *dominates* node *n*, written *d* DOM *n*, if every path from the initial node of the flow graph to *n* goes through *d*. Under this definition, every node dominates itself, and the entry of a loop dominates all nodes in the loop.

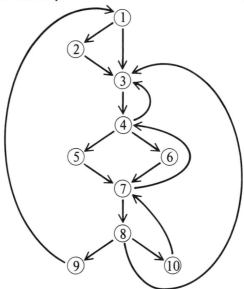

Fig. 13.1. Flow graph.

Example 13.1. Consider the flow graph of Fig. 13.1, with initial node 1. The initial node dominates every node. Node 2 dominates only itself, since control can reach any other node along a path that begins $1 \rightarrow 3$. Node 3 dominates all but 1 and 2. Node 4 dominates all but 1, 2 and 3, since all paths from 1 must begin $1 \rightarrow 2 \rightarrow 3 \rightarrow 4$ or $1 \rightarrow 3 \rightarrow 4$. Nodes 5 and 6 dominate only themselves, since flow of control can skip around either by going through the other. Finally, 7 dominates 7, 8, 9, and 10; 8 dominates 8, 9, and 10; 9 and 10 dominate only themselves.   □

Properties of DOM

Several algebraic properties regarding the dominance relation are readily apparent.

1. Dominance is a reflexive partial order. That is, dominance is reflexive (*a* DOM *a* for all *a*), antisymmetric (*a* DOM *b* and *b* DOM *a* implies that $a = b$), and transitive (*a* DOM *b* and *b* DOM *c* implies that *a* DOM *c*). Note that it is possible that there may be nodes *a* and *b* such that neither *a* DOM *b* nor *b* DOM *a*.

2. The dominators of each node n are linearly ordered by the DOM relation. The dominators of n appear in this linear order on any path from the initial node to n.

Property (1) follows directly from the definition. Property (2) can be seen as follows. Consider $D(n)$, the set of all nodes that dominate a given node n. We must show that the nodes in $D(n)$ can be linearly ordered by DOM. That is, if a and b are in $D(n)$ then either a DOM b or b DOM a. To see this, consider any cycle-free path P from the initial node to n. Both a and b are on P, since they both dominate n. Suppose a appears before b on P. If a does not dominate b, then there is a path Q from the initial node to b that avoids a. Thus we may reach n without going through a by following Q to b, then the remainder of P to n (see Fig. 13.2). But a DOM n, so we have a contradiction and conclude that a DOM b. A similar contradiction occurs if we assume b appears before a on P, so b DOM a must hold in this case.

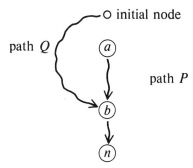

Fig. 13.2. Paths in proof about dominance.

It follows that, given any node n which has a dominator other than itself (i.e., any node but the initial node), there is one dominator of n, other than n, which is in turn dominated by every other dominator of n. We call this node the *immediate dominator* of n. The immediate dominator of n is the closest dominator of n on any path from the initial node to n.

Example 13.2. In Fig. 13.1, the dominators of 9 are 1, 3, 4, 7, 8, and 9. One can check that 1 DOM 3 DOM 4 DOM 7 DOM 8 DOM 9, so 8 is the immediate dominator of 9. □

A useful way of presenting dominator information is in a tree, called the *dominator tree,* in which the initial node is the root, and the parent of each other node is its immediate dominator. All and only the dominators of a node n will be ancestors of n in the tree.

Example 13.3. Figure 13.3 shows the dominator tree for the flow graph of Fig. 13.1. □

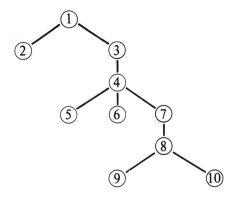

Fig. 13.3. Dominator tree.

Loop Detection

A good way to look for loops is to search for edges in the flow graph whose heads dominate their tails. (If $a \rightarrow b$ is an edge, b is the *head* and a is the *tail.*) We call such edges *back edges.*

Example 13.4. In Fig. 13.1, there is an edge $7 \rightarrow 4$, and 4 DOM 7. Similarly, $10 \rightarrow 7$ is an edge and 7 DOM 10. The other edges with this property are $4 \rightarrow 3$, $8 \rightarrow 3$, and $9 \rightarrow 1$. Note that these are exactly the edges that one would think of as forming loops in the flow graph. □

Given a back edge $n \rightarrow d$, we can find the *natural loop* of the edge by finding those nodes that can reach n without going through d. These nodes, plus d itself, form the loop. Node d is the header of the loop.

Example 13.5. The natural loop containing the edge $10 \rightarrow 7$ consists of nodes 7, 8, and 10, since 8 and 10 are all those nodes which can reach 10 without going through 7. The natural loop of $9 \rightarrow 1$ is the entire flow graph (don't forget the path $10 \rightarrow 7 \rightarrow 8 \rightarrow 9$). □

The natural loop of a back edge is easily constructed by the following algorithm.

Algorithm 13.1. Constructing natural loops.

Input. A flow graph G and a back edge $n \rightarrow d$.

Output. The set LOOP consisting of all nodes in the natural loop.

Method. We use a familiar stacking algorithm to consider each node m in LOOP, other than d, to make sure that m's predecessors are also placed in LOOP. Each node in LOOP, except for d, is placed once on STACK, so its predecessors will be examined. The algorithm is given in Fig. 13.4. □

```
procedure INSERT(m);
if m is not in LOOP then
    begin
        LOOP := LOOP ∪ {m};
        push m onto STACK
    end;
/* main program follows */
STACK := empty;
LOOP := { d };
INSERT(n);
while STACK is not empty do
    begin
        pop m, the first element of STACK, off STACK;
        for each predecessor p of m do INSERT(p)
    end
```

Fig. 13.4. Algorithm for constructing the natural loop.

Finding Dominators

Let us close this section with a technique for computing the dominators of every node n in a flow graph. It is based on the principle that if $p_1, p_2, \ldots, p_k$ are all the predecessors of n, and $d \neq n$, then d DOM n if and only if d DOM p_i for each i. The method is akin to the data-flow analysis technique discussed in the previous chapter, in that we take an approximation to the set of dominators of n and refine it by repeatedly visiting all the nodes in turn. In this case, the initial approximation we choose has only the initial node dominating the initial node, and everything dominating everything besides the initial node.

Algorithm 13.2. Finding dominators.

Input. A flow graph G with set of nodes N, set of edges E and initial node n_0.

Output. The relation DOM.

Method. We compute $D(n)$, the set of dominators of n, iteratively by the procedure in Fig. 13.5. At the end, d is in $D(n)$ if and only if d DOM n. The variable CHANGE is used to record whether convergence has occurred, and NEWD is a set of nodes used to facilitate the check for a change in the value of $D(n)$. □

One can show that NEWD computed at line (7) of Fig. 13.5 is always a subset of the current $D(n)$. Since $D(n)$ cannot get smaller indefinitely, we must eventually terminate the while-loop. A proof that, after convergence, $D(n)$ is the set of dominators of n is left for the interested reader. The

```
          begin
(1)           D(n₀) := {n₀};
(2)           for n in N − {n₀} do D(n) := N;
              /* end initialization */
(3)           CHANGE := true; /* to get the while-loop started */
(4)           while CHANGE do
                  begin
(5)                   CHANGE := false;
(6)                   for n in N − {n₀} do
                          begin
(7)                           NEWD := {n} ∪    ∩    D(p);
                                          p a pred-
                                          ecessor of n
(8)                           if D(n) ≠ NEWD then  CHANGE := true;
(9)                           D(n) := NEWD
                          end
                  end
          end
```

Fig. 13.5. Dominator computing algorithm.

algorithm of Fig. 13.5 is quite efficient, as $D(n)$ can be represented by a bit vector and the set operations of line (7) can be done with logical **and** and **or**. We shall give in the next section an order in which to visit the nodes in the for-loop of line (6) so that usually only one pass through the nodes is necessary, and the while-loop will find no change on the second pass. Let us now close this section with an example of Algorithm 13.2.

Example 13.6. Let us return to the flow graph of Fig. 13.1, and suppose in the for-loop of line (6) nodes are visited in numerical order. Node 2 has only 1 for a predecessor, so $NEWD = \{2\} \cup D(1)$. Since 1 is the initial node, $D(1)$ was assigned $\{1\}$ at line (1). Thus, $D(2)$ is set to $\{1, 2\}$ at line (9) and CHANGE is set to **true** at line (8), since the old value of $D(2)$, from line (2) was $\{1, 2, \ldots, 10\}$.

Then node 3, with predecessors 1, 2, and 8, is considered. Lines (7) and (9) give us $D(3) = \{3\} \cup (\{1\} \cap \{1,2\} \cap \{1,2,...,10\}) = \{1,3\}$. The remaining calculations are:

$$D(4) = \{4\} \cup (D(3) \cap D(7)) = \{4\} \cup (\{1,3\} \cap \{1,2,...,10\}) = \{1,3,4\}$$
$$D(5) = \{5\} \cup D(4) = \{5\} \cup \{1,3,4\} = \{1,3,4,5\}$$
$$D(6) = \{6\} \cup D(4) = \{6\} \cup \{1,3,4\} = \{1,3,4,6\}$$
$$D(7) = \{7\} \cup (D(5) \cap D(6) \cap D(10))$$
$$\quad\quad = \{7\} \cup (\{1,3,4,5\} \cap \{1,3,4,6\} \cap \{1,2,\ldots,10\}) = \{1,3,4,7\}$$
$$D(8) = \{8\} \cup D(7) = \{8\} \cup \{1,3,4,7\} = \{1,3,4,7,8\}$$
$$D(9) = \{9\} \cup D(8) = \{9\} \cup \{1,3,4,7,8\} = \{1,3,4,7,8,9\}$$

$$D(10) = \{10\} \cup D(8) = \{10\} \cup \{1,3,4,7,8\} = \{1,3,4,7,8,10\}$$

The second pass through the while-loop is seen to produce no changes, so the above values yield the relation DOM. □

13.2 Reducible Flow Graphs

There is a special class of flow graphs, called the reducible flow graphs, for which several code-optimization transformations are especially easy to perform. For example, in reducible flow graphs, loops are unambiguously defined, dominators can be efficiently calculated by a variant of Algorithm 13.2, and data-flow analysis problems, such as ud-chaining discussed in Section 12.5, can also be solved efficiently.

An equally important fact about reducible flow graphs is that they occur frequently in practice. Allen [1970] and Knuth [1971b] found that in random samples of FORTRAN programs virtually all programs had reducible flow graphs. Moreover, exclusive use of structured flow-of-control statements such as **if** . . . **then** . . . **else, while** . . . **do, continue**, and **break**, produces programs whose flow graphs are always reducible. These observations indicate that reducible flow graphs occur naturally, even in a language like FORTRAN, which virtually mandates the use of goto's, and even if a programmer has no prior knowledge of structured program design.

A variety of definitions of "reducible flow graph" have been proposed. The one we adopt brings out one of the most important properties of reducible flow graphs; namely, that there are no forward jumps into the middle of loops. The exercises and bibliographic notes contain a brief history of the concept.

Definition. A flow graph G is *reducible* if and only if we can partition the edges into two disjoint groups, *forward* edges and *back* edges, with the following two properties.

1. The forward edges form an acyclic graph in which every node can be reached from the initial node of G.
2. The back edges consist only of edges whose heads dominate their tails.

Example 13.7. The flow graph of Fig. 13.1 is reducible. In general, if we know the relation DOM for a flow graph, we can find and remove all the back edges. The remaining edges are forward edges, and to check whether a flow graph is reducible it suffices to check that the forward edges form an acyclic graph. In the case of Fig. 13.1, it is easy to check that if we remove the five back edges $4 \rightarrow 3$, $7 \rightarrow 4$, $8 \rightarrow 3$, $9 \rightarrow 1$, and $10 \rightarrow 7$, whose heads dominate their tails, the remaining graph is acyclic. □

Example 13.8. Consider the flow graph of Fig. 13.6, whose initial node is 1. This flow graph has no back edges, since no head of an edge dominates the tail of that edge. Thus it could only be reducible if the entire graph

Fig. 13.6. Nonreducible graph.

were acyclic. But since it is not, the flow graph is not reducible. Intuitively, the reason this flow graph is not reducible is that the cycle 2-3 can be entered at two different places, nodes 2 and 3. (Also see Exercise 13.8.)
□

Properties of Reducible Flow Graphs

The key property about reducible flow graphs, as far as loop analysis is concerned, is that every set of nodes that we would informally regard as a loop must contain a back edge. In fact, we need examine only the natural loops of back edges in order to find all loops in a program with a reducible flow graph. In contrast, the flow graph of Fig. 13.6 appears to have a "loop" consisting of nodes 2 and 3, but there is no back edge of which this is the natural loop. In fact, that "loop" has two headers, 2 and 3, making application of the techniques discussed in Chapter 12 for code motion and induction variable removal not directly applicable. Fortunately, nonreducible control flow structures such as that in Fig. 13.6 appear so rarely in most languages as to make the study of loops with more than one header of secondary importance.

If a flow graph is almost reducible, in the sense that only a few cycles remain when back edges are removed, we can still apply the techniques of loop optimization to the natural loops of the back edges. Also, techniques for converting nonreducible flow graphs to reducible ones by "node splitting" exist (see the bibliographic notes).

Another virtue of reducible flow graphs is that one can place a nested structure on loops. Two loops are either disjoint (except possibly for their headers) or one is a subset of the other.

Example 13.9. Returning again to Fig. 13.1, we note that the only "inner loop," that is, a loop with no subloops, is {7,8,10}, the natural loop of back edge 10 → 7. {4,5,6,7,8,10} is the natural loop of 7 → 4. (Note that 8 and 10 can reach 7 via edge 10 → 7.) Our preliminary intuition that {4,5,6,7} forms a loop is wrong, since 4 and 7 would both be entries from outside, violating our single-entry requirement. Put another way, there is no reason to assume that control spends much time going around the set of nodes {4,5,6,7}; it is just as plausible that control passes to 8 from 7 more often than it does to 4. By including 8 and 10 in the loop, we are more certain of having isolated a heavily traveled region of the program.

It is wise to recognize, however, the danger in making assumptions about the frequency of branches. For example, if we moved an invariant statement out of 8 or 10 in loop {7,8,10}, and in fact, control followed edge $7 \rightarrow 4$ more frequently than $7 \rightarrow 8$, we would actually increase the number of times the moved statement was executed. We shall discuss methods to avoid this problem in Section 13.4.

The next loop is {3,4,5,6,7,8,10}, which is the natural loop of both edges $4 \rightarrow 3$ and $8 \rightarrow 3$. As before, our intuition that {3,4} should be regarded as a loop violates the single header requirement. The last loop, the one for back edge $9 \rightarrow 1$, is the entire flow graph.   □

13.3 Depth-First Search

There is a useful ordering of the nodes of a flow graph, known as *depth-first* ordering, which can be used to detect loops in any flow graph. The depth-first ordering is created by starting at the initial node and searching the entire graph, trying to visit nodes as far away from the initial node as quickly as possible (*depth first*). The route of the search forms a tree. Before we give the algorithm, let us consider an example.

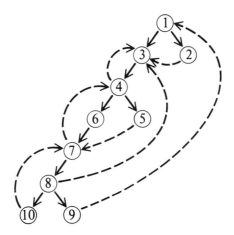

Fig. 13.7. Depth-first presentation of Fig. 13.1

Example 13.10. Figure 13.7 diagrams one possible depth-first search of the flow graph in Fig. 13.1. Solid edges form the tree; dashed edges are the other edges of the flow graph. The search is a preorder traversal of the tree, $1 \rightarrow 3 \rightarrow 4 \rightarrow 6 \rightarrow 7 \rightarrow 8 \rightarrow 10$, then back to 8, then to 9. We go back to 8 once more, retreating to 7, 6, and 4, and thence to 5. We retreat from 5 back to 4, then back to 3 and 1. From 1 we go to 2, then retreat from 2, back to 1, and we have traversed the entire tree in preorder.   □

Depth-First Ordering

The depth-first ordering of the nodes is the *reverse* of the order in which we *last* visit the nodes in the preorder traversal. In Example 13.10, the complete sequence of nodes visited as we traverse the tree is

$$1, 3, 4, 6, 7, 8, 10, 8, 9, 8, 7, 6, 4, 5, 4, 3, 1, 2, 1.$$

In this list, mark the last occurrence of each number to get

$$1, 3, 4, 6, 7, 8, \underline{10}, 8, \underline{9}, \underline{8}, \underline{7}, \underline{6}, 4, \underline{5}, \underline{4}, \underline{3}, 1, \underline{2}, \underline{1}$$

The depth-first ordering is the sequence of marked numbers in reverse order. Here, this sequence happens to be 1, 2, . . . , 10.

Depth-First Spanning Trees

We now give an algorithm which computes a depth-first ordering of a flow graph by constructing and traversing a tree, trying to make paths in the tree as long as possible. Such a tree is called a *depth-first spanning tree* (*DFST*).

Algorithm 13.3. Depth-first spanning tree and depth-first ordering.

Input. A flow graph G.

Output. A DFST T of G and an ordering of the nodes of G.

Method. We use the recursive procedure SEARCH(n) of Fig. 13.8; the algorithm is to initialize all nodes of G to "unvisited," then call SEARCH(n_0), where n_0 is the initial node. When we call SEARCH(n), we first mark n "visited," to avoid adding n to the tree twice. We use i to count from the number of nodes of G down to 1, assigning depth-first numbers DFN(n) to nodes n as we go.   □

Example 13.11. Consider Fig. 13.1. We set i to 10 and call SEARCH(1). At line (2) of SEARCH we must consider each successor of node 1. Suppose we consider $s = 3$ first. Then we add edge $1 \rightarrow 3$ to the tree and call SEARCH(3). In SEARCH(3) we add edge $3 \rightarrow 4$ to T and call SEARCH(4).

Suppose in SEARCH(4) we choose $s = 6$ first. Then we add edge $4 \rightarrow 6$ to T and call SEARCH(6). This in turn causes us to add $6 \rightarrow 7$ to T and call SEARCH(7). Node 7 has two successors, 4 and 8. But 4 was already marked "visited" by SEARCH(4), so we do nothing when $s = 4$. When $s = 8$ we add edge $7 \rightarrow 8$ to T and call SEARCH(8). Suppose we then choose $s = 10$. We add edge $8 \rightarrow 10$ and call SEARCH(10).

Now 10 has a successor, 7, but 7 is already marked "visited," so in SEARCH(10), we fall through to step (6) in Fig. 13.8, setting DFN[10] =

```
        procedure SEARCH(n);
        begin
(1)         mark n "visited";
(2)         for each successor s of n do
(3)             if s is "unvisited" then
                    begin
(4)                     add edge n → s to T;
(5)                     SEARCH(s)
                    end;
(6)         DFN[n] := i;
(7)         i := i−1
        end;
        /* main program follows */
        begin
(8)         for each node n of G do mark n "unvisited";
(9)         i := number of nodes of G;
(10)        SEARCH(n₀)
        end
```

Fig. 13.8. Depth-first search algorithm.

10 and $i = 9$. This completes the call to SEARCH(10), so we return to SEARCH(8). We now set $s = 9$ in SEARCH(8), add edge $8 → 9$ to T and call SEARCH(9). The only successor of 9, node 1, is already "visited," so we set DFN[9] $= 9$ and $i = 8$. Then we return to SEARCH(8). The last successor of 8, node 3, is "visited," so we do nothing for $s = 3$. At this point, we have considered all successors of 8, so we set DFN[8] $= 8$ and $i = 7$, returning to SEARCH(7).

All of 7's successors have been considered, so we set DFN[7] $= 7$ and $i = 6$, returning to SEARCH(6). Similarly, 6's successors have been considered, so we set DFN[6] $= 6$ and $i = 5$, and we return to SEARCH(4). Successor 3 of 4 has been "visited," but 5 has not, so we add $4 → 5$ to the tree and call SEARCH(5), which results in no further calls, as successor 7 of 5 has been "visited." Thus, DFN[5] $= 5$, i is set to 4, and we return to SEARCH(4). We have completed consideration of the successors of 4, so we set DFN[4] $= 4$ and $i = 3$, returning to SEARCH(3). Then we set DFN[3] $= 3$ and $i = 2$ and return to SEARCH(1).

The final steps are to call SEARCH(2) from SEARCH(1), set DFN[2] $= 2$, $i = 1$, return to SEARCH(1), set DFN[1] $= 1$ and $i = 0$. Note that we chose a numbering of the nodes such that DFN[i] $= i$, but that relation need not hold for an arbitrary graph, or even for another depth-first ordering of the graph of Fig. 13.1. □

The Edges in a Depth-First Presentation of a Flow Graph

When we construct a DFST for a flow graph, the edges of the flow graph fall into three categories.

1. There are edges that go from a node m to an ancestor of m in the tree (possibly to m itself). These edges we shall term *retreating* (or *backward*) edges. For example, $7 \to 4$ and $9 \to 1$ are retreating edges in Fig. 13.7. It is an interesting and useful fact that if the flow graph is reducible, then the retreating edges are exactly the back edges of the flow graph, independent of the order in which successors are visited in step (2) of Fig. 13.8. For any flow graph, every back edge is retreating, although if the graph is nonreducible there will be some retreating edges that are not back edges.

2. There are edges, called *advancing edges,* that go from a node m to a proper descendant of m in the tree. All edges in the DFST itself are advancing edges. There are no other advancing edges in Fig. 13.7, but, for example, if $4 \to 8$ were an edge, it would be in this category.

3. There are edges $m \to n$ such that neither m nor n is an ancestor of the other in the DFST. Edges $2 \to 3$ and $5 \to 7$ are the only such examples in Fig. 13.7. We call these edges *cross edges*.

It should be noted that $m \to n$ is a retreating edge if and only if $\mathrm{DFN}[m] \geqslant \mathrm{DFN}[n]$. For if m is a descendant of n in the DFST, then $\mathrm{SEARCH}(m)$ terminates before $\mathrm{SEARCH}(n)$, so $\mathrm{DFN}[m] \geqslant \mathrm{DFN}[n]$. Conversely, if $\mathrm{DFN}[m] \geqslant \mathrm{DFN}[n]$, then $\mathrm{SEARCH}(m)$ terminates before $\mathrm{SEARCH}(n)$, or $m = n$. But $\mathrm{SEARCH}(n)$ must have begun before $\mathrm{SEARCH}(m)$, or else the fact that n is a successor of m would have made n a descendant of m in the DFST. Thus the time $\mathrm{SEARCH}(m)$ is active is a subinterval of the time $\mathrm{SEARCH}(n)$ is active, from which it follows that n is an ancestor of m.

The Depth of a Flow Graph

There is an important parameter of flow graphs called the *depth*. Given a depth-first spanning tree for the graph, the depth is the largest number of retreating edges on any cycle-free path. For example, in Fig. 13.7, the depth is 3, since there is a path $10 \to 7 \to 4 \to 3$ with three retreating edges, but no cycle-free path with four or more retreating edges. It is a coincidence that the "deepest" path here has only retreating edges; in general we may have a mixture of retreating, advancing, and cross edges in a "deepest" path.

We can prove the depth is never greater than what one would intuitively call the depth of loop nesting in the flow graph. If a flow graph is reducible, we may replace "retreating" by "back" in the definition of "depth," since the retreating edges in any DFST are exactly the back edges. The notion of depth then becomes independent of the DFST actually chosen.

Knuth [1971b] measured a parameter called the "interval depth" of a random sample of FORTRAN programs, showing it to be 2.75 on the average, while Hecht and Ullman [1975] showed the depth as defined here to be always equal to or less than the interval depth. Thus, the depth of flow graphs tends to be small, and we can exploit this fact in various algorithms. We give one example here.

Finding Back Edges — An Application of Depth-First Ordering

To begin, we may know *a priori* that a flow graph is reducible. We might, for example, be compiling a language such as BLISS or SIMPL, in which only reducible flow graphs can be obtained from programs. Then we can find the back edges immediately from the depth-first numbering, without computing dominators. To do so, we can use the fact that $m \rightarrow n$ is a retreating edge, or equivalently, a back edge, if and only if $\text{DFN}[m] \geqslant \text{DFN}[n]$.

Even if we do not know flow graphs to be reducible, we can compute dominators efficiently by choosing the ordering in line (6) of Fig. 13.5, the dominator algorithm, to be the depth-first ordering. If the flow graph is reducible, then after one pass of the while-loop of line (4), $D(n)$ will have attained its final value.

The intuitive reason why this is true is that Algorithm 13.2 works by trying to find a path from the initial node to m that avoids n. If there is such a path, there must be a cycle-free one, so we need only consider cycle-free paths. This cycle-free path cannot contain a back edge. Suppose it did contain back edge $r \rightarrow s$. Then s DOM r, so s must precede r on the path, and therefore the path has a cycle containing s. Since all paths without retreating edges, which in the case of reducible flow graphs are back edges, follow nodes with monotonically increasing depth-first numbers (DFN), one pass through the nodes in depth-first order is sufficient to "follow" any such path. While this intuitive argument is not a proof, we invite the interested reader to read further on the subject; the bibliographic notes give sources where more formal proofs may be found.

Even if the graph is not reducible, the number of passes through the while-loop is limited to two more than the depth with respect to DFST T, if the depth-first order according to T is used in line (6) of Fig. 13.5. The intuition here is that if the depth is d, no cycle-free path from the initial node to m may have more than d retreating edges, so $D(m)$ will have converged to its proper value after $d+1$ iterations. One extra iteration is needed to discover that convergence has occurred. The reason this bound on the number of passes is significant is that by the evidence of Knuth [1971b], d tends to be small, less than 3 on the average.

We may also apply a similar argument to data-flow analysis algorithms. For example, in the ud-chaining discussed in Section 12.5, we discovered each definition that reaches a point by discovering a path along which the definition is not killed. Surely if there is such a path there is a cycle-free one. If the depth-first ordering formed from a DFST T is used, and the depth of the flow graph with respect to T is d, then $d+2$ again limits the number of iterations of the while-loop. Unlike the dominator algorithm, where all paths of interest begin at the initial node, we cannot claim convergence of IN and OUT after one pass for reducible flow graphs.

13.4 Loop-Invariant Computations

We now have methods for finding back edges and their natural loops. The task is not hard in any case, but it is especially easy if the flow graph happens to be reducible. We next give algorithms to perform the key optimizations on loops: code motion, induction variabie elimination, and several others. The setting for the remainder of this chapter will be a loop, as we have defined it, having a header which dominates all blocks in the loop.

Several optimizations require us to move statements "before the header." We therefore begin optimization of a loop L by creating a new block, called the *pre-header*. The pre-header has only the header as successor, and all edges which formerly entered the header of L from outside L instead enter the preheader. Edges from inside loop L to the header are not changed. The arrangement is shown in Fig. 13.9. Initially, the preheader is empty, but we shall place statements in it as the optimization of L proceeds.

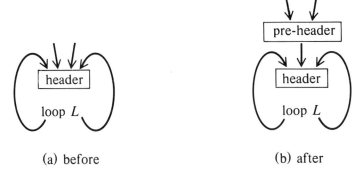

(a) before   (b) after

Fig. 13.9. Introduction of the pre-header.

Detection of Loop-Invariant Computations

Our first algorithm is one which detects those statements in a loop which are loop-invariant. It makes use of ud-chaining information, which we may assume previously calculated by an algorithm such as that of Section 12.5. Specifically, if an assignment A := B + C is at a position in the loop where all possible definitions of B and C are outside the loop (including the special case where B and/or C is constant), then the calculation of B + C will be the same each time encountered, as long as control never leaves the loop. All such assignments are easy to detect, given the ud-chains, that is, a list of all definition points of B and C reaching assignment A := B + C. Having recognized that the value of A computed at A := B + C does not change within the loop, suppose there is another statement D := A + E, where E could only have been defined outside the loop, and A must have been defined at the statement A := B + C just mentioned. Then D is assigned the same value each time the statement D := A + E is executed, as long as control stays within the loop.

It should be clear how we can use the above ideas to make repeated passes over the loop, discovering more and more statements whose value is *loop-invariant,* that is, does not change as long as we stay within the loop. Some of these assignments may be moved to the pre-header.

One requirement for such code motion is that the block containing the statement dominate all *exit* nodes of the loop, where an exit of a loop is a node with a successor not in the loop. We have already seen one justification for the requirement in Example 13.9, where it was observed that moving a statement which need not be executed within the loop, to a position outside the loop could result in an increase in the running time of the program. Worse still, it could change what the program computes, as we see from the next example.

Example 13.11. Consider the portion of a flow graph shown in Fig. 13.10(a). B_2, B_3 and B_4 form a loop with header B_2. Statement I := 2 in B_3 is clearly loop-invariant. However, B_3 does not dominate B_4, the only loop exit. If we move I := 2 to a newly created pre-header B_6, as shown in Fig. 11.10(b), we may change the value assigned to J in B_5, specifically in those cases where B_3 never gets executed. For example, if X = 30 and Y = 25 when B_2 is first entered, Fig. 13.10(a) sets J = 1 at B_5, since B_3 is never entered, while Fig. 13.10(b) sets J = 2. □

We can (and shall) relax the above requirement somewhat if we are willing to take the risk that we may actually increase the running time a bit, without changing what the program computes. The relaxed version is that the block containing the statement to be moved either dominates all exits of the loop or the name assigned is not used outside the loop. For example, if the statement assigns a temporary name, we can be sure (in many compilers) that the value will be used only in its own block.

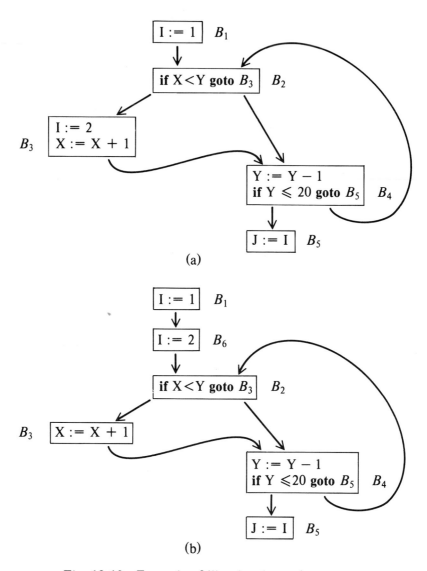

Fig. 13.10. Example of illegal code motion.

In general, we can check whether a name is *live* (has a value which may be used subsequently) by a data-flow analysis technique to be discussed in the next chapter. Specifically, we must check here that the name assigned by the statement to be moved is not live on entering any successor outside the loop of any exit block of the loop.

A second condition we impose to make code motion legal is simply that we cannot move a loop-invariant statement assigning to A into the pre-header if there is another statement in the loop which assigns to A. Again, if A is a temporary assigned only once, this condition is surely satisfied and need not be checked.[†]

Example 13.13. Suppose block B_2 in Fig. 13.10(a) were

$$I := 3$$

if X < Y goto B_3

Now B_2 dominates the exit B_4, so our first prohibition does not apply to moving I := 3 to the pre-header B_6. However, if we do so, we shall set I = 2 whenever B_3 is executed, and I will have value 2 when we reach B_5, even if we follow a sequence such as $B_2 \rightarrow B_3 \rightarrow B_4 \rightarrow B_2 \rightarrow B_4 \rightarrow B_5$. For example, consider what happens if Y = 22 and X = 21 when B_2 is first reached. If I := 3 is in B_2, we set J = 3 at B_5, but if I := 3 is removed to the pre-header, we set J = 2.   □

The third condition we impose on code motion is that we cannot move a statement assigning A to the pre-header if there is a use of A in the loop which is reached by any definition of A other than the statement moved. Let us again remind the reader that the typical temporary, defined and used once each, will surely meet the requirement for code motion.

Example 13.14. Suppose block B_4 in Fig. 13.10(a) were:

$$K := I$$
$$Y := Y - 1$$
if Y ≤ 20 goto B_5

As Fig. 13.10(a) stands, the use K := I is reached by I := 1 in block B_1, as well as by I := 2 in B_3. Thus, we could not move I := 2 to pre-header B_6, because the value of K reaching B_5 would change in the case X = Y = 0. That is, K is set to 1 once and for all before motion of I := 2 to B_6, while after moving I := 2 to B_6, we set K = 2 once and for all.   □

It should be borne in mind that none of the conditions we have imposed is absolutely essential. One could always write a program in which one or even all conditions were violated, yet a code motion could be performed without changing the values computed by the program. As in all aspects of code optimization, we have selected these conditions because they are easy to check and allow us to perform most of the desired optimizations, code motion in this case, for which opportunities occur with regularity in real programs.

[†] We shall see later that an assignment A := B + C can be moved out if we put T := B + C in the preheader and replace A := B + C by A := T, where T is a new temporary.

We now give an algorithm for detecting invariant computations. It will be followed by an algorithm to actually perform the code motion for those invariant computations which one may legally move to the pre-header.

Algorithm 13.4. Detection of Loop-Invariant Computations.

Input. A loop L consisting of a set of basic blocks, each block containing a sequence of three-address statements. We assume ud-chaining information as computed in Section 12.5 is available for the individual statements.

Output. An indication of those three-address statements that will compute the same value each time executed, from the time control enters the loop L until control next leaves L.

Method. We shall give a rather informal specification of the algorithm, trusting that the principles will be clear.

1. Mark "invariant" those statements whose operands are all either constant or have all their reaching definitions outside L.
2. Repeat step (3) until at some repetition no new statements are marked "invariant."
3. Mark "invariant" all those statements not previously so marked whose operands all are either constant, have all their reaching definitions outside L, or have exactly one reaching definition, and that definition is a statement in L marked invariant.   □

Example 13.15. Let us begin a rather elaborate example that will take us through a variety of sample optimizations. The example is essentially the merge routine of a merge-sort in which two sorted arrays A and B, of N words each, are merged to form one sorted array C of 2*N words. To make matters a bit more interesting and exhibit some of the power of code optimization techniques, we assume that A, B, and C are allocated on a stack, although N and index variables I, J, and K (used to index A, B, and C, respectively) are allocated statically.

We suppose there is a name SP which points to the top of the stack.[†] The stack runs down in memory. SP could be a name initialized with each procedure call, but more likely it is a hardware object, such as a base register or a hardware stack pointer. In any event, we shall treat SP as a name initialized outside the loop with which we are dealing and kept constant for the duration of the loop.

Figure 13.11 shows the relevant portion of the activation record. The first words of A, B, and C are addressable by 0[SP], 4[SP] and 8[SP], respectively. We assume the arrays run from 1 up to N (or 2*N in the case

---

† This arrangement differs slightly from that of Sections 10.1 and 10.2, where SP pointed to the bottom of the area for local data. We adopt the convention here to make all offsets positive numbers.

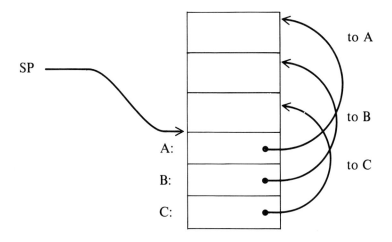

Fig. 13.11. Part of an activation record.

of C). We assume a byte-addressable memory with four bytes/word, so it would turn out to be more efficient if the word 0[SP] held **addr**(A)−4 rather than **addr**(A), and similarly for the next two words. Yet we shall see that this seeming oversight costs little in terms of run-time efficiency.

The flow graph in a high-level language for our routine is shown in Fig. 13.12. The seven blocks can be converted to three-address statements as follows:

(1)	B_1:	I := 1	
(2)		J := 1	
(3)		K := 1	
(4)	B_2:	**if** I > N **goto** B_5	
(5)	B_3:	**if** J > N **goto** B_6	
(6)	B_4:	$T_1 := 0[SP]$	/* address of A */
(7)		$T_2 := T_1 - 4$	
(8)		$T_3 := 4 * I$	
(9)		$T_4 := T_2[T_3]$	/* A[I] */
(10)		$T_5 := 4[SP]$	/* address of B */
(11)		$T_6 := T_5 - 4$	
(12)		$T_7 := 4 * J$	
(13)		$T_8 := T_6[T_7]$	/* B[J] */
(14)		**if** $T_4 \leqslant T_8$ **goto** B_6	
(15)	B_5:	$T_9 := 8[SP]$	/* address of C */

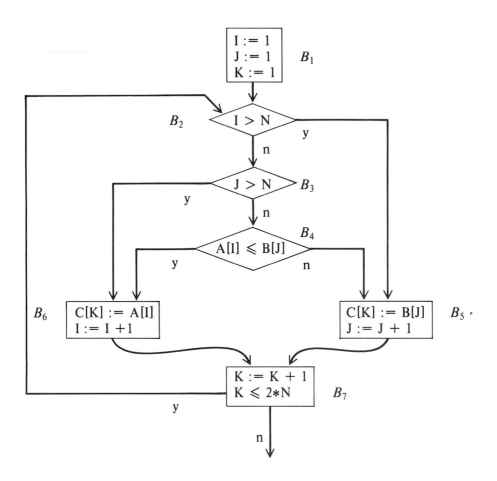

Fig. 13.12. Flow Graph for merge routine.

(16)		$T_{10} := T_9 - 4$	
(17)		$T_{11} := 4 * K$	
(18)		$T_{12} := 4[SP]$	/* address of B */
(19)		$T_{13} := T_{12} - 4$	
(20)		$T_{14} := 4 * J$	
(21)		$T_{15} := T_{13}[T_{14}]$	
(22)		$T_{10}[T_{11}] := T_{15}$	/* C[K] := B[J] */
(23)		$J := J + 1$	
(24)		**goto** B_7	
(25)	B_6:	$T_{16} := 8[SP]$	/* address of C */
(26)		$T_{17} := T_{16} - 4$	
(27)		$T_{18} := 4 * K$	

(28)		$T_{19} := 0[SP]$	/* address of A */
(29)		$T_{20} := T_{19} - 4$	
(30)		$T_{21} := 4 * I$	
(31)		$T_{22} := T_{20}[T_{21}]$	
(32)		$T_{17}[T_{18}] := T_{22}$	/* C[K] := A[I] */
(33)		$I := I + 1$	
(34)	B_7:	$K := K + 1$	
(35)		$T_{23} := 2 * N$	
(36)		**if** $K \leqslant T_{23}$ **goto** B_2	

The loop in question consists of all blocks but B_1; it is the natural loop of edge $B_7 \rightarrow B_2$. Step (1) of Algorithm 13.4 tells us to search the blocks for statements all of whose operands are defined only outside the loop or are constants. Surely N and SP are not defined within the loop, and the contents of 0[SP], 4[SP], and 8[SP] are pointers assigned only by the compiler, so statements 6, 10, 15, 18, 25, 28, and 35 qualify. Then we look for other statements whose operands are either constant, defined outside the loop or are certainly defined at one of the statements just listed.

For example, statement (7), $T_2 = T_1 - 4$ has one constant argument and the other, T_1, which must have been defined at the previous statement (6). Thus, statement (7) qualifies. By a similar argument, statements 11, 16, 19, 26, and 29 qualify. Repeating the procedure with all the statements listed in the previous two groups uncovers no new invariant statements, so the list of invariant statements for the loop of blocks $B_2, B_3, \ldots, B_7$ is 6, 7, 10, 11, 15, 16, 18, 19, 25, 26, 28, 29, and 35. □

Performing Code Motion

We now give two algorithms for doing code motion. The first uses the three conditions we have mentioned; the second uses the relaxed version of the first condition.

Algorithm 13.5. Code Motion I.

Input. A loop L with ud-chaining information and dominator information.

Output. A revised version of the loop with a pre-header and (possibly) some statements moved to the pre-header.

Method.

1. Use Algorithm 13.4 to find loop-invariant statements.
2. For each statement s, say A := B, A := **op** B, or A := B **op** C, found in step (1) check:

      i)   that it is in a block which dominates all exits of L,

      ii)   that A is not defined elsewhere in L, and

      iii)   that all uses in L of A can only be reached by the definition of A in statement s.

3.   Move, in the order found by Algorithm 13.4, each statement s found in (1) and meeting (2i), (2ii), and (2iii) to a newly created pre-header, provided any operands of s which are defined in loop L (in case s were found in step (3) of Algorithm 13.4) have their definition statements moved to the pre-header.   □

To see why no change to what the program computes can occur, conditions (2i) and (2ii) assure that the value of A computed at s must be the value of A after any exit block of L. When we move s to the pre-header, s will still be the definition of A which reaches the end of any exit block of L. Condition (2iii) assures that any uses of A within L did, and will continue to, use the value of A computed by s.

To understand why the transformation cannot increase the running time of the program, we have only to note that condition (2i) assures us that s is executed at least once each time control enters L. After the code motion it will be executed exactly once in the pre-header and not at all in L whenever control enters L.

The order in which the moved statements are placed in the pre-header is the order in which they are found, so if any of them uses a value computed by another, that value will be available in the pre-header when needed.

It is also worth mentioning that the transformation of Algorithm 13.5 does not change ud-chaining information since by conditions (2i), (2ii), and (2iii), all uses of the name assigned by a moved statement s that were reached by s are still reached by s. Definitions of names used by s are either outside L, in which case they reach the preheader, or they are inside L, in which case by step (3) they were moved to the preheader ahead of s.

If the ud-chains are represented by lists of pointers to pointers to statements rather than lists of pointers to statements, we can maintain ud-chains when we move statement s by simply changing the pointer to s when we move it. That is, we create for each statement s a pointer P_s, which always points to s. We put P_s on each ud-chain containing s. Then, no matter where we move s, we have only to change P_s, regardless of how many ud-chains s is on.

If we represent ud-chains by a list of statement addresses (pointers to statements) we can still maintain ud-chains as we move statements. But then we need du-chains, discussed in Chapter 14, which give for each statement s, all uses of the value computed by s. When we move s, we may go down its du-chain, changing the ud-chain of all uses that refer to s.

The dominator information is changed slightly. The pre-header is now the immediate dominator of the header, and the immediate dominator of the pre-header is the node which formerly was the immediate dominator of the header. That is, the pre-header is inserted into the dominator tree as the parent of the header.

Example 13.16. Let us continue with Example 13.15. The only exit of the loop $\{B_2, B_3, \ldots, B_7\}$ in Fig. 13.12 is B_7. It is dominated only by B_2 and B_7 itself. Thus, condition (2i) of Algorithm 13.5 is satisfied only for invariant statement (35) $T_{23} := 2 * N$. The second and third conditions are that T_{23} not be defined elsewhere in the loop (it clearly is not) and that all uses of T_{23} in the loop use the value of T_{23} defined by statement (35). There is only one use of T_{23}, at statement (36), and that statement clearly uses only the value defined at statement (35). Thus all conditions are met, and we may move statement (35) to a newly created pre-header, which we shall refer to subsequently as B_8. All the other invariant statements fail to meet condition (i) and may not be moved. □

A More Powerful Method

The results of applying Algorithm 13.5 were not too satisfactory. The reason that we could not move more of the invariant statements out of the loop is that in the case $N = 0$, blocks B_3, B_4, and B_6 would never be executed. Just looking at the flow graph, ignoring the values that we know I, J and K must have the first time through B_2, it looks as though there is a possible computation in which B_5 never gets executed. There is therefore the appearance that moving invariant statements out of any of B_3, B_4, B_5 or B_6 (those blocks which do not dominate the exit) could increase the number of statements executed, since they are sure be executed in the pre-header, while they might not be executed where they are.

Now the compiler has no way of knowing that we do not intend to use the merge routine with $N = 0$. (In fact it does not even work properly in that case; do you see why?) Moreover, without doing far more work "understanding" what the program is doing than we would normally be willing to put in, the compiler cannot make inferences such as: "If $I \leqslant N$ the first time through B_2 then $N \geqslant 1$, so B_5 will surely be executed, and we cannot lose by moving code out of B_5."

We therefore propose a modification of Algorithm 13.5 that occasionally will increase the running time slightly, but can be expected to do reasonably well on the average. Our new algorithm may move to the pre-header certain computations that might not be executed in the loop. Not only does this risk slowing down the program significantly, it may also cause an error in certain circumstances. For example, the evaluation of A/B in a loop may be preceded in a loop by a test to see whether B = 0. If we move A/B to the pre-header, a division by zero may occur. For this reason, it is wise to use the following algorithm for code motion only if optimization may be inhibited by the programmer.

Algorithm 13.6. Code Motion II.

Input. A loop L with ud-chaining information, dominator information and information as to which identifiers are live immediately after each loop exit.

Output. A revised version of the loop with a pre-header and (possibly) more statements moved to the pre-header.

Method.

1. Use Algorithm 13.4 to find loop-invariant statements.
2. For each statement s found in (1) check that it either

    a) meets the three conditions of step (2) of Algorithm 13.5, or
    b) defines a name A which is not live at entry to any successor of any exit of L if that successor is not in L, and which meets condition (iii) of step (2) of Algorithm 13.5, that is, all uses of A in L can only be reached by the definition of A at statement s.

3. Move, in the order found by Algorithm 13.4, each statement s found in (1) and satisfying the criterion of step (2), to the pre-header, provided any operands of s which are defined in L also have their definitions moved to the pre-header.   □

Example 13.17. Let us return to Example 13.15. As in Example 13.16, we see that criterion (2a) of Algorithm 13.6 is met only by statement (35). However, on the assumption that no temporary T_i is live at the end of an exit from the loop, then all the rest of the invariant statements, 6, 7, 10, 11, 15, 16, 18, 19, 25, 26, 28, and 29 satisfy (2b).

For example, statement (6) is $T_1 = 0[SP]$. T_1 is used only by statement (7), and the value of T_1 used at (7) is clearly the one defined at (6). Statement (7), in turn, defined T_2, which is only used at (9), and (9) clearly uses the value of T_2 defined at (7). Thus we may move all invariant statements to the pre-header in the order in which they were found by Algorithm 11.4. The new contents of the blocks become:

$$
\begin{array}{lll}
(1) & B_1: & I := 1 \\
(2) & & J := 1 \\
(3) & & K := 1 \\
\\
(6) & B_8: & T_1 := 0[SP] \qquad\qquad \text{/* } B_8 \text{ is the pre-header */}\\
(10) & & T_5 := 4[SP] \\
(15) & & T_9 := 8[SP] \\
(18) & & T_{12} := 4[SP] \\
(25) & & T_{16} := 8[SP]
\end{array}
$$

(28)		$T_{19} := 0[SP]$
(35)		$T_{23} := 2 * N$
(7)		$T_2 := T_1 - 4$
(11)		$T_6 := T_5 - 4$
(16)		$T_{10} := T_9 - 4$
(19)		$T_{13} := T_{12} - 4$
(26)		$T_{17} := T_{16} - 4$
(29)		$T_{20} := T_{19} - 4$
(4)	B_2:	**if I > N goto B_5**
(5)	B_3:	**if J > N goto B_6**
(8)	B_4:	$T_3 := 4 * I$
(9)		$T_4 := T_2[T_3]$
(12)		$T_7 := 4 * J$
(13)		$T_8 := T_6[T_9]$
(14)		**if $T_4 \leq T_8$ goto B_6**
(17)	B_5:	$T_{11} := 4 * K$
(20)		$T_{14} := 4 * J$
(21)		$T_{15} := T_{13}[T_{14}]$
(22)		$T_{10}[T_{11}] := T_{15}$
(23)		$J := J + 1$
(24)		**goto B_7**
(27)	B_6:	$T_{18} := 4 * K$
(30)		$T_{21} := 4 * I$
(31)		$T_{22} := T_{20}[T_{21}]$
(32)		$T_{17}[T_{18}] := T_{22}$
(33)		$I := I + 1$
(34)	B_7:	$K := K + 1$
(36)		**if $K \leq T_{23}$ goto B_2**

□

We can see that an application of the DAG construction Algorithm 12.2 will greatly clean up the pre-header B_8, since each value except $2 * N$ is computed twice. In fact, by assumption, none of the temporaries computed in B_8 are used outside of L, so we can identify T_2 with T_{20}, T_6 with T_{13}, and T_{10} with T_{17}. In the next section we assume this elimination of common subexpressions in B_8 has been done, and uses of T_{20}, T_{13}, and T_{17} are replaced by uses of T_2, T_6, and T_{10}, respectively. In Section 14.5 we shall discuss ''hoisting,'' a technique where identical computations such as T_2

and T_{20} would be merged and moved to the header (not pre-header) of the loop even before it was discovered that they were invariant. If all possible "hoists" were done, and then invariant computations were moved to the pre-header, no simplification of the pre-header would have been necessary.

It should be observed that for large N we have effected considerable speed up, since the amount of time spent in the pre-header is negligible compared with the time spent in B_2, B_3, . . . , B_7.

More General Code Motion

Even if none of conditions (2i), (2ii), and (2iii) of Algorithm 13.5 are met by an assignment A := B **op** C, we can still take the computation B **op** C outside a loop. Create a new temporary T, and set T := B **op** C in the pre-header. Then replace A := B **op** C by A := T in the loop. In many cases we can then propagate out the copy A := T, as discussed in Section 14.3. Note that if condition (2iii) of Algorithm 13.5 is satisfied, that is, all uses of A in loop L are defined at A := B **op** C (now A := T), then we can surely remove statement A := T by replacing uses of A in L by uses of T and placing A := T after each exit of the loop. There is still no guarantee that time will not be lost if parts of the loop can be executed zero times.

13.5 Induction Variable Elimination

In Section 12.2 we discussed variables whose values form an arithmetic progression at the loop header. Often these variables are the ones used to count or index an array. In many cases we find that some multiples of these variables are also computed, and it is frequently possible to get rid of a variable and replace it by one of its multiples. While it is often sufficient to look for a name whose values form an arithmetic progression, we shall take a somewhat more general point of view here. We look for *basic induction variables* of a loop L, which are those names I whose only assignments within loop L are of the form I := I $\pm$ C, where C is a constant or a name whose value does not change within the loop. A basic induction variable might form an arithmetic progression at the header; K is an example in Fig. 13.12. However, it might not; I and J in that figure are examples of basic induction variables that do not form arithmetic progressions.

Definition of Induction Variable

Let us define an *induction variable* of loop L to be either a basic induction variable or a name J for which there is a basic induction variable I such that each time J is assigned in L, J's value is the same linear function of the value of I. Referring again to Fig. 13.12, K is a basic induction variable. Since T_{11} is computed in the loop only by statement (17) $T_{11} := 4 * K$, T_{11} is an induction variable.

A common situation is one in which a basic induction variable like K indexes an array, and some other induction variable, which is a linear function of the basic induction variable, is the actual offset used to probe the array. T_{11} is typical. Often, the only use made of the basic induction variable is in the test for loop termination, as K in statement (36). We can then get rid of the basic induction variable by replacing its test by a test on another induction variable.

In our example, since T_{11} is assigned $4 * K$, we can create a new name S_{4*K} whose value will always be $4 * K$. When K is initialized to 1 before the loop, set $S_{4*K} = 4$, and right after K := K + 1, do $S_{4*K} := S_{4*K} + 4$. We could then replace $T_{11} := 4 * K$ by $T_{11} := S_{4*K}$. Even this might be a savings, since we have replaced the multiplication $4 * K$ by an addition and a copy (although in this case, multiplication by a power of 2 can be implemented by a shift, which generally takes less time than a multiplication, and no more than an addition).

However, we can do more in this instance. Since T_{11} is only used in statement (22) of B_5, one can easily check that S_{4*K} still has the same value as it did when T_{11} was computed at statement (17). Thus we can eliminate (17) altogether and replace the lone use of T_{11} by S_{4*K}.

We can do even more. On the assumption that K is not used outside the loop, we need not ever compute it. The test (36) **if** K $\leqslant$ T_{23} **goto** B_2 can be replaced by

$$S_{4*T_{23}} := 4 * T_{23}$$

if S_{4*K} $\leqslant$ $S_{4*T_{23}}$ **goto** B_2

Then statements (3) K := 1 and (34) K := K + 1 can disappear. Note that $S_{4*T_{23}}$ is loop-invariant and its computation can be moved to the pre-header.

Algorithm 13.7. Detection and elimination of induction variables.

Input. A loop L with ud-chaining information, loop-invariant computation information (from Algorithm 13.4) and live variable information.

Output. A revised loop.

Method.

1. Find all basic induction variables by scanning the statements of L. We use the loop-invariant computation information here.

2. Find additional induction variables. Each such variable A is said to belong to the *family* of some basic induction variable B, and there will be a linear function $F_A(B) = C_1B + C_2$, for some loop constants C_1 and C_2, expressing the value of A, at the point p where it is assigned, in terms of the value of B at p. Note C_1 and C_2 could be functions of both constants and loop invariant names. Specifically, we search for names A with a single assignment to A within L having one of the

following forms:

$$A := B * C, \quad A := C * B, \quad A := B / C, \quad A := B \pm C, \quad A := C \pm B$$

where C is a loop constant, and B is an induction variable, basic or otherwise. There are additional requirements, mentioned below, if B is not basic, however.

   If B is basic, the linear function $F_A(B)$ should be obvious, and A is in the family of B. If B is not basic, let B be in the family of D. Then our additional requirements are that (i) there be no assignment to D between the lone point of assignment to B in L and the assignment to A, and (ii) no definition of B outside L reaches A. The usual case will be where the definitions of A and B are in the same block, in which case it is easy to check; but in any event, a data-flow analysis will provide the check we need. If B is not basic, we compute $F_A(B)$ by substituting $F_A(D)$ into the right side of the lone assignment to B.

3.   Consider each basic induction variable B in turn. For every induction variable A in the family of B:

   i)   create a new name $S_{F_A(B)}$ (but if two names A and A′ have $F_A(B) = F_{A'}(B)$, just create one new name for both).
   ii) Replace the assignment to A by $A := S_{F_A(B)}$.
   iii) Set $S_{F_A(B)}$ to $F_A(B)$ at the end of the pre-header. That is, if $F_A(B) = C_1 B + C_2$, append

   $$S_{F_A(B)} := C_1 * B \quad /* \text{ just } S_{F_A(B)} := B \text{ if } C_1 \text{ is } 1 */$$

   $$S_{F_A(B)} := S_{F_A(B)} + C_2 \quad /* \text{ omit if } C_2 \text{ is } 0 */$$

   iv) Immediately after each assignment $B := B + D$, where D is loop-invariant, append:

   $$S_{F_A(B)} := S_{F_A(B)} + C_1 * D$$

   where $F_A(B) = C_1 B + C_2$. If D is a loop-invariant name and $C_1 \neq 1$, create a new loop-invariant temporary for $C_1 * D$.

4.   Then, for each basic induction variable B whose only uses are to compute other induction variables in its family and in conditional branches, take some A in B's family, preferably one such that $F_A(B)$ is as simple as possible, and replace each test of the form **if B relop** X **goto** Y by

   $$R := C_1 * X \quad /* R := X \text{ if } C_1 \text{ is } 1 */$$

   $$R := R + C_2 \quad /* \text{ omit if } C_2 \text{ is } 0 */$$

   if $S_{F_A(B)}$ **relop** R **goto** Y

where $F_A(B) = C_1 B + C_2$ and R is a new temporary. Handle

if X **relop** B **goto** Y analogously. Then delete all assignments to B from the loop, as they will now be useless.

5. Now, consider each induction variable A from step (3). If there can be no assignment to $S_{F_A(B)}$ between the introduced statement $A := S_{F_A(B)}$ of step (3ii) and any use of A (data-flow analysis is needed to tell, but in the usual situation A is used only in the block in which it is defined, so the test is then easy), then replace all uses of A by uses of $S_{F_A(B)}$ and delete statement $A := S_{F_A(B)}$. □

Example 13.18. We shall apply Algorithm 13.6 to the basic blocks created in Example 13.17. In step (1) we find that I, J and K are basic induction variables. In step (2) we find T_3 and T_{21} are induction variables in the family of I, with $F_{T_3}(I) = F_{T_{21}}(I) = 4 * I$. Similarly, T_7 and T_{14} are in the family of J, and their linear functions are both $4 * J$. T_{11} and T_{18} are in the family of K, both with the linear function $4 * K$.

In step (3) we find that the only uses of I, J, and K are in tests and to compute the induction variables in their families. Thus, all our basic induction variables qualify for step (3). We shall discuss the treatment of I; the treatment of J and K in steps (3) and (4) are similar. We create a new name S_{4*I} and replace statements (8) and (30) by $T_3 := S_{4*I}$ and $T_{21} := S_{4*I}$, respectively. In step (3iii), at the end of the pre-header we introduce statement $S_{4*I} := 4 * I$. It happens that the only definition of I reaching this point is $I := 1$ from block B_1. We shall deduce this in Chapter 14 when we discuss constant folding. At that time we shall replace $S_{4*I} := 4 * I$ by $S_{4*I} := 4$. Lastly, in step (3iv) we follow (33) $I := I + 1$ by $S_{4*I} := S_{4*I} + 4$.

In step (4) applied to I, we replace (4) **if** $I > N$ **goto** B_5 by

$$R_1 := 4 * N$$
$$\text{if } S_{4*I} > R_1 \text{ goto } B_5$$

We may move the computation of R_1 to the pre-header, even if we have already done code motion of loop-invariant statements, as we can tell that the introduced computation of R_1 is the only computation of newly created name R_1, and N was found loop-invariant by Algorithm 12.4. We delete statement (33) $I := I + 1$.

Let us now take up step (5) for the family of I. Again, the handling of the families of J and K is similar. The only uses of T_3 and T_{21} are in their respective blocks, B_4 and B_6, and no assignments to S_{4*I} intervene. (In general, a data-flow analysis is needed to make this determination.) We therefore replace (9) $T_4 := T_2[T_3]$ by $T_4 := T_2[S_{4*I}]$ and (31) $T_{22} := T_2[T_{21}]$† by $T_{22} := T_2[S_{4*I}]$, removing statements (8) $T_3 := S_{4*I}$ and (30) $T_{21} := S_{4*I}$.

---

†Recall that T_2 and T_{20} have been identified, as have been $T_{13} - T_6$ and $T_{17} - T_{10}$.

After doing the analogous steps for J and K, we are left with the following contents of blocks. Recall that the preheader B_8 has been cleared of common subexpressions by Algorithm 12.2. Also, copy steps $T_{20} := T_2$, $T_{13} := T_6$ and $T_{17} := T_{10}$ have been removed by an algorithm to be described in Section 14.3.

(1)	B_1:	$I := 1$
(2)		$J := 1$
(3)		$K := 1$
(6)	B_8:	$T_1 := 0[SP]$
(10)		$T_5 := 4[SP]$
(15)		$T_9 := 8[SP]$
(35)		$T_{23} := 2 * N$
(7)		$T_2 := T_1 - 4$
(11)		$T_6 := T_5 - 4$
(16)		$T_{10} := T_9 - 4$
		$S_{4*I} := 4 * I$
		$S_{4*J} := 4 * J$
		$S_{4*K} := 4 * K$
		$R_1 := 4 * N$
		$R_2 := 4 * T_{23}$
(4)	B_2:	**if** $S_{4*I} > R_1$ **goto** B_5
(5)	B_3:	**if** $S_{4*J} > R_1$ **goto** B_6
(9)	B_4:	$T_4 := T_2[S_{4*I}]$
(13)		$T_8 := T_6[S_{4*J}]$
(14)		**if** $T_4 \leqslant T_8$ **goto** B_6
(21)	B_5:	$T_{15} := T_6[S_{4*J}]$
(22)		$T_{10}[S_{4*K}] := T_{15}$
		$S_{4*J} := S_{4*J} + 4$
(24)		**goto** B_7
(31)	B_6:	$T_{22} := T_2[S_{4*I}]$
(32)		$T_{10}[S_{4*K}] := T_{22}$
		$S_{4*I} := S_{4*I} + 4$
	B_7:	$S_{4*K} := S_{4*K} + 4$
(36)		**if** $S_{4*K} \leqslant R_2$ **goto** B_2

To compare the quality of the produced code with that of the original, let us assume N is large, so we may neglect B_1 and B_8, which are outside the loop. If the merge is performed on "random" sorted lists, we may assume that the tests $I > N$ and $J > N$ in blocks B_2 and B_3 will almost never be satisfied, so on the average iteration of the loop we shall execute B_2, B_3, B_4, and B_7 almost always and B_5 and B_6 about half the time. Our figure of merit is thus the sum of the lengths of B_2, B_3, B_4 and B_7 plus one half the lengths of B_5 and B_6. This number for the original code is 23½, while for the optimized code it is 10½. Thus for large sorted lists, the optimized code takes about 45% of the time of the original. □

13.6 Some Other Loop Optimizations

Let us briefly mention some other transformations which can make loops execute more quickly.

Loop Unrolling

The first optimization, called *loop unrolling,* avoids a test at every iteration by recognizing that the number of iterations is constant and replicating the body of the loop.

Example 13.19. Suppose we have a loop like

```
begin
    I := 1;
    while I ≤ 100 do
        begin
            A[I] := 0;
            I := I + 1
        end
end
```

The three-address equivalent will initialize I to 1, and test $I \le 100$ each time through. Replacement of I by another induction variable will not obviate the need for 100 tests. We could do with 50 tests if we converted the code to

```
begin
    I := 1;
    while I ≤ 100 do
        begin
            A[I] := 0;
            I := I + 1;
            A[I] := 0;
            I := I + 1
        end
end                                                        □
```

This transformation could be done either at the source code level or in intermediate code. The problem is how to detect loops that are executed some constant number of times. Part of the problem is to find induction variables whose values form arithmetic progressions, that is, they are incremented once, by the same amount, each time through the loop. We leave an algorithm to detect opportunities for loop unrolling to the reader.

Obviously, one could choose any divisor of the number of times through the loop and replicate the body that number of times, even to the extent of replacing the loop by a straight line sequence of statements. There is clearly a trade-off of space for time here, so it does not pay to unroll too much. Unrolling once (i.e., making two copies of the body) already saves 50% of the maximum possible.

Loop Jamming

A related idea, called *loop jamming,* is to merge the bodies of two loops. It is necessary that each loop be executed the same number of times and that the indices be the same. A sufficient condition for loop jamming to be legal is that no quantity is computed by the second loop at iteration i if it is computed by the first loop at iteration $j \geq i$, nor is a value used by the second loop at iteration i if it is computed by the first loop at iteration $j \geq i$. The reward of loop jamming is that the tests of one loop disappear.

Example 13.20. The two loops which initialize a matrix to be an identity matrix:

```
begin
    for I := 1 to 10 do
        for J := 1 to 10 do
            A[I, J] := 0;   /* zero the matrix */
    for I := 1 to 10 do
        A[I, I] := 1    /* put 1's along the diagonal */
end
```

can be jammed by concatenating the bodies of the two loops on I to form

```
for I := 1 to 10 do
    begin
        for J := 1 to 10 do
            A[I, J] := 0;
        A[I, I] := 1
    end                                                      □
```

We leave to the reader the design of an algorithm to test for the safety and feasibility of loop jamming. We may do the transformation either at the source or intermediate code level.

Exercises

13.1 The program of Fig. 13.13 counts the primes from 2 to N using the sieve method on a suitably large array. Fig. 13.14 gives the flow graph of this program.

```
begin
        read N;
        for i := 2 to N do
            A[i] := true;   /* initialize */
        COUNT := 0;
        for i := 2 to N ** .5 do
            if A[i] then   /* i is a prime */
                begin
                    COUNT := COUNT + 1;
                    for j := 2 * i to N by i do
                        A[j] := false   /* j is divisible by i */
                end;
        print COUNT
end
```

Fig. 13.13. Calculation of primes.

a) Translate the program of Fig. 13.13 into three-address statements assuming A is allocated static storage and the target machine is byte-addressed, with four bytes per word. Show the code for each block of Fig. 13.14.

b) Show the dominator tree for Fig. 13.14.

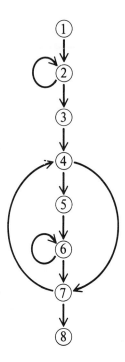

Fig. 13.14. Flow graph for Fig. 13.13.

c) Indicate the back edges of Fig. 13.14 and their natural loops.
d) Move invariant computations out of loops using Algorithm 13.5.
e) Do the same using Algorithm 13.6.
f) Eliminate induction variables wherever possible.
g) Propagate out copy statements wherever possible.
h) Is loop jamming possible? If so, do it.
i) On the assumption that N will always be even, unroll inner loops once each.

13.2 Repeat Exercise 13.1 (d) through (i) on the assumption that A is allocated dynamic storage, with PTR a pointer to the first word of A.

13.3 Is Fig. 13.14 a reducible flow graph?

*13.4 Let G be a flow graph and n a node of G. The *interval with header n,* denoted $I(n)$, is defined as follows.

i) n is in $I(n)$.
ii) If m is not the initial node of G and all predecessors of m are in $I(n)$, then place m in $I(n)$.
iii) Nothing is in $I(n)$ unless it follows from (i) and (ii).

a) Show that the same interval results, no matter in what order we choose the candidates m in rule (ii). *Hint.* Show that if m is at some time a candidate and is not immediately selected, it remains a candidate.

b) Find the interval of each node of Fig. 13.14.

*13.5 The *interval partition* Π of a flow graph G is defined as follows.

i) If n_0 is the initial node of G, then $I(n_0)$ is in Π.

ii) If n is a node of G, n has a predecessor in an interval of Π, but n is not in any interval of Π, then place $I(n)$ in Π.

iii) No interval is in Π unless its being so follows from (i) and (ii).

a) Show that the order in which candidates n are selected in (ii) does not affect the interval partition.

b) Show that the intervals in Π are disjoint and, on the assumption that every node is reachable from the initial node, each node is in one interval of Π.

c) Find the interval partition of Fig. 13.14.

13.6 The *reduced graph* $I(G)$ for a flow graph G has a node for each interval partition of G. If G has an edge $n \rightarrow m$, and n and m are in different intervals (note m must be an interval header; can you prove this?), then $I(G)$ has an edge from the interval containing n to that of m. The initial node of $I(G)$ is the interval of the initial node of G.

a) Find $I(G)$ for G of Fig. 13.14.

b) Find the reduced graph of your answer to (a), and repeatedly take reduced graphs until no changes occur.

**13.7 The result of applying the reduced graph operator to G until no changes occur results in the *limit flow graph* of G, denoted $\hat{I}(G)$. The condition that $\hat{I}(G)$ be a single node is the original definition of a reducible flow graph from Allen [1970]. Prove that this definition is equivalent to the definition of "reducible flow graph" used in this book.

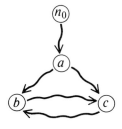

Fig. 13.15. Forbidden subgraph for reducible flow graphs.

**13.8 Show that a flow graph is reducible if and only if it does not have a subgraph of the form shown in Fig. 13.15. Here, n_0 is the initial node, and n_0, a, b, and c are distinct nodes, with the exception that a may be n_0. The wavy lines are mutually node-disjoint paths (except for the endpoints, of course).

Bibliographic Notes

The notion of a loop and the detection of loops has undergone some evolution. Allen [1969] uses a strongly connected component as a model of a loop. Lowry and Medlock [1969] use the dominator idea to discover loops, and Allen [1970] describes intervals, which were introduced in the exercises. All these ideas are essentially the same for reducible flow graphs, although intervals sometimes include acyclic structures that are not really loops.

The use of dominators, both for loop selection and for code motion, was pioneered by Lowry and Medlock [1969], although the general idea is attributed to Prosser [1959]. The dominator-finding algorithm (13.2) is from Purdom and Moore [1972] and Aho and Ullman [1973a]. The dominator algorithm of Section 13.3 can be found in Hecht and Ullman [1975], and the asymptotically most efficient way known to do the job is in Tarjan [1974a].

Reducible flow graphs were defined in Allen [1970]. The characterization used here is from Hecht and Ullman [1974], and other properties of these graphs can be found in Hecht and Ullman [1972], Kasyanov [1973] and Tarjan [1974b]. Exercises 13.7 and 13.8 are from Hecht and Ullman [1974 and 1972, respectively]. The use of "node splitting" to convert nonreducible graphs into reducible ones is from Cocke and Miller [1969].

Gear [1965] introduced the basic loop optimizations of code motion and a limited form of induction variable elimination. Allen [1969] gives the form of induction variable elimination discussed in Chapter 12, while the more complex form discussed in this chapter is modeled after the approach of Lowry and Medlock [1969]. Allen, Cocke, and Kennedy [1975] describe a more general algorithm.

Other loop optimizations are described in Allen [1969] and Allen and Cocke [1972]. Earley [1975b], Fong and Ullman [1976], and Paige and Schwartz [1977] discuss the elimination of induction variables in "very high-level languages." Neel and Amirchahy [1975] discuss an algorithm for loop-invariant code motion.

Wulf et al. [1975], Zelkowitz and Bail [1974], Hecht and Shaffer [1975], and Hecht [1977] discuss loop optimization by "recursive descent" in languages where flow graphs are known to be reducible and the flow graph structure can be easily deduced from a syntactic analysis of the program.

The idea that structured flow of control is modeled by reducible flow graphs is expressed in Kosaraju [1974], Kasami, Peterson, and Tokura [1973] and Cherniavsky, Henderson, and Keohane [1976]. Baker [1977] describes the use of reducible flow graphs in a program structuring algorithm.

CHAPTER 14

More About
Data-Flow
Analysis

This chapter presents the information-gathering algorithms needed to implement safely the optimizations of the previous two chapters. Our first goal is to develop techniques for performing a global data-flow analysis in a single subroutine of a FORTRAN-like language. Then we shall consider the flow of data in the presence of pointers and across subroutine calls.

14.1 Reaching Definitions Again

Let us reconsider ud-chaining, first introduced in Section 12.5. For each node n of a flow graph, we want to determine $IN[n]$, the set of definitions (assignments or reads) that reach the beginning of n. A definition d of name A is said to *reach* node n if there is a path $n_1, n_2, \ldots, n_k, n$ in the flow graph such that

1. d is within n_1,
2. d is not subsequently killed in n_1 (i.e., A is not redefined), and
3. d is not killed in any of $n_2, n_3, \ldots, n_k$.

If conditions (1) through (3) hold, we say that d is *generated* within n_1 and *propagated* along the path $n_1, n_2, \ldots, n_k, n$.

One way of calculating $IN[n]$ is to determine all generated definitions and then to propagate each definition from the point of generation to n. Fortunately, if a definition propagates to n it does so along a cycle-free path. We discussed an easy way to do this propagation by solving the following set of $2N$ simultaneous equations for a flow graph of N nodes.

$$OUT[n] = IN[n] - KILL[n] \cup GEN[n]$$

$$IN[n] = \bigcup_{\substack{p \text{ a pred-} \\ \text{ecessor of } n}} OUT[p] \qquad (14.1)$$

where OUT is analogous to IN, but pertains to the point immediately after the end of basic block n; $KILL[n]$ is the set of definitions which are killed within n, and $GEN[n]$ is the set of definitions generated within n.

Algorithm 12.2 for solving set of equations (14.1) works by starting with the assumption that nothing reaches n and then repeatedly getting a better approximation by computing IN[n] and OUT[n] for all n, using equations (14.1). Recall from Section 12.5 that the solution to (14.1) is not unique, and that we actually want the smallest possible solution. That explains why we should start with the assumption IN[n] = ϕ for all n.

There is one improvement to Algorithm 12.2 that we can make, based on our knowledge of depth-first search from Section 13.3. In particular, as we pass over the nodes computing IN, we do so in a depth-first order. We discussed in Section 13.3 the fact that an average of five passes will be necessary if we choose this order, although there are pathological flow graphs for which a number of passes equal to the number of nodes of the flow graph are necessary. We give the revised algorithm next.

Algorithm 14.1. Reaching definitions using depth-first ordering.

Input. A flow graph G with N nodes with KILL[n] and GEN[n] computed.

Output. IN[n] for each node n.

Method.

1. Compute DFN[n] for each node n, using Algorithm 13.3. We shall assume from here on that the nodes are indexed by their depth-first numbers; that is, DFN[n_i] = i.
2. Execute the propagation algorithm of Fig. 14.1. CHANGE is a Boolean flag indicating whether a change has occurred on the current pass, and NEWIN is a temporary used to check for a change.   □

By this time, we should have a clear idea of how ud-chaining is used in an optimizing compiler. In Section 13.4 we saw that it was used to detect loop-invariant computations and in Section 13.5 we saw how it was used to help perform induction variable removal. We have also mentioned that we can use ud-chaining to detect potentially undefined names by introducing a dummy definition of each name A preceding the initial node of the flow graph, and seeing whether the dummy definition of A reaches any block that has a use of A and does not define A before that use.

Constant Folding

We also alluded in Section 12.5 to the fact that ud-chaining could be used for *constant folding,* that is, replacing expressions by their value if the value can be computed at compile time. For example, in a language without compile-time macros or symbolic constants, one might see the following code.

```
begin
    for i := 1 to N do IN[i] := OUT[i] := φ; /* initialize */
    CHANGE := true; /* to get the iteration started */
    while CHANGE do
        begin
            CHANGE := false;
            for i := 1 to N do
                begin
                    NEWIN :=      ∪      OUT[p];
                             p a pred-
                             ecessor of nᵢ
                    /* nᵢ is the node for which DFN[n] = i */
                    if IN[nᵢ] ≠ NEWIN then
                        begin
                            IN[nᵢ] := NEWIN;
                            OUT[nᵢ] := IN[nᵢ] − KILL[nᵢ] ∪ GEN[nᵢ];
                            CHANGE := true
                        end
                end
        end
end
```

Fig. 14.1. Reaching definitions.

```
SIZE := 100
        .
        .
        .
for I := 0 to SIZE − 1 do
```

In intermediate code partitioned into basic blocks, we might find the situation depicted in Fig. 14.2.

If we determine that the only definition of SIZE that can reach B_3 is SIZE := 100 in B_1, then we can compute T := 99 in B_3. By examining B_3, we can determine that the only definition of T in **if** I ⩽ T **goto** B_2 is T := 99. Thus, we can replace **if** I ⩽ T **goto** B_2 by **if** I ⩽ 99 **goto** B_2, which is less costly to implement in many machine architectures. Moreover, if T is not live on exit from B_3 (a data-flow analysis discussed in Section 14.4 can determine this), we can eliminate T := SIZE − 1 from B_3 altogether. Finally, if all uses of SIZE can be handled in this way, we can eliminate SIZE := 100 from B_1. An algorithm to perform constant folding follows.

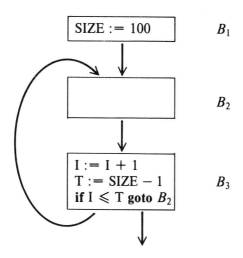

Fig. 14.2. Example of possible constant folding.

Algorithm 14.2. Constant folding.

Input. A flow graph with ud-chaining information computed by Algorithm 14.1.

Output. A revised flow graph.

Method. Execute the program of Fig. 14.3. □

```
while changes occur do /* we elide the detection of changes
        such as the use of CHANGE and NEWIN in Fig. 14.1 */
    for all statements s of the program do
        begin
            for each operand B of s do
                if there is a unique definition of B that reaches s
                    and that definition is of the form B := c for a
                    constant c then replace B by c in s;
                if all operands of s are now constants then
                    begin
                        evaluate the right side of s;
                        replace s by A := e, where A is the name
                            assigned to by s and e is the value of the
                            right side of s
                    end
        end
```

Fig. 14.3. Constant folding.

14.2 Available Expressions

We have seen in Section 12.3 how the DAG representation of a basic block can help us detect *common subexpressions* within the block, that is, two or more statements that compute the same value. We could then eliminate all but one computation of each value. But what if an expression is computed twice, once each in two different blocks, as in Fig. 14.4? First, can we be sure that T_1 in block B_1 and T_2 in B_2 are assigned the same value? If I is assigned a new value along some path from B_1 to B_2, then T_2 will, in general, receive a different value from that of T_1, and $4 * I$ is not really a common subexpression between B_1 and B_2.

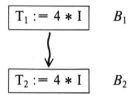

Fig. 14.4. Common subexpression across blocks.

A second potential problem is that there might be some way to get to B_2 without evaluating $4 * I$. In that case, we would have to reevaluate $4 * I$ at B_2 or before reaching B_2, even though it was evaluated along some of the paths to B_2. Supposing none of these problems occur, we can introduce a new name S, replace $T_1 := 4 * I$ in B_1 by

$$S := 4 * I$$
$$T_1 := S$$

and replace $T_2 := 4 * I$ in B_2 by

$$T_2 := S$$

We have thus replaced the computation of $4 * I$ by two copy operations, $T_1 := S$ and $T_2 := S$. Whether we have saved time or space or both depends on the details of the machine and of our code-generation algorithm. For example, is it possible to keep S in a register? If so, then we have surely saved. In many cases, we can improve the situation still further by "copy propagation" as discussed in Section 14.3. That is, uses of T_1 and/or T_2 may be replaced by uses of S in certain circumstances. If we can eliminate even one of the assignments $T_1 := S$ and $T_2 := S$, then a sure savings results.

If T_1 is a temporary name, defined and used once, then we can compute $T_1 := 4 * I$ in B_1 and replace $T_2 := 4 * I$ by $T_2 := T_1$. If T_2 is also defined and used only once, then we can replace the use of T_2 by T_1 and never define T_2. This common situation enables us to eliminate an entire

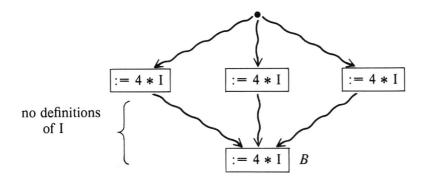

Fig. 14.5. General instance of an available expression.

three-address statement.

In Fig. 14.5 we see a somewhat more general situation. In block B is a computation of $4 * I$, and we imagine that all paths to B from the initial node (including paths with cycles) pass through a block that evaluates $4 * I$, although different paths may pass through different evaluations of $4 * I$. Each path to the use of $4 * I$ in B does not change the value of I after the last evaluation of $4 * I$. In this case we may create a new name S and determine which statements with $4 * I$ on the right reach $4 * I$ in B (reaching definition information is used). We replace each of these statements, say A := $4 * I$, by S := $4 * I$ and A := S. Then we replace the use of $4 * I$ in B by S.

Available Expressions

In order to detect situations like the one above we must solve a data-flow problem called *available expressions.* An expression X **op** Y is *available* at a point p if every path (not necessarily cycle-free) from the initial node to p evaluates X **op** Y, and after the last such evaluation prior to reaching p, there are no subsequent assignments to X or Y.

In computing available expressions, we need to know when a block kills an expression or generates an expression. We say that a block *kills* expression X **op** Y if it assigns X or Y and does not subsequently recompute X **op** Y. A block *generates* expression X **op** Y if it evaluates X **op** Y and does not subsequently redefine X or Y.

Example 14.1. The block

A := B + C
B := D * E
F := B + C
D := D − F

generates B+C because it evaluates B+C at the third statement, and neither the third nor the fourth statement assigns to B or C. The evaluation of B+C at the first statement does not cause B+C to be generated, since B is redefined subsequently, at the second statement. Neither D∗E nor D−F is generated, since D is redefined at the fourth statement, following the evaluation of these two expressions. Note that in an assignment statement, the assignment to the name on the left occurs after the evaluation of the expression on the right.

Any expression involving D is killed in the above block, since an assignment to D is the last thing that happens. Other expressions such as A+G or B−C are also killed since they are not evaluated, and one of their operands is defined in the block.   □

We can find available expressions in a manner reminiscent of the way reaching definitions are computed. Suppose U is the "universal" set of all expressions appearing on the right of one or more statements of the program. For each node n, let IN[n] be the set of expressions in U that are available at the point just before the beginning of n. Let OUT[n] be the same for the point following the end of n. Define $E\_GEN[n]$ to be the expressions generated by n and $E\_KILL[n]$ to be the set of expressions in U killed in n. Note that IN, OUT, E_GEN, and E_KILL can all be represented by bit vectors. The following equations relate the unknowns IN and OUT to each other and the known quantities E_GEN and E_KILL.

$$\text{OUT}[n] = \text{IN}[n] - E\_\text{KILL}[n] \cup E\_\text{GEN}[n]$$

$$\text{IN}[n] = \bigcap_{\substack{p \text{ a pred-} \\ \text{ecessor of } n}} \text{OUT}[p] \quad \text{for } n \text{ not initial} \qquad (14.2)$$

$$\text{IN}[n_0] = \phi \quad \text{where } n_0 \text{ is the initial node.}$$

The equations (14.2) look almost identical to equations (14.1) for reaching definitions. The first difference is that IN for the initial node is handled as a special case. This is justified on the grounds that nothing is available if the program has just begun at the initial node, even though some expression might be available along all paths to the initial node from elsewhere in the program.

The second, and more important, difference is that the operator combining OUT's to form an IN is intersection rather than union. This operator is the proper one because an expression is available at the beginning of a block only if it is available at the end of all its predecessors. In contrast, a definition reaches the beginning of a block whenever it reaches the end of one or more of its predecessors.

The use of the ∩ rather than ∪ makes equations (14.2) behave in a sense backwards from (14.1). While neither set has a unique solution, for (14.1) it is the smallest solution that corresponds to the definition of "reaching," and we obtained that solution by starting with the assumption that nothing reached anywhere, and building up to the solution. In that way, we never assumed that a definition d could reach a point p unless an actual path propagating d to p could be found. In contrast, for equations (14.2) we want the largest possible solution, so we start with an approximation that is too large and work down.

It may not be obvious that by starting with the assumption that "everything is available everywhere" and eliminating only those expressions for which we can discover a path along which it is not available, we do reach a set of truly available expressions. Such is the case, however, and a proof is left to the interested reader. The bibliographic notes contain references on the correctness of this algorithm.

One way to obtain an initial approximation is to set IN of the initial node to ϕ and OUT$[n]$ to $U - E\_KILL[n]$, for n not initial. Here, U is the universal set of expressions.

Algorithm 14.3. Available expressions.

Input. A flow graph G with N nodes with $E\_KILL[n]$ and $E\_GEN[n]$ computed.

Output. IN$[n]$ for each node n.

Method.

1. Compute DFN$[n]$ for each node n using Algorithm 12.4. Store this information as a list of nodes $n_1, n_2, \ldots, n_N$ such that DFN$[n_i] = i$.
2. Execute the algorithm of Fig. 14.6. $\square$

Elimination of Global Common Subexpressions

Let us now see how available expressions are used in common subexpression elimination. The next algorithm formalizes the intuitive ideas presented at the beginning of the section.

Algorithm 14.4. Global Common Subexpression Elimination.

Input. A flow graph with available expression and reaching definitions information.

Output. A revised flow graph.

Method. For every statement s of the form A := B **op** C such that B **op** C is available at the beginning of s's block, and neither B nor C is defined prior to statement s in that block, do the following.

1. Find all definitions which reach s's block and which have B **op** C on the right.

```
begin
   IN[n₁] := φ;
   OUT[n₁] := E_GEN[n₁];
      /* IN and OUT never change for the initial node, n₁ */
   for i := 2 to N do
      begin
         IN[nᵢ] := U;
         OUT[nᵢ] := U − E_KILL[nᵢ]
      end
      /* above initializes to too large a solution */
   CHANGE := true;
   while CHANGE do
      begin
         CHANGE := false;
         for i := 2 to N do
            begin
               NEWIN :=      ∩      OUT[p];
                          p a pred-
                          ecessor of nᵢ
               if IN[nᵢ] ≠ NEWIN then
                  begin
                     IN[nᵢ] := NEWIN;
                     OUT[nᵢ] := IN[nᵢ] − E_KILL[nᵢ] ∪ E_GEN[nᵢ];
                     CHANGE := true
                  end
            end
      end
end
```

Fig. 14.6. Available expressions computation.

2. Create a new name T.
3. Replace each statement D := B **op** C found in (1) by

$$T := B \ op \ C$$
$$D := T$$

4. Replace statement s by A := T.   □

Note that global common subexpression elimination is not a substitute for elimination of subexpressions within a single block; both must be performed. Also, Algorithm 14.4 will not catch deep common subexpressions such as

$$X := A + B \qquad T := A + B$$
$$Y := X * C \quad \text{vs.} \quad S := T * C$$

Kildall [1973] presents a method for catching such expressions on one pass. However, they can be caught with multiple passes of Algorithm 14.4, and one might consider repeating it until no further changes occur. Finally, we should realize that not all changes made by Algorithm 14.4 are improvements. We might wish to limit the number of different expressions reaching s found in step (1), probably to one. However, copy propagation, to be discussed next, often allows benefit to be obtained even when several definitions with B **op** C reach s.

14.3 Copy Propagation

Algorithm 14.4 just presented, and various other algorithms such as Algorithm 13.7 on induction variable elimination, introduce copy steps (*copies*) of the form A := B. Copies may also be directly generated by the intermediate code generator, although most of these have effects local to one block and can be removed by the DAG construction of Algorithm 12.4. It is possible to eliminate statement s: A := B if we determine all places where this definition of A is used. We may then substitute B for A in all these places, provided these conditions are met by every such use u of A:

1. Statement s must be the only definition of A reaching u (that is, the ud-chain for use u consists only of s).
2. On every path from s to u, including paths that go through u several times (but do not go through s a second time), there are no assignments to B.

Condition (1) can be checked using ud-chaining information, but what of condition (2)? We must set up a new data-flow analysis problem in which IN[n] is the set of copies A := B such that every path from the initial node to the beginning of n contains the statement A := B, and subsequent to the last occurrence of A := B, there are no assignments to B. OUT[n] can be defined correspondingly, but with respect to the end of n. We say copy statement s: A := B is *generated* in block n if s occurs in n and there is no subsequent assignment to B within n. We say s: A := B is *killed* in n if A or B is assigned there and s is not in n. The notion that assignments to A "kill" A := B is familiar from reaching definitions, but the idea that assignments to B do so is special to this problem.

Let U be the "universal" set of all copy statements in the program. Define C_GEN[n] to be the set of all copies generated in n and C_KILL[n] to be the set of copies in U which are killed in n. Then the following equations relate the quantities defined:

$$\text{OUT}[n] = \text{IN}[n] - C\_KILL[n] \cup C\_GEN[n]$$

$$\text{IN}[n] = \bigcap_{\substack{p \text{ a pred-}\\ \text{ecessor of } n}} \text{OUT}[n] \quad \text{for } n \text{ not initial} \qquad (14.3)$$

$$\text{IN}[n_0] = \phi \quad \text{where } n_0 \text{ is the initial node}$$

Equations (14.3) are identical to Equations (14.2), if C_KILL is replaced by E_KILL and C_GEN by E_GEN. Thus, (14.3) can be solved by Algorithm 14.3, and we shall not discuss the matter further. We shall, however, give an example which exposes some of the nuances of copy optimization.

Example 14.2. Consider the flowchart of Fig. 14.7. $C\_GEN[n_1]$ = $\{A:=B\}$ and $C\_GEN[n_3]$ = $\{A:=C\}$. $C\_KILL[n_2]$ = $\{A:=B\}$, since B is assigned in n_2. $C\_KILL[n_1]$ = $\{A:=C\}$ since A is assigned in n_1 and $C\_KILL[n_3]$ = $\{A:=B\}$ for the same reason.

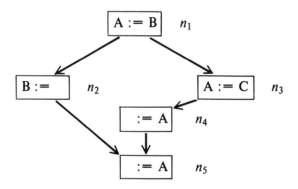

Fig. 14.7. Example flow graph.

Other C_GEN's and C_KILL's are ϕ. $IN[n_1] = \phi$ by Equations (14.3). Algorithm 14.3 in one pass determines that $IN[n_2]$ = $IN[n_3]$ = $OUT[n_1]$ = $\{A:=B\}$. Likewise, $OUT[n_2] = \phi$ and $OUT[n_3]$ = $IN[n_4]$ = $OUT[n_4]$ = $\{A:=C\}$. Finally, $IN[n_5]$ = $OUT[n_2] \cap OUT[n_4]$ = ϕ.

We observe that neither copy $A := B$ nor $A := C$ "reaches" the use of A in n_5, in the sense of Algorithm 14.4. However, both these definitions of A "reach" n_5 in the context of reaching definitions. Thus, neither copy may be optimized, as it is not possible to substitute B (respectively C) for A in all uses of A that definition $A := B$ (respectively $A := C$) reaches. □

We now specify the details of the algorithm to remove copy statements.

Algorithm 14.5. Copy propagation.

Input. A flow graph G, with ud-chaining information represented by sets $R\_IN[n]$ giving the definitions reaching node n, and with $C\_IN[n]$ representing the solution to Equations (14.3), that is, the set of copies $A := B$ that reach node n along every path, with no assignment to A or B following the last occurrence of $A := B$ on the path.

Output. A revised flow graph.

Method. For each copy *s*: A := B do the following.

1. Determine those uses of A which are reached by the definition of A, namely, *s*: A := B.[†]
2. Determine whether for every use of A found in (1), *s* is in C_IN[*n*], where *n* is the block of this particular use, and moreover, no definitions of A or B occur prior to this use of A within *n*.
3. If *s* meets the conditions of (2), then remove *s* and replace all uses of A found in (1) by B.   □

14.4 Backward Flow Problems

Live Variables

There are a number of code optimizations that depend on information computed in the direction opposite to the flow of control in a program. A typical example is live variable analysis. Here we wish to know for name A and point *p* whether the value of A at *p* could be used along some path in the flow graph starting at *p*. If so, we say A is *live* at *p*; otherwise A is *dead* at *p*. In Algorithm 13.5 we saw how it was important to know whether a name was live at points following the exits of a loop.

Another, more important use for live variable information comes when we generate object code. After a value is computed in a register, and presumably used within a block, it is not necessary to store that value if it is dead at the end of the block. Also, if all registers are full and we need another register, we should favor using a register with a dead value since that value does not have to be stored. These matters are discussed more fully in Chapter 15.

Let us define IN[*n*] to be the set of names live at the point immediately before block *n* and define OUT[*n*] to be the same immediately after the block. Let DEF[*n*] be the set of names assigned values in *n* prior to any use of that name in *n*, and let USE[*n*] be the set of names used in *n* prior to any definition thereof. Then the equations relating DEF and USE to the unknowns IN and OUT are:

$$\text{IN}[n] = \text{OUT}[n] - \text{DEF}[n] \cup \text{USE}[n]$$

$$\text{OUT}[n] = \bigcup_{\substack{s \text{ a suc-}\\ \text{cessor of } n}} \text{IN}[s] \tag{14.4}$$

---

† It would be more useful here if ud-chaining information were presented in inverse form (du-chaining) as discussed in the next section. However, this determination can surely be made from R_IN.

The first group of equations say that a name is live coming into a block if it either is used before redefinition in the block or is live coming out of the block and is not redefined in the block. The second group of equations says that a name is live coming out of a block if and only if it is live coming into one of its successors.

The relation between (14.4) and the ud-chaining equations (14.1) should be noticed. Here, IN and OUT have their roles interchanged, and USE and DEF substitute for GEN and KILL, respectively. As for (14.1), the solution to (14.4) is not necessarily unique, and we want the smallest solution. The algorithm used for the minimum solution is akin to Algorithm 14.1. However, to take advantage of the fact that the depth (largest number of retreating edges on a cycle-free path) tends to be small, we must use reverse depth-first ordering for this "backward flowing" problem.

Algorithm 14.6. Live variable analysis.

Input. A flow graph with N nodes.

Output. OUT[n], the set of names live on exit from each block n of the flow graph.

Method.

1. Compute a depth-first ordering of the nodes. Let the nodes be $n_1, n_2, \ldots, n_N$, such that DFN[n_i] = i.

2. Compute IN and OUT by the algorithm of Fig. 14.8. In that algorithm, the mechanism for detecting changes, similar to what was done in previous data-flow algorithms, is elided. □

```
begin
    for i := 1 to N do IN[n] := φ;
    while changes occur do
        for i := n to 1 by −1 do /* in reverse depth-first order */
            begin
                OUT[n_i] :=    ∪    IN[s];
                            s a suc-
                           cessor of n_i
                IN[n_i] := OUT[n_i] − DEF[n_i] ∪ USE[n_i]
            end
end
```

Fig. 14.8. Live variable calculation.

Definition-Use Chains

A calculation done in virtually the same manner as live variable analysis is *definition-use chaining* (du-chaining). We say a name is *used* at statement s if its r-value is required. For example, B and C (but not A) are used in statement A := B + C, A[B] := C and A := B[C]. The du-chaining problem is to compute for a point p the set of uses s of a name, say B, such that there is a path from p to s that does not redefine B. As with live variables, if we can compute OUT[n], the set of uses reachable from the end of block n, for all blocks n, then we can compute the definitions reached from any point p within block n by scanning the portion of block n that follows p. In particular, if there is a definition of name B in the block, we can determine the *du-chain* for that definition, the list of all possible uses of that definition. The method is completely analogous to that of Section 12.5.

The equations for computing du-chaining information look exactly like (14.4) with substitution for DEF and USE. In place of USE[n], take the set of *upwards exposed* uses in n, that is, the set of pairs (s, B) such that s is a statement in n which uses name B and such that no prior definition of B occurs in n. Instead of DEF[n] take the set of pairs (s, B) such that s is a statement which uses B, s is not in n, and n has a definition of B. These equations are solved by the obvious analog of Algorithm 14.6, and we shall not discuss the matter further.

There are a variety of places in which du-chains are useful. For example, we mentioned that Algorithm 14.5, for copy propagation, could make good use of du-chains. As another example, Algorithm 13.8, finding induction variables, added to the set of such variables by finding statements A := B **op** C, where one of B or C was a previously discovered induction variable, and the other was a loop constant. If we have discovered that B is an induction variable, du-chains for the definitions of B within the loop would make it easy to find such statements A := B **op** C.

14.5 Very Busy Expressions and Code Hoisting

Code hoisting is another data-flow problem in which future information is needed. It differs from the problems of the previous section in that the operator that reflects divergence of paths is here intersection rather than union. We define an expression B **op** C to be *very busy* at point p if along every path from p we come to a computation of B **op** C before any definition of B or C. The use of this information is in a space-saving transformation to be discussed subsequently.

If B **op** C is very busy at p, we can compute it at p, even though it may not be needed there, by introducing the statement T := B **op** C. Then we can replace all computations A := B **op** C reachable from p by A := T. To check for safety of the above transformation, we must know, for each use u of B **op** C, that no definition of B or C reaches statement u without first

passing through p. We shall give a method of making this determination
along with the algorithm for detecting very busy expressions.

Since we know B **op** C must be computed once we reach p, we do not
waste time by computing it at p, provided the introduced copies A := T can
be eliminated by copy propagation as discussed in Section 14.3. Then, if
there are two or more uses B **op** C which are eliminated, we have saved in
the space needed for program storage, although we have not necessarily
speeded up the program. Figure 14.9 shows the transformation, called *code
hoisting,* schematically.

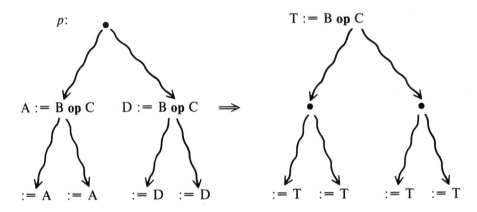

Fig. 14.9. Code hoisting transformation.

Computation of Very Busy Expressions

Let us set up the equations to compute very busy expressions. Let OUT[n]
be the set of very busy expressions at the point following the end of block
n and define IN[n] analogously for the beginning of n. Let U be the
universal set of all expressions computed somewhere in the program.
Define $V\_USE[n]$ to be the set of expressions B **op** C computed in n, with
no prior definition of B or C. Let $V\_DEF[n]$ be the set of expressions B
op C in U for which either B or C is defined in n prior to any computation
of B **op** C. Then:

$$IN[n] = OUT[n] - V\_DEF[n] \cup V\_USE[n]$$

$$OUT[n] = \bigcap_{\substack{s \text{ a suc-} \\ \text{cessor of } n}} IN[s] \qquad (14.5)$$

where an intersection over an empty set of successors is taken to be empty.
Like Equations (14.2) for available expressions, we want the largest solution to Equations (14.5). The approach borrows from Algorithm 14.3, in
that we start with a too-large set of values for IN and OUT and converge to

the desired solution. We also borrow from Algorithm 14.4 (for live variables) in the sense that we use reverse depth-first ordering as we iterate over the nodes of the flow graph.

Algorithm 14.7. Very busy expressions.

Input. A flow graph of N nodes with V_USE and V_DEF computed.

Output. $OUT[n]$ for each node n.

Method.

1. Compute $DFN[n]$ for each node n, using Algorithm 13.5. Let $n_1, n_2, \ldots, n_N$ be a listing of the nodes such that $DFN[n_i] = i$.
2. Execute the algorithm of Fig. 14.10. □

```
begin
    for i := 1 to N do
        IN[n_i] := U;
    /* above initializes to a too-large approximation */
    while changes occur do
        for i := N to 1 by −1 do
            begin
                OUT[n_i] :=    ∩    IN[s];
                            s a suc-
                            cessor of n_i
                IN[n_i] := OUT[n_i] − V_DEF[n_i] ∪ V_USE[n_i]
            end
end
```

Fig. 14.10. Very busy expressions computation.

Code Hoisting

We can now use the information computed in Algorithm 14.7 to hoist certain expressions. The work involved can be immense, since we may have to repeat various data-flow analyses in their entirety to determine the feasibility of a hoist. To simplify matters we need consider only the case in which all computations of an expression such as B **op** C can be hoisted to a point p which dominates all these computations of B **op** C. To move the computation to a point that did not dominate all uses of B **op** C might allow a path along which B **op** C was not available when needed.

The problem of determining the safety of the transformation then reduces to checking that no definition of B or C can reach a use of B **op** C without passing through p. We could do this in a manner akin to copy propagation, but since we are dealing with only one specific expression B **op** C, the problem reduces to reachability in a graph. That is, using a simple stacking algorithm, we trace backwards from statements that use B **op** C to

see what nodes can reach that point, but we exclude the node that has point
p from ever being considered, hence from ever being part of a path. The
transformation is safe if and only if no node which can reach a use of B **op**
C in this way has a definition of B or C.

To check that the transformation does not increase the time spent in
program execution we may use the copy propagation algorithm to check
that for each replacement of A := B **op** C by copy A := T, the latter copy
can be removed. A data-flow analysis or a simple stacking algorithm can be
used.

Algorithm 14.8. Code hoisting.

Input. A flow graph with very busy expressions computed and the dominator relation computed for nodes. This flow graph can be a loop of a larger
flow graph.

Output. A revised flow graph.

Method. For each expression B **op** C that is very busy at the end of one or
more nodes of the flow graph, do the following.

1. Find a node n such that B **op** C is very busy at the end of n (i.e., B **op**
    C is in OUT[n], where OUT is computed by Algorithm 14.7), and n
    dominates all nodes using B **op** C. If there is no such n, skip this
    expression and go on to the next. If there are several choices for n,
    pick one that is dominated by all others.

2. Find each occurrence s: A := B **op** C of the expression B **op** C. Trace
    backwards from the node containing statement s to check that

    i)   there are no definitions of B or C that can reach s without going
         through node n, and
    ii) there is a path from n to s that contains no definition of B or C or
         use of B **op** C.[†]

    Figure 14.11(a) contains an algorithm to test for (i) and 14.11(b) an
    algorithm for (ii). The reader may, as an exercise, combine these two
    algorithms into one. Each algorithm uses a stack to hold nodes
    "reached" whose predecessors have not been checked, and each
    returns "yes" or "no", where "yes" means the condition is met.

3. If all occurrences of B **op** C that meet condition (ii) above (there must
    be at least one occurrence, because B **op** C is very busy at n) also meet
    condition (i), and there are at least two such occurrences of B **op** C,
    then tentatively append T := B **op** C to the end of n (just before the

---

† The condition that no use of B **op** C occurs on the path can be removed, but then we might
find ourselves hoisting to uses of B **op** C that could have been combined by global common
subexpression elimination.

begin
    let *m* be the node containing statement *s*;
    if *m* has a definition of B or C prior to *s* **then return** "no";
    push the predecessors of *m* onto STACK;
    while STACK not empty **do**
        begin
            pop the top node *q* off of STACK;
            if *q* ≠ *n* **then**
                if *q* has a definition of B or C **then return** "no"
                else push onto STACK those predecessors of *q*
                    that have never before been placed on STACK
        end
    return "yes"
end

(a) Test for condition (i).

begin
    let *m* be the node containing statement *s*;
    if *m* has a definition of B or C or a use of B **op** C prior to *s* **then**
       return "no";
    push the predecessors of *m* onto STACK;
        while STACK not empty **do**
            begin
                pop the top node *q* off of STACK;
                if *q* = *n* **then return** "yes"
                else
                    if *q* has no definition of B or C or use of B **op**C
                      then push onto STACK those predecessors
                      of *q* that have never before been on STACK
            end
        return "no"
end

(b) Test for condition (ii).

Fig. 14.11. Testing occurrences of B **op** C.

final jump if there is one), where T is a new name. Then replace each statement *s*: A := B **op** C meeting conditions (i) and (ii) by A := T.

4. Confirm that the transformation of (3) does not slow down the program, by using copy propagation (either Algorithm 14.5 or a graph search test similar to Fig. 14.11) to check that all copies A := T introduced in (3) can be eliminated. If so, eliminate them. If not, restore the changes made in (3) as hoisting is not beneficial for B **op** C. □

Example 14.3. Let us consider the final program in Section 13.5, which was the result of loop optimizations on the program flowcharted in Fig. 13.12. While Algorithm 14.8 was shown as applying to an entire program, it applies as well to a single loop. In fact, it is in inner loops where the most profitable opportunities for hoisting are likely to occur.

We shall examine the expression $T_2[S_{4*I}]$, which appears in statements numbered (9) and (31). This expression is actually the r-value of A[I] from Fig. 13.12. We find that $T_2[S_{4*I}]$ is very busy at the end of B_3. On the assumption that the expression $T_2[S_{4*I}]$ is not used outside the loop, $T_2[S_{4*I}]$ is not very busy at any of the other nodes. For example, at the end of B_2, we could follow the path to B_5, B_7 and out of the loop. Then S_{4*I} is sure to change in B_8 before any use of $T_2[S_{4*I}]$.

Let us consider hoisting $T_2[S_{4*I}]$ to B_3. Clearly, B_3 dominates B_4 and B_6, the blocks in which that expression is used. We must check the conditions of part (2) of Algorithm 14.8. For condition (i) we must find, for the two uses of $T_2[S_{4*I}]$, whether there are definitions of T_2 or S_{4*I} that reach uses of $T_2[S_{4*I}]$ without going through B_3. Now T_2 is assigned only in B_8, and S_{4*I} is assigned in B_8 and B_6. It is easy to see from Fig. 13.12 that to get from the definitions of T_2 and S_{4*I} to the uses of $T_2[S_{4*I}]$ we must go through B_3. Thus condition (i) is met. For condition (ii) the direct paths from B_3 to B_4 and from B_3 to B_6 qualify. Thus we shall attempt to hoist both uses of $T_2[S_{4*I}]$ to B_3.

We may create statement $R_3 := T_2[S_{4*I}]$ and place it before the test in B_3. In B_4, replace $T_4 := T_2[S_{4*I}]$ by $T_4 := R_3$. Since T_4 has only one use, and that use is in B_4, we may surely remove the copy $T_4 := R_3$. Block B_4 becomes

$$T_8 := T_6[S_{4*J}]$$

$$\text{if } R_3 \leqslant T_8 \text{ goto } B_6$$

Similarly, block B_6 becomes

$$T_{10}[S_{4*K}] := R_3$$

$$S_{4*I} := S_{4*I} + 4$$

We should observe that hoisting $T_2[S_{4*I}]$ has saved us the space of one instruction. In fact, it has also saved time on average, since we will almost always execute B_4 on an iteration of the loop, and half the time we would execute B_6 as well. The actual amount of time saved depends on whether we can afford a register for R_3.

As a last note, observe that expression $T_6[S_{4*J}]$, which appears in B_4 and B_5, cannot be hoisted. That is, while B_2 dominates B_4 and B_5, $T_6[S_{4*J}]$ is not very busy at the end of B_2 because of the path $B_2 \rightarrow B_3 \rightarrow B_6 \rightarrow B_7$ out of the loop. □

14.6 The Four Kinds of Data-Flow Analysis Problems

We have seen examples of four varieties of equations solving data-flow analysis problems. These varieties are distinguished by two orthogonal characteristics:

1. Is the operator used to reflect the confluence or divergence of paths in a flow graph union or intersection?

2. Does data flow forward or backward? In forward flowing analyses, like reaching definitions, available expressions, or copy propagation, OUT[n] is a (*transfer*) function of IN[n] and of the statements in node n itself. IN[n] is a function of the OUT[p]'s, where p ranges over the predecessors of n. In backward problems, like du-chaining, live variables, or very busy expressions, IN[n] is a (*transfer*) function of OUT[n] and the statements in n; OUT[n] is a function of the IN[s]'s, where s ranges over the successors of n.

| | | Confluence/divergence operator | |
		$\cup$	$\cap$
Direction	Forward	I Reaching definitions (ud-chaining)	II Available expressions Copy propagation
	Backward	III Live variables du-chaining	IV Very busy expressions

Fig. 14.12. The four types of data-flow analysis problems.

Figure 14.12 shows the four kinds of data-flow problems to which we assign arbitrary group numbers I, II, III, and IV. There are a number of common features among all the problems we have studied. In each case the transfer function is of the form IN[n] = OUT[n] − $S_1[n]$ ∪ $S_2[n]$, for sets S_1 and S_2 (with IN and OUT interchanged for backward problems). For example, S_1 and S_2 were GEN and KILL for reaching definitions. In each case, IN, OUT, S_1, and S_2 were subsets of some universe, such as the set of all names or all expressions used by the program. Thus, they could be represented efficiently by bit vectors. There is no reason why this must be so, and data-flow problems that use other kinds of transfer functions have been used. However, it appears that this type of transfer function and bit vector representable data are sufficient for most common data-flow analysis problems.

There are certain things which the union-type problems, groups I and III, have in common. In each case, the solution to the data-flow equations is not unique, and we want the smallest solution. The equations are solved by starting with the approximation in which all unknowns are ϕ and iterating until the desired solution is reached from below. In contrast, the intersection-type problems, groups II and IV, have equations whose largest solution we want. We start with the unknowns all equal to U, the universal set, and iterate until we reach the solution from above. In the forward-intersection problems (group II), however, IN for the initial node is set to ϕ and remains so.

We should also notice that the forward problems, groups I and II, have something in common. They are all efficiently solved by iterating over nodes in depth-first order. The backward problems, groups III and IV, on the other hand, are efficiently solved by iterating in the reverse of depth-first order.

Interpretation of Data-Flow Equations

The reader should be aware of a subtle point regarding data-flow analysis problems and the solution of data-flow equations. In each case we explained a data-flow problem as calculating something about the set of all paths from the initial node to the beginning or end of each block, or about paths from a block to other blocks. For example, a definition of A was said to reach point p if there was some path which went through that definition of A and thence to p, without redefining A. We then stated categorically that this information about paths could be obtained by solving a set of equations, and we argued that the desired path information was a solution to the equations. We know, however, that the solution to the equations is generally not unique. Therefore, how do we know that the solution we obtain is the one which reflects the path information?

For all the problems we have discussed, we can prove the solution is "correct." But for some problems, the solution to the equations may not be what we really want. We are safe if we have a problem in one of the four groups discussed, where the transfer functions associated with each block are of the form $X = Y - S_1 \cup S_2$. This should cover any data-flow problem where the information being sought is a subset of some universal set. In some situations, especially those associated with optimization of "very high-level languages," one encounters problems where the desired answer is not even a solution to the equations. If we solve the equations iteratively, as we have done, however, the difference is invariably in the nonfatal direction only. That is, the discrepancy could cause us to miss some optimizations but will not lead us to alter the program incorrectly. The bibliographic notes contain pointers to the literature, and we urge anyone attempting to implement data-flow analyses radically different from the ones in this chapter to consult the references, where there is a well-developed theory of what is safe and what isn't.

14.7 Handling Pointers

Until now, we have ignored the role of pointers, subroutine calls and formal parameters in data-flow analysis. This section discusses pointers, and the next covers subroutines and interprocedural data-flow analysis. The basic problem with pointers can be seen in Fig. 14.13. In both n_1 and n_3 the expression B+C is computed. We may suppose that there are no definitions of B or C along any path from n_1 to n_3. However, is B+C available at n_3? It all depends on whether the indirect assignment through pointer P in n_2 could change the value of B or C.

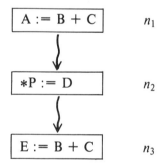

Fig. 14.13. Part of a flow graph with pointer operations.

The only safe assumption if we know nothing about where P can point to is to assume that an indirect assignment through a pointer can potentially change (i.e., define) any name. Thus, B+C is not available at n_3. We must also assume that any use of the data pointed to by a pointer, as in E := *P, can potentially use any name. These assumptions result in more live variables and reaching definitions than is realistic and fewer available expressions than is realistic. Fortunately, we can use data-flow analysis to pin down what a pointer might point to, thus allowing us to get more accurate information from our other data-flow analyses.

A Simple Pointer Language

For specificity, let us consider a language in which there are elementary data types (e.g., integers and reals) requiring one word each, and arrays of these types. Let there also be pointers to these elements and arrays, but not to other pointers. We shall be content to know that a pointer P is pointing somewhere in array A, without concerning ourselves with what particular element of A is being pointed to. This grouping together of all elements of an array, as far as pointer targets are concerned, is reasonable. Typically, pointers will be used as cursors to run through an entire array, so a more detailed data-flow analysis, if we could accomplish it at all, would often tell us that at a particular point in the program, P might be pointing to any one of the elements of A anyway.

We must also make certain assumptions about which arithmetic operations on pointers are semantically meaningful. First, if pointer P points to a primitive (one word) data element, then any arithmetic operation on P produces a value that may be an integer, but not a pointer. If P points to an array, then addition or subtraction of an integer leaves P pointing somewhere in the same array, while other arithmetic operations on pointers produce a value that is not a pointer. While not all languages prohibit, say, moving a pointer from one array A to another array B by adding to the pointer, such action would depend on the particular implementation to make sure that array B followed A in storage. Most high level programming languages do not allow the user to assume any particular order for data in memory. Even in FORTRAN, where COMMON data appears in a fixed order, one is not allowed by the FORTRAN standard to take advantage of juxtaposition of arrays.

While few implementations of languages check that one is not leaving an array boundary, it is poor programming practice to take advantage of situations that depend on particular implementations. It is our point of view that an optimizing compiler should not be prohibited from doing worthwhile optimization because a few programmers may wish to indulge in nonstandard "tricks." Each compiler implementer, however, must make a judgment for himself.

The Effects of Pointer Assignments

Under these assumptions, the only names that could possibly be used as pointers are those declared to be pointers and temporaries that receive a value that is a pointer plus or minus a constant. We shall refer to all these names as pointers. Our rules for determining what a pointer P can point to are as follows.

1. If there is an assignment statement s: P := **addr**(A), then P can point only to A immediately after s. If A is an array, then P can point only to A after any assignment to P of the form P := **addr**(A) + C, where C is a constant. As usual, **addr**(A) is deemed to refer to the location of the first word of array A.

2. If there is an assignment statement s: P := Q + C, where C is an integer other than zero, and P and Q are pointers, then after s, P can point to any array which Q could point to before s.

3. If there is an assignment s: P := Q, then after s, P can point to whatever Q could point to before s.

4. After any other assignment to P, there is no object which P could point to; such an assignment is probably (depending on the semantics of the language) meaningless.

5. After any assignment to a name other than P, P points to whatever it did before the assignment. Note that this rule assumes that no pointer can point to a pointer. Relaxing this assumption does not make matters particularly more difficult, and we leave the generalization to the reader.

We may define IN[n], for node n, to be a datum that gives for each pointer P the set of names to which P could point at the beginning of n. We may think of IN[n] as a set of pairs of the form (P, A), where P is a pointer and A a name, meaning that P might point to A. In practice, IN[n] would be represented as a list for each pointer, the list for P giving the set of A's such that (P, A) is in IN[n]. We define OUT[n] similarly for the end of n.

We shall specify a transfer function TRANS$_n$ which defines the effect of block n. That is, TRANS$_n$ is a function which takes as argument a set of pairs S, each pair of the form (P, A) for P a pointer and A a nonpointer name, and produces as a result another set T. Presumably, the set to which TRANS$_n$ is applied will be in IN[n] and the result of the application will be OUT[n]. We need only tell how to compute TRANS for single statements; TRANS$_n$ will then be composition of TRANS$_s$ for each statement s of block n. The rules for computing TRANS are as follows.

1. If s is P := **addr**(A) or P := **addr**(A) + C in the case A is an array, then TRANS$_s(S) = S - \{(P, B) | $ any B$\} \cup \{(P, A)\}$.

2. If s is P := Q + C for pointer Q and nonzero integer C, then TRANS$_s(S) = S - \{(P, B) | $ any B $\} \cup \{(P, B) | (Q, B)$ is in S and B is an array name $\}$. Note that this rule makes sense even if P = Q.

3. If s is P := Q, then

$$\text{TRANS}_s(S) = S - \{(P, B) \mid \text{any B}\} \cup \{(P, B) \mid (Q, B) \text{ is in } S\}.$$

4. If s is not an assignment to a pointer, then TRANS$_s(S) = S$.

We may now write the equations relating IN, OUT, and TRANS as follows.

$$\text{OUT}[n] = \text{TRANS}_n(\text{IN}[n])$$

$$\text{IN}[n] = \bigcup_{\substack{p \text{ a pred-} \\ \text{ecessor of } n}} \text{OUT}[p] \tag{14.6}$$

where if n consists of statements $s_1, s_2, \ldots, s_k$, then

$$\text{TRANS}_n(S) = \text{TRANS}_{s_k}(\text{TRANS}_{s_{k-1}}(\cdots(\text{TRANS}_{s_2}(\text{TRANS}_{s_1}(S)))\cdots)).$$

Equations (14.6) clearly belong in group I. Since the method of solving group I equations has been covered, we shall not give a formal algorithm for Equations (14.6), but rather go directly to an example.

Example 14.4. Consider the flow graph of Fig. 14.14. We suppose A is an array and B is an integer. P and Q are pointers. Initially, we set $\text{IN}[n_1]$ to ϕ. TRANS_{n_1} has the effect of removing any pairs with first component Q, then adding the pair (Q, B). That is, Q is asserted to point to B. Thus $\text{OUT}[n_1] = \text{TRANS}_{n_1}(\phi) = \{(Q, B)\}$. Then, $\text{IN}[n_2] = \text{OUT}[n_1]$. The effect of P := **addr**(B) is to replace all pairs with first component P by the pair (P, B). The effect of Q := **addr**(A[2]) is to replace pairs with first component Q by (Q, A). Note that Q := **addr**(A[2]) is actually an assignment of the form Q := **addr**(A) + C for a constant C. We may now compute $\text{OUT}[n_2] = \text{TRANS}_{n_2}(\{(Q, B)\}) = \{(P, B), (Q, A)\}$. Similarly, $\text{IN}[n_3] = \{(Q, B)\}$ and $\text{OUT}[n_3] = \{(P, A), (Q, B)\}$.

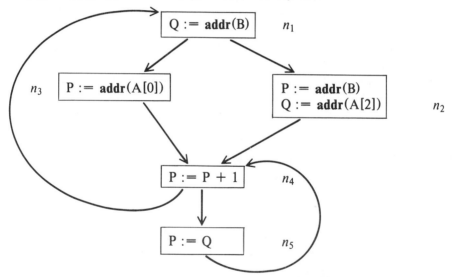

Fig. 14.14. Flow graph with pointer operations shown.

Next, we find $\text{IN}[n_4] = \text{OUT}[n_2] \cup \text{OUT}[n_3] \cup \text{OUT}[n_5]$. Presumably, $\text{OUT}[n_5]$ was initialized to ϕ and has not been changed on this pass yet. However, $\text{OUT}[n_2] = \{(P, B), (Q, A)\}$ and $\text{OUT}[n_3] = \{(P, A), (Q, B)\}$, so $\text{IN}[n_4] = \{(P, A), (P, B), (Q, A), (Q, B)\}$, or put another way, P and Q can each point anywhere. The effect of P := P + 1 is to discard the possibility that P does not point to an array. That is, $\text{OUT}[n_4] =$

$\text{TRANS}_{n_4}(\text{IN}[n_4]) = \{(P, A), (Q, A), (Q, B)\}$. Note that whenever n_2 is executed, making P point to B, a semantically meaningless action takes place if P is used indirectly after $P := P + 1$ in n_4. Thus, this flow graph is not "realistic," but it does illustrate all the inferences about pointers that we are prepared to make.

Continuing, $\text{IN}[n_5] = \text{OUT}[n_4]$, and TRANS_{n_5} copies the targets of Q and gives them to P as well. Since Q can point to A or B in $\text{IN}[n_5]$, $\text{OUT}[n_5] = \{(P, A), (P, B), (Q, A), (Q, B)\}$. On the next pass we find $\text{IN}[n_1] = \text{OUT}[n_4]$, so $\text{OUT}[n_1] = \{(P, A), (Q, B)\}$. This value is also the new $\text{IN}[n_2]$ and $\text{IN}[n_3]$, but these new values do not change $\text{OUT}[n_2]$ or $\text{OUT}[n_3]$, nor is $\text{IN}[n_4]$ changed. We have thus converged to the desired answer. □

Making Use of Pointer Information

We have computed the set of names pointed to by each pointer at the beginning of each block. This information is $\text{IN}[n]$ for each node n. Suppose that we have a reference to pointer P inside block n. Starting with $\text{IN}[n]$, apply TRANS_s for each statement s of block n that precedes the reference to P. This tells us what P could point to at the particular statement where that information is important.

Suppose now that we have determined what each pointer could point to when that pointer is used in an indirect reference, either on the left or right of the assignment symbol. How can we use this information to get more accurate solutions to the usual data-flow problems? In each case we must consider in which direction errors are conservative, and we must utilize pointer information in such a way that only conservative errors are made. To see how this choice is made, let us consider two examples — reaching definitions and live variable analysis.

To calculate reaching definitions we can use Algorithm 14.1, but we need to know the values of KILL and GEN for a block. The latter quantities are computed as usual for statements not assigning indirectly through pointers. An indirect assignment $*P := A$ is deemed to generate a definition of every name B such that P could point to B. This assumption is conservative, because it is conservative to assume definitions reach a point while in reality they do not.

To see that this choice is conservative, we must consider how reaching definitions are used. In all our example uses, such as constant propagation or testing for conditions under which code motion or induction variable elimination is possible, adding to the set of reaching definitions could not cause additional program modifications to be made, but rather, such changes might be inhibited. In principle, one could envision an application of reaching definitions where the more definitions that reached a point, the more program modifications could be made. In this case, an approach other than Algorithm 14.1 would have to be used whether or not there were pointers, since that algorithm does not produce an exact answer, but rather produces an answer which is possibly too large. For example, not all paths in the flow graph may be executable, as we saw in Fig. 12.10.

Finally, let us consider the computation of KILL. We assume that *P := A kills definitions of B only if B is not an array and is the only name P could possibly point to. If P could point to two or more names, then we do not assume definitions of either are killed. If P can point nowhere, there is an error in the program. Again, we are being conservative because we permit definitions of B to pass through *P := A, and thus reach wherever they can, unless we can prove that *P := A redefined B. In other words, when there is doubt, we assume that a definition reaches.

For live variables we may use Algorithm 14.6, but must reconsider how DEF and USE are to be defined for statements of the form *P := A and A := *P. The statement *P := A uses only A and P. We say it defines B only if B is the unique name that P might point to. This assumption allows uses of B to propagate unless they are surely blocked by the assignment *P := A. Thus we can never claim that B is not live at a point when it is in fact alive. The statement A := *P surely represents a definition of A. It also represents a use of any name that P could point to. By maximizing possible uses, we again maximize our estimate of live variables. By maximizing live variables, we are being conservative. For example, we might generate code to store a dead variable, but we shall never fail to store one that was live.

14.8 Interprocedural Data-Flow Analysis

We saw in Fig. 14.13 that an indirect assignment through a pointer could cause uncertainty as to what names can change value in such an assignment. By determining those names to which the pointer might point, however, we can rule out certain names (those certainly not pointed to). Similarly, when we come to a procedure call, we may not have to make our worst-case assumption — that everything can be changed — provided, we can compute the set of names that the procedure might change. Or, if we are computing live variables, we need not assume everything is used by a procedure provided we can compute the set of names that might be used.

As with all code optimizations we may still make errors on the conservative side. That is, the sets of names whose values "may be " changed or used could properly include the names which are actually changed or used in some run of the program. We shall, as usual, simply try to come fairly close to the true sets of changed and used names without working unduly hard or making an error which alters what the program does.

Additional problems occur if we try to compute available expressions involving formal parameters. Suppose we have a procedure P, with two formal parameters X and Y passed by reference. In Fig. 14.15, we see a situation in which B+X is computed in n_1 and n_3.

Suppose that the only paths from n_1 to n_3 go through n_2, and there are no assignments to B or X along any such path. Then, is B+X available at n_3? The answer depends on whether X and Y could denote the same memory address (be *aliases* of one another). For example, there could be a call P(Z, Z), or perhaps a call of P(U, V), where U and V are formal parameters of another procedure Q(U, V), and a call of Q(Z, Z) is possible.

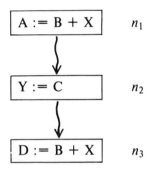

Fig. 14.15. Illustration of aliasing problems.

A Model of Code with Procedure Calls

To illustrate how these issues might be dealt with, let us consider a language which permits recursive procedures, any of which may refer to both local and global names. The data available to a procedure consists of the globals and its own locals only. Parameters are passed by reference.

We require that all procedures have a flow graph with single *entry* (the initial node) and a single *return* node which causes control to pass back to the calling routine. We suppose for convenience that every node lies on some path from the entry to the return.

Now suppose we are in a procedure P and we come upon a call to procedure Q(U, V). If we are interested in computing available expressions (or doing one of a number of other data-flow analyses), we must know whether Q(U, V) might change the value of some name A. Note that we say "might" change, rather than "will" change. As with all data-flow problems, it is impossible to know for sure whether or not the value of a name is changed. We can only find a set which includes all names whose values do change and perhaps some that don't. By being careful, we can cut down on the latter class of names, obtaining a good approximation to the truth and erring only on the conservative side. We might miss a few common subexpressions but should never change the meaning of the program.

The only names whose values the call of Q(U, V) could change are the globals and the names U and V, which might be local to P. Changes to locals of Q are of no consequence after the call returns. Even if Q = P, it will be other copies of Q's locals that change, and these copies disappear after the return. It is easy to determine which globals are changed by Q — just see which have definitions in Q, or are changed in a procedure call made by Q. In addition, U and/or V, which may be global, change if Q has a definition of its first and/or second formal parameter, respectively, or if these formal parameters are passed as actual parameters by Q to another procedure which changes them.

Aliases

If two or more names denote the same memory address, as formals and corresponding actuals do, we say the names are *aliases* of one another. In a sense, we encountered this phenomenon in the previous section, where *P could be an alias for anything that P might point to. As it is not possible for two globals to denote the same memory address, at least one of a pair of aliases must be a formal parameter. Since formals may be passed to procedures, it is possible for two formals to be aliases.

It will turn out in some situations that it is conservative not to regard names as aliases of one another. For example, in reaching definitions, if we wish to assert that a definition of A is killed by a definition of B, we had better be sure that A and B are aliases whenever the definition of B is executed. Other times it is conservative to regard names as aliases of one another whenever there is doubt. Our available-expressions example is one such case. If A+B is not to be killed by a definition of C, we had better be sure neither A nor B is an alias of C. One way to gather all possible aliases is to take the transitive closure of the actual-formal correspondences.

Example 14.5. Consider the sketch of the three procedures shown in Fig. 14.16, where parameters are assumed passed by reference. There are two globals, g and h, and two local names, i for MAIN and k for TWO. Procedure ONE has formals w and x, procedure TWO has formals y and z, and MAIN has no formal parameters. We use the relation $\equiv$ to mean "could be an alias of, in some call of some procedure." We first compute the aliasing due to actual-formal correspondences.

The call of ONE by MAIN makes $h \equiv w$. It also makes $i \equiv x$. The first call of TWO by ONE makes $w \equiv y$ and $w \equiv z$. The second call makes $g \equiv y$ and $x \equiv z$.

The call of ONE by TWO makes $k \equiv w$ and $y \equiv x$. If we take the transitive closure of the alias relationships represented by $\equiv$ (that is, make $a \equiv c$ if we already have $a \equiv b$ and $b \equiv c$ for some b, repeating until no new relationships can be discovered), then we find in this example that all names are possible aliases of one another. $\square$

```
global g, h;
    procedure MAIN( );
    local i;
    g :=  ;
    ONE(h, i)
end;

procedure ONE(w, x);
    x :=  ;
    TWO(w, w);
    TWO(g, x)
end;

procedure TWO(y, z);
    local k;
    h :=  ;
    ONE(k, y)
end
```

Fig. 14.16. Sample procedures.

The aliasing computation suggested by Example 14.5 does not often result in such extensive aliasing. Intuitively, we would not often expect two different names with dissimilar types to be aliases. Moreover, the programmer undoubtedly has conceptual types for his names. For example, if the first formal parameter of a procedure P represents a velocity, it can be expected that the first statement in any call to P will also be thought of by the programmer as a velocity. Thus we may expect most programs to produce small groups of possible aliases. Therefore, while it is not the best we can do, the computation suggested above is reasonable for many purposes.

Data-Flow Analysis in the Presence of Procedure Calls

Let us consider, as an example, how available expressions can be calculated in the presence of procedure calls, where parameters are passed by reference. As in Section 14.2, we must determine when a name could be defined, thus killing an expression, and we must determine when expressions are generated (evaluated).

We may define, for each procedure P, a vector CHANGE[P], whose value is to be the set of global names and formal parameters of P that might be changed during an execution of P. At this point, we do not count a name as changed if a member of its equivalence class of aliases is changed.

Let DEF[P] be the set of formal parameters and globals having explicit definitions within P (not including those defined within procedures called by P). To write the equations for CHANGE[P], we have only to relate the globals and formals of P that are used as actual parameters in calls made by P to the corresponding formal parameters of the called procedures. We may write:

$$\text{CHANGE}[P] = \text{DEF}[P] \cup A \cup G \qquad (14.7)$$

where

1. $A = \{a \mid a$ is a global name or formal parameter of P such that, for some procedure Q and integer i, P calls Q with a as the ith actual parameter and the ith formal parameter of Q is in CHANGE[Q]$\}$
2. $G = \{g \mid g$ is a global in CHANGE[Q] and P calls Q$\}$.

It should come as no surprise that Equations (14.7) may be solved for a set of procedures by an iterative technique. Although the solution is not unique, we only need the smallest one. We may converge to that solution by starting with a too-small approximation and iterating. The logical too-small approximation with which to start is CHANGE[P] = DEF[P].

Calling Graphs

It is worth considering the order in which procedures should be visited in the propagation. For example, if the procedures are not mutually recursive, then we can first visit procedures that do not call any other (there must be at least one). For these procedures, CHANGE = DEF. Next, we can compute CHANGE for those procedures that call only procedures which call nothing. We can apply (14.7) for this next group of procedures directly, since CHANGE[Q] will be known for any Q in (14.7). This idea can be made more precise as follows.

In general, we can draw a *calling graph,* whose nodes are procedures, with an edge from P to Q if P calls Q.[†] A collection of procedures that are not mutually recursive will have an acyclic calling graph. In this case we can visit each node once. A suitable ordering is the reverse of the depth-first ordering one gets by searching the calling graph starting at the "main program." In that order, we will not have to compute CHANGE[P] until we have computed CHANGE for all successors of P in the calling graph, that is, for all procedures called by P. We shall thus choose reverse depth-first ordering whether or not the procedures are recursive, assured that this order will work well at least in the frequently-occurring nonrecursive case.

Algorithm 14.9. Interprocedural analysis of changed variables.

[†] Here we assume no procedure-valued variables. These complicate the construction of the calling graph, as we must determine the possible actuals corresponding to procedure-valued formals at the same time we construct the edges of the calling graph.

Input. A collection of procedures P_1, P_2, . . . , P_N, where i is the depth-first number of P_i in the calling graph of the procedures.

Output. CHANGE[P], the set of global variables and formal parameters of P that are changed by P.

Method.

1. Compute DEF[P] for each procedure P by inspection.
2. Execute the program of Fig. 14.17 to compute CHANGE. □

```
begin
(1)  for i := 1 to N do CHANGE[P_i] := DEF[P_i]; /* initialize */
(2)  while changes occur do
(3)      for i := N to 1 by −1 do
(4)          for each procedure Q called by P_i do
                 begin
(5)                  add any global variables in CHANGE[Q] to CHANGE[P_i];
(6)                  for each formal parameter X (the jth) of Q do
(7)                      if X is in CHANGE[Q] then
(8)                          for each call of Q by P_i do
(9)                              if A, the jth actual parameter of the call,
                                     is a global or formal parameter of P_i then
(10)                                 add A to CHANGE[P_i]
                 end
end
```

Fig. 14.17. Iterative algorithm to compute CHANGE.

Example 14.6. Let us consider Fig. 14.16 again. By inspection, DEF[MAIN] = {g}, DEF[ONE] = {x} and DEF[TWO] = {h}. These are the initial values of CHANGE. The calling graph of the procedures is shown in Fig. 14.18. We may thus take TWO, ONE, MAIN as our reverse depth-first order. Consider P_i = TWO in the program of Fig. 14.16. Then Q can only be procedure ONE in line (4). Since CHANGE[ONE] = {x} initially, nothing is added to CHANGE[TWO] at line (5). At lines (6) and (7) we need consider only the second formal parameter of procedure ONE. In the only call of ONE by TWO, the second actual parameter is y, so we set CHANGE[TWO] to {h, y} at line (10).

We now consider P_i = ONE. At line (4), Q can only be procedure TWO. At line (5), h is a global in CHANGE[TWO], so we set CHANGE[ONE] = {h, x}. At lines (6) and (7), only the first formal parameter of TWO is in CHANGE[TWO], so we must add g and w to CHANGE[ONE] at line (10), these being the two first actual parameters in the calls of procedure TWO. Thus, CHANGE[ONE] = {g, h, w, x}.

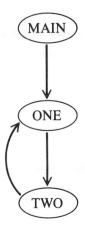

Fig. 14.18. Calling graph.

Now consider MAIN. Procedure ONE changes both its formals, so both *h* and *i* will be changed in the call of ONE by MAIN. However, *i* is a local and need not be considered. Thus we set CHANGE[MAIN] = {*g*, *h*}. Finally, we repeat the while-loop of line (2). On reconsidering TWO, we find that ONE modifies global *g*. Thus the call to ONE(*k*, *y*) causes *g* to be modified, so CHANGE[TWO] = {*g*, *h*, *y*}. No further changes occur in the iteration. □

Conservative Use of CHANGE Information

A word on the use of Algorithm 14.9 is in order. Suppose we are computing available expressions for procedure P, and we want to compute $A\_KILL[n]$ for a node *n*. A definition of name A must be deemed to kill any expression involving A or involving some B that could be an alias of A. A call in *n* to procedure Q cannot kill an expression involving A unless either

i)   A is global and in CHANGE[Q], or
ii) A is passed to Q as the *i*th actual parameter and the *i*th formal parameter of Q is CHANGE[Q], or
iii) A might be an alias of some name satisfying (i) or (ii).

Thus, the information computed by Algorithm 14.9, together with the transitive closure of the formal-actual correspondences (for condition iii), gives us a safe approximation to the set of expressions killed.

Computing Generated Expressions

To compute available expressions in programs with procedure calls, we must also have a conservative way of estimating the set of expressions generated by a procedure call. To be conservative, we may assume A **op** B is generated by a call to Q if and only if, on every path from Q's entry to its return, we find A **op** B with no subsequent redefinition of A or B. When we look for occurrences of A **op** B, we must not accept X **op** Y as such an occurrence unless we are sure that, in every call of Q, X is an alias of A and Y an alias of B.

We make this requirement because it is conservative to err by assuming that an expression is not available when it is. By the same token, we must assume A **op** B is killed by a definition of any Z which could possibly be an alias of A or B, that is, any Z related to A or B by the transitive closure of the formal-actual correspondences. Put another way, when analyzing a procedure for generated expressions, A_KILL must be computed first by the approach described earlier in this section.

That is, we should compute available expressions for all nodes of all procedures on the assumption that a call generates nothing, and that A_KILL[n] for all nodes is as computed above. As one does not expect many expressions to be generated by the typical procedure, this approach is good enough for most purposes.

A more complicated and slightly more accurate alternative approach to the computation of available expressions is to iteratively compute GEN[P] for each procedure P. We may initialize GEN[P] to be the set of expressions available at the end of P's return node according to the method above. That is, no aliasing is permitted for generated expressions; A **op** B represents only itself, even if other names could be aliases of A or B.

Now compute available expressions for all nodes of all procedures again. However, take a call to Q(A, B) to generate those expressions in GEN[Q] with A and B substituted for the corresponding formals of Q. A_KILL remains as before. A new value of GEN[P] can be found by seeing what expressions are available at the end of P's return. This iteration may be repeated until we get no more changes in available expressions at any node. This data-flow process is essentially a group II problem, so we are assured of eventual convergence to a conservative answer.

A variety of extensions to the above methods are possible to handle language features such as EQUIVALENCE statements and block structure.

14.9 Putting it all Together

Having had an overview of what code optimization is about, how are we to put the various algorithms discussed together in an optimizing compiler? There are three issues that we should consider: the internal representation of the program, the order in which to apply the algorithms, and how to minimize the amount of work done by the compiler.

Internal Representations

In answer to the first question, we have used the quadruple or three-address code representation throughout, because we feel it is an aid to perceiving what is going on. The "triples" or syntax tree representation, however, is equally effective and has been used in a number of optimizing compilers, such as BLISS/11. One advantage of triples in an optimizing compiler is that it becomes apparent when a value is used only within a single block, as most temporaries generated for expression evaluation will be. These temporaries can be ignored in all global data-flow analyses.

We can obtain the benefit of triples when using the quadruple notation if temporaries are not entered into the symbol table unless they are mentioned in two or more different blocks. Operands which are local to one block, and their data types, can be encoded by quantities that are distinguishable from pointers to the symbol table. If code motion or another optimization converts a name local to one block into one which spans several blocks, it can be given a new identifier and entered into the symbol table when the optimization occurs. We must also beware of conditional expressions, where a temporary value may span several blocks initially.

Ordering the Optimizations

In what order shall we do the optimizations, and, for that matter, which shall we do? The answer depends to a certain extent on the language at hand. Our first goal should be to compute du- and ud-chaining information; a number of compilers make do with only this information, getting the other data-flow information from this. The POP_10 FORTRAN optimizer (Abel and Bell [1972]) and, to an extent, the SETL optimizer (Schwartz [1975a,b]) are in this category. If our language has pointers, we cannot compute du- and ud-chains until we have first determined what pointers can point to. If the language is one which encourages the use of many small subroutines, then all this information must be done interprocedurally. If the language is not typically used in such a way that procedure calls are frequent, we may be able to do almost as well optimizing each subroutine separately and assuming the worst at each call.

Having obtained du- and ud-chains, we should then compute live variables, either directly, or from ud-chains. We are then in a position to perform the key loop optimizations of code motion and induction variable elimination. If we are concerned with space, hoisting may be performed; we must compute very busy expressions first if we do so.

Then we can turn our attention to some global optimizations. Global common subexpression elimination (after computing available expressions) can be a space saver, although the speedup will not be great, because code motion alone will make sure that many opportunities for global common subexpression elimination have been previously removed from inner loops anyway. Constant folding is worthwhile, although if the language has a preprocessor that substitutes for symbolic constants (like C, or the more general PL/I macro facility), most programmers will not leave much opportunity for global constant folding. If, however, the language has a construct like the for-statement in ALGOL, which requires tests for the sign of the increment within a loop, the compiler itself may generate opportunities to fold constants, namely the constants **true** or **false** resulting from the test on the sign of the increment.

Finally, we can optimize the basic blocks themselves, eliminating local common subexpressions and unnecessary copies within a block. It is good to defer global copy propagation until this point to clean up unnecessary copies generated in the previous steps, including global and local common subexpression elimination, as well as code motion and induction variable elimination. However, the reader should be aware that copy propagation can create more common subexpressions and hoistable expressions, so repeated passes of the various optimizations should be considered.

At this point we have reasonably good intermediate code. The final, important touches of an optimizing compiler come when we generate object code — the subject of the final chapter of this book.

Some Simplifications

Let us now consider the third topic: how to simplify our work and the work of the compiler. First, let us state that the algorithms given in this book are only points in a spectrum ranging from very complicated and very effective optimization algorithms to very trivial and not-so-effective algorithms. We have been biased somewhat towards the latter in the hope that the ideas and philosophies of code optimization would thereby be made more comprehensible. The reader desiring the best possible optimizing compiler may wish instead to increase the amount of work he and his compiler do. The bibliographic notes contain pointers to the literature on the subject, where some algorithms giving closer approximations to the important data obtainable by flow analysis can be found.

One simplification worth mentioning is designed to decrease the amount of information computed by data-flow analysis. Instead of concerning ourselves with all names, look only at those occurring in relatively small loops, ignoring any that are used only outside loops of nesting level three or four, say. For example, FORTRAN H looks at only 128 names, no matter how many there are in a routine (Lowry and Medlock [1969]). Since most of the speedup occurs in the small loops anyway, one might even consider restricting optimization to regions found to lie in these loops.

Another technique which can minimize work is to utilize du- and ud-chaining information to obtain other data-flow analysis information only at the points of interest. For example, suppose we use live variable information only to determine whether a name A must be stored at the end of a block in which it is computed. Then the liveness of A is only important at the end of blocks in which A is defined. We need not compute live variables as suggested in Algorithm 14.6. It is sufficient to consider every definition of every name A and find all uses reached by that definition (du-chaining information tells us what we want to know). For all definitions having a use outside the block, mark A live at the end of the block containing the definition.

Exercises

14.1 For the flow graph of Fig. 14.19 compute:
   a) ud- and du-chains.
   b) live variables at the end of each block.
   c) available expressions.
   d) very busy expressions.

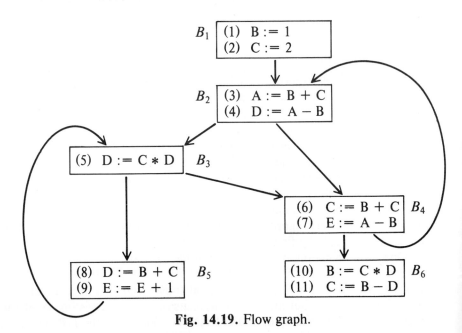

Fig. 14.19. Flow graph.

14.2 Is any constant folding possible in Fig. 14.19? If so, do it.

14.3 Are there any common subexpressions in Fig. 14.19? If so, eliminate them.

14.4 Are there any expressions that may be hoisted in Fig. 14.19? If so, hoist them.

14.5 Where possible, propagate out any copy steps introduced in the modifications of Exercises 14.2 through 14.4.

*14.6 Give algorithms to compute (a) available expressions and (b) live variables for the language with pointers discussed in Section 14.7. Be sure to make conservative assumptions about A_GEN, A_KILL, USE, and DEF in (b).

*14.7 Give an algorithm to compute reaching definitions interprocedurally using the model of Section 14.8. Again, be sure you make conservative approximations to the truth.

*14.8 Suppose parameters are passed by value instead of by reference. Can two names be aliases of one another? What if copy-restore linkage is used?

*14.9 We have mentioned that certain data-flow analysis problems yield solutions to the data-flow equations which are not what one would expect by considering all paths beginning at the initial node. The following is an example, in which we attempt to determine names that have constant values. IN and OUT will be sets of pairs (A, c) with the intended meaning that name A has constant value c at the point in question. We may set up the following data-flow equations.

$$(1) \quad IN[n] = \bigcap_{\substack{p \text{ a pred-}\\ \text{ecessor of } n}} OUT[p]$$

That is, A has constant value c at the beginning of n if and only if A has value c at the end of all predecessors of n.

If block n consists of the assignment A := c, then

$$(2) \quad OUT[n] = IN[n] - \{\text{any pair with A}\} \cup \{(A, c)\}.$$

That is, OUT[n] is IN[n] with pair (A, c) included and any other pair with the first component A removed. If n consists of assignment A := B + C, then OUT[n] = IN[n] = {any pair with A } $\cup$ {(A, $d+e$) if (B, d) and (C, e) are in IN[n]}. That is, OUT[n] is IN[n] with any pair with first component A removed and the pair (A, $d+e$) inserted only in the case that B and C have constant values d and e, respectively. The relation between OUT and IN can be defined by composition of the above transfer functions, for blocks with more than one statement, but this extension need not concern us here.

a) In the flow graph of Fig. 14.20, does Z have a constant value at
    the beginning of B_7, independent of the path taken from B_1,
    on the assumption that $+$ is commutative?

b) Solve the data-flow equations (1) and (2) above. What is
    $IN[B_7]$?

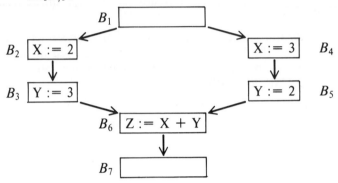

Fig. 14.20. Flow graph.

*14.10 Give an algorithm to compute the calling graph for programs in the
language discussed in Section 14.8, but with procedure-valued
parameters permitted.

Bibliographic Notes

The iterative solution of data-flow equations has been traced to V. Vyssot-
sky and P. Wegner in 1960, who used the method in a FORTRAN compiler. Kildall [1973], Kennedy [1974], Hecht and Ullman [1975], and Kam
and Ullman [1976] discuss the efficiency of the method. Another approach,
based on the interval construction method discussed in the exercises of
Chapter 13, has received consideration in Cocke [1970], Kennedy [1972],
Cocke and Miller [1969], Schaefer [1973], and Earnest [1974]. There is
reason to believe, following Kennedy [1974], that interval-based methods
are somewhat more efficient than iterative ones if the language being
optimized tends to produce few, if any, nonreducible flow graphs.

A modification of the iterative approach having promise of greater
efficiency is "node listing" (Kennedy [1975], Aho and Ullman [1975]).
Graham and Wegman [1976] discuss a variant of interval analysis.

A third method of data-flow analysis, referred to as "recursive descent," takes the loop structure of the flow graph directly from the syntax of
the language. The method is highly efficient but requires a language which
produces only reducible flow graphs, meaning **goto**'s must be forbidden.

This optimization method has been used for BLISS (Wulf *et al.* [1975], Geschke [1972]) and SIMPL (Zelkowitz and Bail [1974]).

The study of aliasing and interprocedural analysis began with Spillman [1971] and Allen [1974]. Recent attempts to handle interprocedural analysis for recursive programs include Rosen [1975], Lomet [1975], Hecht and Shaffer [1975], and Barth [1977].

There have been a number of independent attempts to couch data-flow analysis in greater generality than discussed here. These viewpoints are invariably lattice-theoretic and include Kildall [1973], Tenenbaum [1974], and Wegbreit [1975]. Many of the more general kinds of data-flow analysis proposed, such as Tenenbaum [1974], Schwartz [1975a,b], Graham and Wegman [1976], and Jones and Muchnick [1976], involve the solution of *monotone* data-flow problems, which are a generalization of the four types discussed in Section 14.6. Monotone problems have the interesting property that the solution to the data-flow equations is not necessarily the desired answer to the problem, although it is always a conservative approximation to what we want. Exercise 14.9 gives an example. The theory of monotone data-flow analysis is discussed by Kam and Ullman [1977] and Cousot and Cousot [1977]. Reif and Lewis [1977] present a more efficient implementation of some of Kildall's ideas.

A number of new uses for data-flow analysis have been recently proposed. Fosdick and Osterweil [1976] discuss its use in detecting programming errors. Carter [1975] and Harrison [1977] consider data-flow analysis as a tool in portable compiler implementation. Harrison [1975] and Suzuki and Ishihata [1977] discuss its use in array-bounds checking. Ullman [1975] surveys the subject of data-flow analysis.

CHAPTER 15

Code
Generation

We now turn to code generation, the final phase of compilation. Good code generation is difficult, and not too much can be said without dealing with the details of particular machines. Nevertheless, the subject must be studied because a careful code-generation algorithm can easily produce code that runs perhaps twice as fast as code produced by an ill-considered algorithm.

We begin our study by looking at the problems that arise in generating good code. We initially develop a straightforward algorithm to generate code from a sequence of three-address statements. We progress to more complex algorithms that take into account the flow-of-control structure of a program in assigning registers to names. We then discuss a method for generating reasonably good code, treating a basic block or an expression as the fundamental entity. Finally, we consider various local, machine-dependent optimizations that have been found effective in improving the quality of output code.

15.1 Object Programs

We assume that the input to our code-generation routine is an intermediate language program that can be a sequence of quadruples, a sequence of triples, a tree, or a postfix Polish string. The output of a code generator is the object program. This may take on a variety of forms: an absolute machine-language program, a relocatable machine-language program, an assembly-language program, or perhaps a program in some other programming language.

Producing an absolute machine-language program as output has the advantage that it can be placed in a fixed location in memory and immediately executed. A small program can be compiled and executed in a few seconds. A number of "student-job" compilers, such as WATFIV and PL/C, produce absolute code.

Producing a relocatable machine-language program (object module) as output allows subprograms to be compiled separately. A set of relocatable object modules can be linked together and loaded for execution by a linking loader. Although we must pay the added expense of linking and loading if we produce relocatable object modules, we gain a great deal of flexibility in being able to compile subroutines separately and to call other previously compiled programs from an object module. Many commercial compilers produce relocatable object modules.

Producing an assembly-language program as output makes the process of code generation somewhat easier. We can generate symbolic instructions and use the macro facilities of the assembler to help generate code. The price to be paid is the assembly step after code generation. Nonetheless, since by producing assembly code the compiler will not duplicate the entire task of the assembler, this choice is another reasonable alternative, especially for a machine with a small memory, where a compiler must use several passes.

Producing a high-level language program as output simplifies code generation even further. For example, FORTRAN is the output of the ALTRAN[†] compiler (Brown [1977]) as well as a variety of "Structured FORTRAN" preprocessors such as RATFOR (Kernighan [1975]). Generating FORTRAN as output defers the problems of machine code generation to the FORTRAN compiler, yet allows the compilation of languages that extend FORTRAN in useful ways, as in the cited examples.

The Environment of the Code Generator

We assume that the code generator is presented the intermediate text in one of the forms discussed in Chapter 7; we shall, in our specific algorithms, deal with quadruples or in one case, with parse trees as the intermediate form. We assume that all necessary semantic checking has been done, either during intermediate code generation, in a separate pass, or just before each quadruple is examined by the code generator. Thus the data type of each operator and operand is known, and all necessary type conversions are present in the intermediate text. It is also assumed that data areas and offsets have been determined for each name, as discussed in Chapter 10, and that this information is present in the symbol table.

It is often helpful to imagine that the intermediate text has been partitioned into basic blocks, as in Algorithm 12.1, but with the additional proviso that procedure calls are isolated in blocks by themselves. It is not essential that a data structure representing a flow graph be present. Algorithm 12.1 tells us how to recognize the beginning and end of a basic block as we scan a list of quadruples. Thus our algorithms for code generation are in no way predicated on the existence of an optimization phase in the compiler.

---

† A language for algebraic manipulation.

Run-Time Addresses for Names

The exact nature of the object code is highly dependent on the machine and the operating system. Nevertheless, there are a few general comments we can make. First, suppose the object code is machine language. The encoding of machine operations should pose no problem, once the desired operations are selected. More difficult is the selection of operand addresses. We presume that, prior to code generation, we have determined the data area and offset for each name. In general, if name A has offset f, then a machine instruction I of which A is an operand will have f in its address field. However, depending on the nature of the data area, certain other bits of I may be set as well.

For example, if A is in static storage and we are generating relocatable code, we need only attach to instruction I an indication for the loader that the address of I is to be relocated by adding to f the first machine address used for the procedure to which A belongs. If the target machine uses base registers, however, we do not want I to be relocated, but we must place in the appropriate bits of I the number of the base register selected for the data area. If we are generating absolute code, the compiler must add the address of the beginning of A's data area as instruction I is generated.

If A is allocated on a stack, suppose f is A's offset from the beginning of its activation record. In most implementations of languages with stack allocation there will be a register reserved for what we called SP in Chapter 10, that is, a pointer to the top of the stack. If, as in our discussion of C implementation, A must be in the top activation record when it is accessed, then the machine instruction I referring to A has f in its address field, with an indication that the indexed mode of address is to be used. The index register used is the one reserved for SP, of course. In a language such as ALGOL, where A could be in any activation record on the stack, and a display is used, the same mode of address may be used, with the appropriate display pointer first being brought to an index register if it is not already there.

Whether the object code is machine or assembly language, the code produced from the intermediate language form of each procedure must be followed by words to hold the place for each statically allocated name belonging to that procedure. In assembly language we may generate data-defining "pseudo-operations." In machine language we generate the words themselves, initialized as required. In either case the symbol table must be consulted to determine which names belong to which procedure. If block records, as described in Section 9.3 for block-structured symbol tables, are used, these names can be found directly. Otherwise a scan of the symbol-table is necessary for each procedure, and symbol-table entries must have an indication of the procedure to which each name belongs.

It is worth noting that if machine code is being generated, we have a special problem with statement labels. In the quadruple array, labels refer to quadruple numbers. As we scan each quadruple in turn we can deduce the location of the first machine instruction generated for that quadruple, simply by maintaining a count of the number of words used for the instructions generated so far. This count can be kept in the quadruple array (in an extra field), so if a reference such as j: **goto** i is encountered, and i is less than j, the current quadruple number, we may simply generate the machine jump instruction with address equal to the machine location beginning the code for quadruple i. If, however, the jump is forward, so i exceeds j, we must store on a list for quadruple i the location of the machine instruction generated for quadruple j. Then, when we process quadruple j, we fill in the proper machine location for all instructions that are forward jumps to j. The process is analogous to the "backpatching" discussed in Chapter 7.

If the object code is assembly language, no such problem with addresses arises. In effect, the use of the assembler introduces an extra pass over the code, and an extra pass can always substitute for backpatching.

15.2 Problems in Code Generation

Before we become immersed in details, let us consider, from a general point of view, what is involved in code generation. We assume that the input to the code generator is a sequence of three-address statements as discussed in Chapter 7. Thus, we are assuming that, prior to code generation, the source language has been scanned, parsed, and translated into a reasonably low-level intermediate language, so the values of names appearing in the three-address statements can be represented by quantities that our target machine can directly manipulate (bits, integers, reals, pointers, etc.). We are also assuming that the necessary semantic analysis has taken place, so type-conversion operators have been inserted wherever necessary. Obvious semantic errors (e.g., attempting to index by a floating-point number) have already been detected.

It might appear that the task of code generation is now relatively easy. However, difficulties arise in attempting to perform the computation represented by the intermediate-language program efficiently, using the available instructions of the target machine. There are three main sources of difficulty: deciding what machine instructions to generate, deciding in what order the computations should be done, and deciding which registers to use.

What Instructions Should We Generate?

Most machines permit certain computations to be done in a variety of ways. For example, if our target machine has an "add-one-to-storage" instruction (AOS), then for the three-address statement $A := A + 1$ we might generate the single instruction AOS A, rather than the more obvious sequence

```
LOAD  A
ADD  #1
STORE  A
```

Deciding which machine code sequence is best for a given three-address construct may require extensive knowledge about the context in which that construct appears. We shall have more to say on this matter when we discuss the choice of registers.

In What Order Should We Perform Computations?

The second source of difficulty concerns the order in which computations should be performed. Some computation orders require fewer registers to hold intermediate results than others, as we shall see in Section 15.6. Picking the best order is a very difficult problem in general. Initially, we shall generate code for the three-address statements in the order in which they have been produced by the semantic routines.

What Registers Should We Use?

The final problem that we shall mention is register assignment, that is, deciding in which register each computation should be done. Deciding the optimal assignment of registers to variables is difficult, even with single-register quantities. The problem is further complicated because certain machines require *register-pairs* (an even and next odd-numbered register) for some operands and results.

For example, in the IBM System/370 machines, integer multiplication and integer division involve register pairs. The multiplication instruction is of the form

$$M \quad X, Y$$

where X, the multiplicand, refers to the even register of an even/odd register pair. The multiplicand itself is taken from the odd register of the pair. Y represents the multiplier. The product occupies the entire even/odd register pair.

The division instruction is of the form

$$D \quad X, Y$$

where the 64-bit dividend occupies an even/odd register pair whose even register is X. Y represents the divisor. After division, the even register holds the remainder and the odd register the quotient.

Now consider the two three-address code sequences in Fig. 15.1(a) and (b), in which the only difference is the operator in the second statement.

$$T := A + B$$
$$T := T * C$$
$$T := T / D$$

$$T := A + B$$
$$T := T + C$$
$$T := T / D$$

(a)

(b)

Fig. 15.1 Two three-address code sequences.

Optimal assembly-code sequences for (a) and (b) are given in Fig. 15.2. Ri stands for register i. (SRDA[†] R0, 32 shifts the dividend into R1 and clears R0 to sign bits.) L, ST, and A stand for load, store and add, respectively. Note that the optimal choice for the register into which A is to be loaded depends on what will ultimately happen to T. We shall discuss some strategies for register allocation in Section 15.5.

```
L    R1, A          L     R0, A
A    R1, B          A     R0, B
M    R0, C          A     R0, C
D    R0, D          SRDA  R0, 32
ST   R1, T          D     R0, D
                    ST    R1, T
```

(a)

(b)

Fig. 15.2. Optimal machine code sequences.

15.3 A Machine Model

Good code generation requires an intimate knowledge of the target machine. It is not feasible in a general discussion of code generation to describe all of the nuances that need to be known to generate good code for a complete language on a specific machine. We shall, however, discuss some of the major problems which arise. For this purpose we need to describe some of the features of a typical computer, which we do in this section. Our machine is loosely patterned after the DEC PDP-11.

We assume we have a byte-addressable machine with 2^{16} bytes (2^{15} 16-bit words) of memory. We have eight general-purpose registers R0, R1, . . . , R7 each capable of holding a 16-bit quantity. We have binary operators of the form

---

† Shift Right Double Arithmetic.

OP source, destination

in which OP is a 4-bit op-code, and source and destination are 6-bit fields. Since these 6-bit fields are not long enough to hold memory addresses, certain bit patterns in these fields specify that words following an instruction will contain operands and/or addresses.

The following addressing modes will be assumed. They are given with their assembly-language mnemonic forms.

1. *r* (*register mode*). Register *r* contains the operand.
2. *∗r* (*indirect register mode*). Register *r* contains the address of the operand.
3. *X(r)* (*indexed mode*). Value *X*, which is found in the word following the instruction, is added to the contents of register *r* to produce the address of the operand.
4. *∗X(r)* (*indirect indexed mode*). Value *X*, stored in the word following the instruction, is added to the contents of register *r* to produce the address of the word containing the address of the operand.
5. *#X* (*immediate*). The word following the instruction contains the literal operand *X*.
6. *X* (*absolute*). The address of *X* follows the instruction.

We shall use the following op-codes (among others):

MOV   (move source to destination)
ADD   (add source to destination)
SUB   (subtract source from destination)

Some examples should make clear the meaning and length (in words) of instructions. We consider the length of an instruction to be its cost. Surely if space is important we wish to minimize length, but, since on most machines the time taken to fetch a word from memory exceeds the time spent executing the instruction, by minimizing instruction length we approximately minimize the time taken to perform an instruction as well.[†] Examples of machine instructions follow.

1. The instruction MOV R0,R1 copies the contents of register 0 into register 1. This instruction has cost one, since it occupies only one word of memory.

2. The (store) instruction MOV R5,M copies the contents of R5 into memory location M. This instruction has cost two, since the address of memory location M is in the word following the instruction.

---

† To be more accurate, we should consider whether an instruction requires the value of an operand, as well as its address, to be fetched from memory.

3. The instruction ADD #1,R3 adds the constant 1 to the contents of R3, and has cost 2, since the constant 1 must appear in the next word.

4. The instruction SUB 4(R0),*5(R1) subtracts ((R0)+4) from (((R1)+5)) where (X) denotes the contents of register or location X. The result is stored at the destination *5(R1). The cost of this instruction is 3, since the constants 4 and 5 are stored in the next two words following the instruction.

We should immediately see some of the difficulties in generating code for this machine. For a quadruple of the form A := B + C where B and C are simple variables in distinct memory locations of the same name, we can generate a variety of code sequences:

1. MOV B, R0
    ADD C, R0   cost = 6
    MOV R0, A

2. MOV B, A   cost = 6
    ADD C, A

3. MOV *R1, *R0   cost = 2
    ADD *R2, *R0

assuming R0, R1 and R2 contain the addresses of A, B, and C respectively.

4. ADD R2, R1   cost = 3
    MOV R1, A

assuming R1 and R2 contain the values of B and C respectively, and the value of B is not live after the assignment.

We see that in order to generate good code for this machine, we must utilize its addressing capabilities efficiently. There is a premium on keeping the *l*- or *r*-value of a name in a register, if possible, if it is going to be used in the near future.

15.4 A Simple Code Generator

We shall begin with a rather straightforward strategy to generate assembly or machine code from quadruples. Briefly, we are given a sequence of quadruples; we generate code for each quadruple in turn, remembering if any of the operands of the quadruple are currently in registers, and taking advantage of that fact if possible. For simplicity, we assume that for each operator in a quadruple there is a corresponding machine code operator. We also assume that computed results can be left registers as long as possible, storing them only (a) if their register is needed for another computation or (b) just before a procedure call, jump, or labeled statement.[†]

---

† However, to produce a *symbolic dump*, which makes available the values of memory loca-

Condition (b) implies that everything must be stored just before the end of a basic block.[‡] The reason we must do so is that, after leaving a basic block, we may be able to go to several different blocks, or we may go to one particular block that can be reached from several others. In either case we cannot, without extra effort, assume that a datum used by a block appears in the same register no matter how control reached that block. Thus, to avoid possible error, our simple code-generation algorithm stores everything when moving across basic-block boundaries as well as when procedure calls are made. In the next section we shall consider ways to hold some data in registers across block boundaries.

We can produce better code for a three-address statement $A := B + C$ if we generate the single instruction ADD Rj, Ri (cost = 1) and leave the result A in register Ri. This sequence is possible only if register Ri contains B, Rj contains C, and B is not live after the statement.

If Ri contains B but C is in a memory location (which we shall call C), we can generate the sequence

> ADD C, Ri   (cost = 2)

or

> MOV C, Rj   (cost = 3)
> ADD Rj, Ri

provided B is not subsequently live. The second sequence becomes attractive if this value of C is subsequently used, as we can then take its value from register Rj. There are many more cases to consider, depending on where B and C are currently located and depending on whether the current value of B is subsequently used. We must also consider the cases where one or both of B and C is a constant. The number of cases that need to be considered further increases if we assume that the operator + is commutative. Thus, we see that code generation involves examining a large number of cases, and which case should prevail depends on the context in which a quadruple is seen.

Next-Use Information

To make more informed decisions concerning register allocation we compute the next uses of each name in a quadruple, where *use* is defined as follows. Suppose quadruple *i* assigns a value to A. If quadruple *j* has A as an

---

tions and registers in terms of the source program's names for these values, it may be more convenient to have programmer-defined variables (but not necessarily temporaries) stored immediately upon calculation, should a program error suddenly cause a precipitous interrupt and exit.

‡ Note we are not assuming that the quadruples were actually partitioned into basic blocks by the compiler; the notion of a basic block is useful conceptually in any event.

operand, and control can flow from quadruple i to j along a path that has no intervening assignments to A, then we say quadruple j *uses* the value of A computed at i.

We wish to determine for each quadruple A := B **op** C what the next uses of A, B, and C are. For convenience, we shall not concern ourselves with uses outside the basic block containing this quadruple but we may, if we wish, attempt to determine whether or not there is such a use by live variable analysis.

Our algorithm to determine next uses makes a backward pass over each basic block. We need not assume that basic blocks have been constructed in the code optimization phase, and in fact, no code optimization may have been done. However, we can easily scan a stream of quadruples to find the ends of basic blocks as in Algorithm 12.1. Since procedures can have arbitrary side effects, we assume that each procedure call starts a new basic block.

Having found the end of a basic block, we shall scan backwards to the beginning, recording (in the symbol table) for each name A whether A has a next use in the block and if not, whether it is live on exit from that block. If the data-flow analysis discussed in Section 14.4 has been done, we know which names are live on exit from each block. If no live-variable analysis has been done, we can assume all nontemporary variables are live on exit, to be conservative. If the algorithms generating intermediate code or optimizing the code permit certain temporaries to be used across blocks, these too must be considered live. It would be a good idea to mark any such temporaries, so we do not have to consider all temporaries live.

Suppose in our backward scan we reach quadruple i : A := B **op** C. We then do the following.

1. Attach to quadruple i the information currently found in the symbol table regarding the next use and liveness of A, B, and C.

2. In the symbol table set A to "not live" and "no next use."

3. In the symbol table set B and C to "live" and the next uses of B and C to i. Note that the order of steps (2) and (3) may not be interchanged because A may be B or C.

If quadruple i is of the form A := B or A := **op** B, the steps are the same as above, ignoring C.

Register Descriptors

Having computed next-use information, we are ready to perform a forward pass through the block, selecting the object code as we go. To perform register allocation, we shall maintain a register descriptor that keeps track of what is currently in each register. We shall consult this register descriptor whenever we need a new register. We assume that initially the register descriptor shows that all registers are empty. (If we do register assignment across blocks, this would not be the case.) As the code generation for the block progresses, each register may hold the value of zero or more names.

Address Descriptors

There is one more facility we need. For each name in the block we shall maintain an address descriptor that keeps track of the location (or locations) where the current value of the name can be found at run time. The location might be a register, a stack location, a memory address, or some set of these, since when copied, a value also stays where it was. This information can be stored in the symbol table and is used to determine the accessing method for a name.

The Code-Generation Algorithm

We are now ready to outline the code generation algorithm. We are given a sequence of quadruples constituting a basic block. For each quadruple A := B **op** C we perform the following actions:

1. Invoke a function GETREG( ) to determine the location L where the computation B **op** C should be performed. L will usually be a register, but it could also be a memory location. We shall describe the details of GETREG shortly.

2. Consult the address descriptor for B to determine B', (one of) the current location(s) of B. Prefer the register for B' if the value of B is currently both in memory and a register. If the value of B is not in L, generate the instruction MOV B', L to place a copy of B in L.

3. Generate the instruction OP C', L, where C' is the current location of C. Update the address descriptor of A to indicate that A is in location L. If L is a register, update its descriptor to indicate that it will contain at run time the value of A.

4. If the current values of B and/or C have no next uses, are not live on exit from the block, and are in registers, alter the register descriptor to indicate that, after execution of A := B **op** C, those registers no longer will contain B and/or C, respectively.

If the current quadruple has a unary operator, the steps are analogous to those above, and we omit the details. An important special case is a quadruple A := B. If B is in a register, simply change the register and address descriptors to record that the value of A is now found only in the register holding the value of B. If B has no next use and is not live on exit from the block, the register no longer holds the value of B.

If B is only in memory, we could in principle record that the value of A is in the location of B, but this option would complicate our algorithm, since we could not then change the value of B without preserving the value of A. Thus, if B is in memory we must use GETREG to find a register in which to load B and make that register the location of A. Alternatively, we can generate a MOV B,A instruction, which would be preferable if the value of A has no next use in the block. It is worth noting that most, if not all, copy instructions will be eliminated if we use the block-improving algorithm of Section 12.4 and the copy-propagation algorithm of Section 14.3.

Once we have processed all quadruples in the basic block, we store, by MOV instructions, those names that are live on exit and not in their memory locations. To do this we use the register descriptor to determine what names are left in registers, the address descriptor to determine that the same name is not already in its memory location, and the live variable information to determine whether the name is to be stored.

The Function GETREG

Let us consider one possible version of the function GETREG that returns the location L to hold the value of A for the assignment A := B **op** C. A great deal of effort can be expended in implementing this function to produce a particularly perspicacious choice for L. In this section we shall discuss a simple, easy-to-implement scheme based on the next-use information we have available.

1. If the name B is in a register that holds the value of no other names (recall that copy instructions such as X := Y could cause a register to hold the value of two or more variables simultaneously), and B is not live and has no next use after execution of A := B + C, then return the register of B for L. Update the address descriptor of B to indicate that B is no longer in L.

2. Failing (1), return an empty register for L if there is one.

3. Failing (2), if A has a next use in the block, or **op** is an operator, such as indexing, that requires a register, find an occupied register R. Store the value of R into a memory location (by MOV R, M) if it is not already in the proper memory location M, update the address descriptor for M, and return R. A suitable occupied register might be one whose datum is referenced furthest in the future, or one whose value is also in memory. We shall leave the exact choice unspecified, since there is no one proven best way to make the selection.

4. If A is not used in the block, or no suitable occupied register can be found, select the memory location of A as L.

A more sophisticated GETREG function would also consider the subsequent uses of A and the commutativity of the operator **op** in determining the register to hold the value of A. We leave such extensions of GETREG as interesting exercises.

Example 15.1. The expression W := (A−B) + (A−C) + (A−C) might be translated into the following three-address code sequence

$$T := A - B$$
$$U := A - C$$
$$V := T + U$$
$$W := V + U$$

with W live at the end. The code-generation algorithm given above would produce the code sequence shown in Fig. 15.3 for this quadruple sequence. Shown alongside are the values of the register and address descriptors as code generation progresses. Not shown in the address descriptor is the fact that A, B, and C are always in memory. We also assume that T, U and V, being temporaries, are not in memory unless we explicitly store their values with a MOV instruction.

Statements	Code generated	Register descriptor	Address descriptor
		registers empty	
T := A − B	MOV A, R0 SUB B, R0	R0 contains T	T in R0
U := A − C	MOV A, R1 SUB C, R1	R0 contains T R1 contains U	T in R0 U in R1
V := T + U	ADD R1, R0	R0 contains V R1 contains U	U in R1 V in R0
W := V + U	ADD R1, R0	R0 contains W	W in R0
	MOV R0, W		W in R0 and memory

Fig. 15.3. Code sequence.

The first call of GETREG returns R0 as the location in which to do the computation of T. Since A is not in R0, we generate instructions MOV A, R0 and SUB B, R0. We now update the register descriptor to indicate that R0 contains T.

Code generation proceeds in this manner until the last quadruple W := V + U has been processed. Note that R1 becomes empty because U has

no next use. We then generate MOV R0, W to store the live variable W at
the end of the block.

The cost of the code generated in Fig. 15.3 is 12. We could reduce this
to 11 by generating MOV R0, R1 immediately after the first instruction and
removing the instruction MOV A, R1, but to do so requires a more sophisticated code-generation algorithm. The reason for the savings is that it is
cheaper to load R1 from R0 than from memory. □

Generation of Code for Other Types of Statements

The indexing and pointer operations we introduced into our three-address
repertoire are handled in essentially the same manner as binary operations.
For example, assuming a statically allocated B, the indexed assignment
A:=B[I] can be implemented by selecting a register L for A by GETREG
and then executing

$$
\begin{array}{lll}
\text{MOV} & \text{I}', \text{L} & \text{(cost 4)} \\
\text{MOV} & \text{B(L), L} &
\end{array}
$$

if I is not in a register and I' is a location (memory or stack) for I, and

$$
\begin{array}{lll}
\text{MOV} & \text{B(R), L} & \text{(cost 2)}
\end{array}
$$

if I is in register R. Similarly, A[I] := B is implemented by

$$
\begin{array}{lll}
\text{MOV} & \text{I}', \text{L} & \text{(cost 4)} \\
\text{MOV} & \text{B, A(L)} &
\end{array}
$$

if I is not in a register and I' is a location for I, and

$$
\begin{array}{lll}
\text{MOV} & \text{B, A(R)} & \text{(cost 2)}
\end{array}
$$

if I is in register R. The pointer assignment A:=*P can be implemented
by

$$
\begin{array}{lll}
\text{MOV} & *\text{P, A} & \text{(cost 3)}
\end{array}
$$

or

$$
\begin{array}{lll}
\text{MOV} & \text{P}', \text{L} & \text{(cost 3)} \\
\text{MOV} & *\text{L, L} &
\end{array}
$$

where P' is a location for P, or

$$
\begin{array}{lll}
\text{MOV} & *\text{R, L} & \text{(cost 1)}
\end{array}
$$

if P is in register R. We would prefer to leave A in a register L (by the
second sequence above) if A has a next use in the block and there is an
empty register L available. Similarly, *P:=A can be implemented by

$$
\begin{array}{lll}
\text{MOV} & \text{A, } *\text{P} & \text{(cost 3)}
\end{array}
$$

or

	MOV	A, L	(cost 4)
	MOV	L, *P	

or

	MOV	A, *R	(cost 2)

if P is in register R.

Conditional Statements

Machines generally implement conditional jumps in one of two ways. The first method is to have a collection of conditional jump instructions that jump if the value of a designated register meets one of the six conditions: negative, zero, positive, nonnegative, nonzero, and nonpositive. For example, a three-address statement such as **if** A < B **goto** X could be implemented by subtracting B from A in register r, then jumping to X if register r were negative.

A second approach, found in many modern machines, is to use a *condition code,* which is a hardware indication whether the last quantity computed or loaded into a register is negative, zero, or positive. Often a compare instruction (CMP in our machine) has the desirable property that it sets the condition code without actually computing a value. That is, CMP A, B sets the condition code to positive if A > B, and so on. There is a conditional jump machine instruction which makes the jump if a designated condition ($<$, $=$, $>$, $\leqslant$, $\neq$, $\geqslant$) is met. We have in our machine the instruction CJ$\leqslant$ X for "jump to X if the condition code is negative or zero," and so on. For example, **if** A < B **goto** X could be implemented by

$$\text{CMP A, B}$$
$$\text{CJ< X}$$

If we are generating code for a machine with condition codes it is useful to remember a condition descriptor as we generate code. This descriptor tells the name that last set the condition code, or the pair of names compared, if the condition code was last set that way. Thus we could implement

$$A := B + C$$
$$\textbf{if } A < 0 \textbf{ goto } X$$

by

	MOV	B, R0
	ADD	C, R0
	MOV	R0, A
	CJ<	X

if we were aware that the condition code was determined by A after ADD C, R0.

15.5 Register Allocation and Assignment

As we have seen, instructions involving only register operands are shorter and faster than those involving memory operands. Therefore, efficient utilization of registers is particularly important in generating good code. In this section we shall discuss various strategies for deciding what names in a program should reside in registers, a problem often referred to as *register allocation,* and in which register each should reside (*register assignment*).

One approach to register allocation and assignment is to assign specific types of quantities in an object program to certain registers. For example, a decision can be made to assign subroutine links to one group of registers, base addresses to another, arithmetic computation to another, the run-time stack pointer to a fixed register, and so on.

This approach has the advantage that it simplifies the design of a compiler. Its disadvantage is that, applied too strictly, it uses registers inefficiently; certain registers may go unused over substantial portions of code, while unnecessary loads and stores are generated. Nevertheless, it is reasonable in most computing environments to reserve a few registers for base registers, stack pointers and the like, and to allow the remaining registers to be used by the compiler as it sees fit.

Global Register Allocation

The approach suggested in Section 15.4 served to make use of registers to hold values for the duration of a single basic block. However, we were forced to store values at the end of each block. To save some of these stores and corresponding loads, we must arrange to assign registers to frequently used variables and keep these registers consistent across block boundaries (*globally*). Since programs spend most of their time in inner loops, a natural approach to global register assignment is to try to keep a frequently used name in a fixed register throughout a loop. As we need to know about loops, we must assume that global register assignment is carried out after a flow graph has been constructed for each procedure. We also assume that loops are determined as in Section 12.2, and that live variables have been computed as in Section 14.4.

Thus we might base our global register-handling strategy on the assumption that some fixed number of registers, say three, will be assigned to hold the most active names in each inner loop. The selected names may differ in different loops. Other registers not already dedicated to the purposes mentioned at the beginning of the section may be used to hold values local to one block as was done in Section 15.4. The approach has the drawback that no given number of registers will be universally the right number to make available for global register allocation. Yet the method is far simpler to implement than are some alternative methods. It was used in FORTRAN H, the optimizing FORTRAN compiler for the IBM-360 series machines (Lowry and Medlock [1969]). It is also worth noting that by means of the **register** declaration in the language C, the programmer can choose which names to keep in registers for the duration of a procedure. This ability has been found to speed up many programs by a factor of 2. A similar facility is available in BLISS (Wulf *et al.* [1975]).

Usage Counts

A simple method for determining the savings to be realized by keeping variable A in a register for the duration of loop L is to recognize that in our machine model we save one unit of cost for each reference to A if A is in a register. However, if we use the approach of the previous section to generate code for a block, there is a good chance that after A has been computed in a block it will remain in a register if there are subsequent uses of A in that block. Thus we count a savings of one for each use of A in loop L that is not preceded by an assignment to A in the same block. We also save two units if we can avoid a store of A at the end of a block. Thus if A is allocated a register, count a savings of two for each block of L for which A is live on exit and in which A is assigned a value.

On the debit side, if A is live on entry to the loop header, we must load A into its register just before entering loop L (in the preheader of L). This load costs two units. Similarly, for each exit block B of loop L at which A is live on entry to some successor of B outside of L, we must store A at a cost of two. However, on the assumption that the loop is iterated many times, we may neglect these debits since they occur only once each time we enter the loop.[†] Thus an approximate formula for the benefit to be realized from allocating a register to A within loop L is:

$$\sum_{\substack{\text{blocks} \\ B \text{ in } L}} \text{USES}(A, B) + 2 * \text{LIVE}(A, B) \qquad (15.1)$$

where $\text{USES}(A, B)$ is the number of times A is used in B prior to any definition of A. $\text{LIVE}(A, B)$ is 1 if A is live on exit from B and is assigned a value in B, and $\text{LIVE}(A, B)$ is 0 otherwise. Note that (15.1) is approximate, because not all blocks in a loop are executed with equal frequency and also because (15.1) was based on the assumption that a loop is iterated "many" times. Also, on any machine but the one we use here, a formula analogous to (15.1), but possibly quite different from it, would have to be developed.

Example 15.2. Consider the basic blocks in the inner loop depicted in Fig. 15.4, where jumps and conditional jumps are omitted. We assume registers

---

[†] We would include these debits if space were the only measure of the quality of code, because in that case, the frequency with which an instruction is executed does not matter.

R0, R1, and R2 are allocated to hold names throughout the loop. Variables live on entry into and on exit from each block are shown in Fig. 15.4 for convenience.

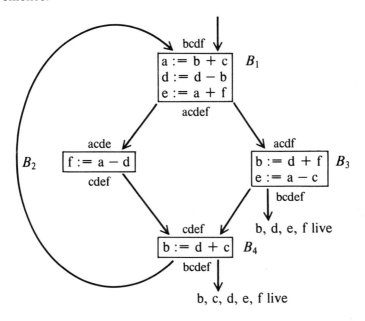

Fig. 15.4. Flow graph of inner loop.

To evaluate (15.1) for A = a we observe that a is live on exit from B_1 and is assigned a value there, but is not live on exit from B_2, B_3, or B_4. Thus $\sum_{B \text{ in } L} 2*\text{LIVE}(a, B) = 2$. Also USE(a, B_1) = 2, since a is defined in B_1 before any use. USE(a, B_2) = USE(a, B_3) = 1 and USE(a, B_4) = 0. Thus $\sum_{B \text{ in } L} \text{USE}(a, B) = 2$. Hence the value of (15.1) for A = a is 4. That is, four units of cost can be saved by selecting a for one of the global registers. The values of (15.1) for b, c, d, e, and f are 5, 3, 6, 4, and 4, respectively. Thus we may select a, b, and d, for registers R0, R1, and R2, respectively. Using R0 for e or f instead of a would be another choice with the same apparent benefit. Figure 15.5 shows the assembly code generated from Fig. 15.4, assuming that the strategy of Section 15.4 is used to generate code for each block. We do not show the generated code for the omitted conditional or unconditional jumps that end each block in Fig. 15.4, and we therefore do not show the generated code as a single stream, as it would appear in practice.

It is worth noting that, if we did not adhere strictly to our strategy of reserving R0, R1, and R2, we could use

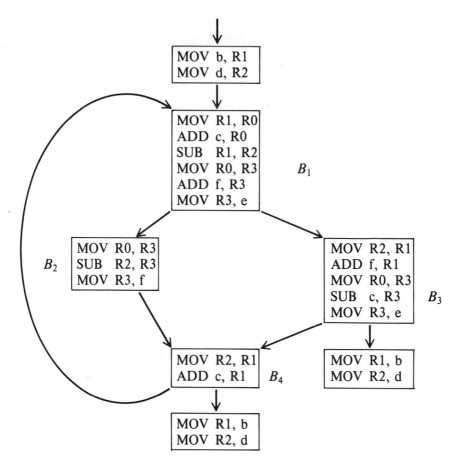

Fig. 15.5. Code sequence using global register assignment.

$$\text{SUB} \quad \text{R2, R0}$$
$$\text{MOV} \quad \text{R0, f}$$

for B_2, saving a unit since a is dead on exit from B_2. A similar saving could be realized at B_3. □

Register Assignment for Outer Loops

Having assigned registers and generated code for inner loops, we may apply the same idea to progressively larger loops. If an outer loop L_1 contains an inner loop L_2, the names allocated registers in L_2 need not be allocated registers in $L_1 - L_2$. However, if name A is allocated a register in loop L_1 but not L_2 we must store A on entrance to L_2 and load A if we leave L_2 and enter a block of $L_1 - L_2$. Similarly, if we choose to allocate A a register in L_2 but not L_1 we must load A on entrance to L_2 and store A on exit from L_2. We leave the formula for selecting names to be allocated registers in an outer loop L, given that choices have already been made for all loops nested within L, as an exercise for the interested reader.

15.6 Code Generation from DAG's

In this section we shall consider generating code for a basic block from its DAG representation (see Section 12.3). The advantage of doing so is that from a DAG we can more easily rearrange the order of the final computation sequence than we can starting from a linear sequence of quadruples. Central to our discussion is the case where the DAG is a tree. For this case we can generate code that we can prove is optimal under such criteria as program length or the fewest number of temporaries used. This algorithm for optimal code generation from a tree is also useful when the intermediate code is a parse tree.

Rearranging the Order

Let us briefly consider how the order in which computations are done can affect the cost of resulting object code. Consider the following quadruple sequence whose DAG representation is shown in Fig. 15.6 (the DAG happens to be a tree).

$$T_1 := A + B$$
$$T_2 := C + D$$
$$T_3 := E - T_2$$
$$T_4 := T_1 - T_3$$

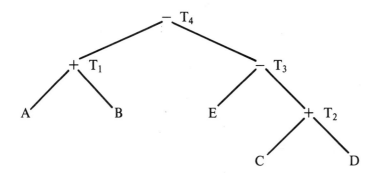

Fig. 15.6. DAG for quadruple sequence.

If we generate code for the quadruples using the algorithm in Section 15.4 we get the code sequence of Fig. 15.7 (assuming two registers R0 and R1 are available, and only T_4 is live on exit).

```
MOV  A, R0
ADD  B, R0
MOV  C, R1
ADD  D, R1
MOV  R0, T₁
MOV  E, R0
SUB   R1, R0
MOV  T₁, R1
SUB   R0, R1
MOV  R1, T₄
```

Fig. 15.7. Code sequence.

On the other hand suppose we rearranged the order of the quadruples so that the computation of T_1 occurs immediately before that of T_4 as:

$$T_2 := C + D$$
$$T_3 := E - T_2$$
$$T_1 := A + B$$
$$T_4 := T_1 - T_3$$

Then, using the code-generation algorithm of Section 15.4, we get the code sequence of Fig. 15.8. (Again, only R0 and R1 are available.) By performing the computation in this order, we have been able to save two instructions, MOV R0, T_1 (which stores the value of R0 in memory location T_1) and MOV T_1, R1 (which reloads the value of T_1 in register R1).

```
MOV  C, R0
ADD  D, R0
MOV  E, R1
SUB   R0, R1
MOV  A, R0
ADD  B, R0
SUB   R1, R0
MOV  R0, T₄
```

Fig. 15.8. Revised code sequence.

A Heuristic Ordering for DAG's

The reason the above reordering improved the code was that the computation of T_4 was made to follow immediately after the computation of T_1, its left operand in the tree. That this arrangement is beneficial should be clear. The left argument for the computation of T_4 must be in a register for efficient computation of T_4, and computing T_1 immediately before T_4 ensures that that will be the case.

In selecting an ordering for the nodes of a DAG we are only constrained to be sure that the order preserves the edge relationships of the DAG. Recall from Section 12.3 that those edges can represent either the operator-operand relationship or implied constraints due to possible interactions between array or pointer assignments. We propose the following heuristic ordering algorithm which attempts as far as possible to make the evaluation of a node immediately follow the evaluation of its leftmost argument. The algorithm of Fig. 15.9 produces the ordering in reverse.

```
(1)     while unlisted interior nodes remain do
            begin
(2)             select an unlisted node n, all of whose parents have
                    been listed;
(3)             list n ;
(4)             while the leftmost child m of n has no unlisted parents
                and is not a leaf do
                    /* since n was just listed, surely m is not yet listed */
                    begin
(5)                     list m ;
(6)                     n := m
                    end
            end
```

Fig. 15.9. Node listing algorithm.

Example 15.3. The algorithm of Fig. 15.9 applied to the tree of Fig. 15.6 yields the order from which the code of Fig. 15.8 was produced. For a more complete example, consider the DAG of Fig. 15.10. Initially the only node with no unlisted parents is 1, so we set $n=1$ at line (2) and list 1 at line (3). Now the left argument of 1, which is 2, has its parents listed, so we list 2 and set $n=2$ at line (6). Now at line (4) we find the leftmost child of 2, which is 6, has an unlisted parent, 5. Thus we select a new n at line (2), and node 3 is the only candidate. We list 3 and then proceed down its left chain, listing 4, 5, and 6. This leaves only 8 among the interior nodes, so we list that. The resulting list is 1234568 so the suggested order of evaluation is 8654321. This ordering corresponds to the sequence of quadruples:

$$T_8 := D + E$$
$$T_6 := A + B$$

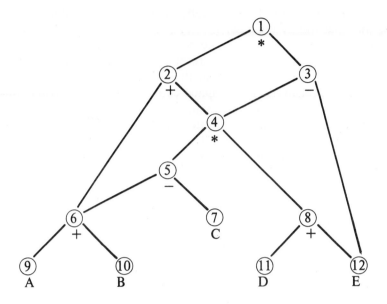

Fig. 15.10. A DAG.

$$T_5 := T_6 - C$$
$$T_4 := T_5 * T_8$$
$$T_3 := T_4 - E$$
$$T_2 := T_6 + T_4$$
$$T_1 := T_2 * T_3$$

which will yield optimal code for the DAG on our machine whatever the number of registers, if the code-generation algorithm of Section 15.4 is used. It should be noted that in this example our ordering heuristic never had any choices to make at step (2), but in general it may have many choices. □

Optimal Ordering for Trees

It turns out that for the machine model of Section 15.3 we can give a simple algorithm to determine the optimal order in which to evaluate a sequence of quadruples when the DAG representation of the quadruples is a tree. Optimal order here means the order that yields the shortest instruction sequence, over all instruction sequences that evaluate the tree. This algorithm, modified as we shall discuss to take into account register pairs and other target-machine vagaries, has been used in a number of compilers, such as ALGOL W, BLISS/11, and the PDP-11 C compiler (see Appendix B).

The algorithm works on the tree representation of the quadruple sequence. It could also be made to work on the parse tree if that were the intermediate code form. The algorithm has two parts. The first part labels each node of the tree, bottom-up, with an integer that denotes the fewest number of registers required to evaluate the tree with no stores of intermediate results. The second part of the algorithm is a tree traversal whose order is governed by the computed node labels. The output code is generated during the tree traversal.

The Labeling Algorithm

We use the term "left leaf" to mean a node that is a leaf and the leftmost descendant of its parent. All other leaves are referred to as "right leaves."

```
(1)      if n is a leaf then
(2)          if n is the leftmost child of its parent then
(3)              LABEL(n) := 1
(4)          else LABEL(n) := 0
         else /* n is an interior node */
             begin
(5)              let n₁, n₂, . . . , nₖ be the children of n ordered by LABEL,
                 so LABEL(n₁) ⩾ LABEL(n₂) ⩾ · · · ⩾ LABEL(nₖ);
(6)              LABEL(n) := max (LABEL(nᵢ)+i−1)
                            1⩽i⩽k
             end
```

$$(5)\quad \text{let } n_1, n_2, \ldots, n_k \text{ be the children of } n \text{ ordered by LABEL,}$$
$$\text{so } LABEL(n_1) \geqslant LABEL(n_2) \geqslant \cdots \geqslant LABEL(n_k);$$
$$(6)\quad LABEL(n) := \max_{1\leqslant i\leqslant k} (LABEL(n_i)+i-1)$$

Fig. 15.11. Label computation.

The labeling can be done by visiting nodes in a bottom-up order so that a node is not visited until all its children are labeled. The order in which parse tree nodes are created is suitable if the parse tree is used as intermediate code, so in this case, the labels can be computed as a syntax-directed translation. Figure 15.11 gives the algorithm for computing the label at node n. In the important special case that n is a binary node and its children have labels l_1 and l_2, the formula of line (6) reduces to

$$LABEL(n) = \begin{cases} \max(l_1, l_2) & \text{if } l_1 \neq l_2 \\ l_1+1 & \text{if } l_1=l_2 \end{cases}$$

Example 15.4. Consider the tree in Fig. 15.6. A postorder traversal[†] of the nodes visits the nodes in the order A B T_1 E C D T_2 T_3 T_4. Postorder is always an appropriate order in which to do the label computations. Node

[†] In a *postorder traversal* we recursively visit the subtrees rooted at children $n_1, n_2, \ldots, n_k$ of a node n, then we visit n. It is the order in which nodes of a parse tree are created in a bottom-up parse.

A is labeled 1 since it is a left leaf. Node B is labeled 0 since it is a right leaf. Node T_1 is labeled 1 because the labels of its children are unequal and the maximum label of a child is 1. Figure 15.12 shows the labeled tree that results. It implies that two registers are needed to evaluate T_4 and, in fact, two registers are needed just to evaluate T_3.   □

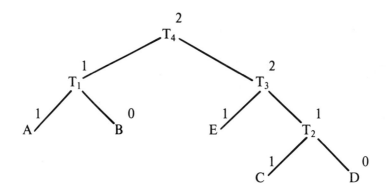

Fig. 15.12. Labeled tree.

Code Generation from a Labeled Tree

We shall now present the algorithm that takes as input a labeled tree T and produces as output a machine code sequence that evaluates T into R0. (R0 can then be stored into the appropriate memory location.) We assume T has only binary operators. The generalization to operators with an arbitrary number of operands is not hard, and is left as an exercise.

The algorithm uses the recursive procedure GENCODE(n) to produce machine code evaluating the subtree of T with root n into a register. GEN-CODE uses RSTACK to allocate registers. Initially RSTACK contains all available registers, which we assume are R0, R1, . . . , R($r-1$), in this order. A call of GENCODE may find a subset of the registers, perhaps in a different order, on RSTACK. When GENCODE returns, it leaves the registers on RSTACK in the same order it found them. The resulting code computes the value of the tree T in the top register on RSTACK.

The function SWAP(RSTACK) interchanges the top two registers on RSTACK. The use of SWAP is to make sure that a left child and its parent are evaluated into the same register.

GENCODE uses a stack TSTACK to allocate temporary memory locations. We assume TSTACK initially contains T0, T1, T2, ... In practice, TSTACK need not be implemented as a list, if we just keep track of that i such that Ti is currently on top. The contents of TSTACK is always a suffix of T0, T1, ...

We use the notation X $\Longleftarrow$ STACK to mean "pop STACK and assign the value popped to X." Conversely, we use STACK $\Longleftarrow$ X to mean "push X onto STACK." TOP(STACK) refers to the value on top of STACK.

The code-generation algorithm is to call GENCODE on the root of T. GENCODE is shown in Fig. 15.13. It can be explained by examining each of the five cases. For case 0 we have a subtree of the form

That is, n is a leaf and the leftmost child of its parent. Therefore we generate just a load instruction.

In case 1 we have a subtree of the form

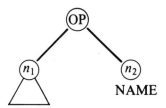

for which we generate code to evaluate n_1 into register R=TOP(RSTACK) followed by the instruction OP NAME, R.

In case 2 we have a subtree of the form

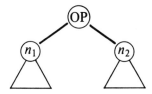

where n_1 can be evaluated without stores but n_2 is harder to evaluate (i.e., requires more registers) than n_1. For this case we swap the top two registers in RSTACK, then evaluate n_2 into R=TOP(RSTACK). We remove R from RSTACK and evaluate n_1 into S=TOP(RSTACK). Note that S was the register initially on top of RSTACK at the beginning of case 2. We then generate the instruction OP R, S, which produces the value of n in register S. Another call to SWAP leaves RSTACK as it was when this call of GENCODE began.

procedure GENCODE(n);
begin
/* case 0 */
if n is a left leaf representing operand NAME and n is
   the leftmost child of its parent **then**
     print 'MOV' || NAME || ', ' || TOP(RSTACK);
if n is an interior node with operator OP and children n_1 and n_2 **then**
/* case 1 */ **if** LABEL(n_2) = 0 **then**
         begin
            let NAME be the operand represented by n_2;
            GENCODE(n_1);
            print OP || NAME || ', ' || TOP(RSTACK)
         end
/* case 2 */ **else if** $1 \leqslant$ LABEL(n_1) $<$ LABEL(n_2)
            and LABEL(n_1) $< r$ **then**
         begin
            SWAP(RSTACK);
            GENCODE(n_2);
            R $\Longleftarrow$ RSTACK; /* n_2 was evaluated into register R */
            GENCODE(n_1);
            print OP || R || ', ' || TOP(RSTACK);
            RSTACK $\Longleftarrow$ R;
            SWAP(RSTACK)
         end
/* case 3 */ **else if** $1 \leqslant$ LABEL(n_2) $\leqslant$ LABEL(n_1)
            and LABEL(n_2) $< r$ **then**
         begin
            GENCODE(n_1);
            R $\Longleftarrow$ RSTACK; /* n_1 was evaluated into register R */
            GENCODE(n_2);
            print OP || TOP(RSTACK) || ', ' || R;
            RSTACK $\Longleftarrow$ R
         end
/* case 4 */ **else** /* both labels $\geqslant r$, the total number of registers */
         begin
            GENCODE(n_2);
            T $\Longleftarrow$ TSTACK;
            print 'MOV' || TOP(RSTACK) || ', ' || T;
            GENCODE(n_1);
            TSTACK $\Longleftarrow$ T;
            print OP || T || ', ' || TOP(RSTACK)
          end
end

Fig. 15.13. Function GENCODE.

Case 3 is similar to case 2 except that here the left subtree is harder and is evaluated first. There is no need to SWAP registers here.

Case 4 occurs when both subtrees require r or more registers to evaluate without stores. Since we must use a temporary memory location, we first evaluate the right subtree into the temporary T, then the left subtree, and finally the root.

Example 15.5. Let us generate code for the labeled tree in Fig. 15.12 with RSTACK = R0, R1 initially. The sequence of calls to GENCODE and code printing steps is shown in Fig. 15.14. Shown alongside in brackets is the contents of RSTACK at the time of each call. The code sequence here is a permutation of that in Fig. 15.8. □

```
GENCODE(T₄)    [R₀R₁]                    /* case 2 */
    GENCODE(T₃)  [R₁R₀]                  /* case 3 */
        GENCODE(E)  [R₁R₀]              /* case 0 */
        print MOV E, R₁
        GENCODE(T₂)  [R₀]              /* case 1 */
            GENCODE(C)  [R₀]           /* case 0 */
            print MOV  C, R₀
            print ADD  D, R₀
        print SUB  R₀, R₁
    GENCODE(T₁)  [R₀]                    /* case 1 */
        GENCODE(A)  [R₀]               /* case 0 */
        print MOV  A, R₀
        print ADD  B, R₀
    print SUB  R₁, R₀
```

Fig. 15.14. Trace of GENCODE routine.

We can prove that GENCODE produces optimal code on expressions for our machine model, assuming that no algebraic properties of operators are taken into account and assuming there are no common subexpressions. The proof, left as an exercise, is based on showing that any code sequence must perform

1. an operation for each interior node,
2. a load for each leaf which is the leftmost child of its parent, and
3. a store for every node both of whose children have labels equal to or greater than r.

Since GENCODE produces exactly these steps it is optimal.

Multiregister Operations

We can modify our labeling algorithm to handle operations like multiplication, division, or a function call, which normally require more than one register to perform. Simply modify step (6) of Fig. 15.11, the labeling algorithm, so LABEL(n) is always at least the number of registers required by the operation. For example, if a function call is assumed to require all r registers, replace line (6) by LABEL$(n) = r$. If multiplication requires two registers, in the binary case use

$$\text{LABEL}(n) = \begin{cases} \max(2, \ l_1, \ l_2) & \text{if } l_1 \neq l_2 \\ l_1 + 1 & \text{if } l_1 = l_2 \end{cases}$$

where l_1 and l_2 are the labels of the children of n.

Unfortunately, this modification will not guarantee that a register-pair is available for a multiplication or division, or for multiple-precision operations. A useful trick implemented in the C compiler for the PDP-11 is to pretend that multiplication and division require three registers. If SWAP is never used in GENCODE, then RSTACK will always contain consecutive high-numbered registers $i, i+1, \ldots, r-1$ for some i. Thus the first three of these are sure to include a register pair. By taking advantage of the fact that many operations are commutative we can often avoid using case 2 of GENCODE, the case that calls SWAP. Also, even if RSTACK does not contain three consecutive registers at the top, we have a very good chance of finding a register-pair somewhere in RSTACK. By being prepared to handle the special case where there are sufficient registers but no register-pair available by introducing extra stores, we can create an algorithm that does multiplicative and multiple-precision operations in a register-pair and is close to optimal.

Algebraic Properties

If we may assume algebraic laws for various operators, we have the opportunity to replace a given tree T by one with smaller labels (to avoid stores in case 4 of GENCODE) and/or fewer left leaves (to avoid loads in case 0). For example, since $+$ is commutative, we may replace the tree of Fig. 15.15(a) by that of Fig. 15.15(b), reducing the number of left leaves by one and possibly lowering some labels as well.

Since $+$ is treated as being associative as well as being commutative, we may take a cluster of nodes labeled $+$ as in Fig. 15.15(c) and replace it by a left chain as in Fig. 15.15(d). To minimize the label of the root we need only arrange that T_{i_1} is one of T_1, T_2, T_3, and T_4 with a largest label and that T_{i_1} is not a leaf unless all of $T_1, \ldots, T_4$ are.

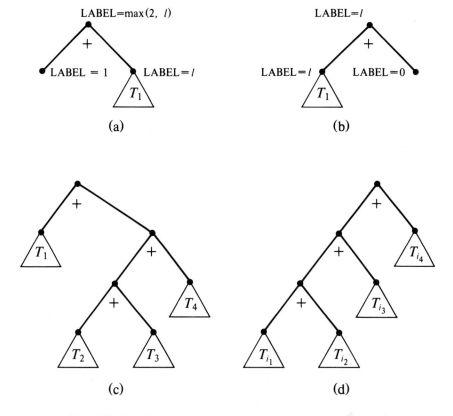

Fig. 15.15. Commutative and associative transformations.

Common Subexpressions

When there are common subexpressions in a sequence of quadruples the corresponding DAG will no longer be a tree. The common subexpressions will correspond to nodes with more than one parent, called *shared nodes*. We can no longer apply the labeling algorithm or GENCODE directly. We can, however, partition the DAG into a set of trees by finding for each root and/or shared node n, the maximal subtree with n as root that includes no other shared nodes, except as leaves.

For example, the DAG of Fig. 15.10 can be partitioned into the trees of Fig. 15.16. Each shared node with p parents appears as a leaf in at most p trees. Nodes with more than one parent in the same tree can be turned into as many leaves as necessary, so no leaf has multiple parents.

Once we have partitioned the DAG into trees in this fashion we can order the evaluation of the trees and use an algorithm similar to the one

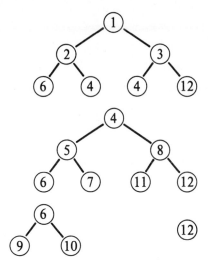

Fig. 15.16. Partition into trees.

just discussed to generate code for each tree. The order of the trees must be such that shared values that are leaves of a tree must be available when the tree is evaluated. The shared quantities can be computed and stored into memory (or kept in registers if enough registers are available). While this process does not necessarily generate optimal code, it will often be satisfactory.

15.7 Peephole Optimization

Peephole optimization is a technique used in many compilers, in connection with the optimization of either intermediate or object code. It is really an attempt to overcome the difficulties encountered in syntax-directed generation of code. Peephole optimization works by looking at the intermediate or object code within a small range of instructions (peephole). The code in the peephole need not be contiguous, although there are some implementations that require this. It is characteristic of peephole optimization that each improvement may spawn opportunities for additional improvements. Thus, repeated passes over the code are necessary to get the maximum benefit from peephole optimization.

Redundant Loads and Stores

For example, if we see the instructions

$$
\begin{array}{lll}
(1) & \text{MOV} & \text{R0, A} \\
(2) & \text{MOV} & \text{A, R0}
\end{array}
\tag{15.2}
$$

we can delete instruction (2) because whenever (2) is executed, (1) will ensure that the value of A is already in register 0. Note that if (2) had a label[†] we could not be sure that (1) was always executed immediately before (2) and so we could not remove (2). Put another way, (1) and (2) have to be in the same basic block for this transformation to be safe.

While code such as (15.2) would not appear if the algorithm suggested in Section 15.4 were used, it might if a more naive algorithm were used. For example, if we always translated A := B **op** C into

$$
\begin{array}{ll}
\text{MOV} & \text{B, R0} \\
\text{OP} & \text{C, R0} \\
\text{MOV} & \text{R0, A}
\end{array}
$$

then we would see pattern (15.2) if we translated

$$
\begin{array}{l}
A := B + C \\
D := A + E
\end{array}
$$

Unreachable Code

Another opportunity for peephole optimization is the removal of unreachable code. An unlabeled instruction immediately following an unconditional jump may be removed. This operation can be repeated to eliminate a sequence of instructions. For example, for debugging purposes, a large program may have within it certain segments that are executed only if DEBUG is 1. The source code might look like:

DEBUG := 0;

.
.
.

if DEBUG = 1 **then**
        sequence of statements to print information
        to aid in debugging

In intermediate code the if-statement might be

$$
\begin{array}{ll}
& \textbf{if } \text{DEBUG} = 1 \textbf{ goto } \text{L1} \\
& \textbf{goto } \text{L2} \\
\text{L1:} & \text{print debugging aids} \\
\text{L2:}
\end{array}
\qquad (15.3)
$$

One immediate peephole optimization is to eliminate jumps over jumps. That is, (15.3) can be replaced by:

---

† One advantage of generating assembly code is that the labels will be present, facilitating peephole optimizations such as this. If machine code is generated, and peephole optimization is desired, we can use a bit to mark the instructions that would have labels.

$$\textbf{if } \text{DEBUG} \neq 1 \textbf{ goto } \text{L2}$$
$$\text{print debugging aids} \qquad (15.4)$$

L2:

Now, since DEBUG is set to 0 at the beginning of the program, constant propagation should replace (15.4) by

$$\textbf{if } 0 \neq 1 \textbf{ goto } \text{L2}$$
$$\text{print debugging aids} \qquad (15.5)$$

L2:

As the argument of the first statement of (15.5) evaluates to a constant **true**, it can be replaced during constant propagation by **goto** L2. Then all the statements that print debugging aids are manifestly unreachable and can be eliminated one at a time.

Multiple Jumps

It is not uncommon for intermediate code-generation algorithms such as those in Sections 7.8 and 7.9 to produce jumps to jumps, jumps to conditional jumps, or conditional jumps to jumps. These can be eliminated in intermediate or object code by replacing

$$\qquad \textbf{goto } \text{L1}$$
$$.$$
$$.$$
$$.$$

L1:   **goto** L2

by

$$\qquad \textbf{goto } \text{L2}$$
$$.$$
$$.$$
$$.$$

L1:   **goto** L2

If there are now no jumps to L1,[†] then it may be possible to eliminate L1: **goto** L2 provided it is preceded by an unconditional jump. Similarly,

$$\qquad \textbf{if } A < B \textbf{ goto } \text{L1}$$
$$.$$
$$.$$
$$.$$

L1:   **goto** L2

can be replaced by

---

† If this peephole optimization is attempted we can count the number of jumps to a label in the symbol-table entry for that label; a search of the code is not necessary.

> **if** A < B **goto** L2
> .
> .
> .

    L1:   **goto** L2

Finally, suppose there is only one jump to L1 and L1 is preceded by an unconditional goto. Then

> **goto** L1
> .
> .
> .

    L1:   **if** A < B **goto** L2
    L3:   (15.6)

may be replaced by

> **if** A < B **goto** L2
> **goto** L3   (15.7)
> .
> .
> .

    L3:

While the number of instructions in (15.6) and (15.7) is the same, we sometimes skip the unconditional jump in (15.7), but never in (15.6). Thus (15.7) is superior to (15.6) in execution time.

Algebraic Simplification

There is no end to the amount of algebraic simplification that can be attempted. A few algebraic identities, however, occur frequently enough that it is worth considering implementing them. For example, statements such as

$$X := X * 1$$

or

$$X := X + 0$$

are often produced by straightforward intermediate code-generation algo-rithms, and they can be eliminated. Multiplication by two could be replaced by an addition (but make sure that $A := 2*A$ is not implemented by ADD Ri, Ri unless the machine permits identical operands) or by a shift if the other operand is fixed-point.

Reduction in Strength

Reduction in strength replaces expensive operations by equivalent cheaper ones. Certain machine instructions are considerably cheaper than others and can often be used as special cases of more expensive operators. For example, X^2 is invariably cheaper to implement as $X*X$ than as a call to an exponentiation routine. Fixed-point multiplication or division by a power of two is cheaper to implement as a shift. Floating-point division by a constant can be implemented (approximated) multiplication by a constant, which may be cheaper.

Use of Machine Idioms

A machine may have hardware instructions to implement certain specific operations efficiently. Detecting situations that permit the use of these instructions can reduce execution time significantly. For example, some machines have auto-increment and auto-decrement addressing modes. These add or subtract one from an operand before or after using its value. The use of these modes greatly improves the quality of code when pushing or popping a stack, as in parameter passing. These modes can also be used in code for statements like A := A + 1.

Exercises

15.1 Suppose R7 is the stack pointer and the display is stored 10 words above the point of the current activation record that is pointed to by R7. Suppose further the nesting level of the current procedure is three. Write instructions or sequences of instructions that will load into register 0 the following quantities. Use whatever addressing modes will make the evaluation most efficient.

  a) The value of name A, where A has offset 23 from the top of the activation record at level 2.
  b) The value of B[I], where I has offset 7 from the top of the activation record at level 2, and a pointer to the base of array B has offset 9 from the top of the activation record at level 1.

15.2 Repeat Exercise 15.1 if the display pointer for level i is stored in register $4+i$.

15.3 If the triples form of intermediate code is used, the temporary values represented by the triples themselves have no memory location. Usually there will be sufficient registers available to hold these values for the typically short time between their computation and single use. However, a code generator using triples must be prepared to store temporary values. Propose an algorithm which allots memory locations to temporaries, being careful not to use the same location for two live temporaries or use a new location when a formerly used one is available.

15.4 Suppose we wish to calculate next-use information for the quadruples of a block, and the DAG for that block is available. Give an efficient algorithm to do so, making use of the DAG.

15.5 Suppose that for the loop of Fig. 15.4 we choose to allocate three registers to hold a, b, and c. Use the approach of Section 15.4 to generate assembly code for the blocks of this loop. How does the code compare in cost with that of Fig. 15.5?

**15.6 Another approach to global-register allocation and assignment is to group definitions and uses into *webs,* which are the transitive closure of ud- and du- chains. For example, Fig. 15.17 shows a web. We might construct this web starting with definition (1). We find, from the du-chain information, that this definition is used by (3) and (4). Then we find from the ud-chains that use (3) could be defined only at (1) but (4) could be defined at (1) or (2). Thus we consider where (2) could be used and find uses (4) and (5). Then we find (5) could only be defined at (2), so no more definitions or uses of A need be added to the web. In essence, we have, starting at (1), found all the definitions and uses we would reach by any sequence of du- or ud- chains in any order.

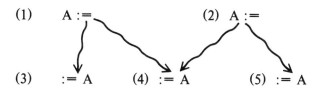

Fig. 15.17. A web.

a) Give an algorithm for taking du- and ud-chains and producing a partition of all definitions and uses into webs.

b) The webs aid register assignment if we allocate some number of registers to hold the values computed by definitions in some subset of the webs. If a web W for variable A is assigned to register i, then whenever we reach a definition of A in web W we evaluate A into Ri. Any use of A in web W refers to Ri. We can assign Ri to hold values for several different webs, as long as at no time are the values for two of these webs simultaneously live. Give an algorithm to determine which pairs of webs can be allocated the same register.

c) Given a fixed number of registers allocated to webs, find an
algorithm to assign webs to these registers until no more webs
can "fit." Suggest a heuristic for ordering the webs so that the
webs which are likely to produce the greatest time savings are
packed first and thus are most likely to be assigned registers.

*15.7 Give an algorithm that adapts the register allocation ideas of Section 15.5 to outer loops.

*15.8 Suppose that for simplicity we automatically store all registers on
the stack (or in memory if a stack is not used) before each procedure call and restore them after the return. How does this affect
the formula (15.1) used to evaluate the utility of allocating a register to a given variable in a loop?

15.9 Modify the procedure GETREG of Section 15.4 to return a
register-pair.

*15.10 The heuristic for ordering the nodes of a DAG given in Fig. 15.9
does not always give the best ordering. Give an example of such a
DAG. *Hint.* Recall that there may be choices at step (2), and not
all choices lead to the best result.

15.11 (a) Label the tree of Fig. 15.18 by the algorithm of Fig. 15.11.

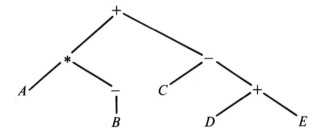

Fig. 15.18. An expression tree.

b) What is the code produced by GENCODE for this tree if two
registers are available? Use NEG for the unary − operator.
c) Use the commutative law to find a tree from which better code
can be produced.
d) Can you think of any other algebraic laws that will improve the
tree of Fig. 15.18?

Bibliographic Notes

The reader interested in a more complete description of code generation issues for an optimizing compiler should consult Waite [1974a,b] or Wulf *et al.* [1975]. A number of the heuristics proposed in this chapter have occurred to many people in various guises. For instance, Freiburghouse [1974] discusses usage counts as an aid to generating good code for basic blocks. He compares the method favorably with others but does not consider reordering of code within a block. The strategy used in GETREG of creating a free register by throwing out of a register the variable whose value will be unused for the longest time was shown optimal in another context (page-swapping strategies) by Belady [1966]. Our strategy in Section 15.5 of allocating a fixed number of registers to hold variables for the duration of a loop was mentioned by Marrill [1962] and implemented by Lowry and Medlock [1969] in FORTRAN H.

Horowitz *et al.* [1966] give an algorithm for optimizing the use of index registers in FORTRAN. Kennedy [1972] considers register allocation in loops.

The labeling algorithm for trees in Section 15.6 was discovered by Ershov [1958] and Nakata [1967], and modified to the present form by Redziejowski [1969]. It was used by Sethi and Ullman [1970] to generate optimal code from trees. This algorithm generalizes the approach of Anderson [1964] and Nievergelt [1965]. It was in turn generalized by Beatty [1972a]. The procedure GENCODE is a modification of Sethi and Ullman's algorithm, due to Stockhausen [1973]. Bruno and Lassagne [1975] give an optimal code-generation algorithm from trees if the target machine has registers that must be used as a stack.

Another approach to optimal code generation for expressions concerns "tiling" of parse trees. For any given machine we can define a set of *templates* which match pieces of a parse tree, perhaps a single node or a cluster of a few nodes with a specified set of operators. An exhaustive algorithm can find a way to cover a tree with the fewest or least costly templates, thus giving machine independence to the code-generation algorithm and enhancing the portability of the compiler. This idea has been discovered independently several times, by Weingart [1973], who implemented code generation for IMP this way, by Wasilew [1971] who did code generation for EPL, and by Johnsson [1975].

Aho and Johnson [1976] showed that a dynamic programming algorithm could be used to generate optimal code for expression trees for a rather general family of machine organizations.

Floyd [1961] gave an algorithm to handle common subexpressions in arithmetic expressions. The partition of DAG's into trees and the use of a procedure like GENCODE on the trees separately is from Waite [1974b]. The papers by Sethi [1975] and Bruno and Sethi [1976] demonstrate that an efficient algorithm (one that is less than exponential in DAG size) to generate optimal code from DAG's is most likely impossible for conventional target machines. The efficiency of code-generation algorithms is also discussed by Aho, Johnson, and Ullman [1976a,b].

Peephole optimization was discussed by McKeeman [1965]. Other local optimizations are discussed by Bagwell [1970] and Frailey [1970]. The web approach to global register assignment is discussed by Day [1970], Beatty [1976], Yhap [1974, 1975], and Harrison [1975a].

APPENDIX A

A Look
at
Some Compilers

This appendix discusses the structure of some existing compilers for three programming languages, C, FORTRAN, and BLISS. C was chosen because it is a "small" but powerful language for which efficient code can be generated simply, by a relatively small compiler. The FORTRAN H compiler was chosen because it had a significant influence in the development of optimization techniques. BLISS/11 was chosen to illustrate the design of a compiler whose goal is to optimize space. Our intent is not to advocate the designs presented here to the exclusion of others, but rather to illustrate the variety that is possible in the implementation of a compiler.

A.1 The C Compilers

C is a general-purpose programming language designed by D. M. Ritchie and is used as the primary programming language on the UNIX operating system (Ritchie and Thompson [1975]). C compilers exist for a number of machines, including the PDP-11, the Honeywell 6070, and the IBM-370 series. This section briefly describes the overall structure of three C compilers, Ritchie's C compiler for the PDP-11, and S. C. Johnson's C compilers for the Honeywell 6070 and IBM-370 machines. All these compilers are essentially two-pass, and the PDP-11 compiler has an optional third pass that does optimization on the assembly-language output, as indicated in Fig. A.1.

Pass I of each compiler does lexical analysis, syntax analysis, and intermediate code generation. The PDP-11 compiler uses recursive descent to parse everything except expressions, for which operator precedence is used. The other two compilers use a lexical analyzer generated by LEX and an LALR(1) parser generated by YACC. In all three compilers the intermediate code consists of parse trees for expressions and assembly code for control-flow statements. In the IBM and Honeywell compilers, relative addresses are substituted for symbol-table pointers in the intermediate code, and the symbol table is not used in Pass II.

557

source code
↓

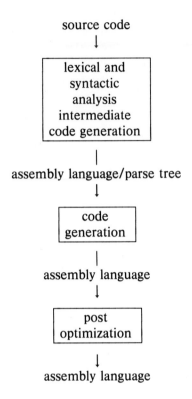

Fig. A.1. The C compiler.

In the PDP-11 compiler, code generation is implemented by a tree walk, using a strategy similar to the labeling algorithm in Section 15.6. Modifications to that algorithm have been made to assure that register pairs are available for operations that need them and to take advantage of operands that are constants. In the other two compilers, the code-generation strategy is to examine a statement at a time, repeatedly finding maximal subtrees that can be computed without stores, using the available registers. Code to evaluate and store the values represented by these sub-trees is generated by the compiler as the subtrees are selected.

The optimization phase performs a variety of transformations designed to eliminate redundant branch instructions, such as inverting the order of tests and eliminating branches to branches. It also does certain other peephole optimizations such as eliminating redundant or inacessible statements.

A.2 The FORTRAN H Compiler

This compiler is an optimizing compiler for the IBM 360 series machines. It can be run with three levels of optimization; we shall describe only its behavior when all optimizations in its repertoire are attempted by the compiler. Further information on this compiler can be found in Lowry and Medlock [1969] and IBM [1968].

The compiler is organized into thirteen major subprograms, called "overlays," which operate on various forms of intermediate text. One overlay is a master routine and four more, called phases 10, 15, 20, and 25, are what we would call "passes." The remaining overlays are brought into main memory for part of one phase, except for the error handler, which follows phase 25 if necessary. The structure of the compiler is shown in Fig. A.2.

Phase 10 performs lexical analysis, producing a list of operator-operand pairs, where "operator" here is interpreted to include punctuation, such as commas and parentheses, as well as the usual operators. For example, A = B(I) + C would be translated into the list of pairs:

"assignment statement"	A
=	B
(s	I
)	—
+	C

In general, the associated operand immediately follows the operator in the source text. Phase 10 distinguishes between a left parenthesis used to introduce actual parameters or subscripts from one used to group operands. The symbol '(s' represents a left parenthesis used as a subscripting operator. The right parenthesis has no associated operand, and the uses of right parentheses as subscripting indicators are not distinguished from other uses. Phase 10 also processes COMMON and EQUIVALENCE statements, so that the various data areas can be mapped.

Phase 15 parses expressions and converts them to quadruple form. Note that as FORTRAN has no structured control statements, such as while- or if-then-else-statements, parsing is easy except for expressions. An operator-precedence parser is used by FORTRAN H. Also in Phase 15, the code is partitioned into basic blocks, and a flow graph is constructed. Each block is examined to determine the names used and defined in the block. Finally, relative addresses are assigned to names.

Phase 20 is the code optimizer. Global common subexpressions are detected and removed, but only in the case that the available expression is either local to the block in which the removable expression is found, or the available expression is evaluated in a dominator of that block. Loops are found by detecting back edges — those whose heads dominate their tails, as described in Section 13.1. Loop-invariant code motion and detection and

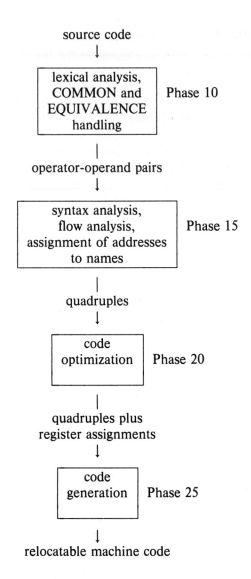

Fig. A.2. The FORTRAN H compiler.

elimination of induction variables are performed for loops roughly as described in Sections 13.4 and 13.5.

Registers are assigned to frequently-used names on a loop-by-loop basis, using an approach similar to that discussed in Section 15.5. Copy statements of the form X = Y are removed from a block if X is not live on exit from the block. Certain subroutine calls to perform built-in mathematical functions are replaced by equivalent code without a subroutine call. Exponentiation by an integer is replaced by a sequence of multiplications, and multiplications or divisions by powers of two are replaced by shifts.

 • Finally, Phase 25 generates a relocatable machine-language program from the quadruples and register assignments produced by the previous phases.

A.3 The BLISS/11 Compiler

This compiler implements BLISS, a systems programming language, on the PDP-11 computer. It is described in detail in Wulf *et al.* [1975]. The compiler works very hard to optimize code, although the goal is not the speed of the object code as we discussed in Chapters 12 through 15. Rather, since the object code must run on a computer with a relatively small main memory, the objective is to produce code that is as small as possible. Space savings usually result in time savings as well, since most space saving transformations leave fewer instructions to execute, on the average.

The compiler operates in a single pass, with one procedure completely processed before the next is read in. The designers view the compiler as composed of five modules, as shown in Fig. A.3.

LEXSYNFLO performs lexical analysis and parsing. A recursive-descent parser is used. As BLISS permits no goto-statements, all flow graphs of BLISS procedures are reducible. In fact, the syntax of the language enables us to build the flow graph, and determine loops and loop entries, as we parse. LEXSYNFLO does so, and also determines common subexpressions and a variant of ud- and du-chains, taking advantage of the structure of reducible flow graphs. Another important job of LEXSYNFLO is to detect groups of similar expressions. These are candidates for replacement by a single subroutine. Note that this replacement makes the program run more slowly but can save space.

The module DELAY examines the parse tree to determine which particular instances of the usual optimizations, such as invariant code motion and elimination of common subexpressions, are actually likely to produce a profit. The order of expression evaluation is determined at this time, based on the labeling strategy of Section 15.6, modified to take into account registers that are unavailable because they are used to preserve the value of common subexpressions. Algebraic laws are used to determine whether reordering of computations should be done. Conditional expressions are evaluated either numerically or by control flow, as discussed in Section 7.9, and DELAY decides which mode is cheaper in each instance.

TNBIND considers which temporary names should be bound to registers. The strategy used is to first group nodes of the parse tree that should be assigned the same register. As discussed in Section 15.6, there is an advantage to evaluating a node in the same register as one of its parents.

Next, the advantage to be gained by keeping a temporary in a register is estimated by a calculation favoring those that are used several times over a short span. Registers are then assigned until used up, packing the most advantageous nodes into registers first. CODE converts the tree, with its ordering and register assignment information, to relocatable machine code.

This code is then repeatedly examined by FINAL which performs peephole optimization until no further improvement results. The improvements made include elimination of (conditional or unconditional) jumps to jumps and complementation of conditionals, as discussed in Section 15.7.

Redundant or unreachable instructions are eliminated (these could have resulted from other FINAL optimizations). Merging of similar code sequences on the two paths of a branch is attempted, as is local propagation of constants. A number of other local optimizations, some quite machine-dependent are attempted. An important one is replacement, where possible, of "jump" instructions, which on the PDP-11 require two words, by "branch" instructions, which require one word but are limited in their range to 128 words.

APPENDIX B

A
Programming
Project

B.1 Introduction

The purpose of this appendix is to present a collection of suggested programming exercises that can be used in a programming laboratory accompanying a compiler-design course based on this book. The exercises consist of implementing the basic components of a compiler for an established programming language. We have chosen a subset of PASCAL (Jensen and Wirth [1975]) as an example. In doing so, we have stripped PASCAL of many of its important features such as record structures. What remains is a minimal, but usable, set of programming-language constructs. Being a subset of an existing language has certain utility. The meaning of programs in our language can be determined by the semantics of PASCAL, and if a PASCAL compiler is available, it can be used as a check on the behavior of the compiler written as an exercise.

B.2 A PASCAL Subset

Listed below is an LALR(1) grammar for our subset of PASCAL. The meanings of the constructs should be familiar not only to PASCAL users but to users of ALGOL, PL/I, and a variety of other related languages. The array declaration (e.g. **array** ABC[3..10]) is perhaps unfamiliar. The constants separated by .. are the lower and upper limits of the array. Our subset permits only one-dimensional arrays.

program →
    program IDENTIFIER (identifier-list) ;
    declarations
    subprogram-declarations
    compound-statement

identifier-list →
     IDENTIFIER
     | identifier-list , IDENTIFIER

declarations →
     declarations **var** identifier-list : type ;
     | ε

type →
     standard-type
     | array-type

standard-type →
     integer
     | **real**

array-type →
     array [CONSTANT .. CONSTANT] **of** standard-type

subprogram-declarations →
     subprogram-declarations subprogram-declaration
     | ε

subprogram-declaration →
     subprogram-head
     declarations
     compound-statement

subprogram-head →
     function IDENTIFIER arguments : **result** standard-type ;
     | **procedure** IDENTIFIER arguments ;

arguments →
     (parameter-list)
     | ε

parameter-list →
     identifier-list : type
     | parameter-list ; identifier-list : type

compound-statement →
     begin
     statement-list
     end

statement-list →
     statement
     | statement-list ; statement

statement →
     elementary-statement

    | **if** expression **then** restricted-statement **else** statement
    | **if** expression **then** statement
    | **while** expression **do** statement

restricted-statement →
    elementary-statement
    | **if** expression **then** restricted-statement **else** restricted-statement
    | **while** expression **do** restricted-statement

elementary-statement →
    variable ASSIGNOP expression
    | procedure-statement
    | compound-statement

variable →
    IDENTIFIER
    IDENTIFIER [expression]

procedure-statement →
    IDENTIFIER
    | IDENTIFIER (expression-list)

expression-list →
    expression
    | expression-list , expression

expression →
    simple-expression
    | simple-expression RELOP simple-expression

simple-expression →
    term
    | sign term
    | simple-expression ADDOP term

term →
    factor
    | term MULOP factor

factor →
    variable
    | CONSTANT
    | (expression)
    | variable [expression]
    | function-reference
    | NOT factor

function-reference →
    IDENTIFIER
    | IDENTIFIER (expression-list)

sign →
    + | −

B.3 Program Structure

A program consists of a sequence of global data declarations, a sequence of procedure and function declarations, and a single compound statement which is the "main program." Global data is to be allocated static storage. Data local to procedures and functions is allocated storage on a stack. Recursion is permitted, and parameters are passed by reference. READ and WRITE procedures are assumed supplied by a library.

Figure B.1 gives an example program. The name of the program is "example," and "input" and "output" are the names of the files used by READ and WRITE, respectively.

```
program example(input, output);
var x, y: integer;
function gcd(a, b: integer): result integer;
begin
        if b = 0 then gcd := a
        else gcd := gcd(b, a mod b)
end

begin
        READ(x, y);
        WRITE(gcd(x, y))
end
```

Fig. B.1. Example program.

B.4 Lexical Conventions

1. Comments are surrounded by '{' and '}'. They may not contain a '}'. Comments may appear after any token.

2. Blanks between tokens are optional, with the exception that keywords must be surrounded by blanks, newlines, or the beginning of the program or the final dot.

3. Identifiers are defined by the following regular expressions:

     letter = 'A' | 'B' | $\cdots$ | 'Z' | 'a' | 'b' | $\cdots$ | 'z'
     digit = '0' | '1' | $\cdots$ | '9'
     identifier = letter (letter | digit)*

The implementer may wish to put a limit on identifier length.

4. Constants are defined by:

   unsigned-integer = digit digit*
   sign = '+' | '−' | ε
   scale-factor = 'E' sign unsigned-integer
   unsigned-real = unsigned-integer (ε | '.' digit*) (ε | scale-factor)
   constant = sign (unsigned-integer | unsigned-real)

5. Keywords are reserved and appear in boldface.

6. The relation operators (RELOP's) are:

   =   < >   <   < =   > =   >

   < > denotes ≠.

7. The ADDOP's are

   + − **or**

8. The MULOP's are

   ∗ / div mod and

9. ASSIGNOP is : =

B.5 Suggested Exercises

One programming exercise suitable for a one-term course is to write an interpreter for the language defined above, or for a similar subset of another high-level language. The project involves translating the source program into quadruples and interpreting the quadruples. We shall propose an order for the construction of the modules. The order is different from the order in which the modules are executed in the compiler because it is convenient to have a working interpreter to debug the other compiler components.

1. *Design a symbol-table mechanism.* Decide on the symbol-table format. Try to decide on what information needs to be collected about names, but leave the symbol-table record structure flexible at this time. Write routines to:

i) Search the symbol table for a given name, create a new entry for that name if none is present, and in either case return a pointer to the record for that name.

ii) Delete from the symbol table all names local to a given procedure.

2. *Write an interpreter for quadruples.* The exact set of quadruples may be left open at this time but they should include the arithmetic and conditional jump statements corresponding to the set of operators in the language. Also include logical operations if conditions are evaluated arithmetically rather than by position in the program. In addition, expect to need

"quadruples" for integer-to-real conversion, for marking the beginning and end of procedures, and for parameter passing and procedure calls.

It is also necessary at this time to design the calling sequence and run-time organization for the programs being interpreted. The simple stack organization discussed in Section 10.1 is suitable for our example language.

For simplicity, another high-level language may be used in place of the interpreter. For example, each quadruple can be a statement of a high-level language such as FORTRAN. The output of the compiler is then a sequence of FORTRAN statements which can be compiled on an existing FORTRAN compiler. This approach enables the implementer to concentrate on the run-time organization.

3. *Write the lexical analyzer.* Select internal codes for the tokens. Decide how constants will be represented in the compiler. Count lines for later use by an error-message handler. Produce a listing of the source program if desired. Write a program to enter the reserved words into the symbol table. Design your lexical analyzer to be a subroutine called by the parser, returning a pair (token type, lexical value). At present, errors detected by your lexical analyzer may be handled by calling an error-printing routine and halting.

4. *Write the semantic actions.* Write semantic routines to generate the quadruples. The grammar may need to be modified in places to make the translation easier. Consult Sections 8.1 and 8.2 for examples of how to modify the grammar usefully. Do semantic analysis at this time, converting integers to reals when necessary.

5. *Write the parser.* If an LALR parser generator is available, this will simplify the task considerably. If you have YACC or another parser generator handling ambiguous grammars, you may wish to combine certain nonterminals such as statement and restricted-statement.

Should another type of parser be desired, some modifications to the grammar will be necessary. For example, to make the grammar suitable for recursive-descent parsing, the left recursion involved in several of the nonterminals will have to be eliminated as described in Section 5.4. Example 5.16 shows how the "dangling-else" can be parsed with a predictive parser.

An operator-precedence parser can easily be constructed for expressions by substituting out for RELOP, ADDOP, and MULOP, and eliminating ϵ-productions.

6. *Write the error-handling routines.* Be prepared to recover from lexical and syntactic errors. Print error diagnostics for lexical, syntactic, and semantic errors.

7. *Evaluation.* Run your compiler through a profiler, if one is available. Determine the routines in which most of the time is being spent. What

modules would have to be modified in order to increase the speed of your compiler?

B.6 Some Extensions

There are a number of features that can be added to our language without greatly increasing the complexity of compilation. Among these are:

1. multidimensional arrays
2. for- and case-statements
3. block structure
4. record structures

If time permits, add one or more of these extensions to your compiler.

Bibliographic Notes

The original definition of PASCAL was published by Wirth [1971]. A revised definition of the language along with a user manual appears in Jensen and Wirth [1975]. A more formal, axiomatic definition of the language is given by Hoare and Wirth [1973]. A critical review of the language is presented by Habermann [1973].

A number of PASCAL compilers are described in the literature. These include Wirth [1971b], Welsh and Quinn [1972], Bron and de Vries [1976], Grosse-Lindemann and Nagel [1976], and Russell and Sue [1976].

Bibliography

Bibliography

Abel, N. E., and Bell, J. R. [1972]. "Global optimization in compilers," *Proc. First USA-Japan Computer Conf.,* AFIPS Press, Montvale, N. J.

Abrahams, P. W. [1974]. "Some remarks on lookup of structured variables," *Comm. ACM* **17:4**, 209-210.

Aho, A. V., and Corasick, M. J. [1975]. "Efficient string matching: An aid to bibliographic search," *Comm. ACM* **18:6**, 333-340.

Aho, A. V., Hopcroft, J. E., and Ullman, J. D. [1974]. *The Design and Analysis of Computer Algorithms,* Addison-Wesley, Reading, Mass.

Aho, A. V., and Johnson, S. C. [1974]. "LR parsing," *Computing Surveys* **6:2**, 99-124.

Aho, A. V., and Johnson, S. C. [1976]. "Optimal code generation for expression trees," *J. ACM* **23:3**, 488-501.

Aho, A. V., Johnson, S. C., and Ullman, J. D. [1975]. "Deterministic parsing of ambiguous grammars," *Comm. ACM* **18:8**, 441-452.

Aho, A. V., Johnson, S. C., and Ullman, J. D. [1977a]. "Code generation for expressions with common subexpressions," *J. ACM* **24:1**, 146-160.

Aho, A. V., Johnson, S. C., and Ullman, J. D. [1977b]. "Code generation for machines with multiregister operations," *Proc. 4th ACM Symposium on Principles of Programming Languages,* 21-28.

Aho, A. V., and Peterson, T. G. [1972]. "A minimum distance error-correcting parser for context-free languages," *SIAM J. Computing* **1:4**, 305-312.

Aho, A. V., and Ullman, J. D. [1972a]. "Optimization of straight line code," *SIAM J. Computing* **1:1**, 1-19.

Aho, A. V., and Ullman, J. D. [1972b]. *The Theory of Parsing, Translation and Compiling,* Vol. I: *Parsing,* Prentice-Hall, Englewood Cliffs, N. J.

Aho, A. V., and Ullman, J. D. [1972c]. "Optimization of LR(k) parsers," *J. Computer and Systems Sciences* **6:6**, 573-602.

Aho, A. V., and Ullman, J. D. [1973a]. *The Theory of Parsing, Translation and Compiling,* Vol. II: *Compiling,* Prentice-Hall, Englewood Cliffs, N. J.

Aho, A. V., and Ullman, J. D. [1973b]. "A technique for speeding up LR(k) parsers," *SIAM J. Computing* **2:2**, 106-127.

Aho, A. V., and Ullman, J. D. [1976]. "Node listings for reducible flow graphs," *J. Computer and Systems Sciences* **13:3**, 286-299.

Allen, F. E. [1969]. "Program optimization," *Annual Review of Automatic Programming* **5**, 239-307.

Allen, F. E. [1970]. "Control flow analysis," *SIGPLAN Notices* **5:7**, 1-19.

Allen, F. E. [1974]. "Interprocedural data flow analysis," *Proc. IFIP Congress 74,* North Holland, Amsterdam, 398-402.

Allen, F. E. [1975a]. "Bibliography on program optimization," RC-5767, IBM T. J. Watson Research Center, Yorktown Heights, N.Y.

Allen, F. E. [1975b]. "Interprocedural analysis and the information derived by it," *Programming Methodology. Lecture Notes in Computer Science* **23**, Springer-Verlag, New York, 291-321.

Allen, F. E., and Cocke, J. [1972a]. "A catalogue of optimizing transformations," in Rustin [1972], pp. 1-30.

Allen, F. E., and Cocke, J. [1972b]. "Graph-theoretic constructs for program control flow analysis," RC-3932, IBM T. J. Watson Research Center, Yorktown Heights, N.Y.

Allen, F. E., and Cocke, J. [1976]. "A program data flow analysis procedure," *Comm. ACM* **19:3**, 137-147.

Allen, F. E., Cocke, J., and Kennedy, K. [1974]. "Reduction of operator strength," TR 476-093-6, Dept. of Mathematical Sciences, Rice Univ., Houston, Tex.

Anderson, J. P. [1964]. "A note on some compiling algorithms," *Comm. ACM* **7:3**, 149-150.

Anderson, T., Eve, J., and Horning, J. J. [1973]. "Efficient LR(1) parsers," *Acta Informatica* **2:1**, 12-39.

ANSI [1966]. "American national standard FORTRAN" (ANS X3.9 - 1966), American National Standards Institute, New York, N. Y.

ANSI [1976a]. "American national standard programming language PL/I" (ANS X3.53 - 1976), American National Standards Institute, New York, N. Y.

ANSI [1976b]. "Draft proposal ANS FORTRAN," (ANS X3J3 - 1976), *SIGPLAN Notices* **11:3**.

Arden, B. W., Galler, B. A., and Graham, R. M. [1961]. "An algorithm for equivalence declarations," *Comm. ACM* **4:7**, 310-314.

Arden, B. W., Galler, B. A., and Graham, R. M. [1962]. "An algorithm for translating Boolean expressions," *J. ACM* **9:2**, 222-239.

Backhouse, R. C. [1976]. "An alternative approach to the improvement of LR parsers," *Acta Informatica* **6:3**, 277-296.

Backus, J. W., Beeber, R. J., Best, S., Goldberg, R., Haibt, L. M., Herrick, H. L., Nelson, R. A., Sayre, D., Sheridan, P. B., Hughes, R. A., and Nutt, R. [1957]. "The FORTRAN automatic coding system," *Proc. AFIPS 1957 Western Joint Computer Conf.,* Spartan Books, Baltimore, Md., 188-198. Also in Rosen [1967], pp. 29-47.

Bagwell, J. T. [1970]. "Local optimizations," *SIGPLAN Notices* **5:7**, 52-66.

Baker, B. S. [1977]. "An algorithm for structuring programs," *J. ACM* **24:1**, 98-120.

Bar Hillel, Y., Perles, M., and Shamir, E. [1961]. "On formal properties of simple phrase structure grammars," *Z. Phonetik, Sprachwissenschaft und Kommunikationsforschung* **14**, pp. 143-172.

Barnard, D. T. [1975]. "A survey of syntax error handling techniques," Computer Science Research Group, Univ. of Toronto, Toronto, Ont., Canada.

Barth, J. M. [1977]. "An interprocedural data flow analysis algorithm," *Proc. 4th ACM Symposium on Principles of Programming Languages,* 119-131.

Batson, A. [1965]. "The organization of symbol tables," *Comm. ACM* **8:2**, 111-112.

Bauer, F. L. [1974]. "Historical remarks on compiler construction," in Bauer and Eickel [1974], pp. 603-621.

Bauer, F. L., and Eickel, J. [1974]. *Compiler Construction: An Advanced Course,* Springer-Verlag, New York, N. Y.

Beatty, J. C. [1972]. "An axiomatic approach to code optimization for expressions," *J. ACM* **19:4**, 613-640. *Errata,* **20:1** (Jan. 1973) 180, and **20:3** (July 1973) 538.

Beatty, J. C. [1974]. "Register assignment algorithm for generation of highly optimized object code," *IBM J. Research and Development* **5:2**, 20-39.

Belady, L. A. [1966]. "A study of replacement algorithms for a virtual storage computer," *IBM Syst. J.* **5:2**, 78-101.

Bell, J. R. [1969]. "A new method for determining linear precedence functions for precedence grammars," *Comm. ACM* **12:10**, 316-333.

Birman, A., and Ullman, J. D. [1973]. "Parsing algorithms with backtrack," *Information and Control* **23:1**, 1-34.

Birtwistle, G. M., Dahl, O.-J., Myhrhaug, B., and Nygaard, K. [1973]. *SIMULA Begin,* Auerbach Press, Philadelphia, Pa.

Bochmann, G. V. [1976]. "Semantic evaluation from left to right," *Comm. ACM* **19:2**, 55-62.

Boyer, R. S., and Moore, J S. [1976]. "A fast string searching algorithm," Technical Report CSL-76-1, Xerox Palo Alto Research Center, Palo Alto, California.

Branquart, P., Cardinael, J.-P., Lewi, J., Delescaille, J.-P., and Vanbegin, M. [1976]. *An Optimized Translation Process and its Application to ALGOL 68, Lecture Notes in Computer Science,* **38**, Springer-Verlag, New York.

Breuer, M. A. [1969]. "Generation of optimal code for expressions via factorization," *Comm. ACM* **12:6**, 333-340.

Bron, C., and de Vries, W. [1976]. "A PASCAL compiler for PDP11 minicomputers," *Software—Practice and Experience* **6:1**, 109-116.

Britton, D. E., Druseikis, F. C., Griswold, R. E., Hanson, D. R. and Holmes, R. A. [1976]. "Procedure referencing environments in SL5," *Proc. 3rd ACM Symposium on Principles of Programming Languages,* 185-191.

Brooker, R. A., MacCallum, I. R., Morris, D., and Rohl, J. S. [1963]. "The compiler-compiler," *Annual Review of Automatic Programming* **3**, 229-275.

Brooker, R. A., and Morris, D. [1962]. "A general translation program for phrase structure languages," *J. ACM* **9:1**, 1-10.

Brosgol, B. M. [1974]. *Deterministic Translation Grammars,* Ph. D. dissertation, Harvard Univ., Cambridge, Mass.

Brown, W. S. [1977]. *ALTRAN Users Manual,* (fourth edition), Bell Laboratories, Murray Hill, N.J.

Bruno, J. L., and Lassagne, T. [1975]. "The generation of optimal code for stack machines," *J. ACM* **22:3**, 382-397.

Bruno, J. L., and Sethi, R. [1976]. "Code generation for a one register machine," *J. ACM* **23:3**, 502-510.

Brzozowski, J. A. [1964]. "Derivatives of regular expressions," *J. ACM* **11:4**, 481-494.

Bullen, R. H. Jr., and Millen, J. K. [1972]. "Microtext - the design of a microprogrammed finite state search machine for full-text retrieval," *Proc. AFIPS 1972 Fall Joint Computer Conf.,* Spartan Books, Baltimore, Md., 479-488.

Busam, V. A., and Englund, D. E. [1969]. "Optimization of expressions in FORTRAN," *Comm. ACM* **12:2**, 666-674.

Carter, J. L. [1975]. "A case study of a new compiling code generation technique," RC-5666, IBM T. J. Watson Research Center, Yorktown Heights, N.Y.

Cheatham, T. E. Jr. [1965]. "The TGS-II translator generator system," *Proc. IFIP Congress 65,* North Holland, Amsterdam, 592-593.

Cheatham, T. E. Jr., and Sattley, K. [1964]. "Syntax directed compiling," *Proc. AFIPS 1964 Spring Joint Computer Conf.,* Spartan Books, Baltimore, Md., 31-57.

Cherniavsky, J. C., Henderson, P. B., and Keohane, J. [1976]. "On the equivalence of URE flow graphs and reducible flow graphs," *Proc. 1976 Conference on Information Sciences and Systems,* Johns Hopkins Univ., pp. 423-429.

Chirica, L. M., and Martin, D. F. [1976]. "An algebraic formulation of Knuthian semantics," *Conf. Record IEEE 17th Annual Symposium on Foundations of Comuputer Science,* 127-136.

Chomsky, N. [1956]. "Three models for the description of language," *IRE Trans. on Information Theory* **2:3**, 113-124.

Chomsky, N. [1959]. "On certain formal properties of grammars," *Information and Control* **2:2**, 137-167.

Chroust, G. [1971]. "Scope conserving expression evaluation," *IFIP71,* TA-3, 178-182.

Cleaveland, J. C., and Uzgalis, R. C. [1977]. *Grammars for Programming Languages,* American Elsevier, New York, N. Y.

Cocke. J. [1970]. "Global common subexpression elimination," *SIGPLAN Notices* **5:7**, 20-24.

Cocke, J., and R. E. Miller [1969]. "Some analysis techniques for optimizing computer programs," *Proc. 2nd Hawaii Intl. Conf. on Systems Sciences,* pp. 143-146.

Cocke, J., and Schwartz, J. T. [1970]. *Programming Languages and Their Compilers, Preliminary Notes, Second Revised Version,* Courant Institute of Mathematical Sciences, New York.

Cohen, D. J., and Gotlieb, C. C. [1970]. "A list structure form of grammars for syntactic analysis," *Computing Surveys* **2:1**, 65-82.

Conway, M. E. [1963]. "Design of a separable transition diagram compiler," *Comm. ACM* **6:7**, 396-408.

Conway, R. W., and Maxwell, W. L. [1963]. "CORC - the Cornell computing language," *Comm. ACM* **6:6**, 317-321.

Conway, R. W., and Wilcox, T. R. [1973]. "Design and implementation of a diagnostic compiler for PL/I," *Comm. ACM* **16:3**, 169-179.

Cousot, P., and Cousot, R. [1977]. "Abstract interpretation: A unified lattice model for the static analysis of programs," *Proc. 4th ACM Symposium on Principles of Programming Languages,* 238-252.

Darlington, J., and Burstall, R. M. [1973]. "A system which automatically improves programs," *Proc. 3rd Intl. Conf. on Artificial Intelligence,* Stanford, California, 537-542.

Day, W. H. E. [1970]. "Compiler assignment of data items to registers," *IBM Syst. J.* **9:4**, 281-317.

DeRemer, F. L. [1969]. *Practical Translators for LR(k) Languages,* Ph. D. dissertation, M. I. T., Cambridge, Mass.

DeRemer, F. L. [1971]. "Simple LR(k) grammars," *Comm. ACM* **14:7**, 453-460.

Demers, A. J. [1974]. "Skeletal LR parsing," *IEEE Conf. Record of 15th Annual Symposium on Switching and Automata Theory,* 185-198.

Demers, A. J. [1975]. "Elimination of single productions and merging of nonterminal symbols in LR(1) grammars," *J. Computer Languages* **1:2**, 105-119.

Dijkstra, E. W. [1960]. "Algol 60 translation," *Supplement ALGOL Bulletin 10.* Also see "Recursive programming," *Numerische Math,* **2**, pp. 312-318 (1960), reprinted in Rosen [1967].

Donegan, M. K. [1973]. "An approach to the automatic generation of code generators," Lab. for Computer Science and Engineering, Rice University, Houston, Texas.

Earley, J. [1970]. "An efficient context-free parsing algorithm," *Comm. ACM* **13:2**, 94-102.

Earley, J. [1975a]. "Ambiguity and precedence in syntax description," *Acta Informatica* **4:2**, 183-192.

Earley, J. [1975b]. "High level iterators and a method of data structure choice," *J. Computer Languages* **1:4**, 321-342.

Earnest, C. [1974]. "Some topics in code optimization," *J. ACM* **21:1**, 76-102.

Eickel, J., Paul, M., Bauer, F. L., and Samelson, K. [1963]. "A syntax controlled generator of formal language processors," *Comm. ACM* **6:8**, 451-455.

El Djabri, N. [1973a]. "Reducing the size of LL(1) parsing tables," TR-119, Dept. of EECS, Princeton Univ., Princeton, N. J.

El Djabri, N. [1973b]. "Extending the LR parsing technique to some non-LR grammars," TR-121, Dept. of EECS, Princeton Univ., Princeton, N.J.

Elson, M. [1973]. *Concepts of Programming Languages,* Science Research Associates, Palo Alto, Calif.

Elson, M., and Rake, S. T. [1970]. "Code generation for large-language compilers," *IBM Syst. J.* **9:3**, 166-188.

Ershov, A. P. [1958]. "On programming of arithmetic operations," *Dokl. A. N. USSR* **118:3**, 427-430. Also in *Comm. ACM* **1:8**, 3-6.

Ershov, A. P. [1966]. "ALPHA — an automatic programming system of high efficiency," *J. ACM* **13:1**, 17-24.

Ershov, A. P. [1971]. *The ALPHA Automatic Programming System,* Academic Press, New York.

Feldman, J. A. [1966]. "A formal semantics for computer languages and its application in a compiler-compiler," *Comm. ACM* **9:1**, 3-9.

Feldman, J. A., and Gries, D. [1968]. "Translator writing systems," *Comm. ACM* **11:2**, 77-113.

Fischer, C. N., Milton, D. R., and Quiring, S. B. [1977]. "An efficient insertion-only error-corrector for LL(k) parsers," *Proc. 4th ACM Symposium on Principles of Programming Languages,* 97-103.

Fischer, M. J. [1972]. "Efficiency of equivalence algorithms," in *Complexity of Computer Computations* (R. E. Miller and J. W. Thatcher, eds.), pp. 153-168, Academic Press, N. Y.

Fleck, A. C. [1976]. "On the impossibility of content exchange through the by-name parameter transmission mechanism," *SIGPLAN Notices* **11:11**, 38-41.

Floyd, R. W. [1961]. "An algorithm for coding efficient arithmetic expressions," *Comm. ACM* **4:1**, 42-51.

Floyd, R. W. [1963]. "Syntactic analysis and operator precedence," *J. ACM* **10:3**, 316-333.

Floyd, R. W. [1964]. "Bounded context syntactic analysis," *Comm. ACM* **7:2**, 62-67.

Fong, A. C. [1977]. "Elimination of common subexpressions in very high-level languages," *Proc. 4th ACM Symposium on Principles of Programming Languages,* 48-57.

Fong, A. C., and Ullman, J. D. [1976]. "Induction variables in very high-level languages," *Proc. 3rd ACM Symposium on Principles of Programming Languages,* 104-112.

Fosdick, L. D., and Osterweil, L. J. [1976]. "Data flow analysis in software reliability," *Computing Surveys* **8:3**, 305-330.

Foster, J. M. [1968]. "A syntax improving device," *Computer Journal* **11:1**, 31-34.

Frailey, D. J. [1970]. "Expression optimization using unary complement operators," *SIGPLAN Notices* **5:7**, 67-85.

Fredman, M. L. [1975]. "On computing the length of the longest increasing subsequence," *Discrete Mathematics* **14:1**, 29-36.

Freeman, D. N. [1964]. "Error correction in CORC—the Cornell computing language," *Proc. AFIPS 1964 Fall Joint Computer Conf.,* Spartan Books, Baltimore, Md., 15-34.

Freiburghouse, R. A. [1969]. "The multics PL/I compiler," *AFIPS Conf. Proc. Fall Joint Computer Conference* **35**, 187-208.

Freiburghouse, R. A. [1974]. "Register allocation via usage counts," *Comm. ACM* **17:11**, 638-642.

Gajeswska, H. [1975]. "Some statistics on the usage of the C language," Bell Laboratories, Murray Hill, N. J.

Galler, B. A., and Fischer, M. J. [1964]. "An improved equivalence algorithm," *Comm. ACM* **7:5**, 301-303.

Galler, B. A., and Perlis, A. J. [1970]. *A View of Programming Languages,* Addison-Wesley, Reading, Mass.

Gates, G., and Poplawski, D. [1973]. "A simple technique for structured variable lookup," *Comm. ACM* **16:9**, 561-565.

Gear, C. W. [1965]. "High speed compilation of efficient object code," *Comm. ACM* **8:8**, 483-488.

Geller, M. M., and Harrison, M. A. [1973]. "Characterizations of LR(0) languages," *IEEE Conf. Record of 14th Annual Symposium on Switching and Automata Theory,* 103-108.

Geschke, C. M. [1972]. *Global Program Optimization,* Ph. D. dissertation, Dept. of Computer Science, Carnegie-Mellon Univ., Pittsburgh, Pa.

Ginsburg, S. [1966]. *The Mathematical Theory of Context-Free Languages,* McGraw-Hill, New York, N. Y.

Graham, R. M. [1964]. "Bounded context translation," *Proc. AFIPS Spring JCC* **40**, pp. 205-217.

Graham, S. L., and Rhodes, S. P. [1975]. "Practical syntactic error recovery in compilers," *Comm. ACM* **18:11**, 639-650.

Graham, S. L., and Wegman, M. [1976]. "A fast and usually linear algorithm for global flow analysis," *J. ACM* **23:1**, 172-202.

Grau, A. A., Hill, U., and Langmaack, H. [1967]. *Translation of ALGOL 60,* Springer-Verlag, New York, N. Y.

Gries, D. [1971] *Compiler Construction for Digital Computers,* John Wiley and Sons, New York, N. Y.

Gries, D., Paul, M., and Wiehle, H. R. [1965]. "Some techniques used in the ALCOR ILLINOIS 7090," *Comm. ACM* **8:8**, 496-500.

Griswold, R. E., Poage, J., and Polonsky, I. [1971]. *The SNOBOL4 Programming Language,* Prentice-Hall, Englewood Cliffs, N. J.

Grosse-Lindemann, C. O., and Nagel, H. H. [1976]. "Postlude to a PASCAL-compiler bootstrap on a DEC System-10," *Software—Practice and Experience* **6:1**, 29-42.

Gudes, R., and Reiter, A. [1973]. "On evaluating Boolean expressions," *Software—Practice and Experience* **3**, 345-350.

Habermann, A. N. [1973]. "Critical comments on the programming language PASCAL," *Acta Informatica* **3:1**, 47-58.

Hansen, G. J. [1974]. *Adaptive Systems for the Dynamic Run-Time Optimization of Programs,* Ph. D. dissertation, Dept. of Computer Science, Carnegie-Mellon University, Pittsburgh, Pa.

Harrison, W. [1975a]. "A class of register allocation algorithms," RC-5342, IBM T. J. Watson Research Center, Yorktown Heights, N.Y.

Harrison, W. [1975b]. "Compiler analysis of the value ranges for variables," RC-5544, IBM T. J. Watson Research Center, Yorktown Heights, N.Y.

Harrison, W. [1977]. "A new strategy for code generation - the general purpose optimizing compiler," *Proc. 4th ACM Symposium on Principles of Programming Languages,* 29-37.

Heaps, H. S., and Radhakrishnan, T. [1977]. "Compaction of diagnostic messages for compilers," *Software—Practice and Experience* **7:1**, 139-144.

Hecht, M. S. [1977]. *Data Flow Analysis of Computer Programs,* American Elsevier, New York, N. Y.

Hecht, M. S., and Shaffer, J. B. [1975]. "Ideas on the design of a 'quad improver' for SIMPL-T, part I: overview and intersegment analysis," TR-405, Dept. of Computer Science, Univ. of Maryland, College Park, Md.

Hecht, M. S., and Ullman, J. D. [1972]. "Flow graph reducibility," *SIAM J. Computing* **1:2**, 188-202.

Hecht, M. S., and Ullman, J. D. [1974]. "Characterizations of reducible flow graphs," *J. ACM* **21:3**, 367-375.

Hecht, M. S., and Ullman, J. D. [1975]. "A simple algorithm for global data flow analysis programs," *SIAM J. Computing* **4:4**, 519-532.

Henderson, P., and Morris, J. H., Jr. [1976]. "A lazy evaluator," *Proc. 3rd ACM Symposium on Principles of Programming Languages,* 95-103.

Hoare, C. A. R. [1969]. "An axiomatic basis for computer programming," *Comm. ACM* **12:10**, 576-580.

Hoare, C. A. R., and Wirth, N. [1973]. "An axiomatic definition of the programming language PASCAL," *Acta Informatica* **2:4**, 335-356.

Hopcroft, J. E., and Ullman, J. D. [1969]. *Formal Languages and Their Relation to Automata,* Addison-Wesley, Reading, Mass.

Hopcroft, J. E., and Ullman, J. D. [1973]. "Set merging algorithms," *SIAM J. Computing* **2:3**, 294-303.

Hopgood, F. R. A. [1969]. *Compiling Techniques,* American Elsevier, New York, N. Y.

Horning, J. J. [1974]. "What the compiler should tell the user," in Bauer and Eickel [1974], pp. 525-548.

Horowitz, L. P., Karp, R. M., Miller, R. M., and Winograd, S. [1966]. "Index register allocation," *J. ACM* **13:1**, 43-61.

Horowitz, E., and Sahni, S. [1976]. *Fundamentals of Data Structures*, Computer Science Press, Woodland Hills, Calif.

Huffman, D. A. [1954]. "The synthesis of sequential switching machines," *J. Franklin Inst.* **257**, pp. 3-4, 161, 190, 275-303.

Hunt, H. B. III, Szymanski, T. G., and Ullman, J. D. [1977]. "Operations on sparse relations," *Comm. ACM* **20:3**, 171-176.

Hunt, J. W., and McIlroy, M. D. [1976]. "An algorithm for differential file comparison," CS Technical Report #41, Bell Laboratories, Murray Hill, N.J.

Hunt, J. W., and Szymanski, T. G. [1977]. "An algorithm for file comparison," *Comm. ACM* **20:5**, 350-353.

IBM [1968]. "FORTRAN IV (H) compiler program logic manual," Form Y28-6642-3, IBM, New York, N. Y.

Ichbiah, J. D., and Morse, S. P. [1970]. "A technique for generating almost optimal Floyd-Evans productions for precedence grammars," *Comm. ACM* **13:8**, 501-508.

Ingerman, P. Z. [1961]. "Thunks," *Comm. ACM* **4:1**, 55-58. Also in Pollack [1972], pp. 457-465.

Ingerman, P. Z. [1966]. *A Syntax Oriented Translator*, Academic Press, New York, N. Y.

Irons, E. T. [1961]. "A syntax directed compiler for ALGOL 60," *Comm. ACM* **4:1**, 51-55.

Irons, E. T. [1963]. "An error correcting parse algorithm," *Comm. ACM* **6:11**, 669-673.

Iverson, K. [1962]. *A Programming Language*, John Wiley and Sons, New York, N. Y.

James, E. B., and Partridge, D. P. [1973]. "Adaptive correction of program statements," *Comm. ACM* **16:1**, 27-37.

James, L. R. [1972]. "A syntax directed error recovery method," CSRG-13, Univ. of Toronto Computer Science Research Group.

Jarvis, J. F. [1976]. "Feature recognition in line drawings using regular expressions," *Proc. 3rd Intl. Joint Conf. on Pattern Recognition.*

Jazayeri, M., Ogden, W. F., and Rounds, W. C. [1975]. "The intrinsically exponential complexity of the circularity problem for attribute grammars," *Comm. ACM* **18:12**, 697-706.

Jensen, K., and Wirth, N. [1975]. *PASCAL User Manual and Report,* Springer-Verlag, New York, N. Y.

Johnson, S. C. [1974]. "YACC—yet another compiler compiler," CSTR 32, Bell Laboratories, Murray Hill, N. J.

Johnson, W. L, Porter, J. H., Ackley, S. I., and Ross, D. T. [1968]. "Automatic generation of efficient lexical analyzers using finite state techniques," *Comm. ACM* **11:12**, 805-813.

Johnsson, R. K. [1975]. *An Approach to Global Register Allocation,* Ph. D. dissertation, Carnegie-Mellon Univ., Pittsburgh, Pa.

Joliat, M. J. [1974]. "Practical minimization of LR(k) parser tables," *Proc. IFIP Congress 74,* North Holland, Amsterdam, 376-380.

Joliat, M. L. [1976]. "A simple technique for partial elimination of unit productions from LR(k) parsers," *IEEE Trans. on Computers,* **C-25:7**, pp. 763-764.

Jones, N. D., and Muchnick, S. S. [1976]. "Binding time optimization in programming languages: Some thoughts toward the design of an ideal language," *Proc. 3rd ACM Symposium on Principles of Programming Languages,* 77-94.

Kam, J. B., and Ullman, J. D. [1976]. "Global data flow analysis and iterative algorithms," *J. ACM* **23:1**, 158-171.

Kam, J. B., and Ullman, J. D. [1977]. "Monotone data flow analysis frameworks," *Acta Informatica* **7:3**, 305-318.

Kasami, T., Peterson, W. W., and Tokura, N. [1973]. "On the capabilities of while, repeat and exit statements," *Comm. ACM* **16:8**, 503-512.

Kasyanov, V. N. [1973]. "Some properties of fully reducible graphs," *Information Processsing Letters* **2:4**, 113-117.

Kennedy, K. [1971]. "A global flow analysis algorithm," *Intl. J. Computer Math.* **3**, 5-15.

Kennedy, K. [1972]. "Index register allocation in straight line code and simple loops," in Rustin [1972], pp. 51-64.

Kennedy, K. [1976]. "A comparison of two algorithms for global flow analysis," *SIAM J. Computing* **5:1**, 158-180.

Kennedy, K. [1975]. "Node listings applied to data flow analysis," *Proc. 2nd ACM Symposium on Principles of Programming Languages,* 10-21.

Kennedy, K., and Warren, S. K. [1976]. "Automatic generation of efficient evaluators for attribute grammars," *Proc. 3rd ACM Symposium on Principles of Programming Languages,* 32-49.

Kernighan, B. W. [1975]. "RATFOR — a preprocessor for a rational FORTRAN," *Software—Practice and Experience* **5:4**, 395-406.

Kernighan, B. W., and Plauger, P. J. [1976]. *Software Tools,* Addison-Wesley, Reading, Mass.

Kernighan, B. W., and Cherry, L. L. [1975]. "A system for typesetting mathematics," *Comm. ACM* **18:3**, 151-156.

Kildall, G. A. [1973]. "A unified approach to global program optimization," *Proc. ACM Symp. on Principles of Programming Languages,* 194-206.

Kim, J., and Tan, C. J. [1976]. "Register assignment algorithm - II," RC-6262, IBM T. J. Watson Research Center, Yorktown Heights, N.Y.

Kleene, S. C. [1956]. "Representation of events in nerve nets," in *Automata Studies* (C. E. Shannon and J. McCarthy, eds.), Princeton Univ. Press, pp. 3-40.

Knuth, D. E. [1965]. "On the translation of languages from left to right," *Information and Control* **8:6**, 607-639.

Knuth, D. E. [1968a]. *The Art of Computer Programming,* Vol. I: *Fundamental Algorithms,* Addison-Wesley, Reading, Mass.

Knuth, D. E. [1968b]. "Semantics of context-free languages," *Math. Systems Theory* **2:2**, 127-145.

Knuth, D. E. [1971a]. "Top down syntax analysis," *Acta Informatica* **1:2**, 79-110.

Knuth, D. E. [1971b]. "An empirical study of FORTRAN programs," *Software—Practice and Experience* **1:2**, 105-133.

Knuth, D. E. [1973]. *The Art of Computer Programming,* Vol. III: *Sorting and Searching,* Addison-Wesley, Reading, Mass.

Knuth, D. E. [1977]. "A generalization of Dijkstra's algorithm," Dept. of Computer Science, Standford University, California.

Knuth, D. E., Morris, J. H. Jr., and Pratt, V. R. [1974]. "Fast pattern matching in strings," TR CS-74-440, Dept. of Computer Science, Stanford Univ., Stanford, Calif. To appear, *SIAM J. Computing, 1977.*

Knuth, D. E., and Trabb Pardo, L. [1976]. "The early development of programming languages," STAN-CS-76-562, Dept. of Computer Science, Stanford Univ., Stanford, Calif.

Korenjak, A. J. [1969]. "A practical method for constructing LR(k) processors," *Comm. ACM* **12:11**, 613-623.

Kosaraju, S. R. [1974]. "Analysis of structured programs," *J. Computer and Systems Sciences* **9:3**, 232-255.

Koster, C. H. A. [1974]. "Using the CDL compiler-compiler," in Bauer and Eickel [1974], pp. 366-426.

LaFrance, J. [1970]. "Optimization of error recovery in syntax-directed parsing algorithms," *SIGPLAN Notices* **5:12**, 2-17.

LaLonde, W. R. [1976]. "On directly constructing LR(*k*) parsers without chain reductions," *Proc. 3rd ACM Symposium on Principles of Programming Languages,* 127-133.

LaLonde, W. R., Lee, E. S., and Horning, J. J. [1971]. "An LALR(*k*) parser generator," *Proc. IFIP Congress 71,* North Holland, Amsterdam, 153-157.

Leavenworth, B. M. [1966]. "Syntax macros and extended translation," *Comm. ACM* **9:11**, 790-793.

Lee, J. A. N. [1974]. *Anatomy of a Compiler,* Van Nostrand, New York.

Leinius, R. P. [1970]. *Error Detection and Recovery for Syntax-Directed Compiler Systems,* Ph. D. dissertation, Univ. of Wisconsin, Madison, Wisc.

Lesk, M. E. [1975]. "LEX—a lexical analyzer generator," CSTR 39, Bell Laboratories, Murray Hill, N. J.

Levy, J. P. [1975]. "Automatic correction of syntax errors in programming languages," *Acta Informatica* **4:3**, 271-292.

Lewis, P. M. II and Rosenkrantz, D. J. [1971]. "An ALGOL compiler designed using automata theory," *Proc. Symp. on Computers and Automata,* Microwave research Inst., Polytechnic Inst. of New York, pp. 75-88.

Lewis, P. M. II, Rosenkrantz, D. J., and Stearns, R. E. [1974]. "Attributed translations," *J. Computer and Systems Sciences* **9:3**, 279-307.

Lewis, P. M. II, Rosenkrantz, D. J., and Stearns, R. E. [1976]. *Compiler Design Theory,* Addison-Wesley, Reading, Mass.

Lewis, P. M. II, and Stearns, R. E. [1968]. "Syntax-directed transduction," *J. ACM* **15:3**, 465-488.

Lomet, D. B. [1975]. "Data flow analysis in the presence of procedure calls," RC-5728, IBM T. J. Watson Research Center, Yorktown Heights, N.Y.

Loveman, D. B. [1976]. "Program improvement by source to source transformation," *Proc. 3rd ACM Symposium on Principles of Programming Languages,* 140-152.

Low, J., and Rovner, P. [1976]. "Techniques for the automatic selection of data structures," *Proc. 3rd ACM Symposium on Principles of Programming Languages,* 58-67.

Lowry, E., and Medlock, C. W. [1969]. "Object code optimization," *Comm. ACM* **12:1**, 13-22.

Lucas, P. [1961]. "Die Structuranalyse von Formelubersetzen," *Electron. Rechenanl.* **3**, 159-167.

Luccio, F. [1969]. "A comment on index register allocation," *Comm. ACM* **12:1**, 13-22.

Lyon, G. [1974]. "Syntax-directed least-errors analysis for context-free languages," *Comm. ACM* **17:1**, 3-14.

Madsen, O. L., and Kristensen, B. B. [1976]. "LR-parsing of extended context-free grammars," *Acta Informatica* **7:1**, 61-74.

Manna, Z. [1974]. *Mathematical Theory of Computation,* McGraw-Hill, New York, N. Y.

Marcotty, M., Ledgard, H. F., and Bochmann, G. V. [1976]. "A sampler of formal definitions," *Computing Surveys* **8:2**, 191-276.

Marrill, T. [1962]. "Computational chains and the simplification of computer programs," *IRE Trans. on Electronic Computers* **EC-11:2**, 173-180.

Martin, D. [1968]. "Boolean matrix method for the detection of simple precedence matrices," *Comm. ACM* **11:10**, 685-687.

Martin, D. [1972]. "A Boolean matrix method for the computation of linear precedence functions," *Comm. ACM* **15:1**, 35-38.

McCarthy, J. *et al.* [1965]. *LISP 1.5 Programmer's Manual,* MIT Press, Cambridge, Mass.

McClure, R. M. [1965]. "TMG—a syntax directed compiler," *Proc. 20th ACM National Conf.,* 262-274.

McClure, R. M. [1972]. "An appraisal of compiler technology," *Proc. AFIPS 1972 Spring Joint Computer Conf.,* Spartan Books, Baltimore, Md., 1-9.

McIlroy, M. D. [1960]. "Macro-instruction extensions of compiler language," *Comm. ACM* **3:4**, 214-220. Also in Pollack [1972], pp. 512-518.

McKeeman, W. M. [1965]. "Peephole optimization," *Comm. ACM* **8:7**, 443-444.

McKeeman, W. M., Horning, J. J., and Wortman, D. B. [1970]. *A Compiler Generator,* Prentice-Hall, Englewood Cliffs, N. J.

McNaughton, R., and Yamada, H. [1960]. "Regular expressions and state graphs for automata," *IRE Trans. on Electronic Computers* **EC-9:1**, 39-47.

Mickunas, M. D., and Schneider, V. B. [1973]. "A parser-generating system for constructing compressed compilers," *Comm. ACM* **16:11**, 669-676.

Miller, P. L. [1970]. "Automatic code-generation from an object-machine description," MAC TM 18, Massachusetts Institute of Technology, Cambridge, Mass.

Minsky, M. [1967]. *Computation: Finite and Infinite Machines,* Prentice-Hall, Englewood Cliffs, N. J.

Moore, E. F. [1956]. "Gedanken experiments on sequential machines," in *Automata Studies,* (C. E. Shannon and J. McCarthy, eds.), Princeton Univ. Press, pp. 129-153.

Morgan, H. L. [1970]. "Spelling correction in systems programs," *Comm. ACM* **13:2**, 90-94.

Morris, R. [1968]. "Scatter storage techniques," *Comm. ACM* **11:1**, 38-43.

Moulton, P. G., and Muller, M. E. [1967]. "DITRAN—a compiler emphasizing diagnostics," *Comm. ACM* **10:1**, 52-54.

Nakata, I. [1967]. "On compiling algorithms for arithmetic expressions," *Comm. ACM* **10:8**, 492-494.

Naur, P. [1976]. "Control record driven processing," in *Structured Programming,* Infotech Intl., Maidenhead, England, pp. 309-322.

Naur P. (ed.) [1963]. "Revised report on the algorithmic language ALGOL 60," *Comm. ACM* **6:1**, 1-17.

Neel, D., and Amirchahy, M. [1975]. "Removal of invariant statements from nested loops in a single effective compiler pass," *SIGPLAN Notices* **10:3**, 87-96.

Newcomer, J. M. [1975]. *Machine-Independent Generation of Optimal Local Code,* Ph. D. dissertation, Computer Science Dept., Carnegie-Mellon U., Pittsburgh, Pa.

Nicholls, J. E. [1975]. *The Structure and Design of Programming Languages,* Addison-Wesley, Reading, Mass.

Nievergelt, J. [1965]. "On the automatic simplification of computer code," *Comm. ACM* **8:6**, 366-370.

Pagan, F. G. [1976]. *A Practical Guide to ALGOL 68.* John Wiley and Sons, New York, N. Y.

Pager, D. [1974]. "On eliminating unit productions from LR(*k*) parsers," *Automata, Languages and Programming* (J. Loeckx, ed.), Springer-Verlag, New York, N. Y.

Pager, D. [1977]. "A practical general method for constructing LR(k) parsers," *Acta Informatica* **7:3**, 249-268.

Paige, R., and Schwartz, J. T. [1977]. "Reduction in strength of high level operations," *Proc. 4th ACM Symposium on Principles of Programming Languages,* 58-71.

Palm, R. C., Jr., [1975]. "A portable optimizer for the language C," M. Sc. Thesis, Massachussets Institute of Technology, Cambridge, Mass.

Peterson, W. W. [1957]. "Addressing for random access storage," *IBM J. Research and Development* **1:2**, 130-146.

Pollack, B. W. [1972]. *Compiler Techniques,* Auerbach Press, Philadelphia, Pa.

Pratt, T. W. [1975]. *Programming Languages: Design and Implementation,* Prentice-Hall, Englewood Cliffs, N. J.

Price, C. E. [1971]. "Table lookup techniques," *Computing Surveys* **3:2**, 49-65.

Prosser, R. T. [1959]. "Applications of Boolean matrices to the analysis of flow diagrams," *Proc. AFIPS 1959 Eastern Joint Computer Conf.,* Spartan Books, Baltimore, Md., 133-138.

Purdom, P. W., and Moore, E. F. [1972]. "Immediate predominators in a directed graph," *Comm. ACM* **15:8**, 777-778.

Rabin, M. O., and Scott, D. [1959]. "Finite automata and their decision problems," *IBM J. Research and Development* **3**, 114-125..

Randell, B., and Russell, L. J. [1964]. *ALGOL 60 Implementation.* Academic Press, New York.

Redziejowski, R. R. [1969]. "On arithmetic expressions and trees," *Comm. ACM* **12:2**, 81-84.

Reif, J. H., and Lewis, H. R. [1977]. "Symbolic evaluation and the global value graph," *Proc. 4th ACM Symposium on Principles of Programming Languages,* 104-118.

Reynolds, J. C. [1965]. "An introduction to the COGENT programming language," *Proc. 20th ACM National Conf.,* 422-436.

Reynolds, J. C. [1972]. "Definitional interpreters for higher-order programming languages," *Proc. 27th ACM National Conf.,* 717-740.

Ritchie, D. M., Kernighan, B. W., and Lesk, M. E. [1975]. "The C programming language," CSTR 31, Bell Laboratories, Murray Hill, N. J.

Ritchie, D. M., and Thompson, K. [1974]. "The UNIX time-sharing system," *Comm. ACM* **17**:7, 365-375.

Rosen, B. K. [1975]. "Data flow analysis for procedural languages," RC-5211, IBM T. J. Watson Research Center, Yorktown Heights, N.Y.

Rosen, S. [1964]. "A compiler building system developed by Brooker and Morris," *Comm. ACM* **7**:7, 403-414.

Rosen, S. [1967]. *Programming Systems and Languages,* McGraw-Hill, New York, N. Y.

Rosenkrantz, D. J., and Stearns, R. E. [1970]. "Properties of deterministic top-down grammars," *Information and Control* **17**:3, 226-256.

Russell, D. L., and Sue, J. Y. [1976]. "Implementation of a PASCAL compiler for the IBM 360," *Software—Practice and Experience* **6**:3, 371-376.

Rustin, R. [1972]. *Design and Optimization of Compilers,* Prentice-Hall, Englewood Cliffs, N. J.

Salomaa, A. [1973]. *Formal Languages,* Academic Press, New York, N. Y.

Samelson, K., and Bauer, F. L. [1960]. "Sequential formula translation," *Comm. ACM* **3**:2, 76-83. Also in Pollack [1972], pp. 439-456.

Sammet, J. E. [1968]. *Programming Languages: History and Fundamentals,* Prentice-Hall, Englewood Cliffs, N. J.

Sammet, J. E. [1972]. "Programming languages: history and future," *Comm. ACM* **15**:7, 601-610.

Schaefer, M. [1973]. *A Mathematical Theory of Global Program Optimization,* Prentice-Hall, Englewood Cliffs, N. J.

Schneck, P. B., and Angel, E. [1973]. "A FORTRAN to FORTRAN optimizing compiler," *Computer J.* **16**:4, 322-330.

Schneider, V. B. [1971]. "On the number of registers needed to evaluate arithmetic expressions," *BIT* **11**:1, 84-93.

Schorre, D. V. [1964]. "META-II: a syntax-oriented compiler writing language," *Proc. 19th ACM National Conf.,* D1.3-1-D1.3-11.

Schwartz, J. T. [1973]. *On Programming: An Interim Report on the SETL Project,* Courant Inst., New York, N. Y.

Schwartz, J. T. [1975a]. "Automatic data structure choice in a language of very high level," *Comm. ACM* **18:12**, 722-728.

Schwartz, J. T. [1975b] "Optimization of very high level languages," *J. Computer Languages,* part I: "Value transmission and its corollaries," **1:2**, 161-194; part II: "Deducing relationships of inclusion and membership," **1:3**, 197-218.

Scott, D. [1970]. "Outline of a mathematical theory of computation," *Proc. 4th Annual Princeton Conf. on Information Sciences and Systems,* pp. 169-176.

Sethi, R. [1975]. "Complete register allocation problems," *SIAM J. Computing* **4:3**, 226-248.

Sethi, R., and Ullman, J. D. [1970]. "The generation of optimal code for arithmetic expressions," *J. ACM* **17:4**, 715-728.

Shaw, M. [1974]. "Reduction of compilation costs through language restriction," *Comm. ACM* **17:5**, 245-250.

Soisalon-Soininen, E. [1977]. "Elimination of single productions from LR parsers in conjunction with the use of default reductions," *Proc. 4th ACM Symposium on Principles of Programming Languages,* 183-193.

Spillman, T. C. [1971]. "Exposing side effects in a PL/I optimizing compiler," *Proc. IFIP Congress 71,* North Holland, Amsterdam, 376-381.

Stearns, R. E. [1971]. "Deterministic top-down parsing," *Proc. 5th Annual Princeton Conf. on Information Sciences and Systems,* pp. 182-188.

Stockhausen, P. F. [1973]. "Adapting optimal code generation for arithmetic expressions to the instruction sets of present day computers," *Comm. ACM* **16:6**, 353-354. *Errata,* **17:10** (Oct. 1974) 591.

Suzuki, N., and Ishihata, K. [1977]. "Implementation of array bound checker," *Proc. 4th ACM Symposium on Principles of Programming Languages,* 132-143.

Szymanski, T. G., and Williams, J. H. [1976]. "Noncanonical extensions of bottom-up parsing techniques," *SIAM J. Computing* **5:2**, 231-250.

Tarjan, R. E. [1972]. "Depth first search and linear graph algorithms," *SIAM J. Computing* **1:2**, 146-160.

Tarjan, R. E. [1974a]. "Finding dominators in directed graphs," *SIAM J. Computing* **3:1**, 62-89.

Tarjan, R. E. [1974b]. "Testing flow graph reducibility," *J. Computer and Systems Sciences* **9:3**, 355-365.

Tarjan, R. E. [1975]. "Efficiency of a good but not linear set union algorithm," *J. ACM* **22:2**, 215-225.

Tarjan, R. E. [1975]. "Solving path problems on directed graphs," Dept. of Computer Science, Stanford University, Stanford, California.

Tennenbaum, A. [1974]. "Compile time type determination in SETL," *Proc. 29th ACM National Conf.,* 95-100. Also see *Type Determination for Very High Level Languages,* Ph. D. dissertation, Courant Institute of Mathematical Sciences, New York, 1974.

Thompson, K. [1968]. "Regular expression search algorithm," *Comm. ACM* **11:6**, 419-422.

Ullman, J. D. [1974]. "Fast algorithms for the elimination of common subexpressions," *Acta Informatica* **2:3**, 191-213.

Ullman, J. D. [1975]. "Data flow analysis," *Proc. 2nd USA-Japan Computer Conference,* pp. 335-342, AFIPS Press, Montvale, N. J.

Urschler, G. [1974]. "Complete redundant expression elimination in flow diagrams," RC-4965, IBM T. J. Watson Research Center, Yorktown Heights, N.Y.

Valiant, L. [1975]. "General context free recognition in less than cubic time," *J. Computer and Systems Sciences* **10:2**, 308-315.

van Wijngaarden, A., Mailloux, B. J., Peck, J. L., Koster, C. H. A., Sintzoff, M., Lindsey, C. H., Meertens, L. G. L. T., and Fisker, R. G. [1975]. "Revised report on the algorithmic language ALGOL 68," *Acta Informatica* **5:1-3**, 1-236.

Vuillemin, J. [1974]. "Correct and optimal implementations of recursion in a simple programming language," *J. Computer and Systems Sciences* **9:3**, 332-354.

Wagner, R. A. [1973]. "Common phrases and minimum-space text storage," *Comm. ACM* **16**, 148-152.

Wagner, R. A. [1974]. "Order-n correction for regular languages," *Comm. ACM* **17:5**, 265-268.

Wagner, R. A., and Fischer, M. J. [1974]. "The string-to-string correction problem," *J. ACM* **21:4**, 168-174.

Waite, W. M. [1974a]. "Code generation," in Bauer and Eickel [1974], pp. 302-602.

Waite, W. M. [1974b]. "Optimization," in Bauer and Eickel [1974], pp. 549-602.

Warshall, S., and Shapiro, R. M. [1964]. "A general purpose table driven compiler," *Proc. AFIPS 1964 Spring Joint Computer Conf.,* Spartan Books, Baltimore, Md., 59-65.

Wasilew, S. G. [1971]. *A Compiler Writing System with Optimization Capabilities for Complex Order Structures,* Ph. D. dissertation, Northwestern Univ., Evanston, Ill.

Wegbreit, B. [1975]. "Property extraction in well-founded property sets," *IEEE Trans. on Software Engineering* **1:3**, 270-285.

Wegbreit, B. [1976]. "Goal-directed program transformation," *Proc. 3rd ACM Symposium on Principles of Programming Languages,* 153-170.

Wegner, P. [1968] *Programming Languages, Information Structures and Machine Organization,* McGraw-Hill, New York, N. Y.

Wegner, P. [1972]. "The Vienna definition language," *Computing Surveys* **4:1**, 5-63.

Weingart, S. [1973]. *A Compiler Building System Based on Formal Machine Description,* Ph. D. dissertation, Yale Univ., New Haven, Conn.

Weingarten, F. W. [1973]. *Translation of Computer Languages,* Holden-Day, San Fransisco, Calif.

Welsh, J., and Quinn, C. [1972]. "A PASCAL compiler for the ICL 1900 series computers," *Software—Practice and Experience* **2:1**, 73-76.

Wharton, R. M. [1976]. "Resolution of ambiguity in parsing," *Acta Informatica* **6:4**, 387-396.

Wilcox, T. R. [1971]. *Generating Machine Code for High-Level Programming Languages,* Ph. D. dissertation, Cornell Univ., Ithaca, N. Y.

Wirth, N. [1968]. "PL360—a programming language for the 360 computers," *J. ACM* **15:1**, 37-74.

Wirth, N. [1971a]. "The programming language PASCAL," *Acta Informatica* **1:1**, 35-63.

Wirth, N. [1971b]. "The design of a PASCAL compiler," *Software—Practice and Experience* **1:4**, 309-333.

Wirth, N., and Weber, H. [1966]. "EULER: a generalization of ALGOL and its formal definition: Part I," *Comm. ACM* **9:1**, 13-23.

Wood, D. [1969]. "The theory of left factored languages," *Computer Journal* **12:4**, 349-356.

Wortman, D. B., Khaiat, P. J., and Laskar, D. M. [1976]. "Six PL/I compilers," *Software—Practice and Experience* **6**:3, 411-422.

Wulf, W., Johnsson, R. K., Weinstock, C. B., Hobbs, S. O., and Geschke, C. M. [1975]. *The Design of an Optimizing Compiler,* American Elsevier, New York, N. Y.

Yhap, E. F. [1974]. "Global register assignment using interval partition and piecewise processing," RC-5015, IBM T. J. Watson Research Center, Yorktown Heights, N.Y.

Yhap, E. F. [1975]. "General register assignment in presence of data flow," RC-5645, IBM T. J. Watson Research Center, Yorktown Heights, N.Y.

Zelkowitz, M. V., and Bail, W. G. [1974]. "Optimization of structured programs," *Software—Practice and Experience* **4**:1, 51-57.

Index

Index